THE ROUGH GUIDE TO

The Netherlands

This seventh edition updated by

Vicky Hampton, Phil Lee, Suzanne Morton-Taylor,
Emma Thomson and Jeroen van Marle

ROUGH
GUIDES

roughguides.com

Contents

Introduction to
The Netherlands

There's nowhere quite like the Netherlands, a country always threatened by the turbulent waters of the North Sea, whose people beat back the ocean to reclaim wide, grassy-green polders from the blue-black depths. That extra space was needed: the Netherlands is one of the most urbanized and densely populated nations on earth, but these crowded flatlands still pack in a wide range of sights and attractions, beginning in the countryside where the fertile, pancake-flat landscape is gridded with drainage ditches and canals set beneath huge open skies, its rural towns and villages often pristine and unchanged places of gabled townhouses and church spires. Despite the country's diminutive size, each town and city is often a profoundly separate place with its own distinct identity – there's perhaps nowhere else in the world where you can hear so many different accents, even dialects, in such a small area. In spring and summer the bulbfields provide bold splashes of colour, and in the west and north the long coastline is marked by mile upon mile of protective dune, backing onto wide stretches of perfect sandy beach.

A major colonial power, the Dutch mercantile fleet once challenged the English for world naval supremacy, and throughout the country's seventeenth-century Golden Age, the standard of living was second to none. There have been a few economic ups and downs since then, but today the Netherlands is one of the most developed countries in the world – and it's an international, well-integrated place too: most people speak English, at least in the heavily populated west of the country; and most of the country is easy to reach on a public transport system of trains and buses, whose efficiency may make British and American visitors weep with envy.

Successive Dutch governments have steered towards political consensus – or at least bearable compromise – and indeed this has been the drift since the Reformation,

ABOVE ERASMUSBRUG, ROTTERDAM **OPPOSITE** BROUWERSGRACHT AND HERENGRACHT CANALS, AMSTERDAM

when the competing pillars of Dutch society learnt to live with – or ignore – each other, at least partly because their minds were focused on trade, which was making most people richer. Almost by accident, Dutch society became tolerant, and, in its enthusiasm to blunt conflict, progressive. These days, many insiders opine that the motive behind liberal Dutch attitudes towards drug use and prostitution isn't freewheeling permissiveness so much as apathy – though this is perhaps a harsh judgement: visit on King's Day, for example, and you'll see the Dutch kitted out in orange to celebrate their country and culture with vim and gusto – unorthodox and incredibly joyous.

Where to go

Mention you're going to the Netherlands and most people assume you're going to **Amsterdam** – and, for that matter, many Amsterdammers can't believe you would want to go anywhere else. Indeed, perhaps surprisingly, given its size and accessibility, the Netherlands outside of the capital is relatively unknown. Some people may confess to a brief visit to Rotterdam or Den Haag (The Hague), but for most visitors Amsterdam *is* the Netherlands. To accept this is to miss much, but there's no doubt that the capital has more cosmopolitan dash than any other Dutch city, both in its restaurant and bar scene and in the pre-eminence of its three great attractions. These are the Anne Frank Huis, where the young Jewish diarist hid during the World War II Nazi occupation; the Rijksmuseum, with its wonderful collection of Dutch paintings, including several of

FACT FILE

• The Netherlands has a **population** of just over 16.8 million people. Of these, some 811,000 live in the capital, Amsterdam, 625,000 in Rotterdam and 515,000 in Den Haag (The Hague). "**Holland**" comprises just two of the twelve Dutch provinces: Noord-Holland around Amsterdam, and Zuid-Holland around Rotterdam and Den Haag.

• One-fifth of the Netherlands is made up of water. Without protection, two-thirds of the country would be regularly flooded. The lowest point in the Netherlands – at seven metres below sea level – is also Europe's lowest point.

• With 20 million bikes in the country – 1.25 for every inhabitant – the Netherlands has the highest level of bicycle usage in the world. However, one bike is stolen every minute of every day – making bike theft much more than a cottage industry.

• The Netherlands is a constitutional **monarchy** presided over by King Willem-Alexander, who was inaugurated as monarch in 2013. The country's bicameral **parliament** sits in Den Haag and comprises Lower House or Second Chamber of 150 directly elected deputies and an Upper House or Senate of 75 senators.

• Every year each Dutch person eats four kilos of Dutch liquorice, or **drop**, which comes in a never-ending supply of sweet, salty and flavoured varieties. Often sold in pharmacies, it was once believed to have medicinal properties, and is as Dutch as tulips and clogs.

Rembrandt's finest works; and the peerless Van Gogh Museum, with the world's largest collection of the artist's work.

In the west of the country, beyond Amsterdam, the provinces of **Noord-** and **Zuid-Holland** are for the most part unrelentingly flat, reflecting centuries of careful reclamation work as the Dutch have slowly pushed back the sea. These provinces are predominantly urban, especially Zuid-Holland, which is home to a grouping of towns known collectively as the Randstad (literally "rim town"), an urban sprawl that holds all the country's largest cities and the majority of its population. Travelling in this part of the country is easy, with trains and buses that are fast, inexpensive and efficient; highlights include easy-going **Haarlem**; the old university town of **Leiden**; **Delft**, with its attractive medieval buildings and diminutive, canal-girded centre; and the gritty port city of **Rotterdam**, festooned with prestigious modern architecture. **Den Haag (The Hague)**, is well worth a visit, too, a laidback and relaxing city, seat of the Dutch government and home to several excellent museums. Nor should you miss the **Keukenhof gardens**, with the finest and most extensive bulbfields in the country. To the north of Amsterdam, the old Zuider Zee ports of **Enkhuizen** and **Hoorn** are very enticing, as are the small villages and unspoilt dunescapes of the **coast**.

Beyond lies a quieter, more rural country, especially in the far north where a chain of low-lying islands – the **Frisian Islands** – separates the North Sea from the coast-hugging Waddenzee. Prime resort territory, the islands possess a blustery, bucolic charm, and thousands of Dutch families come here every summer for their holidays. Apart from **Texel**, the islands lie offshore from the coast of the province of **Friesland**. Friesland's capital, **Leeuwarden**, is a likeable, eminently visitable city, while neighbouring **Groningen** is one of the country's busiest cultural centres.

CLOCKWISE FROM TOP NEMO, AMSTERDAM; CYCLISTS NEAR UTRECHT; ROTTERDAM CARNIVAL

To the south, the provinces of Overijssel and Gelderland are dotted with charming old towns, notably **Deventer** and **Zutphen**, while their eastern portions herald the Netherlands' first few geophysical bumps as the landscape rolls up towards the German frontier. Here also are two diverting towns: **Arnhem**, much rebuilt after its notorious World War II battle, but a hop and a skip from the open heaths of the **Hoge Veluwe National Park**, and the lively college town of **Nijmegen**.

Further south still are the predominantly Catholic provinces of Limburg, Noord-Brabant and Zeeland. The last of these is well named (literally "Sealand"), made up of a series of low-lying islands and protected from the encroaching waters of the North Sea by one of the country's most ambitious engineering plans, the **Delta Project**. Heading east from here, you reach Noord-Brabant, gently rolling scrub- and farmland which centres on the historic cities of **Breda** and **'s-Hertogenbosch**, and the more modern manufacturing hub of **Eindhoven**, home to electronics giant Philips. The hilly province of Limburg occupies the slim scythe of land that reaches down between the Belgian and German borders, with its cosmopolitan capital, **Maastricht**, being one of the Netherlands' most convivial cities.

When to go

The Netherlands enjoys a temperate **climate**, with relatively mild summers and moderately cold winters. Generally speaking, temperatures rise the further south you go. This is offset by the prevailing westerlies that sweep in from the North Sea, making the wetter coastal provinces both warmer in winter and colder in summer than the eastern provinces, where the more severe climate of continental Europe has an influence. As far as rain is concerned, be prepared for it at any time of year.

AVERAGE MONTHLY TEMPERATURES AND RAINFALL

	Jan	Feb	Mar	Apr	May	Jun	Jul	Aug	Sep	Oct	Nov	Dec
AMSTERDAM												
Max/min °C	5/1	6/0	9/2	12/4	17/8	19/10	21/13	22/12	18/10	14/7	9/4	7/2
Max/min °F	41/34	43/32	48/36	54/39	63/46	66/50	70/55	72/54	64/50	57/45	48/39	45/36
Rainfall (mm)	62	43	59	41	48	68	66	61	82	85	89	75
Sun hr/day	2	3	4	6	7	7	7	7	4	3	2	1
MAASTRICHT												
Max/min °C	5/0	6/0	10/2	13/4	18/8	20/11	23/13	23/13	19/10	14/7	9/3	6/1
Max/min °F	41/32	43/32	50/36	55/39	64/46	68/52	73/55	73/55	66/50	57/45	48/37	43/34
Rainfall (mm)	61	51	61	46	64	74	67	58	60	63	66	70
Sun hr/day	2	3	4	5	6	6	6	6	4	4	2	1
GRONINGEN												
Max/min °C	4/-1	5/-1	9/1	12/3	17/7	19/9	21/11	22/11	18/9	14/6	8/3	6/1
Max/min °F	39/30	41/30	48/34	53/37	63/45	66/48	70/52	72/52	64/48	57/43	46/37	43/34
Rainfall (mm)	62	42	59	44	58	67	72	65	68	63	79	78
Sun hr/day	2	3	4	5	7	7	6	6	4	3	2	1

OPPOSITE DUNES, DE COCKSDORP; HILVERSUM RAADHUIS; THE MAURITSHUIS, DEN HAAG

Author picks

We've spent oodles of time in the Netherlands over the years, but there are some things we like to do, or places we have to visit, every time we return. Here's a selection of our favourites.

Carnival chaos Few people realize the Low Countries' capacity for celebrating Carnival – if you don't fancy braving the enormity of King's Day in Amsterdam (see p.95), try the Bergen-op-Zoom Carnival (see p.303), our favourite, where they party better than most.

Classic bike ride Our favourite cycle track is the North Sea Route from Zeeland to Den Helder – you can cycle the whole route if you're lucky enough to have the time, or just pick an individual stretch, from the watery expanses of Zeeland to the dune-side paths further north.

Modernist masters The urinals at Amsterdam's Schiphol airport are etched with a trompe l'oeil fly: the result – sixty percent less "spillage" and another triumph for Dutch design. So much of what you see and use in the Netherlands has been fine-tuned by its designers – as has much of its architecture, from Delft's beehive-like train station (see p.167) to Rotterdam's asymmetrical Erasmusbrug (see p.172), while the Hilversum Raadhuis (see p.139) is a Modernist gem.

Blissful beaches There are great sandy beaches all over the Netherlands, but some of the best are on the islands in the north, where vast areas of golden sand soak up the summer crowds with ease. Try the southwest of Texel (see pp.133–137), or the western end of Schiermonnikoog (see pp.219–221) for the biggest and emptiest stretches. For less solitude, but still wonderful dunes to hike through, make a beeline for Bloemendaal-aan-Zee (see p.109).

The finest fine art Art tourism is a big deal in the Netherlands – and no wonder. The Dutch Golden Age produced a small army of superb painters – Rembrandt, Hals and Vermeer to name but three – and following in their painterly tracks were the likes of van Gogh and Mondriaan. Every major city in the country has at least one good-quality art gallery, each a perfect retreat on a wet and windy day.

Our author recommendations don't end here. We've flagged up our favourite places – a perfectly sited hotel, an atmospheric café, a special restaurant – throughout the guide, highlighted with the ★ symbol.

21
things not to miss

It's not possible to see everything that the Netherlands has to offer in one trip – and we don't suggest you try. What follows is a selective and subjective taste of the country's highlights, in no particular order: cosmopolitan cities, peaceful villages, memorable landscapes and outstanding museums. All entries have a page reference to take you straight into the Guide, where you can find out more. Coloured boxes refer to chapters in the Guide section.

1

1 AMSTERDAM NOORD AND THE EASTERN DOCKLANDS, AMSTERDAM
Page 73

There's plenty to see in the Netherlands apart from Amsterdam, but it would be a strange trip that missed out the capital altogether. It's not all clogs 'n' canals, though – head off the tourist track to the eastern docklands or Amsterdam Noord, newly developed and home to some cutting-edge, Modernist architecture, including the exhilarating EYE.

2 DEN HAAG (THE HAGUE)
Page 151

Den Haag's reputation for dourness is completely undeserved: it boasts a first-rate restaurant scene, smart hotels and enough prime museums to exhaust even the most energetic sightseer – the newly revamped Mauritshuis and the Gemeentemuseum are good reason to visit in themselves.

3 GIETHOORN
Page 248

This inordinately pretty little village is rural Overijssel at its most engaging, with ancient thatched cottages strung along the banks of a narrow canal that is itself crossed by the cutest of wooden bridges.

4 HOGE VELUWE NATIONAL PARK
Page 257

A richly forested swathe of dunes and woodland in the middle of the country. You can cycle your way around thanks to a fleet of free-to-use bicycles and pop into the excellent Kröller-Müller Museum at the heart of the park to admire the fine art and sculpture.

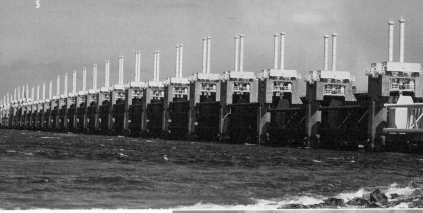

5 DELTA PROJECT
Page 314

A series of huge dykes and flood-barriers in the far-flung western province of Zeeland bear witness to the country's long battle to hold the sea at bay, achievements celebrated in an adjacent exhibition hall.

6 CYCLING
Pages 131, 252, 284, 308, 315

No country in Europe is so kindly disposed towards the bicycle than the pancake-flat Netherlands: you'll find bike paths in and around all towns, plus long-distance touring routes taking you deep into the countryside.

7 ANNE FRANK HUIS, AMSTERDAM
Page 61

A poignant and personal evocation of the German persecution of the Jews. Among the moving exhibits is the bookcase behind which the Frank family and friends hid for two years.

8 FRISIAN ISLANDS
Page 212

Of the string of wild and windswept holiday islands off the northern Dutch coast, Terschelling is the most popular, a fine spot for walks and bike rides amid the swelling dunes.

9 KEUKENHOF GARDENS
Page 149

Literally millions of flowers are on show in these extensive gardens, which specialize in daffodils, narcissi, hyacinths and – of course – tulips.

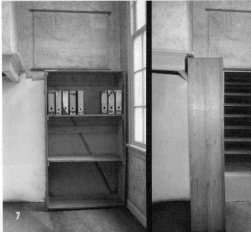

14

10 'S-HERTOGENBOSCH
Page 293

This lively market town features an intricate old quarter of canals and picturesque bridges, plus a simply stunning cathedral.

11 TEXEL
Page 133

With its distinct identity and feel, Texel is the most accessible of the Dutch islands, just a couple of hours north of Amsterdam by train and ferry.

12 VAN GOGH MUSEUM, AMSTERDAM
Page 77

Quite simply the best and most comprehensive collection of van Gogh's work anywhere.

13 FRANS HALS MUSEUM, HAARLEM
Page 107

Hals was one of the finest of the Golden Age painters and this engaging museum has a fine sample of his work, particularly his dark and brooding later canvases.

14 SOUTHWEST FRIESLAND
Page 197

Touring the small towns and villages of this region shows a whole different side to the country from the more urbanized southwest – it's peaceful and charming in equal measure.

15 RIJKSMUSEUM
Page 75

Recently revamped and reconfigured, Amsterdam's Rijksmuseum displays a world-beating collection of Dutch painting with Rembrandt to the fore.

15

16

As an escape from Dutch urban life, the reedy marshes and lagoons of the Biesbosch are hard to beat.

Thanks to the Netherlands' colonial interventions in Southeast Asia, restaurants around the country prepare some of the finest Indonesian cuisine outside Indonesia.

One novel – and strenuous - way of getting to the Frisian Islands is to try guided *wadlopen* or "mud-walking", setting out from the mainland at low tide.

Celebrated by Vermeer, Delft's centre is particularly handsome, and its market square is one of the country's most beguiling.

This atmospheric, laidback city in the far south, squeezed between the porous Belgian and German borders, offers a worldly outlook and a superb old quarter.

This steel-grey inland lake, formerly the Zuider Zee, lies at the heart of the Netherlands and represents the country at its watery best, with fascinating old ports such as Hoorn and Enkhuizen and former islands such as Urk and Schokland to see and explore.

17

Itineraries

The Netherlands beyond Amsterdam is a bit of a mystery to most people, even to those who live there – which, of course, is part of its charm. However, because it can be fun focusing on a particular theme when deciding where to go, we've put together a few itineraries to help you out.

A GRAND TOUR

The Netherlands is a small country, so you can see the best of it within a week or two – that is if you don't linger too long in Amsterdam.

❶ Amsterdam A good place to start, and small enough that you can see its highlights in a day or two. **See pp.44–99**

❷ Haarlem Only fifteen minutes from the capital, but a place apart, with a nice old centre and plenty to see, including the fantastic Frans Hals Museum. **See pp.105–111**

❸ Utrecht Lively student town just half an hour from Amsterdam that retains its cobbled and canalized old centre. **See pp.186–191**

❹ Delft The Netherlands' most appealing provincial town with plenty of historical attractions set amidst a network of pretty canals. **See pp.162–168**

❺ Biesbosch The country's most significant and accessible wetland, readily explorable by boat or bike. **See p.184**

❻ Texel The most accessible of the Dutch islands, and a wonderfully relaxing place of dunes, birds, beaches and gentle cycling, and with some great places to stay. **See pp.133–137**

❼ Enkhuizen Perhaps the most enchanting of the old Zuider Zee ports, its face firmly turned towards the water around its busy inner harbours, and with the excellent Zuider Zee Museum as a bonus. **See pp.121–125**

❽ Groningen The northern part of the country's major urban centre, with a huge university population and a buzzy centre full of bars and restaurants. **See pp.221–226**

THE GREAT OUTDOORS

You don't normally think of the Netherlands as a place to experience the Great Outdoors, but it is a fantastic destination for many outdoor activities, from horseriding and cycling to sailing and some other, more specifically Dutch pursuits.

❶ Wadlopen in Friesland There's nothing more Dutch – or more enjoyable – than the guided walks you can attempt between the north coast and the islands of the Waddenzee. **See p.220**

❷ Sailing The Netherlands is a boaty kind of place all round, but the lakes and waterways of Friesland are the best place to take to the water, and there are plenty of opportunities on the IJsselmeer too. **See p.202**

❸ Skating You can, of course, do this anywhere if the weather is cold enough, but there's nothing better than following at least part of the course of the famous Elfstedentocht race through Friesland. **See p.209**

❹ Horseriding The countryside is well suited to all kinds of equestrian activities, especially the Hoge Veluwe National Park. **See p.257**

❺ Windsurfing and surfing There's no better place for both activities than Renesse in Zeeland's Schouwen-Duiveland, where you can

ABOVE SAILING, FRIESLAND; DELFT POTTERY; VAN GOGH'S *BEDROOM*

rent boards and wet suits and seek out the plentiful waves and wind. **See p.313**

ART AND CULTURE

With every justification, the Netherlands is known for its art and boasts some top-ranking collections. The premier galleries are, as you might expect, in the big cities, but several of the country's smaller towns register excellent art museums too.

❶ **Amsterdam** The capital claims three galleries of international standing: the Rijksmuseum (see p.75) with its wondrous array of Golden Age painting; the Van Gogh Museum (see p.77) with its peerless collection of van Goghs; and the impressive Stedelijk Museum (see p.78) of modern and contemporary art.

❷ **The Frans Hals Musuem** It's worth visiting Haarlem for this museum alone – Frans Hals was one of the most gifted of the Golden Age painters. **See p.107**

❸ **The Mauritshuis** This elegant seventeenth-century mansion in Den Haag is home to one of

the finest concentrations of Dutch Golden Age paintings in the world. **See p.153**

❹ **Museum Beelden aan Zee** In a lovely location, right by the seaside in Scheveningen, this ambitious gallery features a first-rate display of modern and contemporary sculpture. **See p.160**

❺ **Boijmans van Beuningen Museum** A superb collection of Flemish, Dutch and modern art awaits in Rotterdam's prize museum. **See p.173**

❻ **Museum Catharijneconvent** Utrecht's prime gallery features an intriguing sample of medieval religious sculptures and paintings displayed in a spacious former convent. **See p.188**

❼ **Kröller-Muller Museum** One of the country's finest collections of late nineteenth-century and modern paintings and sculptures is housed in a wonderful location in the Hoge Veluwe park. **See p.257**

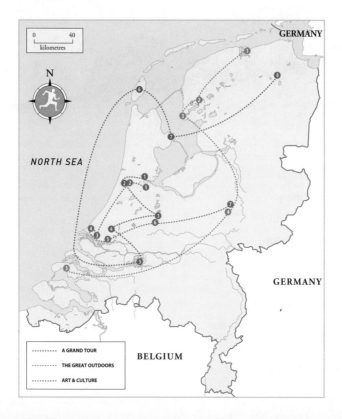

NOVELTY CLOG, AMSTERDAM

Basics

Getting there

There are flights galore from a bevy of UK airports to Amsterdam's Schiphol (pronounced skip-oll) airport as well as a sprinkling of flights to several second-string Dutch airports, primarily Eindhoven and Rotterdam/The Hague. Alternatively, travelling from the UK to the Netherlands by train via the Channel Tunnel is just as easy and about the same price as a flight, and neither, if you live in the southeast of the UK, does it take much longer. You can also get there by long-distance bus, which is usually the most affordable option, though more time-consuming. By car and ferry, deals for drivers on ferry routes into Dutch (and Belgian) ports are particularly competitive.

From North America and Canada the main decision is whether to fly direct – easy enough as Amsterdam's Schiphol is a major international air travel hub – or to route via London, picking up a budget flight onwards from there. From Australia and New Zealand, all flights to Amsterdam require one or two stops on the way; from South Africa, there are direct flights.

Flights from the UK

Amsterdam is one of the UK's most popular short-haul destinations and its international airport, **Amsterdam Schiphol**, is extremely easy to reach. Among many operators, easyJet (Ⓦeasyjet.com), Jet2 (Ⓦjet2.com) and British Airways (Ⓦbritish airways.com) all have flights to Amsterdam, but the two airlines with the widest range of flights are **KLM** (Ⓦklm.com), which flies there direct and nonstop from Aberdeen, Belfast, Birmingham, Bristol, Cardiff, Durham Teesside, Edinburgh, Exeter, Glasgow, Humberside, Inverness, Leeds, London Heathrow, Manchester, Newcastle, Norwich and Southampton; and **Flybe** (Ⓦflybe.com), which flies there direct and

nonstop from some of the same airports as well as Bournemouth, East Midlands, Liverpool and London City Airport. Alternatively, Ryanair (Ⓦryanair .com) flies from London Stansted and Manchester to Eindhoven; CityJet (Ⓦcityjet.com) links London City with Rotterdam/Den Haag; and British Airways (Ⓦbritishairways.com) flies between London Heathrow and Rotterdam/Den Haag.

Prices for flights to Amsterdam vary enormously, but begin at about £180 return from a regional airport, slightly less from London. **Flying times** are insignificant: Aberdeen to Amsterdam is one and a half hours, it's one hour from Norwich and one hour and ten minutes from London.

Flights from Ireland

Flying from Ireland, Aer Lingus (Ⓦaerlingus.com) has daily direct and nonstop flights to Amsterdam from Dublin and Cork; easyJet (Ⓦeasyjet.com) flies there from Belfast; and Ryanair (Ⓦryanair.com) has flights from Dublin to Eindhoven.

Prices for flights vary considerably, but begin at about €170 return from Dublin to Amsterdam. **Flying times** are modest: Dublin to Amsterdam takes one hour and forty minutes.

Flights from the US and Canada

Amsterdam's Schiphol airport is among the most popular and least expensive gateways to Europe from North America, and finding a convenient and good-value flight is rarely a problem. **Direct, nonstop flights from the US** are operated by a number of airlines, including Delta, KLM, Lufthansa and United, but many more airlines fly **via London** and other European centres – and are almost invariably much cheaper because of it. **KLM** (Ⓦklm.com) offers the widest range of flights, with direct or one-stop flights to Amsterdam from several US cities, and connections from dozens more. Return **fares** for direct and nonstop flights from major cities in the US to Amsterdam start at around US$1600. **Flying times** to Amsterdam on nonstop,

---

A BETTER KIND OF TRAVEL

At Rough Guides we are passionately committed to travel. We believe it helps us understand the world we live in and the people we share it with – and of course tourism is vital to many developing economies. But the scale of modern tourism has also damaged some places irreparably, and climate change is accelerated by most forms of transport, especially flying. All Rough Guides' flights are carbon-offset, and every year we donate money to a variety of environmental charities.

direct flights are as follows: New York (7hr 10min), Chicago (8hr 30min), Atlanta (10hr), and Los Angeles (11hr).

From Canada, several airlines, including KLM and Air Canada (Ⓦaircanada.com), fly direct and nonstop to Amsterdam from Toronto (7hr 10min) and KLM offers direct and nonstop flights from Vancouver (9hr 30min). **Return fares** on these direct/nonstop flights from Toronto go for around Can$1500, while from Vancouver you can expect to pay around Can$1800. Less direct routings are characteristically much less expensive.

Flights from Australia and New Zealand

There are no direct/nonstop flights **from Australia** or **New Zealand** to the Netherlands and most itineraries will involve at least one stop in the Far East – Singapore, Bangkok or Kuala Lumpur – before proceeding on to Amsterdam (or the gateway city of the airline you're flying with). You can get tickets to Amsterdam from Sydney, Melbourne or Perth for AUS$1800–2800; it's NZ$2200–3000 from Auckland.

Flights from South Africa

From South Africa, KLM offers **direct/nonstop flights** to Amsterdam from Cape Town and Johannesburg. With most other airlines, you will have to change at a gateway city – for example Lufthansa via Frankfurt – but this is usually much more economical. As for sample **fares**, direct/nonstop return flights with KLM from South Africa begin at about ZAR11000. The **flying time**, direct, is about eleven hours.

By train from the UK

Eurostar trains (Ⓦeurostar.com) departing from London St Pancras (plus Ebbsfleet and Ashford in Kent) reach Brussels via the Channel Tunnel in a couple of hours. In Brussels, trains arrive at Bruxelles-Midi station (Brussel-Zuid in Dutch), from where there are high-speed onward services with **Thalys** (Ⓦthalys.com) to Rotterdam (1hr 10min) and Amsterdam Centraal Station (1hr 50min). Alternatively, **Intercity trains** (Ⓦns.nl), operated by NS International (Ⓦnsinternational.nl) – the international arm of the main Dutch rail company – offer a much slower service between Brussels and several Dutch cities, including Den Haag (2hr 30min), Rotterdam (2hr 10min), Amsterdam (3hr 20min)

and Utrecht (3hr). Eurostar can arrange **through ticketing** from any point in the UK to any point in the Netherlands, as can Rail Europe (Ⓦraileurope.co.uk) and railbookers (Ⓦrailbookers.com), who offer a first-rate range of rail-based holidays and short breaks. A **return fare** from London to Amsterdam using Eurostar and then Thalys can cost as little as £130, but to get the cheapest fares you have to be flexible with dates and times. Obviously enough, **travelling time** from London to Amsterdam depends on how long you have to wait for the connection in Brussels – but five hours in total is about average.

By train and ferry from the UK

Stena Line (Ⓦstenaline.co.uk), in conjunction with Abellio Greater Anglia trains (Ⓦabelliogreateranglia.co.uk), operates the **Dutchflyer**, an inexpensive if somewhat time-consuming rail-and-ferry route from the UK to the Netherlands. **Trains** leave from London's Liverpool Street station bound for Harwich, where they connect with the **ferry** over to the Hook of Holland – the Hoek van Holland – though you can also join the Dutchflyer at stations in between Liverpool Street and Harwich. Beginning in London, the journey to the Hook takes about ten hours during the day, a couple more overnight, including the six- to seven-hour ferry crossing. From the Hook, there are frequent trains on to Rotterdam (every 30min to 1hr; 30min), from where you can reach a host of other Dutch towns. One-way **fares** start at £36 per person, or £75 on an overnight sailing, cabin included – cabins are compulsory on overnight sailings. **Tickets** are available from Abellio Greater Anglia trains.

RAIL PASSES

Pan-European **Inter-Rail** and **Eurail passes** can include the Dutch railway network and there's also a **Holland Rail Pass**, which entitles the holder to between three to five days' unlimited rail travel within one month. The rules and regulations regarding all these passes are complicated – consult the website of the umbrella company, **Rail Europe** (Ⓦraileurope.com). Note that some passes have to be bought before leaving home. Note also that Dutch railways sells a competitively priced, one-day unlimited railcard for €52.

By ferry from the UK

Three companies operate **car ferries** from the UK to the Netherlands. They are Stena Line (Ⓦstenaline.co.uk) with services from Harwich to the Hook of Holland (8–9hr); **DFDS Seaways** (Ⓦdfdsseaways.co.uk) from Newcastle (North Shields) to IJmuiden near Amsterdam (16hr); and **P&O Ferries** (Ⓦpoferries.com) from Hull to the Europoort, 40km west of Rotterdam (12hr). **Tariffs** vary enormously, depending on when you leave, how long you stay, if you're taking a car, what size it is and how many passengers are in it. As a sample **fare**, a weekend excursion from Hull to the Europoort for two adults, a car and a cabin might cost £220 return.

Driving from the UK

To reach the Netherlands **by car or motorbike from the UK**, you can either take a ferry (see opposite) or use **Eurotunnel**'s shuttle train through the Channel Tunnel (Ⓦeurotunnel.com) from Folkestone to Calais. Eurotunnel **fares**, which are charged per vehicle including passengers, depend on the time of year, time of day and length of stay, and the journey takes about 35 minutes. As an example, a five-day return fare in the summer costs in the region of £140. Advance booking is advised. Amsterdam is roughly 370km from the Eurotunnel exit in Calais, Rotterdam 200km, Arnhem 260km.

By bus from the UK

Travelling by **long-distance bus** is generally the least expensive way of reaching the Netherlands from the UK, but it is time-consuming. From London Victoria, there are direct bus services to a clutch of Dutch cities, including Den Haag, Rotterdam, Utrecht and Amsterdam. The journey from London to Amsterdam takes around twelve hours, Utrecht ten hours, Rotterdam eight. There are between two and four buses daily to these key destinations and all services use the Eurotunnel. For timetable details, consult **Eurolines** (Ⓦeurolines.co.uk). One-way **fares** start from as little as £20, £40 return. There are discounts for seniors (60-plus) and the under-26s.

Getting around

Getting around the Netherlands is rarely a problem: it's a small country, and the longest journey you're ever likely to make – say from Amsterdam to Maastricht – takes under three hours by train or car. Furthermore, the public transport system is exemplary, a fully integrated network of trains and buses that brings even the smallest of villages within easy reach, and at affordable prices too. Train and bus stations are almost always next door to each other, and several of the larger cities also have a tram network.

By train

The best way of travelling around the Netherlands is by **train**. The system – one of the best in Europe – is largely, though not exclusively, operated by **Nederlandse Spoorwegen** (NS; Dutch Railways; Ⓦns.nl). NS trains are fast, mostly modern, frequent and very punctual; fares are relatively low; and the network of lines is comprehensive. NS domestic services come in two types: the speedy **Intercity** for city-to-city connections; and the **Sprinter**, which operates on local routes and stops pretty much everywhere. Several other train companies operate a scattering of local lines and both **Thalys** (Ⓦthalys.com) and **ICE** (Ⓦnsinternational.nl/ICE) trains run long-distance/international, high-speed services – Thalys between Amsterdam, Rotterdam and Brussels; ICE linking Amsterdam with Utrecht, Arnhem and ultimately Frankfurt. NS also has an international arm, NS International (Ⓦnsinternational.nl), with a platoon of foreign and domestic

---

PLANNING A JOURNEY

For pre-departure information on your **train journey**, consult the "Journey Planner" feature on the NS website (Ⓦns.nl). Type in your departure and arrival stations and it will not only tell you train times, but also what platform your train leaves from, how many changes to make (and where, with platform numbers), and how much your ticket will cost. Even more comprehensive is the excellent Ⓦ**9292.nl**, which provides detailed advice on any journey you are intending to make, covering every type of public transport and even directions for the walk to the nearest stop or station.

MAJOR RAIL ROUTES

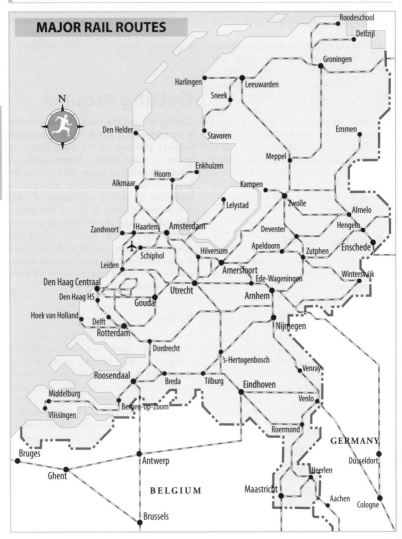

destinations, including Brussels, but its services are not as fast as those of Thalys and ICE, though they are a shade cheaper. At larger train stations in the Netherlands, there are separate high-speed train ticket desks.

Fares and tickets

Ordinary **train fares** are calculated by the kilometre, diminishing proportionately the further you travel: for example, a standard one-way fare from Amsterdam to Maastricht costs €25, Rotterdam €14.80 and Leeuwarden €24.70. A one-way ticket is an *enkele reis*; a return trip is a *retour*. Same-day return tickets (*dagretour*) can knock between ten and forty percent off the price of two one-way tickets for the same journey, but returns are normally double the price of one-way tickets. First-class fares cost about thirty percent on top of the regular fare; holders of plastic OV-chipkaarts (see box opposite) receive a four or five percent discount on standard fares. On certain routes – eg Rotterdam to Amsterdam – there is also a small premium for using high-speed express trains.

Timetables are online and mounds of information on special deals and discounts are available online and at all major train stations. Note that you are not allowed to buy a ticket on the train – travel without a ticket and you can expect to be fined on the spot (€35).

Buying a train ticket

Buying an NS train ticket is not as straightforward as you might expect. There are two types of automatic, **multilingual ticket machine** in every train station concourse, one for passengers with a plastic OV-chipkaart (and signed as such), the other for passengers buying an individual rail ticket – ie a single-use, paper OV-chipkaart (see box below). The latter sport the NS logo (white on a blue background), but some do not accept foreign credit or debit cards – and only a few (around a quarter) accept cash (coins, never notes). NS ticket offices, on the other hand, will almost always accept foreign credit or debit cards, though they do apply a small surcharge per transaction of €0.50. Perhaps surprisingly, NS tickets cannot be bought online with a foreign debit or credit card.

NS discount tickets and deals

NS offers a wide variety of **discount tickets and deals**, perhaps the most useful of which is the **Dagkaart** (Day Travel Card) for unlimited travel on any train in the system and costing just €52 in second-class; first-class is €88. There's also the **Weekendretour** (Weekend Return), which offers significant discounts on the usual return fare; you can also spread your outward and return journeys over a weekend from Friday (7pm+) to Monday (4am) with an added day thrown in when there is a public holiday. A third possibility is the family-orientated **Railrunner**, which charges just €2.50 per journey per child for up to three children aged 4–11 travelling with an adult. All these special-deal tickets can be purchased as one-offs and/or put on a passenger's existing OV-chipkaart (see box below). For further information on deals and discounts, check out ⓦns.nl.

Zonetaxi

With NS's **Zonetaxi scheme**, rail passengers can be assured of a taxi from and/or to around 130 train stations in the NS network. The largest stations – primarily Amsterdam Centraal, Rotterdam and Den Haag CS – are not part of the scheme and it only applies within the city limits of each participating station. To get to the station at the start of your journey, call the national *Zonetaxi* number ☎0900 679 8294 (premium line, only within the Netherlands) at least half an hour in advance. On arrival at your local station, you can either book a *Zonetaxi* for your destination when you buy your ticket, or wait till you get there – and pay the taxi driver direct (for a small extra fee). The **fixed-rate price** per person per *Zonetaxi* ride is €6. Note that *Zonetaxis* are not the same as regular taxis – you may well, for instance, have to share with other people taking a similar route. The cabs are identifiable by a "*Zonetaxi*" sign on the roof and they have a separate rank – usually with summoning buttons – outside train stations.

THE OV-CHIPKAART

The Netherlands has a **nationwide ticketing system** covering all forms of public transport. The ticketing system works via the **OV-chipkaart** (ⓦov-chipkaart.nl), a smart card which needs to be checked against an electronic reader when you enter and leave the public transport system – and also when you change trains, metro, trams or buses etc on the same journey; if you forget, the card soon stops working. The OV-chipkaart comes in two formats – paper and plastic. Paper (disposable) OV-chipkaarts are designed for occasional users of the transport system – whether it be for single journeys or one- or two-day bus or rail passes. They are sold at NS automatic ticket machines and by most tram and bus drivers; however, they are the most expensive way of travelling, at about five percent more than journeys made with a plastic OV-chipkaart.

For extended stays, you might consider purchasing a rechargeable, plastic OV-chipkaart, which come in two main types, personalized and anonymous; both cost €7.50. These are valid for five years and are sold at train and bus stations, including automatic ticketing machines – but not by bus and tram drivers. Before your journey, you load up the card with the required/desired credit – a minimum of €6 for urban transport and €20 for rail. At the end of your visit, any unspent credit can be reclaimed at any public transport ticket office. Bear in mind that most ticket machines do not accept foreign debit or credit cards or cash – but ticket offices do.

By bus and tram

Supplementing the train network are **buses** – run by a patchwork of local companies but again amazingly efficient and reaching into every rural nook and cranny. **Ticketing** is straightforward via the **OV-chipkaart** system (see box, p.7) – and drivers issue paper OV-chipkaarts for single journeys and often 24hr passes too. Bear in mind also that in more remote rural areas some bus services only operate when passengers have made advance bookings: local **timetables** indicate where this applies. Regional bus timetable books, costing around €3, are sold at some train station bookshops, or you can plan your journey **online** at ⓦ 9292.nl.

Within **major towns**, urban public transport systems are extensive, inexpensive and frequent, which makes getting around straightforward and hassle-free; most bus and tram services run from 6am until about midnight and your OV-chipkaart is valid on all services. Urban "**Park and Ride**" (or **Transferium**) schemes are commonplace.

By car

For the most part, **driving** round the Netherlands is pretty much what you would expect: smooth, easy and quick. The country has a uniformly good road network, with most of the major towns linked by some kind of motorway or dual carriageway, though snarl-ups and jams are far from rare. Rules of the road are straightforward: you drive on the right, and **speed limits** are 50kph in built-up areas, 80kph outside, 120kph on motorways – though some motorways have a speed limit of 100kph, indicated by small yellow signs on the side of the road. Drivers and front-seat passengers are required by law to wear seat belts, and penalties for drunk driving are severe. There are no toll roads, and although **fuel** is expensive, currently at around €1.75 per litre (diesel €1.38), the short distances mean this isn't too much of an issue.

Most foreign **driving licences** are honoured in the Netherlands, including all EU, US, Canadian, Australian and New Zealand ones. If you're **bringing your own car**, you must have adequate insurance, preferably including coverage for legal costs, and it's advisable to have an appropriate breakdown policy from your home motoring organization too.

Renting a car

All the major **international car rental agencies** are represented in the Netherlands. To rent a car, you'll have to be 21 or over (and have been driving for at least a year), and you'll need a credit card – though some local agencies will accept a hefty cash deposit instead. **Rental charges** are fairly high, beginning around €290 per week for unlimited mileage in the smallest vehicle, but include collision damage waiver and vehicle (but not personal) **insurance**. **Sat navs** are rarely included in the basic price and cost an exorbitant €7 per day or so extra – take your home sat nav if you can, but make sure the appropriate maps have been updated. To cut costs, watch for special deals offered by the bigger companies. If you go to a smaller, local company (of which there are many), you should proceed with care: in particular, check the policy for the excess applied to claims and ensure that it includes collision damage waiver (applicable if an accident is your fault or the damage is created by an unidentified person/vehicle). If you **break down** in a rented car, you'll get roadside assistance from the particular repair company the rental firm has contracted. The same principle works with your own vehicle's breakdown policy providing you have coverage abroad.

Cycling

One great way to see the Netherlands, whether you're a keen cyclist or an idle pedaller, is to travel by **bike** (*fiets*). Cycle-touring can be a short cut into Dutch culture and you can reach parts of the country – its beaches, forests and moorland – that might otherwise be (relatively) inaccessible. The mostly flat landscape makes travelling by bike an almost effortless pursuit, although you can find yourself battling against a headwind or swallowed up in a shoal of cyclists commuting to work.

The short distances involved make it possible to see most of the country with relative ease, using the nationwide system of well-marked **cycle paths and numbered junctions**: a circular blue sign with a white bicycle on it indicates an obligatory cycle lane, separate from car traffic. Red lettering on signposts gives distances for fairly direct routes; lettering in green denotes a more scenic (and lengthy) mosey. Long-distance (LF) routes weave through the cities and countryside, often linking up to local historic loops and scenic trails. For further tips and hints, check out ⓦ holland-cycling .com and ⓦ nederlandfietsland.nl.

The Dutch as a nation are celebrated touring cyclists, and bookshops are packed with **cycling** books and maps; however, for all but the longest trips the maps and route advice provided by most tourist offices are fine. If you're looking for a **place to stay** after a day in the saddle, the best advice is to visit a member of the **Vrienden op de Fiets** (see p.30).

Bike rental

You can **rent a standard-issue bike** from most NS train stations for €7.50 a day, plus a deposit of anywhere between €50 and €150 depending on the model. Most bikes are single-speed, though there are some three-speeds to be had, and even mountain bikes in the hillier south. You'll also need some form of **ID**. The snag is that cycles must be returned to the station from which they were rented, making onward hops by rented bike impossible. Most **bike shops** – of which there are many – rent bicycles out for around the same amount, and they may be more flexible on deposits: some may accept a passport in lieu of cash. In all cases, advance reservations are advised.

Taking your bike on an NS **train** is allowed – and the bike carriages have a clear cycle symbol on the outside. You'll need to buy a flat-rate ticket for your bike (*dagkaart fiets*; €6), which is valid for the whole day. Space can be limited, despite the variety of ingeniously folding bikes favoured by locals, and because of this you won't be allowed on with your bike during the morning and evening rush hours (6.30–9am & 5.30–6pm), except in July and August.

Note that in the larger cities in particular, but really anywhere, you should never, ever, leave your bike **unlocked**, even for a few minutes – bike stealing is a big deal in the Netherlands. Almost all train stations have somewhere you can store your bike safely for less than a euro.

Accommodation

Inevitably, accommodation is one of the major expenses of a trip to the Netherlands – indeed, if you're after a degree of comfort and style, it's going to be the costliest item by far. There are, however, budget alternatives, principally private rooms (broadly bed and breakfast arranged via the local tourist office), campsites and a scattering of HI-registered hostels. During the summer and over holiday periods vacant rooms can be scarce, so it's wise to book ahead. In Amsterdam, room shortages are commonplace throughout the year, so advance booking is always required; hotel prices are about thirty percent higher here than in the rest of the country.

Hotels

All **hotels** in the Netherlands are graded on a star system. One-star and no-star hotels are rare, and prices for two-star establishments start at around €70 for a double room without private bath or shower, €80 with en-suite facilities. Three-star hotels cost upwards of about €85; for four- and five-star places you'll pay €125-plus. Generally, the stated price includes **breakfast**, except in the very cheapest of hotels.

You can book ahead easily by calling the hotel direct – English is almost always spoken. Within the Netherlands, you can also make same-night bookings in person through any tourist office for a nominal fee. Alternatively, two useful **booking websites** are Ⓦweekendjeweg.nl (Dutch only) and the **Netherlands' Board of Tourism's** Ⓦholland.com.

Private rooms

One way of cutting costs is to use **private accommodation** – rooms in private homes that are let out to visitors on a bed-and-breakfast basis,

---

ACCOMMODATION PRICES

Throughout this Guide we give a **headline price** for every accommodation reviewed. This indicates the lowest price you're likely to pay for a double or twin room in high season (usually June to mid-Aug), barring regularly offered **weekend discounts and special deals**: the price includes breakfast, unless otherwise stated. Single rooms, where available, usually cost between seventy and ninety percent of a double or twin. At **hostels**, we give two prices – the price of a double room, if available, and of a dormitory bed – and at **campsites**, the cost of two people plus car and tent pitch.

sometimes known as **pensions**. Prices are quoted per person and are normally around €25–35 with breakfast usually included. You mostly have to go through the local tourist office to find a private room: they will either give you a list to follow up independently or will book the accommodation themselves and levy a minimal booking fee. Note, however, that not all tourist offices are able to offer private rooms; generally you'll find them only in the larger towns and tourist centres and generally a good way from the centre. In some of the more popular tourist destinations the details of these "B&Bs" are listed in tourist brochures.

Vrienden op de Fiets

If you're cycling or walking round the Netherlands, you will find the organization **Vrienden op de Fiets** (Friends of the Bicycle; ☎088 123 8999, ⓦvriendenopdefiets.nl) an absolute bargain. For an annual joining fee ("donation") of €10, you'll be sent a book with several hundred Dutch addresses where you can stay the night in somebody's home for a fixed tariff of €19 per person; all you have to do is phone/email 24 hours in advance. Accommodation can range from stylish townhouses to suburban semis to centuries-old farmhouses – and staying in somebody's home can give a great insight into Dutch life. Hosts are usually very friendly, offer local information and will provide a breakfast of often mammoth proportions to send you on your way.

TOP 10 HOTELS WITH CHARACTER

The Netherlands has a fantastic range of hotels from grand Art Nouveau buildings to renovated thatched cottages. Here are ten of the country's most individual places to stay.

Abdij van Dokkum, Dokkum. See p.211
Ambassade, Amsterdam. See p.85
De Emauspoort, Delft. See p.167
Grand Hotel Karel V, Utrecht. See p.190
Hotel de Harmonie, Giethoorn. See p.250
Hotel de Mug, Middelburg. See p.308
Paleis Hotel, Den Haag. See p.161
De Posthoorn, Monnickendam. See p.113
Stempels, Haarlem. See p.111
Villa Mar, Makkum. See p.208

Hostels

If you're travelling on a tight budget, an **HI hostel** may well be your accommodation of choice. **Stayokay** (ⓦstayokay.com) is the HI-affiliated Dutch hostelling association and operates 25 hostels across the Netherlands. **Dorm beds** are the norm, in four- to ten-bunk rooms, though the smaller dorms can also be rented as family rooms and some hostels have double and single rooms. For the most part, they represent extremely good value, offering clean and comfortable accommodation at rock-bottom prices.

Dorm beds **cost** €20–35 per person per night including breakfast (€50-plus in the most popular hostels, like Amsterdam), whereas doubles average around €50; rates vary depending on the season and the hostel's facilities; there are no age restrictions. Both city and country locations can get very full between June and September, when you should **book in advance**. Most Stayokay hostels accept online bookings. Inexpensive meals are often available, but there are no self-catering facilities. If you're planning on spending several nights in hostels, it makes sense to join your home HI organization before you leave in order to avoid paying surcharges, though you can join at the first Dutch hostel you stay at instead.

In addition to Stayokay hostels, the larger cities – particularly Amsterdam – have a number of **private hostels** offering dormitory accommodation and almost invariably double- and triple-bedded rooms too. Prices are broadly similar, but standards vary enormously; we've given detailed reviews, where appropriate, in the Guide.

Camping and trekkers' huts

There are plenty of **campsites** in the Netherlands and most of them are well equipped. Prices vary greatly, depending on the facilities available, but in the more deluxe you can expect to pay around €25 for a pitch including electrical hook-up and car parking, plus €3–5 per person. All tourist offices have details of their nearest sites, and we've mentioned a few campsites in the Guide. A list of selected sites is available on the **Eurocampings** website (ⓦeurocampings.co.uk).

If you don't mind having basic facilities, look out also for **minicampings**, which are generally signed off the main roads. These are often family-run – you may end up pitched next to a family's house – and are informal, inexpensive and friendly. Details of registered minicampings can be found in the accommodation section of the provincial guides sold at every tourist office. Some campsites also offer **trekkers' huts** (*trekkershutten*) – frugally furnished wooden affairs that can house a maximum of four people for about €40 a night. You can get details of the national network, with good information in English and a list of sites in each province, from the **Stichting Trekkershutten Nederland** (Ⓦtrekkershutten.nl).

Food and drink

The Netherlands may not be Europe's gastronomic epicentre, but the food in the average Dutch restaurant has improved by leaps and bounds in recent years, and there are any number of places serving a good, inventive take on home-grown cuisine. All the larger cities also have a decent assortment of non-Dutch restaurants, especially Indonesian, Chinese and Thai, plus lots of cafés and bars – often known as eetcafés – that serve adventurous, reasonably priced food in a relaxed and unpretentious setting. The Netherlands is also a great country to go drinking, with a wide selection of bars, ranging from the chic and urbane to the rough and ready. Considering the country's singular approach to the sale and consumption of cannabis, you might choose to enjoy a joint after your meal rather than a beer – for which you will have to go to a "coffeeshop" (see p.36 & p.93).

Food

Dutch **food** tends to be higher in protein content than variety: steak, chicken and fish, along with filling soups and stews, are staples, usually served up in substantial quantities. It can, however, at its best, be excellent and oftentimes good value too.

Breakfast

In all but the cheapest of hotels, **breakfast** (*ontbijt*) will be included in the price of the room. Though usually nothing fancy, it's always substantial: rolls, cheese, ham, hard-boiled eggs, jam and honey or peanut butter are the principal ingredients. Many bars and cafés serve rolls and sandwiches in similar mode, although few open much before 8am or 8.30am.

A standard cup of **coffee** is bitter and strong and served black with *koffiemelk* (evaporated milk) on the side, but lots of places – especially city coffee shops (of the non-dope variety) – have moved up a notch, serving mochas, cappuccinos and so forth. **Tea** generally comes with lemon – if anything; if you want milk you have to ask for it. **Chocolate** (*chocomel*) is also popular, hot or cold; for a real treat, drink it hot with a layer of fresh whipped cream (*slagroom*) on top. Some cafés also sell aniseed-flavoured warm milk (*anijsmelk*).

Snacks

Dutch **fast food** has its own peculiarities. Chips/ fries (*friet* or *patat*) are the most common standby; *vlaamse* or "Flemish" style sprinkled with salt and smothered with huge gobs of mayonnaise (*friete-saus*) are the best, or with curry, satay, goulash or tomato sauce. If you just want salt, ask for *patat zonder*; fries with salt and mayonnaise are *patat met*. You'll also come across *kroketten* – spiced minced meat (usually either veal or beef), covered with breadcrumbs and deep-fried – and *fricandel*, a frankfurter-like sausage. All these are available over the counter at evil-smelling fast-food places, or, for a euro or so, from coin-op heated glass compartments on the street and in train stations.

Much tastier are the **fish specialities** sold by street vendors, which are good as a snack or a light lunch: salted raw herring, rollmops, smoked eel (*gerookte paling*), mackerel in a roll (*broodje makreel*),

---

TOP 5 CAKES AND COOKIES

Dutch cakes and cookies are always good, best eaten in a *banketbakkerij* (patisserie) with a small serving area or bought in a bag and munched on the hoof. Here are some of our favourites.
Amandelkoekjes Cakes with a crisp cookie outside and melt-in-the-mouth almond paste inside.
Appelgebak Chunky, memorably fragrant apple-and-cinnamon pie, served hot in huge wedges, often with whipped cream (*met slagroom*).
Mergpijpjes Soft cakes with a layer of almond on the outside and dipped in chocolate at both ends.
Speculaas Crunchy cinnamon cookie with the texture of gingerbread.
Stroopwafels Butter wafers sandwiched together with runny syrup.

mussels and various kinds of deep-fried fish are all delicious. Look out, too, for "green" or *maatje* herring, eaten raw with onions in early summer: hold the fish by the tail, tip your head back and dangle it into your mouth, Dutch-style. Another snack you'll see everywhere is *shoarma* or **shwarma** – also known as doner kebab, shavings of lamb pressed into a flat pitta bread – sold in numerous Middle Eastern restaurants and takeaways for about €3. Other, less common, street foods include **pancakes** (*pannen-koeken*), sweet or spicy, also widely available at sit-down restaurants; **waffles** (*stroopwafels*), doused with syrup; and, in November and December, *oliebollen*, greasy **doughnuts** sometimes filled with fruit (often apple) or custard (as a *Berliner*) and tradi-tionally eaten on New Year's Eve.

Sandwiches

Bars often serve sandwiches and rolls (*boterham* and *broodjes*) – mostly open, and varying from a slice of tired cheese on old bread to something so embellished it's almost a complete meal – as well as more substantial dishes. A **sandwich** made with French bread is known as a *stokbrood*. In the winter, *erwtensoep* (or *snert*) – thick **pea soup** with smoked sausage, served with smoked bacon on pumper-nickel – is available in many bars, and makes a great buy for lunch, at about €5 a bowl. Alternatively, you can sample the **uitsmijter** (a "kicker-out", derived from the practice of serving it at dawn after an all-night party to prompt guests to depart). Now widely available at all times of day, it comprises one, two or three fried eggs on buttered bread, topped with a choice of ham, cheese or roast beef; at about €5, it's another good budget lunch.

Full meals

Most **cafés**, **bars and café-bars** serve food, every-thing from sandwiches to a full menu – in which case they may be known as an **eetcafé**. This type of place is usually open all day, serving both lunch and an evening meal. Full-blown **restaurants**, on the other hand, tend to open in the evening only, usually from around 5.30 or 6pm until around 10pm. Especially in the smaller towns, the Dutch eat early, around 7.30 or 8pm; after about 10pm you'll find many restaurant kitchens closed.

If you're on a tight budget, stick to the **dagschotel** (dish of the day) wherever possible, for which you'll pay around €12. It's usually a meat or fish dish, heavily garnished with potatoes and other vegetables and salad; note, though, that it's often served at lunchtime or between 6 and 8pm. Otherwise, you can pay up to €25 for a meat or seafood main course in an average restaurant. **Vegetarian** dining isn't a problem. Many eetcafés and restaurants have at least one meat-free menu item, and you'll find a few veggie restaurants in most of the larger towns, offering full-course set meals for €10–15 – although bear in mind that they often close early (7/8pm).

Other cuisines

As for **foreign cuisines**, the Dutch are particularly partial to **Indonesian** food and Indonesian restaurants are commonplace: *nasi goreng* and *bami goreng* (rice or noodles with meat) are good basic dishes, though there are normally more exciting items on the menu, some very spicy; chicken or beef in peanut sauce (*sateh*) is always available. Or you could try a **rijsttafel** – a sampler meal, comprising rice and/or noodles served with perhaps ten or twelve small, often spicy dishes and hot sambal sauce on the side. Usually ordered for two or more people, you can reckon on paying around €25 per person. **Surinamese** restaurants are much rarer, being largely confined to the big cities, but they offer a distinctive, essen-tially Creole cuisine – try *roti*, flat pancake-like

---

DUTCH CHEESE

Dutch cheeses may not be as rich and varied as, say, those of France or Switzerland, but they can certainly be delicious. Most Dutch cheeses are pale yellow, like the most famous of them, **Gouda**, in which differences in taste come with the varying stages of maturity: *jong* (young) cheese has a mild flavour, *belegen* (16–18 weeks old) is much tastier, while *oud* (mature) can be pungent and strong, with a grainy, flaky texture. The best way to eat it is as the Dutch do, in thin slices (cut with a cheese slice, or *kaasschaaf*) rather than large chunks. Among other names to look out for, the best known is **Edam**, semi-soft in texture but slightly creamier than Gouda; it's usually shaped into balls and coated in red wax ready for export, but is not eaten much in the Netherlands. **Leidse** is simply a bland Gouda laced with cumin or caraway seeds; most of its flavour comes from the seeds. **Maasdam** is a Dutch version of Emmental or Jarlsberg, strong, creamy and full of holes, sold under brand names such as Leerdammer and Maasdammer. You'll also find Dutch-made Emmental and Gruyère.

bread served with a spicy curry, hard-boiled egg and vegetables.

Italian food is ubiquitous, with pizzas and pasta dishes starting at a fairly uniform €8 or so in most places.

Drinking

Most **drinking** is done in the laidback surroundings of a brown bar (*bruin kroeg*) – so called because of the colour of the decor – or in more modern-looking places, everything from slick designer bars, minimally furnished and usually catering for a younger crowd, to cosy neighbourhood joints. Most bars **stay open** until around 1am during the week and 2am at weekends, though some don't bother to open until lunchtime, a few not until 4 or 5pm.

Though they're no longer common, you may also come across **proeflokalen** or tasting houses. Originally the sampling premises of small distillers, these are now small, old-fashioned bars that only serve spirits (and maybe a few beers) and sometimes close early (around 8pm).

Beer

The Netherlanders' favourite tipple is **beer**, mostly Pilsener-style lager usually served in a relatively small measure (just under a half-pint, with a foaming head on top) – ask for *een pils*. Away from Amsterdam expect to pay around €2–3, or €3–4 in Amsterdam.

FIVE OF THE BEST: ARTISAN BREWERIES

Brouwerij Brand Limburg Ⓦ brand.nl. The country's oldest brewery turns out a limited range of dark and blond beers plus a particularly tasty, cherry-coloured *Dubbelbock*.

Brouwerij Emelisse Kamperland Ⓦ emelisse.nl. Distinctive stuff – try its Imperial Russian Stout.

Brouwerij de Koningshoeven Tilburg. Ⓦ koningshoeven.nl. The Netherlands' only Trappist brewery produces several strong dark ales, notably *La Trappe Quadrupel*.

Brouwerij de Molen Amsterdam Ⓦ brouwerijdemolen.nl. Several good brews from this tidy little brewery – look out for its *Hemel & Aarde* (Heaven & Earth).

Gulpener Limburg Ⓦ gulpener.nl. Burgeoning brewery noted for its tasty lagers made from prime ingredients; its *Gulpener Oud Bruin* is an especially tangy dark ale.

Predictably, beer is much cheaper from a supermarket, most brands retailing at just under €2 for a half-litre bottle. The most common Dutch brands are Heineken, Amstel and Grolsch, all of which you can find more or less nationwide. Expect them to be stronger and more distinctive than the watery approximations brewed abroad under licence.

For something a little less strong, look out for *donkenbier*, which is about half the strength of an ordinary Pilsener beer. There are also a number of **seasonal beers**: rich, fruity *bokbier* is fairly widespread in autumn, while year-round you'll see *witbier* (a wheaty, white beer) such as Hoegaarden, Dentergems or Raaf – refreshing and potent in equal measure, and often served with a slice of a lemon or lime.

Around the country, you'll also spot plenty of the better-known **Belgian brands** available on tap, like Stella Artois and the darker De Koninck, as well as bottled beers like Duvel, Chimay and various brands of the fruit-flavoured Kriek. There are also an increasing number of local, independent breweries (see box).

Wine and spirits

Wine is reasonably priced – expect to pay around €5 for an average bottle of French white or red in a supermarket, €20 in a restaurant. As for spirits, the indigenous drink is **jenever**, or Dutch gin – not unlike British gin, but a bit weaker and oilier, made from molasses and flavoured with juniper berries. It's served in a small glass (for around €2) and is traditionally drunk straight, often knocked back in one gulp with much hearty back-slapping. There are a number of varieties, principally *Oud* (old), which is smooth and mellow, and *Jong* (young), which packs more of a punch – though neither is extremely alcoholic. The older *jenevers* (including *zeer oude*, very old) are a little more expensive but stronger and less oily. In a bar, ask for a *borreltje* (straight *jenever*) or a *bittertje* (with angostura); if you've a sweet tooth, try a *bessenjenever* (flavoured with blackcurrant). A glass of beer with a *jenever* chaser is a *kopstoot*. Imported spirits are considerably more expensive.

Other drinks include numerous **Dutch liqueurs**, notably *advocaat* (or eggnog), sweet, blue *curaçao* and luminous green *pisang ambon*. There is also an assortment of luridly coloured fruit brandies best left for experimentation at the end of an evening – or perhaps not at all – plus a Dutch-produced brandy, *vieux*, which tastes as if it's made from prunes but is in fact grape-based. Various regional **firewaters** include *elske* from Maastricht – made from the leaves, berries and bark of alder bushes.

The media

English-speakers will find themselves quite at home in the Netherlands as Dutch TV broadcasts a wide range of British programmes, and English-language newspapers are readily available too.

Newspapers and magazines

British newspapers are on sale in every major city on the day of publication. Newsagents located at train stations will almost always have copies if no one else does. Current issues of UK and US magazines are widely available too.

Of the **Dutch newspapers**, *NRC Handels-blad* (Wnrc.nl) is a right-of-centre paper that has perhaps the best international news coverage and a liberal stance on the arts; *De Volkskrant* (Wvolkskrant.nl) is a progressive, leftish daily; the popular right-wing *De Telegraaf* (Wtelegraaf.nl) boasts the highest circulation figures and has a well-regarded financial section; while *Algemeen Dagblad* (Wad.nl) is a right-wing broadsheet. The left-of-centre *Het Parool* ("The Password"; Wparool.nl) and the news magazine *Vrij Nederland* ("Free Netherlands"; Wvn.nl) are the successors of underground Resistance newspapers printed during wartime occupation. The Protestant *Trouw* ("Trust"; Wtrouw.nl), another former underground paper, is centre-left in orientation with a focus on religion.

Television and radio

Dutch TV isn't the best, but English-language programmes and films fill up a fair amount of the schedule – and they are always subtitled, never dubbed. The big global cable and satellite channels are routinely accessible in hotel rooms and most give access to a veritable raft of foreign television channels, including Britain's BBC1 and BBC2.

Dutch radio has numerous stations catering for every niche. Of the **public service stations**, Radio 1 is a news and sports channel, Radio 2 plays AOR music, Radio 3 plays chart music and Radio 4 classical, jazz and world music. Of the **commercial stations**, some of the main nationwide players are Radio 538, Veronica and Noordzee FM; most of them play chart music. The Dutch Classic FM, at 101.2FM, plays mainstream classical music, with jazz after 10pm. There's next to no

English-language programming, apart from the overseas-targeted **Radio Netherlands** (Wrnw.nl), which broadcasts Dutch news in English, with features on current affairs, lifestyle issues, science, health and so on. Frequencies and schedules for the BBC World Service (Wbbc.co.uk/worldservice-radio), Radio Canada (Wrcinet.ca) and Voice of America (Wvoanews.com) are listed on their respective websites.

Festivals and events

Across the Netherlands, most annual festivals are arts- or music-based affairs, confined to a particular town or city, though there is also a liberal sprinkling of folkloric events celebrating one local event or another – the Alkmaar cheese market (see p.129) being a case in point. Most festivals take place during the summer and the local tourist office can be guaranteed to have all the latest details.

JANUARY

Elfstedentocht (Eleven Towns Race) Friesland. Occasional, but theoretically annual, ice-skating marathon along the frozen rivers of Friesland, starting and finishing in Leeuwarden, (cold) weather permitting. Welfstedentocht.nl.

FEBRUARY

Holland Flowers Festival Enkhuizen (late Feb). The world's largest covered flower show held over five days in late February. Whollandflowersfestival.nl.

Lent carnivals Southern Netherlands (late Feb to early March). All sorts of shenanigans at the beginning of Lent in Breda 's-Hertogenbosch, Maastricht and other southern towns.

MARCH

Keukenhof Gardens Lisse (late March to late May). World-renowned floral displays in the bulbfields and hothouses of this large, sprawling park. Wkeukenhof.nl and see p.149.

APRIL

Alkmaar Cheese Market Alkmaar (April–Sept). Held every Friday (10am–12.30pm), from the first Friday in April to the first in September. A herd of large and bright yellow balls of cheese carried round by fancily dressed porters. Wkaasmarkt.nl and see p.129.

Marathon Rotterdam Rotterdam (April). Popular long-distance run beginning in the city centre. Held on a Sunday in April. Wnnmarathonrotterdam.org.

King's Day (Koningsdag) Nationwide (April 27). This is one of the most popular dates in the Dutch diary, a street event *par excellence*. Celebrations in honour of the king take place throughout the Netherlands, but festivities in Amsterdam tend to be the wildest of the lot, with the city's streets and canals lined with people dressed in ridiculous costumes. Anything goes, especially if it's orange – the Dutch national colour. This is also the one day of the year when goods can be bought and sold tax-free to anyone on the streets, and numerous stalls are set up in front of people's houses.

MAY

Herdenkingsdag (Remembrance Day) Nationwide (May 4). There's wreath-laying all over the country and a two-minute silence is widely observed in honour of the Dutch dead of World War II.

Bevrijdingsdag (Liberation Day) Nationwide (May 5). The country celebrates the 1945 liberation from German occupation with music, outdoor festivals and processions.

Breda Jazz Festival Breda (mid- to late May) Open-air concerts and street parades over four days. Ⓦ bredajazzfestival.nl.

Scheveningen Sand Sculpture Festival Scheveningen (May to mid-June). Hard-working teams descend on the resort from all over Europe to create amazing sand sculptures, which are left for three weeks for visitors to admire.

JUNE

Holland Festival Amsterdam (throughout June). This month-long performing arts festival covers all aspects of both national and international music, theatre, dance and the contemporary arts. Ⓦ hollandfestival.nl.

Pinkpop festival Landgraaf, near Maastricht (mid-June). A top-ranking, three-day open-air music festival held in the middle of June. Ⓦ pinkpop.nl and see p.282.

Oerol Festival Terschelling (mid- to late June). A ten-day event featuring theatre and stand-up comedy. Ⓦ oerol.nl.

JULY

Woodstock69 Bloemendaal aan Zee (April–Sept). Festival held on Bloemendaal beach and featuring live percussion, dance acts and plenty of revelry. Begins in April and runs through to September, but July and August are the busiest – and best – months. There are daily shows in high season, weekend shows in the shoulder season. Ⓦ woodstock69.nl.

North Sea Jazz Festival Rotterdam (mid-July). Outstanding three-day jazz festival showcasing international names as well as local talent. Multiple stages and a thousand musicians. Ⓦ northseajazz.com and see p.172.

Internationale Vierdaagse Afstandmarsen Nijmegen (late July). One of the world's largest walking events, with over 30,000 participants walking 30–50km/day over four days. Ⓦ 4daagse.nl.

AUGUST

Sneek Week Sneek (early Aug). International sailing event in Sneek, with around 1000 boats competing in over thirty classes. Ⓦ sneekweek.nl.

Amsterdam Gay Pride Amsterdam (first or second weekend). The city's gay community celebrates with street parties and performances, as well as a "Canal Pride" flotilla of boats parading along the Prinsengracht. Ⓦ amsterdamgaypride.nl.

Grachtenfestival Amsterdam (mid- to late Aug). For nine days, international musicians perform classical music at historic locations in the city centre. Includes the Prinsengrachtconcert, one of the world's most prestigious open-air concerts, featuring a stage over the canal and a promenading audience. Ⓦ grachtenfestival.nl.

SEPTEMBER

Open Monumentendag (Open Monument Day) Nationwide (second weekend). For two days in September, monuments and historical attractions that are normally closed or have restricted opening times throw open their doors to the public for free. Ⓦ openmonumentendag.nl.

OCTOBER

Amsterdam Marathon Amsterdam (early/mid-Oct). Popular city marathon starting and finishing inside the Olympic Stadium and passing through the city centre along the way. Ⓦ tcsamsterdammarathon.nl.

NOVEMBER

Crossing Border Den Haag (second or third week). Four-day festival that aims to cross artistic boundaries with performances by over a hundred international acts presenting the spoken word in various forms, from rap to poetry. Ⓦ crossingborder.nl.

Parade of Sint Nicolaas Amsterdam (second or third Sun). The traditional parade of Sinterklaas (Santa Claus) through the city on his white horse, starting from behind Centraal Station where he arrives by steamboat, before proceeding down the Damrak towards Rembrandtplein accompanied by his helpers, the Zwarte Pieten ("Black Peters") – so called because of their blackened faces – who hand out sweets and little presents. It all finishes on the Leidseplein.

International Documentary Film Festival Amsterdam (mid- to late Nov). Arguably the world's largest documentary film festival, held over ten days in Amsterdam and showing around 250 domestic and international documentaries. Ⓦ idfa.nl.

DECEMBER

Pakjesavond (Present Evening) Nationwide (Dec 5). Pakjesavond, rather than Christmas Day, is when Dutch kids receive their Christmas presents. If you're in the Netherlands on that day and have Dutch friends, it's worth knowing that it's traditional to give a present together with an amusing poem you have written caricaturing the recipient. For the children, legend asserts that presents are dropped down the chimney by Zwarte Pieten (Black Peters) as Sinterklaas rides across the rooftops on his white horse. Traditionally, kids sing songs to make Sinterklaas happy in the weeks before Pakjesavond as there is always the chance of being caught by the Zwarte Pieten (if you haven't been good) and sent to Spain – where Sinterklaas lives – in a brown bag.

Sports and outdoor activities

Most visitors to the Netherlands confine their exercise to cycling (see p.28) and walking, both of which are ideally suited to the flatness of the terrain and, for that matter, the excellence of the public transport system. The Netherlands also offers all the sporting facilities you would expect of a prosperous, European country, from golf to gymnasia, swimming pools to horseriding, plus one or two more distinctive activities: these include Korfball, canal ice skating, though this is of course dependent on the weather being cold enough, and the idiosyncratic pole sitting, whereby participants literally sit on top of a pole for as long as possible.

Beaches and watersports

The Netherlands possesses some great **sandy beaches** on both its western and northern coasts, although it has to be admitted that the weather is notoriously unreliable – some say bracing – and the North Sea is really rather murky. There are a number of fully fledged seaside resorts – such as Zandvoort (see p.109) and Scheveningen (see p.159) – but there are nicer, quieter stretches of coast, most notably amid the wild dunes and beaches that make up the **Nationaal Park Zuid-Kennemerland** near Haarlem (see p.109). There are also long, sandy strands right across the islands of the Waddenzee from Texel to Schiermonnikoog and these beaches are popular for **windsurfing** and **kitesurfing**. The lakes of Friesland and the IJsselmeer are good for **sailing**, particularly the yachting centre of Sneek (see p.201).

Spectator sports

The chief spectator sport is **football** (soccer) and the teams that make up the country's two professional leagues attract a fiercely loyal following. Big-deal clubs include PSV Eindhoven (W psv.nl), Feyenoord from Rotterdam (W feyenoord.nl) and Amsterdam's Ajax (W ajax.nl). The football season runs from September to May, and matches are traditionally held on Sunday at 2.30pm, with occasional games at 8pm on Wednesday. Tickets for key matches are notoriously hard to come by.

Korfball

Played from one end of the Netherlands to the other, **Korfball** (W korfball.com) is a home-grown sport cobbled together from netball, basketball and volleyball, and played with mixed teams and a high basket. To watch a game, ask for fixture details at the local tourist office.

Culture and etiquette

The stereotypical view of the Netherlands is of a liberal country, where drugs and prostitution are both legal and homosexuality is widely accepted. In fact, many Netherlanders deplore prostitution and fret about the decriminalization of drugs, while the gay and lesbian scene flourishes in Amsterdam above everywhere else.

Drugs

Thousands of visitors come to the Netherlands in general, and Amsterdam in particular, just to get **stoned**. In the Netherlands, the purchase of **cannabis** is decriminalized and this has proved to be a real crowd puller, though it's not without its problems: many Amsterdammers, for instance, get mightily hacked off with "**drug tourism**", as do folk in border towns, who have to deal with tides of people popping over the international frontier to visit the first **coffeeshop** they see – coffeeshops being the licensed premises where you can buy the stuff. The irritation is such that there have been moves to both reduce the number of coffeeshops and restrict access to Dutch citizens only, who will have to show a valid "weed card" to get served – but at time of writing, the politicians seemed to have kicked these plans into the long grass.

In essence, the Dutch government's attitude to soft drugs remains unchanged: the use of cannabis is tolerated but not condoned, resulting in a rather complicated set of rules and regulations. These permit users to buy very small amounts for **personal use only** – which means possession of up to 5g and sales of up to 5g per purchase in coffeeshops are OK. Needless to say, never, ever buy dope on the street and don't try to take any form of cannabis out of the country. A surprising number of people think (or claim to think) that if it's bought legally in Amsterdam it can be taken back home legally; this story won't wash with customs officials and drug enforcement officers, who will happily add your stash to the statistics of national drug seizures, and charge you into the bargain.

As far as **other drugs** go, a series of serious incidents prompted the Dutch government to ban the sale of **magic mushrooms**, making them just as illegal as hard drugs. That said, you can still purchase the "grow-your-own" kits or buy truffles, which are claimed to have a similar effect. Despite the existence of a lively and growing trade in cocaine and heroin, possession of either could mean a stay in one of the Netherlands' lively and ever-growing jails. Ecstasy, acid and speed are as illegal in the Netherlands as they are anywhere else.

Coffeeshops

When you first walk into a **coffeeshop**, how you buy the stuff isn't immediately apparent – it's illegal to advertise cannabis in any way, which includes calling attention to the fact that it's available at all. What you have to do is ask to see the **menu**, which is normally kept behind the counter. This will list all the different hashes and grasses on offer, along with (if it's a reputable place) exactly how many grams you get for your money. The in-house dealer will be able to help you out with queries. Current **prices** per gram of hash and marijuana range from €8 for low-grade stuff up to €25 for top-quality hash and a bit more for really strong grass.

The **hash** you come across originates in various countries and is much like you'd find anywhere, apart from **Pollem**, which is compressed resin and stronger than normal. **Marijuana** is a different story, and the old days of imported Colombian, Thai and sensimelia are fading away. Taking their place are limitless varieties of "Nederwiet", Dutch-grown under UV lights and more potent than anything you're likely to have come across. Skunk, Haze and Northern Lights are all popular types of Dutch weed, and should be treated with caution – a smoker of low-grade British draw will be laid low (or high) for hours by a single spliff of skunk. You would be equally well advised to take care with **space-cakes** (cakes or biscuits baked with hash), which are widely available: you can never be sure exactly what's in them; they tend to have a delayed reaction (up to two hours before you notice anything strange – don't get impatient and gobble down another one); and once they kick in, they can bring on an

extremely intense, bewildering high (10–12hr is common). You may also come across **cannabis seeds** for growing your own: while locals are permitted to grow a small amount of marijuana for personal use, the import of cannabis seeds is illegal in any country, so don't even think about trying to take some home.

Finally, one oddity is that in July 2008, **smoking tobacco** was banned in coffeeshops (as well as bars and restaurants), though smoking hash remained perfectly permissible: there has been some backtracking on this, however, and some places now have separate smokers' dens, though the majority do not – hence the pile-up on the pavement outside.

LGBT travellers

The Netherlands ranks as one of the top **gay-friendly** countries in Europe, with the superstar of the country's LGBT scene being, of course, Amsterdam – here attitudes are tolerant, bars are excellent and plentiful, and support groups and facilities unequalled. In the other major cities of the Netherlands, the scene isn't anywhere near as extensive, but it's well organized: Rotterdam, Den Haag, Nijmegen and Groningen, for example, all have a visible and enjoyable gay nightlife. The native **lesbian** scene is smaller and more subdued: many politically active lesbians move in close-knit communities, and it takes time for foreign visitors to find out what's happening.

The **COC** (W coc.nl), the national organization for gay men and women, dates from the 1940s and is actively involved in gaining equal rights for gays and lesbians, as well as informing society's perceptions of gayness. Every city of any size has a branch office, which can offer help, information on events and promotions – and many have a sociable coffee bar too. **Gay legislation** is particularly progressive – for example same-sex marriage and adoption by same-sex partners were legalized in 2001 ahead of every other country. The age of consent is 16.

Consider timing your visit to coincide with **Amsterdam's Gay Pride** (W amsterdampride.nl) on the first or second weekend in August. Celebrations are unabashed, with music, theatre, street parties and floats parading through the streets. The other major deal for the gay scene is **King's Day** – a goodly part of which, at least in Amsterdam, mirrors the city's Gay Pride, but is held on April 27.

TOP 5 KIDS' ATTRACTIONS

Artis Royal Zoo, Amsterdam. See p.72
De Efteling, Noord-Brabant. See p.299
Miffy Museum, Utrecht. See p.189
NEMO, Amsterdam. See p.74
Wadlopen (mud-flat walking), Friesland.
See p.220

Children

In general terms at least, Dutch society is sympathetic to its **children** and the tourist industry follows suit. Extra beds in hotel rooms are usually easy to arrange; many restaurants (though not the very smartest) have children's menus; concessions for children are the rule, from public transport through to museums; and baby-changing stations are commonplace. Pharmacists (*apotheken*) carry all the kiddy stuff you would expect – nappies, baby food and so forth.

Travel essentials

Addresses

These are written, for example, as Haarlemmerstraat 15 III, meaning the third-floor (US fourth-floor) apartment at no. 15 Haarlemmerstraat. The ground floor is indicated by **hs** (*huis*, "house") after the number; the basement is **sous** (*sousterrain*). The figures **1e**, **2e**, **3e** and **4e** before a street name are abbreviations for Eerste, Tweede, Derde and Vierde, respectively – the first, second, third and fourth streets of the same name. Some **side streets**, rather than have their own name, take the name of the street that they run off, with the addition of the word *dwars*, meaning crossing – so Palmdwarsstraat is a side street off Palmstraat. **T/O** (*tegenover*, "opposite") in an address shows that the address is a boat: hence "Prinsengracht T/O 26" would indicate a boat to be found opposite building Prinsengracht 26. Dutch postcodes are made up of four figures and two letters.

Concessions

Concessionary rates apply at almost every sight and attraction as well as on public transport. Rates vary, but usually children under 5 go free and kids over 5 and under 15/16 get a substantial discount. There are senior discounts too, but the age of eligibility is rising in increments from 65 to 67 by 2023. Family ticket deals are commonplace. See also "Museum cards" (p.41).

Crime and personal safety

By comparison with many other parts of Europe, the Netherlands is relatively free of **crime**, so there's little reason why you should ever come into contact with the Dutch police. However, there is more **street crime** than there used to be and wherever you go at night it's always better to err on the side of caution. Using public transport any time of the day or night isn't usually a problem, but if in doubt take a taxi, and if you're on a bike, make sure it is well locked up – bike theft and resale is a major industry here. Be especially vigilant in the big cities, especially in Rotterdam and Amsterdam, where the Red Light District can have an unpleasant, threatening undertow (although the crowds of people act as a deterrent). In Amsterdam, there has also been a spate of street crimes in which thieves impersonate plain-clothes police, flashing false IDs: only very rarely will genuine non-uniform officers stop you in the street, so be sceptical if you are stopped in this manner.

If you do have to approach the Dutch police, you'll mostly find them courteous, concerned and usually able to speak English. If you have something stolen, make sure you get a copy of the **police report** or its number – essential if you are to make a claim against your insurance.

As for **offences you might commit**, drinking and driving is treated harshly and although you're allowed to be in possession of cannabis for personal use (up to 5g), anything more can result in confiscation by the police. It's not illegal to smoke cannabis in public, but it is frowned upon and you can be fined – stick to the coffeeshops (see p.37). If you're **detained by the police**, you don't automatically have the right to a phone call, although in practice they'll probably phone your consulate for you – not that consular officials have a reputation for excessive helpfulness. If your alleged offence is a minor matter, you can be held for up to six working hours with or without questioning (though note that midnight to 9am is not counted – tough luck if you are arrested at 11.59pm).

Electricity

The current is 220 volts AC, with standard European-style two-pin plugs. British equipment needs only a plug adaptor; American apparatus requires a transformer and an adaptor.

Entry requirements

Citizens of the EU/EEA, including the UK and Ireland, plus citizens of Australia, New Zealand, Canada and the US do not need a **visa** to enter the Netherlands if staying for ninety days or less, but they do need a current **passport**. Travellers from South Africa, on the other hand, need a passport and a tourist visa for visits of less than ninety days; visas must be obtained before departure for the Netherlands and are available from the Dutch embassy (see below).

For stays in the Netherlands of **longer than ninety days**, EU/EEA residents will have few problems, but everyone else needs a mix of **visas and permits. In all cases,** consult your Dutch embassy at home before departure.

DUTCH EMBASSIES ABROAD

Australia ⓦ netherlands.org.au
Canada ⓦ canada.nlembassy.org
Ireland ⓦ ireland.nlembassy.org
New Zealand ⓦ newzealand.nlembassy.org
South Africa ⓦ southafrica.nlembassy.org
UK ⓦ dutchembassyuk.org
US ⓦ the-netherlands.org

Health

Under **reciprocal health arrangements**, all citizens of the EU and EEA (European Economic Area) are entitled to free or discounted medical treatment within the Dutch public health-care system. Non-EU/EEA nationals are not entitled to free or discounted treatment and should, therefore, take out their own medical insurance – though some countries, for example Australia, do have limited mutual agreements. EU/EEA citizens may want to consider private health insurance too, in order to cover the cost of the discounted treatment as well as items not within the EU/EEA's scheme, such as dental treatment and repatriation on medical grounds. Note also that the more worthwhile policies promise to sort matters out before you pay (rather than after) in the case of major expense; if you do have to pay upfront, get and keep the receipts. For more on insurance policies and what they cover, see below.

Health care in the Netherlands is of a high standard and rarely will **English speakers** encounter language problems – if the doctor or nurse can't speak English themselves (which is unlikely) there will almost certainly be someone at hand who can. If necessary, your local pharmacy, tourist office or hotel should be able to provide the address of an English-speaking doctor (or dentist).

If you're **seeking treatment under EU/EEA reciprocal public health agreements**, double-check that the medic is working within (and seeing you as) a patient of the public health-care system. This being the case, you'll receive reduced-cost/government-subsidized treatment just as the locals do; any fees must be paid upfront, or at least at the end of your treatment, and are non-refundable. Sometimes you will be asked to produce documentation to prove you are eligible for EU/EEA health care, sometimes no one bothers, but technically at least you should have your passport and your **European Health Insurance Card (EHIC)** to hand. If, on the other hand, you have a **travel insurance policy covering medical expenses**, you can seek treatment in either the public or private health sectors, the main issue being whether – at least in major cases – you have to pay the costs upfront and then wait for reimbursement or not.

Anyone planning to stay in the Netherlands for **more than ninety days** (even when coming from another EU/EEA member state) is required by Dutch law to take out private **health insurance**.

Pharmacies

Minor ailments can be remedied at a **drugstore** (*drogist*). These sell non-prescription drugs as well as toiletries, tampons, condoms and the like. A **pharmacy** (*apotheek*) – generally open Monday to Friday 9.30am to 6pm, but often closed Monday mornings – is where you go to get a prescription filled. There aren't many 24-hour pharmacies, but the local tourist office, as well as most of the better hotels, will supply addresses of ones that stay open late.

Insurance

Prior to travelling, it's a good idea to take out **travel insurance** to cover against theft, loss and illness or injury. Before paying for a new policy, however, it's worth checking whether you already have some degree of cover: for instance, EU/EEA health-care privileges apply in the Netherlands (see above), some all-risks home insurance policies may cover your possessions when overseas, and many private medical schemes include cover when abroad.

A typical **insurance policy** usually provides cover for loss of baggage, tickets and – up to a certain limit – cash and cards, as well as cancellation or curtailment of your journey and medical costs.

ROUGH GUIDES TRAVEL INSURANCE

Rough Guides has teamed up with WorldNomads.com to offer great travel insurance deals. Policies are available to residents of over 150 countries, with cover for a wide range of adventure sports, 24hr emergency assistance, high levels of medical and evacuation cover and a stream of travel safety information. Roughguides.com users can take advantage of their policies online 24/7, from anywhere in the world – even if you're already travelling. And since plans often change when you're on the road, you can extend your policy and even claim online. Roughguides.com users who buy travel insurance with WorldNomads.com can also leave a positive footprint and donate to a community development project. For more information, go to ⓦ roughguides.com/travel-insurance.

Most of them exclude so-called **dangerous sports** – horseriding, windsurfing and so forth – unless an extra premium is paid. Many policies can be chopped and changed to exclude coverage you don't need – for example, sickness and accident benefits can often be excluded or included at will. If you do take **medical coverage**, ascertain whether benefits will be paid as treatment proceeds or only after your return home, and whether the policy has a 24-hour medical emergency number. When securing **baggage cover**, make sure that the per-article limit will cover your most valuable possessions. If you need to **make a claim**, keep receipts for medicines and medical treatment. In the event you have anything stolen, you should obtain a crime report statement or number.

Internet

Almost all the country's hotels, B&Bs and hostels provide **wi-fi** for their guests either free or at minimal charge. Most cafés, restaurants and bars offer free wi-fi too, as does every library and all NS Intercity trains. Tourist hotspots – for example all of central Delft – are another source of free wi-fi.

Mail

The Dutch postal system has been privatized and is now run by TNT as **PostNL** (ⓦ postnl.nl). Since privatization, many of the old post offices have been closed and replaced with counters within large stores and supermarkets, though these can be difficult to track down. Fortunately, **stamps** are sold at a wide range of outlets, including shops and hotels, and TNT has not reduced the number of **postboxes**, which are legion.

Maps

There are lots of Netherlands **road maps** on the market and for the most part they are widely available both at home and in the Netherlands. The **Hallwag** (ⓦ hallwag.com) map is particularly good and is also one of the more detailed (at 1:200,000), a feat it accomplishes by being double-sided; it also includes an index. The problem – and this even applies to the Hallwag – is that the Netherlands is such a crowded country that following any fold-out road map can be very difficult: if you're doing any serious driving, you're best off investing in a Road Atlas. The best is the **Nederland Road Atlas** (1:100,000) produced by **ANWB** (ⓦ anwb.nl), the main Dutch touring organization; it includes an index and has detailed insets of major Dutch towns and cities. ANWB also publishes a whole raft of **specialist/regional maps**, including waterproof maps specifically designed for cyclists. It might also be worth equipping yourself with a **sat nav.** As for **city maps**, your first port of call should be the local tourist office, which will almost invariably supply free, reasonably good-quality maps.

Money

The **currency** of the Netherlands is the **euro** (€), divided into 100 cents. There are euro **notes** of €500, €200, €100, €50, €20, €10 and €5, and **coins** of €2, €1, 50c, 20c, 10c, 5c, 2c and 1c, but note that many retailers will not touch the €500 and €200 notes with a bargepole – you have to break them down into smaller denominations at the bank. The **exchange rate** for one euro at time of writing was €0.73 to the British pound; €1.11 to the US dollar; €1.38 to the Canadian dollar; €1.43 to the Australian dollar; €1.55 to the New Zealand dollar; and €13.60 to the South African Rand.

To give an idea of currency fluctuations, the exchange rate three years ago were: €0.84 to the British pound; €1.34 to the US dollar; €1.33 to the Canadian dollar; €1.24 to the Australian dollar; €1.59 to the New Zealand dollar; and €10.02 to the South African Rand.

ATMs are liberally distributed around every city, town and large village in the Netherlands – and they accept a host of debit cards without charging a transaction fee. Credit cards can be used in ATMs too, but in this case transactions are treated as loans, with interest accruing daily from the date of withdrawal. All major **credit/debit cards**, including American Express, Visa and especially MasterCard, are widely accepted in most shops, restaurants and cafés, as well as in ATMs. Typically, Dutch ATMs give instructions in a variety of languages.

An alternative is a **cash passport**, onto which you pre-load a certain amount of cash before your trip commences. There are scores of different suppliers, including the UK's Post Office and all the major credit card companies. The cash passport works pretty much the same as a debit/credit card – and can be used at ATMs – but you can only spend the amount you have pre-loaded on it. The supplier makes a profit on the differential currency rates – so check out the relevant rates before you get one.

You can change **foreign currency** into euros at most banks, which are ubiquitous; banking hours are Monday to Friday 9am to 4pm, with a few big-city banks also open Thursday until 9pm or on Saturday morning. All are closed on public holidays (see box below).

Mosquitoes

These pesky blighters thrive in the country's canals and can be a real handful (or mouthful) if you are camping. An antihistamine cream such as Phenergan is the best antidote, although this can be difficult to find – in which case preventative sticks like Autan or Citronella are the best (if perhaps somewhat forlorn) bet.

Museum cards

If you're planning to visit more than just a couple of Dutch museums, you'll save money with a **Museumkaart** (Museum Card; Ⓦ museumkaart.nl), which gives free entry to over four hundred museums and galleries nationwide. It costs €60 for a year (less if you're 18 or under) and you can purchase one at any participating museum – most major museums are in the scheme.

Opening hours

The Dutch weekend fades painlessly into the working week with many smaller shops and businesses, even in Amsterdam, staying closed on Monday mornings until noon. **Normal opening hours** are, however, Monday to Friday 8.30/9am to 5.30/6pm and Saturday 8.30/9am to 4/5pm, and many places open late on Thursday or Friday evenings. **Sunday** opening is becoming increasingly common, with many stores and shops in every city open between 11am/noon and 5pm. In addition, many supermarkets stay open until about 8pm every night and in the cities **night shops** – *avondwinkels* – stay open into the small hours or round the clock. Out in the sticks, on the other hand, Saturday afternoon can be a retail desert with just about everywhere closed.

Most **restaurants** open for dinner from about 6 or 7pm, and though many close as early as 9.30pm, a few stay open past 11pm. **Bars**, **cafés and coffeeshops** are either open all day from around 10am or don't open until about 5pm; all close at 1am during the week and 2am at weekends. **Nightclubs** generally function from 11pm to 4am during the week, though a few open every night, and some stay open until 5am at the weekend.

Phones

Almost all of the Netherlands has **mobile phone** (**cell phone**) coverage at GSM900/1800, the band common to the rest of Europe, Australia and New Zealand. Mobile/cell phones bought in North

---

PUBLIC HOLIDAYS

Public holidays (*Nationale feestdagen*) provide the perfect excuse to take to the streets. The most celebrated of them all is **King's Day** – *Koningsdag* – on April 27, which is celebrated everywhere but with particular abandon in Amsterdam.

January 1 New Year's Day
Good Friday (although many shops are open)
Easter Sunday
Easter Monday
April 27 King's Day
May 5 Liberation Day
Ascension Day (40 days after Easter)
Whit Sunday & Monday
December 25 & 26 Christmas
December 31 New Year's Eve

EMERGENCY NUMBER

In an emergency – police, fire or ambulance – call ☏ 112.

INTERNATIONAL CALLS

PHONING HOME FROM THE NETHERLANDS

To make an **international phone call from the Netherlands**, dial the appropriate international access code as below, then the number you require, omitting the initial zero where there is one.

Australia ☎0061
Canada ☎001
New Zealand ☎0064
Republic of Ireland ☎00353
South Africa ☎0027
UK ☎0044
USA ☎001

PHONING THE NETHERLANDS FROM ABROAD

To call a number in the Netherlands **from abroad**, dial the local international access code, then ☎31, followed by the number you require, omitting the initial zero where there is one. Note that numbers with certain prefixes – for example, ☎0800 and ☎0900 – cannot be dialled from outside the Netherlands; frustratingly, a number of tourist offices have telephone numbers with this type of prefix. Within the Netherlands, ☎0800 is toll free, ☎0900 premium-rated – a (Dutch) message before you're connected tells you how much you will be paying for the call.

America will need to be able to adjust to this GSM band. If you intend to use your mobile/cell phone in the Netherlands, note that call charges can be excruciating – particularly irritating is the supplementary charge you often have to pay on incoming calls – so check with your supplier before you depart. You may find it cheaper to buy a **Dutch SIM card**, though this can get complicated: many mobiles/cells will not permit you to swap SIM cards and the connection instructions for the replacement SIM card can be in Dutch only. If you overcome these problems, you can buy SIM cards at high-street phone companies, which offer myriad deals beginning at about €5 per SIM card. **Text messages**, on the other hand, are normally charged at ordinary or at least bearable rates – and with your existing SIM card in place. The Dutch **phone directory** is available (in Dutch) at ⓦ detele-foongids.nl.

Shopping

The Netherlands has a flourishing **retail sector** and each of its large towns and cities is jammed with department stores and international chains. More distinctively, the big cities play host to scores of **specialist shops** selling everything from condoms to beads. There are certain obvious Dutch goods – tulips, clogs and porcelain windmills to name the big three – but it's the Dutch flair for **design** that is the most striking feature, whether it's reflected in furniture or clothes. Most towns have a **market day**, usually midweek (and sometimes Saturday morning), and this is often the liveliest time to visit, particularly when the stalls fill the central square, the *markt*.

Smoking

In 2008, **smoking tobacco** was prohibited inside all public buildings, including train and bus stations, as well as in restaurants, clubs, bars and cafés. It was also banned in (dope-smoking) coffeeshops – which created some rather odd situations. Since then, there has been some zigging and zagging but in 2013 the Dutch parliament confirmed a total ban in the hospitality sector, though there are still outside smoking areas on train station platforms – and of course you can still smoke on the street. One in four Netherlanders continues to puff away.

Time zones

The Netherlands is on **Central European Time** (**CET**) – one hour ahead of Greenwich Mean Time, six hours ahead of US Eastern Standard Time, nine hours ahead of US Pacific Standard Time, nine hours behind Australian Eastern Standard Time and eleven hours behind New Zealand. There are,

CLOGS

You'll see **clogs** – or *klompen* – on sale in all the main tourist centres, usually brightly painted and ready for the nearest mantelpiece or even wall. They are not typical: about three million wooden clogs are made in the Netherlands every year and the unpainted variety are the chosen footwear of thousands of Dutch workmen, who swear they are safe and sound – apparently they pass all European safety standards with flying colours.

however, minor variations during the changeover periods involved in **daylight saving**. The Netherlands operates daylight saving time, moving clocks forward one hour in the spring and one hour back in the autumn.

Tipping

Tipping isn't quite as routine a matter as it is in the US or even in the UK. However, you are expected to leave something if you have enjoyed good service – up to around ten percent of the bill should suffice in most restaurants, while taxi drivers may expect a euro or two on top of the fare.

Tourist information

The **Netherlands' Board of Tourism and Conventions** (NBTC) operates an all-encompassing website (Ⓦholland.com), which highlights upcoming events and is particularly strong on practical information. It also publishes a wide range of brochures and guides. Once in the Netherlands, almost every place you visit will have a **tourist office**. Until recently, these were all known by the acronym **VVV** (pronounced *fay-fay-fay*), with a distinctive triangular logo, but with privatisation the VVV is now just one brand of tourist office with many others now called **TIP** (Tourist Information Points). Whatever the branding, staff are nearly always enthusiastic and helpful, and speak excellent English. In addition to handing out basic maps (usually for free) and English-language information on the main sights, many tourist offices keep lists of local accommodation, which they can book for a small fee. Most tourist offices sell **province guides** listing every type of accommodation, from plush hotels to campsites, albeit almost always in Dutch. However, establishments must pay for inclusion, so the listings are not comprehensive.

Travellers with disabilities

Despite its general social progressiveness, the Netherlands is only just getting to grips with the requirements of people with **mobility problems**. In Amsterdam and most of the other major cities, the most obvious difficulty you'll face is in negotiating the cobbled streets and narrow, often broken pavements of the older districts, where the key sights are often located. Similarly, provision for people with disabilities on the country's urban **public transport** is only average, although improving – many new buses, for instance, are wheelchair-accessible.

Practically all **public buildings**, including museums, theatres, cinemas, concert halls and hotels, are obliged to provide access, and do. Places that have been certified wheelchair-accessible now bear the **International Accessibility Symbol** (IAS). If you're planning to use the **Dutch train network** and would like assistance on the platform, phone the Bureau Assistentieverlening Gehandicapten (Disabled Assistance Office; daily 7am–11pm) on ☎030 235 7822 at least 24 hours before your train departs, and there will be someone to help you at the station. NS, the main train company, publishes information about train travel for people with disabilities at Ⓦns.nl and in various leaflets, stocked at main stations.

Amsterdam

THE SINGEL CANAL

1

Amsterdam

With every justification, AMSTERDAM is one of Europe's top short-break destinations. It's a compact, instantly likeable city that's appealing to look at and pleasant to walk around. An intriguing mix of the parochial and the international, it has a welcoming attitude towards visitors and a uniquely youthful orientation, shaped by the liberal counter-culture that took hold in the 1960s. Also engaging are the buzz of its open-air summer events and the intimacy of its clubs and bars, not to mention the Dutch facility with languages: just about everyone you meet in Amsterdam will be able to speak near-perfect English, on top of their own native Dutch and often French and German too.

Amsterdam has three world-famous sights, the **Anne Frank Huis**, the **Van Gogh Museum** and the **Rijksmuseum**, with its wonderful collection of Rembrandt paintings. In addition, there is a slew of lesser-known attractions, from the Resistance Museum through to the Royal Palace on Dam square, though for many visitors the city's **canals** are its main draw – take a cruise or a stroll around the **Grachtengordel** and you'll see why. Beyond the sights, Amsterdam also boasts an unparalleled selection of drinking places, be it a traditional, bare-floored **brown café** or one of the city's many designer bars and grand cafés. The city's **nightlife** and **cultural events** have a similarly innovative edge, with offerings that are at the forefront of contemporary European film, dance, drama and music. In addition, Amsterdam boasts one of the world's leading classical **orchestras**, a platoon of great **clubs** and one of Europe's liveliest and largest **gay scenes**.

The Old Centre

The **Old Centre** was where Amsterdam began, starting out as a fishing village at the mouth of the River Amstel and then, after the river was dammed in about 1270, flourishing as a trading centre. Thereafter, the city developed in stages, each of which was marked by the digging of new canals and, after a particularly severe fire in 1452, by the abandonment of timber for stone and brick as the main building materials. Today, it's the handsome stone and brick buildings of subsequent centuries, especially the seventeenth, which provide the Old Centre with most of its architectural highlights.

Strolling across the bridge from **Centraal Station** brings you onto **Damrak**, the spine of the Old Centre and the thoroughfare that once divided the **Oude Zijde** (Old Side) of the medieval city to the east from the smaller **Nieuwe Zijde** (New Side) to the west. Damrak culminates in **Dam square**, flanked by two of Amsterdam's most impressive

THE CITIZEN'S HALL AT THE KONINKLIJK PALEIS

Highlights

❶ The Koninklijk Paleis See Amsterdam in its full Golden Age glory at the Royal Palace, which began life as the city's Stadhuis (Town Hall). **See p.53**

❷ Grachtengordel Amsterdam's "girdle" of canals is the city at its most beautiful. **See p.59**

❸ Anne Frank Huis A poignant memorial to the Holocaust, this is Amsterdam's most visited sight by a country mile. **See p.61**

❹ Museum Willet-Holthuysen Amsterdam's merchant class lived in style and comfort – as the interior of this opulent canal house reveals. **See p.67**

❺ Hortus Botanicus Amsterdam's botanical gardens offer a welcome splash of tropical greenery. **See p.71**

❻ De Hollandsche Schouwburg Of the several memorials to the Jews of Amsterdam, this is perhaps the most moving. **See p.72**

❼ Rijksmuseum World-beating collection of Dutch paintings from the Golden Age including Rembrandt's superb *Night Watch*. **See p.75**

❽ Van Gogh Museum The world's largest collection of van Gogh's paintings, shown to fine advantage and full effect. **See p.77**

HIGHLIGHTS ARE MARKED ON THE MAP ON PP.48–49

1

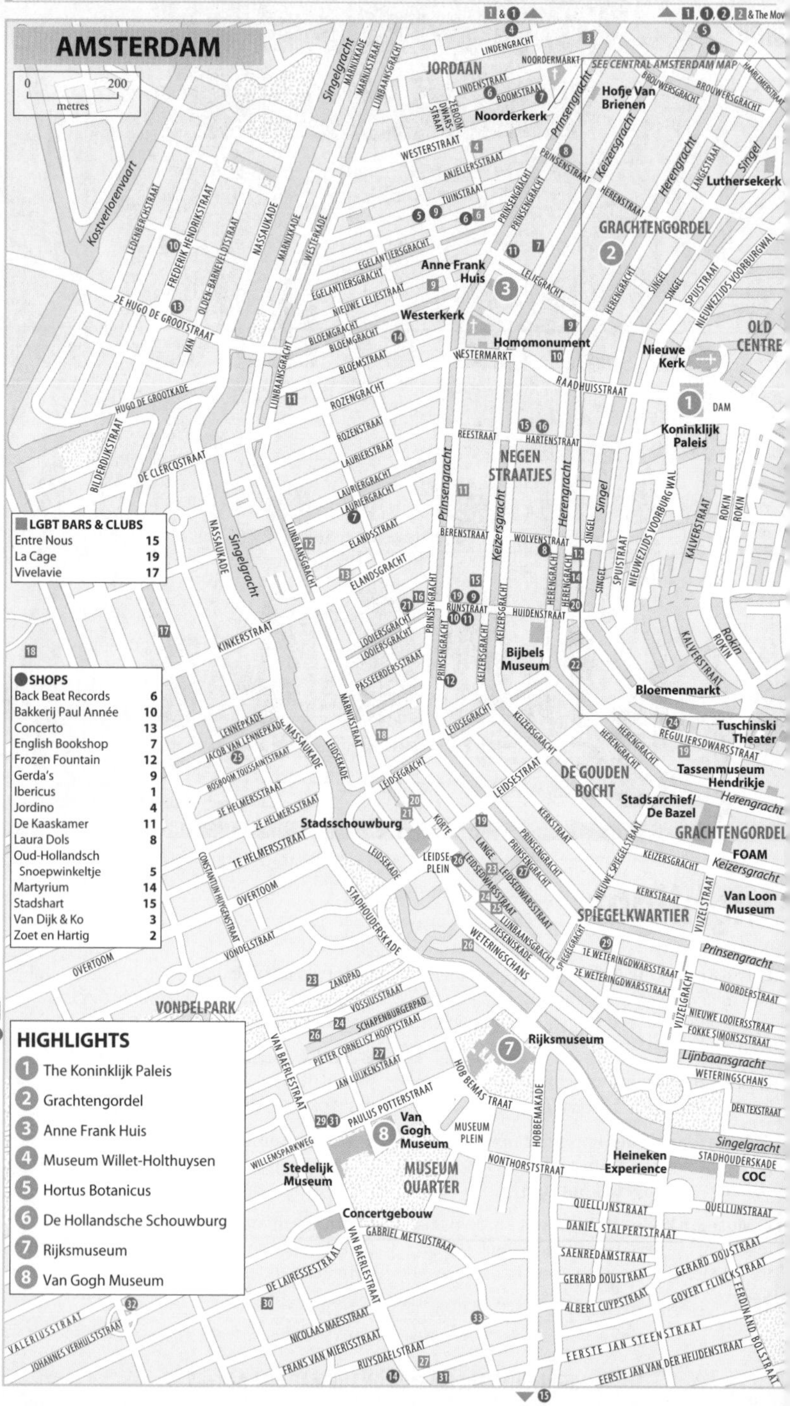

AMSTERDAM
0 200 metres
SEE CENTRAL AMSTERDAM MAP
LGBT BARS & CLUBS
Entre Nous 15
La Cage 19
Vivelavie 17
SHOPS
Back Beat Records 6
Bakkerij Paul Année 10
Concerto 13
English Bookshop 7
Frozen Fountain 12
Gerda's 9
Ibericus 1
Jordino 4
De Kaaskamer 11
Laura Dols 8
Oud-Hollandsch Snoepwinkeltje 5
Martyrium 14
Stadshart 15
Van Dijk & Ko 3
Zoet en Hartig 2
HIGHLIGHTS
1 The Koninklijk Paleis
2 Grachtengordel
3 Anne Frank Huis
4 Museum Willet-Holthuysen
5 Hortus Botanicus
6 De Hollandsche Schouwburg
7 Rijksmuseum
8 Van Gogh Museum
JORDAAN
Noorderkerk
Hofje Van Brienen
Luthersekerk
GRACHTENGORDEL
Anne Frank Huis
Westerkerk
Homomonument
Nieuwe Kerk
OLD CENTRE
DAM
Koninklijk Paleis
NEGEN STRAATJES
Bijbels Museum
Bloemenmarkt
Tuschinski Theater
Tassenmuseum Hendrikje
DE GOUDEN BOCHT
Stadsarchief/ De Bazel
FOAM
Van Loon Museum
SPIEGELKWARTIER
Stadsschouwburg
LEIDSEPLEIN
VONDELPARK
Rijksmuseum
Van Gogh Museum
MUSEUM PLEIN
Stedelijk Museum
MUSEUM QUARTER
Heineken Experience
COC
Concertgebouw
Prinsengracht
Keizersgracht
Herengracht
Singel
Singelgracht
Lijnbaansgracht
Kostverlorenvaart
Rokin

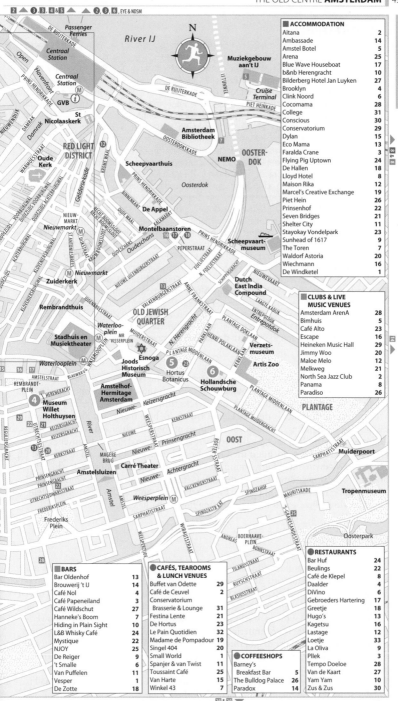

ACCOMMODATION

Aitana	2
Ambassade	14
Amstel Botel	5
Arena	25
Blue Wave Houseboat	17
b&b Herengracht	10
Bilderberg Hotel Jan Luyken	27
Brooklyn	4
Clink Noord	6
Cocomama	28
College	31
Conscious	30
Conservatorium	29
Dylan	15
Eco Mama	13
Faralda Crane	3
Flying Pig Uptown	24
De Hallen	18
Lloyd Hotel	8
Maison Rika	12
Marcel's Creative Exchange	19
Piet Hein	26
Prinsenhof	22
Seven Bridges	21
Shelter City	11
Stayokay Vondelpark	23
Sunhead of 1617	9
The Toren	7
Waldorf Astoria	20
Wiechmann	16
De Windketel	1

CLUBS & LIVE MUSIC VENUES

Amsterdam ArenA	28
Bimhuis	5
Café Alto	23
Escape	16
Heineken Music Hall	29
Jimmy Woo	20
Maloe Melo	12
Melkweg	21
North Sea Jazz Club	2
Panama	8
Paradiso	26

BARS

Bar Oldenhof	13
Brouwerij 't IJ	14
Café Nol	4
Café Papeneiland	3
Café Wildschut	27
Hanneke's Boom	7
Hiding in Plain Sight	10
L&B Whisky Café	24
Mystique	22
NJOY	25
De Reiger	9
't Smalle	6
Van Puffelen	11
Vesper	1
De Zotte	18

CAFÉS, TEAROOMS & LUNCH VENUES

Buffet van Odette	29
Café de Ceuvel	2
Conservatorium Brasserie & Lounge	31
Festina Lente	21
De Hortus	23
Le Pain Quotidien	32
Madame de Pompadour	19
Singel 404	20
Small World	1
Spanjer & van Twist	11
Toussaint Café	25
Van Harte	15
Winkel 43	7

COFFEESHOPS

Barney's Breakfast Bar	5
The Bulldog Palace	26
Paradox	14

RESTAURANTS

Bar Huf	24
Beulings	22
Café de Klepel	8
Daalder	4
DiVino	6
Gebroeders Hartering	17
Greetje	18
Hugo's	13
Kagetsu	16
Lastage	12
Loetje	33
La Oliva	9
Pllek	3
Tempo Doeloe	28
Van de Kaart	27
Yam Yam	10
Zus & Zus	30

1

ORIENTATION

Amsterdam's layout is determined by its **canals**. The oldest part of the city is the **Old Centre**, an oval-shaped area dating from the thirteenth century and featuring a jumble of antique streets and narrow little canals. It's here that you'll find two of the city's most historically important buildings – the Koninklijk Paleis (Royal Palace) and the Oude Kerk – as well as the industrialized eroticism of the **Red Light District**. Encircling the Old Centre are the canals of the **Grachtengordel** – or "Girdle of Canals" – the Singel, followed by Herengracht, Keizersgracht and Prinsengracht, the last three dug in the seventeenth century as part of a planned expansion to create a uniquely elegant urban environment. This is Amsterdam at its prettiest and it is here that the city's upper bourgeoisie built their grand mansions, typified by tall, graceful, decorated gables, whose fine proportions are reflected in the olive-green waters below. The Grachtengordel is also home to the city's most famous sight, the **Anne Frank Huis**.

Beyond the Grachtengordel, the **Jordaan** to the west remains the traditional heart of working-class Amsterdam, although it has experienced a degree of gentrification: its maze of streets and narrow canals make it a pleasant area to wander. On the east side of the centre is the **old Jewish quarter**; since the German occupation of World War II, this area has changed more than any other – its population gone and landscape altered – but there are several poignant reminders of earlier times, most notably the first-rate **Jewish Historical Museum** and the Hollandsche Schouwburg. Beyond the southern boundary of the Grachtengordel lies **the Oud-Zuid**, a well-to-do residential area, its working-class equivalent, **De Pijp**, and the **Museum Quarter**, which holds three top-ranking museums: the **Rijksmuseum**, internationally famous for its Rembrandts, the **Van Gogh Museum**, with its peerless collection of van Goghs, and the **Stedelijk Museum** of modern and contemporary art. Together, these form a cultural prelude to the sprawling greenery of the nearby **Vondelpark**, Amsterdam's loveliest park. Finally, two resurgent areas of former dockland chip in with several attractions and a scramble of modern architecture, **Amsterdam Noord** on the far side of the River IJ from the city, and the **eastern docklands** stretching east from Centraal Station.

buildings, the Koninklijk Paleis (Royal Palace) and the Nieuwe Kerk. From here, it's a brief ramble south to both the **Spui**, one of the city's most engaging open spaces, and the first-rate **Amsterdam Museum**, which tracks through the city's eventful history.

To the east of Damrak is the **Red Light District**. It's here that you'll find many of the district's finest buildings, though the seediness of the tentacular red-light zone tends to dull their charms. That said, be sure to spare time for two delightful churches – the Ons' Lieve Heer Op Solder and the Oude Kerk. Just beyond the reach of the Red Light District is **Nieuwmarkt**, a fairly mundane start to the **Kloveniersburgwal**, which forms one of the most beguiling parts of the Old Centre, with a medley of handsome old houses lining the prettiest of canals. From here, it's a short walk west to **Muntplein**, a busy junction where you'll find the floating flower market.

Centraal Station

Stationsplein

With its high gables and cheerful brickwork, the neo-Renaissance **Centraal Station** is an imposing prelude to the city. At the time of its construction in the 1880s, it aroused much controversy because it effectively separated the centre from the River IJ, source of the city's wealth, for the first time in Amsterdam's long history. There was controversy about the choice of architect too: the man selected, **Pierre Cuypers**, was Catholic, and in powerful Protestant circles there were mutterings about the vanity of his designs (he had recently completed the Rijksmuseum) and their unsuitability for Amsterdam. In the event, the station was built to Cuypers' design, but it was to be his last major commission; thereafter he spent most of his time building parish churches. Whatever you think about the building it's certainly a nice place to arrive: its grand arches and cavernous main hall have a suitable sense of occasion, and from here all of the city lies before you.

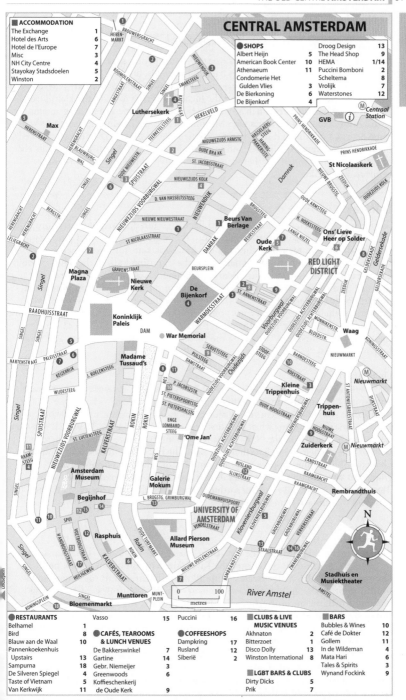

CENTRAL AMSTERDAM

1

St Nicolaaskerk

Prins Hendrikkade 73 • Mon & Sat noon–3pm, Tues–Fri 11am–4pm • Free • ⓦ nicolaas-parochie.nl

Across the water from Stationsplein rise the twin towers and dome of **St Nicolaaskerk**, the city's foremost Catholic church, dedicated to the patron saint of sailors – and of Amsterdam. Like the station, it dates back to the 1880s, but here the cavernous interior holds some pretty dire religious murals, mawkish concoctions only partly relieved by swathes of coloured brickwork. Above the high altar is the crown of the Habsburg Emperor Maximilian, very much a symbol of the city and one you'll see again and again. Amsterdam had close ties with Maximilian – in the late fifteenth century he came here as a pilgrim and stayed on to recover from an illness. The burghers funded many of his military expeditions, and in return he let the city use his crown in its coat of arms, a practice which – rather surprisingly – survived the seventeenth-century revolt against Spain.

Damrak

A wide but unenticing avenue lined with tacky restaurants and souvenir shops, **Damrak** slices south from Stationsplein into the heart of the city, first passing an inner harbour crammed with the bobbing canal boats of Amsterdam's considerable tourist industry. Just beyond the harbour is the imposing bulk of the **Beurs**, the old Stock Exchange – known as the "Beurs van Berlage" – a seminal work designed at the turn of the last century by the leading light of the Dutch Modern movement, **Hendrik Petrus Berlage** (1856–1934). It's used for concerts and occasional exhibitions these days, so you can't often get in to see the graceful exposed ironwork and shallow-arched arcades of the main hall, but you can pop into its café, round the corner on Beursplein, to admire the tiled scenes of the past, present and future by Jan Toorop.

De Bijenkorf

Dam 1 • Mon & Sun 11am–8pm, Tues & Wed 10am–8pm, Thurs & Fri 10am–9pm, Sat 9.30am–8pm ⓣ 0800 0818, ⓦ debijenkorf.nl

Something of a city institution, **De Bijenkorf** – literally "beehive" – is a large department store that stretches south along Damrak. Curiously, it posed all sorts of problems for the Germans when they first occupied the city in World War II. The store was a Jewish concern, so the Nazis didn't really want their troops shopping here, but it was just too popular to implement a total ban. The bizarre solution was to prohibit German soldiers from shopping on the ground floor, where the store's Jewish employees were concentrated, as they always had been, in the luxury goods section. These days it's a good all-round department store, with the usual floors of designer-wear and well-known brands.

The Dam

Situated at the very heart of the city, **Dam** square – or **the Dam** – gave Amsterdam its name: in the thirteenth century the River Amstel was dammed here, hence "Amstelredam". Originally, boats could sail down Damrak into the square and unload right in the middle of the settlement, which soon prospered by trading herrings for Baltic grain. In the early fifteenth century, the building of Amsterdam's principal church, the Nieuwe Kerk, and thereafter the town hall (now the Royal Palace), formally marked the Dam as Amsterdam's centre, but since World War II it has lost much of its dignity. Today it's open and airy but somehow rather desultory, despite – or perhaps partly because of – the presence of the main municipal **war memorial**, a prominent stone tusk adorned by bleak, suffering figures and decorated with the coats of arms of each of the Netherlands' provinces (plus the ex-colony of Indonesia).

The Koninklijk Paleis

Dam • April–Sept daily 10am–5pm; Oct–March daily 11am–5pm; closed on state occasions – check website • €10 • ☎ 020 620 4060,
ⓦ paleisamsterdam.nl

Dominating Dam square is the sturdy bulk of the **Koninklijk Paleis** (Royal Palace),
although the title is deceptive, given that this vast sandstone structure was built as the city's
Stadhuis (Town Hall), and only had its first royal occupant when Louis Bonaparte moved
in during the French occupation (1795–1813). The **exterior** of the palace is very much to
the allegorical point: twin tympana a depict Amsterdam as a port and trading centre, the
one at the front presided over by a female representation of the city with Neptune and a
veritable herd of unicorns at her feet. Above these tympana are representations of the
values that the city council espoused – at the front, Prudence, Justice and Peace, to the rear
Temperance and Vigilance on either side of a muscular, globe-bearing Atlas. One
deliberate precaution, however, was the omission of a central doorway – just in case the
mob turned nasty (as it was wont to do) and stormed the place.

The interior

The palace **interior** proclaims the pride and confidence of Amsterdam's Golden Age,
principally in its lavish **Citizen's Hall**, an extraordinarily handsome, arcaded marble
chamber. Here, the enthroned figure of Amsterdam looks down on the earth and the
heavens, which are laid out before her in three circular, inlaid marble maps, one each of
the eastern and western hemispheres, the other of the northern sky. Other allegorical
figures ram home the municipal point: flanking "Amsterdam" to the left and right are
Wisdom and Strength, while the reliefs to either side of the central group represent
good governance – on the left is the demigod Amphion, who plays his lyre to persuade

---

THE KONINKLIJK PALEIS: STADHUIS (TOWN HALL) TO ROYAL PALACE

At the time of the **Stadhuis**'s construction in the mid-seventeenth century, **Amsterdam**
was at the height of its powers. The city was pre-eminent among Dutch towns, and the
council craved a residence that proclaimed their extraordinary success. They opted for a
startlingly progressive design by **Jacob van Campen**, who proposed a Dutch interpretation
of the classical principles revived in Renaissance Italy. Initially, there was opposition to the
plan from the council's Calvinist minority, who pointed out that the proposed building
would dwarf the neighbouring Nieuwe Kerk (see p.54). However, the Calvinists fell into line
after being promised a new church spire (which was never built), and work started in 1648
on what was then the largest town hall in Europe. Supported by no fewer than 13,659
wooden piles driven into the Dam's sandy soil – a number every Dutch schoolchild
remembers by adding a "1" and a "9" to the number of days in the year – the new building
was called "The world's Eighth Wonder/With so much stone raised high and so much timber
under", by the poet Constantijn Huygens.

The Stadhuis received its **royal designation** in 1808, when **Louis Bonaparte**, who had
recently been installed as "king of Holland" by his brother Napoleon, commandeered it as his
residence. Louis took his new job seriously enough, but an initial gaffe set the scene when he
declared himself the "Konijn van 'Olland" (Rabbit of 'Olland) rather than the "Koning van
Holland" (King of Holland). Lonely and unpopular, Louis was deposed by his brother in 1810
and left the country, leaving the Netherlands to the despotic mercies of Napoleon himself.
After Napoleon's defeat, possession of the palace became something of a sore point between
the Dutch royal family and the city: an initial compromise allowed the royals to keep the
building provided they stayed here for part of the year. However, the Oranges failed to do this,
which irritated many Amsterdammers, and in the 1930s the royal family offered the city fifteen
million guilders to build a new city hall. Ownership of the Stadhuis passed to the state (as
distinct from the city) in return for a new agreement allowing the Oranges to use the Palace
whenever they wanted. A new town hall was finally built in the 1980s on Waterlooplein (see
p.70) and nowadays the Dutch royals live down in the Huis ten Bosch, near Den Haag, and only
use the Royal Palace for state occasions (of which there are many).

1

the stones to pile themselves up into a wall, and to the right Mercury attempts to lull Argos to sleep, stressing the need to be vigilant. All this is part of a good-natured and witty symbolism that pervades the hall and its surrounding galleries: in the top left gallery, cocks fight above the entrance for the Commissioner of Petty Affairs, while in the gallery to the right of the main hall, above the door of the Bankruptcy Chamber, a medallion shows the Fall of Icarus below marble carvings depicting hungry rats scurrying around an empty money chest and nibbling at unpaid bills.

High Court of Justice

The decorative whimsy fizzles out in the narrow and cramped **High Court of Justice** at the front of the building, close to the entrance. Inside this intimidating chamber, the judges sat on marble benches overseen by heavyweight representations of Righteousness, Wisdom, Mercy and so forth as they passed judgement on the hapless criminal in front of them; even worse, the crowd on Dam square could view the proceedings through barred windows, almost always baying for blood. They usually went home contented; as soon as the judges had passed the death sentence, the condemned were whisked up to the wooden scaffold attached to the front of the building and promptly dispatched.

The Nieuwe Kerk

Dam • Hours and admission vary with the exhibition, but usually daily 10am–5pm • €8–15 • ☎ 020 638 6909, ⓦ nieuwekerk.nl

Vying for importance with the Royal Palace is the **Nieuwe Kerk** (New Church), which – despite its name – is an early fifteenth-century structure built in a late flourish of the Gothic style, with a forest of pinnacles and high, slender gables. Nowadays it's deconsecrated and used for temporary exhibitions, but its hangar-like interior is worth investigating for its decorative details, principally the seventeenth-century tomb of Dutch naval hero **Admiral Michiel de Ruyter**, complete with trumpeting angels, conch-blowing tritons and cherubs all in a tizzy. Ruyter trounced in succession the Spanish, the Swedes, the English and the French, and his rise from deck hand to Admiral-in-Chief is the stuff of national legend. The church is still used for state occasions: the coronations of queens Wilhelmina, Juliana and, in 1980, Beatrix, were all held here.

Rokin and Kalverstraat

Rokin picks up where Damrak leaves off, cutting south from Dam square in a wide sweep that follows the former course of the River Amstel. This was the business centre of the nineteenth-century city, and although it has lost much of its prestige it is still flanked by an attractive medley of architectural styles incorporating everything from grandiose nineteenth-century mansions to more utilitarian modern buildings. Rokin culminates at the **Muntplein**, a dishevelled traffic junction overlooked by the sturdy, late medieval **Munttoren**, which was originally a strategic point in the old city wall. Later, the tower was adopted as the municipal mint – hence its name – and Hendrick de Keyser, in one of his last commissions, added a flashy spire in 1620. Running parallel to Rokin, pedestrianized **Kalverstraat** is a busy shopping street that has been a commercial centre since medieval times, when it was used as a calf market; today, it's home to many of the city's chain stores – you could be anywhere in Holland really.

The Allard Pierson Museum

Oude Turfmarkt 127 • Tues–Fri 10am–5pm, Sat & Sun 1–5pm • €10 • ☎ 020 525 2556, ⓦ allardpiersonmuseum.nl

The **Allard Pierson Museum** is a good, old-fashioned archeological museum in a solid Neoclassical building. The collection is spread over two floors and although it is not an

CLOCKWISE FROM TOP LEFT THE KONINKLIJK PALEIS (P.53); BLOEMENMARKT (P.56); CENTRAAL STATION (P.50); THE STEDELIJK MUSEUM (P.78) >

1

especially large museum, it covers a lot of ground. A particular highlight is the museum's Greek pottery, with fine examples of both the black- and red-figured wares produced in the sixth and fifth centuries BC. Look out also for the Roman sarcophagi, especially a marble whopper decorated with Dionysian scenes, several rare Etruscan funerary urns and a platoon of Egyptian mummies.

Bloemenmarkt

South side of the Singel between Muntplein and Koningsplein • Mon–Sat 9am–5.30pm & Sun 11am–5.30pm.

Popular with locals and tourists alike, the floating **Bloemenmarkt** (flower market) is one of the main suppliers of flowers to central Amsterdam, though its blooms and bulbs now share stall space with souvenir clogs, garden gnomes and Delftware. Come early for the pick of the flowery crop.

Spui

One of Amsterdam's most appealing streets, **Spui** begins as a narrow alley running west off the Rokin, but soon widens out into an amiable wedge-shaped square. Dotted with bookshops and popular café-bars, it's home to an innocuous-looking statue of a young boy, known as **'t Lieverdje** ("Little Darling" or "Lovable Scamp"), a gift to the city from a cigarette company in 1960. It was here in the mid-1960s, with the statue seen as a symbol of the addicted consumer, that the playful Sixties pressure group, the **Provos** (see box, p.330) organized some of their most successful *ludiek* ("pranks").

The Begijnhof

Spui • There are two entrances: a side entrance on Spui, and the main entrance, 100m north of Spui on Gedempte Begijnensloot • Daily 8am–5pm • Free • ☎ 020 622 1918, 🖰 begijnhofamsterdam.nl

Accessed via a fancy little gateway on the north side of Spui, the **Begijnhof** consists of a huddle of immaculately maintained old houses looking onto a central green – their backs turned firmly against the outside world. The Begijnhof was founded in the fourteenth century as a home for the *beguines* – members of a Catholic sisterhood living as nuns, but without vows and with the right of return to the secular world. The original medieval complex comprised a series of humble brick cottages, but these were mostly replaced by the larger, grander houses of today shortly after the Reformation, though the secretive, enclosed design survived. A couple of pre-Reformation buildings remain, including the **Houten Huys**, at no. 34, whose wooden facade, the oldest in Amsterdam, dates from 1477 – before the city forbade the construction of timber houses as an essential precaution against fire.

Engelse Kerk

Begijnhof • Free, but no admission except during church services on Sundays at 10.30am

The **Engelse Kerk** (English Reformed Church), beside the central green, is of medieval construction, but it was taken from the *begijns* and given to Amsterdam's English community during the Reformation. Plain and unadorned, the church is of interest for its carefully worked pulpit panels, several of which were designed by a youthful **Piet Mondriaan** (1872–1944), of De Stijl fame and fortune – although to see them you'll have to attend a church service on Sundays at 10.30am.

Begijnhofkapel

Begijnhof • Mon 1–6.30pm, Tues–Fri 9am–6.30pm, Sat & Sun 9am–6pm • Free

Amsterdam's *begijns* may have lost their original church, but in keeping with the terms of the *Alteratie* (the city's switch from Catholicism to Protestantism in 1578), they were allowed to celebrate Mass inconspicuously in the clandestine Catholic **Begijnhofkapel**, which they established in the house just opposite. It's still used today, a homely little place with some terribly sentimental religious paintings.

Amsterdam Museum

Kalverstraat 92 & Sint Luciënsteeg 27 • Daily 10am–5pm • €12 • Be sure to collect a museum map at reception • ☎ 020 5231 822, ⓦ amsterdammuseum.nl

Occupying the rambling seventeenth-century buildings of the former municipal orphanage, the **Amsterdam Museum** traces the city's development from its origins as an insignificant fishing village to its present incarnation as a major metropolis and trading centre. The first section provides an overview by means of a series of short films and a selection of prime artefacts. Thereafter, the museum gets rather more confusing as you negotiate its many levels and corridors. Broadly, the ground floor concentrates on the "Golden Age"; the first floor focuses on the eighteenth and nineteenth centuries; and the second floor deals with the modern era, from 1940 onwards. This last is perhaps the most intriguing section, covering a wide range of topics, notably the German occupation of World War II.

Schuttersgalerij

Gedempte Begijnensloot • Daily 10am–5pm • Free • ☎ 020 5231 822, ⓦ amsterdammuseum.nl

An adjunct to the Amsterdam Museum, the **Schuttersgalerij** – the Civic Guard Gallery – is part glassed-in passageway, part art gallery. Traditionally, it was hung with huge group portraits of the **Amsterdam militia**, but nowadays the paintings are regularly rotated and feature more modern groups – ballet choreographers and Ajax football stars for example.

The Red Light District

The whole area to the east of Damrak, between Warmoesstraat, Nieuwmarkt and Damstraat, is the **Red Light District**, known locally as "De Walletjes" (Small Walls) on account of the series of low brick walls that contains its canals. By and large, the area is pretty seedy, though the legalized prostitution here has long been one of the city's most distinctive and popular draws. It wasn't always so: the handsome facades of **Oudezijds Voorburgwal** in particular recall ritzier days, when this was one of the wealthiest parts of the city, richly earning its nickname, the "Velvet Canal".

Nowadays, both Oudezijds Voorburgwal and its twin **Oudezijds Achterburgwal**, along with their narrow connecting passages, are thronged with "**window brothels**", and at busy times the on-street haggling over the price of various sex acts is drowned out by a surprisingly festive atmosphere – entire families grinning more or less amiably at the women in the windows or discussing the specifications (and feasibility) of the sex toys in the shops. In recent years, the city council has made determined efforts to sanitize the area, so the hang-around junkies, dealers and hawkers who once infested it are far less prominent, but there's still an uneasy undertow that might put you off dawdling here. And don't even think about taking a picture of a window brothel unless you're prepared for some major grief from the camera-shy prostitutes, or their pimps. Window brothels and sex shops aside, the district does contain two prime attractions, the medieval **Oude Kerk** and the clandestine Catholic church of **Ons' Lieve Heer Op Solder**.

Warmoesstraat

Soliciting hasn't always been the principal activity on sleazy **Warmoesstraat**. It was once one of the city's most fashionable streets, home to Holland's foremost poet, **Joost van den Vondel** (1587–1679), who ran his hosiery business from no. 110 in between writing and hobnobbing with the Amsterdam elite – a **plaque** on the Art Nouveau

1

building that now stands here marks the spot. Vondel is a kind of Dutch Shakespeare: his *Gijsbrecht van Amstel*, a celebration of Amsterdam during its Golden Age, is one of the classics of Dutch literature, and he wrote regular, if ponderous, official verses, including well over a thousand lines on the inauguration of the new town hall. He had more than his share of hard luck too. His son frittered away the modest family fortune and Vondel lived out his last few years as doorkeeper of a pawn shop, dying of hypothermia at what was then the remarkable age of 92.

The Oude Kerk

Oudekerksplein · Mon–Sat 10am–6pm, Sun 1–5pm · €10 · ☎ 020 625 8284, ⓦ oudekerk.nl

In the midst of the Red Light District, the Gothic **Oude Kerk** (Old Church) is the city's most appealing church. There's been a church on this site since the middle of the thirteenth century, but most of the present building dates from a century later, funded by the pilgrims who came here in their hundreds following a widely publicized **miracle**. The story goes that in 1345 a dying man regurgitated the Host he had received here at Communion and when it was thrown on the fire afterwards, it did not burn. The un-burnable Host was placed in a chest and eventually installed here: although the Host itself disappeared during the Reformation, thousands of the faithful still come to take part in the annual commemorative **Stille Omgang** in mid-March, a silent nocturnal procession terminating at the Oude Kerk. Inside the church, you can see the unadorned **memorial tablet** of Rembrandt's first wife, Saskia van Uylenburgh, beneath the smaller of the organs, and, beside the ambulatory, three beautiful sixteenth-century **stained-glass windows**. They depict, from left to right, the Annunciation, the Adoration of the Shepherds and the Assumption of the Virgin. The church is also regularly used for art displays and concerts.

Ons' Lieve Heer Op Solder

Oudezijds Voorburgwal 40 · Mon–Sat 10am–5pm, Sun 1–5pm · €9 · ☎ 020 624 6604, ⓦ opsolder.nl

The northern reaches of **Oudezijds Voorburgwal** are home to the **Ons' Lieve Heer Op Solder** (Our Dear Lord in the Attic), which was momentarily the city's principal Catholic place of worship and is now one of Amsterdam's most enjoyable museums. The church dates from the early seventeenth century when, with the Protestants firmly in control, the city's Catholics were only allowed to practise their faith in private – such as here in this clandestine church (*schuilkerk*), which occupies the loft of an old merchant's house. The church's narrow nave has been skilfully shoehorned into the available space and, flanked by elegant balconies, there's just enough room for an ornately carved organ at one end and a mock-marble high altar, decorated with Jacob de Wit's mawkish *Baptism of Christ*, at the other. The rest of the house is similarly untouched, its original furnishings reminiscent of interiors by Vermeer or de Hooch.

The Zeedijk

Curving round the northern edge of the Red Light District is the **Zeedijk**, which was originally just that – a dyke to hold back the sea. A couple of decades ago this narrow thoroughfare was the haunt of drug addicts and very much a no-go area at night, but it's been spruced up and now forms a lively route from Stationsplein through to Nieuwmarkt as well as being the main hub of Amsterdam's pint-sized Chinatown. Its seaward end is home to a couple of the oldest bars in the city and the jazz trumpeter **Chet Baker** famously breathed his last here in 1988, when he either fell or threw himself out of the window of the *Prins Hendrik Hotel* – an event remembered by an evocative plaque of the man in full blow.

Nieuwmarkt

Just clear of the Red Light District, **Nieuwmarkt** was long one of the city's most important market squares and the place where Gentiles and Jews from the nearby

1

Jewish Quarter – just southeast along St Antoniebreestraat – traded. All that came to a traumatic end during World War II, when the Germans cordoned off the Nieuwmarkt with barbed wire and turned it into a holding pen. After the war, the square's old exuberance never quite returned and these days its focus is the sprawling multi-turreted **Waag**, dating from the 1480s and with a chequered history. Built as one of Amsterdam's fortified gates, the city's expansion soon made it obsolete and the ground floor was turned into a municipal weighing-house (*waag*), with the rooms upstairs taken over by the surgeons' guild. It was here that the surgeons held lectures on anatomy and public dissections, the inspiration for Rembrandt's *Anatomy Lesson of Dr Tulp*, displayed in the Mauritshuis collection in Den Haag (see p.153). Abandoned by the surgeons and the weigh-masters in the nineteenth century, the building eventually fell into disuse, until being renovated to house a café-bar and restaurant, *In de Waag*.

Kloveniersburgwal

With Nieuwmarkt at its head, **Kloveniersburgwal** is one of the city's most charming canals, a long, dead-straight waterway framed by a string of old and dignified facades. One of the most imposing, the **Trippenhuis**, at no. 29, is a huge overblown mansion complete with Corinthian pilasters and a grand frieze built for the Trip family in 1662. Almost directly opposite, on the west bank of the canal, the **Kleine Trippenhuis**, at no. 26, is, by contrast, one of the narrowest houses in Amsterdam, albeit with a warmly carved facade. Legend asserts that Mr Trip's coachman was so taken aback by the size of the new family mansion that he exclaimed he would be happy with a home no wider than the Trips' front door – which is exactly what he got. His reaction to his new lodgings is not recorded.

The Zuiderkerk

Zuiderkerkhof 72 • Open for special events and concerts only • ☎ 020 308 0399, ⓦ zuiderkerkamsterdam.nl

Dating from 1614, the **Zuiderkerk** was the first Amsterdam church to be built specifically for the Protestants. It was designed by the prolific architect and sculptor **Hendrick de Keyser**, whose distinctive and very popular style extrapolated elements of traditional Flemish design with fanciful detail and frilly towers added wherever possible. The basic design of the Zuiderkerk is firmly Gothic, but the soaring **Zuidertoren** (tower) is a fine illustration of de Keyser's work with balconies and balustrades, arches, urns and columns. The church was deconsecrated in the 1930s and today it's used for special events, concerts and conferences, which are the only times when you can actually get in.

The Grachtengordel

Medieval Amsterdam was enclosed by the **Singel**, part of the city's protective moat, but this is now just the first of five canals that reach right around the city centre, extending anticlockwise from Brouwersgracht to the River Amstel in a "girdle of canals" or **Grachtengordel**. This is without doubt the most charming part of the city, its lattice of olive-green waterways and dinky humpback bridges overlooked by street upon street of handsome seventeenth-century canal houses, almost invariably undisturbed by later development. It's a subtle cityscape – full of surprises, with a bizarre carving here, an unusual facade there – but architectural peccadilloes aside, it is the district's overall atmosphere that appeals rather than any specific sight, with the notable exception of the **Anne Frank Huis**. There's no obvious walking route around the Grachtengordel, and indeed you may well prefer to wander as the mood takes you, but the description we've

1

THE CANALS OF THE GRACHTENGORDEL

The three main **canals of the Grachtengordel** – Herengracht, Keizersgracht and Prinsengracht – were dug in the seventeenth century as part of a comprehensive plan to extend the boundaries of a city no longer able to accommodate its burgeoning population. Increasing the area of the city from two to seven square kilometres was a monumental task, and the conditions imposed by the council were strict: **Herengracht**, **Keizersgracht** and **Prinsengracht** were set aside for the residences and businesses of the richer and more influential Amsterdam merchants, while the radial cross-streets were reserved for more modest artisans' homes; meanwhile, immigrants, newly arrived to cash in on Amsterdam's booming economy, were assigned, albeit informally, the Jodenhoek (see p.68) and the Jordaan (see p.68). Of the three main canals, **Herengracht**, the "Gentlemen's Canal", was the first to be dug, followed by the **Keizersgracht**, the "Emperor's Canal", named after the Holy Roman Emperor and fifteenth-century patron of the city, Maximilian. Further out still, the **Prinsengracht**, the "Princes' Canal", was named in honour of the princes of the House of Orange.

In the Grachtengordel, everyone, even the wealthiest merchant, had to comply with a set of detailed **planning regulations**. In particular, the council prescribed the size of each building plot – the frontage was set at thirty feet, the depth two hundred – and although there was a degree of tinkering, the end result was the loose conformity you can see today: tall, narrow residences, whose individualism is mainly restricted to the stylistic permutations among the gables. The earliest extant **gables**, dating from the early seventeenth century, are **crow-stepped** but these were largely superseded from the 1650s onwards by **neck gables** and **bell gables**. Some are embellished, others aren't, many have decorative cornices, and the fanciest, which almost invariably date from the eighteenth century, sport full-scale balustrades. The plainest gables are those of former **warehouses**, where the deep-arched and shuttered windows line up on either side of loft doors, which were once used for loading and unloading goods, winched by pulley from the street down below. Indeed, outside **pulleys** remain a common feature of houses and warehouses alike, and are often still in use as the easiest way of moving furniture into the city's myriad apartments.

given below goes from north to south, taking in all the highlights on the way. On all three of the main canals – **Herengracht**, **Keizersgracht** and **Prinsengracht** – street numbers begin in the north and increase as you go south.

Brouwersgracht

Running east to west along the northern edge of the three main canals is leafy **Brouwersgracht**, one of the most picturesque waterways in the city. In the seventeenth century, Brouwersgracht lay at the edge of Amsterdam's great harbour. This was where ships returning from the East unloaded their silks and spices, and as one of the major arteries linking the open sea with the city centre it was lined with storage depots and warehouses. Breweries flourished here too, capitalizing on their ready access to shipments of fresh water. Today, the harbour bustle has moved elsewhere, and the **warehouses**, with their distinctive spout-neck gables and shuttered windows, formerly used for the delivery and dispatch of goods by pulley from the canal below, have been converted into chi-chi apartments. There are handsome merchants' houses here as well, plus moored houseboats and a string of quaint little swing bridges.

The Noordermarkt

Flea market Mon 9am–1pm; Boerenmarkt Sat 9am–4pm • ⓦ boerenmarktamsterdam.nl, ⓦ jordaanmarkten.nl/noordermarkt.html

Dominated by its hulking church, the **Noordermarkt** is a large if somewhat inconclusive square located just south of Brouwersgracht, along the west side of

Prinsengracht. The square comes to life on market days: there's a general household goods and **flea market** on Mondays, plus a popular farmers' market, the **Boerenmarkt**, on Saturdays. The latter is an especially lively affair with organic fruit and vegetables, freshly baked breads and a plethora of oils and spices for sale – plus general household and clothing stalls where the food stalls fizzle out.

The Noorderkerk

Noordermarkt • Mon 10.30am–12.30pm & Sat 11am–1pm • Free • ☎ 020 626 6436, ⓦ noorderkerk.org

Cramped and ungainly, the **Noorderkerk** was the architect Hendrick de Keyser's last creation and perhaps his least successful, finished two years after his death in 1623. Unsuccessful perhaps, but the building did represent a radical departure from the conventional church designs of the time, having a symmetrical Greek-cross floor plan, with four equally proportioned arms radiating out from a steepled centre. The design was an attempt to reformulate religious worship, making it more democratic with the congregation sitting on sets of wooden pews that face inward rather than to any altar - a symbolic break with the Catholic past. The pews are also overseen by the **pulpit**, a fancy affair with a large carved sounding board, from where Calvinist preachers would sermonize for several hours at a time.

Just in front of the church's west door is a **statue** of three figures bound to each other, a poignant tribute to the bloody Jordaanoproer riot of 1934, part of a successful campaign to stop the government cutting unemployment benefits during the Depression; the inscription reads: "The strongest chains are those of unity."

The Anne Frank Huis

Prinsengracht 263–267 • April–June & Sept–Oct daily 9am–9pm, Sat till 10pm; July & Aug daily 9am–10pm; Nov–March daily 9am–7pm, Sat till 9pm; closed Yom Kippur • €9, 10- to 17-year-olds €4.50, under-10s free • ☎ 020 556 7100, ⓦ annefrank.org • Tickets can be bought at reception or online, but try to visit early or late to avoid the crowds, which can be almost overwhelming • The bookshop sells Anne's *Diary* and related texts

In 1957, the Anne Frank Foundation set up the **Anne Frank Huis** in the premises on Prinsengracht where the young diarist and her family hid from the Germans during World War II (see box, p.62). Since the posthumous publication of her diaries, Anne Frank has become extraordinarily famous, in the first instance for recording the iniquities of the Holocaust, and latterly as a symbol of the fight against oppression in general and racism in particular.

A **visit** begins in the main body of the building with several well-chosen displays setting the historical scene. You then proceed through the premises of what was once the Frank business, beginning with the ground-floor warehouse and continuing with the old offices, before reaching a series of exhibits providing brief biographies of those who sought refuge here. Filmed interviews with some of the leading characters, including Anne's friend Hanneli Goslar and Otto Frank, fill out more of the background, and there are also displays on the persecution of the Jews – from arrest and deportation through to the concentration camps. Further sections are devoted to Anne as a writer/diarist; information on the Franks' Dutch helpers; and the importance of Anne's diary to other prisoners, most notably Nelson Mandela.

Ultimately, you arrive at the entrance to the **Secret Annexe**, or *achterhuis*, which was separated from the rest of the house by a **false bookcase**. The Secret Annexe was stripped of furniture long ago, but it still bears traces of its former occupants – such as the movie-star pin-ups in Anne's bedroom and the marks on the wall recording the children's heights. Anne Frank was only one of about 100,000 Dutch Jews who died during World War II, but this, her final home, provides one of the most enduring testaments to its horrors and, despite the number of visitors, most people find a visit very moving.

1

THE STORY OF ANNE FRANK

The story of **Anne Frank**, her family and friends is well known. Anne's father, **Otto Frank**, was a well-to-do Jewish businessman, who fled Germany in December 1933 after Hitler came to power, moving to Amsterdam, where he established a successful spice-trading business on the Prinsengracht. After the German occupation of the Netherlands, Otto felt – along with many other Jews – that he could avoid trouble by keeping his head down. However, by 1942 it was clear that this was not going to be possible: Amsterdam's Jews were isolated and conspicuous, being confined to certain parts of the city and forced to wear a yellow star, and roundups were increasingly common. In desperation, Otto Frank decided to move the family into the unused back rooms of their Prinsengracht premises, first asking some of his Dutch office staff if they would help him with the subterfuge – they bravely agreed.

The Franks went into hiding in July 1942, along with a Jewish business partner and his wife and son, the van Pels (renamed the van Daans in the *Diary*). Their new "home" was separated from the rest of the building by a **bookcase** that doubled as a door. As far as everyone else was concerned, they had fled to Switzerland. So began a two-year incarceration in the **achterhuis**, or Secret Annexe, and the two families were joined in November 1942 by a dentist friend, Fritz Pfeffer (the *Diary*'s Albert Dussel), bringing the number of occupants to eight. Otto's trusted office staff continued working in the front part of the building, regularly bringing supplies and news of the outside world. In her **diary** Anne Frank describes the **day-to-day lives** of the inhabitants of the annexe: the quarrels, frequent in such a claustrophobic environment, the celebrations of birthdays, or of a piece of good news from the Allied Front; and of her own, slightly unreal, growing up (some of which, it's been claimed, was later deleted by her father prior to publication).

In 1944, the atmosphere was optimistic; the Allies were clearly winning the war and liberation seemed within reach – but it wasn't to be. One day in the summer of that year, a Dutch collaborator betrayed the Franks and the Gestapo arrived and forced open the bookcase. The occupants of the secret annexe were arrested and dispatched to **Westerbork** – the transit camp in the north of the country where all Dutch Jews were processed before being moved to Belsen or Auschwitz. Of the eight who had lived in the annexe, only Otto Frank survived; Anne and her sister died of typhus within a short time of each other in **Belsen**, just one week before the German surrender. Remarkably, Anne's **diary** survived the raid, with one of the family's Dutch helpers handing it to Otto on his return from Auschwitz. In 1947, Otto decided to publish his daughter's diary and, since its appearance, the *Diary of a Young Girl* has been translated into over sixty languages and sold millions of copies worldwide.

The Westerkerk

Prinsengracht 281 • **Church** Mon–Fri 10am–3pm, plus April–Oct Sat 11am–3pm • Free • ☎ 020 624 7766, ⓦ westerkerk.nl • **Westertoren** (tower) April–Sept daily 10am–8pm, Oct daily 10am–6pm • €7.50 • ☎ 020 689 2565, ⓦ westertorenamsterdam.nl

Trapped in the *achterhuis*, Anne Frank liked to listen to the bells of the **Westerkerk** until they were taken away to be melted down for the German war effort. The church still dominates the district, its 85m tower, the **Westertoren** – without question Amsterdam's finest – soaring graciously above its surroundings. On its top perches the crown of the Emperor Maximilian, a constantly recurring symbol of Amsterdam and the finishing touch to what was only the second city church to be built expressly for the Protestants. The church was designed by **Hendrick de Keyser** and completed ten years after his death in 1631. Its construction was part of the general enlargement of the city, but whereas the exterior is all studied elegance, the interior – as required by the Calvinist congregation – is bare and frugal. Nonetheless, though the merchant elite may have set their minds against "idolatrous" adornment, they were certainly not averse to asserting status: the boxed-in benches at the base of several of the nave's stone columns were **gentleman's pews**, reserved for – and rented by – the wealthy. The Westerkerk is also the last resting place of **Rembrandt**, though the location of his pauper's tomb is not known. Instead, a small **plaque** in the north aisle commemorates the artist and nearby, in the floor of the nave, is the **tomb** of his son, **Titus** (Grave No.143). Rembrandt adored his son – as evinced by numerous portraits – and the

DESCARTES: SPY OR PHILOSOPHER?

The French philosopher **René Descartes** (1596–1650) once lodged at **Westermarkt 6**. Apparently happy that the Dutch were indifferent to his musings – and that therefore he wasn't going to be persecuted – he wrote: "Everybody except me is in business and so absorbed by profit-making that I could spend my entire life here without being noticed by a soul." However, this declaration may itself have been a subterfuge: it's quite possible that Descartes was spying on the Dutch for the Habsburg King Philip II of Spain, a theory explored in detail in A.C. Grayling's book, *Descartes: The Life and Times of a Genius*. In the event, Descartes spent twenty years in the Netherlands before accepting an invitation from Queen Christina of Sweden to go to Stockholm in 1649. It was a poor choice: no sooner had he got there, than he caught pneumonia and died.

boy's death dealt a final crushing blow to the ageing artist, who died just over a year later. In summertime, you can clamber up the **Westertoren** (tower) for a view over this part of the city.

Westermarkt

Westermarkt, an open square in the shadow of the Westerkerk, is home to two evocative statues. The first of the two, standing just to the south of the church entrance, by Prinsengracht, is a small but beautifully crafted **statue of Anne Frank** by the gifted Dutch sculptor Mari Andriessen (1897–1979). The second, at the back of the church, beside Keizersgracht, consists of three pink granite triangles (one each for the past, present and future), which together comprise the **Homomonument**. The world's first memorial to persecuted gays and lesbians, commemorating all those who died at the hands of the Nazis, it was designed by Karin Daan and recalls the pink triangles that homosexuals were forced to display on their clothes during the occupation. The monument's inscription, by the Dutch writer Jacob Israel de Haan, translates as "Such an infinite desire for friendship".

De Negen Straatjes (The Nine Streets)

Westermarkt flows into **Raadhuisstraat**, the principal thoroughfare into the Old Centre, running east to Dam square. South of here, the narrow cross-streets of the Grachtengordel are named after animals whose pelts were used in the local tanning industry – Reestraat ("Deer Street"), Hartenstraat ("Hart Street") and Berenstraat ("Bear Street"), to name but three. The tanners are long gone, but they've been replaced by some of the most pleasant shopping streets in the city, known collectively as **De Negen Straatjes** ("The Nine Streets"), selling everything from carpets and handmade chocolates to designer toothbrushes and beeswax candles. The area's southern boundary is marked by **Leidsegracht**, a mostly residential canal, overseen by a medley of handsome gables.

The Bijbels Museum

Herengracht 366–368 · Tues–Sun 11am–5pm · €8 · ☎ 020 624 8355, ⓦ bijbelsmuseum.nl

The graceful and commanding **Cromhouthuizen**, at Herengracht 364–370, consist of four matching stone mansions, embellished with tendrils, garlands and scrollwork, all finessed by charming little bull's-eye windows and elegant neck gables. Built in the 1660s for one of Amsterdam's wealthy merchant families, the Cromhouts, the houses were designed by **Philip Vingboons** (1607–78), the most inventive of the architects who worked on the Grachtengordel during the city's expansion.

Two of the houses have now been adapted to hold the **Bijbels Museum** (Bible Museum), which is named after the antique Bibles displayed on the top floor (Floor 3).

1

The most important are two early versions of the official **Statenvertaling** (literally State's Translation), published in 1637. Key to the development of Dutch Protestantism, the Statenvertaling was the result of years of study by leading scholars, who returned to the original Greek and Hebrew texts for this translation; it sold by the cartload. Much stranger, and also on the top floor, are the idiosyncratic models of the Jewish **Tabernacle** and **Jerusalem's Temple Mount** made by a Protestant vicar by the name of **Leendert Schouten** (1828–1905). Attempts to reconstruct biblical scenes were something of a cottage industry in the Netherlands in the late 1800s, with scores of Dutch antiquarians beavering away, but Schouten went one step further, making it his lifetime's work. It was a good move; Schouten became a well-known figure and his models proved a popular attraction, drawing hundreds of visitors to his home. Floor 2 is mostly devoted to temporary exhibitions and, rounding off the museum, the ground floor (Floor 1) holds a small "Aroma Cabinet" of biblical fragrances – palm, almond and so forth.

Leidseplein and around

Lying on the edge of the Grachtengordel, **Leidseplein** is the bustling hub of Amsterdam's nightlife, a rather cluttered and disorderly open space that has never had much character. The square once marked the end of the road in from Leiden and, as horse-drawn traffic was banned from the centre long ago, it was here that the Dutch left their horses and carts – a sort of equine car park. Today, it's quite the opposite: continual traffic made up of trams, bikes, cars and pedestrians gives the place a frenetic feel, and the surrounding side streets are jammed with bars, restaurants and clubs in a bright jumble of jutting signs and neon lights, though, on a good night, Leidseplein can still feel like Amsterdam at its carefree, exuberant best. Running northeast from the Leidseplein is busy **Leidsestraat,** a crowded shopping street full of fashion and shoe shops of little distinction which leads across the three main canals up towards the Singel.

Stadsschouwburg

Leidseplein 26 • ☎ 020 624 2311, ⓦ stadsschouwburgamsterdam.nl

The grandiose **Stadsschouwburg**, a neo-Renaissance edifice dating from 1894, was so widely criticized for its clumsy vulgarity that the city council of the day temporarily withheld the money for decorating the exterior. Formerly home to the National Ballet and Opera, it is now used for theatre, dance and music performances, but its most popular function is as the place where the Ajax football team gather on the balcony to wave to the crowds whenever they win anything – as they often do.

American Hotel

Leidsekade 97 • ☎ 020 556 3000, ⓦ edenamsterdamamericanhotel.com

The **American Hotel**, just off Leidseplein, is one of the city's oddest buildings, a monumental and slightly disconcerting rendering of Art Nouveau, complete with angular turrets, chunky dormer windows and fancy brickwork. Completed in 1902, the present structure takes its name from its demolished predecessor, which was adorned with statues and murals of North American scenes. Inside, the hotel's *Café Americain* was once the haunt of Amsterdam's literati, but today is a mainstream location for coffee and lunch. The Art Nouveau decor is well worth a peek – an artful combination of stained glass, shallow arches and geometric patterned brickwork.

The Golden Bend

Overlooked by a long sequence of double-fronted mansions, some of the most opulent dwellings in the city, **De Gouden Bocht** (the **Golden Bend**) stretches along the Herengracht from Leidsegracht to the River Amstel. Most of the houses here were

CLOCKWISE FROM TOP LEFT AMSTERDAM CAFÉ (P.88); BROUWERSGRACHT (P.60); GRACHTENGORDEL (P.59) >

1

extensively remodelled in the late seventeenth and eighteenth centuries, with double stairways leading up to the main entrance – and the small door beneath reserved for servants. Classical references are common, both in form – pediments, columns and pilasters – and decoration, from scrolls and vases through to geometric patterns inspired by ancient Greece. One of the first buildings to look out for is **Herengracht 475**, an extravagant edifice decorated with allegorical figures and surmounted by a slender balustrade. Typically, the original building was a much more modest affair, but in the 1740s, a new owner created the ornate facade of today. **Herengracht 493** is similarly grand, and completed with a carved pediment. Equally imposing is the nearby **Herengracht 507**: all Neoclassical pilasters and slender windows, it was once the home of Jacob Boreel, a one-time major whose attempt to impose a burial tax prompted a riot during which the mob ransacked his house. Boreel escaped by climbing over his garden fence, quite an achievement for a man known to be very tubby.

The Stadsarchief

Vijzelstraat 32 • **Conference Centre** ☎ 020 251 1800, ⓦ debazelamsterdam.nl • **Stadsarchief (City Archives)** Tues–Fri 10am–5pm, Sat & Sun noon–5pm • Free • ☎ 020 251 1510, ⓦ stadsarchief.amsterdam.nl

The **Stadsarchief** (City Archives) are housed within one of Amsterdam's weirdest and most monumentally incongruous buildings, a mammoth edifice of broadly Expressionist design that stretches down Vijzelstraat from Herengracht to Keizersgracht. Dating from the 1920s, the building started out as the headquarters of a Dutch shipping company, the Nederlandsche Handelsmaatschappij, before falling temporarily into the hands of the ABN-AMRO bank, then becoming home to the city's archives in 2007. The building is commonly known as **De Bazel** after its architect Karel de Bazel (1869–1923), whose devotion to theosophy formed and framed his design. Founded in the late nineteenth century, theosophy combined metaphysics and religious philosophy, and every facet of de Bazel's building reflects the cult's belief in order and balance, from the pink and yellow brickwork of the exterior (representing male and female respectively) to the repeated use of motifs drawn from the Middle East, the source of much of the cult's spiritual inspiration.

The Schatkamer

Tues–Fri 10am–5pm, Sat & Sun noon–5pm • Free, but some temporary exhibitions attract an admission fee • ☎ 020 251 1510, ⓦ stadsarchief.amsterdam.nl

At the heart of De Bazel is the magnificent **Schatkamer** (Treasury), a richly decorated Art Deco extravaganza that feels rather like a royal crypt. Exhibited here is an intriguing selection of photographs and documents drawn from the city archives – anything from 1970s squatters occupying City Hall to hagiographic tracts on the virtues of the Dutch naval hero, Admiral de Ruyter and, perhaps best of the lot, photos of miscreants (or rather the poor and the desperate) drawn from police records. The exhibits are changed regularly and an adjoining film studio shows documentaries about the city, both past and present.

The Museum van Loon

Keizersgracht 672 • Daily 10am–5pm • €9 • ☎ 020 624 5255, ⓦ museumvanloon.nl

The **Museum van Loon** has perhaps the finest accessible canal-house interior in the whole of Amsterdam. In the 1670s, the first tenant of the property was the artist Ferdinand Bol, who married an exceedingly wealthy widow and promptly hung up his easel for the rest of his days. The last owners were the van Loons, co-founders of the East India Company and long one of the city's leading families, though they came something of a cropper at the end of World War II. One of the clan, Thora van Loon-Egidius, the wife of Willem van Loon, was proud of her German roots and allegedly entertained high-ranking Nazi officials here during the occupation – a charge of collaboration that led to the van Loons being shunned by polite society.

In recent years, the house has been returned to something akin to its eighteenth-century appearance, with oodles of wood panelling and fancy stuccowork. Look out also for the ornate copper balustrade on the **staircase**, into which is worked the name "Van Hagen-Trip" (after a one-time owner of the house); the van Loons later filled the spaces between the letters with iron curlicues to prevent their children falling through. The **top-floor** landing has several pleasant paintings sporting classical figures, and one of the bedrooms – the "painted room" – is decorated with a Romantic painting of Italy, a motif favoured by Amsterdam's bourgeoisie from around 1750 to 1820. The oddest items are the **fake bedroom doors**: the eighteenth-century owners were so keen to avoid any lack of symmetry that they camouflaged the real bedroom doors and created imitation, decorative doors in the "correct" position instead.

FOAM

Keizersgracht 609 • Mon–Wed & Sat–Sun 10am–6pm, Thurs & Fri 10am–9pm • €10, plus additional charge for some exhibitions • ☎ 020 551 6500, ⓦ foam.org

In a large and thoroughly refurbished canal house, Amsterdam's leading photography museum, **FOAM** (short for Fotografiemuseum), is achingly fashionable, its temporary exhibitions – of which there are usually four at any one time – featuring the best (or most obscure) of contemporary photographers. FOAM prides itself on its internationalism, though it does give space to leading and/or up-and-coming Dutch photographers. FOAM also offers guided, walk-through tours and photography workshops, both of which have proved extremely popular.

The Tassenmuseum Hendrikje

Herengracht 573 • Daily 10am–5pm • €9.50; ☎ 020 524 6452, ⓦ tassenmuseum.nl

The delightful **Tassenmuseum Hendrikje** is home to a superb collection of handbags, pouches, wallets, bags and purses from medieval times onwards, exhibited on three floors of a sympathetically refurbished grand old mansion. Highlights include examples of several types of bag that preceded the purse – portefeuilles, chatelaines, frame-bags and reticules to name but four – as well as a number of beautiful Art Nouveau handbags. There is also a separate display on handbags made from animal skins – check out the eel, crocodile, python and lizard bags, though the armadillo bag is really rather gruesome. A final floor is given over to temporary displays usually featuring contemporary bags and purses.

The Museum Willet-Holthuysen

Herengracht 605 • Mon–Fri 10am–5pm, Sat & Sun 11am–5pm • €8.50 • ☎ 020 523 1822, ⓦ museumwilletholthuysen.nl

The **Museum Willet-Holthuysen** offers an insight into the life and tastes of one of Amsterdam's leading families, the coal-trading Holthuysens, who occupied this elegant, late seventeenth-century mansion until the last of the line, Louisa Willet-Holthuysen, gifted her home and its contents to the city in 1895. The museum is entered via the old servants' door, which leads into the basement, where a small collection of porcelain, glass and silverware is on display. Above are the family rooms, most memorably the **Men's Parlour** (or Blue Room), which has been returned to its nineteenth-century Rococo appearance – a flashy and ornate style copied from France and held to be the epitome of refinement and good taste by local merchants. The **Ballroom**, all creams and gilt, is similarly opulent and the **Dining Room** is laid out for dinner as if Louisa and her hubby, Abraham (1825–88), were about to entertain. The top floor displays the fine and applied art collection assembled by Abraham, principally Dutch ceramics, pewter

1

and silverware. At the back of the house lie the formal **gardens**, a geometric pattern of miniature hedges graced by the occasional stone statue.

The River Amstel

The main canals come to an abrupt halt beside the wide and windy **River Amstel**, long the main route into the interior, with goods arriving by barge and boat to be traded for the materials held in Amsterdam's many warehouses. Several bridges span the river, including the **Blauwbrug** ("Blue Bridge"), leading to the old Jewish quarter (see below), and the **Magere Brug** ("Skinny Bridge"), arguably the cutest of the city's many swing bridges, which leads over to the Hermitage Amsterdam (see p.71). Near the Magere Brug are the **Amstelsluizen**, or Amstel locks, which play an integral part in refreshing the city's canal water. Every night, the municipal water department closes these locks to begin the process of **sluicing** out the city's canals. A huge pumping station on an island out to the east of the city then pumps fresh water from the IJsselmeer into the canal system; similar locks on the west side of the city are left open for the surplus to flow into the IJ and, from there, out to sea via the North Sea Canal.

The old Jewish quarter and Plantage

Once one of the marshiest parts of Amsterdam, prone to regular flooding, the narrow slice of land sandwiched between the curve of the River Amstel, Oudeschans and Nieuwe Herengracht was the home of Amsterdam's **Jews** from the sixteenth century up until World War II. By the 1920s, this **old Jewish quarter**, or **Jodenhoek** ("Jews' Corner"), was crowded with tenement buildings and smoking factories, but in 1945 it lay derelict – and postwar redevelopment has not treated it kindly either. Its focal point, **Waterlooplein**, has been overwhelmed by a whopping town hall and concert hall complex, and the once-bustling Jodenbreestraat – the "Broad Street of the Jews" – is now bleak and very ordinary, with Mr Visserplein, at its east end, one of the city's

---

A SCENIC JAUNT AROUND THE JORDAAN

The **Jordaan** is a likeable and easily explored area of slender canals and narrow streets lying to the west of the city centre, its boundaries clearly defined by the Prinsengracht and the Lijnbaansgracht. Traditionally, the Jordaan was the home of Amsterdam's working class, but in recent years it has been transformed by a middle-class influx, with the district now one of the city's most sought-after **residential neighbourhoods**. The streets and canals extending north from **Rozengracht to Egelantiersgracht** form the heart of the Jordaan and provide the district's prettiest moments. Cream of the scenic crop is **Bloemgracht** (Flower Canal), a leafy waterway dotted with houseboats and traversed by dinky little bridges, its network of cross-streets sprinkled with cafés, bars and quirky shops. There's a warm, relaxed community atmosphere here which is really rather beguiling, not to mention a clutch of fine old canal houses. Pride of architectural place goes to **Bloemgracht 87–91**, a sterling Renaissance building of 1642 complete with mullion windows, three crow-step gables, brightly painted shutters and distinctive facade stones, representing a *steeman* (city-dweller), a *landman* (farmer) and a *seeman* (sailor). **Nos. 83 and 85** next door were built a few decades later – two immaculately maintained canal houses adorned by the bottleneck gables typical of that period.

The further east you go on **Egelantiersgracht** (Rose-Hip Canal) the prettier it becomes, and here at no. 12 – as you near Prinsengracht – is the street's most interesting feature, **Café 't Smalle** (see p.92). An antique bar with a canal-side terrace, 't Smalle opened in 1786 as a *proeflokaal* – a tasting house for the (long-gone) gin distillery next door. At the time, when quality control was erratic to say the least, each batch of *jenever* (Dutch gin) could turn out very differently, so customers insisted on a taster before they splashed out. As a result, each distillery ran a *proeflokaal* offering free samples, and this is a rare survivor.

busiest traffic junctions. Picking your way round these obstacles is not much fun, but persevere – among all the cars and concrete are several moving reminders of the Jewish community that perished in the war, most memorably the imposing **Esnoga** (Portuguese synagogue) and the fascinating **Joods Historisch Museum** (Jewish Historical Museum). There's a Rembrandt connection here too: in 1639 the artist moved into a house on the Jodenbreestraat and this has been restored as the **Rembrandthuis**, which displays a fine collection of the great man's etchings. From the Rembrandthuis, it's a brief stroll south to **Hermitage Amsterdam**, an art gallery used for lavish temporary exhibitions of fine and applied art on loan from the Hermitage Museum in St Petersburg.

Immediately east of the old Jewish quarter lies the **Plantage**, a well-heeled residential area centred around **Plantage Middenlaan** and home to the city's botanical gardens - the **Hortus Botanicus** - as well as the **Artis Zoo** and the excellent **Verzetsmuseum** (Dutch Resistance Museum).

The Rembrandthuis

Jodenbreestraat 4 • Daily 10am–6pm • €12.50 • ☎ 020 520 0400, ⓦ rembrandthuis.nl

One of the city's key attractions, the **Rembrandthuis** (Rembrandt House) boasts an intricate facade decorated by pretty wooden shutters and a fancy pediment. Rembrandt bought this house in 1639 at the height of his fame and popularity, living here for over twenty years and spending a fortune on furnishings – an expense that ultimately contributed to his bankruptcy (see box, p.337). An inventory made at the time details the huge collection of paintings, sculptures and art treasures he'd amassed, almost all of which were confiscated after he was declared insolvent and forced to move to a more modest house on Rozengracht in the Jordaan in 1658. The city council bought the Jodenbreestraat house in 1907 and has subsequently revamped the premises on several occasions.

The interior

Entry to the Rembrandthuis is via the modern annexe, but you're soon into the old house, where several rooms have been restored to something resembling their appearance when the artist lived here – the reconstruction being based on the inventory. The period furniture is appealing enough, especially the dinky box-beds, and the great man's **studio** is surprisingly large and well lit, but it's the collection of **seventeenth-century Dutch paintings** that grabs most of the attention. They do vary in quality and interest, but in the Old Entrance Hall look out for several paintings by Rembrandt's master in Amsterdam, **Pieter Lastman** (1583–1633) – not because of their brilliance, but rather because their sheer mawkishness demonstrates just how far Rembrandt soared above his artistic milieu. On the same floor, in the **Salon**, is the museum's one and only Rembrandt painting, his *Portrait of the Preacher Eleazer Swalmius*, an early work currently on long-term loan from Antwerp. The subject's straggly beard and twinkling eyes get the full Rembrandt treatment, though the painting was not attributed to him for many years largely because its intricacies were hidden by a thick layer of varnish, which has now been removed.

The Art Cabinet and beyond

The intriguing "**Art Cabinet**" is a room crammed with *objets d'art* and miscellaneous rarities reassembled here in line with the original inventory. There are African spears and shields, Pacific seashells, Venetian glassware and even busts of Roman emperors, all of which were meant to demonstrate Rembrandt's wide interests and eclectic taste. Beyond the Art Cabinet, the rest of the Rembrandthuis is usually given over to temporary exhibitions on the artist and his contemporaries. Here also, space permitting, is the museum's own collection of **Rembrandt's etchings**, as well as several of the original copper plates on which he worked.

1

Waterlooplein

A rectangular parcel of land that was originally swampy marsh, **Waterlooplein** was the site of the first Jewish quarter, but by the late nineteenth century it had become an insanitary slum, home to the poorest of the Ashkenazi Jews. The slums were cleared in the 1880s and thereafter Waterlooplein (and its open-air market) became the centre of Jewish life in the city. During the war, the Germans used the square to round up their victims, but despite these ugly connotations Waterlooplein was revived in the 1950s as the site of the city's main **flea market** – and remains so to this day, albeit on a much smaller scale thanks to the domineering **Stadhuis en Muziektheater** (Town and Concert Hall), a sprawling and distinctly underwhelming modern complex. The Muziektheater is home to the Nationale Opera & Ballet (see p.95) and in its foyer is a forceful **memorial** to the district's Jews, in which a bronze violinist bursts through the floor tiles.

Mr Visserplein

Mr Visserplein, metres from Waterlooplein, is a busy junction for traffic speeding towards the IJ tunnel. It takes its name from **Lodewijk Ernst Visser**, president of the Supreme Court of the Netherlands in 1939. He was dismissed the following year when the Germans occupied the country, and became an active member of the Jewish resistance, working for the illegal underground newspaper *Het Parool* ("The Password"). He consistently denounced all forms of collaboration and refused to wear the yellow Star of David, but died from a heart attack shortly after he was threatened with deportation to a concentration camp.

The Esnoga

Mr Visserplein 3 • March–Oct Mon–Thurs & Sun 10am–5pm, Fri 10am–4pm; Nov–Feb Mon–Thurs & Sun 10am–4pm & Fri 10am–2pm; closed Sat, Yom Kippur and Rosh Hashanah • €15 for combined ticket with Joods Historisch Museum (see below) • ☎ 020 624 5351, ⓦ esnoga.com

Unmissable on the corner of Mr Visserplein is the brown and bulky brickwork of the **Esnoga** or **Portuguese synagogue**, completed in 1675 for the city's Sephardic Jews. One of Amsterdam's most imposing buildings, the synagogue, with its grand pilasters and blind balustrade, was built in the broadly Neoclassical style then fashionable in Holland. Barely altered since its construction, the synagogue's lofty interior follows the Sephardic tradition in having the *hechal* (the Ark of the Covenant) and *tebah* (from where services are led) at opposite ends. Also traditional is the seating, with two sets of wooden benches (for the men) facing each other across the central aisle – the women have separate galleries up above. A set of superb brass chandeliers holds the candles, which remain the only source of artificial light. When it was completed, the synagogue was one of the largest in the world, its congregation almost certainly the richest; today, the Sephardic community has dwindled to just 250 families, most of whom live outside the city centre.

The surrounding **outhouses**, where the city's Sephardim have fraternized for centuries, illustrate different aspects of the Sephardic tradition – from the mourning room and the rabbi's room to the treasure room with its assortment of ritual vestments and silverware. There's also the intimate **winter synagogue** converted from a classroom in the late 1940s after the disasters of World War II. The mystery to the whole complex is quite why the Germans left it alone – no one knows for sure, but it seems likely that they intended to turn it into a museum once all of the Jews had been deported and slaughtered.

The Joods Historisch Museum

Nieuwe Amstelstraat 1 • Daily 11am–5pm; closed Yom Kippur and Rosh Hashanah• €15 for combined ticket with the Esnoga (see above) • ☎ 020 531 0310, ⓦ jhm.nl

The **Joods Historisch Museum** (Jewish Historical Museum) is cleverly shoehorned into four adjacent Ashkenazi synagogues dating from the late seventeenth century.

For years after World War II these buildings lay abandoned, but they were finally refurbished – and connected by walkways – in the 1980s, to accommodate a Jewish resource and exhibition centre. The first major display area, just beyond the reception desk on the ground floor of the **Nieuwe Synagoge**, features temporary exhibitions on Jewish life and culture with vintage photographs usually to the fore. Moving on, the ground floor of the capacious, late seventeenth-century **Grote Synagoge** holds an engaging display on Jewish life and faith in the Netherlands. There is a fine collection of religious silverware here, plus all manner of antique artefacts illustrating religious customs and practices, alongside a scattering of paintings and portraits. The gallery up above, reached via a spiral staircase, holds a finely judged social history of the country's Jewish population from 1600 to 1900, with an assortment of bygones, documents and paintings tracing their prominent role in a wide variety of industries. A complementary history of the Jews in the Netherlands from 1900 onwards occupies the upper level of the neighbouring Nieuwe Synagoge. Inevitably, attention is given to the trauma of World War II, but there is also a biting display on the indifferent/hostile reaction of many Dutch men and women to liberated Jews in 1945.

Hermitage Amsterdam at the Amstelhof

Amstel 51 • Daily 10am–5pm • €15 • ☎ 020 530 7488, ⓦ hermitage.nl

Built in the 1680s on behalf of the Dutch Reformed Church, the large and stern-looking **Amstelhof** started out as a *hofje* or almshouse for the care of elderly women. In time, it grew to fill most of the chunk of land between Nieuwe Herengracht and Nieuwe Keizersgracht, becoming a fully fledged hospital in the process, but in the 1980s it became clear that its medical facilities were out of date and it went up for sale. Much municipal debate ensued until it was finally agreed to convert it into a museum, **Hermitage Amsterdam**, to display items loaned from the Hermitage in St Petersburg. It was – and is – a very ambitious scheme and has proved extremely popular, so popular in fact that although the Russian "imports" provide the bulk of the exhibits, they are often boosted by works from elsewhere. These exhibitions usually last about five months and have included a "Portrait Gallery of the Golden Age" and "1917: From Romanov to Revolution". These headline exhibitions only occupy a part of the Amstelhof, which also musters a few **additional galleries** exploring the institution's history – modest stuff perhaps, but still of some interest: the pick are the eighteenth-century kitchen and the old chapel with its mini-organ and twin balconies.

Hortus Botanicus

Plantage Middenlaan 2a • Daily Feb–Nov 10am–5pm; Dec & Jan 10am–4pm • €8.50 • ☎ 020 625 9021, ⓦ dehortus.nl

The lush **Hortus Botanicus**, the city's botanical gardens, were founded in 1682 for medicinal purposes after an especially bad outbreak of the plague. Thereafter, many of Amsterdam's merchants made a point of bringing back exotic plants from the East, the result being the six thousand-odd species exhibited here today – both outside and in a series of hothouses. The gardens are divided into several distinct sections, each clearly labelled, its location pinpointed on a map available at the entrance kiosk. The outdoor sections are mainly devoted to temperate and Arctic plants, trees and shrubs, while the largest of the hothouses, the **Three-Climate Glasshouse**, is partitioned into separate climate zones: subtropical, tropical and desert. The gardens also hold a **butterfly house** and a capacious **palm house** with a substantial collection of cycad palms. It's all very low-key – and none the worse for that – and the gardens make a relaxing break on any tour of central Amsterdam, especially as the **café**, in the old orangery, serves tasty lunches and snacks.

1

The Hollandsche Schouwburg

Plantage Middenlaan 24 • Daily 11am–5pm, closed Yom Kippur and Rosh Hashanah • Free • ☎ 020 531 0310,
ⓦ hollandscheschouwburg.nl

A sad relic of the war, **De Hollandsche Schouwburg** was a one-time Jewish
theatre, which was turned into the main assembly point for Amsterdam
Jews prior to their deportation in 1942. Inside, there was no daylight and families
were interned in conditions that foreshadowed those of the camps they would soon
be taken to. The front of the building has been refurbished to display a list of the
dead and an eternal flame along with a small exhibition on the plight of the city's
Jews, but the old auditorium out at the back has been left as an empty, roofless
shell. A memorial **column** of basalt on a Star of David base stands where the
stage once was, an intensely mournful monument to suffering of unfathomable
proportions.

Artis Royal Zoo

Plantage Kerklaan 38–40 • Daily March–Oct 9am–6pm; Nov–Feb 9am–5pm; June–Aug till sundown on Sat with special activities •
Adults €19.95, 3–9-year-olds €16.50, under 2s free

Opened in 1838, this is the oldest zoo in the country, and it's one of the city's top
attractions for kids, though thankfully its layout and refreshing lack of bars and
cages mean that it never feels overcrowded. Highlights include an African savanna
environment, huge aquariums and an aviary. In addition to the usual lions,
monkeys and creepy-crawlies, there's also a children's farm where kids come
nose-to-nose with sheep, calves, goats, etc. Feeding times always draw a crowd
and take place as follows: 10.45am birds of prey; 11.30am and 3.45pm seals
and sea lions; 12.30pm crocodiles (Sun only); 2pm pelicans; 3pm lions and tigers
(not Thurs); 3.30pm penguins. The on-site **Planetarium** has five or six shows
daily, all in Dutch, though you can pick up a leaflet with an English translation
from the desk.

The Verzetsmuseum

Plantage Kerklaan 61 • Mon, Sat & Sun 11am–5pm, Tues–Fri 10am–5pm • €10 • ☎ 020 620 2535, ⓦ verzetsmuseum.org

The excellent **Verzetsmuseum** (Dutch Resistance Museum) details the development
of the Dutch Resistance from the German invasion of the Netherlands in May 1940
to the country's liberation in 1945. Thoughtfully presented, the main gangway
examines the experience of the majority of the population, dealing honestly with
the fine balance between cooperation and collaboration. Side rooms are devoted to
different aspects of the resistance, from the brave determination of the Communist
Party, who went underground as soon as the Germans arrived, to more ad hoc
responses like the so-called **Melkstaking** (Milk Strike) of 1943, when hundreds of
milk producers refused to deliver in protest at the Germans' threatened deportation
of 300,000 former (demobilized) Dutch soldiers to labour camps in Germany.
Fascinating old photographs illustrate the (English and Dutch) text along with a
host of original artefacts, from examples of illegal newsletters to signed German
death warrants and, perhaps most moving of all, farewell letters thrown from the
trains to Auschwitz. Interestingly, the Dutch Resistance proved especially adept at
forgery, forcing the Germans to make the identity cards they issued more and more
complicated. Aside from the treatment of the Jews, perhaps the most chilling
feature of the occupation was the use of indiscriminate reprisals to terrify the
population. The museum has dozens of little metal sheets providing biographical
sketches of the members of the Resistance – and it's this mixture of the general and
the personal that is its real strength.

The eastern docklands and Amsterdam Noord 1

The reclaimed islands of the **Oosterdok** stretching east from Centraal Station as well as those of **Amsterdam Noord**, across the River IJ from the city centre, were dredged out to accommodate warehouses, docks and shipyards from the seventeenth century onwards. They once formed part of a vast maritime complex that spread right along the river, but industrial decline set in during the 1880s and only recently have both areas been subject to a massive redevelopment programme. The outer parts of the Oosterdok are now dotted with upmarket housing, whilst its inner reaches hold several attractions, most notably an excellent children's science centre **NEMO** and the popular **Scheepvaartmusuem** (Maritime Museum). Amsterdam Noord, easily reachable by means of a short (free) ferry ride from behind Centraal Station (see p.81), is still in the early stages of redevelopment, but it does boast the city's proudest new building and best cinema at the **EYE Film Institute** (see p.96). Also here is the sprawling former **NDSM Shipyard**, which is in the process of being turned into a creative arts and events hub, with some good bars and restaurants.

The Oosterdok

There are several ways to explore the **Oosterdok**: the easiest is by tram, the most diverting is via the footbridge that spans the canal near the Verzetsmuseum (see opposite) to reach **Entrepotdok**. A good second bet begins near Centraal Station, where an elevated walkway spans the greasy waters of the harbour to link the city's brand-new **Bibliotheek** (library), on Oosterdokskade, with **NEMO**.

Entrepotdok

The most interesting of the **Oosterdok** islands is **Entrepotdok**, where old brick warehouses stretch along much of the quayside, distinguished by their spout gables, multiple doorways and overhead pulleys. Built by the **Dutch East India Company** in the eighteenth century, they were once part of the largest warehouse complex in continental Europe, a gigantic customs-free zone established for goods in transit. On the ground floor, above the main entrance, each warehouse sports the name of a town or island; goods for onward transportation were stored in the appropriate warehouse until there was enough to fill a boat or barge. The warehouses have been tastefully converted into offices and apartments, a fate they share with the central East India Company compound, whose chunky Neoclassical entrance is at the west end of Entrepotdok on Kadijksplein.

Scheepvaartmuseum

Kattenburgerplein • Daily 9am–5pm • €15 • ☎ 020 523 2222, ⓦ scheepvaartmuseum.nl

One of the city's most popular attractions, the **Scheepvaartmuseum** (Maritime Museum) occupies the old arsenal of the Dutch navy, an imposing sandstone structure built on its own Oosterdok mini-islet in the 1650s. It's underpinned by no fewer than 18,000 wooden piles driven deep into the riverbed at enormous expense, a testament to the nautical ambitions of the emergent nation. Visitors get their bearings in the central **courtyard** from where you can enter any one of three display areas – labelled "West", "Noord" and "Oost". Of the three, the "**West**" displays are the most gimmicky and child-orientated, the "**Oost**" the most substantial, including garish ships' figureheads, examples of early atlases, globes and navigational equipment. There are many nautical paintings in this section too, some devoted to the achievements of Dutch trading ships, others showing heavy seas and shipwrecks and yet more celebrating the successes of the Dutch navy. Honed by the long and bloody struggle with Habsburg Spain, the navy was the most powerful fleet in the world for about thirty years from the 1650s to the 1680s. **Willem van de Velde II** (1633–1707) was the most successful of the Dutch marine painters of the period and there's a good sample of his work here – canvases that emphasize the strength and power of the Dutch warship, often depicted in battle.

The "**Noord**" section gives access to the 78m **De Amsterdam**, a full-scale replica of an East Indiaman merchant ship. The original vessel first set sail in 1748, but came to an ignominious end, getting stuck on the British coast near Hastings. Visitors can wander the ship's decks and galleys, storerooms and gun bays at their leisure.

NEMO

Oosterdok • Tues–Sun 10am–5.30pm, plus May–Aug & all school holidays Mon 10am–5.30pm• €15, under-4s free • ☎ 020 531 3233, ⓦ e-nemo.nl

Resembling the prow of a ship, the massive, copper-green elevated hood that rears up above the entrance to the River IJ tunnel was designed by the Italian architect Renzo Piano in the 1990s. Inside is **NEMO**, a large and popular science and technology centre whose various interactive exhibits combine to create a (pre-teenage) kids' attraction *par excellence*. Spread over three main floors, there is all sorts of stuff here, such as "Dissecting Light Waves" in the Phenomena section and the nature of the universe in "The Search for Life" area.

De Appel

Prins Hendrikkade 142 • Tues–Sun 11am–6pm • €7 • ☎ 020 625 5651, ⓦ deappel.nl

A self-styled international institution for contemporary art, **De Appel** arts centre offers an ambitious programme of temporary exhibitions in a variety of media – from film through to sculpture, installations and paintings. The nineteenth-century premises are large enough to showcase several exhibitions at any one time and there are also performances, lectures and discussions. De Appel sets out to stimulate/shock, so don't be surprised if you are bemused by what's on display.

EYE Film Institute

IJpromenade 1 • Exhibition space: daily 11am–6pm, Fri till 9pm • €9, €15 combi ticket with a film • ☎ 020 589 1400, ⓦ eyefilm.nl • Take the GVB Buiksloterwegveer passenger ferry service across the River IJ from the back of Centraal Station to the Buiksloterweg quay (daily 6.30am–11pm, till 9pm from Buiksloterweg; every 10–15min; 10min; passengers and cycles free), and it's a 5min walk

Clearly visible from the south side of the River IJ – including parts of Centraal Station – the **EYE Film Institute** occupies a superb new building, a graceful shimmering structure whose sleek, angular lines were designed by a Viennese architectural company, Delugan Meissi. The EYE offers engaging views back over both the river and the city centre from all its three floors, which hold a bar-restaurant, a store, a film-focused library and four cinema screens showing an enterprising programme of classic and cult films (see p.96). There is also an **Exhibition** area offering four major exhibitions each year with two favourite themes being the interface between film and the visual arts and the evolution of Dutch film and cinematography. The archive of Jean Desmet (1875–1956), a leading film maker in the 1910s, gets a regular run-out as it comprises one of the key components of the EYE collection.

Oud-Zuid, De Pijp and the Museum Quarter

During the late nineteenth century, Amsterdam burst out of its restraining canals, gobbling up the surrounding countryside with a slew of new residential suburbs. Leading the charge was the **Oud-Zuid**, whose well-appointed boulevards have become home to many of the city's wealthier citizens, though the money fades away as you enter **De Pijp** ("The Pipe"), a working-class area named after its canyon-like brick tenements, which were said to resemble pipe-drawers. Both the Oud-Zuid and De Pijp have a flourishing bar and restaurant scene (see p.91 & p.93), but only one main sight – the **Heineken Experience**, in the former Heineken brewery, whereas the neighbouring **Museum Quarter** holds three outstanding museums. Top of the trio is the **Rijksmuseum,** which occupies an imposing edifice designed in an inventive and especially attractive historic style by Pierre Cuypers, the creator of Centraal Station – and is now home to a world-beating collection of paintings from Amsterdam's seventeenth-century Golden Age with Rembrandt to the fore. Equally enticing is the neighbouring **Van Gogh Museum**, which boasts a superb collection of van Gogh paintings with important works representative of all his artistic periods. Taken together, the two museums form one of Amsterdam's biggest draws – and they are supplemented by the modern and contemporary art of the **Stedelijk Museum**. From here, it's a brief walk northwest along van Baerlestraat to the sprawling greenery of the **Vondelpark**, Amsterdam's loveliest park.

The Rijksmuseum

Museumstraat 1 • Daily 9am–5pm • €17.50 for permanent collection, temporary exhibitions extra • ☎ 0900 0745 (premium line), ⓦ rijksmuseum.nl

The **Rijksmuseum** is without question the country's foremost art museum, with an extravagant collection of Dutch paintings, as well as a vast hoard of applied art and sculpture. In the last few years, the museum has been thoroughly refurbished and is now equipped with a capacious and singularly impressive **entrance area**, though the very height of this has interfered with the building's original floor plan and as a consequence getting from one section to another can be a tad confusing. **Floor 0** holds the most diverse part of the museum with early Flemish paintings (1100–1600) on one side and discrete collections of, amongst much else, Delftware, armaments, jewellery, silverware and model

REMBRANDT'S "DE NACHTWACHT"

Pride of place in the **Rijksmuseum** goes to Rembrandt's **De Nachtwacht** (*The Night Watch*). Dated to 1642, it's a group portrait of a **militia company**, the Kloveniersdoelen, one of the armed bands formed in the sixteenth century to defend the United Provinces (later the Netherlands) against Spain. As the Habsburg threat receded, so the militias became social clubs for the wealthy, who were eager to commission their own group portraits as signs of their prestige. Rembrandt charged the princely sum of one hundred guilders to each member of the company who wanted to be in the picture; sixteen – out of a possible two hundred – stumped up the cash, including the company's moneyed captain, **Frans Banning Cocq**, whose disapproval of Rembrandt's live-in relationship with **Hendrickje Stoffels** was ultimately to tarnish their friendship. Curiously, *The Night Watch* is, in fact, a misnomer – the painting got the tag in the eighteenth century when the background darkness was misinterpreted. There were other misconceptions too, most notably that it was this work that led to the downward shift in Rembrandt's standing with the Amsterdam elite; in fact, there's no evidence that the militiamen weren't pleased with the picture, nor that Rembrandt's commissions dwindled after it was completed. Though not as subtle as much of the artist's later work, *The Night Watch* is an adept piece, full of movement and carefully arranged. Paintings of this kind were collections of individual portraits as much as group pictures, and for the artist their difficulty lay in doing justice to every single face while simultaneously producing a coherent group scene. Abandoning convention in vigorous style, Rembrandt opted to show the company preparing to march off – a snapshot of military activity in which banners are unfurled, muskets primed and drums rolled. There are a couple of **allegorical figures** as well, most prominently a young, spotlit woman with a bird hanging from her belt, a reference to the Kloveniersdoelen's traditional emblem of a claw. Militia portraits commonly included cameo portraits of the artist involved, but in this case it seems that Rembrandt didn't insert his likeness, though some art historians insist that the pudgy-faced figure peering out from the back between the gesticulating militiamen is indeed the artist himself.

1

ships on the other. **Floor 1**, arguably the Rijksmuseum's weakest floor, features Dutch art from the eighteenth and nineteenth centuries, with a handful of lesser van Goghs and a healthy sample of the Hague School of landscape artists being the high points. Up above, **Floor 3** does a quick tour of twentieth-century art and applied art with Dutch figures such as Karel Appel and Gerrit Rietveld taking prominence. In between, **Floor 2** holds the kernel of the collection, the **Golden Age** paintings, which deservedly attract most visitor attention, with key works displayed in the long and wide **Eregalerij** (Gallery of Honour). Temporary exhibitions are held in a separate wing.

In the permanent collection, there is some **rotation** of the paintings, but you can count on seeing all the leading Rembrandts plus a healthy sample of canvases by Steen, Hals, Vermeer and their leading contemporaries; be sure to pick up a **free plan** at reception. Bear in mind also that the Rijksmuseum is extremely popular so it's a good idea to come early in the day, especially during major exhibitions.

Floor 2: The Eregalerij (Gallery of Honour)

At the start of the **Eregalerij**, you can expect to see the expansive and finely observed *Marriage Portrait of Isaac Massa and Beatrix Laen* by **Frans Hals** (c.1580–1666). Relaxing beneath a tree, a portly Isaac glows with contentment as his new wife sits beside him in a suitably demure manner. An intimate scene, the painting also carries a detailed iconography: the ivy at Beatrix's feet symbolizes her devotion to her husband, the thistle faithfulness, the vine togetherness and in the fantasy garden behind them the peacock is a classical allusion to Juno, the guardian of marriage.

Jan Steen

The prolific **Jan Steen** (1625–79) is well represented here in the Eregalerij by the drunken waywardness of his *Merry Family*, the anarchy of the *Family Scene* and his *Feast of St Nicholas*, which, with its squabbling children, makes the festival a celebration of disorderly greed. Steen knew his bourgeois audience well: his caricatures of the proletariat blend humour with moral condemnation – or at least condescension – a mixture perfectly designed to suit their tastes. Steen was also capable of more subtle works, a famous example being his *Woman at her Toilet*, which is full of associations, referring to sexual pleasures just had or about to be taken.

Pieter de Hooch

The paintings of **Pieter de Hooch** (1629–84) are less symbolic than those of Steen – more exercises in lighting – but they're as good a visual guide to the everyday life and habits of the seventeenth-century Dutch bourgeoisie as you'll find: witness both his curious *A Mother's Duty* in which the mother is delousing the child's head and his *Interior with Women beside a Linen Basket*, showing the women of the house changing the linen while a series of doorways reveals the canal bank in the background.

Johannes Vermeer

The canvases of Pieter de Hooch bear comparison with, and are usually displayed near, the work of **Johannes Vermeer** (1632–75), whose *The Love Letter* reveals a tension between servant and mistress – the lute on the woman's lap was a well-known sexual symbol – while *The Kitchen Maid* (sometimes *The Milk Maid*) is an exquisitely observed domestic scene, right down to the nail – and its shadow – on the background wall. Similarly, in the precise *Woman in Blue Reading a Letter*, the map behind her hints at the far-flung places her lover is writing from. What you won't get, however, is Vermeer's *Girl with a Pearl Earring* – this is on display in the Mauritshuis in Den Haag (see p.153).

Rembrandt

For many, **Rembrandt van Rijn** (1606–69) is the star turn and the museum owns several of his early paintings, most memorably an exquisite *Portrait of Maria Trip*, depicting an

Amsterdam oligarch kitted out in all her pearls and lace finery. Of Rembrandt's later work, look out for the celebrated *Members of the Clothmakers Guild* and a late *Self-Portrait*, with the artist caught in mid-shrug as the Apostle Paul, a self-aware and defeated old man. Also here are the artist's touching depiction of his cowled son, *Titus*, and *The Jewish Bride*, one of his very last pictures, finished in 1667. No one knows who the couple are, nor whether they are actually married (the title came later), but the painting is one of Rembrandt's most telling, the paint dashed on freely and the hands touching lovingly – as the art historian Kenneth Clark wrote, in "a marvellous amalgam of richness, tenderness and trust". But there's no mistaking the culmination of the Eregalerij – it's Rembrandt's **The Night Watch** (*De Nachtwacht*; see box, p.75).

The Van Gogh Museum

Paulus Potterstraat 7 • Daily 9am–6pm, Fri until 10pm • €17 • ☎ 020 570 5200, ⓦ vangoghmuseum.nl

Vincent van Gogh (1853–90) is arguably the most popular, most reproduced and most talked-about of all modern artists, so it's not surprising that the **Van Gogh Museum**, comprising a fabulous collection of the artist's work, is one of Amsterdam's top attractions. The museum occupies two modern buildings that back onto the northern edge of Museumplein, with the key paintings housed in an angular building designed by a leading light of the De Stijl movement, **Gerrit Rietveld** (1888–1964), and opened to the public in 1973. This part of the museum provides an introduction to the man and his art based on paintings that were mostly inherited from Vincent's art-dealer brother Theo. To the rear of Rietveld's building, connected by a ground-floor escalator, is the ultramodern annexe, which provides temporary exhibition space. As you might expect, the museum can get very crowded, and the **queues** can be long, so come early to avoid the crush or book online.

Before Arles

Inside the Rietveld building, a flight of stairs leads up to three floors, where the paintings of van Gogh are presented in broadly chronological order with temporary displays providing extra contextual or artistic ballast. The first paintings go back to the artist's **early years** in Holland and Belgium – dark, sombre works in the main, ranging from an assortment of drab grey and brown still lifes to the gnarled faces and haunting, flickering light of *The Potato Eaters*, the culmination of hundreds of studies of the local peasantry. Further along, the sobriety of these early works is easily transposed onto the urban landscape of **Paris** (1886–88), particularly in the *View of Paris*, where the city's domes and rooftops hover below Montmartre under a glowering, blustery sky. But before long, under the sway of fellow painters and the sheer colour of the city, van Gogh's approach began to change. This is most noticeable in two of his many self-portraits and in the pictures from **Asnières**, just outside Paris, where the artist used to go regularly to paint.

Arles

In February 1888 van Gogh moved to **Arles**, inviting Gauguin to join him a little later (see box, p.78). With the change of scenery came a heightened interest in colour, and the predominance of **yellow** as a recurring motif; it's represented most vividly in the disconcerting juxtapositions of *Bedroom in Arles*. Also from this period comes a striking canvas from the artist's *Sunflowers* series, intensely – almost obsessively – rendered in the deepest oranges, golds and ochres he could find.

St Rémy and after

During his time at the asylum in **St Rémy**, van Gogh's approach to nature became more abstract, as evidenced by his unsettling *Wheatfield with a Reaper*, the dense, knotty *Undergrowth* and his palpable *Irises*. Van Gogh is at his most expressionistic here, the paint

1

VAN GOGH'S EAR

In February 1888, **Vincent van Gogh** (1853–90) left Paris for **Arles**, a small town in the south of France, where he warmed to the open vistas and bright colours of the Provençal countryside. In September he moved into the house he called the "**Yellow House**", where he hoped to establish an artists' colony – though only **Gauguin**, who arrived in Arles in late October, stayed for any length of time. Initially the two artists got on well, hunkering down together in the Yellow House and sometimes painting side by side, but the bonhomie didn't last. They argued long and hard about art, with van Gogh complaining, "Sometimes we come out of our arguments with our heads as exhausted as a used electric battery." Later, Gauguin claimed that van Gogh threatened him during several of these arguments; true or not, it is certainly the case that Gauguin had decided to return to Paris by the time the two had a ferocious quarrel on the night of December 23. The argument was so bad that Gauguin left to stay at the local hotel, and when he returned in the morning, he was faced by the police. After Gauguin's hasty exit, a deeply disturbed van Gogh had taken a razor to his **ear**, severing part of it before presenting the selected slice to a prostitute at the local brothel. Presumably, this was not an especially welcome gift, but in van Gogh's addled state he may well have forged some sort of connection with bullfighting, where the dead bull's ears are cut off and given as a prize to the bullfighter. Hours after Gauguin's return, van Gogh was admitted to hospital, the first of several extended stays before, fearing for his sanity, he committed himself to the asylum of **St Rémy** in May 1889. Here, the doctor's initial assessment described him as suffering from "**acute mania**, with hallucinations of sight and hearing"; van Gogh attributed his parlous state to excessive drinking and smoking, though he gave up neither during his year-long stay.

In May 1890, feeling lonely and homesick, van Gogh discharged himself from St Rémy and headed north to Paris before going on to the village of **Auvers-sur-Oise**. At first, his health improved and he even began to garner critical recognition for his work. However, his twin ogres of **depression and loneliness** soon returned to haunt him and, in despair, van Gogh shot himself in the chest. This wasn't, however, the end; he didn't manage to kill himself outright, but took 27 hours to die, even enduring a police visit when he refused to answer any questions, pronouncing: "I am free to do what I like with my own body."

applied thickly, often with a palette knife, a practice he continued in his final, tortured works painted at **Auvers-sur-Oise**, where he lodged for the last three months of his life. It was at Auvers that he painted the frantic *Wheatfield with Crows*, in which the fields swirl and writhe under weird and dark skies, as well as the organized chaos of *Tree Roots*.

The Stedelijk Museum

Museumplein 10 • Daily 10am–6pm, Thurs until 10pm • €15 for permanent collection, temporary exhibitions extra • ☎ 020 573 2911, ⓦ stedelijk.nl

The **Stedelijk Museum** has long been Amsterdam's number one venue for modern and contemporary art dating from the 1870s onwards. It's housed in a big old building that has recently undergone a complete refurbishment, though the end result – to a design by Benthem Crouwel Architects – has not been to everyone's liking: the facade looks like a giant bath tub. The museum focuses on cutting-edge, temporary exhibitions of **modern art** – from photography through to sculpture and collage – and these are supplemented by a regularly rotated selection from the museum's large and wide-ranging **permanent collection**. Among many highlights, the latter includes a particularly large sample of the work of **Piet Mondriaan** (1872–1944), Karel Appel (1921–2006), Theo van Doesburg (1883–1931) and **Kasimir Malevich** (1878–1935). Other high spots include a number of pictures by American abstract Expressionists Mark Rothko, Ellsworth Kelly and Barnett Newman, plus the odd work by Lichtenstein, Warhol, Robert Ryman and Jean Dubuffet. Furthermore, the Stedelijk was the first European museum to start collecting video art, of which it has an extensive range.

The Concertgebouw

Concertgebouwplein 10 • Regular guided tours (90min; €10) with advance booking required • ☎ 0900 671 8345 (premium line within the Netherlands), ☎ 0031 20 671 8345 (from abroad), ⓦ concertgebouw.nl • Further concert and orchestra details appear in Entertainment and nightlife listings (see p.95)

The **Concertgebouw** (Concert Hall) is home of the famed – and much recorded – **Koninklijk Concertgebouworkest** (Royal Concertgebouw Orchestra). When the German composer Brahms visited Amsterdam in the 1870s he was scathing about the locals' lack of culture and in particular their lack of an even halfway suitable venue for his music. In the face of such ridicule, a consortium of Amsterdam businessmen got together to fund the construction of a brand-new concert hall and the result was the Concertgebouw, completed in 1888. Since then it has become renowned among musicians and concertgoers for its marvellous acoustics, and after a facelift in the early 1990s it is looking and sounding better than ever. The **guided tour** takes in the Grote Zaal and Kleine Zaal auditoriums, as well as various behind-the-scenes activities – control rooms, piano stores, artistes' dressing rooms and the like.

The Vondelpark

Multiple entrances, but main entrance on Stadhouderskade • Open access • Free

Central Amsterdam is short of green spaces, which makes the leafy expanse of the **Vondelpark** doubly welcome. This is easily the largest and most popular of the city's parks, its network of footpaths used by a healthy slice of the city's population. The park dates back to 1864, when a group of leading Amsterdammers clubbed together to transform the soggy marshland that lay beyond the Leidseplein into a landscaped park. The group, who were impressed by the contemporary English fashion for natural (as distinct from formal) landscaping, gave the park commission to the Zocher family, big-time gardeners who set about their task with gusto, completing the work in 1865. Named after the seventeenth-century poet **Joost van den Vondel**, the park proved an immediate success and was expanded to its present size (45 hectares) in 1877. It's now home to over one hundred species of tree, a wide variety of local and imported plants, and – among many incidental features – a **bandstand**, an excellent **rose garden** and a grand **statue** of a pensive Vondel, shown seated with quill in hand, near the park's main entrance. Neither did the Zochers forget their Dutch roots: the park is latticed with ponds and narrow waterways, home to many species of wildfowl, though it's the large colony of (very noisy) bright green parakeets that grabs the attention. The Vondelpark has several different children's play areas and during the summer regularly hosts free concerts and theatrical performances, mostly in its **open-air theatre**.

The Heineken Experience

Stadhouderskade 78 • Jan–June & Sept–Dec Mon–Thurs 10.30am–7.30pm, Fri–Sun 10.30am–9pm; July & Aug daily 10.30am–9pm • Last admission 2hr before closing; allow 1hr 30min for the self-guided tour • €18 • ☎ 020 523 9222, ⓦ heinekenexperience.com • Tram #16 or #24 from Centraal Station to Stadhouderskade tram stop

The **Heineken Experience** is housed in the former Heineken brewery, a whopping building that was the company's headquarters from 1864 to 1988, at which time the firm restructured and moved the brewing out of town. Since then, Heineken has developed the site as a tourist attraction, with displays on the history of beer-making in general and Heineken in particular. Considering it's not a real brewery any more, Heineken makes a decent stab at both entertaining and informing – as well as promoting the brand. You get a free drink at two bar stops along the way.

1

ARRIVAL AND DEPARTURE

AMSTERDAM

Schiphol, Amsterdam's international airport, is a quick and convenient train ride from Amsterdam Centraal Station, the city's international train station, which is itself just a 10min metro ride from Amstel Station, the terminus for long-distance and international buses. Centraal Station is also the hub of an excellent **public transport** network, whose trams, buses and metro combine to delve into every corner of the city and its suburbs.

BY PLANE

Schiphol airport (☎ 0900 0141, premium line reachable from within the Netherlands only, ⓦ schiphol.nl) is located about 15km southwest of the city centre. The taxi fare from the airport to the city centre is about €50.

TRAINS TO THE CITY

There are fast and frequent trains from the airport to Centraal Station (6am–midnight every 10min, midnight–6am hourly; 15min; €4.10 one way; ⓦ ns.nl).

BUSES TO THE CITY

Connexxion runs a shuttle-bus service between the airport and most of the city's hotels (every 30min; 6am–9.30pm; €17 one way, €27 return; ☎ 088 339 4741, ⓦ schipholhotelshuttle.nl). It's best to book online in advance, though tickets are available from the Connexxion desk in the arrivals hall. Shuttle buses depart platform A7 at Schiphol Plaza outside the Arrivals/Departures halls; journey times vary considerably depending on the hotel. Alternatively, the Airport Express bus #197 (ⓦ bus197.nl) departs every 15min for the city centre, from platform B9 at Schiphol Plaza to Museumplein, the Rijksmuseum or Leidseplein; tickets cost €4.75 one way, €9 return.

BY TRAIN

Centraal Station (CS) is conveniently located right in the city centre, and has services to and from every other Dutch city as well as from several key cities in Germany, France and Belgium. Domestic trains are operated by NS (ⓦ ns.nl), international services by several companies (see p.24). The station has all the facilities you would expect, including ATMs, a bureau de change and coin-operated luggage lockers. Just outside the station on Stationsplein, to the right, there is a taxi rank and, directly opposite the station exit, a branch of the tourist office – the VVV (see below). Stationsplein is also the hub of the city's public transport system with multiple tram and bus stops.

DESTINATIONS

Alkmaar (every 15min; 36min); Apeldoorn (every 30min; 1hr 10min); Arnhem (every 30min; 1hr 5min); Den Helder (every 30min; 1hr 15min); Dordrecht (every 10min; 1hr 30min); Eindhoven (every 20min; 1hr 20min); Enkhuizen (every 30min; 1hr); Groningen (every 20min; 2hr 7min); Den Haag (every 15min; 50min); Haarlem (every 10min; 15–19min); Hoorn (every 20min; 32–42min); Leeuwarden (every 20min; 2hr 15min); Leiden (every 10–15min; 35–45min); Maastricht (every 30min; 2hr 30min); Nijmegen (every 20min; 1hr 34min); Rotterdam (every 15min; 1hr 11min); Schiphol Airport (every 10min; 15min); Utrecht (every 5–15min; 30min); Vlissingen (every 30min; 2hr 30min–3hr); Zwolle (every 20min; 1hr 8–11min).

BY BUS
AMSTEL STATION

Long-distance, international buses to Amsterdam, including services operated by Eurolines (ⓦ eurolines.nl), arrive at Amstel Station, about 3.5km to the southeast of Centraal Station. The metro journey from here to Centraal Station takes about 10min.

CENTRAAL STATION

Amsterdam's Centraal Station is the hub of the city's excellent public transport system (see opposite): trams and buses depart from Stationsplein, which is also the location of a metro station and a GVB public transport information office. Buses to Noord-Holland destinations, such as Edam (#314; every 10min; 50min); Marken (#315; every 30min; 45min); Monnickendam (#316; every 10min; 26min) and Volendam (#316; every 20min; 40min), run by several different companies, also leave from Stationsplein.

BY CAR

Arriving by car on either the A4/E19 from Den Haag or the A2/E35 from Utrecht, you should experience few traffic problems, and the city centre is clearly signposted as soon as you approach Amsterdam's southern reaches. Both roads feed onto the A10 ring road; on its west side, leave the A10 at either the Osdorp or Geuzenveld exits for the city centre. However, be warned that driving in central Amsterdam – never mind parking – is extremely difficult (see box opposite).

INFORMATION

Tourist office The main information desk of the VVV, Amsterdam's official tourist bureau, is located on Stationsplein, across from the entrance to Centraal Station (Mon–Sat 9am–5pm, Sun 9am–4pm) and there's one at Schiphol Airport Arrivals 2 at Schiphol Plaza (daily 7am–10pm). These two offices share one premium-rate information line on ☎ +32 (0)20 702 6000, and a website: ⓦ iamsterdam.com. They take bookings in person (and online) for canal cruises and other organized excursions and operate an extremely efficient accommodation reservation

1

PARKING IN AMSTERDAM

On-street parking in Amsterdam is limited and expensive. Every city-centre street where parking is permitted is **metered** between 9am and midnight from Monday to Saturday, from midday to midnight on Sunday, with a standard cost of €5 an hour, €30–45 a day, and €20 for the evening (7pm to midnight). **Tickets** are available from meters, which give instructions in several languages. If you overrun your ticket, you can expect to be clamped and fined. **Car parks** in the centre charge comparable rates to the metered street spaces. Much cheaper and easier is the Park+Ride scheme: large car parks on the outskirts of town serviced regularly by metro trains, buses and trams that ferry you into the city centre. It costs €8 for 24hr. Look for the blue P+R logo on the A10 or A2 motorways. Note also that some of the better hotels either have their own parking spaces or offer special deals with nearby car parks.

service, though at peak times the wait can be long. At the time of writing, a sleek new I amsterdam store (daily 8am–11pm) was being constructed inside the northern hall of IJ-hal above Centraal Station, to act as a visitor centre and sell tickets, regional products and gifts.

Tickets Tickets for most concerts and events can be bought from the I amsterdam visitor centres (see p.80). The Last Minute Ticket Shop (ⓦ lastminuteticketshop.nl) sells half-price seats from 10am on the day of performance; you can buy them online, from the I amsterdam stores, the Stadsschouwburg on Leidseplein or the OBA Central Bibliotheek on Oosterdokskade.

Discount cards and passes The VVV's much-touted I amsterdam card is valid for 24, 48 or 72 hours and costs €49/59/69; you can purchase one online, or from the tourist office on arrival (see p.80). It includes a city map, a free canal cruise, unlimited use of the GVB public transport system, including trams, buses (not Connexxion airport shuttles) and metros, free entrance to various museums (but not the Anne Frank Huis, and there's only a €2.50 saving on Rijksmuseum tickets); there's also a 25 per cent discount on bike rental, tours, concert performances and some restaurants. Alternatively, a Museumkaart (see p.41) is good value at €60 for a year, especially if you're travelling elsewhere in the country, as it allows free entry to over four hundred museums and galleries nationwide.

GETTING AROUND

BY PUBLIC TRANSPORT

Amsterdam has a first-rate **public transport system** run by GVB, comprising trams, buses, a one-line metro and four passenger ferries across the River IJ to the northern suburbs. Centraal Station is the hub of the system, with a multitude of trams and buses departing from outside on Stationsplein, which is also the location of a metro station and the main GVB information/ ticketing office (Mon–Fri 7am–9pm, Sat & Sun 8am–9pm; ☎ 0900 8011, ⓦ gvb.nl); here they also issue free transit maps. Trams, buses and the metro operate daily between 6am and midnight, supplemented by a limited number of night buses (*nachtbussen*) on major routes. Almost all tram and bus stops display a detailed map of the network.

TICKETS AND FARES

OV-chipkaart To travel on Amsterdam's GVB network, you will need an electronic OV-chipkaart of one type or another (see box, p.27). Bus and tram drivers issue disposable, paper OV-chipkaarten – single-journey tickets (valid 1hr) at €2.90, or 24hr (€7.50), 48hr (€12) or 72hr (€16) versions, with children aged 4–11 eligible for a Children's Day Card (€2.50/24hr). These are also available from the GVB office on Stationsplein, at metro stations and at many hotels. Both plastic and paper OV-chipkaarten must be scanned as you enter and leave the GVB network – if you forget, it will stop working.

I amsterdam card As part of its provision, the VVV's I amsterdam card (see above) includes unlimited travel on all GVB trams, buses and the metro for a period of 24, 38 or 72 hours.

Fare-dodging The GVB tries hard to keep fare-dodging to a minimum, and wherever you're travelling, and at whatever time of day, there's a reasonable chance you'll have your ticket checked. If you are caught without a valid ticket, you risk an on-the-spot fine of €35.

BY CANAL

Canal Bus (☎ 020 217 0500, ⓦ canal.nl). A good way to get around Amsterdam's waterways, the Canal Bus operates on three circular routes, coloured green, red and orange, which meet at various places: the jetty outside Centraal Station; on the Singelgracht opposite the Rijksmuseum; and by the Stadhuis on Waterlooplein. There are sixteen stops in all and together they give easy access to all the major sights. Boats leave every 30min or so during high season between 9.15am and 7.25pm, and a day ticket for all three routes, allowing you to hop on and off as many times as you like, costs €25/adult, €12.50 for kids 4–12 years; it's also worth considering the 48hr ticket, which costs €35. Online discounts apply, and there's a 25 percent discount with an I amsterdam card.

1

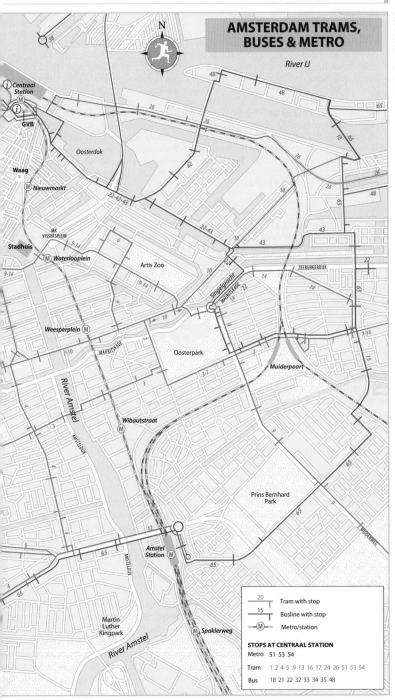

AMSTERDAM TRAMS, BUSES & METRO

River IJ

STOPS AT CENTRAAL STATION

Metro	51 53 54
Tram	1 2 4 5 9 13 16 17 24 26 51 53 54
Bus	18 21 22 32 33 34 35 48

Legend:
- 20 — Tram with stop
- 15 — Busline with stop
- M — Metro/station

1

CITY CANAL TOURS

No one could say the Amsterdam tourist industry doesn't make the most of its canals, with a veritable armada of glass-topped **cruise boats** shuttling along the city's waterways, offering everything from quick hour-long excursions to fully fledged dinner cruises. There are several major operators and they occupy the prime pitches, either the jetties near Centraal Station on Stationsplein or beside the first part of Damrak. Despite the competition, **prices** are fairly uniform with a one-hour tour costing around €16 per adult, €8 per child (4–12 years old). The big companies, for example **Lovers** (see below), also run a lot of different themed cruises – candlelight cruises, cocktail cruises, etc – with tickets in the region of €37 – though dinner cruises will cost you about €75. All the basic cruises are extremely popular and long queues are common throughout the summer. One way of avoiding much of the crush is to walk down Damrak from Centraal Station to the jetty at the near end of the Rokin, where **Reederij P. Kooij** (☎020 623 3810, ⓦrederijkooij.nl) offers all the basic cruises at cheaper prices.

Lovers Canal Cruises (☎020 530 1090, ⓦlovers.nl). Operates a hop on-hop off sightseeing route with seven stops at or near many of the city's major attractions. It departs from opposite Centraal Station (every 25min; 10am–5pm) and a day ticket costs €19, children (4–12 years old) €9.50.

Canal Bikes (☎020 217 0500, ⓦcanal.nl). These four-seater pedalos take a lifetime to get anywhere but are nevertheless good fun. You can rent them – only if the weather is good – at three locations: on the Singelgracht opposite the Rijksmuseum; at Westerkek near the Anne Frank Huis; and behind Leidseplein. Rental prices are €24 (3–4 persons) or €8/person for an hour, plus a refundable deposit of €20. Pedalos can be picked up at one location and left at any of the others (daily 10am–5.30pm, July & Aug until 10pm); there's a 25 percent discount with an I amsterdam card.

BY BIKE

One of the most agreeable ways to explore Amsterdam is by bicycle. The city has an excellent network of designated bicycle lanes (*fietspaden*) and for once cycling isn't a fringe activity – there are cyclists everywhere. Indeed, much to the chagrin of the city's taxi drivers, the needs of the cyclist take precedence over those of the motorist and by law if there's a collision it's always the driver's fault.

BIKE RENTAL

Bike rental is straightforward. There are lots of rental companies (*fietsenverhuur*), including Bike City, Bloemgracht 68–70 (☎020 626 3721, ⓦbikecity.nl); Rent-a-Bike, Damstraat 20–22 (☎020 625 5029, ⓦrentabike.nl); Yellow Bikes, Nieuwezijds Kolk 29 (020 620 6940, ⓦyellowbike.nl); and MacBike (ⓦmacbike.nl) at Stationsplein 5 (☎020 624 8391), Waterlooplein 199 (☎020 428 7005), Weteringschans 2 (☎020 528 7688), and Marnixstraat 220 (☎020 626 6964). Standard bicycles cost around €7.50 for 3hr, €12 for a day, €20 for two days. All rental companies ask for some type of security, usually in the form of a cash deposit (some will take credit card imprints) or passport.

BY CAR

Driving Central Amsterdam is geared up for trams and bicycles rather than cars; motorists have to negotiate a convoluted one-way system, avoid getting boxed onto tram lines, and steer round herds of cyclists.

Car rental Europcar, Overtoom 197 ☎020 683 2123; Hertz, Overtoom 333 ☎020 612 2441.

BY TAXI

Taxis Taxi ranks are liberally distributed across the city centre and cabs can also be hailed on the street. If all else fails, call Taxicentrale on ☎020 777 7777.

Fares Taxi fares are tightly regulated with a maximum start price of €2.83 and maximum price per minute of €0.34.

ACCOMMODATION

Amsterdam's accommodation options are among the most exciting in Europe: take your pick from handsomely converted old canal houses, sleek and chic boutique B&Bs, houseboats, a converted train depot and even a crane, as well as a good array of **hostels**. It's essential to pre-book at peak times – July and August, Easter and Christmas – and indeeed, such is the city's popularity as a short-break destination that you'd be well advised to make an **advance reservation** at any time of the year, either direct or via the VVV's website (ⓦiamsterdam.com). Most hotels only charge the full quoted rates at the very busiest times, which means that you'll often pay less than the peak-season prices quoted in this book, and **breakfast** is included (unless otherwise indicated) as is, in most cases, free wi-fi. Another bonus is that the city's compactness means that you're pretty much bound to end up somewhere within easy reach of the centre.

HOTELS

THE OLD CENTRE

The Exchange Damrak 50 ☎020 523 0080, ⓦhoteltheexchange.com; map p.51. Rooms at this boutique hotel in the heart of the Old Centre are dressed with all manner of fashiony details. Options range from tiny, pared-back one-star rooms to spacious, five-star rooms with great city views (€273). €̄110

Hotel des Arts Rokin 154–156 ☎020 620 1558, ⓦhoteldesarts.nl; map p.51. This seventeenth-century townhouse started life as an orphanage for Catholic girls, and is now a two-star hotel with 22 classical-style rooms. Wi-fi is available only in the lounge, and guests are charged a set fee of €12.50 for access. €̄158

Hotel de l'Europe Nieuwe Doelenstraat 2–14 ☎020 531 1777, ⓦleurope.nl; map p.51. This elegant old-timer has a wonderful *fin-de-siècle* charm and an attractive and central riverside location. The large, opulent rooms each feature a replica Dutch Master painting, chosen by the Rijksmuseum, and there's also a two-Michelin-star restaurant, *Bord'Eau*, a spa and the glamorous *Freddy's Bar*. Last-minute bargains are plentiful. €̄449

Misc Kloveniersburgwal 20 ☎020 330 6241, ⓦmisceatdrinksleep.com; map p.51. Very friendly hotel on the edge of the Red Light District with six good-sized rooms, each elegantly decorated in a different theme. The bright breakfast area overlooks the canal and is great for peoplewatching. Canal-view rooms cost roughly €30 more. €̄225

NH City Centre Spuistraat 288–292 ☎020 420 4545, ⓦnh-hotels.com; map p.51. Well situated for the cafés and bars of the Spui and the Museum Quarter, this appealing hotel occupies a sympathetically renovated 1920s Art Deco building that was once the HQ of the Gerzon fashion house. Rooms vary in size, some have canal views, and all boast comfy beds and good showers. Bike rental available. Breakfast costs extra. €̄150

Winston Warmoesstraat 129 ☎020 623 1380, ⓦwinston.nl; map p.51. This self-consciously young and cool budget hotel has rooms and dorms individually decorated with wacko art, a busy ground-floor bar and restaurant and the *Winston Kingdom* nightclub next door. It's a formula that works a treat: the *Winston* is popular and often full – though this is probably also due to its low prices. Rooms are light and airy, some en suite, some with a communal balcony. Erotic images adorn some, so if you're travelling as a family you might want to check first. Lift and full disabled access. Dorms €̄42, doubles €̄67

THE GRACHTENGORDEL

★**Ambassade** Herengracht 341 ☎020 555 0222, ⓦambassade-hotel.nl; map pp.48–49. Eminently appealing hotel that occupies a series of cleverly renovated seventeenth-century canal houses. There are sixty-odd rooms, each decorated in period-meets-country-house style, mostly in pastel shades and with big beds and high-spec bathrooms. There's also a well-stocked library and a study with modern art. Breakfast is taken in an elegant panelled room; a restaurant is in the offing. Guests get discounts at a "Float & Massage" centre a few doors away. €̄250

★**Dylan** Keizersgracht 384 ☎020 530 2010✉ ⓦdylanamsterdam.com; map pp.48–49. Hip without being pretentious, the *Dylan* has earned itself many repeat guests. This stylish hotel is housed in a seventeenth-century building that centres on a beautiful courtyard and terrace. The 41 sumptuous rooms come in shades of white and oatmeal, and have flat-screen TV, Illy espresso maker and Bose stereo, and there's a Michelin-star restaurant serving up modern French cuisine. Breakfast costs extra. €̄495

Prinsenhof Prinsengracht 810 ☎020 623 1772, ⓦhotelprinsenhof.com; map pp.48–49. This place has been offering bed and board since 1813. Today, rooms are tastefully decorated, making it one of the city's top budget options, but with only eleven spacious rooms, booking ahead is essential. Rooms don't have TV, but there is wi-fi. €̄80

Seven Bridges Reguliersgracht 31 ☎020 623 1329, ⓦsevenbridgeshotel.nl; map pp.48–49. Excellent value for money, this hotel takes its name from its canal-side location and is beautifully decorated in antique style, its spotless rooms regularly revamped. It's small and popular, so advance reservations are pretty much essential. Breakfast is served in the rooms. €̄195

★**The Toren** Keizersgracht 164 ☎020 622 6352, ⓦthetoren.nl; map pp.48–49. Cosy, retro-chic boutique hotel, converted from two elegant canal houses (one of which was once the home of the Dutch prime minister), with an emphasis on intimacy and comfort. There's also a sumptuous bar/breakfast room downstairs and snacks for lunch and dinner. Very attentive and friendly staff too. €̄270

Waldorf Astoria Herengracht 542–556 ☎020 718 4600, ⓦwaldorfastoria3.hilton.com; map pp.48–49. The iconic *Waldorf Astoria* set up shop in Amsterdam in 2014, within a series of conjoined seventeenth-century canal houses in one of the city's most prestigious neighbourhoods. The 93 rooms and suites come in tasteful, calming neutral shades, with either canal or garden views.

TOP 5 CANAL-SIDE HOTELS

Staying in a renovated canal house, with a view over the water is one of the real treats of Amsterdam. Here's our favourite canal-side accommodation:

Ambassade See above
Seven Bridges See above
The Toren See above
Waldorf Astoria See above
Wiechmann See p.86

1

There's a variety of dining options, including the two-Michelin-star *Librije's Zusje*, plus a chic Guerlain spa. It's hard to fault, except for the eye-watering cost. **€630**

Wiechmann Prinsengracht 328–332 ☏ 020 626 3321, ⊛ hotelwiechmann.nl; map pp.48–49. Family-run for over fifty years, this medium-sized hotel occupies an attractively restored canal house close to the Anne Frank Huis, with dark wooden beams and homely style throughout. The large, bright rooms – with TV and shower – are a bit bare, but very clean. **€140**

THE JORDAAN

★**De Hallen** Bellamyplein 47 ☏ 020 8208 670, ⊛ hoteldehallen.com; map pp.48–49. A stunningly converted 1902 tram depot, with original features, such as the rails in the dining-room floor and the vaulted glass ceiling. The 55 small but smart rooms – all fresh green tones and white linens – are split over two floors, and arranged around a central area decorated with sofas and modern art from the owner's private collection. The bar and *Remise47* restaurant are good too. Six apartments are also available. **€150**

THE OLD JEWISH QUARTER AND PLANTAGE

Arena 's-Gravesandestraat 51 ☏ 020 850 2400, ⊛ hotelarena.nl; map pp.48–49. A little way east of the centre, in a renovated former orphanage on the edge of the Oosterpark, this hip four-star hotel has split-level rooms in tranquil grey or cream. There's a lovely, relaxed vibe in the bar and intimate restaurant with garden terrace, and a lively late-night club (Fri & Sat) located within the former chapel. Bike rental and in-room massages are also available. Breakfast costs extra. **€129**

AMSTERDAM NOORD AND THE EASTERN DOCKLANDS

Aitana IJDok 6 ☏ 020 891 4800, ⊛ aitana.room-matehotels.com; map pp.48–49. Built on an artificial island just metres from Centraal Station, this ultra-modern hotel has light, bright rooms that come with LCD TV and rainshower, and access to the on-site gym. The breakfast buffet doesn't finish until noon – perfect for late-risers. **€239**

Amstel Botel Moored at NDSM Pier 3 ☏ 020 626 4247, ⊛ www.amstelbotel.com; map pp.48–49. This three-star floating hotel in the NDSM district has 175 en-suite rooms, "waterside" or "landside", with TV and free in-house movies. Rooms are fairly functional – staying here might feel like spending your holiday on a cross-Channel ferry – but the bar has internet access, a pool table, juke box and pinball machine. **€120**

Brooklyn NDSM-Plein 28 ☏ 020 722 0666, ⊛ brooklynhotel.nl; map pp.48–49. The first hotel to set up in the hip NDSM district, this plush boutique option may have icy front-desk staff, but the luxurious rooms, fitness centre, brasserie and bar more than make up for it. **€230**

Faralda Crane NDSM-Plein 78 ☏ 020 760 6161, ⊛ faralda.com; map pp.48–49. Ever slept 50 metres in the air? The world's first hotel in a crane offers three ultra-contemporary suites with knee-buckling city views. Bungee jumping from the top costs €85 a go, or there's the more relaxing spa pool. As you'd expect, there's a long waiting list, so book well in advance. **€435**

★**Lloyd Hotel** Oostelijke Handelskade 34 ☏ 020 561 3607, ⊛ lloydhotel.com; map pp.48–49. This ex-prison has been renovated to become a "cultural embassy", with an arts centre that puts on regular exhibitions and performances. The hotel serves all kinds of travellers, with rooms ranging from one-star, shared-bath affairs to five-star suites. Some rooms are great, others less so, so don't be afraid to ask to change. The pleasantly bustling, airy restaurant and lobby area on the ground floor is a bonus. **€176**

OUD-ZUID, DE PIJP AND THE MUSEUM QUARTER

Bilderberg Hotel Jan Luyken Jan Luykenstraat 58 ☏ 020 573 0730, ⊛ bilderberg.nl; map pp.48–49. A please-all boutique hotel whose smart rooms all have the same cream linens and wood finish. There's a nice lounge and bar downstairs. Pets allowed. **€169**

★**College** Roelof Hartstraat 1 ☏ 020 571 1511, ⊛ thecollegehotel.com; map pp.48–49. Converted from an old nineteenth-century schoolhouse, the *College* is an elegant boutique hotel run by hotel-school students. It has tasteful modern rooms, a first-rate restaurant, a swanky bar and a chic terrace planted with olive trees – perfect for sunny days. **€234**

★**Conscious** De Lairessestraat 7 ☏ 020 671 9596, ⊛ conscioushotels.com; map pp.48–49. Right in the heart of the museum district, this hotel is 100 percent sustainable, from the living plant wall by reception to the 36 rooms, which feature photographic forest wallpaper, Mongolian goat-hair carpet that's anti-static (and good for your feet, apparently), desks made out of recycled yoghurt pots and ergonomic beds. Other pluses are the scrumptious organic breakfast, bike rental and hotel garden. **€140**

★**Conservatorium** Van Baerlestraat 27 ☏ 020 570 0000, ⊛ conservatoriumhotel.com; map pp.48–49. The capital's most jaw-dropping hotel, this heritage building – once the Sweelinck Music Conservatorium – has been transformed into a contemporary design wonderland. Standard guestrooms come with Nespresso machine and free newspapers, plus access to Akasha – the city's largest and most opulent spa. There's a great on-site brasserie too (see p.91). Check website for packages. **€375**

Piet Hein Vossiusstraat 51–53 ☏ 020 662 7205, ⊛ hotelpiethein.nl; map pp.48–49. This sleek three-star has large rooms with views over the entrance to the Vondelpark; the slightly pricier rooms in the modern annexe overlook its peaceful back garden. There's also a comfy bar that's normally open until 1am, and a smart garden. **€176**

B&BS

★**b&nb Herengracht** Herengracht 176, Grachtengordel ☎020 612 0120, ⊛bandnbherengracht .com; map pp.48–49. Owned by the same entrepreneur responsible for *De Hallen* (see opposite), this oh-so-central bed (and no breakfast) has three double rooms: subterranean bolthole, canal view or garden view. They're all snug, but come with an en-suite rainshower, Nespresso coffee machine and flatscreen TV with DVD player. Check-in is at the *Hotel Vondel* on Vondelstraat; you'll then be taken by taxi to the Herengracht. **€150**

Blue Wave Houseboat De Costakade 342 ☎020 427 8968, ⊛bluewavehouseboat.com; map pp.48–49. Hosts Elizabeth, Hans and daughter Maya rent out a double bedroom with en-suite mosaic-tiled bathroom aboard their houseboat. The floating terrace has serene canal views and there's internet, a piano, guitar and a DVD collection for entertainment too. **€180**

★**Maison Rika** Oude Spiegelstraat 12, Grachtengordel ☎020 330 1112, ⊛rikaint.com; map pp.48–49. Housed in a former art gallery, this boutique option has two beautifully furnished queen-size bedrooms on the second and third floors and is owned by fashion designer Ulrika Lundgren, who has a shop across the street. There's free water, chocolates, tea and coffee, but no breakfast. **€250**

Marcel's Creative Exchange Leidsestraat 87, Grachtengordel ☎020 622 9834, ⊛marcelamsterdam .nl; map pp.48–49. Named after owner and graphic designer Marcel van Woekkom, this stylishly restored house has regulars returning year after year, so you'll need to book well in advance in high season. Three en-suite doubles, including one with private patio garden, are available for two, three or four people sharing. No breakfast, but tea- and coffee-making facilities. **€160**

Sunhead of 1617 Herengracht 152, Grachtengordel ☎020 626 1809, ⊛sunhead.com; map pp.48–49. Very popular thanks to its seventeenth-century charm and prime location, this guesthouse offers two rooms, of which the Tulip is the pick, with 6m-high ceiling and canal views. No breakfast but rooms are stocked with muesli bars and a Nespresso machine. Wine-and-cheese evenings are in the pipeline too. **€169**

De Windketel Watertorenplein 8c ⊛windketel.nl; map pp.48–49. A unique chance to stay in an octagonal 1890s converted water tower. Split over three floors, there's a well-equipped kitchen on the ground floor, a living room with floor-to-ceiling windows on the second floor, and in the eaves a bedroom with built-in bathtub and wooden ceiling. Minimum two-night stay. **€325**

HOSTELS

ClinkNoord Badhuiskade 3, Amsterdam Noord ☎020 214 9730, ⊛clinkhostels.com; map pp.48–49. This brand-new hostel housed in the 1920s former headquarters of Shell, offers four- to ten-bed dorms (including women-only dorms) and private en-suite rooms. Facilities include a free cinema, self-catering kitchen, café, library and bar with live music. Dorms **€25**

★**Cocomama** Westeinde 18 Grachtengordel ☎020 627 2454, ⊛cocomama.nl; map pp.48–49. Amsterdam's first boutique hostel, with upmarket two- to six-bed wooden-bunk dorms, four double rooms, and a family room planned. There's also a super-communal kitchen, a lounge with movies and games and a lush garden. Dorms **€38**, doubles **€131**

★**Eco Mama** Valkenburgerstraat 124, Eastern Docklands ☎020 770 9529, ⊛ecomamahotel.com; map pp.48–49. Superb light, bright eco hostel with green roof, water-saving system and rooms that range from "El Cheapo" twelve-bed dorms to very stylish private en-suite doubles; there's a women-only dorm too. Dorms **€42**, doubles **€142**

Flying Pig Uptown Vossiusstraat 46–47, Museum Quarter ☎020 400 4187, ⊛flyingpig.nl; map pp.48–49. The better of the city's two Flying Pig hostels, this one is immaculately clean and well maintained by a staff of travellers. Dorms sleep from four to fourteen, and a few have queen-size bunks that can be shared. There's free use of kitchen facilities, no curfew and good tourist information, as well as a strong party atmosphere – they serve the cheapest beer in town. Dorms **€16**, doubles **€45**

Shelter City Barndesteeg 21, Old Centre ☎020 625 3230, ⊛shelter.nl; map pp.48–49. A non-evangelical Christian youth hostel smack in the middle of the Red Light District. You might be handed a booklet on Jesus when you check in, but you'll get a quiet night's sleep, the sheets are clean and they cook pancakes for breakfast. Dorms are single-sex and require a €15 key deposit; towel rental costs €1. There's a second *Shelter* in the Jordaan. Dorms **€31**

Stayokay Stadsdoelen Kloveniersburgwal 97, Old Centre ☎020 624 6832, ⊛stayokay.com; map p.51. The closest to Centraal Station of the city's three *Stayokay* hostels. There are private twins as well as dorm rooms, and the price includes linen, breakfast and locker, plus use of communal kitchen. There's a good bar with pool table downstairs, and guests get a range of discounts on activities in the city too. Dorms **€39.50**, doubles **€115**

Stayokay Vondelpark Zandpad 5, Museum Quarter ☎020 589 8996, ⊛stayokay.com; map pp.48–49. With 536 beds, this is one of the largest hostels in Europe, with good facilities such as a bar, restaurant, secure lockers, and bike rental and shed, plus various discounts on tours and museums and no curfew. To be sure of a place in high season (when there's a minimum stay of two nights if you want to stay on a Sat), you'll need to book at least two months ahead. Members receive €2.50 discount on every night's stay, plus ten percent discount on bar orders and bike rental. Rates vary enormously, but include use of all facilities, shower (though not towels), sheets and breakfast. Dorms **€39.50**, doubles **€115**

1

EATING

Traditionally at least, Amsterdam has never been one of Europe's culinary hotspots, but there has been a resurgence of interest in Dutch cooking in recent years and the city has accumulated a string of excellent home-grown **restaurants**. It also boasts tremendous gastronomic diversity – as well as having some of the best Indonesian food outside Indonesia, there are lots of ethnic restaurants, from French, Iberian and Italian, to Thai, Middle Eastern and Indian. Amsterdam also excels in the quantity and variety of its **cafés, tearooms and lunch venues**, many of which serve increasingly adventurous and inexpensive food in a wide range of settings. These establishments are generally open all day, might serve alcohol (in which case they are often very similar to bars), but don't allow dope-smoking – and are not to be confused with the city's druggy "**coffeeshops**" (the signage is very different).

THE OLD CENTRE
CAFÉS, TEAROOMS AND LUNCH VENUES

De Bakkerswinkel Warmoesstraat 69 ☎020 489 8000, ⌨bakkerswinkel.nl; map p.51. Part of an immensely popular chain where you can expect to queue for a table at lunchtime. Mouthwatering home-made scones with lemon curd and jam, muffins, cakes, quiches and pies for €5–10. Other branches at Roelof Hartstraat in the Oud-Zuid and at the Westergasfabriek complex in Westerpark. Mon–Fri 8am–5.30pm, Sat & Sun 9am–6pm.

★**Gartine** Taksteeg 7 ☎020 320 4132, ⌨gartine.nl; map p.51. Tucked down an alleyway just off the Kalverstraat shopping street, *Gartine* is an oasis of civilized calm, and most of the ingredients in its delicious sandwiches, salads and afternoon teas are grown in its own allotment. Wed–Sun 10am–6pm.

★**Gebr. Niemeijer** Nieuwendijk 35 ☎020 707 6752, ⌨gebroedersniemeijer.nl; map p.51. A great spot for a continental breakfast before hitting the shops, *Gebr. Niemeijer* serves wonderful pastries and bread (also available to take away) with top-quality organic hams, cheeses, jams and more. The coffee is excellent too. Tues–Fri 8.15am–6.30pm, Sat 8.30am–5pm, Sun 9am–5pm.

Greenwoods Singel 103 ☎020 623 7071, ⌨greenwoods.eu; map p.51. Pocket-sized, English-style tearoom serving up a tasty line in salads, omelettes and cakes. Look out for the daily specials and order an über-English pot of tea, perhaps with some scones and jam? Second branch at Keizersgracht 465. Mon–Thurs 9.30am–6pm, Fri–Sun 9.30am–7pm.

Koffieschenkerij de Oude Kerk Oudekerksplein 27 ☎06 4129 8114, ⌨oudekerk.nl; map p.51. Located in a converted part of the Oude Kerk (see p.58), this café exudes tranquillity. It has a beautiful little garden outside for sunny days, too. The sandwich selection is small but home-made, and the coffee and cakes are delicious. Mon–Sat 10am–6pm, Sun 1–5.30pm.

Puccini Staalstraat 21 ☎020 620 8458, ⌨puccini.nl; map p.51. This lovely café serves great salads, sandwiches, cakes and pastries, a few doors down from its sister chocolate shop (see p.98). Mon–Fri 8.30am–6pm, Sat & Sun 10am–6pm.

RESTAURANTS

Bird Zeedijk 72–74 ☎020 620 1442, ⌨thai-bird.nl; map p.51. This Thai restaurant is always packed, and rightly so, drawing people from far and wide for its authentic Thai fare. Its sister snack bar across the road (also called *Bird*) serves much the same food but in cheap-and-cheerful snack-bar surroundings. Daily 5–11pm; snack bar daily 1–10pm.

★**Blauw aan de Wal** Oudezijds Achterburgwal 99 ☎020 330 2257, ⌨blauwaandewal.com; map p.51. A haven of peace amid the hustle and bustle of the Red Light District, *Blauw aan de Wal* lies down an alleyway in the heart of De Wallen. It serves tremendous French-Dutch food that's a little on the pricey side (three courses at €55) but absolutely worth it. Tues–Sat 6–11.30pm.

★**Lastage** Geldersekade 29 ☎020 737 0811, ⌨restaurantlastage.nl; pp.48–49. Awarded a Michelin star in 2011 (and deservedly so), *Lastage* is serving up some of the most creative, modern Dutch food in Amsterdam. Prices range from €40 for three courses, to €89 for a "flight" of courses that lets you try pretty much the entire menu. Needless to say, booking well in advance is essential. Tues–Sun 6.30–9pm.

Pannenkoekenhuis Upstairs Grimburgwal 2 ☎020 626 5603, ⌨upstairspannenkoeken.nl; map p.51. Minuscule place in a tumbledown house opposite the university buildings, accessible via an extraordinarily steep staircase (think: ladder!), and with dozens of teapots hanging from the ceiling. It serves hearty sweet and savoury pancakes at low prices. Wed–Sun noon–6pm.

Sampurna Singel 498 ☎020 625 3264, ⌨sampurna.com; map p.51. Intimate but relaxed, *Sampurna* has been serving classic Indonesian dishes for decades in its cosy location just off the flower market. Satay skewers are under €10, main dishes are around €20–25, or you can order a bunch of small dishes to share in the form of a *rijsttafel*. Daily noon–11pm.

De Silveren Spiegel Kattengat 4 ☎020 624 6589, ⌨desilverenspiegel.com; map p.51. There's been a restaurant in this location since 1614, and "The Silver Mirror" is one of the best in the city, with a delicately balanced menu of Dutch cuisine. The proprietor lives on the coast and brings in the fish himself. Spectacular food, with a cellar of 350 wines. The tasting menus range from €40 to

€112 depending on number of courses and whether you choose the paired wines to go with them. Mon–Sat 5.30–10.30pm.

Van Kerkwijk Nes 41 ☎020 620 3316, ⓦcaferestaurantvankerkwijk.nl; map p.51. It looks like a café but is more of a restaurant these days, serving steaks, fish and so on, from an ever-changing menu that isn't written down, but heroically memorized by the attentive waiting staff. Good food, and reasonably priced – mains around €15. Daily 11am–1am.

Vasso Roozenboomsteeg 10–14 ☎020 626 0158, ⓦvasso.nl; map p.51. Genuine, creative Italian food served in three curvy, sixteenth-century buildings off a corner of the Spui. Polite and attentive service and semi-steep prices – around €24 for a main course. Mon–Sat 5–11pm.

THE GRACHTENGORDEL
CAFÉS, TEAROOMS AND LUNCH VENUES

Buffet van Odette Prinsengracht 598 ☎020 423 6034, ⓦbuffet-amsterdam.nl; map pp.48–49. Neat little place decorated in attractive, modern style and serving tasty snacks and light meals, from home-made quiches, soups and pastas through to fruit tarts; cheese omelettes are the house speciality. Daily 10am–10pm.

Madame de Pompadour Huidenstraat 12 ☎020 623 9554, ⓦpompadour-amsterdam.nl; map pp.48–49. This patisserie and chocolatier sells dozens of different sorts of bonbon as well as a mouthwatering selection of cakes and candied fruits – take out or eat in. Mon–Fri 10am–6pm, Sat 9am–5pm, Sun noon–6pm.

★ **Singel 404** Singel 404 ☎020 428 0154; map pp.48–49. A favourite among students for decades, *Singel 404* serves arguably *the* best sandwiches in Amsterdam. Try the smoked chicken, avocado, sun-dried tomatoes and Brie – lunch heaven. Get there early or be prepared to wait for a table. Daily 10am–6pm.

Spanjer & van Twist Leliegracht 60 ☎020 639 0109, ⓦspanjerenvantwist.nl; map pp.48–49. Hip café-bar with an arty air and brisk modern fittings. Tasty snacks and light meals, including daily specials of soups, quiches and pasta. The terrace right on the canal is a gorgeous place to people-watch during the summer. Daily 10am–1am.

Van Harte Hartenstraat 24 ☎020 625 8500, ⓦvanharte.com; map pp.48–49. Crowded and cheerful spot for lunch, dinner and drinks with tasty sandwiches, a large tea selection, home-made pies and bonbons from *Pompadour* (see above). Good pan-European, three-course dinner menu for €25. Mon & Sun 10am–6pm, Tues–Thurs 10am–11pm, Fri & Sat 10am–midnight.

RESTAURANTS

Bar Huf Reguliersdwarsstraat 43 ☎020 303 9561, ⓦbarhuf.nl; map pp.48–49. A handy place for late-night dining, *Bar Huf* is Amsterdam's answer to a gastropub. Burgers, ribs, mac 'n' cheese and salads are all on the menu, but given a modern, creative twist that elevates them above their humble origins. Main courses average around €10–15. Mon–Thurs & Sun 4pm–1am, Fri & Sat 4pm–3am.

Belhamel Brouwersgracht 60 ☎020 622 1095, ⓦbelhamel.nl; map p.51. Beautiful restaurant where the Art Nouveau decor makes a delightful setting and the menu is extremely well chosen, mixing French and Italian dishes with Dutch influences. Main courses at around €22–25. The prime tables have charming canal views, and the overall experience makes for a very romantic evening. Mon–Thurs & Sun noon–4pm & 6–10pm, Fri & Sat noon–4pm & 6–10.30pm.

★ **Beulings** Beulingstraat 9 ☎020 320 6100, ⓦbeulings.nl; map pp.48–49. Perfect for a special occasion, *Beulings* is a sophisticated but intimate place serving elegant French food. Five-course chef's tasting menu for €55. Mon & Thurs–Sun 7–11pm.

★ **Café de Klepel** Prinsenstraat 22 ☎020 623 8244, ⓦcafedeklepel.nl; map pp.48–49. Brown café turned gorgeous restaurant, *Café de Klepel* serves up delicious French-inspired dishes with an extensive wine list. The menu is short but perfectly balanced, and the venue itself has an airy but intimate atmosphere. Good choice for a delightful evening out. Mon–Fri 6pm–midnight, Sat 4pm–midnight, Sun 4–10pm.

Kagetsu Hartenstraat 17 ☎020 427 3828, ⓦkagetsu .nl; map pp.48–49. Excellent Japanese restaurant in the Negen Straatjes for sushi and other traditional Japanese dishes. The freshness of *Kagetsu's* fish is second to none. Two other branches at Van Woustraat 29 and Kastelenstraat 268. Daily noon–10.30pm.

Taste of Vietnam Herenstraat 28 ☎020 358 6715, ⓦthetasteofvietnam.nl; map p.51. Vietnamese restaurants have recently taken off in Amsterdam, and this is one of the finest – albeit also one of the more expensive. The fresh spring rolls, soups and noodle dishes are all delightful, and you can also order a chef's tasting menu for €34.50 per person. Tues–Sun 4.30–10.30pm.

Tempo Doeloe Utrechtsestraat 75 ☎020 625 6718, ⓦtempodoeloerestaurant.nl; map pp.48–49. A buzzing place packed full of tables serving excellent *rijsttafels* whose component parts come in several spice levels. Beware the "very hot" dishes – they can be eye watering. Reservations are a must, but don't expect to get seated on time. Mon–Sat 6–11.30pm.

Van de Kaart Prinsengracht 512 ☎020 625 9232, ⓦvandekaart.com; map pp.48–49. Excellent French/ Mediterranean basement restaurant decorated in minimalist style and featuring an inventive, ever-changing menu, with excellent service. Three courses for €37.50. Mon–Sat from 5.30pm, but it's also a catering business so opening times vary – call ahead to check.

1

THE JORDAAN

CAFÉS, TEAROOMS AND LUNCH VENUES

Festina Lente Looiersgracht 40b ☎020 638 1412, ⓦ cafefestinalente.nl; map pp.48–49. Relaxed, neighbourhood café-bar with mismatched furniture and armchairs to laze in. The outside tables overlooking the canal are a suntrap in the summer when the locals come out to relax with friends for the afternoon; inside is cosy in the winter, and has a good selection of board games. Mon & Sun noon–1am, Tues–Thurs 10.30am–1am, Fri & Sat 10.30am–3am.

Small World Binnen Oranjestraat 14 ☎020 420 2774, ⓦ smallworldcatering.nl; map pp.48–49. Tiny, Australian-run café and deli with a few chairs inside and a few more on the pavement outside. Amazing sandwiches, salads, savoury pies and juices, as well as a selection of cakes and muffins that's as delicious as it is varied. Tues–Fri 10.30am–7pm, Sat 10.30am–6pm, Sun noon–6pm.

Winkel 43 Noordermarkt 43 ☎020 623 0223, ⓦ winkel43.nl; map pp.48–49. Queue up along with the rest of Amsterdam (or so it seems) for what's often reputed to be the best apple pie in Amsterdam, home-made in the basement of this sober but agreeable lunchroom-cum-restaurant. Great coffee and fresh mint tea to go with it. Mon 7am–1am, Tues–Thurs 8am–1am, Fri 8am–3am, Sat 7am–3am, Sun 10am–1am.

RESTAURANTS

★**Daalder** Lindengracht 90 ☎020 624 8864, ⓦ daalderamsterdam.nl; map pp.48–49. *Daalder* may look like a brown café, but behind the scenes is a seriously ambitious chef turning out exquisite modern European food. Despite its recent Michelin-starred status, a three-course menu sets you back just €36.50 at the time of writing. Mon–Fri & Sun noon–1am, Sat 10am–1am.

DiVino Boomstraat 41a ☎020 845 2207, ⓦ wijnbar divino.nl; map pp.48–49. Although it calls itself a wine bar, *diVino* is as much a simple Italian restaurant as it is a bar – perfect for *aperitivo* o'clock. Order some of its cured meats and cheeses as *antipasti*, and then move onto the delicious but affordable fresh pasta. Mon–Thurs 5pm–midnight, Fri 5pm–2am, Sat 4pm–2am, Sun 4pm–midnight.

Hugo's Hugo de Grootplein 10 ☎020 751 6633, ⓦ barhugo.nl; map pp.48–49. A creative European kitchen serving up three courses for €32 or à la carte mains such as steak, fish and gnocchi for around €20. The bar staff also mix up tasty cocktails – ask for the Hugo the Great. Tues–Thurs 6pm–1am, Fri & Sat 5pm–3am.

La Oliva Egelantiersstraat 122–124 ☎020 320 4316, ⓦ laoliva.nl; map pp.48–49. This sleek Jordaan establishment specializes in *pintxos*, the delectable Basque snacks on sticks that make Spanish bar-hopping such a delight. With a nod to Dutch tastes perhaps, this is more of a restaurant than a bar, and the *pintxos* anything but bite-sized. But you're more than welcome to sit at the bar and sample one or two with a drink. Mon–Wed & Sun noon–10pm, Thurs–Sat noon–11pm.

YamYam Frederik Hendrikstraat 88-90 ☎020 681 5097, ⓦ yamyam.nl; map pp.48–49. Top pizzeria and *trattoria* in a simple, traditional dining room with an open kitchen. It attracts the couples and hip young parents of the neighbourhood with its excellent pizza toppings, including fresh *rucola* and truffle sauce. Pizzas €8–13. Booking strongly advised. Tues–Sat 6–10pm, Sun 5.30–10pm.

THE OLD JEWISH QUARTER AND PLANTAGE

CAFÉS, TEAROOMS AND LUNCH VENUES

De Hortus Plantage Middenlaan 2a ☎020 625 9021, ⓦ dehortus.nl; map pp.48–49. The pleasant café in the orangery of the Hortus Botanicus (see p.71) serves a good range of tasty sandwiches and rolls – plus cakes and tarts supplied by the famous Patisserie Kuyt. Unfortunately, you do have to pay entry for the gardens (€8.50) to get to the café. Daily 10am–5pm.

RESTAURANTS

Gebroeders Hartering Peperstraat 10 ☎020 421 0699 ⓦ gebrhartering.nl; map pp.48–49. Run by two brothers, *Gebroeders Hartering* serves up a feast for a special occasion. Choose from four courses for €40 up to nine courses for €75. Menus are always seasonal and frequently adventurous, with offal and unpasteurized cheeses frequently appearing. Tues & Wed 6–10.30pm, Thurs–Sat 6–11pm, Sun 6–10pm.

★**Greetje** Peperstraat 23–25 ☎020 779 7450, ⓦ restaurantgreetje.nl; map pp.48–49. A cosy, busy restaurant serving traditional Dutch dishes with a modern twist. A changing menu reflects the seasons and the favourite dishes of the owner's mother – a native of the southern Netherlands. Superb home cooking with great service. Daily 6–10pm.

THE EASTERN DOCKLANDS AND AMSTERDAM NOORD

CAFÉS, TEAROOMS AND LUNCH VENUES

★**Café de Ceuvel** Korte Papaverweg 4 ☎020 229 6210, ⓦ cafedeceuvel.nl; map pp.48–49. This genial vegetarian café, opened in June 2014, is well worth the walk. The friendly owners have transformed a polluted shipyard into a sustainable green "business" park, of which the café – constructed entirely from recycled materials – forms the hub. The quiches, salads and sandwiches (€8) include ingredients and herbs grown from their converted houseboat garden; don't miss the home-made lemonade. Mon–Thurs & Sun noon–midnight, Fri & Sat noon–2am; closed Mon in winter.

1

RESTAURANTS

★**Pllek** Tt. Neveritaweg 59 ☎020 290 0020, ⓦpllek
.nl; map pp.48–49. One of several hip venues to have
sprung up at the NDSM wharf, *Pllek* is arguably the best.
Dishes are inventive, international and affordable: mains
like wild boar stew will set you back around €19. Mon–
Thurs & Sun 9.30am–1am, Fri & Sat 9.30am–3am.

OUD-ZUID, DE PIJP AND THE MUSEUM QUARTER

CAFÉS, TEAROOMS AND LUNCH VENUES

Conservatorium Brasserie & Lounge Van Baerlestraat
27 ☎020 570 0000, ⓦconservatoriumhotel.com; map
pp.48–49. Inside the gorgeously renovated *Conservatorium
Hotel*, the *Brasserie* serves an all-day dining concept including
salads, sandwiches and seasonal daily meals at lunchtime. It
may not be cheap, but it's worth it for the amazing glass-
roofed courtyard venue. Daily 6.30am–1am.

Le Pain Quotidien Johannes Verhulststraat 104 ☎020
379 5900, ⓦlepainquotidien.nl; map pp.48–49. A
small but growing chain of French bakeries and cafés, *Le
Pain Quotidien* is popular with foodies and families alike.
The bread and pastries are all super-fresh, and come
topped with continental staples like ham, cheese or jam, or
more adventurous choices like hummus, smoked salmon or
avocado and tomato salsa. Daily 8am–6pm.

Toussaint Café Bosboom Toussaintstraat 26 ☎020
685 0737, ⓦbosboom-toussaint.nl; map pp.48–49.
This cosy, very friendly café not far from the Vondelpark is a
pleasant spot for lunch – excellent sandwiches, toasties
and *uitsmijters*, as well as tapas-style options. Mon–Thurs
& Sun 9am–midnight, Fri & Sat 9am–1am.

RESTAURANTS

★**Loetje** Johannes Vermeerstraat 52 ☎020 662 8173,
ⓦloetje.com; map pp.48–49. Excellent steaks, fries and
salads are the order of the day at this *eetcafé*. The pleasant
outdoor terrace in the summer is a bonus. This is the
original of four branches in Amsterdam, the others being at
Central Station (Stationsplein 10), Werfkade 14 and
Ruyschstraat 15. Daily 10am–10.30pm.

Zus & Zus Overtoom 548 ☎020 616 5825,
ⓦrestaurantzusenzus.nl; map pp.48–49. This family-
run restaurant serves a monthly-changing seasonal menu
of Mediterranean-inspired meat, fish and vegetarian
dishes. Though it's a little off the beaten track when coming
from the centre, it's is well worth the tram ride – friendly
and affordable with mains at €12–17. Mon–Sat 6–11pm.

DRINKING

Amsterdam's selection of **bars and café-bars** is one of the real pleasures of the city. There are, in essence, two main kinds
of bar: the traditional, old-style bar or brown café – a *bruin café* or *bruine kroeg* – cosy, intimate places so called because of
the colour of their walls, stained by years of tobacco smoke; and the slick, self-consciously modern designer bars, which
tend to be as un-brown as possible and geared towards a younger crowd. Another type of drinking spot – though there are
very few of them left – is the tasting house (*proeflokalen*), originally the sampling room of small private distillers, now tiny,
stand-up places that concentrate on selling spirits – mainly Dutch gin or *jenever*.

THE OLD CENTRE

Bubbles & Wines Nes 37 ☎020 422 3318,
ⓦbubblesandwines.com; map p.51. More than fifty
wines available by the glass in this intimate and elegant
wine and champagne bar. The knowledgeable staff will
advise you on drinks to suit your taste. Mon–Sat
3.30pm–1am, Sun 2–9pm.

Café de Dokter Roozenboomsteeg 4 ☎020 626 4427,
ⓦcafe-de-dokter.nl; map p.51. Small, dark, brown café
with stained glass and furnishings that all look like they've
been there for centuries – which they probably have, given
that *Café de Dokter* has been in business since 1798. Liqueurs
fill the shelves behind the tiny bar, and the *ossenworst* (raw
smoked beef sausage) is to die for. Tues–Sat 4pm–1am.

★**Gollem** Raamsteeg 4 ⓦcafegollem.nl; map p.51.
Small, cosy, split-level bar with rickety furniture, wood
panelling and a comprehensive selection of Belgian beers,
plus a few Dutch brews for variety – and with the correct
glasses to drink them from. Three other branches at
Overtoom 160, Daniel Stalpertstraat 74 and Amstelstraat
34. Mon–Fri 4pm–1am, Sat & Sun noon–3am.

★**In de Wildeman** Kolksteeg 3 ☎020 638 2348,
ⓦindewildeman.nl; map p.51. This lovely old-fashioned
watering-hole has a barely changed wood-and-tile interior
that still boasts its original low bar and shelving: a peaceful
escape from the loud, tacky shops of nearby Nieuwendijk.
One of the centre's most appealing beer-tasting houses.
Mon–Thurs & Sun noon–1am, Fri & Sat noon–2am.

Mata Hari Oudezijds Achterburgwal 22 ☎020 205 0919,
ⓦmatahari-amsterdam.nl; map p.51. A breath of fresh air
at the northern end of the seedy Red Light District, *Mata Hari*
is a spacious, trendy bar with vintage/retro styling that's
popular with locals as well as tourists. Also does good food.
Mon–Thurs & Sun noon–1am, Fri & Sat noon–3am.

Tales & Spirits Lijnbaanssteeg 5 ☎06 5535 6467,
ⓦtalesandspirits.com; map p.51. Down an alleyway just
off the Singel canal, *Tales & Spirits* does a delicious line in
unique cocktails, which make a delicious pre-dinner
aperitif or a great start to a night out on the town. The food
is also creative and not too pricey for its central location,
with dishes coming in at around €9–15. Tues–Thurs
5.30pm–1am, Fri & Sat 5.30pm–3am.

1

★**Wynand Fockink** Pijlsteeg 31 ☎020 639 2695, ⓦwynand-fockink.nl; map p.51. This small, intimate bar, hidden just behind the *Krasnapolsky* hotel off Dam square, is one of the city's oldest *proeflokalen*, and it offers a vast range of its own flavoured *jenevers* that were once distilled down the street. It's standing room only here – you bend down at the counter and sip your *jenever* from a glass filled to the brim. Daily 3–9pm.

THE GRACHTENGORDEL

Café Papeneiland Prinsengracht 2 ☎020 624 1989, ⓦpapeneiland.nl; map pp.48–49. With its wood panelling, antique Delft tiles and ancient stove, this rabbit warren of a place is one of the cosiest (and oldest, founded in 1642) bars in the Grachtengordel. Jam-packed late at night with a garrulous crew of locals and tourists alike. Mon–Thurs & Sun 10am–1am, Fri & Sat 10am–3am.

L&B Whisky Café Korte Leidsedwarsstraat 82 ☎020 625 2387, ⓦwhiskyproeverijen.nl/cafe; map pp.48–49. With literally hundreds of whiskies on offer, *L&B* has the biggest selection anywhere in the Netherlands. From Scotch to Irish whiskies, and from bourbon to Japanese varieties, you'll find it all here. Mon–Thurs & Sun 8pm–3am, Fri & Sat 8pm–4am.

Mystique Utrechtsestraat 30 ☎020 330 2994, ⓦmystiqueamsterdam.nl; map pp.48–49. While upstairs is an Asian-fusion restaurant, downstairs is a swanky cocktail bar. The lighting is low, the decor designed to seduce. The cocktails are fantastic, and the list changes regularly – try one of the punch bowls if they're on offer. Tues–Thurs 5pm–1am, Fri & Sat 5pm–3am.

★**NJOY** Korte Leidsedwarsstraat 93 ⓦnjoycocktails .com; map pp.48–49. You have to ring a buzzer and follow the dress code to get into *NJOY* (so make sure you're not wearing trainers or a baseball cap) but for all that, once you're inside it's not at all pretentious. A lively spot near the Leidseplein for a few excellently made cocktails. Be warned: the Cosmopolitans are *very* strong. Mon–Thurs & Sun 5pm–3am, Fri 4pm–4am, Sat 5pm–4am.

Van Puffelen Prinsengracht 377 ☎020 624 6270, ⓦrestaurantvanpuffelen.com; map pp.48–49. This long-established and popular spot is divided into two, with a brown café-bar on one side and an eetcafé on the other. The café-bar is an appealing place to drink, with a good choice of international beers, while the restaurant side concentrates on Dutch(ish) dishes with occasional Mediterranean leanings. Main courses average around €18–20. Mon–Thurs from 4pm, Fri–Sun from noon till late.

★**De Zotte** Raamstraat 29 ☎020 626 8694, ⓦdezotte .nl; map pp.48–49. Down a tiny street tucked behind the Leidseplein, this laidback bar specializes in Belgian beer, of which it has dozens of varieties. The chips and mayo are pretty amazing too. Daily 4pm–1am.

THE JORDAAN

★**Bar Oldenhof** Elandsgracht 84 ☎020 751 3273, ⓦbar-oldenhof.com; pp.48–49. Beautiful old-fashioned bar, decorated with opulent velvet, leather armchairs and deer antlers on the wall. *Oldenhof* does a great line in cocktails, as well as single malt whiskies and fine wines. Settle in for an evening, and leave feeling like Ernest Hemingway himself. Tues–Thurs 7pm–1am, Fri & Sat 7pm–3am, Sun 4–11pm.

Café Nol Westerstraat 109 ☎020 624 5380, ⓦcafenol-amsterdam.nl; map pp.48–49. Raucous but jolly Jordaan singing bar, this luridly lit dive closes late, especially at weekends, when the back-slapping joviality and drunken sing-alongs keep you rooted until the small hours. Wed, Thurs & Sun 9pm–3am, Fri & Sat 9pm–4am.

De Reiger Nieuwe Leliestraat 34 ☎020 624 7426, ⓦdereigeramsterdam.nl; map pp.48–49. Situated in the thick of the Jordaan, this is one of the area's many meeting places: an old-style café-bar filled with modish Amsterdammers, and with faded portraits on the walls. Mains for around €20. Tues–Thurs 5pm–10.30pm, Fri–Sun noon–4pm & 5pm–10.30pm.

★**'t Smalle** Egelantiersgracht 12 ☎020 623 9617, ⓦt-smalle.nl; map pp.48–49. Candlelit and comfortable café-bar, with a pontoon on the canal out front for relaxed summer afternoons. In winter, be sure to try the *gluhwein*. Mon–Thurs & Sun 10am–1am, Fri & Sat 10am–2am.

Vesper Vinkenstraat 57 ⓦvesperbar.nl; map pp.48–49. On a quiet street sandwiched between the lovely Brouwersgracht canal and the Haarlemmerdijk shopping street, *Vesper* is an intimate little cocktail bar that's perfect for a pre-dinner aperitif or a late-night tipple. Try the Vesper Martini – cocktail heaven. Tues–Thurs 8pm–1am, Fri & Sat 5pm–3am, Sun 7pm–1am.

THE OLD JEWISH QUARTER AND PLANTAGE

★**Brouwerij 't IJ** Funenkade 7 ☎020 622 8325, ⓦbrouwerijhetij.nl; map pp.48–49. Long-established brewery in the old public baths adjoining the Gooyer windmill. Serves up an excellent range of its own home-made beers and ales, from the thunderously strong (nine percent) Columbus amber ale to the easier-drinking Natte (6.5 percent). Daily 2–8pm.

Hanneke's Boom Dijksgracht 4 ☎020 419 9820, ⓦhannekesboom.nl; map pp.48–49. Right on the waterfront between Central Station and NEMO science centre, this hipster hangout is especially popular in summer. Grab a beanbag or a bench and get working on that tan . . . Mon–Thurs & Sun 11am–1am, Fri & Sat 11am–3am.

★**Hiding in Plain Sight** Rapenburg 18, ☎06 2529 3620, ⓦhpsamsterdam.nl; map pp.48–49. Arguably the best cocktail bar in Amsterdam, decorated in the style of an old American speakeasy. The drinks menu is ever-changing, but if you find it impossible to choose then just ask the extremely knowledgeable bar staff what they recommend. Also has a large selection of mescal. Mon–Thurs 6pm–1am, Fri, Sat 6pm–3am.

THE OUD-ZUID, DE PIJP AND THE MUSEUM QUARTER

Café Wildschut Roelof Hartplein 1–3 ☎ 020 676 8220, ⓦ cafewildschut.nl; map pp.48–49. Just around the corner from the *College Hotel*, this busy bar-café is famous for its congenial, spacious Art Deco interior and outdoor seating in summer. By far the nicest place to drink in the area, with a decent menu too. Mon–Fri from 9am, Sat & Sun from 10am till late.

COFFEESHOPS

In Amsterdam a "**coffeeshop**" is advertising just one thing: **cannabis**. You might also be able to get coffee and a slice of cake, but the main activity in a coffeeshop is, predictably enough, dope smoking. In recent years, the number of coffeeshops has reduced dramatically due to a number of laws and regulations coming into force. Coffeeshops are no longer allowed to operate within a few hundred metres of schools, "grow shops" (shops selling the wherewithal to grow marijuana) have been banned, and tobacco is not allowed to be smoked inside coffeeshops. The laws are tightening all the time, so make sure you do your research before lighting up.

Barney's Breakfast Bar Haarlemmerstraat 102 ☎ 020 625 9761, ⓦ barneys.biz; map pp.48–49. This extremely popular café-cum-coffeeshop is one of the most civilized places in town to enjoy a big hit with a fine breakfast – at any time of day. A few doors down, at no. 98, *Barney's Farm* affords a nice sunny spot in the morning and serves alcohol, and across the street *Barney's Uptown* has good cocktails in a trendier environment. Daily 8am–1am.

The Bulldog Palace Leidseplein 15 ☎ 020 422 3444, ⓦ thebulldog.com; map pp.48–49. The biggest and most famous of the coffeeshop chains, and a long way from its poky Red Light District origins, the main branch of *The Bulldog* is here on the Leidseplein, housed in a former police station. It has a large cocktail bar, coffeeshop, juice bar and souvenir shop, all with separate entrances. It's big and brash, not at all the place for a quiet smoke, though the dope they sell (packaged up in neat little brand-labelled bags) is reliably good. Mon–Thurs 10am–1am, Fri & Sat 10am–3am, Sun 10am–2am.

Dampkring Handboogstraat 29 ☎ 020 638 0705, ⓦ dampkring-coffeeshop-amsterdam.nl; map p.51. Colourful coffeeshop with loud music and a laidback atmosphere, known for its good-quality hash. A second branch, also popular, has opened on Haarlemmerstraat, just west of Central Station. Daily 10am–1am.

Paradox 1e Bloemdwarsstraat 2 ☎ 020 623 5639, ⓦ paradoxcoffeeshop.com; map pp.48–49. If you're fed up with the usual coffeeshop food offerings, *Paradox* satisfies the munchies with outstanding natural food, including spectacular fresh fruit smoothies and veggie burgers. Daily 10am–8pm.

★ **Rusland** Rusland 16 ☎ 020 627 9468, ⓦ coffeeshop-rusland-amsterdam.com; map p.51. One of the first Amsterdam coffeeshops, a cramped but vibrant place that's a favourite with both dope fans and tea addicts (it has forty different kinds). A cut above the rest. Daily 8am–12.30am.

★ **Siberië** Brouwersgracht 11 ☎ 020 623 5909, ⓦ coffeeshopsiberie.nl; map p.51. Bright, modern coffeeshop set up by former *Rusland* (see above) staff and notable for having avoided the over-commercialization of the larger chains. Very relaxed, very friendly, and worth a visit whether you want to smoke or not; has a good selection of magazines and a chessboard. Mon–Thurs 9am–11pm, Fri & Sat 9am–midnight, Sun 10am–11pm.

ENTERTAINMENT AND NIGHTLIFE

Amsterdam offers a broad range of **music, dance and film**, partly due to its relatively youthful population and partly to government subsidies. Indeed, the city is often at the cutting edge of the arts and its frequent **festivals** and fringe events provide plenty of offbeat/exciting entertainment. It's also something of a magnet for **clubbers**, with numerous venues clustered around Leidseplein and its environs buzzing into the small hours, and more late-night haunts among the narrow lanes and alleys around Rembrandtplein.

ROCK, JAZZ AND FOLK VENUES

Amsterdam is a regular tour stop for many major artists, and something of a testing ground for current rock bands. Alongside the main venues, the city's clubs, bars and multimedia centres host live bands on a regular basis.

Akhnaton Nieuwezijds Kolk 25, Old Centre ☎ 020 624 3396, ⓦ akhnaton.nl; map p.51. This crowded, lively, soi-disant "Centre for World Culture" is your best bet for Latin

music, hosting a wide-ranging programme of events, from salsa nights to Turkish dance parties. Mon–Thurs & Sun 9pm–4am, Fri–Sat 5pm–5am.

Amsterdam ArenA ArenA Blvd 1, Oud-Zuid ☎ 020 311 1333, ⓦ amsterdamarena.nl; map pp.48–49. The Ajax soccer stadium also plays host to world-class music acts.

Bimhuis Piet Heinkade 3, eastern docklands ☎ 020 788 2150, ⓦ bimhuis.nl; map pp.48–49. The city's

1

WHAT'S ON WHERE AND WHEN

The quickest way to find up-to-date listings of events is to visit ⓦ iamsterdam.com, or you can pop into the new I amsterdam store and the visitor centres (see p.80) for information about what's on, as well as tickets and copies of listings magazines. You can buy the excellent English-language *A-mag*, published every two months, from visitor centres too (€3.50), as well as free copies of the Dutch-only *Uitkrant*, which has comprehensive listings of all concerts, festivals and theatre events. You could also try the Wednesday entertainment supplement of the daily newspaper *Het Parool*. Tickets for most concerts and events can be bought from the visitor centres or The Last Minute Ticket Shop (see p.81)

premier jazz and improvised music venue is located right next to the Muziekgebouw, beside the River IJ to the east of Centraal Station. There are gigs from Dutch and international artists throughout the week, as well as jam sessions and workshops, plus a bar and restaurant for concertgoers, with pleasant views over the river. Mon–Thurs & Sun 6.30pm–1am, Fri & Sat 6.30pm–3am.

Café Alto Korte Leidsedwarsstraat 115, Grachtengordel ☎ 020 626 3249, ⓦ jazz-cafe-alto.nl; map pp.48–49. It's worth hunting out this legendary little jazz bar just off Leidseplein for its quality modern jazz every night; though slightly cramped, it's high on atmosphere. Entry is free, and you don't have to buy a beer to hang out and watch the band. Mon–Thurs & Sun 9pm–3am, Fri & Sat 9pm–4am.

Heineken Music Hall ArenA Blvd 590, Oud-Zuid ☎ 020 311 1333, ⓦ heineken-music-hall.nl; map pp.48–49. This hi-tech music venue attracts international pop stars and bands, as well as hosting music festivals and football matches.

Maloe Melo Lijnbaansgracht 163, Jordaan ☎ 020 420 4592, ⓦ www.maloemelo.com; map pp.48–49. You can catch lively local blues acts every day of the week in the small back room of this dimly lit, low-ceilinged bar. €5 entry Fri & Sat. Mon–Thurs & Sun 9pm–3am, Fri & Sat 9pm–4am.

★Melkweg Lijnbaansgracht 234a, Grachtengordel ☎ 020 531 8181, ⓦ melkweg.nl; map pp.48–49. The Melkweg ("Milky Way") is probably Amsterdam's most respected entertainment venue. A former dairy (hence the name) just round the corner from Leidseplein, it has two separate halls for live music, hosting a broad range of genres, from reggae to rock. There's also a café-restaurant (Marnixstraat entrance; Wed–Sun noon–9pm).

North Sea Jazz Club Pazzanistraat 1, Jordaan ☎ 020 722 0980, ⓦ northseajazzclub.com; map pp.48–49. Exactly what a jazz club should be: low-lit, intimate and with a superb roster of top musicians. Three-course dinner concerts are available too. Daily 7pm–5am.

Winston International Warmoesstraat 123, Old Centre ☎ 020 623 1380, ⓦ winston.nl; map pp.48–49. Part of the arty *Winston Hotel* (see p.85), this adventurous small venue attracts an eclectic crowd and offers a mix of live bands, electro, drum'n'bass and cheesy pop nights. Mon–Thurs 9pm–late, Fri & Sat 11pm–late, Sun 10pm–late.

CLUBS

Amsterdam's full-throttle club scene ranges from standard-issue meat markets to the cool, the rough, the ready, the rough and ready and the super groovy. DJs, both domestic stars and big-name imports, have headline status and most play variations on house, trance, garage and techno. As you might expect, it's a late-night scene too – arrive before 11pm and you'll wonder where everyone is. Most clubs charge for entry, with ticket prices between €15 and €20 at weekends and around €10 during the week. A singular feature of Amsterdam clubbing, however, is that you should tip the bouncer if you want to return to the same place next week; €1 or €2 in the palm of his hand will do. Drinks are only slightly more expensive than in cafés, though you'll usually pay a bit more for spirits.

Bitterzoet Spuistraat 2, Old Centre ☎ 020 421 2318, ⓦ bitterzoet.com; map p.51. Spacious but cosy two-floor bar and theatre hosting a mixed bag of events: DJs playing punk, hip-hop, r'n'b, reggae and disco, film screenings and occasional urban poetry nights. Mon–Thurs & Sun 8pm–3am, Fri & Sat 8pm–4am.

Disco Dolly Handboogstraat 11, Old Centre ☎ 020 620 1779, ⓦ discodolly.nl; map p.51. The reincarnation of the *Dansen bij Jansen* club, this two-floor disco-ball club plays a soundtrack of soul, boogie-woogie, disco, deep house and occasional hip-hop. Very popular with students. Mon–Thurs 10pm–4am, Fri–Sun 10pm–5am.

Escape Rembrandtplein 11, Grachtengordel ☎ 020 622 1111, ⓦ escape.nl; map pp.48–49. A feature of Amsterdam's clubbing scene since the 1980s, this vast club can hold two thousand people. It has undergone renovations to stay modern, with an impressive sound system and visuals, and the new café and lounge should pull in the crowds. Thurs 11pm–4am, Fri & Sat 11pm–5am, Sun 11pm–4.30am.

Jimmy Woo Korte Leidsedwarsstraat 18, Grachtengordel ☎ 020 626 3150, ⓦ jimmywoo.com; map pp.48–49. This exclusive club is spread over two floors: upstairs, the black lacquered walls, Japanese lamps and cosy booths with leather couches have an intimate, sexy vibe, while downstairs a packed dancefloor throbs under the oscillating light from hundreds of light bulbs studded into the ceiling. It's popular with young, well-dressed locals, so look smart if you want to join in. Wed–Thurs & Sun 11pm–3am, Fri & Sat 11pm–4am.

Melkweg Lijnbaansgracht 234a, Grachtengordel ☏ 020 531 8181, ⓦ melkweg.nl; map pp.48–49. After the bands have finished (see opposite), excellent, offbeat disco sessions go on well into the small hours, sometimes featuring the best DJs in town, with anything from dancehall to indie pop. The *Melkweg* also plays host to some of the most enjoyable theme nights around, from African dance to experimental jazz-trance. There's also a café-restaurant (Marnixstraat entrance; Wed–Sun noon–9pm). Opening times vary; check the website.

★**Panama** Oostelijke Handelskade 4, eastern docklands ☏ 020 311 8686, ⓦ panama.nl; map pp.48–49. One of Amsterdam's coolest clubs, *Panama* overlooks the River IJ and plays host to top-name international DJs (Thurs–Sun). Dress to impress. There's also a restaurant, *Mercat*. Mon–Wed noon–1am, Thurs & Sun noon–3am, Fri & Sat noon–4am.

★**Paradiso** Weteringschans 6–8, Grachtengordel ☏ 020 626 4521, ⓦ paradiso.nl; map pp.48–49. One of the principal venues in the city, this converted church just around the corner from the Leidseplein is popular with an alternative crowd. On Wed and Thurs eclectic dance night "Noodlanding" continues to draw in the crowds, and look out for DJ sets featuring live performances on Sat. Hours vary.

CLASSICAL MUSIC AND OPERA

There's no shortage of classical music concerts in Amsterdam, with two major orchestras based in the city, plus regular visits by other touring orchestras. Amsterdam's Koninklijk Concertgebouworkest (Royal Concertgebouw Orchestra; ⓦ concertgebouworkest.nl) is one of the most dynamic in the world, and occupies one of Europe's finest concert halls to boot, sharing its premises with the other resident orchestra, the Nederlands Philharmonisch Orkest (Dutch Philharmonic; ⓦ orkest.nl). There's also the internationally renowned Nationale Opera & Ballet (ⓦ operaballet.nl), which joined forces with the closely associated Muziektheater in 2013.

Carré Theater Amstel 115–125, Grachtengordel ☏ 0900 252 5255, ⓦ carre.nl. A chunky old building on the eastern bank of the Amstel which, aside from its folk associations, hosts all kinds of top international acts, with an emphasis on hit musicals.

Concertgebouw Concertgebouwplein 2–6, Museum Quarter ☏ 0900 671 8345, ⓦ concertgebouw.nl. One of the most impressive venues in the city, with a star-studded international programme, yet very reasonable prices (€15–50). Free 30min Wednesday lunchtime concerts are held from September to May (doors open 12.15pm; arrive early), and in July and August there's a heavily subsidized series of summer concerts.

Muziekgebouw aan't IJ Piet Heinkade 1, eastern docklands ☏ 020 788 2000, ⓦ muziekgebouw.nl. Amsterdam's first new concert hall in over a hundred years, opened in 2005, has two medium-sized concert halls, state-of-the-art acoustics and a café and bar. Its top-quality programme of contemporary music, opera and orchestral music draws a highbrow crowd, but it's worth a visit for the building alone; the café offers great views over the water. The same development also includes the Bimhuis (see p.93). Box office Mon–Sat noon–6pm.

Nationale Opera & Ballet Amstel 3, old Jewish quarter ☏ 020 551 8117, ⓦ operaballet.nl. The Nationale Opera & Ballet offers the fullest, and most reasonably priced, programme of opera in Amsterdam; not surprisingly, tickets go very quickly.

Stadsschouwburg Leidseplein 26, Grachtengordel ☏ 020 624 2311, ⓦ stadsschouwburgamsterdam.nl. Connected to the *Melkweg*, the municipal theatre stages significant opera, theatre and dance performances. Thursday performances are subtitled in English. Box office Mon–Sat noon–6pm.

CABARET AND COMEDY CLUBS

Surprisingly for a city that functions so much in English, there is next to no English-language theatre – though English-speaking touring companies do regularly visit. English-language comedy, on the other hand, has become

---

AMSTERDAM'S FESTIVALS

The city's festival calendar starts proper with a celebration of the King's birthday (also referred to as **King's Day**) on April 27, with a large portion of the city given over to an impromptu flea market and lots of street parties – straight and gay. Then comes June's annual **Holland Festival** (ⓦ hollandfestival.nl), which attracts the best domestic mainstream and fringe performers in all the performing arts, as well as an exciting international line-up. Otherwise, one of the more interesting, music-oriented events is the popular **Grachtenfestival** (ⓦ grachtenfestival.nl), held at the end of August, a week-long classical music festival which concludes with a piano recital on a floating stage outside the *Pulitzer Hotel* on the Prinsengracht. Amsterdam's only regular film event is the top-ranking **International Documentary Film Festival**, held in November (ⓦ idfa.nl), during which two hundred documentaries from all over the world are shown in ten days.

1

a big thing here, spearheaded by the resident and extremely successful Boom Chicago comedy company.

★ **Boom Chicago** Rozengracht 117, Jordaan ☏ 020 217 0400, ⊛ boomchicago.nl. Something of a phenomenon in Amsterdam, this rapid-fire improv comedy troupe hailing from the US performs nightly to crowds of both tourists and locals, and receives rave reviews. Inexpensive food, cocktails and beer served in pitchers.

Comedy Café Rozengracht 117, Jordaan ☏ 020 638 3971, ⊛ comedycafe.nl. Held upstairs at the Rozentheater, the Comedy Café puts on stand-up four nights a week. Tuesday is open mic night – a good chance to spot new talent.

FILM

Most of Amsterdam's cinemas are huge, multiplex picture palaces where you can watch a selection of general releases, but there is also a scattering of film houses (*filmhuizen*) showing revival and cult films along with occasional retrospectives and themed nights. All foreign movies playing in Amsterdam are shown in their original language (OV) and subtitled in Dutch.

Cinecenter Lijnbaansgracht 236, Grachtengordel ☏ 020 623 6615, ⊛ cinecenter.nl. Opposite the *Melkweg*, this cinema shows independent and quality commercial films, the majority originating from non-English-speaking countries, shown with an interval.

★ **EYE** IJpromenade 1, Amsterdam Noord ☏ 020 589 1400, ⊛ eyefilm.nl. The stunning EYE centre, across the water from Centraal Station, screens a mixture of blockbusters and arthouse films every other day or so.

Melkweg Lijnbaansgracht 234a, Grachtengordel ☏ 020 531 8181, ⊛ melkweg.nl; map pp.48–49. As well as music, art and dance, the *Melkweg* manages to maintain a consistently good monthly film programme, ranging from mainstream fodder through to more obscure imports. There's also a café-restaurant (Marnixstraat entrance; Wed–Sun noon–9pm).

The Movies Haarlemmerdijk 161–163, Jordaan ☏ 020 638 6016, ⊛ themovies.nl. This beautiful Art Deco cinema is a charming setting for independent films, but it's worth visiting for the bar and restaurant alone, fully restored to their original appearance. "Filmdinner" nights include a three-course meal and film from €35, and there are late showings (11.45pm) of classic or cult films at weekends.

Tuschinski Theater Reguliersbreestraat 26–34, Grachtengordel ☏ 0900 1458, ⊛ pathe.nl/bioscoop/ tuschinski. This fabulous Art Deco theatre, famous for its hand-woven carpet and hand-painted wallpaper, shows the artier offerings from the mainstream list.

LGBT AMSTERDAM

Amsterdam boasts one of the most dynamic **LGBT scenes** in Europe, with a liberal sprinkling of advice centres, bars and clubs. The city has four main LGBT areas, beginning with **Reguliersdwarsstraat**, where the bars and clubs tend to attract a young and trendy crowd, and quieter **Kerkstraat**, which is populated as much by locals as visitors. The streets just **north of Rembrandtplein** and along the Amsel are a camp focus, while **Warmoesstraat**, in the heart of the Red Light District, is cruisey and mainly leather- and denim-oriented. Many bars and clubs have **darkrooms**, which are legally obliged to provide safe-sex information and condoms. The **bars and clubs** listed below cater either predominantly or exclusively to a gay clientele. Some venues have both gay-only and mixed gay/straight nights; there are, however, very few **lesbian**-only nights or clubs and bars. The city also has its own LGBT radio station, **MVS Radio** (⊛ mvs.nl).

INFORMATION AND BOOKSHOPS

COC ⊛ cocamsterdam.nl. COC (pronounced "say-oh-say"), the Netherlands' national LGBT pressure group, is one of the oldest, and largest, groups of its kind in the world. Its website offers advice and provides contacts.

Gay, Lesbian & Transgender Switchboard ☏ 020 623 6565, ⊛ switchboard.coc.nl. An English-speaking phone service and online "live chat" which provides help and advice. Mon & Wed–Fri 2–6pm, Tues 1–4pm & 7–9pm, Thurs 7–9pm, Sat 2–5pm.

Pink Point Westermarkt, corner of Raadhuisstraat and Keizersgracht, Jordaan ☏ 020 428 1070, ⊛ pinkpoint.org. This free advice and information kiosk, run by a team of knowledgeable volunteers, offers practical information about where to go and what to do in the city, and is stocked with flyers and brochures, also souvenirs and T-shirts. Also publishes the excellent *Bent Guide*. Daily 10am–6pm.

Vrolijk Paleisstraat 135, Old Centre ☏ 020 623 5142, ⊛ vrolijk.nu. "The largest gay and lesbian bookstore on the continent", with a vast stock of new and secondhand books and magazines, as well as music and DVDs. Mon–Sat 11am–6pm, Sun noon–6pm.

BARS AND CLUBS

Dirty Dicks Warmoesstraat 86 ☏ 06 4787 7614, ⊛ dirtydicksamsterdam.com; map p.51. One of the city's oldest fetish bars, it's been enlivened by the new dress code, which stipulates something in leather, latex, or shirtless. On Thursdays beer costs €2 all night. Mon–Thurs & Sun 8pm–3am, Fri & Sat 8pm–4am.

Entre Nous Halvemaansteeg 14 ☏ 020 623 1700; map pp.48–49. Camp brown café that's packed at peak times, when everyone joins in the singalongs to cheesy Eighties music. Women welcome. Mon–Thurs & Sun 8pm–3am, Fri & Sat 8pm–4am.

La Cage Regulierdwarsstraat 44 ☎020 320 9108, ⓦ lacageamsterdam.nl; map pp.48–49. The *Arc* bar that once stood here burnt down and this is its glamorous reincarnation. Lots of mood lighting, fancy snacks and first-rate drinks, plus a "Happy Oyster Hour" on Fridays from 5pm. Mon–Thurs & Sun 4pm–1am, Fri & Sat 4pm–3am.

Prik Spuistraat 109 ☎020 320 0002, ⓦ prikamsterdam .nl; map p.51. Voted the Netherlands' best gay bar of 2015

by Rainbow Awards, with tasty cocktails, smoothies and snacks, plus DJs on weekends. Mon–Thurs 4pm–1am, Fri & Sat 4pm–3am, Sun 3pm–1am.

Vivelavie Amstelstraat 7 ☎020 624 0114, ⓦ vivelavie .net; map pp.48–49. Casual lesbian bar, but gay men are very welcome. Quiet during the week, but packed at the weekends. Mon–Thurs & Sun 4pm–3am, Fri & Sat 3pm–4am.

SHOPPING

Amsterdam has some excellent and unusual **speciality shops** as well as a handful of great **street markets**. Where the city scores most though is in its convenience – the centre concentrates most of what's interesting within its tight borders – and, as an added bonus, the majority of shops are still individual businesses rather than chains, which makes a refreshing change from many big cities.

BOOKS AND MAGAZINES

★ **American Book Center** Spui 12, Old Centre ☎020 625 5537, ⓦ abc.nl; map p.51. This store has a vast stock of books in English, as well as lots of imported US magazines and books. Mon noon–8pm, Tues, Wed & Fri 10am–8pm, Thurs 10am–9pm, Sun 11am–6.30pm.

Athenaeum Spui 14–16, Old Centre ☎020 514 1460, ⓦ athenaeum.nl; map p.51. Perhaps the city's most appealing bookshop, and although it's relatively short on stuff in English, its array of books about Amsterdam is always current, and its selection of international newspapers and magazines is one of the best in the city. Mon 11am–6pm, Tues, Wed & Fri–Sat 9.30am–6pm, Thurs 9.30am–9pm, Sun noon–5.30pm.

The English Bookshop Lauriergracht 71, Jordaan ☎020 626 4230, ⓦ shop.englishbookshop.nl; map pp.48–49. A small, quirky collection of titles on a wide range of subjects – in particular literature, but also cookery, travel and children's books. Tues–Sat 11am–6pm.

Martyrium Van Baerlestraat 170–172, Oud-Zuid ☎020 673 2092, ⓦ hetmartyrium.nl; map pp.48–49. Good general bookshop with lots of material in English. Mon–Fri 9am–6pm, Sat 9am–5pm, Sun noon–5pm.

★ **Scheltema** Rokin 9–15, Old Centre ☎020 523 1411,

ⓦ scheltema.nl; map p.51. Amsterdam's biggest and arguably best bookshop. Six floors of absolutely everything (mostly in Dutch). Mon 11am–7pm, Tues, Wed & Fri–Sat 10am–7pm, Thurs 10am–9pm, Sun noon–6pm.

Waterstones Kalverstraat 152, Old Centre ☎020 638 3821, ⓦ waterstones.com; map p.51. Amsterdam branch of the UK high-street chain, with four floors of books and magazines. Prices are sometimes cheaper here than elsewhere. Mon & Sat 10am–6.30pm, Tues, Wed & Fri 9.30am–6.30pm, Thurs 9.30am–9pm, Sun 11am–6.30pm.

DEPARTMENT STORES

De Bijenkorf Dam 1, Old Centre ☎088 245 3333, ⓦ debijenkorf.nl; map p.51. Dominating the northern corner of Dam square, this is the city's top department store with an interesting history (see p.52), a huge bustling place, spread over six floors, whose name means "beehive". It's good for designer clothes, accessories and kids' stuff. Free wi-fi throughout. Mon & Sun 11am–8pm, Tues & Wed 10am–8pm, Thurs & Fri 10am–9pm, Sat 9.30am–8pm.

HEMA Nieuwendijk 174–176, Old Centre ☎020 623 4176, ⓦ hema.nl, map p.51. Great for stocking up on all the important things you need – underwear, toiletries and other essentials, plus occasional designer delights. There's

WHERE TO SHOP

Broadly speaking, the **Nieuwendijk/Kalverstraat** strip, **Damstraat** and **Rokin** are where you'll find the usual high-street fashion and mainstream department stores. Elsewhere, the expensive end of Amsterdam's renowned antiques trade is clustered around the smart and chic **Spiegelkwartier** (ⓦ spiegelkwartier.nl) – it's a great district to browse, with one local speciality being antique Dutch tiles. The **Grachtengordel** is home to **Negen Straatjes** (Nine Streets; ⓦ theninestreets.com), an area spanning off from the Herengracht – Amsterdam's version of New York's Fifth Avenue – and lined with upmarket boutiques, affordable antiques and quirky independent shops. Similar in style is **Haarlemmerstraat**, running west from Centraal Station, in the Jordaan district. Nearby **Leidsestraat** offers a good selection of affordable designer clothes and shoe stores, while the new **De Hallen** complex (see p.86) has a lovely peaceful covered arcade of independent clothing shops and intriguing knick-knacks.

1

another branch at Kalverstraat 212 (Old Centre; ☎ 020 422 8988). Mon–Wed & Fri 9am–7pm, Thurs 9am–9pm, Sun 11am–6pm.

Stadshart Rembrandtweg 37, Amstelveen ☎ 020 426 5800, ⓦ stadhartamstelveen.nl; map pp.48–49. Large covered shopping centre south of the city with 200 luxury shops, restaurants and bars, plus an organic market on Tues. Mon noon–6pm, Tues–Wed & Fri–Sat 9.30am–6pm, Thurs 9.30am–9pm, Sun noon–6pm.

FOOD AND DRINK

Albert Heijn NZ Voorburgwal 226, Old Centre ☎ 020 421 8344, ⓦ ah.nl; map p.51. Located just behind Dam square, this is the biggest of the city's forty-odd Albert Heijn supermarkets. Daily 8am–10pm.

Bakkerij Paul Année Bellamystraat 8, Jordaan ☎ 020 618 3113, ⓦ bakkerijpaulannee.nl; map pp.48–49. The best wholegrain and sourdough breads in town, bar none – all made from organic grains. Mon 9am–5pm, Wed–Sat 9am–5pm.

De Bierkoning Paleisstraat 125, Old Centre ☎ 020 625 2336, ⓦ bierkoning.nl; map p.51. The "Beer King" is aptly named: 950 different beers, with the appropriate glasses to drink them from. Mon–Sat 11am–7pm, Sun 1–6pm.

Ibericus Haarlemmerstraat 93, Jordaan ☎ 020 223 6573; map pp.48–49. Great thighs of high-quality Spanish cured hams hang from the ceiling of this atmospheric shop run by Paul Gonzalez. If you're feeling peckish he offers sampler menus for €9.50. Otherwise try-before-you-buy tastings are encouraged. Mon–Sat 10am–6pm, Sun 11am–5pm.

Jordino Haarlemmerdijk 25a, Old Centre ☎ 020 420 3225, ⓦ jordino.nl; map pp.48–49. You can sample some of Amsterdam's best ice cream and chocolates at this Haarlemmerdijk institution. Mon & Sun 1–6.30pm, Tues–Sat 10am–6.30pm.

De Kaaskamer Runstraat 7, Grachtengordel ☎ 020 623 3483, ⓦ kaaskamer.nl; map pp.48–49. Friendly shop with a comprehensive selection of Dutch cheeses, plus international wines, cheeses and olives. Mon noon–6pm, Tues–Fri 9am–6pm, Sat 9am–5pm, Sun noon–5pm.

Oud-Hollandsch Snoepwinkeltje Tweede Egelantierdwarsstraat 2, Jordaan ☎ 020/420 7390, ⓦ snoepwinkeltje.com; map pp.48–49. All kinds of mouthwatering Dutch sweets, piled up in glass jars and attracting hordes of neighbourhood kids. The ideal place to try the typical Dutch liquorice (*drop*). Tues–Sat 11am–6.30pm.

Puccini Bomboni Staalstraat 17, Old Centre ☎ 020 626 5474, ⓦ puccinibomboni.com; map p.51. Arguably the best chocolatier in town, selling a wonderfully creative range of chocolates in all shapes and sizes. There's a second

---

AMSTERDAM MARKETS

A visit to one of Amsterdam's **open-air markets** is a must. There's a first-rate flea market on Waterlooplein, several lively street markets selling everything from fresh veg to clothes, plus smaller, specialist markets devoted to everything from books to flowers.

Albert Cuypmarkt Albert Cuypstraat, De Pijp ⓦ albertcuypmarkt.nl. In existence since 1905, this is the city's principal street market with more than 260 stands selling everything from luggage to fish, with some great bargains to be had – including clothing and shoes. Mon–Sat 9am–5pm.

Biologische Borenmarkt Haarlemmerplein ⓦ biologischemarkt.nl. Organic farmers' market selling all kinds of produce, including amazing fresh bread, wine, cheese and meat. Wed from 9am.

Bloemenmarkt Singel, between Koningsplein and Muntplein, Grachtengordel. Raft of barges selling tulips aplenty. Locals have all but abandoned Amsterdam's famous flower market because the choice and quality have wilted considerably over the years, but at least you'll know where to find it. Daily from 11am.

IJHallen Vlooienmarkt TT Neveritaweg 15, NDSM ⓦ ijhallen.nl. Housed in a huge warehouse in the trendy NDSM district, this is one of Europe's biggest and best flea markets with over 750 stalls. You won't leave empty-handed. There's a €5 entrance fee; €2 for kids under 11. Twice a month; check website for dates.

Noordermarkt Next to the Noorderkerk, Grachtengordel. Part organic food market, part junk-lover's gold mine. It's full of all kinds of bargains – oriental rugs, jewellery, old books, etc – tucked away beneath piles of seemingly useless rubbish. Get there early. Sat from 9am.

Sunday Market Cultuurpark Westergasfabriek, Westerpark ⓦ sundaymarket.nl; tram #10 stop Van Hallstraat. A monthly art, fashion and design market where designers sell their own wares such as jewellery, customized T-shirts, ceramics and art. Interesting food stalls, too. First Sun of month noon–6pm.

Waterlooplein Waterlooplein, behind the Stadhuis, old Jewish quarter ⓦ waterloopleinmarkt.nl. A real Amsterdam institution, and the city's best central flea market by far. Sprawling and chaotic, with wonderful antique/junk stalls to root through. Some second-hand vinyl too. Mon–Sat from 9am.

branch at Singel 184, Grachtengordel. Mon & Sun noon–6pm, Tues–Sat 9am–6pm.

★**Zoet en Hartig** Haarlemmerdijk 158, Jordaan ☎020 767 0434, ⓦchcocompany.com; map pp.48–49. Rustic chocolate shop famous for its handcrafted chocolates and signature "hotchocspoon" available in sixty flavours. There are also home-made cheese biscuits and sausage rolls for those less sweet of tooth. Mon & Sun 11am–6.30pm, Tues–Sat 9.30am–6.30pm.

HOME

Droog Design Staalstraat 7b, Old Centre ☎020 523 5050, ⓦdroogcom; map p.51. Founded in 1993, Droog Design has made a serious contribution to the contemporary design market. Some of its products, such as its milk bottle chandelier, have ended up in museum collections; this is its gallery, café and shop. Tues & Wed 11am–6pm, Thurs–Sun 11am–7pm.

★**Frozen Fountain** Prinsengracht 645, Grachtengordel south ☎020 622 9375, ⓦfrozenfountain.nl; map pp.48–49. Contemporary furniture and interior design with the emphasis on all things Dutch. Mon 1–6pm, Tues–Sat 10am–6pm, Sun noon–5pm.

Gerda's Runstraat 16, Grachtengordel ☎020 624 2912, ⓦgerdasflowers.com; map pp.48–49. Amsterdam is full of flower shops, but this one is the most imaginative and sensual, with bouquets to melt the hardest of hearts. Mon–Fri 9am–6pm, Sat 9am–5pm.

★**Van Dijk & Ko** Papaverweg 46, NDSM ☎020 684 1524, ⓦvandijkenko.nl; map pp.48–49. This antiques warehouse is a treasure trove of reasonably priced vintage furniture, books, school supplies, glassware – you name it. Can deliver internationally. Tues–Sat 10am–6pm, Sun noon–6pm.

MUSIC

Back Beat Records Egelantiersstraat 19, Grachtengordel ☎020 627 1657, ⓦbackbeat.nl; map pp.48–49. Small specialist in soul, blues, jazz, funk, etc, with a helpful and enthusiastic owner. Mon–Sat 11am–6pm.

Concerto Utrechtsestraat 52–60, Grachtengordel ☎020 624 5467, ⓦconcerto.amsterdam; map pp.48–49. Around since the 1950s, Concerto sells new and used records and CDs in all categories; equally good on Baroque as on grunge with the option to listen before you buy. Mon–Wed & Sat 10am–6pm, Thurs–Fri 10am–7pm, Sun noon–6pm.

VINTAGE

★ **Laura Dols** Wolvenstraat 7, Grachtengordel ☎020 624 9066, ⓦlauradols.nl; map pp.48–49. Queen of the vintage fashion scene, *Laura Dols* is split into two shops opposite each other on Wolvenstraat. There is a multitude of pieces for both women and men, including some stunning printed fabrics from the 1950s and 1960s, piles of pillowcases, tablecloths, tea towels, and even a superb selection of children's and baby clothes. Mon–Wed & Fri–Sat 11am–6pm, Thurs 11am–7pm, Sun noon–6pm.

MISCELLANEOUS

★ **Condomerie Het Gulden Vlies** Warmoesstraat 141, Old Centre ☎020 627 4174, ⓦcondomerie.com; map p.51. This shop sells condoms of every shape, size and flavour imaginable (and unimaginable) – all in the best possible taste. Mon–Wed & Fri 11am–6pm, Thurs & Sat 11am–9pm, Sun 1–6pm.

The Head Shop Kloveniersburgwal 39, Old Centre ☎020 624 9061, ⓦheadshop.nl; map p.51. Every dope-smoking accessory you could possibly need, along with assorted marijuana ephemera. Mon–Fri 11am–6pm, Sat 11am–7pm, Sun noon–7pm.

DIRECTORY

Doctor Your hotel/hostel or the VVV should have the address of an English-speaking doctor. Otherwise, call the Centraal Doktorsdienst ☎088 003 0600.

Left luggage At Centraal Station – near platform 2b (follow the suitcase signs) – you'll find bankcard-operated left-luggage lockers (daily 7am–11pm), which cost €5.10/24hr for a small one, €7.95/24hr for a larger one.

Library The city's deluxe library, the Amsterdam Bibliotheek is at the heart of a massive docklands redevelopment programme at Oosterdokskade 143 (daily 10am–10pm; ⓦoba.nl).

Lost property For items lost on the trams, buses or metro, contact GVB Head Office, Arlandaweg 100 (Mon–Fri 9am–6.30pm; ☎0900 8011). For property lost on an NS train, first go to the service office at Centraal Station at Stationplein 15 (☎0900 321 2100). Schiphol Airport's lost and found desk is in the Arrivals Hall (☎0900 0141; daily 7am–6pm).

Pharmacies Pharmacies are legion and are usually open Mon–Fri 9am–6pm, though some are closed on Monday mornings.

Post Amsterdam's main post office is at Singel 250 (Mon–Fri 7.30am–6.30pm, Sat 9am–5pm; ⓦpostnl.nl). Otherwise postal transactions can be carried out at stores with the PostNL logo. Stamps are sold at a wide range of outlets including many supermarkets, shops and hotels.

Noord-Holland

BEACH HUTS, TEXEL

2

Noord-Holland

Stretching north from Amsterdam to the island of Texel, the province of Noord-Holland is largely rural, its polder landscapes of green, pancake-flat fields intersected by hundreds of drainage canals and ditches, and its wide horizons only interrupted by the odd farmhouse or windmill. The province's west coast is defended from the ocean by a long belt of sand dunes, which is itself shielded by long and broad sandy beaches, and it's these that attract holidaying Netherlanders. Much of the east coast has been reclaimed from what was once the saltwater Zuider Zee and is now, after the construction of two complementary dykes, the freshwater Markermeer and IJsselmeer. Here, along this deeply indented coast, lies a string of old seaports which flourished from the fourteenth to the eighteenth century on the back of the sea trade with the Baltic, Asia and the Americas.

Noord-Holland's principal urban highlight is **Haarlem**, an easy-going town with more than its fair share of Golden Age buildings, the province's best art gallery, and ready access to some wild stretches of dune and beach in the **Nationaal Park Zuid-Kennemerland**. Northeast of Amsterdam, the old Zuider Zee ports of **Marken**, **Volendam** and **Edam** are a bit touristy in summer, but have considerable charm if you visit off-season. Further north, **Hoorn** and **Enkhuizen** were once major Zuider Zee ports, and their historic wealth is reflected in a scattering of handsome old buildings. Enkhuizen, in particular, is very attractive and has one of the country's best open-air museums. A short train ride north of Amsterdam is the **Zaanstad** conurbation, whose chief attraction is the antique windmills and canals of **Zaanse Schans**. Further up the line, the pleasant provincial town of **Alkmaar** has a much-touted summer cheese market, and makes a good base for exploring two protected coastal zones, the **Noordhollands Duinreservaat** (North Holland Dune Reserve) and the **Schoorlse Duinen** nature reserve. Beyond, in the far north of the province, the island of **Texel** is the most accessible of the Waddenzee islands. It can get crowded in summer, but don't be put off: with a bit of walking or cycling you can easily find some solitude.

Most of Noord-Holland is located north of Amsterdam, though the borders of the province also dip round the city, taking in an area known as **Het Gooi**, where the highlights are the small town of **Muiden** with its castle and the old fortified town of **Naarden**.

GETTING AROUND

By public transport Getting around Noord-Holland by public transport is easy, with trains linking all the major centres – Haarlem, Alkmaar, Hoorn, Enkhuizen and Den Helder (for Texel) – and buses filling in the gaps. Distances are small and frequencies regular so the majority of Noord-Holland is easily visited on day-trips from Amsterdam, but to make the most of the province you're better off staying over at least a couple of nights.

By car If you want to continue north or east, the two dykes that enclose the Markermeer and the IJsselmeer carry handy road links. The former, the Markerwaarddijk, connects Enkhuizen with Lelystad on the reclaimed Flevoland polders (see p.245), while the latter, the Afsluitdijk, makes the 30km trip from Den Oever to the province of Friesland (see Chapter 4).

THE COSTER STATUE AND GROTE KERK, HAARLEM

Highlights

❶ Haarlem This good-looking old town is home to the outstanding Frans Hals and Teylers museums and makes a lovely base for exploring the southern part of the province and the nearby coast. **See p.105**

❷ Dunes The dunes of Noord-Holland's west coast are the closest the country gets to hills, and exploring them by bike or on foot is a joy. **See p.109 & p.131**

❸ Edam Archetypal Dutch country town of narrow canals and quaint houses – one of them with a unique floating cellar. **See p.114**

❹ Enkhuizen This handsome old Zuider Zee port of slender waterways is worth a visit in its own right, but it has the excellent Zuiderzeemuseum thrown in too. **See p.121**

❺ Zaanse Schans A lively open-air museum with crafts demonstrations and several impressive working windmills, just thirty minutes from Amsterdam. **See p.127**

❻ Texel Just twenty minutes from the mainland by regular ferry, but with a real island feel – not to mention good places to stay and eat and some magnificent sandy beaches. **See p.133**

HIGHLIGHTS ARE MARKED ON THE MAP ON P.104

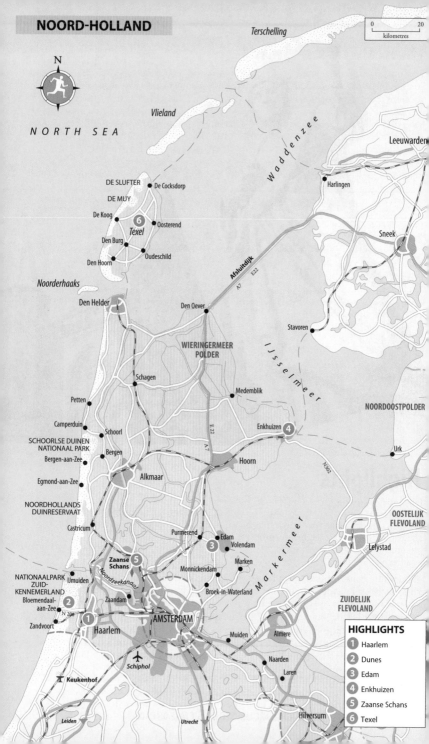

NOORD-HOLLAND

Terschelling

Vlieland

NORTH SEA

Leeuwarden

W a d d e n z e e

Harlingen

Sneek

DE SLUFTER
De Cocksdorp
DE MUY
De Koog
Texel **6** Oosterend
Den Burg
Afsluitdijk
A7 E22
Den Hoorn
Oudeschild

Noorderhaaks

Den Helder

Den Oever

Stavoren

**WIERINGERMEER
POLDER**

IJsselmeer

Schagen

Medemblik

NOORDOOSTPOLDER

Petten

Camperduin
Schoorl
**SCHOORLSE DUINEN
NATIONAAL PARK**
Bergen-aan-Zee
Bergen

E22
A7

Enkhuizen **4**

Urk

Hoorn

N302

Egmond-aan-Zee

Alkmaar

**NOORDHOLLANDS
DUINRESERVAAT**

Castricum

**OOSTELIJK
FLEVOLAND**

Purmerend
3 Edam
Volendam

Lelystad

M a r k e r m e e r

**Zaanse
Schans** **5**
Marken

Monnickendam

**NATIONAALPARK
ZUID-
KENNEMERLAND**
IJmuiden
Bloemendaal-
aan-Zee **2**
N200
Zaandam

Broek-in-Waterland

**ZUIDELIJK
FLEVOLAND**

Noordzeekanaal

AMSTERDAM

1 **Haarlem**

Muiden
Almere

Zandvoort

Naarden
Laren

Schiphol

Keukenhof

Leiden

Utrecht

Hilversum

HIGHLIGHTS	
1	Haarlem
2	Dunes
3	Edam
4	Enkhuizen
5	Zaanse Schans
6	Texel

0   20
kilometres

N

Haarlem and around

It's only fifteen minutes from Amsterdam by train, but **HAARLEM** has a very different pace and feel from its neighbour. A former cloth-making centre, it's an easy-going, medium-sized town of around 150,000, with a good-looking centre that is easily absorbed in a few hours or on an overnight stay. In 1572, the townsfolk sided with the Protestant rebels against the Habsburgs, a decision they must have regretted when a large Spanish army besieged them later the same year. The siege was a desperate affair that lasted for eight months, but finally the town surrendered after receiving various assurances of good treatment – assurances the Spanish commander, Frederick of Toledo, promptly broke, massacring over two thousand of the Protestant garrison. Recaptured five years later, Haarlem went on to enjoy its greatest prosperity in the seventeenth century and was home to a flourishing school of **painters**, whose canvases are displayed at the outstanding **Frans Hals Museum**, located in the almshouse where Hals spent his last and, according to some, his most brilliant years.

Haarlem is also within easy striking distance of the **coast**: every fifteen minutes trains make the ten-minute trip to the modern resort of **Zandvoort-aan-Zee**, while frequent buses serve the huddle of beach bars and fast-food joints that make up **Bloemendaal-aan-Zee** just to the north. Neither is particularly endearing in itself, but both are redeemed by long sandy beaches and the pristine stretches of the dune and lagoon, crisscrossed by footpaths and cycling trails, that make up the nearby **Nationaal Park Zuid-Kennemerland**.

Grote Markt

At the heart of Haarlem is the **Grote Markt**, an attractive open space flanked by an appealing ensemble of Gothic and Renaissance architecture, including an intriguing if garbled **Stadhuis**, whose turrets and towers, balconies and galleries were put together between the fourteenth and the seventeenth centuries. At the other end of the Grote Markt stands a **statue** of Laurens Coster (1370–1440), who, Haarlemmers insist, is the true inventor of printing. Legend tells of Coster cutting a letter "A" from the bark of a tree, dropping it into the sand by accident, and, hey presto, realizing how to create the printed word. The statue shows him earnestly holding up a printing letter, but most historians agree that it was the German Johannes Gutenberg who invented printing, in the early 1440s.

De Hallen Museum

Grote Markt 16 • Tues–Sat 11am–5pm, Sun noon–5pm • €10 or less, depending on the exhibition • ⓦ dehallen.nl

Opposite the Stadhuis, the rambling **De Hallen Museum** is located inside the old meat market, the **Vleeshal**, which boasts a flashy Dutch Renaissance facade. It houses the town's museum of modern and contemporary art, with a special focus on photography and video, and occasionally hosts additional exhibitions for the Frans Hals Museum.

The Grote Kerk

Grote Markt • Mon–Sat 10am–5pm • Organ recitals mid-May to mid-Oct Tues at 8.15pm; July & Aug also Thurs at 4pm; carillon concerts Mon noon–1pm & Fri 12.45–1.15pm, plus July–Aug Tues 7.15pm • €2.50; recitals and concerts free

Dominating Haarlem's Grote Markt is the **Grote Kerk**, a soaring Gothic structure supported by mighty buttresses that dwarfs the surrounding clutter of ecclesiastical outhouses. Dedicated to St Bavo, the church was finished in 1538, after 150 years in the making, and is surmounted by a good-looking lantern tower, which perches above the transept crossing and hosts carillon concerts. Inside, the towering beauty of the nave is enhanced by the creaminess of the stone and the bright simplicity of the whitewashed walls. The Protestants cleared the church of most of its decoration during the Reformation, but the splendid wrought-iron **choir screen** has survived, as have the

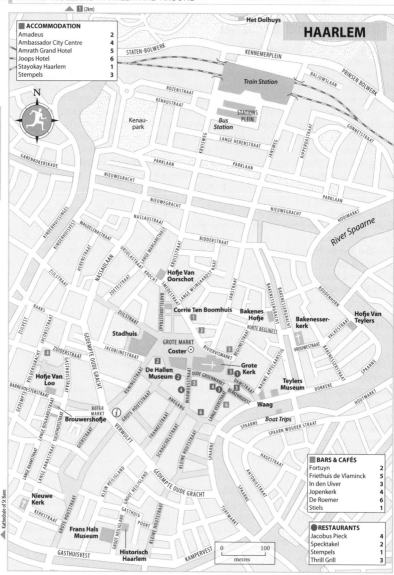

ACCOMMODATION

Amadeus	2
Ambassador City Centre	4
Amrath Grand Hotel	5
Joops Hotel	6
Stayokay Haarlem	1
Stempels	3

BARS & CAFÉS

Fortuyn	2
Friethuis de Vlaminck	5
In den Uiver	3
Jopenkerk	4
De Roemer	6
Stiels	1

RESTAURANTS

Jacobus Pieck	4
Specktakel	2
Stempels	1
Thrill Grill	3

choir's wooden **stalls** with their folksy misericords. In front of the screen is the conspicuous Neoclassical **tomb** shared by Christiaan Brunings and Frederik Conrad, much-lauded hydraulic engineers and founders of the national water board. The entire floor of the church is made of around 1500 tombstones.

The chapels

Next to the south transept is the **Brewers' Chapel**, where the central pillar bears two black markers – one showing the height of a local giant, the 2.64m-tall Daniel Cajanus, who died in 1749, the other the 0.84m-high Simon Paap from Zandvoort

(1789–1828). In the middle of the nave, the pulpit's banisters are in the form of snakes – fleeing from the word of God – while on the other side the pocket-sized **Dog Whippers' Chapel** was built for the men employed to maintain order and keep dogs out of the church, as evidenced by the rings there to tether them to.

The Christian Müller organ

At the west end of the church, the mighty Christian Müller **organ** is one of the biggest in the world, with over five thousand pipes and loads of snazzy Baroque embellishment. Manufactured in Amsterdam in the 1730s, it is said to have been played by both Handel and Mozart – you can still hear it at one of the free organ recitals held in the summer. Beneath it, Jan Baptist Xavery's lovely group of draped marble figures represent Poetry and Music offering thanks to the town, which is depicted as a patroness of the arts – in return for its generous support in the purchase of the organ.

The Corrie Ten Boomhuis Museum

Barteljorisstraat 19 • 1hr guided tours only; English tours April–Oct at 10am, 11.30am, 1.30pm & 3pm, Nov–March by appointment • Free • Booking recommended on Ⓦ corrietenboom.com

Two minutes from the Grote Markt, the **Corrie Ten Boomhuis** is where a Dutch family – the Ten Booms – hid fugitives, resistance fighters and Jews alike above their jeweller's shop during World War II. There isn't actually much to look at in the house, but the guided tour is instructive and moving. The family, whose bravery was inspired by their Christian faith, was betrayed to the Gestapo in 1944, and only one member, Corrie Ten Boom, survived – as does the jeweller's itself, still doing business at street level.

The Frans Hals Museum

Groot Heiligland 62 • Tues–Sat 11am–5pm, Sun noon–5pm • €12.50 • Ⓦ franshalsmuseum.nl

Haarlem's biggest draw, the **Frans Hals Museum**, is a five-minute stroll south of the Grote Markt, housed in the almshouse complex where the aged Hals lived out his last destitute years. The collection comprises a handful of prime works by Hals along with an eclectic sample of Dutch paintings from the fifteenth century onwards, all immaculately presented and explained on the free audioguide or app, which can also be used during the fifteen-minute film presentation.

Sixteenth- and seventeenth-century paintings

The museum has a small group of early sixteenth-century paintings, the most prominent of which is a triptych from the School of **Hans Memling**, but otherwise focuses on work by Haarlem artists. The most notable works are a couple of paintings by **Jan van Scorel** (1495–1562), and **Cornelius Cornelisz van Haarlem's** (1562–1638) giant *Wedding of Peleus and Thetis*, an appealing rendition of what was then a popular subject. This marriage precipitated civil war among the gods and was used by the Dutch as an emblem of warning against discord, a call for unity during the long war with Spain. Similarly, the same artist's *Massacre of the Innocents* connects the biblical story with the Spanish siege of Haarlem in 1572. Opposite, three accomplished pictures by **Hendrik Goltzius** (1558–1616) depict Hercules, Mercury and Minerva.

Look out also for *Adam and Eve* by **Maerten van Heemskerck** (1498–1574), whose work dominates one room, in particular a brutal and realistic *Christ Crowned with Thorns* and a painting of St Luke with the Virgin and Infant Jesus. There are also several rooms of paintings by the **Haarlem Mannerists**, including two tiny and precise works by **Karel van Mander** (1548–1606), leading light of the Haarlem School and mentor of many of the city's most celebrated painters, including Hals; genre works by **Adriaen** (1610–85) and **Isack van Ostade** (1621–49); and depictions of the Grote Kerk by **Gerrit**

2

THE PAINTER WITH 27 KINDS OF BLACK

Little is known about **Frans Hals** (c.1580–1666), born in Antwerp, the son of Flemish refugees who settled in Haarlem in the late 1580s. His extant oeuvre is relatively small – some two hundred paintings, and nothing like the number of sketches and studies left behind by his contemporary, Rembrandt. His outstanding gift was as a portraitist, showing a sympathy for his subjects and an ability to capture fleeting expression that some say even Rembrandt lacked. Seemingly quick and careless flashes of colour characterize his work, but they are always blended into a coherent and marvellously animated whole. He is perhaps best known for his civic guard portraits – group portraits of the militia companies initially formed to defend the country from the Spanish, but which later became social clubs for the gentry. Getting a commission to paint one of these portraits was a well-paid privilege – Hals got his first in 1616 – but their composition was a tricky affair and often the end result was dull and flat. With great flair and originality, Hals made the group portrait a unified whole instead of a static collection of individual portraits, his figures carefully arranged, but so cleverly as not to appear contrived. Hals's later paintings are darker, more contemplative works, closer to Rembrandt in their lighting and increasingly sombre in their outlook, giving meaning to van Gogh's remark that "Frans Hals had no fewer than 27 blacks."

Berckheyde (1638–98) and others. Look out also for **Pieter Bruegel the Younger**'s (1564–1638) berserk *Dutch Proverbs*, illustrating a whole raft of contemporary proverbs – a touchscreen gives the lowdown.

Frans Hals paintings

The **Hals paintings** begin in earnest in **Room 14** with a set of five "Civic Guard" portraits. For a time, Hals himself was a member of the Company of St George, and in the *Officers of the Militia Company of St George* he appears in the top left-hand corner – one of his few self-portraits. See also Hals's Haarlem contemporary Johannes Cornelisz Verspronck's (c.1600–62) *Regentesses of the Holy Ghost Orphanage* – one of the most accomplished pictures in the gallery, which echoes Hals's own *Regents of St Elizabeth Gasthuis*, a serious but benign work of 1641. Perhaps the museum's most valuable and impressive works, however, are Hals's famous twin portraits, *Regents* and *Regentesses of the Oudemannenhuis*, which depicts the people who ran the almshouse when Hals was there – a collection of cold, self-satisfied faces staring out of the gloom, the women reproachful, the men only marginally more affable. There are those who claim Hals had lost his touch by the time he painted these pictures, yet their sinister, almost ghostly, power suggests quite the opposite.

The Teylers Museum

Spaarne 16 • Tues–Sat 10am–5pm, Sun noon–5pm • €12 • ⓦ teylersmuseum.nl

It's a short stroll from the Grote Markt to the **River Spaarne**, whose wandering curves mark the eastern periphery of the town centre, and are home to the country's oldest museum, the **Teylers Museum**. Founded in 1774 by a wealthy local philanthropist, one **Pieter Teyler van der Hulst**, the museum is delightfully old-fashioned, its wooden cabinets crammed with fossils and bones, crystals and rocks, medals and coins, all displayed alongside dozens of antique scientific instruments of lugubrious appearance and uncertain purpose. Pride of the collection is the world's largest electrostatic plate generator, from 1791. The finest room is the **rotunda** – Ovale Zaal – a handsome, galleried affair with splendid wooden panelling, and there is also a room of nineteenth-century and early twentieth-century Dutch paintings, featuring the likes of Breitner, Israëls, Weissenbruch and Wijbrand Hendriks. There's an English-language audioguide.

Het Dolhuys

Schotersingel 2 • Tues–Fri 10am–5pm, Sat & Sun noon–5pm • €8.50 • ⓦ hetdolhuys.nl

Perhaps Haarlem's strangest attraction is **Het Dolhuys**, an imaginative and thought-provoking museum of madness and psychiatric care throughout the ages, housed in a converted lunatic asylum. There are isolation cells, exhibits which tell the stories of "mad" people who have done extraordinary things, as well as displays which show different attitudes to mental illness over the years – from medieval imbalances to possession. The central Zorgzaal is the hub of the exhibition, with films, pictures and artefacts from asylums around Holland. A helpful English-language booklet on loan from the reception translates the most important captions. The museum is just a five-minute stroll from the train station.

Zandvoort-aan-Zee

The suburbs of Haarlem ramble out almost as far as **ZANDVOORT-AAN-ZEE**, a major seaside resort just 5km to the west. As Dutch resorts go, Zandvoort is pretty standard – packed in summer, dead and gusty in winter – and its agglomeration of modern apartment blocks hardly cheers the heart, but its **beach** is wide and sandy, it musters up a casino and a car-racing circuit and it is one of the few places in the Netherlands where the rail network reaches the coast: there's a service every fifteen minutes from Haarlem, and Zandvoort train station is just a few minutes' walk from the beach. Bus #81 also runs hourly from Haarlem bus station, via Bloemendaal-aan-Zee (see below), to Zandvoort bus station, on Louis Davidsstraat, a short, signposted walk from the train station.

Nationaal Park Zuid-Kennemerland

The pristine woods, dunes and lagoons of the **NATIONAAL PARK ZUID-KENNEMERLAND** (ⓦnp-zuidkennemerland.nl) stretch north from Zandvoort up to the eminently missable industrial town of IJmuiden, at the mouth of the Nordzeekanaal. Bus #81 leaves Haarlem bus station every thirty minutes to cross the national park via the N200 before reaching the coast at the minuscule beachside settlement of **Bloemendaal-aan-Zee**. En route, several bus stops give access to the clearly marked **hiking and cycling**

HAARLEM'S HOFJES

You could do worse than spend a day exploring Haarlem's **hofjes** – small, unpretentious complexes of public housing built for the old and infirm in the seventeenth century. The best known and perhaps most accessible is the one that was home to Frans Hals in the last years of his life and now houses the Frans Hals Museum. But there are others dotted around town, most of them still serving their original purpose but with their gardens at least open to the public. The most grandiose is the riverside **Hofje van Teylers,** a little way east of the museum of the same name around the bend of the Spaarne at Koudenhorn 64. Unlike many of the other *hofjes*, which are decidedly cosy, this is a Neoclassical edifice dating from 1787 with solid columns and cupolas. To the west, the elegant fifteenth-century tower of the **Bakenesserkerk** on Vrouwestraat is a flamboyant, onion-domed affair soaring high above the Haarlem skyline, that marks the nearby **Bakenes Hofje**, at Wijde Appelaarsteeg 11: founded in 1395, it is Haarlem's (and indeed the country's) oldest *hofje*, with a delightful enclosed garden. Five minutes' walk away, the **Hofje van Oorschot**, at the junction of Kruisstraat and Barteljorisstraat, dates from 1769 and is also rather grand. To the south of here, the **Brouwershofje**, just off Botermarkt, is a small, peaceful terrace of housing with a courtyard behind, and windows framed by brightly painted red and white shutters, while the nearby **Hofje van Loo**, on nearby Barrevoetstraat, is equally diminutive, and open to view from the street.

2

HANS BRINKER

Given that the Dutch have spent most of their history struggling to keep the sea from flooding their land, it's hardly surprising that their folklore abounds with tales of watery salvation, either by luck or the bravery of its inhabitants. One well-known hero is **Hans Brinker**, a young lad who supposedly saved the Haarlem area from disaster by sticking his finger into a hole in the dyke. The village of **Spaarndam**, just north of Haarlem, has a statue in his honour, but in fact the tale is fictitious – invented by the American writer Mary Mapes Dodge in her 1873 children's book, *The Silver Skates*. The monument to the boy was unveiled in 1950, more, it seems, as a tribute to the opportunistic Dutch tourist industry than anything else.

trails that pattern the national park, but the best option is to alight at the **Koevlak** entrance – ask the driver to let you off. Maps of the park are available at Haarlem tourist office, and there are colour-coded **hiking routes** posted at all entrances. The most appealing is the 4–5km (1hr) jaunt west through pine woods and dunes to the seashore, where the *Parnassia* **café** (April–Nov) provides refreshments with a view of the North Sea. From here, it's a 1.5km walk back to Bloemendaal-aan-Zee, where you can catch bus #81 back to Haarlem (or of course you can do the whole thing in reverse).

Museum de Cruquius

Cruquiusdijk 27, Cruquius • Mon–Fri 10am–5pm, Sat & Sun 11am–5pm • €7 • ⓦ museumdecruquius.nl • Bus #340 from Haarlem to the Ringvaartbrug stop (every 5–10min; 15min)

Five kilometres south of Haarlem, **De Cruquius** is the world's largest steam pumping station, one of three built in the 1850s to pump dry the Haarlemmermeer lake. The eight beams sticking out of the elegant Gothic Revival building are connected to pistons that can each take 64,000 litres of water up five metres in one go. Inside the venerable industrial monument there's a small museum about the Dutch system of dykes, polders and canals, with a particular focus on the role of the pumping station. It can regularly be seen in action – in 2002 it was restored, powered by modern hydraulics instead of steam. The quaint *theehuis* café in the adjacent former superintendent's house is great for lunch.

ARRIVAL AND DEPARTURE
HAARLEM

By train Haarlem's train station is just north of the city centre, about a 10min walk from the Grote Markt.
Destinations Alkmaar (every 30min; 30min); Amsterdam (every 10min; 15min); Hoorn (every 30min; 1hr).

By bus Buses stop on Stationsplein, just in front of the train station.
Destinations Bloemendaal (every 30min; 15min); Zandvoort (every 30min; 20min).

INFORMATION

Tourist office The VVV is in the Stadhuis at Grote Markt 2 (April–Sept Mon–Fri 9.30am–5.30pm, Sat 9.30am–5pm, Sun noon–4pm; Oct–March Mon 1–5.30pm, Tues–Fri 9.30am–5pm, Sat 10am–5pm; ⓣ 023 531 7325, ⓦ vvvhaarlem.nl). It has details of a small number of rooms in private houses, mostly on the outskirts of town.

ACCOMMODATION

Amadeus Grote Markt 10 ⓣ 023 532 4530, ⓦ amadeus-hotel.com. The town centre's cheapest option and right on Haarlem's main square. The rooms here are a bit tatty but nice enough. The downstairs restaurant serves a cheap international menu. **€81**

Ambassador City Centre Oude Groenmarkt 20 ⓣ 023 512 5300, ⓦ acc-hotel.nl. Haarlem's best budget option, this modern hotel couldn't be more central, with its eccentrically decorated lobby and heavy antique furniture. Double rooms are simply but well furnished, a few with

four-posters, and although bathrooms are on the small side, the welcome is warm. **€89**

Amrath Grand Hotel Frans Hals Damstraat 10 ⓣ 023 518 1818, ⓦ hotelfranshals.nl. Plumb in the centre of town, this modern chain hotel has 79 good-sized rooms with bathrooms, decent enough, if a bit lacking in character. The lobby at least tries hard to be memorable, with its spiral steel staircase and stained-glass dome. **€135**

Joops Hotel Lange Veerstraat 36 ⓣ 023 512 5300, ⓦ joopshotel.nl. A mixture of large antique-filled and slightly more expensive rooms as well as good-value, functionally furnished apartments for up to four people. Check in at the sister hotel *Ambassador*. Rooms €90, apartments €149

Stayokay Haarlem Jan Gijzenpad 3 ☎ 023 537 3793, ⓦ stayokay.com. Spick-and-span modern hostel near the sports stadium, about 3km north of the town centre. To get there, take bus #2 from the station – a 10min journey. Dorms €33, doubles €115

★**Stempels** Klokhuisplein 9 ☎ 023 512 3910, ⓦ stempelsinhaarlem.nl. Housed in a former printworks behind the Grote Kerk, Haarlem's best boutique hotel has a variety of rooms, all of them simply and comfortably furnished with a contemporary restraint that suits the building. The nicest tend to be in the grander end, where the printing family lived, and which dates from the 1700s. The restaurant is excellent and there's an all-day brasserie too. €140

EATING AND DRINKING

BARS, CAFÉS AND TAKEAWAYS

Fortuyn Grote Markt 23, ⓦ fortuynhaarlem.nl. A popular café-bar with modern decor and a menu of organic meals. Meat and fish dishes are prepared in a coal-fired Josper oven; these hover around €12–20. Mon–Wed & Sun 10am–midnight, Thurs–Sat 10am–1am.

Friethuis de Vlaminck Warmoesstraat 3, ⓦ friethuisdevlaminck.nl. It may just be a snack bar, but this is a decent and very central *friterie*, great if you fancy lunch on the go. It serves excellent, freshly made frites with all the usual toppings. Mon–Wed & Fri–Sun 11am–7pm, Thurs 11am–9pm.

In den Uiver Riviervismarkt 13 ☎ 023 532 5399 ⓦ indenuiver.nl. Just off the Grote Markt, this lively and extremely appealing brown bar, housed in an old fish shop, is decked out in traditional Dutch-café style; it has occasional live music too. Mon–Wed 4pm–1am, Thurs–Sat 4pm–2am, Sun 2pm–midnight.

Jopenkerk Gedempte Voldersgracht 2 ☎ 023 533 4114, ⓦ jopenkerk.nl. Haarlem used to be known for its beer, and this converted old church is home to the Jopen microbrewery, bar and restaurant. It's very nicely done, with long benches, comfy sofas and its own cloudy, unfiltered beer. The food is simple rather than splendid, but you should at least try one of the dozen or so Jopen brews at the bar. Daily 10am–1am; lunch noon–3pm; dinner 5.30–8pm.

De Roemer Botermarkt 17 ☎ 023 532 5267, ⓦ cafederoemer.nl. Cosy bar with a covered outside terrace, tucked away on the edge of the old centre. It serves excellent, mainly Dutch food, with sandwiches and salads (€5–9) at lunchtime, and a great-value evening menu, including decent burgers and excellent steaks at dinner.

Mon–Thurs 10am–1am, Fri & Sat 10am–2am, Sun noon–1am.

Stiels Smedestraat 21 ☎ 023 531 6940, ⓦ stiels.nl. A lively bar that's locally famous for live pop, jazz and blues concerts. Mon–Wed & Sun 8pm–2am, Thurs–Sat 8pm–4am.

RESTAURANTS

Jacobus Pieck Warmoesstraat 18 ☎ 023 532 6144, ⓦ jacobuspieck.nl. Welcoming café-restaurant that's a good bet for either lunch or dinner, with sandwiches for €7, burgers and salads for €9, and a short menu of more substantial main courses in the evenings for €17–20. Tues–Sat 11am–4pm & 5.30–10pm.

Specktakel Spekstraat 4 ☎ 023 532 3841, ⓦ specktakel.nl. Inventive little place that tries its hand at an international menu, dishing up everything from kangaroo through to antelope – it's better than you might think. Starters cost €14, main courses €22, though if you're hungry enough it's better to choose three courses for €35. Daily 5.30–10pm.

★**Stempels** Klokhuisplein 9 ☎ 023 512 3910, ⓦ stempelsinhaarlem.nl. Not a cheap option by any means, but you do feel you're eating in one of the grander spaces in the city, and the four-course menu at €43 has to be one of Haarlem's greatest food bargains: very high-quality cooking, with great fish and meat laced with innovative blends of flavours and ingredients. Daily 5.30–10pm.

Thrill Grill Oude Groenmarkt 26 ☎ 023 202 4047, ⓦ thrillgrill.nl. Gourmet hamburgers with unusual ingredients such as salmon, chicken and hot dogs, served in this bustling restaurant overlooking the Grote Kerk. Mon–Fri noon–11pm, Sat & Sun 9am–11pm.

Marken

Until its road connection to the mainland in 1957, the village of **MARKEN** was an almost entirely closed island community in the Zuider Zee, supported by a small fishing industry. Today, it mainly lives off its tourist industry, and can get pretty busy on summer weekends, though it's of the day-tripping, coach-driven variety, and when the crowds have left, or out of season, it's a rather special place, very peaceful and remote, despite being within just a few miles of Amsterdam's urban sprawl.

2

HOW THE ZUIDER ZEE BECAME THE IJSSELMEER

The towns and villages that string along the east coast of **Noord-Holland** flourished during Amsterdam's Golden Age, their economies buoyed up by shipbuilding, the Baltic Sea trade and the demand for herring. They had access to the open sea via the waters of the **Zuider Zee** (Southern Sea, counterpart to the North Sea) and the connecting **Waddenzee (Mud Flat Sea)**. The business was immensely profitable and its proceeds built a string of prosperous seaports – most notably Volendam, Hoorn and Enkhuizen – and nourished market towns like Edam, while the Zuider Zee itself supported a batch of fishing villages such as Marken and Urk. In the eighteenth century, however, the Baltic trade declined and the harbours silted up, leaving the ports economically stranded.

The Zuider Zee continued to provide a livelihood for local fishermen, but most of the country was more concerned by the danger of flooding it posed, as time and again storms and high tides combined to breach the east coast's defences. The first plan to seal off and reclaim the Zuider Zee was proposed in 1667, but the rotating-turret windmills that then provided the most efficient way of drying the land were insufficient for the task and matters were delayed until suitable technology arrived – in the form of the steam-driven pump. In 1891, **Cornelis Lely** (1854–1929) proposed a retaining dyke and his plans were finally put into effect after devastating floods hit the area in 1916. Work began on this dyke, the **Afsluitdijk**, in 1920 and, on May 28, 1932, the last gap in it was closed and the Zuider Zee simply ceased to exist, replaced by the freshwater **IJsselmeer**.

The original plan was to reclaim all the land protected by the Afsluitdijk, turning it into farmland for settlers from the country's overcrowded cities, starting with three large-scale land-reclamation schemes that were completed over the next forty years: the **Noordoostpolder** in 1942 (480 square kilometres), **Oostelijk Flevoland** in 1957 (540 square kilometres) and **Zuidelijk Flevoland** in 1968 (440 square kilometres). In addition, a complementary dyke linking Enkhuizen with Lelystad was finished in 1976, thereby creating lake **Markermeer** – a necessary prelude to the draining of another stretch of the IJsselmeer. The engineers licked their contractual lips, but they were out of sync with the majority of the population, who were now opposed to any further draining of the lake. Partly as a result, the grand plan was abandoned and, after much governmental huffing and puffing, the Markermeer was left alone and thus most of the old Zuider Zee remained water.

There were many economic benefits to be had in the closing of the Zuider Zee, not least great chunks of new and fertile farmland, while the roads that were built along the top of the two main retaining dykes brought Noord-Holland within twenty minutes' drive of Friesland. The price was the demise of the old Zuider Zee **fishing fleet**, and today these placid, steel-grey lakes are popular with day-tripping Amsterdammers, who come here in their droves to sail boats, observe the waterfowl and visit a string of dinky towns and villages that pretty much rely on tourism to survive. These begin on the coast just a few kilometres north of Amsterdam with the picturesque old fishing village of **Marken** and the former seaport of **Volendam**, just up the coast. From here, it's a couple of kilometres further to **Edam**, the pick of the local bunch, a small and infinitely pretty little town of narrow canals and handsome old houses.

The village

There's no denying the picturesque charms of Marken, where the immaculately maintained houses, mostly painted in deep green with white trimmings, cluster on top of artificial mounds raised to protect them from the sea. There are two main parts to the village: **Havenbuurt**, around and behind the harbour, is the bit you see in most of the photographs, where many of the waterfront houses are raised on stilts. Although these are now panelled in, they were once open, allowing the sea to roll under the floors in bad weather, enough to terrify most people half to death. One or two of the houses are open to visitors, proclaiming themselves to be typical of Marken, and the waterfront is lined by snack bars and souvenir shops, often staffed by locals in traditional costume. Still you do get a hint of how hard life used to be – both here and in **Kerkbuurt**, five minutes' walk from the harbour around the **church**, an ugly 1904 replacement for its sea-battered predecessor. Kerkbuurt is quieter and less touristy than Havenbuurt, its narrow lanes lined by ancient dwellings and a row of old eel-smoking houses, one of which is now the **Marker**

Museum at Kerkbuurt 44 (April–Sept Mon–Sat 10am–5pm, Sun noon–4pm; Oct Mon–Sat 11am–4pm, Sun noon–4pm; €2.50; ⓦmarkermuseum.nl), furnished as an old fishermen's cottage and devoted to the history of the former island and its fishing industry.

ARRIVAL AND DEPARTURE

MARKEN

By bus Marken is accessible direct from Amsterdam on bus #315, departing from outside Centraal Station every 30min; the journey takes 40min. The bus drops passengers beside the car park on the edge of Marken village, from where it's a 5min walk to the shore.

By ferry The Marken Express ferry (☎0299 363 331,

ⓦmarkenexpress.nl) sails between Volendam and Marken every 15–45min (March–Oct daily 11am–5pm; 25min; €9.95 return, €7.50 one-way, €1.50 for a bike single).

Tourist office The VVV is at Havenbuurt 19 (Thurs–Sun noon–4pm; ☎0299 602 184, ⓦvvvwaterland.nl).

ACCOMMODATION AND EATING

★ **Hof van Marken** Buurt II 15 ☎0299 601 300, ⓦhofvanmarken.nl. This small hotel, tucked away in the backstreets from Marken's harbour, has seven simple but stylish rooms, with a homely yet contemporary feel. Its elegant dining room serves great food with three-course menus priced from €35 featuring the likes of steamed turbot, sea bass or leg of lamb. Mon, Thurs & Fri

6–10pm, Sat & Sun noon–10pm. **€95**

Land en Zeezicht Havenbuurt 6 ☎0299 601 302. Right on the north side of the harbour, this old-fashioned place serves a decent smoked eel sandwich as well as more substantial, mainly traditional Dutch dishes. Mon–Thurs 11am–8pm, Fri 10am–8.30pm, Sat & Sun 9am–10pm.

Monnickendam

The former port of **MONNICKENDAM** was named by a group of Benedictine monks, who built a dam here in the fourteenth century. There's not much to it now, but it has the same sleepy charm of the other old Zuider Zee ports to divert you on your way to Volendam and Edam. The harbour repays a wander too. It has a more rough-and-ready air than that of its neighbours and a more authentically nautical one too, with herring smokehouses and lots of rugged sailing barges alongside the pleasureboats of its marina – all pleasingly not spruced up for tourists.

ARRIVAL AND INFORMATION

MONNICKENDAM

By bus Monnickendam is pretty easy to reach, with regular buses between Amsterdam and the Zuider Zee towns of Volendam and Edam stopping on the outskirts of town –

principally the #314, #315 and #316.

Tourist office The VVV is at Zuideinde (April–Oct daily 10am–5pm; ☎0299 820 046, ⓦvvvwaterland.nl).

ACCOMMODATION

★ **De Posthoorn** Noordeinde 43 ☎0299 654 598, ⓦposthoorn.eu. This boutique hotel brilliantly mixes the traditional and contemporary in its five large rooms and suites, with flat-screen TVs, DVD players and sumptuously

equipped bathrooms merging seamlessly with the beams, old-fashioned beds, paintings and fabrics that show off this seventeenth-century mansion at its best. Very comfy, and the service is charming. **€155**

EATING AND DRINKING

De Koperen Vis Havenstraat 1 ☎0299 650 627, ⓦdekoperenvis.nl. Right by the water, this cosy restaurant is maybe Monnickendam's friendliest place for a drink and a bite to eat. You can sit outside on sunny days and watch the boats coming and going. It serves a good menu of hot and cold sandwiches for around €5, *uitsmijters* (€7 or so) and delectable Dutch bar snacks. The three-course menu is just €29.50 on Mon, Wed and Thurs. 11am–10pm; closed Tues.

★ **De Posthoorn** Noordeinde 43 ☎0299 654 598,

ⓦposthoorn.eu. With one Michelin star, this refined hotel restaurant has a lovely dining room, with a terrace out the back in the summer, and service that is impeccable without being showy. You can choose à la carte – mains are €30 – or from one of three menus which range from €55 to €85. The food won't disappoint, whether you choose succulent veal roulade with Russian salad and piccalilli, or creamy Zeeland oysters with fingers of bread and butter. A feast for the senses. Tues–Sun 10am–11pm.

2

Volendam

The former fishing village of **VOLENDAM** is the largest of the Markermeer towns and has had, by comparison with its neighbours, some rip-roaring times. In the early years of the twentieth century it became something of an artists' retreat, with both Picasso and Renoir spending time here, along with their assorted acolytes. Evidence of the town's artistic connections can be seen in the antique-filled public rooms of the **Hotel Spaander** on the waterfront, whose collection of paintings and sketches was given to the hotel by various artists in lieu of their lodgings. The hotel opened in 1881 and its first owner, Leendert Spaander, had seven daughters, quite enough to keep a whole bevy of artists in lust for a decade or two. The artists are, however, long gone and today Volendam is more or less a tourist target, crammed in season with day-trippers running the gauntlet of the souvenir stalls arranged along the length of the cobbled main street, whose perky gables line the picturesque yet workaday harbour.

Volendams Museum

Zeestraat 41 • Mid-March to mid-Nov daily 10am–5pm • €3 • ⓦ volendamsmuseum.nl

While it's pleasant enough to wander the harbour and the streets behind, Volendam's only real sight is the **Volendams Museum**, which has displays of paintings by the artists who have come here over the years. Exhibits also include mannequins in local costumes and several interiors – a shop, school, and living room – although the museum's crowning glory is a series of mosaics made from eleven million cigar bands: the bizarre lifetime project of a local artist.

ARRIVAL AND INFORMATION   VOLENDAM

By bus Bus #316 from Amsterdam and Monnickendam drops passengers on Zeestraat, just across the street from the tourist office. From here, it's a 5min walk to the waterfront.

By ferry The Marken Express passenger ferry (ⓣ 0299 363 331, ⓦ markenexpress.nl), links Volendam and Marken

(every 15–45min; 25min; €9.95 return, €7.50 one-way, €1.50 for a bike single). Ferries depart from the eastern part of the harbour.

Tourist office The VVV is at Zeestraat 37 (mid-March to Oct Mon–Sat 10am–5pm; Nov to mid-March Mon–Sat 10am–3pm; ⓣ 0299 363 747, ⓦ vvv-volendam.nl).

ACCOMMODATION AND EATING

Spaander Haven 15–19 ⓣ 0299 363 595, ⓦ hotelspaander.com. If you want to stay in Volendam, there's no better place than this wonderfully old-fashioned hotel, whose maze of corridors and creaking old floors harbours decently furnished rooms, most of which overlook the water. Choose from "classic" or "luxury" – the latter are larger and with bathtubs. **€89**

Van den Hogen Haven 106 ⓣ 0299 363 775, ⓦ hogen.nl.

Five simply furnished but good-value rooms above an enticing restaurant and bar. This is the best of Volendam's harbourside restaurants, with a good selection of local fish specialities, like sole, mussels and cod. Try the three small fried Volendam soles for €20, mussels for €18.50 or the cod with mustard sauce for €22. Or if you're feeling more adventurous, the stewed pike with shrimps is very good. Mon–Fri 11am–9pm, Sat & Sun 11am–9.30pm. **€85**

Edam

You might expect **EDAM** to be jammed with tourists, considering the international fame of the rubbery red balls of cheese that carry its name. In fact, Edam usually lacks crowds and remains a delightful, good-looking and prosperous little town of neat brick houses, high gables, swing bridges and slender canals. Founded by farmers in the twelfth century, it experienced a temporary boom in the seventeenth as a shipbuilding centre with river access to the Zuider Zee. Thereafter, it was back to the farm – the excellent pastureland surrounding the town is still grazed by large herds of cows,

2

though nowadays most Edam cheese is produced elsewhere, even abroad ("Edam" is the name of a type of cheese and not its place of origin). This does, of course, rather undermine the authenticity of Edam's open-air **cheese market**, held every Wednesday morning in July and August, but it's still a popular attraction and the only time the town heaves with tourists. From here, it's a couple of hundred metres south to the fifteenth-century **Speeltoren**, an elegant, pinnacled tower with a carillon from 1516, that is all that remains of Edam's second most important medieval church, and roughly the same distance again – south along Lingerzijde – to the impossibly picturesque **Kwakelbrug** bridge.

Damplein

At the heart of Edam is **Damplein**, a pint-sized main square. Alongside it, an elongated, humpbacked bridge vaults the Voorhaven canal, which now connects the town with the Markermeer and formerly linked it to the Zuider Zee. The bridge stopped the canal flooding the town, which occurred with depressing regularity, but local shipbuilders hated the bridge, as it restricted navigation, and on several occasions they launched night-time raids to break it down, though eventually they bowed to the will of the local council.

Edams Museum

Damplein 1 & 8 • April–Oct Tues–Sat 10am–4.30pm, Sun 1–4.30pm • €5 • ⓦ edamsmuseum.nl

Facing the bridge is the **Edams Museum**, which occupies an attractive old house whose crow-stepped gables date back to 1530. Inside, a series of cramped and narrow rooms holds a modest display on the history of the town as well as an assortment of local bygones, including a couple of splendid box beds. The museum's pride and joy is its **floating cellar**, effectively a stone boat, built to store food at cool temperatures in a town with very high and fluctuating ground-water levels. There's a good English audio guide you can use. The second part of the museum (same times and ticket) is housed in Edam's eighteenth-century **Stadhuis**, just across the bridge. A severe Louis XIV-style structure whose plain symmetries culminate in a squat little tower, the Stadhuis has a handful of old Dutch paintings; the most curious is the portrait of **Trijntje Kever** (1616–33), a local girl who grew to over 2.5m tall – displayed in front of the portrait is a pair of her specially made shoes.

The Grote Kerk

Kerkepad • April–Oct daily 1.30–5pm • Free, tower €2

From Damplein, it's a short walk to the rambling **Grote Kerk**, on the edge of the fields to the north of town. This is the largest three-ridged church in Europe, a handsome, largely Gothic structure whose strong lines are disturbed by the almost comically stubby spire, which was shortened to its present height after lightning started a fire in 1699. The church interior is distinguished by its magnificent stained-glass windows – which date from the early seventeenth century and sport both heraldic designs and historical scenes – and by its whopping **organ** from 1663, but don't miss the sight of cheese stored in the southern portal.

The Cheese Market

Jan Nieuwenhuizenplein • July to mid-Aug Wed 10.30am–12.30pm

Stroll back from the church along Matthijs Tinxgracht, just to the west of Grote Kerkstraat, and you soon reach Jan Nieuwenhuizenplein, site of the summer **cheese market**. It's overlooked by the **Kaaswaag,** where they used to weigh the cheese, whose decorative panels feature the town's coat of arms, a bull on a red field with three stars. It's a good deal humbler than Alkmaar's market (see p.129), but follows the same format, with the cheeses laid out in rows before buyers sample them. Once a cheese has been purchased, the cheese porters, dressed in traditional white costumes and straw boaters, spring into action, carrying them off on their gondola-like trays.

ARRIVAL AND DEPARTURE — EDAM

By bus Edam's bus station is on the southwest edge of town, on Singelweg, a 5–10min walk from Damplein. Buses #312, #314 and #316 run between Amsterdam and Edam every 10min or so; the journey takes 40min.

By bike Bikes can be rented from Ronald Schot, at Grote Kerkstraat 7 in the town centre (Tues–Fri 8.30am–6pm & Sat 8.30am–4pm; ☎0299 372 155, ⓦronaldschot.nl); one-day bike rental costs from €9.50, and customers get free parking nearby.

INFORMATION

Tourist office The VVV is in the Stadhuis on Damplein (mid-March to Nov Mon–Sat 10am–5pm, in July & Aug also Sun 11am–4pm; Nov to mid-March Mon noon–4pm, Tues–Thurs 10am–3pm, Fri & Sat 10–4pm; ☎0299 315 125, ⓦvvv-edam.nl). There's an informative city walk (€4) every Sat at 2pm; English speakers should book in advance. The VVV has details of – and take bookings for – local boat trips along the town's canals (on cheese market days even in a traditional "cow boat") and out into the Markermeer, and can book rooms in private houses (averaging €40–50 for a double).

ACCOMMODATION

Camping Strandbad Zeevangszeedijk 7a ☎0299 371 994, ⓦcampingstrandbad.nl. East of town on the way to the lakeshore, Edam's nearest campsite is a 20min walk along the canal from the north side of Damplein. Also has cabins, sleeping two, for €37 a night. April–Sept. **€14**

Damhotel Keizersgracht 1 ☎0299 371 766, ⓦdamhotel.nl. Edam is a great place to spend a night or two, and this is perhaps the nicest place to do it – a boutique-style hotel with an emphasis on old-style opulence, with bunched curtains, statues of angels and luxurious fabrics. Each room is different, but all have up-to-date facilities. **€125**

De Fortuna Spuistraat 3 ☎0299 371 671, ⓦfortuna-edam.nl. Just round the corner from the Damplein and a butting a narrow canal, this attractive three-star hotel is the epitome of cosiness, its 23 guest rooms distributed among two immaculately restored old houses and three cottage-like buildings round the back. The rooms are simply but very nicely furnished, all with baths. It's a lovely spot with good organic food and chairs and tables set out by the canal. **€112**

EATING AND DRINKING

L'Auberge Damhotel Keizersgracht 1 ☎0299 371 766, ⓦdamhotel.nl. The bar here is a cosy place for a drink, and it has a terrace in an outside loggia facing the town hall, where you can get a decent lunch of sandwiches, salads and pancakes for €6–10 and light mains for €16–18. There's also the upmarket but excellent-value *Auberge* restaurant, which serves a fantastic and quite ambitious menu; reckon on paying around €22–27 for halibut with caramelized leek or sauteed pork chop. Daily noon–10pm.

De Fortuna Spuistraat 3 ☎0299 371 671, ⓦfortuna-edam.nl. This first-rate restaurant is a lively and eminently agreeable spot decorated in traditional style and serving a slightly fussy, French-Dutch menu featuring local ingredients; starters go for €10–12, main courses €20–25. Reservations, especially at the weekend, are essential. Daily lunch noon–3pm; Mon–Sat dinner from 6pm, Sun from 5.30pm.

Hoorn

The old Zuider Zee port of **HOORN**, 15km north of Edam, "rises from the sea like an enchanted city of the east, with its spires and its harbour tower beautifully unreal". So wrote the English travel writer E.V. Lucas, who passed through here in 1905, and Hoorn is still a place that is best approached from the water. During the seventeenth century this was one of the richest of the Dutch ports, referred to by the poet Vondel as the "trumpet" of the Zuider Zee, handling the important Baltic trade and that of the Dutch colonies. The Dutch East India Company had one of its centres of operation here; *The Tasman* left Hoorn to "discover" Tasmania and New Zealand; and in 1616 William Schouten sailed out of Hoorn to navigate a passage around South America,

2

De Halve Maen, Museum van de Twintigste Eeuw, **3**, **5** & ⓘ ▼

calling its tip "Cape Hoorn" after his native town – reason for a year of celebrations and special events on the 400th anniversary in 2016. The good times ended in the early eighteenth century when the harbour silted up, strangling the trade on which the town was reliant and turning Hoorn into one of the so-called "dead cities" of the Zuider Zee – a process completed with the creation of the IJsselmeer in 1932.

Rode Steen

The centre of Hoorn is **Rode Steen**, literally "red stone", an unassuming square that used to hold the town scaffold and now zeroes in on a swashbuckling **statue** of Jan Pieterszoon Coen (1587–1629), founder of the Dutch East Indies Empire and one of the town's big shots in its seventeenth-century heyday. Coen was a headstrong and determined leader of the Dutch imperial effort and under him the country's Far East colonies were consolidated, and rivals, like the English, kept at bay. His settling of places like the Moluccas and Batavia was something of a personal crusade, and his austere, almost puritanical way of life was in sharp contrast to the wild and unprincipled behaviour of many of his fellow colonialists. On one side of Rode Steen stands the early seventeenth-century **Waag**, whose handsome stone symmetries were designed by Hendrick de Keyser (1565–1621), one of the leading architects of his day. The Waag now houses a café, which is enjoyable for its setting amid the ponderous wood and iron appliances that once weighed the cheese here – and is in fact a good place from which to watch the summer **cheese market**. The market takes place twice on Thursdays (mid-June to Aug 12.30pm & 8.30pm), though like Alkmaar's it's basically laid on for tourists.

The Westfries Museum
Rode Steen 1 • Mon–Fri 11am–5pm, Sat & Sun 1–5pm • €8 • ⓦ wfm.nl

On the opposite side of the square from the Waag, the **Westfries Museum** is housed in the former West Friesland government building of 1632, an imposing stone structure whose facade is decorated with the coats of arms of the house of Orange-Nassau and the region's towns. Now a district within the province of Noord-Holland, West Friesland incorporates the chunk of land between Alkmaar, Hoorn and Enkhuizen, but its origins were much grander. The **Frisians**, who speak a distinctive German dialect, once controlled a narrow sliver of seaboard stretching west from Bremerhaven in Germany to Belgium. Charlemagne conquered them in the 780s and incorporated their territory into his empire, chopping it down in size and dividing the remainder into seven regions, two of which – West Friesland and Friesland – are now in the Netherlands.

The ground floor and basement
Inside the museum, with English labelling throughout, the ground floor holds a string of period rooms that re-create the flavour of the seventeenth- and eighteenth-century seaport, with paintings, silverware, antique furniture and other objects. Most notable of the numerous paintings are the militia portraits of **Jan Rotius** (1624–66) in the old Council Chamber – walk past the figure in the far right of the central painting opposite the fireplace and you'll see his foot change position from left to right, a nifty little trick that was much admired by Rotius's contemporaries. A large model representing Hoorn around 1650 – with 150 ships in the harbour – can be viewed in the basement.

The upper floors
Upstairs, the **Chirurgijnskamer** (literally Surgeon's Room, but also, in medieval times, the barber's, the alchemist's and the pharmacist's), holds a mock-up of a seventeenth-century "medical" workshop, complete with skeletons, skulls and pickled specimens, while another room has a splendid wooden fireplace carved with scenes of a whaling expedition – Hoorn was once a whaling port of some importance. There's a focus on Coen and the Dutch East India Company too.

Around the harbour
East of Rode Steen, **Grote Oost** is shadowed by fine, decorated old mansions, some

---

THE STOOMTRAM
Hoorn is the home of the **Museumstoomtram**, across the rail tracks from the town's main station, which is the starting point for the Stoomtram, an antique steam train that chugs north out of Hoorn across open countryside to Medemblik, 14km away (see p.125). It's a popular family excursion and you can pick up a leaflet from the tourist office for the rather complicated schedule, or book direct in advance (recommended) on ☎0229 214 862 or ⓦ museumstoomtram.nl. There are between one and three departures a day in late July and early August, and one departure a day (Tues–Sun) the rest of the year. The journey takes 1hr 15min and a return ticket costs €21 (children aged 4–12 €15.80), including an optional excursion by passenger ferry to Enkhuizen (see p.121), from where you can either come back the same way or take the half-hourly train service directly back to Hoorn (an additional €5).

of which house antique shops and art galleries, and one of which, the newly renovated **Affiche Museum**, just off Rode Steen at Groot Oost 2 (Tues–Fri 11am–5pm, Sat & Sun noon–5pm; €3.50), sports a frieze of the cheese market as well as housing a modest permanent display of political and commercial posters – a treat for students of graphic design. At the far end of Groot Oost, on the corner of Slapershaven, the **Bossuhuizen** have facades decorated with a long and slender frieze depicting the Zuider Zee sea battle of 1573 in which the Spanish Admiral Bossu was defeated. **Slapershaven** itself has some of the most comfortable houseboats imaginable and leads to Hoorn's inner harbour, the **Binnenhaven**, with its clutter of sailing boats and antique barges alongside **Oude Doelenkade**.

Veermanskade
Just over the swing bridge, **Veermanskade** is fringed by elegant merchants' houses mostly dating from the seventeenth century: look out, in particular, for the birthplace of **Willem Ysbrantzoon Bontekoe** (1587–1657), set back from the quay at Veermanskade 15, whose stone facade shows a particularly ugly spotted cow (his name translates as "spotted cow"). A sea captain with the East India Company, Bontekoe published his journals in 1646, a hair-raising and very popular account of his adventures in which he portrayed himself as astute and brave in equal measure. Almost at the end of Veermanskade, the solid brick **Hoofdtoren**, a defensive watchtower from 1532, is now a restaurant and has nearby a bronze sculpture of three little boys looking out to sea that also recalls Bontekoe – it's based on the 1924 classic Dutch novel by Johan Fabricius, *The Cabin Boys of Bontekoe*.

The Oostereiland
Across the bridge south of the Hoofdtoren, the **Oostereiland** holds a prison that was recently converted into a hotel and arthouse cinema (see opposite) and two worthwhile sights.

De Halve Maen
Schuijteskade 22 • March–Oct hourly tours daily between 11am–4pm • €8.50 • ⓦ halvemaenhoorn.nl

The **Halve Maen** is an impressive full-scale and operating replica of the ship that sailed around Cape Hoorn in 1615, on loan from the New Netherlands Museum in New York and centrepiece of the 2016 celebrations marking the 400th anniversary of the voyage. Guided 45-minute tours (advance booking required) take in the history and all decks of the surprisingly compact ship. The Centrum Varend Erfgoed (Centre for Sailing Heritage) where she's moored has other historical ships from 1850–1950 that are often used for trips, and a working shipyard too.

Museum van de Twintigste Eeuw
Krententuin 24 • Mon–Fri 10am–5pm, Sat & Sun noon–5pm • €8 • ⓦ museumhoorn.nl

The **Museum van de Twintigste Eeuw** (Museum of the Twentieth Century) is basically a collection of nostalgia that documents life during the twentieth century with products and objects set up in engaging tableaux of everyday life. There are living rooms from the 1940s, 1950s and 1960s, a mock-up of Jacob Blokker's first housewares store at Breed 14 (it's now a nationwide chain), an old school room and a room full of Barbies and Kens.

ARRIVAL AND DEPARTURE	**HOORN**

By train Hoorn's train station is on the northern edge of the town centre about a 10min walk from Rode Steen. Regular trains serve Hoorn from Amsterdam (every 30min; 30min).
By bus Regional buses stop just outside the train station.

Bus #239 runs from Medemblik to Hoorn every 30min–1hr, and the journey takes 40min; bus #314 runs from Edam bus station to Hoorn every 15min (every 30min on Sun), and takes 35min.

INFORMATION

Tourist office The small VVV **desk** is in the Westfries Museum at Rode Steen 1 (April–Oct Tues–Fri 11am–5pm, Sat 1–5pm; Nov–March Tues–Sat 10am–5pm; ☎072 511 4284, ⓦvvvhoorn.nl), and has the usual info plus a small supply of rooms to rent in private houses. There's an additional VVV information point on Oostereiland (Schuijteskade 1; March–Sept daily 10am–5pm, Oct–Feb Sat & Sun 10am–5pm).

ACCOMMODATION

Gevangenishotel Oostereiland Schuijteskade 5 ☎0229 820 246, ⓦgevangenishotelhoorn.nl. Cells of the old prison on Oostereiland have been converted into a dozen compact but comfortable en-suite hotel rooms (some equipped with bunk beds), where anyone can become an inmate for the night. There are more new rooms in the attic – ask for one with views of the lake. **€80**

De Magneet Kleine Oost 5 ☎0229 215 021, ⓦhoteldemagneet.nl. Friendly long-established small hotel that's the best option if you want to stay down by the harbour. Well-kept and recently renovated rooms in both the main building and a series of annexes in the garden behind. **€100**

Petit Nord Kleine Noord 53 ☎0229 212 750, ⓦhotelpetitnord.nl. Very well-kept and decently furnished rooms, most of which have baths, and with two Asian restaurants on the premises. A 2min walk from the station. **€78**

EATING AND DRINKING

Brasserie Oostereiland Schuijteskade 5 ☎0229 820 246, ⓦgevangenishotelhoorn.nl. The modern restaurant inside the former prison has a small menu of tapas, burgers (€14.50), salads and a three-course menu for €25. Great for a meal before catching an arthouse film on one of the three cinema screens in the complex. Daily noon–10pm.

Charlie's Dubbele Buurt 4 ☎0229 217 798, ⓦcharlies.nl. One of several places on this short yet lively street, just off Grote Noord, this is a great, very friendly bar, where there's always something going on. There's a good selection of Belgian and Dutch beers, and an €11 two-course menu on Wednesday nights, when they also show films. Wed–Sat 4pm–1am, Sun 2–10pm.

De Hoornse Kogge Nieuwendam 2 ☎0229 210 574, ⓦdehoornsekogge.nl. In a sympathetically revamped old building right on the harbour, this relatively upscale restaurant offers a selection of small dishes for around €11 that you can combine and share around the table; pick three – for example oysters, tataki beef and smoked eel – and you have a full meal. Thurs–Sun 5–10.30pm.

De Korenmarkt Korenmarkt 1 ☎0229 279 826, ⓦdekorenmarkt.nl. Mainly Dutch staples at this relaxed and informal brasserie with lots of outside seating right on the harbour quay. It serves everything from lunchtime salads and toasted sandwiches (from €5), to good fish soup, usually a catch of the day, and the standard steak, chicken and spare ribs options for €15–20. Noon–10pm; closed Tues.

D'Oude Waegh Rode Steen 8 ☎0229 215 195, ⓦoudewaegh.nl. Café-restaurant fashioned out of the antiquated paraphernalia of the old municipal weigh-house, and with tables outside to watch the action on the square. All-day food, from club sandwiches, burgers and pasta dishes for €7.50–10.50, to beef bourgignon and steaks for €19–24. Mon–Thurs & Sun 8am–1am, Fri & Sat 8am–2am.

Enkhuizen

Like Hoorn, **ENKHUIZEN**, just 19km to the east, was once one of the country's most important seaports. From the fourteenth to the early eighteenth century, when its harbour silted up, it prospered from both the Baltic sea trade and the North Sea herring fishery – and indeed its maritime credentials were second to none: Enkhuizen was home to Holland's largest fishing fleet and its citizens were renowned for their seamanship, with the Dutch East India Company always keen to recruit here. Enkhuizen was also the first town in Noord-Holland to rise against Spain, in 1572, but unlike many of its Protestant allies it was never besieged – its northerly location kept it safely out of reach of the Habsburg army. Subsequently, Enkhuizen slipped into a long-lasting economic lull, becoming a remote and solitary backwater until tourism revived its fortunes. It's not a big place – about twenty minutes' walk from end to end – but the town centre, with its ancient streets, slender canals and pretty harbours, is wonderfully well preserved, a rough

2

circle with a ring of bastions and moat on one side, and the old sea dyke on the other. It also has a major attraction in the excellent **Zuiderzeemuseum** and is a good place to visit for its summer passenger **ferry** connections across the IJsselmeer to Stavoren (see p.203) and Urk (see p.245).

The Oude Haven

A good place to start an exploration of Enkhuizen's compact centre is the **Oude Haven**, which stretches east in a gentle curve to the conspicuous **Drommedaris**, a heavy-duty brick watchtower built in 1540 to guard the harbour entrance, and now in use as a theatre. On the green by the tower there's a modern statue of the seventeenth-century artist **Paulus Potter**, who was a native of Enkhuizen, painting one of the farm animals he was most famous for. Beyond the Drommedaris is the picturesque Buitenhaven, a jangle of sailing boats and barges, while immediately to the east is the oldest part of town, an extraordinarily pretty lattice of alleys, quays, canals and antique houses.

Flessenscheepjesmuseum

Zuiderspui 1 • Feb–Oct daily noon–5pm; Nov–Jan Mon & Sat–Sun noon–5pm • €4 • ⓦ flessenscheepjesmuseum.nl

The pocket-sized **Flessenscheepjesmuseum** is built above the lock gates at the end of the Zuiderhaven canal – ask and they'll show you the water flowing beneath the house. The museum itself is devoted to that ubiquitous maritime curiosity, the ship-in-a-bottle, and is a well-presented and -labelled collection, with vessels ranging from East Indiamen to steamboats, and containers from light bulbs, even fuses, to a thirty-litre wine flagon. There's also a short film introducing you into the ingenious mysteries of how it's done.

Westerstraat and around

Walk north from the Flessenscheepjesmuseum along Zuider Havendijk and turn left at the end of the canal to get to the **Zuiderkerk**, a hulking Gothic pile with a massive brick tower that was erected in 1518 – the octagon and then the cupola on top were added later. Close by, just to the east, is the solid, classically styled mid-seventeenth-century **Stadhuis**, an elegant and imposing Neoclassical edifice that still houses the city council. From here stroll up to the end of Enkhuizen's main street, **Westerstraat**, the town's spine, and a busy pedestrianized street that is home to most of its shops. About halfway along stands the **Westerkerk**, an early fifteenth-century, red-brick Gothic church with a free-standing wooden tower. The bare interior of the church, with its three naves of equal height, is distinguished by its **rood screen**, a mid-sixteenth-century extravagance whose six intricately carved panels show biblical scenes in dramatic detail – Moses with the Tablets, St John on Patmos and so forth.

Sprookjeswonderland

Kooizandweg 9 • April–Oct daily 10am–6pm • €9.50 • ☎ 0228 317 853

Just five to ten minutes' walk from the eastern end of Westerstraat, there's a little stretch of sandy **beach**; a shallow spot that's perfect for kids. Right by here, you'll also find **Sprookjeswonderland**, a modest theme park with gnome houses, rides, a mini railway, boats and a children's farm.

The Zuiderzeemuseum

Wierdijk 12–22 • Daily 10am–5pm; Museumpark April–Oct only • €15, children €10 • ⓦ zuiderzeemuseum.nl

It's a short walk from the centre of Enkhuizen to the **Binnenmuseum**, the landbound part of the **Zuiderzeemuseum**, around a dozen rooms devoted to changing annual exhibitions on different aspects of the Zuider Zee. At its heart is the impressive ship hall, where you can get up close and personal with a number of traditional sailing barges and other craft. There is an ice-cutting boat from Urk, once charged with the responsibility of keeping the shipping lanes open between the island and the mainland; a dinghy for duck-hunting, complete with shotgun; and some wonderful fully rigged and highly varnished sailing vessels.

Buitenmuseum

The museum's highlight, however, is the open-air **Buitenmuseum** section, whose main entrance is about 100m to the north along Wierdijk, and which stretches north along the seaward side of the old dyke that once protected Enkhuizen from the Zuider Zee. It's a fantastically well-put-together collection of over 130 dwellings, stores, workshops and even streets that have been transported here from every part of the region, and which together provide the flavour of life hereabouts from 1880 to around 1932. There are many highlights, and just about everything is worth seeing, but the best include a reconstruction of Marken harbour as of 1900, a red-brick chapel and assorted cottages from Den Oever, old fishermen's houses from Urk, an Amsterdam tattoo parlour and a pharmacy, which has a marvellous collection of "gapers" – painted wooden heads with their tongues out, which were the traditional pharmacy's sign. There's even a traditional tourist shop – for over ninety years foreigners have been dressing up in local Volendam costume for photos.

2

The museum works very hard to be authentic: sheep and goats roam the surrounding meadows and its smokehouses smoke (and sell) real herring and eels, the sweetshop sells real old-fashioned sweets, the beautifully kept schoolrooms offer geography and handwriting classes and there's even a woman in a 1930s furnished house who will make you a traditional Dutch lunch. There's also a **nature reserve**, where you can take a picnic and walk through the woods, and a water-themed playground. All in all not be missed, especially if you have children. A ferry to the Buitenmuseum, included in the ticket price, departs from the large car park at the western entrance of town at Sluisweg 1, stopping off at the train station as well (April–Oct; every 20min).

ARRIVAL AND DEPARTURE   ENKHUIZEN

By train Enkhuizen is at the end of the line, and the station is right opposite the head of the main harbour – the Buitenhaven – at the southern end of town. There are regularly connections to Hoorn (25 min) and to Amsterdam (1hr).

By bus Buses stop beside the train station, with connections roughly every 30min to Hoorn (20min) and Medemblik (1hr).

By ferry In summer, passenger ferries run east across the IJsselmeer to and from Stavoren (mid-April

Tues–Sun 1 daily; May–Sept 3 daily; Oct 2 daily; 1hr 20min; €11, children €7; day-return €15, children €8.50; ☎0228 326 006, ⓦveerboot.info). There are also summer sailings to Urk on a three-masted schooner (July to mid-Aug 2 daily Mon–Sat; 2hr 30min; €20, children €16; day-return €30, children €24; bikes €5, €7 return; ⓦveerdienst-urk-enkhuizen.nl). Ferries arrive and depart from the jetty behind the train station, and you can buy tickets from the tourist office, which also has timetables.

INFORMATION

Tourist office The VVV is opposite the train station, on the harbourfront at Tussen Twee Havens 1 (daily 9am–5pm ☎0228 313 164, ⓦvvvenkhuizen.nl). It sells

maps and town brochures and has details of local boat trips and rooms to rent in private houses.

ACCOMMODATION

HOTELS

De Koepoort Westerstraat 294 ☎0228 314 966, ⓦhoteldekoepoort.com. On the edge of the centre, but its wide range of rooms are handy if everywhere else is full. There's a pleasant bar and restaurant downstairs, though the welcome is businesslike rather than friendly. **€99**

Port van Cleve Dijk 74 ☎0228 312 510, ⓦdeportvancleve.nl. Elegant and central hotel with 22 rooms in a seventeenth-century house overlooking the harbour. There's a good restaurant with French and international dishes and a summer terrace too. **€98**

★Recuerdos Westerstraat 217 ☎0228 562 469, ⓦrecuerdos.nl. Enkhuizen's best accommodation option, this immaculate Victorian house has three doubles and one single in a series of chalets in a peaceful and elegant garden. The rooms are clean and comfortable, with well-appointed showers, and there are regular Spanish guitar and other concerts in the hotel's purpose-built music salon – reflecting the owner's occupation as a classical guitar teacher. **€88**

Suydersee Koltermanstraat 7 ☎0228 316 381, ⓦsuyderseehotel.nl. Right on the canal, in a very peaceful location, this has good-sized if plainly furnished rooms and apartments in a slightly faded 1960s building. Quite a large hotel but it's a friendly place. **€99**

CAMPING

Enkhuizer Zand Kooizandweg 4 ☎0228 317 289, ⓦcampingenkhuizerzand.nl. The closest of Enkhuizen's two campsites, on the far side of the Zuiderzeemuseum, a 10–15min walk from the station, and very handy for the beach. Facilities include a well-stocked shop, snack bar and indoor swimming pool. April–Sept. **€19**

De Vest Noorderweg 31 ☎0228 321 221, ⓦcampingdevest.nl; bus #138 from the station drops you nearby. The slightly plainer of Enkhuizen's two campsites, fitting snugly onto an old bastion. If you don't get the bus, follow Vijzelstraat north off Westerstraat, continue along Noorderweg, and turn left by the old town ramparts – a 15min walk. April–Oct. **€16**

EATING AND DRINKING

't Ankertje Dijk 6 ☎0228 315 767, ⓦcafe-ankertje.nl. An atmospheric, old-fashioned kind of place for a drink, with nautical knick-knacks hanging on the walls and lots of

tables outside on the quay. It serves food too, from simple lunchtime menus of soup and sandwiches, a few mains at dinner, like spare ribs, satay pork or catch of the day for around €15, and a short list of tapas. Daily 10am–2am.

★**Die Drie Haringhe** Dijk 28 ☎0228 318 610, ⓦdrieharinghe.nl. Housed in an immaculately renovated seventeenth-century building on the harbour, with tables in the courtyard garden outside and by the canal, this is perhaps the town's best restaurant, with a French-inspired menu that's strong on seafood. Main courses are in the region of €25 – though the three-course set dinner menu is worth trying at €40 (four courses €45). Wed–Sun 5–10pm; lunch by reservation only.

De Mastenbar Compagnieshaven 3 ☎0228 313 691, ⓦdemastenbar.nl. Down in the marina, this place is great both for a drink or a full meal, lunch or dinner, with sandwiches, burgers and *uitsmijters*, soups and big salads for lunch and a nice shortish dinner menu of meat and fish dishes for €15–20, along with three-course menus for €29.95. It's cosy enough inside, but the outside terrace, from which you can watch the yachts chugging by after a long day on the IJsselmeer, is about as good an end to a summer's day in Enkhuizen as it gets. Daily 10am–11.30pm.

De Smederij Breedstraat 158–160 ☎0228 314 604, ⓦrestaurantdesmederij.nl. Inventive, modern French-Mediterranean cuisine in a smartly renovated building a block back from the harbour, with starters for €15, main courses around €25. Mon, Tues & Fri–Sun 5–10pm.

Theo Schilder Dijk 48 ☎0228 317 809. A great fish shop with a pint-sized café attached and tables outside. Serves a wide variety of fish and seafood snacks for around €5–7. Mon–Sat 9am–7pm, Sun noon–7pm.

Van Bleiswijk Westerstraat 84–86 ☎0228 325 909, ⓦvanbleiswijk.nl. Grand café with two large rooms that stay open all day for drinks, lunch and dinner. The lunch menu takes in sandwiches, soup, salads and good burgers, while the dinner menu features international staples for €13–20. Daily 10am–midnight.

Medemblik and around

Nautical **MEDEMBLIK**, just over 20km north along the coast from Enkhuizen is one of the oldest towns in the Netherlands, a seat of Frisian kings until the seventh century and later a Zuider Zee port of some importance. Unfortunately, there's not a great deal to entice you here nowadays unless you're into yachts: the town's several waterways, harbour and marina are jam-packed with leisure craft. The main drag, **Nieuwstraat**, is wide and bustling, with the dinky Kasteel Radboud, perched at the end of the harbour.

Kasteel Radboud

Oudevaartsgat 8 • May to mid-Sept Mon–Thurs & Sat 11am–5pm, Sun 2–5pm; mid-Sept–April Sun 2–5pm • €6 • ⓦkasteelradboud.nl

A handsome, gabled, fortified manor house, **Kasteel Radboud**, is named after the last Frisian king to hold sway here, although the structure that survives is not his at all, but a much-modified thirteenth-century fortress built by a count of Holland, **Floris V** (1254–96), one of the most celebrated of the country's medieval rulers. Nicknamed "God of the Peasants" (Der Keerlen God) for his attempts to improve the lot of his humbler subjects, Floris spent most of his time fighting his enemies, both the nobles within his territories and his arch-enemy, the duke of Flanders. In the end, it was his own nobles who did for him, capturing Floris when he was out hunting and then murdering him during a skirmish when the peasantry came to the rescue. As for the castle itself, it owes much of its present appearance to Pierre Cuypers (1827–1921), who repaired and rebuilt what had by then become a dilapidated ruin; Cuypers was a leading architect of his day, who was also responsible – among many other commissions – for Amsterdam's Centraal Station and the Rijksmuseum. Inside the castle, exhibits outline the fort's turbulent history and there's a ragbag of archeological finds from local sites.

The Wieringermeer Polder and the Afsluitdijk

North of Medemblik, the **Wieringermeer Polder** was reclaimed in the 1920s, filling in the gap between the former Zuider Zee island of Wieringen and the mainland. Towards the end of World War II, just three weeks before their surrender, the Germans flooded the polder, boasting they could return the Netherlands to the sea if they so wished. After the war, it was drained again, leaving a barren, treeless terrain that had to be totally replanted. Almost sixty years later, it's indistinguishable from its surroundings, a familiar landscape of flat, geometric fields highlighted by neat and trim farmhouses. The polder leads north to the **Afsluitdijk** highway over to Friesland. The sluices on this side of the Afsluitdijk are known as the **Stevinsluizen**, after **Hendrick Stevin**, the seventeenth-century engineer who first had the idea of reclaiming the Zuider Zee. At the time, his grand plan was impracticable – the technology wasn't up to it – but his vision lived on, to be realized by **Cornelis Lely** (see box, p.112), though he too died before the dyke was completed. There's a **statue** of Lely by the modern Dutch sculptor Mari Andriessen at the west end of the dyke. Further out along the dyke, at the point where the barrier was finally closed, there's an observation point on which an inscription reads "A nation that lives is building for its future" – a linking of progress with construction that read well in the 1930s, but seems rather more dubious today.

ARRIVAL AND INFORMATION   MEDEMBLIK

By bus Buses to Medemblik, as well as the Stoomtram from Hoorn (see p.119), pull in on the Dam, at the north end of the town centre, and at the top of Nieuwstraat.
Tourist office The VVV is just off the Nieuwstraat at

Kaasmarkt 1 (daily: April & Sept–Oct 11am–3pm; May–June 11am–4pm; July–Aug 10am–5pm; ☎ 0229 547 997, ⓦ hartvannoordholland.nl). It has town maps and a small supply of rooms in private houses.

ACCOMMODATION AND EATING

Medemblik Oosterhaven 1 ☎ 0227 543 844, ⓦ hetwapenvanmedemblik.nl. This central hotel is the obvious place to stay in Medemblik, with comfortable if characterless rooms and a decent

restaurant downstairs. There's a simple lunch menu of sandwiches and *uitsmijters* from €5, while the short dinner menu features steaks and fish mains from about €21. Daily noon–9pm. **€105**

Zaandam

Largely a dormitory suburb of Amsterdam, the modern town of **ZAANDAM** is not especially alluring, though it does deserve a brief stop. The town was a popular tourist hangout in the nineteenth century, when it was known as "La Chine d'Hollande" for the faintly oriental appearance of its windmills, canals and row upon row of brightly painted houses. Monet spent some time here in the 1870s and, despite being under constant police surveillance as a suspected spy, went on to immortalize the place in a series of paintings.

The Czaar Peterhuisje

Krimp 23 • Tues–Sun 10am–5pm • €3 • A 10min walk east from the train station

Zaandam's one historical curiosity is the **Czaar Peterhuisje**, where the Russian Tsar Peter the Great stayed incognito in 1697. Earlier that year, Peter had attached himself to a Russian trade mission to Holland as an ordinary sailor, Peter Mikhailov. The Russians came to Zaandam, which was then an important shipbuilding centre, and the tsar bumped into a former employee, one Gerrit Kist. Swearing Kist to the utmost secrecy, the tsar moved into Kist's simple home and worked at a local shipyard where he learnt as much as he could about shipbuilding – although he was, in fact, only here for just over a week. Kist's old home is these days a tottering wooden structure, enclosed within a brick museum erected in 1895 – itself now also a registered monument – and comprises just two small rooms, decorated with a handful of portraits of a benign-looking emperor and the graffiti of tourists going back to the mid-nineteenth century. You can see the cupboard bed in which the tsar is supposed to have slept, together with the calling cards of various visiting Russian delegations, while around the outside of the house displays tell the story of Peter and his Western aspirations, and give background on the shipbuilding industry in Zaandam and the modest house itself. As Napoleon is said to have remarked on visiting the building, "Nothing is too small for great men."

Zaanse Schans

Schansend 7 • Hours of attractions vary, but most are open 10am–5pm • The Zaanse Schans Pass includes entry to the museum and at least one windmill €11.50, children €7, or you can pay per attraction; museum €10; windmills €4 each • ☎ 075 681 0000, ⓦ zaanseschans.nl

About 4km north of Zaandam, **Zaanse Schans** is a re-created Dutch village whose antique houses, shops, warehouses and windmills, mostly dating from the eighteenth century, were brought here from all over the region half a century ago and re-erected amid a network of narrow canals. It's a popular day-trip from Amsterdam and can get very crowded in summer, but it's a real village too – all the businesses are real, even though they derive most of their income from tourists, and all the houses are lived in year-round by people who have opted to move and work here. It's also the closest place to Amsterdam to see fully functioning windmills – pick a blowy day to visit.

The museum and Verkade Paviljoen

The main building beside the car park houses an information and ticket desk, shop and the **Zaanse Schans Museum**, which has well-displayed and engaging collections relating to the history of the area, including pictures of all the folk who live in the village and some information in English; it also incorporates the **Verkade Paviljoen**, a separate space devoted to the history of the local manufacturing company, who made chocolate and biscuits in Zaandam until the 1990s, when the company was sold to a conglomerate (its mostly female workforce was famously known for years as the "Verkade Girls"). There are lots of buttons for kids to press as they watch the chocolate biscuits coming out of the 1950s-era machines.

The village and windmills

The village itself, across the car park from the museum, is very quaint, basically a string of attractions, focused on old **crafts** – a clog-making workshop, bakery and cheese farm – and throwback nostalgia: there's a museum of old clocks, an old-style Albert Heijn grocery and even a B&B. But the real highlight of Zaanse Schans is the **windmills** themselves, eight in all, strung along the River Zaan, giant, insect-like affairs still used – among other things – to cut wood, grind mustard seeds and produce oil.

ARRIVAL AND DEPARTURE   **ZAANDAM**

By train Zaandam is just a 15min train ride from Amsterdam CS, while the nearest train station to Zaanse Schans is Koog-Zaandijk, two stops up the line from Zaandam. From the station, it's a 15min walk east to the river, where regular ferries take you across to Zaanse Schans.
By bus Bus #391 runs direct to Zaanse Schans every 15min from Amsterdam CS, and takes 40min.
By ferry The Zaanhopper ferry runs every 2hr between 10am and 4pm (Fri, Sat & Sun May–Oct) between Wilhelminahuis in Zaandam to Zaanse Schans and beyond to Wormerveer (5 stops in all, €1.50 per stop); ☎ 06 3053 9468, ⓦ varenopdezaan.nl.

Alkmaar and around

The engaging and attractive little town of **ALKMAAR** has preserved much of its medieval street plan, its compact centre surrounded by what was once the town moat and laced with spindly canals. The town is also dotted with fine old buildings, but is best known for its much-touted **cheese market**, an ancient affair that these days ranks as one of the most extravagant tourist spectacles in Noord-Holland. Alkmaar was founded in the tenth century in the middle of a marsh. Just like Haarlem, the town was besieged by Frederick of Toledo, but heavy rain flooded its surroundings and forced the Spaniards to withdraw in 1573, an early Dutch success in their long war of independence. At the time, Alkmaar was small and comparatively unimportant, but the town prospered when the surrounding marshland was drained in the 1700s and it received a boost more recently when the northern part of the old moat was incorporated into the Noordhollandsch Kanaal, itself part of a longer network of

ALKMAAR

Alkmaar station

■ ACCOMMODATION	
Grand Hotel Alkmaar	2
King's Inn Hotel & Hostel	1

● RESTAURANTS, CAFÉS & BARS	
De Boom	3
De Buren	5
Heeren van Sonoy	2
De Pilaren	6
Samen	4
Zegels	1

De Kraak Bike Rental

Biermuseum de Boom.

Kaas-Markt

Waag

Stadhuis

Rent-a-Scooter

Stedelijk Museum

St Laurenskerk

waterways running north from Amsterdam to the open sea. Alkmaar is also within easy striking distance of **Bergen**, a pretty little village halfway between Alkmaar and the North Sea coast, whose immediate hinterland, with its woods and dunes, is protected in the **Noordhollands Duinreservaat** (North Holland Dune Reserve) and, just to the north, the **Schoorlse Duinen** (Schoorl Dunes). Both areas are latticed by hiking and cycling routes, with bike rental available at Alkmaar and Bergen.

Waagplein and around

Alkmaar's main square is Waagplein, where the **Waag** or Weigh House was originally a chapel – hence the imposing tower – dedicated to the Holy Ghost; it was converted shortly after the town's famous victory against the Spanish, when it was given its delightful **gable** – an ostentatious Dutch Renaissance affair bedecked with allegorical figures and decorated with the town's militant coat of arms. The Waag holds the tourist office and the **Hollands Kaasmuseum** (April–Oct Mon–Sat 10am–4pm; Nov–March Sat 10am–4pm; €4; ⓦkaasmuseum.nl) with displays on – predictably enough – the history of cheese, cheese-making equipment and the like. At the far end of the Waagplein, the modest **Biermuseum de Boom** (June–Aug Mon–Sat 10.30am–4.30pm; Sept–May Mon–Sat 1–4pm; €4; ⓦbiermuseum.nl) above the *De Boom* bar, has three floors devoted to the art of making and distributing beer.

In the other direction, at the south end of Mient, the open-air **Vismarkt** (Fish Market) marks the start of the **Verdronkenoord** canal, whose attractive medley of facades and gables leads east to the spindly **Accijenstoren** (Excise Tower), part harbour master's office, part fortification built in 1622 during the long struggle with Spain. Turn left at the tower along Bierkade and you'll soon reach **Luttik Oudorp**, another attractive corner of the old centre, its slender canal jammed with antique barges.

Langestraat and the St Laurenskerk

One block south of Waagplein, pedestrianized **Langestraat** is Alkmaar's main and mundane shopping street, whose only notable building is the **Stadhuis**, a florid edifice, half of which (the Langestraat side) dates from the early sixteenth century. At the west end of Langestraat lurks **St Laurenskerk**, a de-sanctified Gothic church from the late fifteenth century whose pride and joy is its **organ**, commissioned at the suggestion of the diplomat and political bigwig Constantijn Huygens in 1645. The case was designed by Jacob van Campen, the architect who was later to design Amsterdam's town hall (see box, p.53), and decorated with paintings by **Caesar van Everdingen** (1617–78). The artist's seamless brushstrokes – not to mention his willingness to kowtow to the tastes of the burgeoning middle class – were to make van Everdingen a wealthy man. In the apse is the **tomb** containing the intestines of the energetic Count Floris V of Holland, who improved the region's sea defences, succoured the poor and did much to establish

---

ALKMAAR'S CHEESE MARKET

Cheese has been sold on Alkmaar's main square since the 1300s, and although it's no longer a serious commercial concern, the **kaasmarkt** (cheese market; April to early Sept Fri 10am–12.30pm) continues to pull the crowds – so get there early if you want a good view. The ceremony starts with the buyers sniffing, crumbling and finally tasting each cheese, followed by intensive bartering. Once a deal has been concluded, the cheeses – golden discs of local Beemster mainly, laid out in rows and piles on the square – are borne away on ornamental carriers by groups of four **porters** (*kaasdragers*) for weighing. The porters wear white trousers and shirt plus a straw hat whose **coloured bands** – green, blue, red or yellow – represent the four companies that comprise the cheese porters' guild. Payment for the cheeses, tradition has it, takes place in the cafés around the square.

the independence of the towns hereabouts, until his untimely demise at the hands of his own nobles; the rest of him ended up in Rijnsburg, near Leiden.

The Stedelijk Museum

Canadaplein 1 • Tues–Sun 10am–5pm • €13 • ⓦ stedelijkmuseumalkmaar.nl

Across from St Laurenskerk, Alkmaar's cultural centre holds a theatre, offices and a mildly diverting local museum, the **Stedelijk Museum**, whose three floors focus on the history of the town. Well displayed, the collection has a short film on the history of the town (in English), paintings, maps and models of Alkmaar during its seventeenth-century glory years. The many paintings include a typically precise interior of Alkmaar's St Laurenskerk by Pieter Saenredam (1597–1665), a striking *Holy Family* by the Mannerist Gerard van Honthorst (1590–1656) and a huge canvas by the medievalist Jacobus Hilverdink (1809–64) depicting the bloody siege of 1573. The top floor explores the history of the town during the twentieth century and hosts a large and well-displayed collection along with pictures by local artist Charley Toorop (1891–1955), daughter of the Dutch Impressionist Jan Toorop.

ARRIVAL AND DEPARTURE ALKMAAR

By train There are trains at least every 30min from Amsterdam, Haarlem and Hoorn to Alkmaar's train station, which is a 10min walk from the centre of town.

By bus All buses stop outside the train station, with bus #6 departing to Bergen every 30min.

INFORMATION AND TOURS

Tourist office The VVV is housed in the Waag at Waagplein 2 (April–Oct Mon–Sat 10am–4pm, Fri 9am–4pm on cheese market days; Nov–March Mon 1–4pm, Tues–Sat 10am–4pm; ☎ 072 511 4284, ⓦ vvvalkmaar.nl). It sells a useful town brochure, has details of the area's walking and cycling routes, and plenty of rooms in private houses for around €40 per double per night, including breakfast, though most places are on the outskirts of town.

Bike rental Bikes can be rented from the train station and in the centre of town at De Kraak, Verdronkenoord 54 (€8.50/day; book ahead at ☎ 072 512 5840, ⓦ dekraak.nl;

May Mon–Fri 11am–6pm, Sat & Sun 10am–8pm; June–Aug daily 10am–9pm); it also rents canoes and rowing boats. Electric bikes and scooters can be rented from Rent-a-Scooter at Molenbuurt 21 (from €12/4hr; ☎ 072 562 8530, ⓦ ras-alkmaar.nl; April–June & Sept–Nov Tues–Sun 9am–5pm, July & Aug 9am–9pm).

Canal trips Boats leave from the jetty on Mient for a quick zip round the town's central waterways – an enjoyable way to spend 45min (hourly 11am–5pm: April–Oct Mon–Sat; May–Sept also Sun; €6; ☎ 072 512 5840, ⓦ rondvaartalkmaar.nl); tickets are on sale at the VVV or on board.

ACCOMMODATION

Grand Hotel Alkmaar Gedempte Nieuwesloot 36 ☎ 072 576 0970, ⓦ grandhotelalkmaar.nl. This boutique-style hotel has been stylishly converted from a post office and has 42 sleek modern rooms, plus an inviting bar, which serves a brasserie menu as well as the posher *Zegels* restaurant (see opposite). **€90**

King's Inn Hotel & Hostel Koningsstraat 6 ☎ 072 511 0112, ⓦ kings-inn.com. Set in two buildings near Waagplein, this budget hotel has 25 basic dorm and private rooms and a lively bar, as well as fourteen elegant hotel rooms in an old canal-side warehouse around the corner. There's bike rental too. Dorms **€28**, doubles **€80**

EATING AND DRINKING

De Boom Houttil 1 ☎ 072 511 5547, ⓦ proeflokaaldeboom.nl. Right in the centre of town, this small unpretentious bar has a museum of beer upstairs (see p.129). Mon & Sun 2pm–midnight, Tues & Wed 1pm–midnight, Thurs–Sat 1pm–2am.

De Buren Mient 37 ☎ 072 512 0308, ⓦ restaurant-deburen.nl. Busy and fashionable bistro and bar that makes the most of its position on the corner of two canals. The dinner menu incorporates a bit of everything,

such as pork satay, burgers, cannelloni and Thai green curry: mains start at €15 and go up to €27. Daily 10am–10pm.

Heeren van Sonoy Hof van Sonoy 1 ☎ 072 512 1222, ⓦ heerenvansonoy.nl. A delightfully restored medieval nunnery just off Gedempte Nieuwesloot, this is pretty good for both lunch and dinner, with inexpensive omelettes, sandwiches and pancakes at lunch, and tasty Dutch cuisine at night with main courses averaging €15–20; there's an outside terrace too. Mon–Thurs 4pm–midnight, Fri & Sat 10am–midnight, Sun 11am–midnight.

De Pilaren Verdronkenoord 129 ☎072 511 4997, ⓦcafedepilaren.nl. A youthful brown cafe catering to a lively crowd, some of whom take refuge in the *Café Stapper* next door if the music gets too much. Upstairs, simple meals are served at *Heerlijk Nel*. Daily 2pm–2am.

Samen Houttil 34 ☎072 511 3283, ⓦgrandcafesamen.nl. Nice, relaxed, child-friendly bar-café with an array of well-priced lunch options and a

slightly rowdier feel at night. Mon & Tues 10am–midnight, Wed & Thurs 10am–1am, Fri & Sat 10am–2am, Sun noon–midnight.

Zegels Gedempte Nieuwsloot 36 ☎072 576 0970, ⓦgrandhotelalkmaar.nl. The upmarket restaurant in the *Grand Hotel* is named after the stamps that were once sold in this former post office. Besides the regular meals of duck breast, local veal and vegetarian tagliatelle (starting around €19), there's a choice of two- (€29) to six-course (€63) set menus. Daily 10am–10pm.

Bergen and Bergen-aan-Zee

Out towards the coast, just 5km northwest of Alkmaar, the village of **BERGEN** is a cheerful sort of place that has been something of a retreat for artists since the late nineteenth century. Its centre is a pleasant place for a wander, with a leafy church square and plenty of cafés and restaurants, all focused on the amiable main square – intersection, really – of Plein. With a nod to the village's artistic heritage, the local council organizes all sorts of cultural events in Bergen, including open-air sculpture displays and concerts, and the village also boasts a scattering of chi-chi commercial galleries.

Museum Kranenburgh

Hoflaan 26 • Tues–Sun 11am–5pm • €8 • ☎072 589 8927, ⓦmuseumkranenburgh.nl

Bergen's main sight, the **Museum Kranenburgh**, in a Neoclassical villa five minutes' walk from the Plein, features the work of the Expressionist Bergen School, which was founded here in 1915. The group was greatly influenced by the Post-Impressionists, especially Cézanne, and, though none of the group is original enough to stand out, taken as a whole it's a delightful collection and one that is supported by an imaginative programme of temporary exhibitions. These often focus on the two contemporaneous Dutch schools that were to have much more artistic impact – De Ploeg and De Stijl (see p.344).

Museum Het Sterkenhuis

Oude Prinsweg 21 • May–Nov Tues–Sat 1–5pm • €2 • ⓦmuseumhetsterkenhuis.nl

Bergen's other museum of note is **Museum Het Sterkenhuis**, housed in a step-gabled manor house dating from 1655 right by the church. It holds regular exhibitions of work by contemporary Dutch artists, has a string of period rooms and features a local history section, including a display on a largely forgotten episode in the Napoleonic Wars, when a combined army of 30,000 English and Russian soldiers were defeated by a Franco-Dutch force here in 1799.

Bergen-aan-Zee and the dunes

It's just 5km across the dunes from Bergen to **BERGEN-AAN-ZEE**, a sprawling, modern resort that's of little interest beyond its first-rate **beach**, a strip of golden sand extending both north and south as far as the eye can see, and a small **sea aquarium** on the seafront at Van der Wijckplein 16 (April–Sept daily 10am–6pm; Nov–March daily 11am–5pm; €9.50, children €7.50; ☎072 581 2928, ⓦzeeaquarium.nl). The village also marks the northerly limit of the **Noordhollands Duinreservaat** (North Holland Dune Reserve), whose bumpy sand dunes stretch north from IJmuiden, and the southern boundary of the **Schoorlse Duinen** (Schoorl Dunes), where a band of sweeping, wooded dunes, up to 5km wide, extends north as far as Camperduin – one of the widest undeveloped portions of the whole Dutch coastline. The dune reserve and the national park are both crisscrossed by footpaths and cycling trails, but the most lauded is the well-signposted, 42km-long **Brede Duinen route** that takes cyclists on a loop through Alkmaar, Bergen, Bergen-aan-Zee, Schoorl and Camperduin, passing the highest sand dunes (54m) on

2

the way. Both Bergen and Alkmaar tourist offices sell detailed **maps** of local hiking and cycling routes but if you just want a taster of the landscape, there's a car park and access to marked trails halfway between Bergen and Bergen-aan-Zee on Uilenvangerweg.

ARRIVAL AND INFORMATION — BERGEN AND BERGEN-AAN-ZEE

By bus Bus #6 leaves Alkmaar train station every 30min for the 10min ride to Bergen, dropping passengers in the centre on Plein, 600m east of Museum Kranenburgh and the VVV.

Tourist office The Bergen VVV is inside the Museum Kranenburgh (same hours) at Hoflaan 26 (☎ 072 589 8927 ⓦ vvvbergen.com). It sells maps of hiking and cycling

routes in the Noordhollands Duinreservaat and the Schoorlse Duinen.

Bike rental There are several places in Bergen to rent bikes, and it's much the best way to get around – try Fietsverhuur Bergen, just north of Plein at Breelaan 46 (☎ 06 2319 9841, ⓦ bergenfietsverhuur.nl).

Den Helder

The gritty port, oil supply centre and naval base of **DEN HELDER**, some forty minutes north from Alkmaar by train, was little more than a fishing village until 1811, when Napoleon, capitalizing on its strategic position at the very tip of Noord-Holland, built a fortified dockyard here. It's still the principal home of the Dutch navy, and **navy days**, or **Marinedagen**, are held in the harbour on one weekend in July every second and third year – when you can check out the bulk of the Dutch navy. Otherwise, the town holds little of interest beyond its ferry connections to the island of Texel (see opposite), and the redeveloped old dockyard complex of Willemsoord, which stretches down to the ferry terminal for Texel. Probably the most interesting part of Den Helder, it's a decent place to spend an hour or two while waiting for a ferry, and is home to a few places to eat, the tourist office and the excellent **Marinemuseum**, right by the ferry port.

The Marinemuseum

Hoofdgracht 3 • May–Oct Mon–Fri 10am–5pm, Sat & Sun noon–5pm; Nov–April Tues–Fri 10am–5pm, Sat & Sun noon–5pm • €6 • ☎ 0223 657 534, ⓦ marinemuseum.nl

Den Helder's **Marinemuseum** does justice to the town's role as home of the Dutch navy in a series of buildings and craft scattered around the seaward end of the Willemsoord complex. The building by the ferry terminal houses a series of well-presented and entertaining exhibits tracking the history of the Dutch navy – in particular look out for the stuff on the naval heroes of yesteryear, especially Admiral Michiel de Ruyter (1607–76), who trounced in succession the Spaniards, the Swedes, the English and the French. His most daring exploit was a raid up the River Thames to Medway in 1667 and the seizure of the Royal Navy's flagship, *The Royal Charles*, an act that drove Charles II almost to distraction. There's lots of technical information too – on shipbuilding techniques and the like – and, perhaps most interestingly, several decommissioned vessels, including the 1960s diesel electrical submarine, the *Tonijn*, and the veteran World War II minesweeper, the *Abraham Crijnssen*, which famously escaped the Japanese by disguising itself as a tropical island and hotfooting it to Australia. You can also clamber around the bridge of a warship and stand below a fast-spinning radar.

ARRIVAL AND INFORMATION — DEN HELDER

By train Den Helder train station is a 10min walk from Willemsoord – follow Beatrixstraat and cross the canal – and around 25min from the ferry terminal; alternatively, there's a direct bus between the train station and the ferry dock. There are two trains an hour to Amsterdam (1hr 15min).

By ferry Car and passenger ferries run between Den Helder and Texel island hourly, and the journey takes 20min. See p.135.

Tourist office The VVV is in the Willemsoord complex at Willemsoord 52a (Mon–Fri 10am–4pm, Sat 10am–3pm; ☎ 0223 674 694, ⓦ vvvkopvannoordholland.nl).

Texel

Stuck out in the Waddenzee, **Texel** (pronounced "tessel") is the westernmost of the string of islands that band the northern coast of the Netherlands. Some 25km long and up to 9km wide, Texel is a mixture of natural island – in its southwest reaches – and reclaimed polder, mostly on the eastern side. Overall it's a flat landscape of green pastureland dotted with chunks of woodland, speckled with small villages and protected by long sea defences. The west coast boasts magnificent stretches of sand that reach from one end of the island to the other, its numbered markers (*palen*)– from *paal* 6 in the south to *paal* 33 in the north – distinguishing one section from another. Behind the beach, a belt of sand dunes widens as it approaches both ends of the island. In the north it spreads out into two nature reserves – **De Muy** and **De Slufter** – the latter incorporates Texel's finest scenery in a tidal inlet where a deep cove of salt marsh, lagoon and dune has been left beyond the sea defences, exposed to the ocean. It's this landscape, and of course the beaches, combined with the island's laidback rural charms, that attracts holidaying Dutch and Germans by the ferryload in summer, and the island has scores of holiday bungalows and cottages, plus a scattering of hotels and campsites. The island's **villages** are fairly humdrum

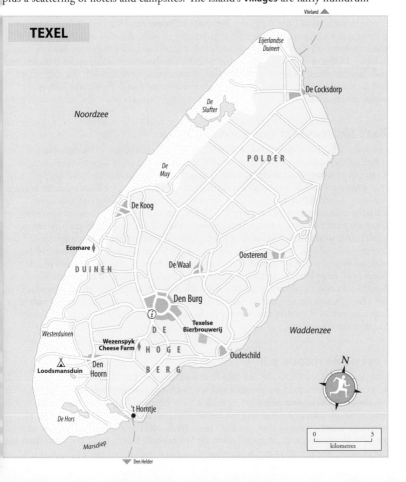

places, though the "capital", Den Burg, has its lively moments. **Den Hoorn**, is probably the prettiest place on the island, while **Oudeschild** still boasts a working harbour with a twenty-ship fishing fleet, best observed on Friday afternoon when it arrives home from a week on the North Sea. Other ships offer regular Waddenzee cruises with seal-spotting and shrimp-fishing for around €11; some include short excursions on the exposed sandbanks at low tide. Overall, Texel is a bit of an untouched gem.

Den Burg

DEN BURG is the island's main village and home to the tourist office, a Monday morning market and the island's best range of shops. There's little else of interest, the only sight being the **Oudheidkamer** local museum at Kogerstraat 1 (April–Oct Mon–Fri 11am–5pm, Sat 2–4pm; €3), whose period interiors show how life was on Texel in times gone by.

Wezenspyk Cheese Farm

Hoornderweg 29, Den Burg • April–Oct Tues–Sat 9.30am–5pm; Nov–March Tues, Thurs, Fri, Sat 9.30am–5pm; tours Tues & Fri at 2pm • €5.50 • ☏ 0222 315 090, ⓦ wezenspyk.nl

To the southwest of Den Burg, the **Wezenspyk Cheese Farm** has been going for around 35 years, having revived the island's ancient sheep's milk cheese. Today, they make cheese using milk from both the island's many sheep and the farm's own herd of Friesian-Holstein cows. The farm tour takes half an hour and includes the cowshed and milking parlour, the cheese-making room and the storeroom beyond. The salty Texel soil is said to import a special flavour and certainly the cheese they make here is especially delicious.

Kaap Skil Museum van Jutters & Zeelui

Heemskerckstraat 9, Oudeschild • April–Oct Mon–Sat 10am–5pm, Sun noon–5pm • €8.50 • ☏ 0222 314 956, ⓦ kaapskil.nl

Right by the harbour in the village of **OUDESCHILD**, 3km from Den Burg, is the new **Kaap Skil Museum van Jutters & Zeelui**. The wonderfully ramshackle collection of maritime junk which was its core collection in days gone by, is still its most interesting feature – a shed full of beachcombed items from around the island, including an amazing collection of bottles stacked as high as the ceiling. There's a small open-air museum with cottages, shops, a functioning windmill, an eighteenth-century ship's garden and an exhibition on today's fishing industry. In the main building is an impressive model of Oudeschild in the seventeenth century, when its offshore waters were an important stopping-off point for navy and merchant ships; upstairs plastic boxes hold what remains of the dozens of ships that never made it out to the North Sea. There's also a café on the ground floor. Nearby, the lovely **Skillepaadje** footpath to Den Burg passes the restored wells that provided long-lasting drinking water with high iron content to ships that sometimes purchased over 100,000 litres for trips to the Cape or the Americas.

Texelse Bierbrouwerij

Schilderweg 214, Oudeschild • Tours Tues–Fri 2pm & 3pm, Sat 2pm, 3pm & 4pm • €9.50 • ☏ 0222 313 229, ⓦ speciaalbier.com

Just outside Oudeschild on the road to Den Burg, the **Texelse Bierbrouwerij** offers regular tours of its premises, starting with a short film and finishing up in the cosy *proeflokaal* to taste its unique and excellent brews. It's a great small business, and produces around ten so-called "special" beers (it doesn't do straight lager), from its popular Skuumkoppe to an award-winning Stormbock. You can also try them from the bottle or on draught all over the island.

Den Hoorn

The hamlet of **DEN HOORN** is the nearest village to the ferry dock on the southern side of the island. It's a leafy little place whose rustic cottages, some of which date back to the eighteenth century, string along the main street, Herenstraat, and out towards the dunes, just 2km away to the west: the beach is a further 2km (at *paal* 10). There's nothing to see in the village, but it does have a couple of good places to stay and to eat (see p.136).

De Koog

Northwest of Den Burg, **DE KOOG** is Texel's busiest resort, equipped with lots of restaurants and hotels and a small army of campsites. The village centre is entirely given over to shops and places to eat and the only sight as such is the Ecomare complex, 1.5km south of the village.

Ecomare

Ruijslaan 92, De Koog • €9.75, joint ticket with Oudeheidkamer & Kaap Skil €15 • ☎ 0222 317 741, ⓦ ecomare.nl

Less than two kilometres outside De Koog, amid the dunes, **Ecomare** is a sealife and marine centre devoted to the wildlife and history of Texel. There are tanks of seals and porpoises, displays on the history of the island that sport some great skeletons of locally found turtles and humpback whales, and tanks devoted to the island's various habitats. It's also the headquarters of the **Duinen van Texel** national park, which comprises pretty much all of the dunes on the west side of the island. The road leads beyond Ecomare to the beach, where there's a café and, of course, unlimited opportunities for duney walks.

De Slufter

North of De Koog, the coastal road north leads after about 4km past the first of two turnings that cut down to the sea wall behind **De Slufter** nature reserve, a beautiful tidal inlet whose assorted lagoons, marshes and dunes are exposed to the ocean's tides. Steps enable visitors to clamber up and over the sea wall to the footpaths beyond: it is perhaps the prettiest spot on the island.

De Cocksdorp

Near the northern tip of Texel, **DE COCKSDORP** is a middling sort of village (named after the Belgian banker De Cock, who funded the draining of these northwestern polders), whose wedge of mostly modern houses trails along a slender inlet, protected by a sea wall. Across the sea wall is a lighthouse (April–Oct daily 10am–5pm, Nov–March Wed, Sat & Sun 10am–5pm; €4; ⓦ vuurtorentexel.nl), whose red shape is the iconic image of Texel. Ferries to the island of Vlieland leave from the jetty about 1km north of the village, with an hourly **bus** running between De Cocksdorp, De Koog and the ferry dock.

ARRIVAL AND DEPARTURE   TEXEL

By ferry Car ferries, run by Teso (Mon–Sat 6.30am–9.30pm, Sun 7.30am–9.30pm; ☎ 0222 369 600, ⓦ teso.nl), leave Den Helder for Texel hourly on the half-hour with extra departures in high season, and the journey takes about 20min. Return tickets cost €2.50 for foot passengers, plus €2.50 for a bike or moped; cars including passengers cost €37 at peak times, which includes most weekend sailings, €25 at other times. Ferries dock at the southern end of the island, pretty much in the middle of nowhere, but the Texelhopper bus services reach all Texel's villages, and connect with each ferry arrival. There's also a seasonal passenger ferry to Vlieland, the next island along, which docks just outside De Cocksdorp, at the northern tip of the island. Operated by De Vriendschap (☎ 0222 316 451, ⓦ waddenveer.nl), the ferry runs May–Sept, with two services daily every day in July and Aug, and two services daily on Tues, Wed and Thurs in May, June and Sept. The journey takes an hour and tickets cost €18.50 one-way, €27.50 return, including a drive across the sandbanks in a special truck when it's low tide.

2

By bus Texelhopper bus #28 from Den Helder's train station uses the ferry to cross to Texel and then drives on to Den Burg and De Koog. It departs at twelve minutes past the hour and the tickets (€5.50 to anywhere on the island, €3 on the way back, OV-chipkaart not valid) include the ferry.

INFORMATION

Tourist office Texel VVV is on the southern edge of Den Burg at Emmalaan 66 (June–Oct Mon 9am–9pm, Tues–Fri 9am–5.30pm, Sat 9am–5pm, Sun 6–9pm; Nov–May Mon–Fri 9am–5.30pm, Sat 9am–5pm; ☎ 0222 314 741, Ⓦ vvv.texel.net). It has a wide range of island information, including booklets detailing cycling routes as well as the best places to view the island's many bird colonies – for example De Slufter and the De Hors area south of the ferry terminal. The VVV operates an online accommodation service, which is especially useful in the height of the summer when spare rooms can be thin on the ground.

GETTING AROUND

By bus Pick up a Texelhopper bus timetable on the ferry. All rides on the island cost €3. Bus #28 runs from De Koog via Den Burg to Den Helder every hour; for all other destinations there's the Texelhopper minibuses which must be booked at least an hour in advance at ☎ 0222 784 000 or online at Ⓦ texelhopper.nl.

By taxi There are also usually plenty of taxis, or you can call Taxi Texel (☎ 0222 315 555).

By bike The best way to get around the island is by bike – Texel has about 130km of cycle paths. Bike rental is available at a number of locations across the island, but there is a very convenient outlet beside the Texel ferry dock: Fietsverhuur Veerhaven Texel (daily 8.30am–6pm; ☎ 0222 319 588 Ⓦ fietsverhuurtexel.nl; from €7.50/day, €25.50/week); reservations aren't necessary. Alternatively, you can rent bikes in Den Hoorn at Vermeulen Bikes, Herenstraat 69 (☎ 0222 319 213), for €7.50/day (Mon–Fri 8.30am–12.30pm & 1.30–6pm, Sat 9am–5pm). Especially on windy days, renting a bike with gears is a good idea.

ACCOMMODATION AND EATING

DEN BURG

★ **De Smulpot** Binnenburg 5 ☎ 0222 312 756, Ⓦ smulpot.nl. You couldn't be more central in Den Burg, and this cosy bar-restaurant has seven rooms upstairs, nicely finished with driftwood furniture. The food served downstairs is tasty and plentiful, with most mains under €20, including excellent steaks, pork satay and ribs. There's also an impressive breakfast included. €115

Vincent City Lounge Binnenburg 8 ☎ 0222 320 240, Ⓦ vincentcitylounge.nl. An excellent place to try classic regional dishes with a modern twist – and with some unusual island ingredients such as salty samphire. Mon & Wed–Sun noon–10pm.

OUDESCHILD

't Pakhuus Haven 8 ☎ 0222 313 581, Ⓦ pakhuus .com. Right on the fishing harbour, this is one of the nicest restaurants on this side of the island, serving a lovely lunch menu of fish soup, open sandwiches and more substantial offerings (a three-course lunch fixed-price menu costs €35) and an array of great fish dishes in the evening – reckon on paying €25–35 for a main course. They also have three beautifully designed and very comfortable contemporary suites upstairs. Tues & Wed 5–9.30pm, Thurs–Sun noon–9.30pm. €118

Van der Star Heemskerckstraat 15 ☎ 0222 312 441, Ⓦ vispaleistexel.nl. A good alternative to the posh fish restaurants down by Oudeschild's harbour, a seafood and fish café with lots of baked and smoked marine delights, fish soup and salads – all delicious. Mon–Sat 8.30am–6pm.

DEN HOORN

Bij Jef Herenstraat 34 ☎ 0222 319 623, Ⓦ bijjef.nl. In an old building right on the main street, this place is one of the island's most enticing prospects, with stylish and very comfortable rooms. The restaurant is one of Texel's best, with crisp white tablecloths and white leather chairs, and with an excellent reputation for its excellent Franco-Dutch cuisine: the four-course menu is €75. July & Aug daily 6–10pm; May–June & Sept–Nov Wed–Fri & Sun 6–10pm. €214

Klif 23 Klif 23 ☎ 0222 319 515, Ⓦ klif23.nl. On the west side of the village on the road that runs towards the dunes, this simple café specializes in pancakes: it serves up more than 150 varieties, along with Texel lamb dishes. In spring the terrace has amazing views of the adjacent tulip fields. Tues–Sun 11am–9pm.

Loodsmans Welvaren Herenstraat 12 ☎ 0222 319 228, Ⓦ welvaarttexel.nl. Nine spick-and-span, modern double rooms, all decorated with naval scenes, in a sympathetically modernized old building. The decent restaurant downstairs continues the nautical theme. €94

Loodsmansduin Rommelpot 19 ☎ 0222 317 208, Ⓦ rsttexel.nl. Large campsite with plenty of space for tents and caravans on the edge of the dunes just to the southwest of Den Hoorn – about a 10min walk. April–Oct. €24

DE COCKSDORP

Anker van Texel Kikkertstraat 22 ☎0222 316 274, ⓦhotelhetankervantexel.nl. An unassuming little place in a pair of oldish cottages on the main street. It offers a cosy downstairs sitting room, nice rooms and a good breakfast with home-made bread. €93

Pangkoekehuus Kikkertstraat 9 ☎0222 316 441, ⓦpangkoekehuus.nl. They serve a great line in pancakes here – both sweet and savoury – and you can sit outside on the large terrace and watch the world go by. Prices start at around €4. Daily noon–8.30pm, July–Aug until 9pm.

Het Gooi

Known collectively as **Het Gooi**, the sprawling suburbs that spread southeast from Amsterdam towards Amersfoort and Utrecht are interrupted by open heaths, lakes, canals and woods, reminders of the time when this was a sparsely inhabited district largely devoted to sheep farming. The turning point was the construction of the Amsterdam–Amersfoort railway in 1874, which allowed hundreds of middle-class Amsterdammers to build their country homes here, nowhere more so than in well-heeled **Hilversum**, long the area's main settlement and nowadays pretty much a dormitory town despite the best efforts of the Dutch media, many of which are based here. Hilversum is a possible target for a day-trip on account of its modern architecture, most notably the work of Willem Dudok, although Het Gooi's two other prime attractions, the immaculate star-shaped fortifications of **Naarden** and the handsome medieval castle at **Muiden**, are frankly more appealing.

GETTING AROUND   **HET GOOI**

By train The most useful train line across Het Gooi passes through Weesp, where there are connecting buses on to Muiden, and then to Naarden-Bussum (for Naarden) and Hilversum.

Muiden

Just to the north of the A1 motorway about 10km southeast of Amsterdam, **MUIDEN** straddles the River Vecht as it approaches the Markermeer, its several waterways crowded with pleasure boats and yachts. At the far end of the town on the old ramparts is the **Muiderslot**, one of the country's most visited castles.

The Muiderslot

Herengracht 1 • April–Oct Mon–Fri 10am–5pm, Sat & Sun noon–5pm; Nov–March Sat & Sun noon–5pm • €13.50 • ☎0294 256 262, ⓦmuiderslot.nl

The **Muiderslot** is a handsome, red-brick structure whose imposing walls are punctuated by mighty circular towers, all set behind a reedy moat. Originally built by Count Floris V of Holland, it has been rebuilt or remodelled on several occasions, most recently after World War II when the interior was returned to its seventeenth-century appearance in honour of the poet Pieter Hooft, one of its most celebrated occupants. Hooft was chatelain here from 1609 to 1647, a sinecure that allowed him to entertain a group of artistic and literary friends who were known as the Muiderkring or Muiden Circle.

In order to see certain parts of the castle, you have to join one of the half-hourly guided tours, which take you through a series of period rooms, among them the large Ridderzaal, which has a painting showing Hooft and his most famous cronies – Vondel, Huygens, Jacob Cats, Maria Tesselschade and others – although it's is something of a fake in that not all the people in the painting were alive at the same time. But really the best bits of the building can be seen on your own, whether it's the chapel which shows a short film about Muiden, Hooft's study and en-suite loo, good views over what would have been the Zuider Zee, or the suits of armour and knightly bits and pieces in one of the towers. Kids may also enjoy the chance to joust or dress in a jester's suit, but the best thing is the wonderful view over the Markerwaard from the bastions. Bear in mind that the entrance ticket also includes the gardens, and the regular falconry displays that take place nearby.

2

By train and bus To get to Muiden, take the train from Amsterdam Centraal Station to Weesp (every 15min; 15min) where you catch the hourly local bus #110 to Muiden: it's a 5min journey. In Muiden, the bus drops you on the edge of town, a short, signposted walk from the centre and the Muiderslot.

By ferry In summer the castle can be reached by ferry from Amsterdam's IJburg harbour, near the terminus of tram #26 (April–Oct Tues–Sun 11am, Sat & Sun also 1.30pm; €20 including castle admission; ⓦveerdienstamsterdam.nl).

EATING AND DRINKING

Ome Ko Herengracht 71, ☎0294 262 333, ⓦcafeomekomuiden.nl. Right by the lock gates in the centre of Muiden, this is a pleasant eetcafé with a terrace overlooking the canal – it's a good lunch or drink stop, serving *uitsmijters*, sandwiches and the like. Mon–Thurs & Sun 8am–2am, Fri & Sat 8am–3am.

Naarden

Look at a postcard of **NAARDEN**, about 8km east along the A1 from Muiden, and it seems as if the old town was created by a giant pastry-cutter, its gridiron of streets encased within a double ring of ramparts and moats that were engineered with geometrical precision between 1675 and 1685 to defend the eastern approaches to Amsterdam. Within the ramparts, Naarden's attractive and architecturally harmonious centre mostly dates from the late sixteenth century, its small, low houses erected after the Spanish sacked the town in 1572, including the elaborately step-gabled **Stadhuis**, built in 1601 and still in use by the town council today. Naarden's old town is readily explored on foot – it's only 1km long and about 800m wide.

Nederlands Vestingmuseum

Westwalstraat 6 • Tues–Fri 10.30am–5pm, Sat & Sun noon–5pm • €7 • ☎ 035 694 5459, ⓦ vestingmuseum.nl

Naarden's formidable defences were used right up until the 1920s, and one of the fortified spurs is now the wonderful **Nederlands Vestingmuseum**, on whose grassy forks you can clamber around among the cannons. It's great to explore and its claustrophobic casemates demonstrate how the garrison defended the town for nigh-on 300 years.

The Grote Kerk

Marktstraat 15 • Free • Tower tours May–Sept Wed, Sat & Sun at 2pm & 3pm • €3 • ☎ 035 694 9873, ⓦ grotekerknaarden.nl

One building that was spared by the Spaniards was the late Gothic **Grote Kerk**, whose superb vault paintings, based on drawings by Dürer, are the town's other main sight. These 22 rectangular wooden panels were painted between 1510 and 1518 and show Old Testament scenes on the south side, New Testament scenes on the north; there are also five triangular panels at the east end of the church. To study the paintings without cricking your neck, borrow a mirror at the entrance. The church is also noted for its wonderful acoustics: every year there are several acclaimed performances of Bach's *St Matthew Passion* in the Grote Kerk in the days leading up to Easter. A haul up the 235 steps of the Grote Kerk's massive square **tower** gives the best view of the fortress.

Comenius Museum

Kloosterstraat 33 • Tues–Sun noon–5pm • €5 • ☎ 035 694 3045, ⓦ comeniusmuseum.nl

The mildly absorbing **Comenius Museum** is the third of Naarden's trio of sights. Jan Amos Komenski, his name latinized as Comenius, was a seventeenth-century philosopher, cartographer and educational reformer who was born in Moravia, today part of the Czech Republic. A Protestant, he was expelled for his religious beliefs in 1621 and spent the next 36 years wandering round Europe preaching and teaching before finally settling in Amsterdam. The museum outlines Comenius' life and times and takes a stab at explaining his work, notably his plan to improve the Swedish educational system and his 1658 *Orbis Pictus* ("The World in Pictures"), the first-ever picture-book for children. Comenius was buried here in Naarden, and the museum incorporates his **mausoleum**, a remarkable affair with an ornamental screen and engraved glass panels decorated with scenes from his life, in what was once the chapel of a Franciscan convent. In the 1930s the Dutch authorities refused the Czechoslovak government's request for the repatriation of the philosopher's remains, and instead rented them the building for the symbolic price of one guilder per year.

ARRIVAL AND INFORMATION NAARDEN

By train and bus There are up to three trains hourly from Amsterdam Centraal Station to Naarden-Bussum train station, with local buses linking the train station with the old town 4km away.

Tourist office The VVV is at the south end of the main Marktstraat at Ruijsdaelplein 6 (April–Oct Tues–Sun 11am–4pm; Nov–March Wed, Sat & Sun noon–3pm; ☎035 694 2673, ⓦ vvvnaarden.nl), and provides maps of the town.

EATING AND DRINKING

Het Arsenaal Kooltjesbuurt 1 ☎035 694 9148, ⓦ paulfagel.nl. Housed in the old arsenal shopping complex across the canal from Naarden's main street, this is without doubt the town's best restaurant, home base of the well-known Dutch chef Paul Fagel, who cooks excellent French food for both the restaurant and a more informal brasserie. Restaurant Mon–Fri noon–10pm, Sat 6–10pm, Sun 1–10pm; brasserie Mon–Sat 10am–5pm.

Hilversum

Sprawling, leafy **HILVERSUM** is the main town of Het Gooi and a prosperous, commuter suburb with a population of around 90,000. Many locals love the place, but for the casual visitor, Hilversum is mainly of interest for its modern architecture – or to be precise the work of **Willem Marinus Dudok** (1884–1974), the director of public works and town architect for over thirty years. Hilversum possesses several dozen buildings by Dudok, who was much influenced by the American Frank Lloyd Wright.

Raadhuis and DAC

Dudokpark 1 • DAC Dudok Architectuur Centrum: Thurs–Sun 11am–4pm; building tour at 1.30pm; €8.50 • ☎035 629 2826, ⓦ dudok100jaar.nl

Pride of place among Hilversum's Dudok buildings goes to the **Raadhuis**, about 700m northwest of the train station – follow Stationsstraat and then Melkpad from the station; it's a fifteen-minute walk. Dating from 1931, the design of the building was based on a deceptively simple progression of straw-coloured blocks rising to a clock tower, with long, slender bricks giving it a strong horizontal emphasis. The interior is well worth seeing too: essentially a series of lines and boxes, its marble walls are margined with black, like a monochrome Mondriaan painting, all coolly and immaculately proportioned. Dudok also designed the interior decorations, and though some have been altered, his style prevails, right down to the ashtrays and lights. The **Dudok Architectuur Centrum (DAC)**, in the basement of the Raadhuis, presents an overview of Dudok's life and work and has ninety-minute tours of the building and its tower (ask in advance about English tours).

Singer Museum

Oude Drift 1, Laren • Tues–Sun 11am–5pm • €15 • ⓦ singerlaren.nl • Bus #108 runs here every 30min from Hilversum station, bus #109 every 30min from Naarden-Bussum station

It's a short trip from Hilversum to the quaint village of **LAREN**, where the **Singer Museum** houses an impressive collection of mainly late nineteenth-century paintings by both local artists and the Hague School, as well as the French Barbizon painters and American Impressionists – in a beautiful, well-lit modern space. It was established in the 1950s by the widow of the American artist William Henry Singer and is well worth the trip.

ARRIVAL AND INFORMATION HILVERSUM

By train Trains leave Amsterdam's Centraal Station twice an hour for Hilversum, and take about 20min to get there. Hilversum also has regular train connections with Utrecht (every 15min; 20min).

Tourist office It's a 10min walk from the train station to the VVV at Kerkbrink 6 (Mon–Sat 10am–5pm; ☎035 544 6971, ⓦ vvvhilversum.nl) – follow Spoorstraat and then Kerkstraat.

Zuid-Holland and Utrecht

WINDMILLS AT KINDERDIJK

Zuid-Holland and Utrecht

Zuid-Holland (South Holland) is the most densely populated province of the Netherlands, incorporating a string of towns and cities that make up the bulk of what is commonly called the Randstad (literally "Rim-Town"). By and large, careful urban planning has succeeded in stopping this from becoming an amorphous conurbation, however, and each town has preserved a pronounced identity.

It's a short hop from Amsterdam to **Leiden**, a university town *par excellence*, its antique centre patterned by canals and dotted with fine old buildings. Moving on, it's another brief step to **Den Haag** (The Hague), a likeable city with a string of good museums and an appealing bar and restaurant scene. Similarly enticing is neighbouring **Delft**, a much smaller place, with just 100,000 inhabitants, but one that possesses an inordinately pretty centre replete with handsome seventeenth-century buildings. In stark contrast is the rough and tumble of big-city **Rotterdam**, one of the world's largest ports, where an adventurous city council has redefined the city's appearance with a platoon of striking modern buildings that add to a string of first-rate attractions, most memorably the fine art of the Museum Boijmans van Beuningen. From here, it's a short journey inland to **Gouda**, a good-looking country town historically famed for its cheese market, and to the somnambulant charms of rural **Oudewater**. Back on the coast, **Dordrecht** marks the southern edge of the Randstad and is of mild interest as an ancient port and for its location, within easy striking distance of the windmills of the **Kinderdijk** and the creeks and marshes of the **Biesbosch**. Finally, the province of **Utrecht** is distinguished by its capital city, Utrecht, a sprawling city with a dramatic history and a bustling, youthful centre.

The region's coastal cities – especially Leiden and Den Haag – are only a short bus or tram ride from the wide sandy **beaches** of the North Sea coast, while the pancake-flat Randstad landscape is brightened by rainbow flashes of **bulbfields** in spring with the **Keukenhof gardens**, near Leiden, having the finest display. A fast and efficient rail network makes travelling around Zuid-Holland extremely easy, and where the trains fizzle out, buses take over.

Brief history

Historically speaking, **Zuid-Holland** is part of what was once simply **Holland**, the richest and most influential province in the country. Throughout the Golden Age, Holland dominated the political, social and cultural life of the republic, overshadowing its neighbours, their economies dwarfed by its success. There are constant reminders of this pre-eminence in the province's buildings: elaborate town halls proclaim civic importance and even the usually sombre Calvinist **churches** allow themselves decorative excesses – the later windows of Gouda's Janskerk being a case in point. Many of the great Dutch **painters** either came from, or worked here, too – Rembrandt, Vermeer, Jan

Highlights

❶ Den Haag Often underrated, Den Haag is one of the country's most enjoyable cities and its prime attraction, the Mauritshuis art gallery, boasts a simply wonderful collection of Dutch paintings. **See p.151**

❷ Delft A lovely little town with a postcard-pretty Markt, its beguiling centre graced by a brace of handsome church towers and a lattice of slender canals. **See p.162**

❸ Rotterdam This boisterous port city has reinvented itself in flashy modern style after extensive war damage and comes complete with a batch of cultural attractions and a vibrant nightlife. **See p.168**

❹ Gouda Archetypal Dutch country town, home of the famous cheese and a splendid set of stained-glass windows in St Janskerk. **See p.177**

❺ Utrecht Lively university town that winds itself around a tight skein of narrow canals, with the Domtoren – the highest Gothic church tower in the Netherlands – soaring high above its crowded centre. **See p.186**

HIGHLIGHTS ARE MARKED ON THE MAP ON P.144

Steen – a tradition that continued well into the nineteenth century with the paintings of the Hague School. Today, Zuid-Holland remains an economic powerhouse, its success crucial to the prospects of the Netherlands as a whole.

Leiden and around

Just twenty minutes by train from Amsterdam's Schiphol airport, **LEIDEN** is a lively and energetic city of around 120,000 souls – and one that makes for an enjoyable day-trip or overnight stay. At its heart, the city's antique, sometimes careworn, centre is a maze of narrow lanes wriggling and worming their way around a complicated network of canals, one of which marks the line of the medieval walls. It's all very appealing and unfussy, with Leiden's multitude of bars and cafés kept afloat by the thirsty students of the city's great institution, its **university** – one of Europe's most prestigious seats of learning. The obvious place to start an exploration of the city centre is the **Beestenmarkt**, a large and really rather plain open space that's long been the town's major meeting point. As for specific sights, top billing amongst a small army of museums goes to the splendid ancient Egyptian and Roman collections in the **Rijksmuseum van Oudheden** (National Museum of Antiquities) and the seventeenth-century Dutch paintings of the **Museum de Lakenhal**, though, perhaps surprisingly, given that this was his home town, the Lakenhal is very short of Rembrandts. Leiden is also within easy striking distance of both the Dutch **bulbfields**, including the showpiece **Keukenhof gardens,** and the pleasant North Sea resort of **Katwijk-aan-Zee** with its long sandy beach.

Brief history

It may well have been the **Romans** who founded Leiden as a forward base on an important trade route running behind the dunes, but, whatever the truth, it was certainly fortified in the ninth century when a local lord built a **castle** here on an artificial mound. Flemish weavers migrated to Leiden in the fourteenth century and thereafter the town prospered as a minor cloth-making centre, but things didn't really take off until the foundation of its **university** in 1575. It was **William the Silent** who chose Leiden to be the home of the university as a reward for the city's bravery during the rebellion against Spain: Leiden had declared for William in 1572, but a Habsburg army besieged the city in October 1573. The **siege**, which lasted a whole year, was a desperate affair during which **Pieter van der Werff**, the heroic burgomaster, famously offered up his own body to be eaten. Fortunately for der Werff, the invitation was declined, but it inspired new determination in the town's flagging citizens. Finally, William the Silent sailed to the rescue on October 3, 1574, cutting through the dykes around the town and vanquishing the Spaniards in one fell swoop. The event is still commemorated with an annual fair, fireworks and the consumption of two traditional dishes: herring and white bread, which the fleet brought with them, and *hutspot*, a vegetable and potato stew, a cauldron of which was found simmering in the abandoned Spanish camp outside the walls.

Rijksmuseum van Oudheden

Rapenburg 28 • Tues–Sun 10am–5pm, plus Mon 10am–5pm in school hols • €9.50 • ☎ 071 516 3163, ⓦ rmo.nl

A gentle, curving canal flanked by some of Leiden's grandest mansions, the Rapenburg is also home to the town's most important museum, the **Rijksmuseum van Oudheden** (National Museum of Antiquities), which holds an outstanding range of Egyptian and Roman artefacts. The museum spreads over three floors, its permanent collection supplemented by an ambitious programme of temporary exhibitions.

3

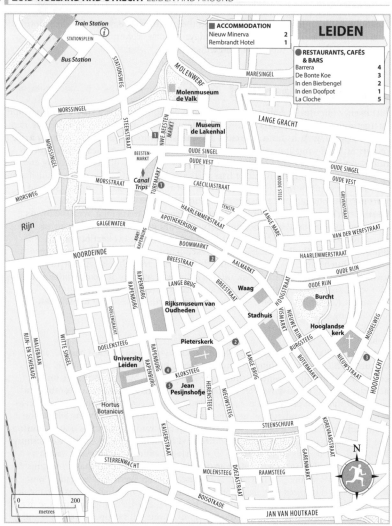

ACCOMMODATION	
Nieuw Minerva	2
Rembrandt Hotel	1

LEIDEN

RESTAURANTS, CAFÉS & BARS	
Barrera	4
De Bonte Koe	3
In den Bierbengel	2
In den Doofpot	1
La Cloche	5

The ground floor

In the ground-floor foyer, the museum kicks off in style with the squat and sturdy **Taffeh Temple**, a present from the Egyptian government: in the 1960s, the construction of the Aswan Dam – and the rising waters of the Nile – threatened scores of ancient monuments; the Dutch lent a helping hand and this was their reward. Dating back to the first century AD, the Taffeh Temple was originally part of a fortress that guarded the southern border of the Roman province of Egypt. Initially, it was dedicated to Isis, the goddess of love and magic, but in the fourth century it was turned into a Christian church.

Beyond, the rest of the ground floor showcases the **Egyptian collection**, which includes wall reliefs, statues, stelae and sarcophagi from a variety of tombs and temples, plus a set of mummies as complete as you're likely to see outside Egypt. Particular highlights include magnificent stelae from the temple at Abydos and the exceptionally well-preserved double-tomb sculpture of Maya and Merit, Maya being the minister of finance under Tutankhamen, Merit his wife.

The upper floors

The next floor up exhibits oodles of classical **Greek and Roman sculptures**, notably stolid busts, sarcophagi, statues and friezes from imperial Rome as well as a scattering of Etruscan artefacts. Moving on, the top floor displays an intriguing **Netherlands archeological section**, which has a selection of Roman stone altars and inscribed tombstones, some of them retrieved from the waters of Zeeland in the 1970s. Here also is a remarkable gilded silver helmet and an eerie Roman horse-rider's mask.

Hortus Botanicus

Rapenburg 73 • April–Oct daily 10am–6pm; Nov–March Tues–Sun 10am–4pm • €7 • ☎ 071 527 7249, ⓦ hortusleiden.nl

Leiden's botanical gardens, the **Hortus Botanicus**, are approached through a three-sided courtyard complex, which includes – on the left – the building that became the university's first home, after previously being part of a medieval monastery. First planted in 1587, this is one of the oldest botanical gardens in Europe, a mixture of carefully tended beds of shrubs, ancient gnarled trees and hothouses full of tropical foliage, all stretching out beside the Witte Singel canal.

Pieterskerk

Kloksteeg 16 • Entry through Pieterskerkcafé • Daily 11am–6pm • €2 • ☎ 071 512 4319, ⓦ pieterskerk.com

Just to the east of Rapenburg lies an ancient network of narrow streets that converges on the Gothic **Pieterskerk**, an ungainly-looking structure that was long Leiden's principal church. Now deconsecrated, the church has a magnificent nave with a veritable forest of stone columns plus a rare set of ornately written guild signs – essentially replacements for the guild altars that the Protestants had ripped out as sacrilegious. A host of **memorials** marks the passing of the sundry notables who are interred here, including Carolus Clusius, the man who brought the first tulip bulb over from Vienna (see box, p.149), and **John Robinson** (1575–1625), leader of the Pilgrim Fathers. A curate in England at the turn of the seventeenth century, Robinson was suspended from preaching in 1604, later fleeing with his congregation to pursue his Puritanism in the more amenable atmosphere of Calvinist Holland. Settling in Leiden, Robinson acted as pastor to growing numbers, but even here he found himself at odds with the religious establishment. In 1620, one hundred of his followers – the **Pilgrim Fathers** – sailed via Plymouth for the untrammelled wilderness of America, though Robinson died before he could join them. Robinson lived across from Pieterskerk at what is now the **Jean Pesijnshofje**, at Kloksteeg 21, and there's a memorial plaque to him there too.

The Stadhuis and around

From Pieterskerk, it's a short stroll east to **Breestraat**, which marks the southern edge of Leiden's present commercial centre, but is undistinguished except for the **Stadhuis**, an imposing edifice whose Renaissance facade is a copy of the late sixteenth-century original destroyed by fire in 1929. Behind the Stadhuis are the canals that cut Leiden's centre into pocket-sized segments that converge at the busiest point in town, tiny **Hoogstraat**, the focus of a vigorous general **market** on Wednesdays and Saturdays (9am–5pm). Around Hoogstraat, a tangle of narrow bridges is flanked by a number of fetching buildings, ranging from overblown Art Nouveau department stores to modest

3

terrace houses. Here also, on Vismarkt, is the **Waag**, built to a design by Pieter Post (1608–69) and fronted with a naturalistic frieze showing a merchant watching straining labourers.

The Nieuwe Rijn and around

Stretching southeast from the Vismarkt is the **Nieuwe Rijn**, one of the town's prettiest canals, the first of its several bridges topped off by a matching pair of Neoclassical porticoes dating from 1825. Nearby, on the north side of the Nieuwe Rijn at the end of **Burgsteeg**, go through the fancy gateway and down the alley to reach the steps up to the top of the **Burcht** (daily 10m–10pm; free), the artificial mound where Leiden's first castle stood. The castle is long gone and the circular stone wall which occupies the site today is disappointingly paltry, but the view over the city centre is first-rate. At the far end of the alley is the **Oude Rijn** canal, on the other side of which lies the blandly pedestrian **Haarlemmerstraat**, the town's main shopping street.

The Museum de Lakenhal

Oude Singel 32 • Tues–Fri 10am–5pm, Sat & Sun noon–5pm • €7.50 • ☎ 071 516 5360, ⓦ lakenhal.nl

Housed in the former Cloth Hall, Leiden's rambling **Museum de Lakenhal** spreads over three large and two small floors, its permanent collection supplemented by an ambitious programme of temporary exhibitions. Of most interest is the **ground floor**, which holds a lively sample of local sixteenth- and seventeenth-century paintings, including the alarming and spectacularly unsuccessful *Last Judgement* triptych by Lucas van Leyden (1489–1533) and a splendid *View of Leiden* by Jan van Goyen (1596–1656). There are also several canvases by Jacob van Swanenburgh (1571–1638), Rembrandt's first teacher, and Jan Lievens (1607–74), with whom Rembrandt shared a studio, but **Rembrandt** (1606–69) himself, though a native of Leiden, is poorly represented; he left his home town at the tender age of 14, and although he returned in 1625, he was off again six years later, this time to settle permanently in Amsterdam. Only a handful of his Leiden paintings survive, but there are two here, *The Glasses' Salesman* and *Agamemnon before Palamedes*, a stilted and rather unsuccessful rendition of the classical tale, painted in 1626. By comparison, Rembrandt's first pupil, Gerrit Dou (1613–75) is well represented by his exquisite *Astrologer*. Dou began by imitating his master but soon developed his own style, pioneering the Leiden tradition of small, minutely detailed pictures of enamel-like smoothness. Look out also for several paintings by the earthy Jan Steen (1625–79) and, among several works recalling the siege of 1573 (see p.145), Gustave Wappers' (1803–74) large and melodramatic *The Self-sacrifice of Burgomaster Pieter van der Werff*.

Up above, the museum's first floor has several period rooms and an extensive display on the town's woollen industry, and the top floor concentrates on the siege of 1573.

Molenmuseum de Valk

2e Binnenvestgracht 1 • Tues–Sat 10am–5pm, Sun 1–5pm • €4 • ☎ 071 516 5353, ⓦ molenmuseumdevalk.nl

A restored grain mill, the **Molenmuseum de Valk** (Falcon Windmill Museum) is the last survivor of the twenty-odd windmills built on the town's outer fortifications in the eighteenth century. On the ground floor are the miller's musty living quarters, furnished in simple late nineteenth-century style, and then it's up the stairs for a short video recounting the history of Dutch windmills. Up yet more stairs are a series of displays that give the lowdown on the hard life of the average Dutch miller, who had to be incredibly nimble to survive if the cramped conditions here are anything to go by. The miller was rarely paid in cash, but took a scoop from each sack instead. He was supposed to pay tax on this – some windmills even had a taxman's kiosk next door

– but evasion was widespread and many windmills, including this one, had a so-called smuggler's cupboard where the miller could hide the proceeds.

The Keukenhof gardens

Stationsweg 166, Lisse • Mid-March to mid-May daily 8am–7.30pm • €16• ⓦ keukenhof.nl • Bus #54 runs from Leiden bus station direct to the main entrance (mid-March to mid-May daily every 15min; 30min)

If you're after bulbs, then make a beeline for the bulb growers' showcase, the **Keukenhof gardens**, located on the edge of the little town of **LISSE**, beside the N208 about 15km north of Leiden. The largest flower gardens in the world, dating back to 1949, the Keukenhof was designed by a group of prominent bulb growers to convert people to the joys of growing flowers from bulbs in their own gardens. Literally the "kitchen garden", its site is the former estate of a fifteenth-century countess, who used to grow herbs and vegetables for her dining table. Several million flowers are on show for their full flowering period, complemented, in case of especially harsh winters, by thousands of square metres of glasshouse holding indoor displays. You could easily spend a whole day here, swooning with the sheer abundance of it all, but to get the best of it you need to come early, before the tour buses descend on the place. There are several restaurants in the grounds, and a network of well-marked footpaths explores every horticultural nook and cranny.

Katwijk-aan-Zee

From Leiden bus station, take bus #31 to the Boulevard bus stop by the beach in Katwijk-aan-Zee (every 30min; 20min)

Leiden is just a few kilometres from the North Sea coast, where the prime target is **KATWIJK-AAN-ZEE**, a pleasant little resort whose low-slung houses string along behind a wide sandy beach, with a pristine expanse of beach and dune beckoning beyond – and stretching south towards Scheveningen (see p.159). Here and there, a row of cottages

THE BULBFIELDS

The pancake-flat fields stretching north from Leiden towards Haarlem (see p.105) are the heart of the Dutch **bulbfields**, whose bulbs and blooms support a billion-euro industry and some ten thousand growers, as well as attracting tourists in their droves. Bulbs have flourished here since the late sixteenth century, when one **Carolus Clusius**, a Dutch botanist and one-time gardener to the Habsburg emperor, brought the first **tulip bulb** over from Vienna, where it had – in its turn – been brought from Asia Minor by an Austrian aristocrat. The tulip flourished in Holland's sandy soil and was so highly prized that it fuelled a massive **speculative bubble**. At the height of the boom – in the mid-1630s – bulbs were commanding extraordinary prices: the artist Jan van Goyen paid 1900 guilders and two paintings for ten rare bulbs, while a bag of one hundred bulbs was swapped for a coach and horses. When the government finally intervened in 1636, the industry returned to reality with a bang, leaving hundreds of investors ruined – much to the satisfaction of the country's Calvinist ministers, who had long railed against such excesses.

Other types of bulbs apart from the tulip have also been introduced, and nowadays the spring flowering season begins in mid-March with **crocuses**, followed by **daffodils** and yellow **narcissi** in late March, **hyacinths** and **tulips** from mid-April through to May, and **irises** and **gladioli** in August. The views of the bulbfields from any of the trains heading southwest from Schiphol airport can often be sufficient in themselves, the fields divided into stark geometric blocks of pure colour, but, with your own transport – either bicycle or car – you can take in their particular beauty by way of special routes marked by conspicuous signposts; local tourist offices sell pamphlets describing the routes in detail (see above). You could also drop by the bulb growers' showpiece, the **Keukenhof** gardens (see above). Bear in mind also that there are any number of local flower festivals and parades in mid- to late April; every local VVV has the details of these too.

recalls the time when Katwijk was a busy fishing village, but there are no real sights as such, with the possible exception of the **Katwijk sluices**, on the north side of Katwijk. Completed in 1807, this chain of sluice gates regulates the flow of the Oude Rijn as it approaches the sea. Around high tide, the gates are closed, and when they are reopened the pressure of the accumulated water brushes aside the sand deposited at the mouth of the river. This simple system has effectively fixed the course of the Oude Rijn, which for centuries had been continually diverted by its sand deposits, flooding the surrounding area with depressing regularity.

ARRIVAL AND DEPARTURE

By train Leiden's ultramodern train station is on the northwest edge of town on Stationsplein, a 5min walk from the Beestenmarkt at the west end of the centre.
Destinations Amsterdam (every 10min; 35min); Amsterdam Schiphol (every 10min; 20min); Den Haag CS (every 10min; 15min); Rotterdam (every 15min; 35min).

By bus Leiden's bus station is adjacent to the train station on Stationsplein.
Destinations Katwijk-aan-Zee (bus #31 to the beachside Boulevard bus stop: every 30min; 20min); Keukenhof gardens (mid-March to mid-May bus #54 every 15min; 30min).

INFORMATION AND TOURS

Tourist office Leiden's helpful VVV, serving the city and its immediate surroundings, is at Stationsweg 41 (Mon–Fri 7am–7pm, Sat 10am–4pm, Sun 11am–3pm; ☎071 516 6000, ⓦvvvleiden.nl).

Canal trips Beestenmarkt is the starting point for enjoyable canal trips around the city centre (March–Oct hourly between 10am–4pm; 50min; €10).

ACCOMMODATION

Nieuw Minerva Boommarkt 23 ☎071 512 6358, ⓦnieuwminerva.nl. Easily the most appealing hotel in town – a cosy, very Dutch place that occupies a sequence of old canal-side houses right in the centre. The tiled breakfast room is particularly pleasant and all the guest rooms are spacious and comfortable, in an undemanding sort of way, though the "honeymoon room" is up a notch, boasting a four-poster bed and fancy drapes. **€100**

Rembrandt Hotel Nieuwe Beestenmarkt 10 ☎071 514 4233, ⓦrembrandthotel.nl. Medium-sized, competitively priced hotel with twenty rooms decorated in spick-and-span modern style. The central location could not be handier and some of the higher (slightly larger) rooms have views over the Valk windmill. **€105**

EATING AND DRINKING

Leiden's crowded centre heaves with inexpensive cafés and café-bars, and there's a cluster of top-flight restaurants too. Many of the more interesting places are concentrated in the immediate vicinity of Pieterskerk, amidst the ancient brick houses that make up this especially pretty part of the city.

Barrera Rapenburg 56 ☎071 514 6631 ⓦcafebarrera .nl. A fashionable café-bar and student favourite with a traditional brown interior. Has a great canal-side location, a good, long beer menu and a pavement terrace. Also many wines by the glass and filling bar food – try the Rapenburger for €7.50. Mon–Sat 10am–1am, Sun 11am–1am.

★De Bonte Koe Hooglandsekerkkoorsteeg 13 ☎071 514 1094, ⓦcafedebontekoe.net. One of the grooviest café-bars in Leiden, "The Colourful Cow" occupies vintage premises – apparently it was kitted out as a butcher's shop (hence the tiles) that never quite managed to open. Serves a good range of beers on draught and an especially tasty home-made burger. Mon–Thurs 4pm–1am, Fri 4pm–3am, Sat 12.30pm–3am & Sun 1.30pm–1am

In den Bierbengel Langebrug 71 ☎071 514 8056, ⓦindenbierbengel.nl. Inhabiting an old building in an attractive corner of the town centre, this popular, bistro-style restaurant has a short but well-chosen menu covering all the Dutch basics. Mains such as grilled butterfish or steak with Calvados go for around €20. Daily 5–10pm.

In den Doofpot Turfmarkt 9 ☎071 512 2434, ⓦindendoofpot.nl. Smooth and polished restaurant of minimalist persuasion offering an extremely creative, international menu – from pork belly through to razor clams. Large wine cellar and attentive service. Mains from around €25. Mon–Fri noon–10pm, Sat 5–10pm.

La Cloche Kloksteeg 3 ☎071 512 3053, ⓦlaclocheleiden.nl. Small and smart French restaurant with a well-chosen menu featuring local ingredients – try the Texel lamb. Mains €20–25 and a daily changing, three-course set menu for €35. Tues–Sat 6–10.30pm.

Den Haag

DEN HAAG (**The Hague** formerly 's-Gravenhage) is markedly different from any other Dutch city. In a country built on municipal independence, it's been the focus of national institutions since the sixteenth century, but is not – curiously enough – the capital, which is Amsterdam. Frequently disregarded until the development of central government in the 1800s, Den Haag's older buildings are comparatively modest with little of Amsterdam's flamboyance. Indeed, the majority of the canal houses are demurely classical and exude that sense of sedate prosperity which prompted Matthew Arnold's harsh estimation of 1859: "I never saw a city where the well-to-do classes seemed to have given the whole place so much of their own air of wealth, finished cleanliness, and comfort; but I never saw one, either, in which my heart would so have sunk at the thought of living."

Fortunately, much has changed since Arnold's day. His "well-to-do-classes" – now mostly diplomats and top-ranking executives – are still in evidence and parts of the centre are festooned with new government high-rises, but the city also holds a slew of lively restaurants and bars, offers a lively programme of concerts and events, boasts a veritable battery of outstanding museums, principally the wonderful Dutch paintings of the **Mauritshuis**, and is a brief tram ride from the long beach of kiss-me-quick **Scheveningen**.

The Binnenhof

Binnenhof • Open access • Free • Guided tours of the Binnenhof and the adjacent Parliament leave from the ProDemos visitor centre, Hofweg 1 (☏ 070 757 0200, ⊚ prodemos.nl); check its website for hours and reservations; tours €5–€10 depending on itinerary

The prettiest spot in Den Haag – and the logical place to start a visit – is the north side of the **Hofvijver** (Court Pond), a placid lakelet that mirrors the attractive, vaguely Ruritanian symmetries of the extensive **Binnenhof** (Inner Court), the one-time home of the country's bicameral parliament. The Binnenhof is at the very heart of the city and it occupies the site of the medieval castle where Den Haag began. The first fortress was raised by William II, Count of Holland (1227–56) – hence the city's official name, 's-Gravenhage, literally "Count's Hedge", but more precisely "Count's Domain". William's descendants became the region's most powerful family, simultaneously acting as Stadholders (effectively provincial governors) of most of the seven United Provinces, which rebelled against the Habsburgs in the sixteenth century. In due course, one of the family, **Prince Maurice of Orange-Nassau** (1567–1625), established his main residence in Den Haag, which had effectively become the country's political capital. As the embodiment of central rather than municipal power, the Binnenhof was at times fêted, at others virtually ignored, until the nineteenth century when Den Haag officially shared political capital status with Brussels during the uneasy times of the United Kingdom of the Netherlands (1815–30). Thereafter it became the seat of government and home to a functioning legislature. However, the lack of prestige in the low-slung brick buildings of the Binnenhof long irked Dutch parliamentarians and finally, in 1992, they moved into a flashy new extension next door. Without the politicians, the original Binnenhof became somewhat redundant, but it's still an eye-pleasing architectural ensemble, comprising a broadly rectangular complex built around two connecting courtyards.

The Riderzaal

The Binnenhof's main sight as such is the **Ridderzaal** (Knights' Hall), an imposing twin-turreted structure that looks distinctly church-like, but was actually built as a banqueting hall for Count William's son, Floris V, in the thirteenth century. Now used for state occasions, it's been a courtroom, market and stable, and so often renovated that little of the original remains. Unless you are on a guided tour, the only part you can visit is the vaulted basement, which is used for modest temporary displays on the Binnenhof as a whole and the state ceremonies that have been held here.

3

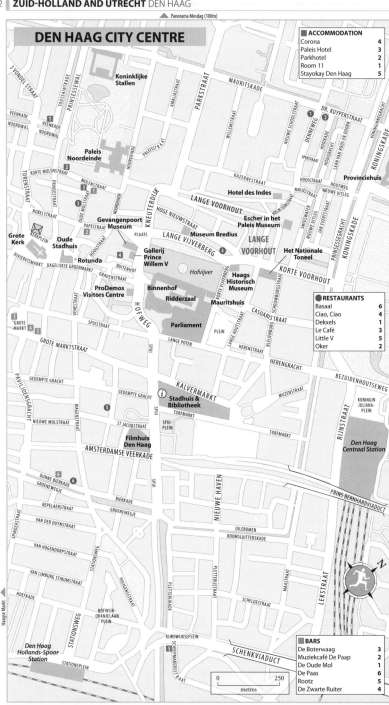

Panorama Mesdag (100m)

DEN HAAG CITY CENTRE

■ ACCOMMODATION

Corona	4
Paleis Hotel	3
Parkhotel	2
Room 11	1
Stayokay Den Haag	5

● RESTAURANTS

Basaal	6
Ciao, Ciao	4
Dekxels	1
Le Café	3
Little V	5
Oker	2

■ BARS

De Boterwaag	3
Muziekcafé De Paap	2
De Oude Mol	1
De Paas	6
Rootz	5
De Zwarte Ruiter	4

0 — 250
metres

The Mauritshuis

Plein 29 • Mon 1–6pm, Tues–Sun 10am–6pm, Thurs till 8pm • €14 • ☎ 070 302 3456, ⓦ mauritshuis.nl

Handily located next door to the Binnenhof, the **Mauritshuis** holds a world-famous collection of Flemish and Dutch paintings from the fifteenth to the eighteenth century, based on the hoard accumulated by Prince William V of Orange (1748–1806). The permanent collection is exhibited in an elegant seventeenth-century mansion, whose two floors – and sixteen rooms – are easily digestible, whilst an ambitious programme of temporary exhibitions is hosted in a second building across the street – and connected via the museum's underground foyer. The permanent collection is not arranged thematically or chronologically, which can be a tad confusing, but although the paintings are rotated you can still expect to see the works mentioned below. Be sure to pick up a **plan** at reception.

Level 1 (Rooms 1–8)

On Level 1, Rooms 6 and 7 usually display a small but exquisite sample of late medieval Flemish art, including a *Portrait of a Man* by **Hans Memling** (1440–94), a typically observant work, right down to the scar on the nose, and *The Lamentation of Christ* by **Rogier van der Weyden** (1400–64), a harrowing picture of death and sorrow. Weyden has Christ's head hanging down toward the earth, surrounded by the faces of the mourners, each with a particular expression of anguish and pain. Look out also for Look out also for an especially heartfelt Virgin and Child by **Quentin Matsys** (1465–1530), in which baby Jesus reaches out to his mother in the tenderest of gestures. An influential figure, Matsys was the first major artist to work in Antwerp, where he was made a Master of the Guild in 1519.

Hans Holbein

Normally displayed in Room 6 or 7 also are two fine canvases by **Hans Holbein the Younger** (1497–1543): a striking *Portrait of Robert Cheseman*, where all the materials – the fur collar, the falcon's feathers and the cape – seem to take on the appropriate texture; and a *Portrait of Jane Seymour*, one of several pictures commissioned by Henry VIII, who sent Holbein to paint matrimonial candidates. Holbein's vibrant technique was later to land him in hot water: an over-flattering portrait of Anne of Cleves swayed Henry into an unhappy marriage with his "Flanders mare" that was to last only six months.

Rubens

Peter Paul Rubens (1577–1640) is perhaps best remembered for his giant-sized religious paintings, but he was a dab hand at portraiture as demonstrated here at the Mauritshuis in his exquisitely detailed *Portrait of Michael Ophovius*, a Catholic bishop, and his *Old Woman* with its dappled and evocative use of shade and light. Rubens was so successful that he was able to set up his own studio, where he gathered a team of talented artists, thereby ensuring a high rate of productivity and a degree of personal flexibility: the degree to which Rubens personally worked on a canvas would vary – and would determine its price. A case in point is the florid *Garden of Eden with the Fall of Man*, a collaboration between himself and **Jan Brueghel the Elder** (1568–1625): Rubens painted the figures and Brueghel the landscape and assorted animals.

Level 2 (Rooms 9–16)

The Mauritshuis owns no fewer than twelve paintings by **Rembrandt** (1606–69). Pride of place amongst them goes to the *Anatomy Lesson of Dr Tulp*, the artist's first commission in Amsterdam, dating from 1632. The peering pose of the students who lean over the corpse solved the problem of emphasis falling on the body rather than the subjects of the portrait, who were members of the surgeons' guild. Hopefully Tulp's skills as an anatomist were better than his medical advice, which included the recommendation that his patients drink fifty cups of tea a day. Very different are two later Rembrandt paintings, his hauntingly gloomy *Saul and David* and his *Homer*; both are deeply contemplative works shrouded in a mist of brown.

Fabritius and Hals

Carel Fabritius (1622–54), a pupil of Rembrandt and (possibly) a teacher of Vermeer, was killed in a gunpowder explosion at Delft when he was only 22. Few canvases of his survive but an exquisite exception is *The Goldfinch*, a curious, almost impressionistic work, with the bird reduced to a blur of colour – and recently popularized by Donna Tartt's eponymous novel. By comparison, **Frans Hals** (c.1582–1666) lived to a ripe old age – not that his last years in Haarlem were much fun (see p.107) – and of the five Hals portrait paintings in the Mauritshuis, easily the most original is his *Laughing Boy*, completed in 1625.

Vermeer

One of the museum's most trumpeted paintings is *Girl with a Pearl Earring* by **Johannes Vermeer** (1632–75), which is not – as is often thought – a portrait, but a "tronie", that is an illustration of a mood or emotion based on a real-life model. In this particular case, the girl looks back over her shoulder expectantly, wide-eyed and with her lips parted, the turban on her head and the sheer size of her earring suggesting her exoticism – as distinct from the rest of her attire, which is ordinary and workaday: Dutch women of the time just did not wear turbans or large pearl earrings. The second Vermeer, the superb and somehow thrilling *View of Delft*, is similarly deceptive: the fine lines of the city are pictured beneath a cloudy sky, a patchwork of varying light and shade, but once again all is not quite what it seems. The painting may look like the epitome of realism, but in fact Vermeer doctored what he saw to fit in with the needs of his canvas, straightening here, lengthening there, to emphasize the horizontal. Interestingly, the detached vision implicit in the painting has prompted some experts to suggest that Vermeer viewed his subject through a fixed reducing lens or maybe even a mirror.

Other genre paintings

Amongst the gallery's other **genre paintings**, high points include the work of **Jan Steen** (1625–79), most memorably a wonderfully riotous picture carrying the legend "*As the Old Sing, so Pipe the Young*" (a parable on the young learning bad habits from the old), and two typically salacious paintings featuring oysters – *Girl Eating Oysters* and *Man and Woman Eating Oysters* in which the man has a truly horrible leer. The talented **Gerard ter Borch** (1617–81) chose to concentrate on domestic scenes with a sentimental undertow, as in the *Lice Hunt* and *Woman Writing a Letter*, while Delft's **Gerard Houckgeest** (1600–61) specialized in church interiors, notably *The Tomb of William of Orange*, a minutely observed study of architectural lines lightened by expanses of white marble. **Paulus Potter** (1625–54), on the other hand, specialized in cattle and his most successful canvas, *The Bull*, is a massive affair that includes the smallest of details, from the exact hang of the testicles to the dung at the rear end.

The Haags Historisch Museum

Korte Vijverberg 7 • Tues–Fri 10am–5pm, Sat & Sun noon–5pm • €7.50 • ☏ 070 364 6940, ⓦ haagshistorischmuseum.nl

The mildly enjoyable **Haags Historisch Museum** (City Historical Museum) occupies an imposing Neoclassical mansion that was originally home to the city's leading militia company, the Guild of St Sebastian. The most interesting part of the permanent collection is concentrated on the ground floor in Rooms 1 and 2. Room 1 provides a potted history of the city illustrated by several fine paintings, most memorably *A View of Den Haag from the Southeast*, a large and simply wonderful tonal landscape by that pioneer of realistic landscape painting, Jan van Goyen. Room 2 warms to the same historical theme, though here the prime exhibits are a portrait of a lantern-jawed Johan de Witt in all his magisterial pomp and, by way of contrast, a mummified piece of his tongue and a finger from Cornelis, his brother, both rescued from the mob that chopped the brothers to pieces in 1672 (see p.326). Other parts of the museum are used for temporary exhibitions and to display a number of fine, seventeenth-century Civic Guard group portraits.

Lange Voorhout

Just north of the Binnenhof are the trees and cobblestones of **Lange Voorhout**, a wide L-shaped street-cum-square overlooked by a string of ritzy Neoclassical mansions, many of which are now embassies and consulates. Most conspicuous is the *Hotel des Indes*, an opulent hotel where the ballerina Anna Pavlova died in 1931 and where today you stand a fair chance of being flattened by a chauffeur-driven limousine.

Escher in het Paleis

Lange Voorhout 74 • Tues–Sun 11am–5pm • €9 • ☎ 070 427 7730, Ⓦ escherinhetpaleis.nl

The work of the Dutch graphic artist Maurits Cornelis Escher (1898–1972) is celebrated in the **Escher in het Paleis**, a museum housed in a grand mansion that was a favourite royal residence in the early decades of the twentieth century. Escher churned out dozens of very precise, often disconcerting, lithographs and engravings and a sizeable collection is on display, but the most appealing part of the museum is the top floor, which is given over to several hands-on **optical illusions**, all based on Escher's work.

Museum Bredius

Lange Vijverberg 14 • Tues–Sun 11am–5pm • €6 • ☎ 070 362 0729, Ⓦ museumbredius.nl

The delightful **Museum Bredius** displays the collection of paintings bequeathed to the city by art connoisseur and one-time director of the Mauritshuis, Abraham Bredius, in 1946. Squeezed together in this fine old house, with its stuccowork and splendid staircase, are some exquisite paintings, notably **Rembrandt**'s *Head of Christ*, all smooth browns and yellows with the face of Jesus serene and sensitive; interestingly, Rembrandt was the first Dutch artist to use a Jewish model for a portrait of Christ. Among the genre paintings, there are several canvases by **Jan Steen**, including the fruity *Couple in a Bedchamber* and the curious *Satyr and the Peasant*, a representation of a well-known Aesop fable in which the satyr, sitting at the table with his hosts, is bemused by human behaviour: the creature's confusion is symbolically represented by the surrounding figures – the man blowing on his soup to cool it down, the woman with the basket of fruit on her head. Look out also for a charming interior with a toddler and two women by **Pieter de Hooch** (1629–84) and a characteristic *Boar Hunt* by **Roelandt Savery** (1576–1639), all green foliage and fighting beasts, but rather oddly displayed high up above a cabinet.

Museum Gevangenpoort

Buitenhof 33 • Tues–Fri 10am–5pm, Sat & Sun noon–5pm • €7.50, including guided tour; combined ticket with the Galerij Prins Willem V €10 • ☎ 070 346 0861, Ⓦ gevangenpoort.nl.

The **Museum Gevangenpoort** (Prison Gate Museum) on the west side of the Hofvijver, is sited in the old town prison, which is itself squeezed into one of Den Haag's medieval fortified gates. The big pull here is the museum's collection of instruments of torture, interrogation and punishment, which goes down a storm with visiting school parties. Several of the prison's old cells have survived too, including the *ridderkamer* for the more privileged captives. It was here that Cornelis de Witt, burgomaster of

Dordrecht, was imprisoned before he and his brother Johan, another staunch Republican and leading politician, were murdered by an Orangist mob in 1672.

Galerij Prince Willem V

Buitenhof 33 • Tues–Sun noon–5pm • €5, combined ticket with the Gevangenpoort €10 • Free, illustrated guides are available in the gallery • ☎ 070 302 3456, ⊛ mauritshuis.nl

Sharing its entrance with the Museum Gevangenpoort, the **Galerij Prins Willem V** was created in 1773 as the private picture gallery of the eponymous prince and Stadholder of the United Provinces. It holds a wide-ranging collection of seventeenth-century paintings exhibited in the style of an eighteenth-century "cabinet" gallery, with the paintings crowded together from floor to ceiling. There is some pretty average stuff here, but there are highlights, notably a superb *Portrait of a Woman* by Rubens; a delightful *River Landscape* by Jacob van Ruysdael (c.1628–82); a charming Frans Snijders (1579–1657), *Still Life with Huntsman*; and – amongst several canvases by Jan Steen – the cautionary *As the Old Sing, so Twitter the Young*.

The Oude Stadhuis

The cobweb of narrow, mostly humdrum streets and squares stretching west of the Binnenhof shelters the flamboyant Dutch Renaissance facade of the **Oude Stadhuis** (Old City Hall), a good-looking, sixteenth-century affair complete with mullioned windows, shutters and decorative carvings. To the rear of the Oude Stadhuis are the plodding symmetries of a later extension and across the street is the imposing bulk of the Grote Kerk.

Grote Kerk

Rond de Grote Kerk 12 • Mid-May to late Aug Tues–Sat 11am–5pm, Sun 2–5pm • Free • ☎ 070 302 8630, ⊛ grotekerkdenhaag.nl

Easily the pick of Den Haag's old churches, the deconsecrated **Grote Kerk** – or St Jacobskerk – dates from the middle of the fifteenth century, its cavernous interior, with its three naves, possessing an exhilarating sense of breadth and handsome timber vaulting. Like most Dutch churches, it's short on decoration, but there are one or two high points, especially the **stained-glass windows** of the choir. Of the two windows right at the back of the church, one depicts the Nativity, while the other shows the Virgin descending from heaven to show the Infant Jesus to a kneeling Emperor Charles V, who footed the glaziers' bill. To either side are three other key windows, an Annunciation, a Christ in the Temple with the Pharisees and a modern Prophet Zachariah in the Temple. Also at the back of the church stands a fancy **memorial** to a bewigged Admiral Jacob van Opdam, who died during the little-remembered naval battle of Lowestoft in 1665. Opdam and his fleet were at the receiving end of a real drubbing by the English, though Opdam himself may have been spared knowledge of the full disaster: a cannon ball swept him off his deck before his ship blew up.

The Paleis Noordeinde

On the northwest side of the city centre is the sixteenth- and seventeenth-century **Paleis Noordeinde** (no public access), the grandest of several royal buildings in and around Den Haag. Outside the palace's main entrance, on Noordeinde, is a jaunty/haughty equestrian statue of the country's principal hero, William the Silent – outside the palace to represent his failure to secure full control before his assassination – and with the whopping testicles of his steed presumably designed to emphasize his manliness.

North of the city centre

Den Haag's suburbs canter north towards Scheveningen and the North Sea in an apparently haphazard sequence of long boulevards intercepted by patches of woodland. For the most part, this is a prosperous part of town and embedded in it are a string of museums, the most important of which are the **Panorama Mesdag**, a tribute to the endeavours of the nineteenth-century landscape painter H.W. Mesdag (1831–1915), and the **Gemeentemuseum Den Haag**, with its enormous collection of fine and applied art. The area's attractions are widely dispersed, but it's easy to get around by **tram**.

Panorama Mesdag

Zeestraat 65 • Mon–Sat 10am–5pm, Sun 11am–5pm • €10 • ☎ 070 310 6665, ⓦ panorama-mesdag.nl • A 10min walk north of the Paleis Noordeinde (see opposite), and accessible by tram #1 from Kneuterdijk – get off at Mauritskade

The **Panorama Mesdag** was designed in the late nineteenth century by Hendrik Mesdag, banker-turned-painter and local citizen-turned-Hague School luminary. For the most part, Mesdag painted unremarkable seascapes tinged with bourgeois sentimentality, but there's no denying the achievement of his panorama, a delightful depiction of Scheveningen in 1881. Completed in four months with help from his wife and George Hendrik Breitner (1857–1923), the painting is so naturalistic that it takes a few moments for the skills of lighting and perspective to become apparent as you stand on the viewing platform with the painting all around. Before you get to the

3

DEN HAAG (NORTH) & SCHEVENINGEN

■ ACCOMMODATION	
Carlton Ambassador Hotel	2
Jorplace Beach Hostel	1
Residenz Stadslogement	3

Pier

N

NORTH SEA

Kurhaus

Sea Life Scheveningen

Museum Beelden aan Zee

Casino

Harbour

SCHEVENINGEN

Nieuwe Scheveningse Bosjes

Westbroek Park

Madurodam

Scheveningse Bosjes

GEM/ Fotomuseum

Gemeente-Museum

Omniversum

Museon

Vredespaleis

Bosjes van Poot

Panorama Mesdag

Mesdag Collectie

Westduin Park

WESTDUIN PARK

0   600
metres

● RESTAURANTS	
Catch by Simonis	2
Simonis aan de Haven	1

Panorama, you pass through three small rooms showing a selection of Mesdag's other **paintings**, including a veritable battery of boats on Scheveningen beach beneath cotton-wool skies.

The Mesdag Collectie

Laan van Meerdervoort 7-F • Wed–Sun noon–5pm • €9 • ☎ 070 362 1434, ⓦ demesdagcollectie.nl • A 10min walk north of the Mesdag Panorama and accessible by tram #1 from Kneuterdijk – get off at the Peace Palace

When Hendrik Mesdag bought the house that became his home and gallery in the middle of the nineteenth century, it had a view over the dunes, the inspiration for many of his canvases, but the house and its environs were gobbled up by the city long ago. More recently, the house was turned into the **Mesdag Collectie** (Mesdag Collection) to hold a few bits and pieces surviving from the Mesdags' assorted baubles – tapestries, Chinese vases and so forth – and an easily assimilated collection of late nineteenth- and early twentieth-century paintings. Pride of place goes to the paintings of the Hague School, whose artists – such as Mesdag, Mauve and Breitner – took local land and seascapes as their favourite subject.

The Vredespaleis (Peace Palace)

Carnegieplein 2 • Visitor centre: May–Oct Tues–Sun 10am–5pm; Nov–April Tues–Sun 10am–4pm • Free • Check the website for details of guided tours • ☎ 070 302 4242, ⓦ vredespaleis.nl • Tram #1 from Kneuterdijk

Flanking the Carnegieplein, the conspicuous, neo-Renaissance **Vredespaleis** (Peace Palace) is home to several international judicial institutions and, by accident, a monument to the addiction to war – as is explained in the pocket-sized **visitor centre**. Towards the end of the nineteenth century, Tsar Nicholas II called an international conference for the peaceful reconciliation of national problems. The result was the First Hague Peace Conference of 1899, which led to the formation of a **Permanent Court of Arbitration (PCA)** housed obscurely in Den Haag until the far-minded American industrialist Andrew Carnegie gave $1.5 million for a large new building – the Peace Palace. These honourable aims came to nothing with the onset of World War I: just as the donations of tapestries, urns, marble and stained glass were arriving from all over the world, so Europe's military commanders were preparing their offensives. After the war, in 1922, the PCA was joined in the Palace by the forerunner of the **International Court of Justice**, which sits here still and is the principal judicial organ of the United Nations. Backed by a massive law library, fifteen judges sit at the court, conducting trade matters in English and diplomatic affairs in French. Widely respected and generally considered neutral, their judgments are nevertheless not binding.

Gemeentemuseum Den Haag

Stadhouderslaan 41 • Tues–Sun 11am–5pm • €13.50 • ☎ 070 338 1111, ⓦ gemeentemuseum.nl • Tram #17 from Centraal Station and the Buitenhof

The **Gemeentemuseum Den Haag** is easily the largest and most diverse of Den Haag's many museums. Designed by Hendrik Petrus Berlage (1856–1934) and completed in 1935, the building itself is often regarded as his masterpiece, an austere but particularly appealing structure with brick facings superimposed on a concrete shell. Inside, the museum displays a regularly rotated selection from its vast permanent collection and also offers an ambitious, headline-making programme of temporary exhibitions. Among much else, the museum's permanent collection includes a large and diverting array of **Delft pottery**, a platoon of period rooms, a fashion section and a wide selection of drawings, prints and posters from the nineteenth and twentieth centuries. The **modern art** section outlines the development of painting since the early nineteenth century and although the bulk of the paintings are Dutch, there's a liberal sprinkling of international artists too. The museum is especially strong on the land and seascape painters of the **Hague School**, which flourished here in the city from 1860 to 1900.

De Stijl

The museum has a fine collection of works by the **De Stijl** movement, that loose but influential group of Dutch painters, sculptors, designers and architects who developed their version – and vision – of modern art and society between the two world wars. On display is the world's largest collection of paintings from the most famous member of the group, **Piet Mondriaan** (1872–1944), and although much of it consists of unfamiliar early works, painted before he evolved the abstraction of form into geometry and pure colour for which he's best known, it does include *Victory Boogie Woogie*, his last and – some say – finest work.

The Gemeentemuseum campus

GEM Stadhouderslaan 43 • Tues–Sun noon-6pm • €8, including Fotomuseum • ☎ 070 338 1133, ⓦ gem-online.nl • **Fotomuseum** Stadhouderslaan 43 • Tues–Sun noon–6pm • €8, including GEM • ☎ 070 338 1144, ⓦ fotomuseumdenhaag.nl • **Museon** Stadhouderslaan 37 • Tues–Sun 11am–5pm • €11.50 • ☎ 070 338 1338, ⓦ museon.nl • Tram #17 from Centraal Station and the Buitenhof

There are three other museums on the Gemeentemuseum campus. First up is **GEM**, **Museum voor Actuele Kunst**, a gallery of contemporary art featuring an enterprising programme of temporary exhibitions. In the same building, the **Fotomuseum** puts on a minimum of four exhibitions a year and in between times displays photographs from the Gemeentemuseum's permanent collection. Nearby is the **Museon**, a sequence of non-specialist exhibitions dealing with human activities and the history of the earth – everything from rock formations to what dinosaurs had for supper. Self-consciously internationalist, it's aimed principally at school parties.

Scheveningen

Scheveningen is best visited on a day-trip from Den Haag: take tram #9 from Central Station or tram #1 from Kneuterdijk – it's a 15min journey

Wedged against the seashore about 4km north of the centre of Den Haag, the fishing port and harbour of **SCHEVENINGEN** now doubles up as the Netherlands' biggest coastal resort, a sometimes tacky, often breezy place that attracts more than nine million visitors a year. It also has one curious claim to fame: during World War II, resistance groups tested suspected Nazi infiltrators by getting them to say "Scheveningen" – an impossible feat for Germans, apparently, and not much easier for English-speakers either (try a throaty *s-khay-ve-ning-uh*). A thick strip of forested dune once separated Den Haag from Scheveningen, but nowadays it's hard to know where one ends and the other begins. There is, however, no mistaking Scheveningen's principal attraction, its **beach**, a long expanse of golden sand that is hard to resist on a warm day. Scheveningen is also home to an outstanding sculpture museum, **Beelden aan Zee**, and hosts a lively programme of special events, most memorably an international **sand sculpture** competition held in May.

The Kurhaus and around

Scheveningen's most central tram stop (*Kurhaus*) is a couple of hundred metres from the resort's most impressive building, the **Kurhaus**, a grand hotel of 1885 – now the *Amrâth Kurhaus* – built when this was one of the most fashionable spots in Europe. Pop inside for a peek at its central hall, a richly decorated affair with pendulous chandeliers and rich frescoes bearing mermaids and semi-clad maidens cavorting high

---

A BEACH WITHOUT CROWDS

Scheveningen's sandy beach is easily long enough to absorb the heaving crowds that arrive here every sunny weekend, but to find an unhurried spot, just walk west from the centre along the seaside promenade-cum-sea wall. Even better, take tram #12 from Den Haag HS train station to Markenseplein, its Duindorp terminus, from where it's a 5min walk through the dunes to the long, quiet and peaceful **Zuiderstrand** beach, to the west of Scheveningen's harbour.

above the coffee-drinkers. From the Kurhaus, it's a short stroll either east to the **pier** or west to the **Museum Beelden aan Zee**.

Museum Beelden aan Zee

Harteveltstraat 1 • Tues–Sun 10am–5pm • €12, plus small additional fee for some exhibitions • ☏ 070 358 5857, ⊛ beeldenaanzee.nl

Scheveningen's excellent **Museum Beelden aan Zee** occupies a modern concrete building that burrows and bores into the sand dunes above the beach, with the royal pavilion built by King William I (1772–1843) for his ailing wife, Wilhelmina, in clear view immediately behind. The museum specializes in temporary exhibitions of modern sculpture and although Dutch sculptors are often to the fore, the displays feature an international crew. These exhibitions are supplemented by the permanent collection – with works by the likes of Karel Appel, Man Ray, Nik Jonk and Fritz Koenig – and by a set of larger, playful pieces, the *Fairy Tale Sculptures*, that line up outside the museum above the beachside boulevard, all the work of the American Tom Otterness (b.1952).

ARRIVAL AND DEPARTURE   DEN HAAG

By train The city has two train stations: Den Haag HS (Hollands Spoor) on Stationsplein and the recently revamped and enlarged Den Haag CS (Centraal Station) on Koningin Julianaplein. Of the two, Den Haag CS is the more convenient, a 5–10min walk from the town centre; Den Haag HS is 1km to the south. There are frequent rail services between the two - or you can catch tram #1 from Den Haag HS direct to the city centre.

Destinations Den Haag CS to Amersfoort (every 30min; 1hr); Amsterdam CS (every 30min; 50min); Delft (every 15min; 12min); Dordrecht (every 30min; 35min); Gouda (every 20min; 20min); Leiden (every 30min; 20min); Rotterdam (every 15min; 25min); Utrecht (every 15min; 40min).

INFORMATION

Tourist office Den Haag's main VVV is in the centre of the city, a 5–10min walk west from Den Haag CS inside the public library at Spui 68 (Mon noon–8pm, Tues–Fri 10am–8pm, Sat 10am–5pm, Sun noon–5pm; ☏ 070 361 8860, ⊛ denhaag.com).

GETTING AROUND

By tram and bus The main hub of the public transport system is Centraal Station, though perhaps the most useful tram, tram #1 (which runs through the city centre on its way between Scheveningen and Delft), bypasses Centraal Station. There is also a mini-metro with some of the trams going underground to the west of Centraal Station underneath Grote Marktstraat and part of Prinsegracht.

Tickets Den Haag's transport network is operated by HTM (⊛ htm.nl). Single tickets, valid for one hour, cost €3.50, a day pass (*dagkaart*) €6.50, three days €16.50 – less in all cases if you have an OV-chipkaart (see box, p.27). Note that the day passes are valid for days rather than hours – thus the one-day pass is only valid on the day it is first used. Tickets can be purchased at the HTM service points in both the city's train stations; in addition, bus and tram drivers sell single tickets, but not the day passes – except for drivers on Trams #1, #9 and #11, who can.

By bike Cycle rental is available at the Rijwiel outlets at both train stations for €7.50/day.

Taxis Call HTMC on ☏ 070 390 7722.

ACCOMMODATION

Den Haag has a good supply of central **hotels**, with many of the more comfortable (and sometimes luxurious) dotted within hollering distance of the Binnenhof, to the west of Den Haag CS. Advance reservations are always a good idea as conferences and events can push hotel prices way up. There is a complete list of accommodation on the VVV's website (⊛ denhaag.com).

HOTELS

Carlton Ambassador Hotel Sophialaan 2 ☏ 070 363 0363, ⊛ carlton.nl; tram #1 from Kneuterdijk to the Mauritskade stop; map p.157. Deluxe four-star hotel with every mod con, located in an attractively maintained nineteenth-century mansion on a smart residential avenue about 1km north of the centre. The rooms are large, well appointed and decorated in plush, traditional style. The breakfasts are banquet-like and there's an open-air terrace. **€100**

Corona Buitenhof 39 ☏ 070 363 7930, ⊛ corona.nl; map p.152. In a great location just across the street from the Binnenhof, this chain hotel has a good-looking frontage and an attractive period foyer. The rooms beyond, with their surfeit of browns and creams, are less distinctive, but they are very comfortable. Prices vary enormously, but at quiet times a double here is a snip. **€110**

★**Paleis Hotel** Molenstraat 26 ☏070 362 4621, ⓦpaleis-hotel.nl; map p.152. This charming, privately owned hotel is in an old, mostly eighteenth-century townhouse. Each of the twenty bedrooms is decorated with style and panache – antique furniture, French fabrics and so forth. Great central location as well. **€120**

★**Parkhotel** Molenstraat 53 ☏070 362 4371, ⓦparkhoteldenhaag.nl; map p.152. From the outside, the four-star *Parkhotel* doesn't look anything special, but the interior is graced by all sorts of charming Art Deco flourishes and has spacious public rooms to boot. There are over one hundred well-appointed rooms decorated in brisk modern style both in the main building and the garden annexe, but if you are a light sleeper, think twice about a room at the front – Molenstraat can get noisy. Central location with some rooms overlooking the Paleis Noordeinde gardens. **€120**

Residenz Stadslogement Sweelinckplein 35 ☏070 364 6190, ⓦresidenz.nl; tram #17 from Den Haag CS to the Groot Hertoginnelaan (Oost) stop; map p.157. In a creatively remodelled late nineteenth-century villa, this boutique hotel is slick and smart in equal measure with shades of grey, brown and white to the fore. Sweelinckplein itself is an attractive garden square to the

north of the centre near the Laan van Meerdervoort boulevard. **€170**

Room 11 Veenkade 6 & 7–9 (reception is at the Café de Bieb, Veenkade 7) ☏070 346 3657, ⓦhotelroom11.nl; tram #17 from Den Haag CS to the Noordwal tram stop; map p.152. This small, bargain hotel holds ten rooms spread over the upper floors of three three-storey terrace houses. All the rooms are en suite and although they are far from luxurious, they are pleasant enough and very affordable. A handy location, too, and organic breakfasts. **€70**

HOSTELS

Jorplace Beach Hostel Keizerstraat 296 ☏070 338 3270, ⓦjorplace.nl; tram #1 from map p.157. Within easy walking distance of the beach, Scheveningen's well-equipped beach hostel offers bunk-bed accommodation and shared facilities in ten- to 24-bunk dorms. Also has several double rooms, including a camper van in the back garden. There's a café and a bar, plus bike and longboard rental. Dorms **€22**, doubles **€50**, camper van **€30**

Stayokay Den Haag Scheepmakersstraat 27 ☏070 315 7888, ⓦstayokay.com; map p.152. This large and comfortable HI hostel is located just 400m northeast of – and across the canal from – Den Haag HS station. A good range of facilities includes luggage and bicycle storage, bike rental, a café and a small library. Dorms **€19**, doubles **€60**

EATING AND DRINKING

Den Haag has an excellent range of **restaurants**, and although some are aimed squarely at the expense account, many more are very affordable. Some of the good spots are concentrated along and around Denneweg and Molenstraat, but the liveliest **bars** are clustered on and in the vicinity of the Grote Markt, south of the Grote Kerk, and on the Plein, near the Mauritshuis.

RESTAURANTS

Basaal Dunne Bierkade 3 ☏070 427 6888, ⓦbasaal.net; map p.152. With its crisp, modern decor, this charming restaurant has a short but sharp menu featuring local ingredients – like the catch of the day. Main courses – for example, lemon dab and saffron potatoes – average €22. Tues–Sun 6–11pm.

Catch by Simonis Dr Lelykade 43, Scheveningen ☏070 338 7609, ⓦcatch-bysimonis.nl; take tram #11 from Den Haag HS to the Willem de Zwijgerlaan stop and it's a 5min walk; map p.157. Cousin to the other *Simonis* (see p.162), this fills out some of the decorative gaps – it occupies a smart, glassy building beside the marina and has a loungey terrace with sofas. The seafood is just as good, but you pay a little extra. Daily noon–10pm.

Ciao, Ciao Tournooiveld 1 ☏070 345 9037, ⓦciaociao.nl; map p.152. Buzzy and engaging, bistro-style Italian restaurant (shame about the naff name) that covers all the basics from pizza upwards, though it's the fresh pasta that takes the gastronomic crown. Has a large pavement terrace

and is handily located near the Hofvijver. Competitively priced with main courses averaging €14. Daily 11am–11pm.

Dekxels Denneweg 130 ☏070 365 9788, ⓦdekxels.nl; map p.152. This coolly decorated, chic restaurant serves a first-rate range of international and Dutch dishes. Dishes – such as truffle risotto or Peking-style duck – are starter-sized and average around €9. Mon–Sat 5.30–10pm.

★**Le Café** Oude Molenstraat 26a ☏070 360 4055; map p.152. This engagingly informal restaurant, with its boho furniture and vintage photos, offers a short and simple French-influenced menu, whose filling and satisfying main courses feature the likes of beef bavette with shallots in a red wine jus (€23). Daily 5pm–1.30am, kitchen till 10pm.

Little V Rabbijn Maarsenplein 21 ☏070 392 1230, ⓦlittlev.nl; map p.152. Smart and fashionable Vietnamese restaurant on a pleasant square near Chinatown. Mains such as caramelized sea bass or chicken in curry-coco sauce average €8–14. Tues–Sat noon–10pm, Sun noon–9.30pm.

Oker Denneweg 71 ☎ 070 364 5453, ⓦ restaurantoker .nl; map p.152. Popular tapas-style restaurant with imaginative pick-and-mix decor – and an equally imaginative menu featuring the likes of quail and artichokes, scallops with broccoli and truffle. Two tapas should be enough for most – and each will cost around €13. Daily 11.30am–10pm, bar till 1am.

★ **Simonis aan de Haven** Visafslagweg 20 ☎ 070 350 0042, ⓦ simonisvis.nl; take tram #11 from Den Haag HS station to the Vuurbaakstraat stop and it's a 10min walk through old dockers' terraces; map p.157. Few would argue that this place, located out amongst the clutter of Scheveningen's harbour, is the best seafood restaurant in town, a canteen-style affair whose garish decor – think nautical knick-knacks – somehow adds to the atmosphere. The seafood is invariably delicious, served in generous portions and inexpensive – sole for €17, sea bass for €17 – and the fish soup is outstanding. Daily 8am–9pm.

CAFÉ-BARS AND BARS

De Boterwaag Grote Markt 8a ☎ 070 365 9686, ⓦ gmdh.nl; map p.152. Immensely appealing café-bar lodged in an old and cavernous brick-vaulted weigh house. It's very popular with a youthful crowd and offers a wide range of beers as well as inexpensive bar food, though this hardly inspires the palate. Large terrace, which fills up quickly when the sun comes out. Daily 10am–1.30am.

Muziekcafé de Paap Papestraat 32 ☎ 070 365 2002, ⓦ depaap.nl; map p.152. Dark and raucous bar with live music most nights showcasing the best of local talent. A favourite with the locals. Thurs 7pm–4am, Fri & Sat 7pm–5am.

★ **De Oude Mol** Oude Molstraat 61 ☎ 070 345 1623; map p.152. Good old traditional bar and neighbourhood joint down a narrow side street. Oodles of atmosphere and an enjoyable range of beers. Upstairs is a tiny tapas bar. Daily from 5pm; kitchen Wed–Sat from 5.30pm.

De Paas Dunne Bierkade 16a ☎ 070 360 0019, ⓦ depaas.nl; map p.152. Traditional brown bar a short walk south of the centre, with lots of zip and over 150 beers to sample. Canal-side with an inviting boat-terrace in summer and an ample whisky collection. Mon–Thurs & Sun 3pm–1am, Fri & Sat 3pm–1.30am.

★ **Rootz** Grote Marktstraat 14 ☎ 070 363 9988, ⓦ rootz.nl; map p.152. Accusations that Den Haag is a little staid are comprehensively debunked at this large and heaving café-bar, whose attractive shuttered facade and pavement terrace serve as a prelude to a saloon-style interior with bare-brick walls and a wood-beamed ceiling. The place prides itself on its range of Dutch and mainly Belgian beers – over two hundred and counting. Mon–Thurs & Sun 10am–12.30am, Fri & Sat 10am–1am.

De Zwarte Ruiter Grote Markt 27 ☎ 070 364 9549, ⓦ gmdh.nl; map p.152. This fashionable bar boasts a good selection of beers and ales, and positively heaves at the weekend. There's a large terrace too, with picnic tables under a comfortable heater for chilly evenings. Daily 11am–1am.

DIRECTORY

Cinema The well-regarded Filmhuis Den Haag, Spui 191 (☎ 070 365 6030, ⓦ filmhuisdenhaag.nl) is the city's prime arthouse cinema.

Embassies and consulates Australia, Carnegielaan 4 ☎ 070 310 8200; Canada, Sophialaan 7 ☎ 070 311 1600; Ireland Scheveningseweg 112 ☎ 070 363 0993; New Zealand, Eisenhowerslaan 77N ☎ 070 346 9324; UK, Lange Voorhout 10 ☎ 070 427 0427; US, Lange Voorhout 102 ☎ 070 310 2209.

Markets Antiques, books and curios markets are on Lange Voorhout (mid-May to late Sept Thurs & Sun 10am–6pm) and on Plein (Oct–May Thurs 10am–6pm). The city's largest outdoor market is the Haagse Markt (Mon, Wed, Fri & Sat 9am–5pm), where you'll find everything from cheap veg to colourful clothing, but it is off the beaten track on De Heemstraat (tram #6 from the Spui – direction Leyenburg; get off at the Hobbemaplein stop).

Pharmacy Hofstad Apotheek, in the centre at Korte Poten 7a (Mon–Fri 8.30am–6pm, Sat 10am–4pm; ☎ 070 346 4748).

Post office Kerkplein 6 (Mon–Fri 7.30am–6.30pm; Sat 9am–5pm).

Delft

DELFT, in between Den Haag and Rotterdam, has the most beguiling of centres, a medley of ancient red-tiled houses set beside tree-lined canals intercepted by the cutest of humpback bridges. It's no surprise, then, that the town is one of the most visited spots in the Netherlands, but most tourists come here for the day, and in the evening, even in the summer, the town can be surprisingly – and mercifully – quiet. Delft boasts a clutch of handsome old buildings, most notably two fine churches – the **Nieuwe Kerk** and the **Oude Kerk** - a fascinating museum, the **Prinsenhof**, which holds an enjoyable collection of Golden Age paintings, and the imaginative **Vermeercentrum**, celebrating

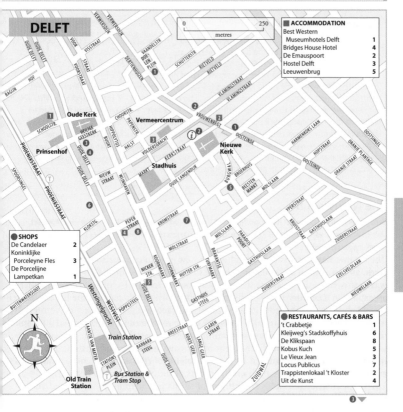

ACCOMMODATION	
Best Western	
Museumhotels Delft	1
Bridges House Hotel	4
De Emauspoort	2
Hostel Delft	3
Leeuwenbrug	5

● **SHOPS**	
De Candelaer	2
Koninklijke	
Porceleyne Fles	3
De Porcelijne	
Lampetkan	1

● **RESTAURANTS, CAFÉS & BARS**	
't Crabbetje	1
Kleijweg's Stadskoffyhuis	6
De Klikspaan	8
Kobus Kuch	5
Le Vieux Jean	3
Locus Publicus	7
Trappistenlokaal 't Kloster	2
Uit de Kunst	4

3

the life and times of Delft's best-known son, **Johannes Vermeer** (see box, p.164). And then there is the **Delftware**, the blue and white ceramics for which the town is famous: more than anything else, it's this that pulls in the day-trippers, who throng a battery of souvenir shops and a factory or two.

Markt

The obvious place to start an exploration of Delft is the **Markt**, a good-looking square and central point of reference with the Stadhuis at one end and the Nieuwe Kerk at the other, and with cafés and souvenir shops and a **statue** of Delft's own Hugo Grotius lined up in between. A well-known scholar and statesman, **Grotius** (1583–1645) was sentenced to life imprisonment by Maurice of Orange-Nassau during the political turmoil of the 1610s, but was subsequently rescued by his wife who smuggled him out of jail in a chest. Unfortunately, it didn't save Grotius from a sticky end – he died of exposure after being shipwrecked near Danzig.

The Stadhuis

At the west end of the Markt is the **Stadhuis**, whose delightful facade of 1618 is equipped with dormer windows, shutters, fluted pilasters and shell decoration. Most of its medieval predecessor was incinerated in the fire of 1536, but the stern stone tower of the earlier building survived and was incorporated – none too successfully – into the later design.

JOHANNES VERMEER

Precious little is known about **Johannes Vermeer** (1632–75), but he was certainly born in Delft and died here too, leaving a wife, eleven children and a huge debt to the local baker. He had given the baker two pictures as security, and his widow subsequently bankrupted herself trying to retrieve them. Vermeer's most celebrated painting is his 1661 *View of Delft*, now exhibited at the Mauritshuis in Den Haag (see p.153), but nowadays if you're after a townscape that even vaguely resembles the picture, you'll be disappointed – it doesn't exist and in a sense it never did, no matter how many "Vermeer walks" Delft lays on. Vermeer made no claim to be a realist and his *View* accorded with the landscape traditions of his day, presenting an idealized Delft framed by a broad expanse of water and dappled by a cloudy sky. There is a cool detachment here that Vermeer also applied to those scenes of contemporary domestic life which are more typical of his oeuvre – though only 37 Vermeers survive – as exemplified by *The Love Letter*, in Amsterdam's Rijksmuseum (see p.75).

---

3 The Nieuwe Kerk

Markt • Jan Mon–Fri 11am–4pm, Sat 10am–5pm; Feb–March Mon–Sat 10am–5pm; April–Oct Mon–Sat 9am–6pm; Nov & Dec Mon–Fri 10am–4pm, Sat 10am–5pm • €3.75; combined ticket with Oude Kerk €6.50; Nieuwe Kerk tower €3.75 extra • ☎ 015 212 3015, ⓦ oudeennieuwekerkdelft.nl

The **Nieuwe Kerk**, opposite the Stadhuis, is new only in comparison with the Oude Kerk, as there's been a church on this site since 1381. Most of the original structure was destroyed in the great fire that swept through Delft in 1536, and the remainder in an explosion a century later – a disaster, incidentally, which claimed the life of the artist Carel Fabritius, Rembrandt's greatest pupil and (debatably) the teacher of Vermeer. The most striking part of the rebuilding is one of the most recent, the church's 100m **spire**, replaced in 1872 and from whose summit there's a great view over the town.

Otherwise, apart from the sheer height of the nave and its imposing columns, the interior is mainly distinguished by the **mausoleum of William the Silent**, a prodigiously elaborate marble structure built on the orders of the States General between 1614 and 1623. The mausoleum holds two effigies of William, one in his pomp, seated and dressed in his armour, the other showing him recumbent on his deathbed. This second carving is exquisite, down to the finest details of his face, and at his feet is his faithful dog, who – so legend has it – refused to eat or drink after William's death, thereby rejoining his master in double-quick time. The two effigies are surrounded by bronze allegorical figures, representing the likes of Liberty and Justice. The statue of **Fame**, standing on tiptoe behind the recumbent William, caused all sorts of problems: it fell over and the cost of the repairs pushed the whole project way over budget. Look out also for the seventeen **stained-glass windows**. The explosion of 1654 took care of the medieval originals and for centuries most of the windows were bricked up, but in the 1920s new windows were commissioned on a piecemeal basis. In quality and subject matter they are a mixed bunch, but although some illustrate biblical themes, most sing the praises of the House of Orange, many of whom are interred in the **burial vault** beneath the nave (no public access).

The Vermeercentrum

Voldersgracht 21 • Daily 10am–5pm • €8 • ☎ 015 213 8588, ⓦ vermeerdelft.nl

Since the **Vermeercentrum** doesn't actually own any of the great man's paintings, you might be loath to part with the admission fee, but in fact the Centre takes a more than decent stab at exploring the life, times and work of Delft's most famous son, **Johannes Vermeer** (see box above). The Centre has three smallish floors with the lowest devoted to the "World of Vermeer", featuring a short film and reproductions of all the 37 paintings currently attributed to him arranged chronologically. As the explanatory panels point out, at least three have long been the subject of intense artistic debate, the

HAN VAN MEEGEREN AND THE FORGED VERMEERS

During the German occupation of World War II, the Dutch art forger **Han van Meegeren** (1889–1947) sold a "previously unknown" Vermeer to a German art dealer working for Herman Goering – a religious painting from Vermeer's "early period"; what neither the agent nor Goering realized was that Meegeren had painted it himself. A forger *par excellence*, Meegeren had developed a sophisticated ageing technique in the early 1930s. He mixed his paints with phenol formaldehyde resin dissolved in benzene and then baked the finished painting in an oven for several hours; the end result fooled everyone, including the curators of the Rijksmuseum, who had bought another "Vermeer" from him in 1941.

The forgeries might well have never been discovered but for a strange sequence of events. In May 1945 a **British captain** by the name of Harry Anderson discovered Meegeren's "Vermeer" in Goering's art collection. Meegeren was promptly arrested as a collaborator and, to get himself out of a pickle, he soon confessed to this and other forgeries, arguing that he had duped and defrauded the Nazis rather than helping them – though he had, of course, pocketed the money. It was a fine argument and his reward was a short prison sentence – but in the event he died from a heart attack before he could be locked up.

3

difficulty being that Vermeer's religious paintings – for example *Christ in the House of Martha and Mary* – are so very different from the intense bourgeois interiors and views for which Vermeer is famous; it was this stylistic gap that the forger Han van Meegeren exploited (see box above). Up above, a second floor examines Vermeer's art, especially his use of light and perspective, and the top floor takes a fascinating look at Vermeer's themes, notably lust and love, both attainable and unattainable.

The Oude Kerk

Heilige Geestkerkhof 25 • Feb–March Mon–Sat 10am–5pm; April–Oct Mon–Sat 9am–6pm; Nov–Jan Mon–Fri 11am–4pm, Sat 10am–5pm; • €3.75, combined ticket with Nieuwe Kerk €6.50 • ☎ 015 212 3015, ⓦ oudeennieuwekerkdelft.nl

The discordant lines of the **Oude Kerk**, a rambling Gothic pile, are redeemed by the most magnificent of church towers – a soaring cluster of turrets rising high above the town. Despite its dense buttressing, the tower has long been subject to subsidence and the angle of its lean has been measured by generations of worried town architects. Indeed, there have been periodic panics about its safety, not least in the 1840s when the council almost decided to pull it down; the last repairs were undertaken in the 1990s. Inside, the church boasts a splendid vaulted timber ceiling and a fine set of modern **stained-glass windows** which mostly depict biblical scenes, the key exception being the crowded "Liberation Window", installed in the north transept in 1956 to celebrate the expulsion of the German army at the end of World War II. Also of interest is the main **pulpit**, whose five intricately carved panels depict John the Baptist and the four Evangelists in false perspective; dating from 1548, the pulpit did well to survive the attentions of the Protestants when they ransacked the church in the Iconoclastic Fury of 1565.

The tombs

Among the assorted **tombs** there is a plain floor plaque in honour of Vermeer just to the west of the main pulpit and a flashy marble memorial to **Admiral Maarten Tromp** (1598–1653) close by, next to the north transept. One of the country's most successful admirals, Tromp was captured twice at sea – once by the English and once by Tunisian Arabs – but survived to lead the Dutch fleet at the start of the First Anglo-Dutch War (1652–54). Tromp famously hoisted a broom at his masthead to "sweep the seas clear of the English", but the Royal Navy had its revenge, gunning him down during a sea battle off Scheveningen in 1653. It's this last battle that is depicted on Tromp's tomb alongside an effigy of the man himself, dressed up in his armour beneath a flock of

3

DELFTWARE DELIGHTS

Delftware traces its origins to fifteenth-century Mallorca, where craftsmen had developed **majolica**, a type of porous pottery that was glazed with bright metallic oxides. During the Renaissance, these techniques were exported to Italy from where they spread north, first to Antwerp and then to the United Provinces. Initially, Delft pottery **designs** featured landscapes, portraits and biblical scenes, while the top end of the market was dominated by more ornate Chinese porcelain imported by the Dutch East India Company. However, when a prolonged civil war in China broke the supply line, Delft's factories picked up the slack, taking over the luxury end of the market by copying Chinese designs. By the 1670s, Delft was churning out blue-and-white tiles, plates, panels, jars and vases by the boatload, even exporting to China, where they undercut Chinese producers. In the event, their success was short-lived: a century later, the Delft factories were themselves undercut by the British and the Germans, and by the time Napoleon arrived they had all but closed down. There was a modest revival of the industry in the 1870s and there are several local producers today, but it's mostly mass-produced stuff of limited originality, though there are exceptions.

BUYING DELFTWARE

De Candelaer Kerkstraat 13a ☎015 213 1848, ⓦcandelaer.nl. You can avoid the tourist throngs at Royal Delftware and still buy good – and certainly more creative – Delftware at this shop-cum-mini-factory in the shadow of the Oude Kerk. You can see the painters and potters at work here too. Mon–Sat 9.30am–5pm.

Koninklijke Porceleyne Fles Rotterdamseweg 196 ☎015 251 2030, ⓦroyaldelft.com. Delft's souvenir shops are jam-packed with Delftware but Royal Delftware is the leading local manufacturer, producing a wide range of hand-painted pieces. Entrance to the factory shop is free, but the frequent guided tours (€12.50), which include a "journey through" the history of Royal Delft and a visit to the factory itself, are pricey – and attract day-trippers by the coach load. From Delft train station, it's a good 20min walk south, or you can take bus #40 and get off on Rotterdamseweg at the Jaffalaan stop; incidentally, there's a good chance that Royal Delft will move its showroom to the town's old and empty train station sometime in the future. Mid-March to Oct daily 9am–5pm; Nov to mid–March Mon–Sat 9am–5pm, Sun noon–5pm.

De Porcelijne Lampetkan Just behind the Nieuwe Kerk at Vrouwenregracht 5 ☎065 1066 824, ⓦantiquesdelft.com. Conveniently located, this appealing little shop sells an excellent range of antique Delftware at (comparatively) reasonable rates. Mon 1–5pm, Tues–Sat 10.30am–5.30pm.

bawling, trumpeting cherubs. The marble carving depicting the battle, which shows the British fleet burning away, was much admired by no less than Samuel Pepys, who wrote "the smoke [was] the best expressed that ever I saw".

Museum Prinsenhof

Sint Agathaplein 1 • Tues–Sun 11am–5pm, plus June to late Aug Mon 11am–5pm • €12.50 • ☎015 260 2358, ⓦprinsenhof-delft.nl

Tucked away down a passageway opposite the Oude Kerk, in what was originally a convent, **the Museum Prinsenhof** served as the main residence of William the Silent of Orange-Nassau from 1572 to 1584. A sprawling, somewhat confusing building spread over two main floors, it was here that William coordinated the Dutch resistance to the Habsburgs and it was here too that he was assassinated. Today, the museum has three principal sections – one celebrating the William connection, a second concentrating on Delft in the Golden Age, and a third devoted to the town's most famous product, Delftware. There are also regular temporary exhibitions, most of which attract a supplementary entry fee; free **plans** are issued at reception.

Rooms 3–7

At the start of the museum, **Rooms 3–7** focus on the life and turbulent times of **William the Silent** (1533–84), illustrated by paintings of the leading protagonists, most notably a finely observed portrait of a careworn William by Delft's own Michiel Jansz. van

Mierevelt (1566–1641). Moving on, the foot of the old wooden staircase in Room 7 marks the spot where William the Silent was **assassinated** on July 10, 1584. Two of the assassin's three bullets passed right through William, doing him untold damage and lodging in the wall behind – the **bullet holes** are now protected by a Perspex sheet, put there to stop curious fingers further enlarging them. The murderer was a Habsburg agent by the name of **Balthazar Gérard**, who had managed to inveigle himself into William's household. According to legend, William's last words were "Lord have mercy upon me, and remember thy little flock"; no mercy was extended to Gérard, who died after four days of torture.

The rest of the museum
Rooms 8–17 hold the bulk of the municipal art collection, an appealing jumble of works mostly dating from the sixteenth and seventeenth centuries. In **Room 8**, highlights include a small selection of **militia paintings**, the pick of which is *The Officers of the White Company* by Jacob Willemsz (1619–61). During the long war with Spain, every Dutch city had its own militia, but as the Habsburg threat diminished so the militias devolved into social clubs, each of them keen to immortalize their particular company in a group portrait like this one produced in 1648. In **Room 15**, there are three superbly executed anatomy paintings, with *The Anatomy Lesson* by Cornelis de Man (1621–1706) being especially striking, while Room 16 has a particularly interesting section on Delft as a centre of Golden Age portrait painting: Michiel Jansz. Miereveld (1567–1641), for one, made a handsome living from what amounted to his own portrait factory – hence the four almost identical paintings of Maurits, Prince of Orange. **Rooms 18–24** are stuffed to the gunnels with Delftware (see box oppposite), with explicatory panels exploring the local ceramics industry in considerable detail.

3

ARRIVAL AND INFORMATION DELFT

By train Delft's glassy new train station is handily located a 10min walk from the Markt. The platforms are now underground and are reached via tunnels that make passengers feel like bees entering a hive, which is really rather delightful. The old train station, itself a good-looking Neo-Gothic structure built in the late nineteenth century, is just a few metres away and is currently empty – though it may at some point house Royal Delftware (see box opposite). **Destinations** Amsterdam (every 15min; 1hr); Den Haag CS (every 10min; 10min); Dordrecht (every 10min; 30min); Rotterdam (every 5min; 10min).

By bus Delft bus station is in front of the train station. Services depart hourly for Rotterdam (45min).

By tram Tram #1 links Scheveningen, Den Haag and Delft. In Den Haag, it has several stops, including Kalvermarkt and Den Haag HS train station; in Delft it rattles along Phoenixstraat/Westvest on the west side of the town centre; for the centre of Delft, get off at the Prinsenhof tram stop. **Destinations** Den Haag HS (every 15min; 25min); Scheveningen (every 15min; 40min).

Tourist office Delft's Toeristen Informatie Punt (TIP) is just off the Markt at Kerkstraat 3 (April–Sept Mon & Sun 10am–4pm, Tues–Sat 10am–5pm; Oct–March Tues–Sat 10am–4pm; Sun 11am–3pm; ☎015 215 4051, ⓦdelft.nl).

ACCOMMODATION

Best Western Museumhotels Delft Oude Delft 189 ☎015 215 3070, ⓦmuseumhotels.nl. There are two separate sections to this four-star hotel – one in an eighteenth-century building, the other in its grander, seventeenth-century neighbour. Great location, beside the Oude Delft canal just along from the Prinsenhof, though the bedrooms themselves are uninspiringly modern. **€110**

★**Bridges House Hotel** Oude Delft 74 ☎015 212 4036, ⓦbridgeshouse.nl. This medium-sized, privately owned hotel occupies an old townhouse that was once the home of the artist Jan Steen. There's no chain-hotel

standardization here and the best guest rooms are large, well equipped and have good views of the Oude Delft canal. It's in an ideal location, too, the shortest of walks from the Markt. **€110**

★**De Emauspoort** Vrouwenregracht 9 ☎015 219 0219, ⓦemauspoort.nl. Medium-sized, family-owned, three-star hotel in a great location just behind the Nieuwe Kerk. The rooms are inordinately cosy, cleverly shoehorned into a pair of old cottage-like houses and the garden courtyard round the back. Competitively priced. **€110**

Hostel Delft Voldersgracht 17a ☎061 649 6621, ⓦhosteldelft.nl. Recently revamped and reopened, this bright and breezy city-centre hostel ambles and rambles round three old buildings, its six en-suite rooms accommodating between four and sixteen guests in tidy bunk beds. The six-bunk attic room is especially convivial. Has a communal kitchen, a TV lounge and four rooftop terraces. Free wi-fi, but no breakfasts. Dorms **€22**

Leeuwenbrug Koornmarkt 16 ☎ 015 214 7741, ⓦ leeuwenbrug.nl. Pleasant, medium-sized, three-star hotel occupying attractively renovated, canal-side premises – nothing fancy, just cosy and homely. The bedrooms are perhaps a little spartan, but those at the front have nice views and the breakfasts are very good. **€90**

EATING AND DRINKING

Many of Delft's cafés, bars and restaurants are geared up for day-trippers and serve some pretty routine stuff, but there are also several excellent places dotted within easy strolling distance of the Markt.

RESTAURANTS AND CAFÉS

★**'t Crabbetje** Verwersdijk 14 ☎ 015 213 8850, ⓦ crabbetjedelft.nl. Delightful seafood restaurant with a friendly atmosphere and spick-and-span modern decor. The well-considered menu offers half a dozen seafood dishes, each of which is served with tasty garnishes and accoutrements – the halibut with shrimp croquettes and a dill dressing is especially tasty. Mains average €25. Wed–Sun 5.30–10pm.

★**Kleijweg's Stadskoffyhuis** Oude Delft 133 ☎ 015 212 4625, ⓦ stads-koffyhuis.nl. Charming little café that regularly wins awards for its inventive range of sandwiches (€6–9) and also serves the best pancakes in town (€6–12). Very popular with tourists both inside, in a cosily kitted-out old terrace house, and outside, on a patio-barge. Mon–Fri 9am–8pm & Sat 9am–6pm.

De Klikspaan Koornmarkt 85 ☎ 015 214 1562, ⓦ klikspaandelft.nl. Smart and polished restaurant in an old canal-side townhouse just south of the Markt. The food is broadly French, though Dutch dishes do pop up now and then, and you can eat outside on their patio-barge in summer. Mains average €27. Wed–Sun 5.30–11pm.

Kobus Kuch Beestenmarkt 1 ☎ 015 212 4280, ⓦ kobuskuch.nl. Located on one of Delft's most atmospheric squares, this café is famous for its home-baked apple pie with whipped cream – an absolute hit – served in an old-fashioned wood-panelled setting. Great terrace too. Mon–Thurs 9.30am–1am, Fri & Sat 9.30am–2am, Sun 10am–1am.

Le Vieux Jean Heilige Geestkerkhof 3 ☎ 015 213 0433, ⓦ levieuxjean.nl. Smart but informal French restaurant in old, vaguely rustic premises serving nouvelle cuisine (read small portions) with care and precision. Main courses are around €26, and there's an excellent cellar too. Tues–Fri noon–2pm & 6–10pm, Sat 6–10pm.

Uit de Kunst Oude Delft 140 ☎ 015 212 1319, ⓦ uitdekunstdelft.nl. Cute-meet-artsy coffee house with an inviting canal-side terrace away from the tourist crowds (just about). Scrumptious sandwiches and great coffee, as well as a nice covered courtyard patio presided over by a pair of parrots. Wed–Sat 10am–5.30pm, Sun 11am–5.30pm.

BARS

Locus Publicus Brabantse Turfmarkt 67 ☎ 015 213 4632, ⓦ locuspublicus.nl. You don't come to Delft for the nightlife, but this is one of the town's busier bars, a traditional sort of place offering a dozen beers on tap, a couple of hundred different sorts of bottled beer plus some simple bar food. Mon–Thurs 11am–1am, Fri & Sat 11am–2am, Sun noon–1am.

★**Trappistenlokaal 't Klooster** Vlamingstraat 2 ☎ 015 212 1013, ⓦ trappistenlokaal.nl. Smashing little bar with traditional decor and an excellent range of beers, mainly Belgian but also from Scandinavia, Germany and the US, both on tap and bottled. They often organize beer tastings and have a great whisky selection too. Mon–Thurs & Sun 4pm–1am, Fri 4pm–2am, Sat 2pm–2am.

Rotterdam

One of the largest ports in the world, **ROTTERDAM** lies at the heart of a maze of rivers and artificial waterways where the Rijn (Rhine) and Maas (Meuse) approach the sea. In essence, Rotterdam is a no-nonsense, working-class city, whose tough grittiness is part of its appeal, but in the last decade or so it has also flourished as a creative centre, becoming a vibrant, forceful metropolis dotted with first-division cultural attractions. Leading the artistic way are the **Kunsthal**, exhibiting contemporary art, and the **Museum Boijmans van Beuningen**, which holds an outstanding collection of Dutch painting. Both are in the city's designated culture zone, the **Museumpark**, but be sure to venture further afield: exploring Rotterdam's pattern of seaway and reconfigured

3

RESTAURANTS

Bazar	2
HMB	5
Look's	3
Oliva	1
Zeezout	4

BARS & CLUBS

Club Vie	5
Rotown	1
Sijf	2
Stadsbrouwerij De Pelgrim	6
Toffler	4
Café De Witte Aap	3

ROTTERDAM

■ ACCOMMODATION	
Bazar	1
Citizen M	4
King Kong Hostel	2
New York	8
NHOW	7
Room	5
SS Rotterdam	9
Stayokay Rotterdam	3
Stroom	6

THE NORTH SEA JAZZ FESTIVAL

Held every year in mid-July, the **North Sea Jazz Festival** (ⓦnorthseajazz.com) is the country's most prestigious jazz event, attracting international media coverage and the world's most famous jazz musicians. For many years, the festival was held in Scheveningen near Den Haag, but in 2006 it transferred to Rotterdam's **Ahoy** centre, about 4km south of the city centre at Ahoy'-weg 10. To get there by metro, take the D/E Line to Zuidplein. Details of performances are available online and from the VVV, which will also reserve accommodation – virtually impossible to find after the festival has begun. Various tickets can be purchased; a *dagkaart*, for example, valid for an entire day, costs around €85.

dockland can be a real pleasure – take for example the antique harbour of **Delfshaven** or the harmonious architecture edging the **Veerhaven**. Rotterdam also boasts a string of outstanding **festivals**, including the much-lauded **North Sea Jazz Festival** (see box, above) and the colourful **Summer Carnival** (ⓦcarnifest.com)

Brief history

An important **port** as early as the fourteenth century, Rotterdam was one of the major cities of the United Provinces and shared its periods of fortune and decline until the nineteenth century when it was caught unawares. The city was ill prepared for the industrial expansion of the Ruhr, the development of larger ships and the silting up of the Maas, but prosperity did finally return in a big way with the digging of an entirely new ship canal (the "Nieuwe Waterweg") between the city and the North Sea in the 1860s. Rotterdam has been a major seaport ever since, though it has had difficult times, especially during World War II, when the Nazis **bombed** the city centre in 1940 and, in retreat, destroyed much of the harbour four years later, with Allied bombing doing much damage in between.

The postwar period saw the rapid reconstruction of the **docks** and, when huge container ships and oil tankers made the existing port facilities obsolete, Rotterdammers promptly built an entirely new deep-sea port, the **Europoort**, jutting out into the North Sea some 25km to the west of the old town. Completed in 1968, the Europoort can accommodate the largest of ships with more than half of all goods heading into Europe passing through it. The same spirit of enterprise was reflected in the council's plans to rebuild the devastated **city centre**. There was to be no return to the crowded terrace houses of yesteryear; instead the centre was to be a modern extravaganza of concrete and glass, high-rise and pedestrianized areas. Decades in the making, parts of the plan worked – and work – very well indeed, nothing more so than the Erasmusbrug, but others – such as the Lijnbaan – dated badly, prompting another bout of intensive construction and reconstruction which continues today: the new glassy and glossy **Centraal Station** was one of the most recent schemes to be completed and now serves as a particularly impressive introduction to the city.

Coolsingel and around

Coolsingel and its southerly continuation, **Schiedamsedijk**, spine the centre of the city, running south from the modern skyscrapers of the Hofplein to the asymmetrical beauty of the cable-stretching **Erasmusbrug**, spanning the River Maas and completed in 1996. The district to either side of Coolsingel was heavily bombed in World War II, nowhere more so than **Blaak**, a compact, former working-class district, which has been rebuilt in the full flush of modern design. The architectural high points here are the **Markthal** (Mon–Sat 10am–8pm, Sun noon–6pm; free) a glassy, remarkably curvaceous structure with apartments constructed on top of a hoop-like market hall, and the idiosyncratic *kubuswoningen*, cube-shaped houses built in 1984 to a design by the architect Piet Blom: one of them, the **Kijk-Kubus**, at Overblaak 70 near Blaak station (daily

THE SHOCK OF THE NEW: A TOP FIVE OF ROTTERDAM'S PROUDEST BUILDINGS

Calypso Mauritsweg 6. A shimmering tower block that steals the show from its skyrise neighbours. Alsop Architects; 2012.

Erasmusbrug Willemsplein. A stunningly handsome bridge spanning the River Nieuwe Maas. UNStudio; 1996. See p.172.

Kubuswoningen (Cube Houses) Overblaak. Modern design at its most idiosyncratic. Piet Blom; 1984. See p.172.

Markthal Dominee Jan Scharpstraat. Aesthetically imposing structure in the heart of the city. MVRDV; 2014. See p.172

Rotterdam Centraal Station Stationsplein. The worker bees congregate here in this handsome, glassy and glossy new station. Maarten Struijs and Benthem Crouwel; 2014.

11am–5pm; €2.50; ☎010 414 2285, ⓦkubuswoning.nl), is open to visitors, offering a somewhat disorientating tour of what amounts to an upside-down house. Behind the cube houses is the **Oude Haven**, built in 1325, and now flanked by cafés and crowded with antique barges and boats – and there's a slice of 1930s Rotterdam down amongst the old shipping offices of the **Veerhaven**, on the west side of the Erasmusbrug.

Museum Rotterdam

Meent 115 · ☎010 217 6767, ⓦmuseumrotterdam.nl · Times and admission tbc

At time of writing, the lavish new **Museum Rotterdam** is under construction, its avowed intention to provide both an overview of the city's history and to reflect its multi-cultural, international present. One leading historical display will feature original footage of the bombing of the city by the Germans in 1940.

Nederlands Fotomuseum

Wilhelminakade 332 · Tues–Fri 10am–5pm, Sat & Sun 11am–5pm · €9 · ☎010 203 0405, ⓦnederlandsfotomuseum.nl

The enterprising **Nederlands Fotomuseum** (Netherlands Museum of Photography) spreads over three floors of a modern, warehouse-like block within shouting distance of the Erasmusbrug. The museum hosts a lively programme of temporary exhibitions – two or three at any one time – and more often than not at least one of the exhibitions draws extensively from the museum's large photographic and cinematic archive whose particular forte is Rotterdam, both past and present.

Museumpark

Kunsthal Westzeedijk 341 · Tues–Sat 10am–5pm, Sun 11am–5pm · €12 · ☎010 440 0301, ⓦkunsthal.nl · Tram #8 (direction Spangen) to the Kievitslaan stop · **Het Nieuwe Instituut** Museumpark 25 · Tues–Sat 10am–5pm, Sun 11am–5pm · €10 · ☎010 440 1200, ⓦhetnieuweinstituut.nl · Eendrachtsplein metro station

Known as the **Museumpark**, Rotterdam's designated cultural zone comprises a string of museums that fringe a narrow slab of parkland between Rochussenstraat and Westzeedijk. Pride of place by a country mile goes to the **Museum Boijmans van Beuningen** (see below), but spare time also for the **Kunsthal**, which showcases imaginative exhibitions of modern and contemporary art, photography and design, and **Het Nieuwe Instituut** (The New Institute), housed in a modern glassy and partly moated building, an appropriate setting for an ambitious schedule of temporary exhibitions featuring sketches, models and photos by prominent Dutch architects and urban planners.

Museum Boijmans van Beuningen

Museumpark 18 · Tues–Sun 11am–5pm · €15 · ☎010 441 9400, ⓦboijmans.nl · Eendrachtsplein metro station

The much-vaunted **Museum Boijmans van Beuningen** spreads over two floors with temporary exhibitions on both and a selection of key works from the permanent collection displayed on Floor 1. The older paintings are in one wing of Floor 1, and those from the late nineteenth century onwards in another. The information desk provides an updated and simplified diagrammatic **plan** of the museum, necessary as the exhibits are frequently rotated.

Flemish and Netherlandish paintings

The museum's rewarding early **Flemish and Netherlandish** section holds no fewer than four works by **Hieronymus Bosch** (1450–1516). Usually considered a macabre fantasist, Bosch was actually working at the limits of oral and religious tradition, where biblical themes were depicted as iconographical representations, laden with explicit symbols. In his *St Christopher*, the dragon, the hanged bear and the broken pitcher lurk in the background, representations of danger and uncertainty, whereas the Prodigal Son's attitude to the brothel behind him in *The Peddler* is deliberately ambivalent. Bosch's technique never absorbed the influences of Renaissance Italy, and his figures in the *Marriage Feast at Cana* are static and unbelievable, uncomfortably arranged around a distorted table. Other works in this section include paintings by **Jan van Scorel** (1495–1562), who was more willing to absorb Italianate styles as in his *Young Scholar in a Red Cap*; the mysterious, hazy *Tower of Babel* by **Pieter Brueghel the Elder** (c.1525–69); and **Geertgen tot Sint Jans**' (c.1460–90) beautiful, delicate *Glorification of the Virgin*.

The Golden Age

A fascinating selection of **Dutch genre** paintings reflects the tastes of the emergent seventeenth-century middle class. The idea was to depict real-life situations overlaid with a symbolic moral content as typified by *Easy Come, Easy Go* by Jan Steen (1625–79). There's also *The Quack* by Gerrit Dou (1613–75), ostensibly just a passing scene, but littered with small cameos of deception – a boy catching a bird, the trapped hare – that refer back to the quack's sham cures. In this section also are several **Rembrandts**, including the analytic *Portrait of Aletta Adriaensdr*, her ageing illuminated but softened by her white ruff, and a gloomy, powerfully indistinct *Blind Tobias and his Wife* painted twenty years later. Most of the work of Rembrandt's pupil **Carel Fabritius** was destroyed when he was killed in a Delft gunpowder explosion in 1654; an exception is his *Self-Portrait*, reversing his master's usual technique by lighting the background and placing the subject in shadow.

Modern paintings

The museum's collection of **modern paintings** is perhaps best known for its **Surrealists**. It's difficult to appreciate Salvador Dalí's *Spain*, de rigueur for student bedrooms in the 1970s, as anything more than the painting of the poster, but other works by the likes of René Magritte, Max Ernst and Giorgio de Chirico still have the power to surprise. Dutch artists never adopted Surrealism, though the **Magic Realism** of Carel Willink (1900–83) has its similarities in the precise, hallucinatory technique he uses to distance the viewer in *Self-Portrait with a Pen*. *Three Generations* by Charley Toorop (1891–1955) is also Realism with an aim to disconcert: the huge bust of her father, Jan, looms in the background and dominates the painting. Here also are paintings by a brigade of Europe's most famous artists, including Monet, van Gogh, Picasso, Gauguin, Cézanne and Munch, as well as a representative sample of the Barbizon and Hague schools, notably *Strandgezicht* by J.H. Weissenbruch (1824–1903), a beautiful gradation of radiant tones.

Delfshaven

Voorhaven • 2km southwest of Centraal Station • From the city centre, either take the metro to Delfshaven or tram #8 (direction Spangen) and get off at the Spanjaardstraat tram stop

If little in Rotterdam's city centre can exactly be called picturesque, **Delfshaven** goes part of the way there. Once the harbour that served Delft, it was from here that the **Pilgrim Fathers** set sail in 1620, changing to the more reliable *Mayflower* in Plymouth before continuing onward to the New World. Nevertheless, despite this substantial claim to fame, Delfshaven was long a neglected corner of the city until finally, in the 1970s, the council recognized its tourist potential and set about conserving and restoring. The focus of interest is Delfshaven's engaging **Voorhaven**, whose ensemble of eighteenth- and nineteenth-century warehouses and high-gabled houses lines up on either side of the main canal with its flotilla of boats and barges.

ARRIVAL AND DEPARTURE ROTTERDAM

By plane Rotterdam/Den Haag airport (ⓦrotterdamthehagueairport.nl) is just 10km or so northwest of Centraal Station on Airportplein; bus #33 (every 10–20min; 20min) links the two. A taxi from the airport to Rotterdam's Centraal Station costs about €30.
By train Rotterdam has several train stations, but the one you want for the centre is Centraal Station, on

Stationsplein. Be warned, however, that Centraal Station and its immediate surroundings can be intimidating late at night.
Destinations (from Rotterdam Centraal) Delft (every 5min; 10min); Den Haag CS (every 10min; 25min); Dordrecht (every 10min; 15min); Gouda (every 10min; 20min); Utrecht (every 15min; 40min).

INFORMATION

Tourist offices Rotterdam Info has an information desk on the main concourse at Centraal Station (daily 9am–5.30pm), but its main office is a 10min walk away at Coolsingel 195–197 (daily 9.30am–6pm; ☎010 790 0185, ⓦrotterdam.info).
Discount cards The Rotterdam Welcome Card

(ⓦrotterdamwelcomecard.com), giving you up to fifty-percent discount on many key attractions and unlimited access to the city's public transport network, comes in three versions: one day (€10), two days (€13.50) or three days (€17.50).

GETTING AROUND

By public transport Operated by RET (☎0900 500 6010, ⓦret.nl), Rotterdam's public transport system is fast and efficient and comprises an extensive bus, tram and metro network; the hub is Centraal Station.
Tickets and passes A 1hr single ticket on any part of the system costs €3 and can be bought from bus and tram drivers and from the ticketing machines at metro stations. Other types of ticket – 2hr (€3.50), one day (€7.50), two days (€12.50) or three days (€16.50) – can only be purchased from either the ticketing machines or an RET sales point (there is one in Centraal Station); costs are less if

you have your own OV-chipkaart (see p.27).
Spido boat cruises Leaving from beside the Erasmusbrug, Spido cruises (☎010 275 9988, ⓦspido.nl) offer tours of Rotterdam's assorted waterways and port facilities. The standard **harbour tour** costs €12 per person (April–Oct 5–11 daily; Nov–March Mon–Wed 1 daily, Thurs–Sun 4 daily; 1hr 15min), while the longer version, which includes a closer look at the port, cost €20 (July Thurs–Sat 2 daily, Aug Thurs, Fri & Sun 2 daily; 2hr 30min).
Taxis RTC ☎010 462 6060.

ACCOMMODATION

Predictably, Rotterdam has a slew of big chain **hotels**, but it also possesses a clutch of much less expensive places, occasionally in – or at least near – the centre, including an HI **hostel** in one of Rotterdam's distinctive *kubuswoningen* (see p.176).

HOTELS

Bazar Witte de Withstraat 16 ☎010 206 5151, ⓦbazarrotterdam.nl. Lively, central, very agreeable two-star hotel with gaudy-kitsch rooms decorated in African,

South American and Middle Eastern style and an excellent café-restaurant downstairs (see p.176). A bargain. €80
Citizen M Hotel Gelderse Plein 50 ☎010 810 8100, ⓦcitizenm.com. "We've drowned hotel clichés in the

---

LEAVING ROTTERDAM ON THE WATERBUS

Departing from beside Rotterdam's Erasmusbrug, the **Waterbus passenger ferry** (ⓦwaterbus.nl) takes an hour to zip down the rivers Nieuwe Maas and Noord en route to Dordrecht (see p.180). It's a great way to see this part of the country and fares are very reasonable – a single to Dordrecht, for instance, costs just €4.70; boats leave every half-hour from 7am to 8pm on weekdays, 8am to 8pm on Saturdays and 11am to 7.30pm on Sundays. Furthermore, connecting ferries make side journeys to – among several places – the Kinderdijk (see p.185) and the Biesbosch (see p.184).

3

River Maas", proclaims the hotel's website – a catchy line to be sure and it's true that all the rooms here are splendidly modern in design with large and comfortable beds, wall-to-wall windows and free movies – plus the public areas are particularly inviting. It's in a central location too – in a fairly routine modern block that has been cannily revived. €80

★**New York** Koninginnenhoofd 1 ☎010 439 0500, ⓦhotelnewyork.com. This distinctive, four-star hotel occupies the grand and sympathetically modernized early twentieth-century former head office of a shipping line. All the rooms are well appointed and many have smashing river views. It's situated across from the city centre on the south bank of the Nieuwe Maas – a 10min walk from Wilhelminaplein metro station. Incidentally, the hotel restaurant may be very popular, but the food is only average. €100

NHOW Wilhelminakade 137 ☎010 206 7600, ⓦnhow-rotterdam.com; a 5min walk from Wilhelminaplein metro station. Inhabiting one of the city's newest and glitziest skyscrapers, this large chain hotel offers superb views over the Erasmusbrug from its best rooms, but the bargain-rated rooms look directly into the office block next door. Splash out for the view. All the rooms are decorated in crisp, modern style and the beds are noticeably comfortable. €125

SS Rotterdam 3e Katendrechtsehoofd 25 ☎010 297 3090, ⓦssrotterdam.nl; bus #77 from Rijnhaven metro station. Built in the 1950s, the *SS Rotterdam* once shuttled across the North Atlantic, but it's now berthed here in Rotterdam and has been turned into a hotel. The ship has the graceful lines of its time – and none of the ugliness of modern cruise ships – and although the cabins vary in size

and comfort, nearly all are decorated in period style and are none the worse for that. You are, however, stuck out a good way southwest from the centre. €90

Stroom Lloydstraat 1 ☎010 221 4060, ⓦstroomrotterdam.nl; tram #8 (direction Spangen) to the Pieter de Hooghweg stop, or a 10min walk from Coolhaven metro. Twenty-three hi-tech studios – all varying in size – located in a former power station, which gives them an urban-industrial feel. All the studios on the second floor are split-level and there's also a modish bar-lounge downstairs. €100

HOSTELS

King Kong Hostel Witte de Withstraat 74 ☎010 818 8778, ⓦkingkonghostel.com. In a handy location, on one of Rotterdam's most fashionable streets, this bright and breezy hostel has a cool and arty vibe with hammocks in the dormitories and (private) rain showers in the single/double rooms. Dorms €26, doubles €100

Hostel Room Van Vollenhovenstraat 62 ☎010 282 7277, ⓦroomrotterdam.nl. Funky hostel in bright orange and purple colours, accommodating up to a hundred people in dorms with themes such as art, festival, port and zoo. There's a busy bar downstairs and the hostel has a central location. Dorms €16, doubles with shared facilities €43

Stayokay Rotterdam Overblaak 85 ☎010 436 5763, ⓦstayokay.com. It was an inspired idea to run an HI hostel in one of Rotterdam's cube houses – the *kubuswoningen* (see p.172). It opened in 2009 and has a handy central location, but the facilities, which include luggage storage and bike rental, are fairly basic. Dorms €21, doubles €60

EATING AND DRINKING

Rotterdam's grooviest street just has to be **Witte de Withstraat**: the architecture is nothing special, but it's flanked by a long line of boho-chic café-bars and restaurants, and its pavement terraces heave whenever the sun pops out. The **Oude Haven** is also a lively spot in summer, its outdoor terraces overlooking the glutinous waters of the old harbour.

RESTAURANTS

Bazar Witte de Withstraat 16 ☎010 206 5151, ⓦbazarrotterdam.com. Big and bustling North African/Middle Eastern restaurant with strikingly vivid decor and a good variety of vegetarian dishes. Mains such as couscous or chicken kebab cost around €13, but you can also opt for the daily special for a mere €9. Laidback (some would say cool) atmosphere. Mon–Fri 8am–1am, Sat 9am–2am, Sun 9am–midnight.

HMB Holland Amerika Kade 104 ☎010 760 0620, ⓦhmb-restaurant.nl. Sharp, modern restaurant on the ground floor of one of the tower blocks overlooking the River Nieuwe Maas. A well-conceived menu features such delights as halibut with shrimps and chorizo (€18). Tues–Fri 11am–midnight & Sat 5.30pm–midnight; kitchen Tues–Fri noon–3.30pm & 5.30–10pm, Sat 5.30–10pm.

Look's 's-Gravendijkwal 140B ☎010 436 7000,

ⓦrestaurantlook.nl. As the name would suggest, garlic is the big deal here (*look* is Flemish for "garlic"), in everything from the creamy garlic soup to the garlic-vanilla ice cream. Tasty surprises at affordable prices, with a three-course set menu costing just €30. Wed–Sun 5.30–10.30pm.

Oliva Witte de Withstraat 15A ☎010 412 1413, ⓦrestaurantoliva.nl. All the ingredients in this smart, bistro-style restaurant are directly imported from Italy and most are organic. The main courses are written out on a blackboard, guaranteeing you the freshest seasonal produce, and a three-course meal will set you back just €34. Daily 5.30–10pm.

Zeezout Westerkade 11 ☎010 436 5049, ⓦrestaurantzeezout.nl. In a prime location, beside one of Rotterdam's several mini-harbours, this chic little restaurant specializes in seafood, expertly cooked and beautifully presented. Reckon on €30 for a main course. Tues–Sat noon–2.30pm & 6–9.30pm, Sun 5.30–8.30pm.

CAFÉ-BARS AND BARS

Café de Witte Aap Witte de Withstraat 78 ☎010 414 9565, ⓦdewitteaap.nl. Funky little café-bar with faded furniture, an arty clientele and displays of modern art on the walls. Occasional DJ sounds too – and a lively spill-out pavement terrace. Daily 1pm–4am.

Rotown Nieuwe Binnenweg 19 ☎010 436 2669, ⓦrotown.nl. Lively café-bar attracting an alternative crew and serving up a wide variety of snacks and light meals from as little as €5. Regular live music too, showcasing mainly local talent. Daily 11am–2am.

Sijf Oude Binnenweg 115 ☎010 433 2610, ⓦsijf.nl.

Downbeat café-bar with appealing Art Deco decor; serves filling snacks and light meals such as wild salmon or satay for around €14. Intimate little French-style terrace, great for people-watching. Mon & Sun 10am–midnight, Tues–Sat 10am–1am; kitchen till 10pm, 11pm on the weekend.

Stadsbrouwerij De Pelgrim Aelbrechtskolk 12 ☎010 477 1189, ⓦpelgrimbier.nl. Rotterdam's most popular brewery is located in the old Delfshaven council house, which dates back to 1580 and has an attractive terrace overlooking the harbour. Its Mayflower Tripel beer with a hint of caramel is especially tasty. Wed–Sun noon–midnight.

NIGHTLIFE AND ENTERTAINMENT

Rotterdam has a vibrant **club** and **live music** scene – your best bet for finding up-to-date listings is to check Rotterdam Info's website (ⓦrotterdam.info).

Cinema Lantaren Venster, Otto Reuchlinweg 996 (☎010 277 2277, ⓦlantarenvenster.nl), is the best arthouse cinema in the city. A 5min walk from the Wilhelminaplein metro station.

Club Vie Maasboulevard 300 ☎010 280 0238, ⓦclubvie.com. A stylish venue hosting regular R&B,

hip-hop and dance-classic nights as well as many international DJs. Tickets from €10 upwards. Every other Mon 10pm–5am, plus Fri & Sat 10.30pm–4/5am.

Toffler Weena-Zuid 3, just off Hofplein ⓦtoffler.nl. Grungy house and techno club with great lighting and an army of boisterous, youthful clubbers. Fri & Sat 11pm–6am.

DIRECTORY

Football Feyenoord (ⓦfeyenoord.com) is Rotterdam's famous football team and rival to Amsterdam's Ajax.

Markets The largest market is on the Binnenrotte in the city centre (Tues & Sat 8am–5pm), with several hundred

stalls selling everything from food to cheap clothing.

Pharmacy BENU Apotheek Erasmus can be found at West-Kruiskade 21a (Mon–Fri 8.30am–5.30pm; ☎010 412 9331).

Gouda

GOUDA, a pretty little place some 20km northeast of Rotterdam, is everything you'd expect of a Dutch country town, with its ring of canals encircling ancient buildings set amidst a tangle of narrow lanes and alleys. More surprisingly, its **Markt** is the largest in the Netherlands, a wide and airy piazza that remains an attractive reminder of the town's prominence as a centre of the medieval cloth trade, and later of its success in the manufacture of cheeses and that old Dutch favourite, the clay pipe. The weekly **cheese market** held here is mercilessly milked by tour operators who herd their crowds here – but don't let this put you off, since Gouda's real charms lie elsewhere, especially in the splendid stained-glass windows of **St Janskerk**, and the winsome jumble of old canal-side buildings that rambles off along **Westhaven** towards the Hollandsche IJssel River, on the southern edge of the town centre.

The Stadhuis and the Goudse Waag

Goudse Waag Markt 35 · April–Oct daily 10am–5pm · Free · **Museum** April–Oct noon–5pm, Thurs from 10am · €4.50 · ☎0182 529 996, ⓦgoudsewaag.nl

Slap-bang in the middle of the **Markt** is the **Stadhuis**, an elegant Gothic structure whose soaring stonework, with its spiky towers and dinky dormer windows, dates from 1450. Statues of Burgundian counts and countesses decorate the building's facades and on its east side is the cheeriest of carillons, where the tiny figures perform an elaborate little ritual every half-hour. Opposite, on the north side of the square, is the **Goudse Waag**

3

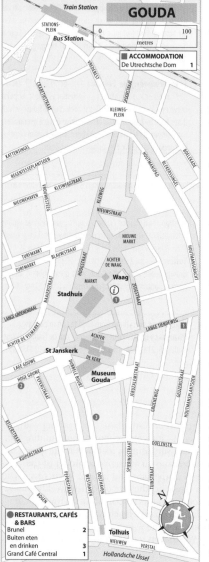

(Gouda Weigh House), a tidy seventeenth-century building adorned by a detailed relief of cheese-weighing – and now home to a moderately interesting cheese museum.

St Janskerk

Achter de Kerk 16 • March–Oct Mon–Sat 9am–5pm; Nov–Feb Mon–Sat 10am–4pm • €3.50 • ☎ 0182 512 684, ⊛ sintjan .com • All the windows are numbered and a detailed guide and audioguide are available at the entrance

Just to the south of the Markt, the lumpy **St Janskerk** was founded in 1280, though the present structure mostly dates from the second half of the sixteenth century, when it was rebuilt following a fire. The church is famous for its magnificent and stunningly beautiful **stained-glass windows**, which bear witness to the move from Catholicism to Calvinism. The biblical themes executed by **Dirk and Wouter Crabeth** between 1555 and 1571, when Holland was still Catholic, are traditional in content, but they have an amazing clarity of detail and richness of colour. Their last work, *Judith Slaying Holofernes* (Window no. 6), is perhaps the finest, the story unfolding in intricate perspective – and a gruesome tale it was too. The Assyrian general Holofernes made the mistake of sharing his tent with Judith, a Jewish woman from Bethulia, the town he was besieging; he made things worse by drinking himself into a stupor and Judith, not one to look a gift horse in the mouth, lopped off his head and carried it back home in triumph.

By comparison, the **post-Reformation windows**, which date from 1594 to 1603, adopt an allegorical and heraldic style typical of a more secular art. A prime illustration is *The Relief of Leiden* (Window no. 25), which shows William the Silent retaking the town from the Spanish, though Delft and its burgomasters take prominence – no doubt because they footed the bill for the window's manufacture.

Museum Gouda

Achter de Kerk 14 • Tues–Sun 11am–5pm • €8 • ☎ 0182 331 000, ⊛ museumgouda.nl

By the south side of St Janskerk, the fancily carved **Lazarus Gate** of 1609 was once part of the town's leper hospital until it was moved here to form the back entrance to the

> **GOUDA'S CHEESE**
>
> Gouda's main claim to fame is its **cheese market**, held on the Markt every Thursday morning (10am–1pm) from April to late August. Traditionally, a thousand or so local farmers brought their home-produced cheeses here to be weighed, tested and graded for moisture, smell and taste. These specifications were marked on the cheeses and formed the basis for negotiation between buyer and seller, the exact price confirmed by an elaborate code of handclaps. Today, however, the cheese market is a shadow of its former self, comprising a few locals in traditional dress standing outside the Goudse Waag with their cheeses, all surrounded by modern, open-air stands.

Catharina Gasthuis, a hospice till 1910 and now the **Museum Gouda**. The collection, which spreads over two floors, is really rather confusing and short of major paintings, but the Gasthuiskapel does hold a pleasant assortment of sixteenth- and seventeenth-century Dutch paintings, notably a sterling biblical triptych by Dirck Barendsz (1534–92), and, in the corridor between Rooms 10 and 11, a set of four striking Civic Guard group portraits. Upstairs, a modest selection of Hague and Barbizon School canvases is given a bit of artistic sparkle by four small paintings of rural idylls by Anton Mauve (1838–88).

ARRIVAL AND INFORMATION GOUDA

By train Gouda's train station is located to the immediate north of the town centre on Stationsplein, a 5–10min walk from the Markt.

Destinations Den Haag Centraal (every 20 min; 20min); Rotterdam (every 10 min; 20min); Utrecht (every 15 min; 20min).

By bus The bus station is adjacent to the train station. There's a regular service to Oudewater (every 30min, hourly on Sun; 20min).

Tourist office The VVV is inside the Goudse Waag, at Markt 35 (April–Oct daily 10am–5pm, Nov–March Tues–Sun 10am–2pm; ☎ 0182 589 110, ⓦ welkomingouda.nl).

ACCOMMODATION

De Utrechtsche Dom Geuzenstraat 6 ☎ 0182 528 833, ⓦ hotelgouda.nl. Gouda is short of places to stay, but this modest little place, in an airy and pleasantly renovated building a 5min walk from the Markt, will do very nicely – and it's good value too. In summer, breakfast is served in a pleasant little garden. **€67** with shared facilities, **€87** en suite

EATING AND DRINKING

Brunel Hoge Gouwe ☎ 0182 518 979, ⓦ restaurant brunel.nl. Probably the best restaurant in town, this smart Franco-Dutch split-level joint serves up main courses such as deer steak or guinea fowl for around €20. Daily 5.30–10pm.

Buiten eten en drinken Oosthaven 23a ☎ 0182 524 884, ⓦ buitenetenendrinken.nl. Cosy and very agreeable restaurant with a boho-meets-artsy interior and a well-conceived menu that features local, seasonal ingredients. All the main courses cost the same (€19) – try the organic chicken breast with pearl barley and corn

risotto. Daily 5–11pm.

Grand Café Central Markt 22 ☎ 0182 512 576, ⓦ grandcafecentral.nl. Gouda's old-time favourite, where they rustle up a tasty and filling range of home-made Dutch staple dishes in resolutely old-fashioned premises – there's been no tacky modernization here, witness the wood panelling. Main courses average around €17, salads and snacks €8, and they serve great pancakes too. Mon 9am–5.30pm, Tues–Sat 9am–11.30pm, Sun 10am–11pm.

Oudewater

Pocket-sized **OUDEWATER**, deep in the countryside about 11km east of Gouda, is a compact and delightful little town that holds a unique place in the history of Dutch witchcraft (see box, p.180). Apart from the Heksenwaag, there's not much else to see, but it's a pleasant place, whose old brick houses spread out along the River Hollandsche IJssel as it twists its way through town.

3

WITCH HUNTS AND OUDEWATER

Over one million European women were burned or otherwise killed in the widespread **witch hunts** of the sixteenth century – and not just from quasi-religious fear and superstition: anonymous accusation was an easy way of removing a wife, at a time when there was no divorce. Underlying it all was a virulent misogyny and an accompanying desire to terrorize women into submission. There were three main methods for investigating accusations of witchcraft: in the first, **trial by fire**, the suspect had to walk barefoot over hot cinders or have a hot iron pressed into the back or hands. If the burns blistered, the accused was innocent, since witches were supposed to burn less easily than others; naturally, the (variable) temperature of the iron was crucial. **Trial by water** was still more hazardous: dropped into water, if you floated you were a witch, if you sank you were innocent – though those deemed innocent often drowned before being rescued. The third method, **trial by weight**, presupposed that a witch would have to be unduly light to fly on a broomstick, so many Dutch towns – including Oudewater – used the Waag (town weigh house) to weigh the accused. If the weight didn't accord with a notional figure derived from a person's height, the woman was burned. The last Dutch woman to be burned as a witch was a certain Marrigje Ariens, a herbalist from Schoonhoven in Zuid-Holland, whose medical efforts, not atypically, inspired mistrust and subsequent persecution; she was killed in 1597.

The **Emperor Charles V** (1516–52) made **Oudewater** famous after seeing a woman accused of witchcraft in a nearby village. The weigh-master there, who'd been bribed, stated that the woman weighed only a few pounds, but Charles was dubious and ordered the woman to be weighed again in Oudewater, where the officials proved unbribable, pronouncing a normal weight and acquitting her. The probity of Oudewater's weigh-master impressed Charles, and he granted the town the privilege of issuing **certificates**, valid throughout the empire, stating: "The accused's weight is in accordance with the natural proportions of the body." Once in possession of the certificate, a woman could never be brought to trial for witchcraft again. Not surprisingly, thousands of women came from all over Europe for this life-saving piece of paper, and, much to Oudewater's credit, no one was ever condemned here.

Heksenwaag

Leeuweringerstraat 2 • April–Oct Tues–Sun 11am–5pm • €4.25 • ☎ 034 856 3400, ⓦ heksenwaag.nl

Pride of place in Oudewater goes to the town's sixteenth-century Waag, which has been turned into the curious **Heksenwaag** (Witches' Weigh House), where many medieval women were weighed and saved from certain death when it was "proved" they were not witches. Today, it's a family-run affair where you can be weighed on the original rope and wood balance with the owners dressed up in national costume to issue a certificate in olde-worlde English that states nothing much in particular, but does so very prettily.

ARRIVAL AND DEPARTURE   OUDEWATER

By bus Bus #107 links Gouda train station with Oudewater (every 30min, hourly on Sun; 20min); get off at the Molenwal stop, a 5min walk from the Heksenwaag – just follow the signs.

EATING

Lumière Eetcafé Markt Westzijde 7 ☎ 034 856 0004, ⓦ eetcafe-lumiere.nl. An extremely cosy old place with a tiled fireplace and oodles of wood panelling just opposite the Heksenwaag. It serves traditional, home-made Dutch food – and very tasty it is too; mains average €19 at dinner, less at lunch. 10am–10pm; kitchen from noon; closed Wed.

Dordrecht and around

Lying about 25km southeast of Rotterdam, the ancient port of **DORDRECHT**, or "Dordt" as it's often called, sits beside one of the busiest waterway junctions in the world, where tankers and containers from the north pass the waterborne traffic of the Maas and Rijn. Eclipsed by the expansion of its larger neighbour – and barely touched by World War II – Dordrecht's **old centre** has survived in relatively good fettle, its medley of warehouses, townhouses and workers' terraces intercepted by the three concentric waterways that once protected the town from assault. Sights as such are thin on the ground, but it's the flavour of Dordrecht's old centre – and its watery location – that appeal most, its narrow streets and harbours jutting out into the River Maas. The town is also the obvious base from which to explore the sprawling marshes and tidal flats of the wilderness **Nationaal Park de Biesbosch** just to the south and a possible starting point for the other main pull hereabouts, the windmills of the **Kinderdijk**.

Brief history

Granted a town charter in 1220, **Dordrecht** was the most important and powerful town in the Province of Holland until well into the sixteenth century. One of the first cities to declare against the Habsburgs (in 1572), it was the obvious site for the first meeting of the Free Assembly of the United Provinces, and for a series of doctrinal conferences that tried to solve a whole range of theological differences among the various Protestant sects. The Protestants may have hated the Catholics, but they inherited the medieval church's enthusiasm for theological debate: in 1618, at the **Synod of Dordt**, the Remonstrants argued with the Calvinists over the definition of predestination – pretty weighty stuff compared with the Synod of 1574, when one of the main rulings demanded the dismantling of church organs. From the 1690s, Dordrecht lost ground to its great rivals to the north, slipping into comparative insignificance, though it did manage to hold onto enough trade and industry to keep its economy afloat – as is the case today, helped by its popularity as a minor tourist destination.

The Grote Kerk

Groenmarkt • **Church** April to late Oct Tues–Sat 10.30am–4.30pm, Sun 10am–4pm • Free **Tower** April to late Oct Tues–Sat 10.30am–4.30pm, Sun noon–4pm • €1 • ☏ 078 614 4660, ⦿ grotekerk-dordrecht.nl

The Gothic **Grote Kerk** is easily the most impressive building in Dordrecht, its truncated, fourteenth-century tower – topped with incongruous, seventeenth-century clocks –visible from all over town. One of the largest churches in the country, it was built to emphasize Dordrecht's wealth and importance, but although the exterior is suitably imposing, the interior, stripped of its ornamentation by the Protestants long ago, is somewhat disappointing, though there is aesthetic consolation in the fancy pulpit, the occasional stained-glass window and, best of all, the intricately carved **choir stalls** with their folksy misericords. Climb the **tower** for a great view over the town and its surrounding waterways.

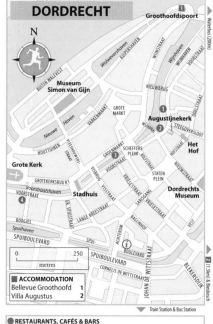

Voorstraat

Three canals parcel up Dordrecht's old centre and the middle one runs beside **Voorstraat**, the main shopping street. Here, at the junction of Voorstraat and Visstraat, sitting on the **Visbrug** (bridge), is a lugubrious **monument** to the de Witt brothers, Johan and Cornelis, prominent Dutch Republicans who paid for their principles when they were torn to pieces by an Orangist mob in Den Haag in 1672. To the right of the Visbrug, Voorstraat wends its way northeast, a chaotic mixture of the old, the new and the restored, intersected by a series of tiny alleys that once led down to a set of jetties.

The Wijnhaven and the Groothoofdspoort

Leading off Voorstraat, the Wijnbrug spans the **Wijnhaven**, the harbour where the city's merchants kept a beady eye on the import and export of wine, for which they had a state monopoly from the fourteenth to the seventeenth century. The narrow channel at the entrance to the Wijnhaven is guarded by the **Groothoofdspoort**, formerly the main city gate, its grand brick and stone facade of 1618, complete with a bronze-green cupola and clock tower, staring down at the barges and boats that shuttle across the adjacent waterways.

The Dordrechts Museum

Museumstraat 40 • Tues–Sun 11am–5pm • €12 • ☏ 078 770 8708, ⓦ dordrechtsmuseum.nl

The **Dordrechts Museum** is the town's premier art gallery, with a lively programme of temporary exhibitions and an enjoyable permanent collection focused on local artists from the seventeenth century onwards. High points include a couple of finely drawn portraits by Jacob Cuyp (1594–1651) and *De Dordtse Vierling* (The Dordt Quadruplets), an unusual, unattributed seventeenth-century painting of a dead child and her three siblings, who are safely wrapped in swaddling clothes – a simple, moving tribute to a lost daughter. **Jan van Goyen** (1596–1656), one of the country's finest landscape painters, is well represented by the detailed realism of his exquisite *View of Dordrecht*, the city flat and narrow beneath a wide, cloudy sky. Goyen's vision of Dordrecht bears interesting comparison with Adam Willaertz's (1577–1664) massive *Gezicht op Dordt* (View of Dordt), in which the painter abandons proper scale to emphasize the ships in front of the city. There's also a selection of work by the later and lesser Ary Scheffer (1795–1858), who was born in Dordrecht, but lived in Paris from 1811. His much-reproduced *Mignon Pining for her Native Land* struck a chord in the sentimental hearts of the nineteenth-century bourgeoisie. Lastly, *Midday Meal at the Inn*, a scream against poverty by Jozef Israëls (1826–1911), and *Amsterdam's Lauriergracht* by G.H. Breitner (1857–1923) are among a small selection of Hague School paintings.

ARRIVAL AND INFORMATION · DORDRECHT

By train Dordrecht's train station is on Stationsplein, a 10min walk from the town centre: head straight down Stationsweg/Johan de Wittstraat.

Destinations Delft (every 10min; 30min); Den Haag CS (every 20min; 45min); Rotterdam (every 10min; 15min).

By bus The bus station is adjacent to the train station on Stationsplein.

Destinations Biesboschcentrum Dordrecht (hourly; 15min) on Belbus #501 – you need to call at least an hour in advance to confirm on ☏ 0900 1961. In summer school holidays, there is an hourly service that does not need advance confirmation – Dordrecht VVV (see below) has the details; Kinderdijk (bus #19; hourly; 35min).

Tourist office The VVV is at Spuiboulevard 99 (Mon noon–6pm, Tues–Fri 9am–6pm, Sat 10am–5pm; also mid–April to Oct Mon 10am–6pm; ☏ 0900 463 6888, ⓦ vvvdordrecht.nl). It carries a good range of information about the town and its surroundings – including the Biesbosch and the Kinderdijk.

ACCOMMODATION

Bellevue Groothoofd Boomstraat 37 ☎ 078 633 2500 3111, ⓦ bellevuegroothoofd.nl. In a prime location overlooking the waterways at the very tip of the old town, this smart chain hotel has slick (if mildly self-conscious) rooms decorated in shades of black and white. Be sure to get a room with a river view – and/or relax in the enclosed gallery terrace. There are two restaurants here too – one a smart affair, the other bistro-like, where they specialize in steaks. **€150**

Villa Augustus Oranjelaan 7 ☎ 078 639 3111, ⓦ villa-augustus.nl; about 1.5km east of the centre, reachable on bus #3 (every 15min; 10min). Handsomely converted, this former water tower and pumping station has a grand waterside location and sits in its own carefully maintained garden grounds. Its 37 rooms, of modern demeanour and varying size, all have appealing stylistic flourishes, and there's a restaurant. **€125**

EATING AND DRINKING

Knollen & Citroenen Groenmarkt 8 ☎ 078 614 0500, ⓦ knollen-citroenen.nl. Traditional Dutch stews, soups and veggie dishes from – as they say – grandma's kitchen, with decor to match. Main courses average around €20. Wed–Fri 6–10pm, Sat 5–10pm, Sun 5–9pm.

Nobel's Brood Grotekerksbuurt 53 ☎ 078 737 0377, ⓦ nobelsbrood.nl. Pocket-sized café with a handful of tables in sympathetically modernized old premises near the Grote Kerk. Serves light snacks and the best coffee in town, but its speciality is its range of breads, organic, speciality, nut – you name it and they seem to have it. Mon–Sat 7.30am–5pm, Sun 9am–noon.

Rood, Wit & Rose Voorstraat 227 ☎ 06 1535 1817, ⓦ roodwitenrose.nl. An original *vinoteca* specializing in

European wines, and serving fifty-odd wines by the glass, many more by the bottle. Little appetizers such as wild salmon, cheese or farmer's pâté are matched with each wine. Try the Champagne brunch (€22.50) for a truly decadent experience. Thurs–Sat noon–7pm, plus first & last Sun of the month noon–7pm.

De Stroper Wijnbrug 1 ☎ 078 613 0094, ⓦ destroper.com. A smart seafood restaurant occupying modern, well-turned-out premises; main courses such as halibut, cod or bouillabaisse cost around €25. It also offers several types of set menu – for example the good-value, four-course "Stropermenu" for €27.50. Mon–Fri noon–2pm & 5–10pm, Sat & Sun 5–10pm.

The Nationaal Park de Biesbosch

The **Biesbosch** (Reed Forest) is one of the Netherlands' larger national parks and one of the few remaining freshwater tidal areas in Europe. Located on the border of the provinces of Noord-Brabant and Zuid-Holland, it covers around fifteen square kilometres of river, creek, marsh and reed to the south and east of Dordrecht and divides into two main sections, north and south of the Nieuwe Merwede waterway. The undeveloped heart of the park is the **Brabantse Biesbosch**, the chunk of land to the south, while almost all the tourist facilities have been carefully confined to the north on a strip just east of Dordrecht, along the park's perimeter. A wetland habitat, the park offers a perfect breeding ground for many species of birds such as kingfishers, bluethroats and assorted waterfowl. Best explored by **boat**, the park makes for a pleasant day-trip from Dordrecht.

Inundated twice daily by the tide, the Biesbosch produced a distinctive **reed culture**, its inhabitants using the plant for every item of daily life, from houses to baskets and boats, and selling excess cuttings at the local markets. It was a harsh existence that lasted well into the nineteenth century, when machine-manufactured goods rendered the reeds pretty much redundant. Now protected as a national park, the Biesbosch's delicate ecosystem is, oddly enough, threatened by the very scheme that aims to defend the province from flooding: the dams of the Delta Project (see p.314) have controlled the rivers' flow and restricted the tides' strength, forcing the reeds to give ground to other forms of vegetation incompatible with the area's bird and plant life. Large areas of reed have disappeared, and no one seems to know how to reconcile the nature reserve's needs with those of the seaboard cities, but vigorous attempts are being made.

ARRIVAL AND DEPARTURE   NATIONAAL PARK DE BIESBOSCH

By bus Belbus #501 links Dordrecht bus station with the Biesboschcentrum Dordrecht (hourly; 15min), though

you'll need to call at least an hour in advance to confirm the bus on ☎ 0900 1961. In summer school holidays, there is an hourly service that does not need advance confirmation – Dordrecht VVV (see p.182) has the details.

By boat The Waterbus passenger ferry service from Rotterdam (see p.175) docks on the edge of the centre, about 200m from the Groothoofdspoort.

By bike The other way to visit the park is by cycling:

bikes are available to rent for approx €7.50/day from Dordrecht train station. Dordrecht VVV sells detailed maps of the park and brochures with suggested cycle routes. The cycle ride from town to the Kop van 't Land dock, where ferries shuttle over to the Brabantse Biesbosch, takes about half an hour.

INFORMATION AND TOURS

Information The Biesboschcentrum Dordrecht, Baanhoekweg 53, is at the main entrance to the national park, 10km or so east of Dordrecht (Visitor Centre: April–June & Sept–Oct Tues–Sun 9am–5pm; July & Aug daily 9am–5pm; Nov–March Tues–Sun 10am–4pm; ☎078 770 5353, ⊛biesboschcentrumdordrecht.nl). It has some pretty routine displays on the flora and fauna of the region and a beaver observatory, as well as being the departure point for the boat trips that are the best way of seeing the park.

Boat trips Exploring by boat takes you into the untouched reaches of the park, where deep and dense tracts of forest are crisscrossed by narrow waterways. Prices vary according to the itinerary, starting at €8 for an hour-long excursion ("Rondvaarten"); check what's on offer – and make an advance booking – at Dordrecht VVV (see p.182) before you set out. If you fancy doing it under your own steam, there is boat and kayak rental here too – but again make a booking at Dordrecht VVV.

ACCOMMODATION

Hostel Dordrecht Baanhoekweg 25 ☎078 621 2167, ⊛stayokay.com; Belbus #501 from Dordrecht bus station stops outside (hourly; 15min), though you'll need to call at least 1hr in advance to confirm on ☎0900 1961. In spacious modern premises, this

well-equipped hostel is located in its own grounds about 6km east of Dordrecht on the edge of the Biesbosch. Has bicycle rental, a café, a laundry, and en-suite bedrooms of various sizes and with bunk beds. Dorms €28, doubles €60

The Kinderdijk

The much-publicized **Kinderdijk** (Child's Dyke) sits at the end of a long drainage channel that feeds into the River Lek about halfway between Rotterdam and Dordrecht. Sixteenth-century legend asserts that it takes its name from the time when a cradle, complete with cat and kicking baby, was found at the precise spot where the dyke had held during a particularly bad storm. Encompassing a mixture of symbols – rebirth, innocence and survival – the story encapsulates the determination with which the Dutch have fought the floods since time immemorial. Today, the Kinderdijk is famous for its picturesque, quintessentially Dutch **windmills**, all nineteen lining the main channel and its tributary for some 3km. They vary slightly in purpose and design, but the majority were built to drive water from the Alblasserwaard polders in around 1740. The windmills stand in a slab of open countryside that is best explored by bike – and you might try to coordinate your visit with the times when the windmills are put into operation, every Saturday afternoon in July and August, weather permitting. You might also pop into the **Molenmuseum** at Nederwaard 5 (April–Oct daily 9.30am–5.30pm; Nov–March Sat & Sun 11am–4pm; €6; ☎078 691 2830, ⊛kinderdijkinfo.nl/museummolen) for some background information.

ARRIVAL AND DEPARTURE

THE KINDERDIJK

By bus Arriva bus #19 connects Dordrecht bus station with the Kinderdijk (hourly; 35min).

By boat Take the Waterbus passenger ferry (see p.175) from Rotterdam and get off at the Ridderkerk de Schans stop to transfer to the connecting ferry (the *Driehoeksveer* to the Kinderdijk. Frequencies vary with the season, but are every hour or so; the ferry from

Rotterdam to Ridderkerk de Schans takes 30min, the *Driehoeksveer* just 5min. Bikes are carried free on both ferries.

By bike Easily the best way to get to – and around – the Kinderdijk is by bike; rent one at Dordrecht station, then simply follow the signs.

Utrecht

First impressions of **UTRECHT** are rarely positive: the mammoth shopping centre that encloses the city's train station is not encouraging (though there are plans to make it more bearable) and neither is its tangle of busy dual carriageways. But persevere: much of Utrecht's old centre has survived intact, with its network of canals, cobbled lanes and old gabled houses at their prettiest around the **Domkerk**, the city's landmark cathedral. It's the general appearance and university atmosphere of Utrecht that is the city's main appeal rather than any specific sight, but the place does possess two especially enjoyable museums, the **Speelklok** collection of street organs and musical boxes and the **Catharijneconvent**, which has a particularly fine collection of medieval sculptures and paintings. Utrecht was also the long-time home of the De Stijl luminary **Gerrit Rietveld**, with examples of his furniture at the **Centraal Museum**, and, on the outskirts of Utrecht,

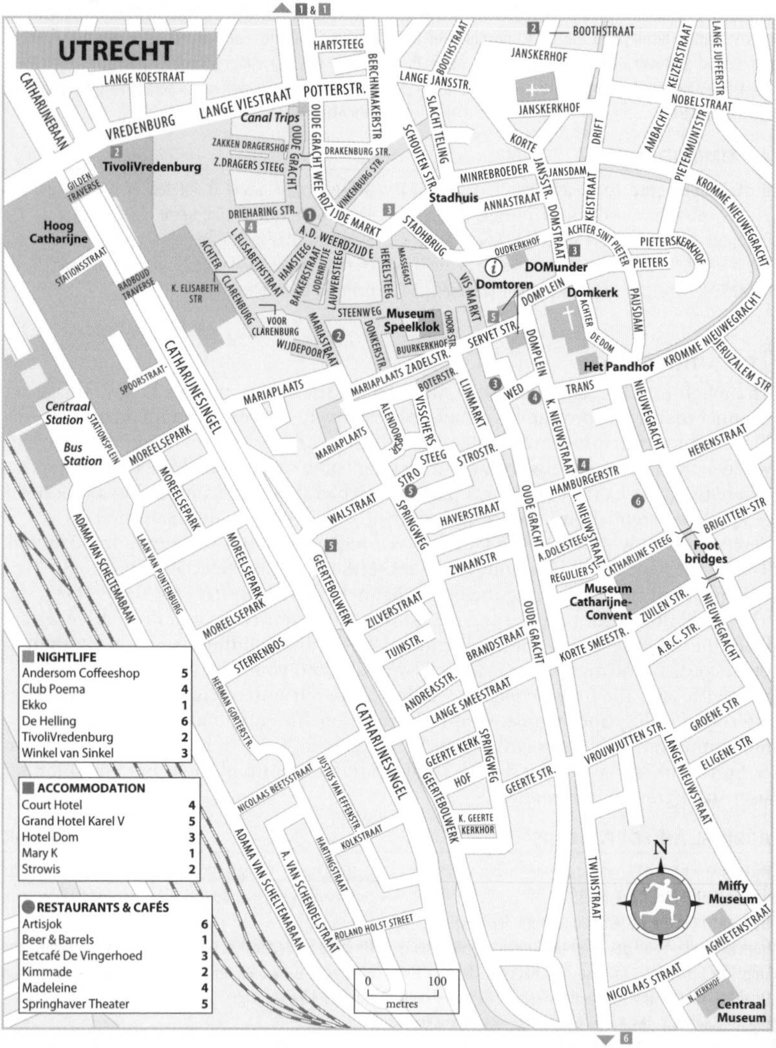

3

UTRECHT

NIGHTLIFE
Andersom Coffeeshop	5
Club Poema	4
Ekko	1
De Helling	6
TivoliVredenburg	2
Winkel van Sinkel	3

ACCOMMODATION
Court Hotel	4
Grand Hotel Karel V	5
Hotel Dom	3
Mary K	1
Strowis	2

RESTAURANTS & CAFÉS
Artisjok	6
Beer & Barrels	1
Eetcafé De Vingerhoed	3
Kimmade	2
Madeleine	4
Springhaver Theater	5

0   100
metres

N

Miffy
Museum

Centraal
Museum

there's also the house that Rietveld built – the **Rietveld Schröderhuis**. Further De Stijl treasures can be seen at the **Mondriaanhuis** in the nearby town of Amersfoort.

As you might expect of a university town, Utrecht has a vibrant café, bar and restaurant scene and its students ensure that prices are kept competitive. One of the best times to visit is during the **Netherlands Film Festival**, ten days of cinematic inspiration held every year at the end of September (⊕filmfestival.nl).

Brief history

Founded by the **Romans** in the first century AD, Utrecht only came to prominence in the eighth century after the consecration of its first **bishop**. Thereafter, a long line of powerful bishops made Utrecht an independent city-state, albeit under the auspices of the German emperors, extending and consolidating their control over the surrounding region. In 1527, the bishop, seeing which way the historical wind was blowing, sold off his secular rights to the Habsburg Emperor Charles V, and shortly afterwards the town council enthusiastically joined the revolt against Spain. Indeed, the **Union of Utrecht**, the agreement that formalized the opposition to the Habsburgs, was signed here in 1579. The seventeenth century witnessed the foundation of **Utrecht University** and the eighteenth saw Utrecht pop up again as the place where the **Treaty of Utrecht** was signed in 1713, thereby concluding decades of dynastic feuding between Europe's rulers. Fifty years later, it was also the object of one of James Boswell's harsher judgements: "I groaned with the idea of living all winter in so shocking a place," he moaned, which said more about his homesickness – he had just arrived here from England to study law – than it did about the city. Today, with a population of around three hundred thousand, Utrecht is one of the country's most important cities, its economy buoyed by light industry, academia and IT.

The Domtoren

Domplein • Beginning at the adjacent VVV (see p.190), 1hr guided tours (April–Sept Mon & Sun hourly noon–4pm, Tues–Sat hourly 11am–4pm; Oct–March Mon–Fri & Sun 3 daily, Sat hourly noon–4pm); Advance booking advised; €9; ☎ 0900 128 8732, ⊕ domtoren.nl • **DOMunder** 1hr guided tours: Tues–Sun hourly 11am–4pm • €10; ☎ 030 233 9999, ⊕ domunder.nl

The logical place to start a visit to the city is the mighty **Domtoren**, which soars above its surroundings and is, at 112 metres, the highest church tower in the country. It's one of the most beautiful, too, its soaring columns and arches rising to a delicate, octagonal lantern, which was added in 1380 some sixty years after the rest of the tower was completed. The Domtoren is, however, no longer attached to its church, the Domkerk (see below): the church nave that stood in what is now the empty space on the east side of the tower was brought tumbling during a violent storm in 1674. **Guided tours** of the tower take you unnervingly near to the top, from where on a clear day you can see Rotterdam and Amsterdam, or you can investigate the subterranean foundations of the nave in the **DOMunder** tourist attraction just next to the tower.

The Domkerk

Achter de Dom 1 • May–Sept Mon–Sat 10am–5pm & Sun 2–4pm; Oct–April Mon–Sat 11am–4pm & Sun 2–4pm • Free • ☎ 030 231 0403, ⊕ domkerk.nl.

The **Domkerk**'s nave may be long gone, but the monumental transepts and chancel have survived in good condition, the strong Gothic vaulting more than hinting at what the church must originally have looked like. The Domkerk also possesses a platoon of funerary monuments, the high point being the exquisitely carved marble sarcophagus of a certain Admiral Willem Joseph van Gendt, who came a cropper at the long-forgotten sea battle of Solebay in 1672.

Around the Domkerk

Kromme Nieuwegracht, just to the east of the Domkerk, is one of the city's most delightful streets, its medley of fine old buildings overlooking a slender canal and a string of mini-footbridges. Follow the street and canal heading north and you soon reach Jansdam, from where it's the briefest of strolls through to the **Stadhuis**, whose grandiose Neoclassical facade dates from 1826. The Stadhuis stands on a bend of the **Oude Gracht**, a pretty canal where, most unusually, the cellar-like warehouses down by the water have been turned into bars, cafés and restaurants with the street level one storey up above.

Museum Speelklok

Steenweg 6 • Tues–Sun 10am–5pm • €11 • ☎ 030 231 2789, ⓦ museumspeelklok.nl

Perhaps the most enjoyable attraction in Utrecht is the unusual **Museum Speelklok**, where a collection of fully operational street organs, orchestrions (self-playing orchestras), musical clocks and ingenious musical boxes chime and chirp their way through their assorted tunes. Incidentally, the museum is housed in the **Buurkerk**, once the home of one Sister Bertken, who was so ashamed of being the illegitimate daughter of a priest that she hid away in a small cell here for 57 years, until her death in 1514.

The Museum Catharijneconvent

Lange Nieuwstraat 38 • Tues–Fri 10am–5pm, Sat & Sun 11am–5pm • €12.50 • ☎ 030 231 3835, ⓦ catharijneconvent.nl

The excellent **Museum Catharijneconvent** holds a delightful sample of medieval religious sculptures and paintings, all superbly exhibited in an imaginatively recycled former convent named after St Catherine of Alexandria, who came to a particularly gruesome end at the hands of the Romans in the early fourth century. The museum's labelling is almost exclusively in Dutch, but an English "highlights" booklet is available at reception. A visit begins in the **basement** with the Catharina Gallery, where an assortment of ecclesiastical artefacts includes a striking *Man of Sorrows*, by Geertgen tot Sint Jans (c.1460–90), and St Martin's hammer, which the eponymous patron saint of Utrecht is supposed to have used to smash up Frankish idols in the fourth century. Next door, the **Schatkamer** (Treasury) displays reliquaries, monstrances, vestments, chalices and other Catholic artefacts, whilst the former **refectory** on the floor above (Floor 0) holds a superb selection of medieval religious sculpture, most notably a charming *St Ursula and her Travelling Companions* and an exquisitely carved *St Christopher*. The adjacent **Utrecht Galleries** have a mix of sculptures and paintings, the pick of which is Jan van Scorel's *Triptych with Crucifixion*, painted for a local monastery in the 1530s. There follows a large and somewhat confusing display on "Christianity in the Netherlands", a kind of religious potpourri of sculptures and paintings including an early *Baptism of the Eunuch* by Rembrandt. Up above, the top floor (Floor 1) is given over to temporary displays.

Centraal Museum

Nicolaaskerkhof 10 • Tues–Sun 11am–5pm • €11 including same-day admission to Miffy Museum (see opposite) and Rietveld Schröderhuis (see opposite) • ☎ 030 236 2310, ⓦ centraalmuseum.nl

Housed within a rambling brick building and currently being revamped, Utrecht's **Centraal Museum** holds a significant collection of Dutch art, which it supplements with a lively range of temporary exhibitions. Amongst early paintings, look out for the canvases of **Jan van Scorel** (1495–1562), who lived in Utrecht before and after he visited Rome, from where he brought the influence of the Renaissance back home to his fellow painters. Prime examples of this mix of native Dutch observation and Renaissance style are Scorel's rosy and Italianate *Madonna with Wild Roses* and his vivid *Five Members of Utrecht's Jerusalem Brotherhood*, an early – and seminal – group portrait. Scorel is also thought to have made a trip to Jerusalem sometime in the 1520s and this may well account for his unusually accurate depiction of the city in the central panel of the Lokhorst Triptych showing *Christ's Entry into Jerusalem* on Palm Sunday.

The Utrecht School

A later generation of city painters known as the **Utrecht School** fell under the influence of Italian art in general and Caravaggio (1571–1610) in particular. One of the group's leading practitioners was **Gerard van Honthorst** (1590–1656), whose *Procuress* adapted Caravaggio's chiaroscuro technique to a genre subject and also developed an erotic content that would itself influence later genre painters like Jan Steen and Gerrit Dou. Even more skilled and realistic is **Hendrik Terbrugghen**'s (1588–1629) *The Calling of St Matthew*, a beautiful balance of gestures dramatizing Christ summoning the tax collector to become one of the twelve disciples.

Gerrit Rietveld

Gerrit Rietveld (1888–1964), the celebrated De Stijl architect and designer, lived and worked in Utrecht, and the museum has a fine collection of his furniture, especially the brightly coloured geometrical chairs for which he is perhaps best known. The chairs are quite simply beautiful, but although part of the De Stijl philosophy stressed the need for universality, they are undoubtedly better to look at than to actually sit on.

Miffy Museum

Agnietenstraat 1 • Tues–Sun 11am–5pm • €11 including same-day admission to Centraal Museum (see opposite) & Rietveld Schröderhuis (see below) • ☎ 030 236 2310, ⓦ centraalmuseum.nl.

A long-time resident of Utrecht, the Dutch graphic designer, illustrator and writer Dick Bruna (b.1927) has established an international reputation for his children's picture-books in general and for his star creation, *Miffy*, in particular – hence the **Miffy Museum**, which celebrates his life and work. Created in 1955, the Miffy books have been translated into over fifty languages, making Miffy one of the world's best-known rabbits. The appeal lies in the simplicity of the illustrations, using primary colours and simple lines. Mainly aimed at children, the museum displays an ample collection of Bruna's work, and often puts on activities and workshops for kids.

The Rietveld Schröderhuis

Prins Hendriklaan 50 • Fixed entry times: Wed–Sun at 11am, noon, 2pm, 3pm & 4pm • Reservations required online or by phone • €11 including same-day admission to Centraal Museum (see opposite) and Miffy Museum (see above) • ☎ 030 236 2310, ⓦ centraalmuseum.nl. • Bus #8 from Centraal Station (direction Wilhelminapark) – get off at De Hoogstraat. A 20min walk from Centraal Museum

Designed and built by Rietveld in the early 1920s, the **Rietveld Schröderhuis** is hailed as one of the most influential pieces of modern architecture in Europe, demonstrating the organic union of lines and rectangles that was the hallmark of the De Stijl movement. The ground floor is the most conventional part of the building, since its design had to meet the rigours of the building licence, but Rietveld was able to let his imagination run riot with the top-floor living space, creating a flexible environment where only the outer walls are solid – indeed the entire top floor can be subdivided in any way, simply by sliding the modular walls.

The Mondriaanhuis

Kortegracht 11, Amersfoort • Tues–Fri 11am–5pm, Sat & Sun noon–5pm • €8 • ☎ 033 460 0170, ⓦ mondriaanhuis.nl • By train from Utrecht Centraal to Amersfoort station (every 15min; 15min), then bus #5 (every 20min; 4min) to the Varkensmarkt stop and it's a 5min walk

The **Mondriaanhuis** comprises the house where the artist **Piet Mondriaan** (1872–1944), the leading light of De Stijl, was born and raised, along with the adjacent school where his father was the head teacher. The museum holds an enjoyable retrospective of the artist's life and work, and although the exhibits are regularly rotated, you can expect to see prime examples of the geometric, non-representational paintings for which Mondriaan was internationally famous. There is also an interesting reconstruction of the five-sided studio Mondriaan had built for himself in Paris in the 1920s.

ARRIVAL AND INFORMATION

By train and bus Utrecht's train and several bus stations are all enmeshed within the mammoth Hoog Catharijne shopping centre, on the western edge of the city centre. Destinations (train) Amersfoort (every 15min; 15min); Amsterdam CS (every 15min; 30min); Arnhem (every 30min; 40min); Den Haag (every 15min; 40min); Leeuwarden (hourly; 2hr); Rotterdam (every 15min; 45min); Zwolle (every 30min; 1hr).

Destinations (bus) Kinderdijk (bus #90 every 30min; 25min)

Tourist office The VVV is beside the Domtoren at Domplein 9 (Mon & Sun noon–5pm, Tues–Sat 10am–5pm ☎ 030 236 0000, ⓦ visit-utrecht.com). It offers all the usual services and also organizes tours of the Domtoren (see p.187).

GETTING AROUND

Canal trips Schuttevaer (☎ 030 231 9377, ⓦ schuttevaer .com) operates enjoyable, hour-long canal trips around the city centre (April–Sept daily, hourly on the hour 11am–5pm; €10); departures are from Oude Gracht, just south of the Viebrug (bridge).

ACCOMMODATION

Court Hotel Korte Nieuwstraat 14 ☎ 030 233 0033, ⓦ courthotel.nl. The city's former courthouse, dating from the 1950s, has been turned into a slick, modern hotel with around thirty well-appointed rooms, all decorated in pastel shades and with pictures of famous "inmates" on the walls. Handy location too. **€110**

★**Grand Hotel Karel V** Geertebolwerk 1 ☎ 030 233 7555, ⓦ karelv.nl. This delightful five-star hotel occupies the site of what was, in medieval times, the headquarters of the Knights of the Teutonic Order. The main building has been cleverly modernized and there's a contemporary wing – the Roman wing – too; in between are attractive gardens. All the rooms are well appointed and extremely comfortable, but the mostly split-level suites in the Roman wing are somewhat larger and more luxurious. **€190**

Hotel Dom Domstraat 4 ☎ 030 232 4242, ⓦ hoteldom .nl. Luxurious and happening hotel located above a trendy cocktail bar and restaurant - and offering the city's best views of the Domtoren from its eleven suites. Regular DJs at weekends make this the place to be for style-conscious visitors, while lonely sleepers can even rent a goldfish for some company.

★**Mary K** Oudegracht 25 ☎ 030 230 4888, ⓦ marykhotel.com. A funky little art hotel located in an eighteenth-century canal house, with only nine rooms, all decorated in different styles. The concept is simple, making guests feel like they're staying with relatives, and being part of a cosy household. The hotel is eco-friendly, so breakfast, coffee and bed linen are all organic. **€120**

Strowis Budget Hostel Boothstraat 8 ☎ 030 238 0280, ⓦ strowis.nl. This pleasant hostel, in a seventeenth-century townhouse on a tatty side street, has a good range of facilities including a small library, bike rental, a self-catering kitchen and free wi-fi. The good-value bedrooms, which range from single rooms to large dorms, are well kept and painted in cheerful colours. The *Strowis* is situated in the old centre near St Janskerk. Breakfast €6. Dorms **€20**, doubles **€65**

EATING AND DRINKING

Downtown Utrecht literally heaves with inexpensive cafés, bars and restaurants, especially along the Oudegracht canal, where tourists and shoppers congregate as soon as the sun pops out. As you might expect of a big city, there is also a platoon of more upmarket restaurants, where reservations are recommended, especially at the weekend.

Artisjok Nieuwegracht 33 ☎ 030 231 7494, ⓦ deartisjok.nl. Cosy little place with an imaginative menu featuring variations on a Dutch theme. Main courses such as duck breast in Japanese herbs or monkfish with cauliflower hover around €20. In a nice canal-side location. Mon–Sat 5–10.30pm.

Beers & Barrels Oudegracht aan de Werf 125 ☎030 236 8744, ⓦbeersbarrels.nl. The old brick cellars that line up along the Oude Gracht canal have been turned into bars and restaurants – and this is the pick: deep and dark, busy and atmospheric with a great range of local and foreign beers, some brewed on the premises, and inexpensive barbecue food, from pulled pork (€7.50) through to burgers (€12). Daily 4pm–midnight; kitchen till 10pm, 11pm Thurs–Sat.

Eetcafé de Vingerhoed Donkere Gaard 11 ☎030 231 9659, ⓦeetcafedevingerhoed.nl. Near the Domtoren, this bustling, brown eetcafé offers a wide range of Dutch dishes, not haute cuisine perhaps but certainly filling. Daily specials cost around €15, regular main courses such as lamb chops or steak go for a little more. Mon–Sat 10am–1.30am, Sun noon–7pm; kitchen Mon–Fri 5–9.30pm.

Kimmade Mariastraat ☎030 737 0993, ⓦkimmade nl. Arguably the best Vietnamese restaurant in town, this cosy, well-established place offers a prime range of main courses – from honey pork through to fried tofu – with a minimum of fuss and at excellent prices; mains are around €7. Mon–Sat noon–10pm, Sun 1–8pm.

Madeleine 't Wed 3a ☎030 231 0100, ⓦmadeleine-utrecht.nl. Lively restaurant in inventively reconfigured premises, from bespoke wooden cabinets through to soft lighting. A fairly short menu is creative and inviting in equal measure – try, for example, the ravioli with a salad of chestnuts, scallops and radishes. Main courses average €20. Mon 5pm–1am, Tues–Sat noon–1am & Sun 1pm–1am; kitchen till 9.30pm

Springhaver Theater Springweg 46 ☎030 231 3789, ⓦspringhaver.nl. Groovy, pint-sized cinema-cum-bar-cum-restaurant that attracts a varied, arty crew. The food isn't brilliant, but the atmosphere is – and there's a pavement terrace too. Daily 11.30am–4.30pm & 5–9pm.

NIGHTLIFE

Andersom Vismarkt 23 ☎030 232 8665. There aren't too many coffeeshops in the centre of Utrecht, but this well-established place fits the bill – and it's metres from the Domtoren. Mon–Sat 10am–11pm, Sun noon–11pm.

Club Poema Drieharingstraat 22 ☎030 232 2673, ⓦclubpoema.nl. For a city not known for its heavy clubbing, *Poema* might be your best bet for some serious dancing with well-known Dutch DJs spinning the wheel in an up-to-the-minute setting. Check the website, but usually Thurs–Sat 11pm–3/4am.

Ekko Bemuurde Weerd WZ 3 ☎030 231 7457, ⓦekko nl. Alternative rock and dance venue with live performances by a wide range of artists and DJs. Check the website for the schedule of gigs.

De Helling Helling 7 ☎030 231 4544, ⓦdehelling.nl. Out in the boondocks to the south of the city centre, this is the city's main underground music venue showcasing many international and upcoming artists as well as regular dance nights. Check the website for gigs.

TivoliVredenburg Vredenburgkade 11 ☎030 231 4544, ⓦtivolivredenburg.nl. Opened in 2014, this is the city's main concert hall, a gleaming new block offering a wide-ranging programme in its five auditoriums.

Winkel van Sinkel Oude Gracht 158 ☎030 230 3030, ⓦdewinkelvansinkel.nl. This is one of the city's liveliest and most distinctive bars attracting a diverse crew who throng the spacious interior, whose gallery and mirrors date from its previous incarnation as a ballroom. There's a canal-side terrace too and the occasional club night – check the website for details. Daily 11am–midnight/1am.

3

The north and the Frisian Islands

HINDELOOPEN, FRIESLAND

The north and the Frisian Islands

Until the early twentieth century, the north of the Netherlands was a remote area, a distinct region of small provincial towns far removed from the mainstream life of the Randstad. Yet, in 1932, the opening of the Afsluitdijk, a 30km-long sea wall bridging the mouth of the Zuider Zee, changed the orientation of the country once and for all: the Zuider Zee, once a corridor for great trading ships, became the freshwater IJsselmeer and the cultural gap between the north and west narrowed almost immediately.

One of the three northern provinces, **Friesland**, is a deservedly popular tourist stopover, with its cluster of dune-swept **islands**, a likeable capital in **Leeuwarden** and a chain of eleven immaculate, history-steeped "cities" (villages really), each with a distinct charm: **Harlingen** is noted for its splendid merchant houses; **Hindeloopen**, with its cobbled streets and pin-neat canals, encapsulates the antique prettiness of the region; while **Makkum** was a focus for tile manufacture and is known for its role as a sailing centre. As for the islands, each is barely more than an elongated sandbank, parts of which can be reached by indulging in **wadlopen**, hearty walks along (or ankle-deep in) the mud flats that flank the islands to the south. In the north stretches kilometre after kilometre of hourglass-fine sandy beach and a network of cycleways. Like much of the Netherlands, the scenery of the mainland is predominantly green, bisected by canals and dotted with black-and-white cattle – Friesians, of course – and pitch-black Frisian horses. Breaking the pancake-flat monotony of the landscape, sleek wind turbines make the most of the strong westerlies, a modern counterpart to the last working windmills in the area.

East of Friesland, the province of **Groningen** has comparatively few attractions, but the university town of Groningen more than makes up for this with a vibrant ambience, contemporary fashions, range of affordable bars and restaurants, a growing international performance-art festival and the best nightlife in the region. It's also home to the **Groninger Museum**, a striking and controversial vision of urban architecture and art, and a definite highlight of the region.

South of Groningen lies **Drenthe**, little more than a barren moor for much of its history. During the nineteenth century, the face of the province was changed by the founding of peat colonies, whose labourers drained the land and dug the peat to expose the subsoil below. As a result, parts of Drenthe are given over to prosperous farmland, with agriculture the dominant industry. Sparsely populated and the least visited of the Dutch provinces, Drenthe is now popular with home-grown tourists, who are drawn by its quiet natural beauty, swathes of woodland, wide cycling paths and abundant walking trails, although many come here to visit Drenthe's most original feature – its *hunebeds*, or megalithic tombs.

Highlights

❶ Sneek Week This prosperous shipbuilding town of old is now famous as the location of the annual Sneek Week sailing regatta, held every August. **See p.202**

❷ The Eleven Towns Touring this historic chain of towns in southwest Friesland is really one of the best introductions to the region – and overall they are as enticing a group of places as you'll find anywhere in the country. **See p.209**

❸ The Frisian Islands The most popular spots often get busy in high summer, but for much of

the year these offshore dunescapes can feel as remote and unspoilt as anywhere in Europe. **See p.212**

❹ Wadlopen The best way to experience the northern landscapes is to copy the Dutch and take a guide for *wadlopen* – mud-flat walking. **See p.220**

❺ Groningen Dynamic university town in the far north, with a great nightlife and the memorable Groninger Museum of art and culture. **See p.221**

HIGHLIGHTS ARE MARKED ON THE MAP ON P.196

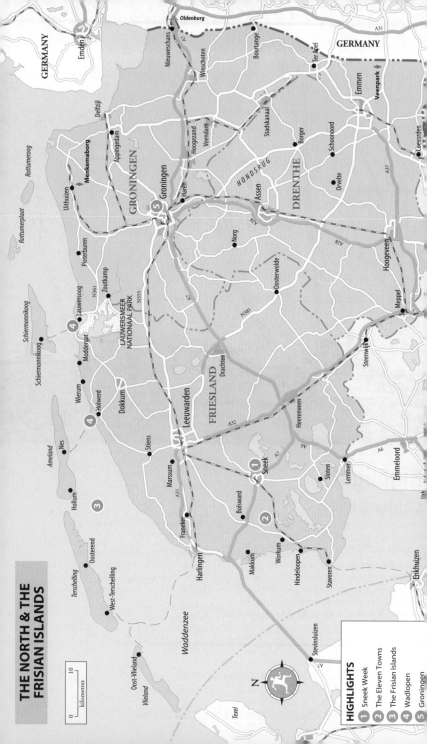

THE NORTH & THE FRISIAN ISLANDS

HIGHLIGHTS

1. Sneek Week
2. The Eleven Towns
3. The Frisian Islands
4. Wadlopen
5. Groningen

FRIESLAND: A LAND APART?

A region that prospered during the sixteenth-century heyday of the Zuider Zee trade, **Friesland** is focused around eleven historic cities and seven lakes, the latter symbolized by the seven red hearts on the province's flag, which proudly flutters in many a back garden. Friesland once occupied a much larger chunk of the north and, in the eighth century, Charlemagne recognized three parts: West Frisia, equivalent to today's West Friesland, across the IJsselmeer; Central Frisia, today's Friesland; and East Frisia, now Groningen province. From earliest times, much of the region was prey to inundation by the sea and the inhabitants built their settlements on artificial mounds (*terpen*) in a frequently forlorn attempt to escape the watery depths. It was a tough existence, but over the centuries the Frisians finessed their skills, extending their settlements by means of a complex network of dykes. You can still see what's left of some of the mounds around the area, though in large settlements they're mostly obscured. Always a maverick among Dutch provinces, the area that is now Friesland proper remained independent of the rest of Holland until it was absorbed into the Habsburg Empire by Charles V in 1523.

Since the construction of the Afsluitdijk, Friesland has relied on holidaymakers drawn to its rich history, picturesque lakes and immaculate villages to replace the trading routes and fishing industries of yesteryear. Grand old farmhouses define the region: their thatched roofs slope almost to the ground and are crowned with *ûleboerden,* white gables in the form of a double swan once used as a deterrent to evil spirits. Boating is one way of getting around and Friesland is also an ideal province to visit by bicycle. The best loop, which takes in all of the Eleven Towns, follows the 220km-long route of the **Elfstedentocht**, a marathon ice-skating race held during winters cold enough for the canals to freeze over (see p.209). Most tourist offices stock maps and guides for cycling, in-line skating, driving or sailing the route all year round.

Finally, the Frisians have several unusual **sports and traditions** that can still raise eyebrows in the rest of the country. Using a large pole to jump over wet obstacles was once a necessity in the Frisian countryside, but the Frisians turned it into a sport: **fierljeppen**. Today Frisian and Dutch pole jumpers compete during the annual Frisian championships held in Winsum, on the second Saturday of August.

Skûtsjesilen, a fourteen-day sailing race held throughout Friesland in July or August, is another regional oddity. *Skûtjes* are large cargo vessels, but they went out of use after World War II and are now only used for contests and recreational purposes: the tourist office in Sneek can give information on where to see the races. Last but not least is **kaatsen**, a Frisian version of tennis, with over 2000 contests held every year. Instead of a racket a *kaatser* uses a handmade glove to hit the handmade ball; a team of *kaatsers* comprises three players. There's a small museum devoted to *kaatsen* in Franeker, (see p.210).

4

Leeuwarden

An old market town lying at the heart of an agricultural district, **LEEUWARDEN** was formed from the amalgamation of three *terpen* that originally stood on an expanse of water known as the Middelzee. Later it was the residence of the powerful Frisian Stadholders, who vied with those of Holland for control of the United Provinces. These days it's Friesland's capital, a university town with a laidback provincial air, its centre a haphazard blend of modern glass and traditional gabled terraces overlooking canals. It perhaps lacks the concentrated historic charm of many other Dutch towns, but it's an amiable old place, with a couple of decent museums. Its most appealing feature is its compact and eminently strollable old centre, almost entirely surrounded and dissected by water. Leeuwarden is a real student town too, so it has a bit of life about it, not to mention a decent array of good-value places to eat and drink.

Waagplein and around

The southern part of Leeuwarden's centre, near the station, is an indeterminate and careless mixture of the old and new, high-rise blocks and shopping centres lining

LEEUWARDEN

RESTAURANTS & CAFÉS
Eetcafé 't Goede	6
Eetcafé Spinoza	3
Eindeloos	5
De Lachende Koe	4
Le Sandre	2
De Vliegende Hollander	7
De Walrus	1

BARS
Fire Café	2
Oranje Bierhuis	1
Paddy O'Ryan	3

ACCOMMODATION
't Anker	2
Grand Hotel Post Plaza	4
De Kleine Wielen	1
Oranje Leeuwarden	5
Stadhouderlijk Hof	3

Wirdumerdijk as far as the central **Waagplein**, a long, narrowing open space cut by a canal and flanked by cafés and large department stores with a fresh produce and household market on Monday and Saturday. The **Waag** itself, now converted into a restaurant, dates from 1598. The Friday market is located at the modern **Wilhelminaplein**, just to the south, home to the **Zaailand** shopping centre and spectacular **Fries Museum** (see opposite).

Oldehoofster Kerkhof and around

Walking west, **Nieuwestad** is Leeuwarden's main shopping street, from where Kleine Kerkstraat leads to the featureless **Oldehoofster Kerkhof**, a large and recently refurbished square near the old city walls, at the end of which stands the precariously leaning **Oldehove**. Something of a symbol for the city, this is part of a cathedral started in 1529 but never finished because of subsidence, the end result being a lugubrious mass of disproportion that defies all laws of gravity and geometry. To the right stands a statue of the Frisian politician and trade unionist P.J. Troelstra, who looks on impassively, no doubt admonishing the city fathers for their choice of architects. For a better view, climb the 40m-high tower (April–Oct daily 1–5pm; €3.50).

The town's most central square, **Hofplein**, lies just a short stroll from the Oldehoofster Kerkhof. This enclosed open space is home to the sedate, eighteenth-century Stadhuis, topped with a clock tower and, opposite, the **Stadhouderlijk Hof**, the original seat of the Frisian Stadholders, now a hotel.

Het Princessehof

Grote Kerkstraat 11 • Tues–Sun 11am–5pm • €8.50, joint ticket with the Fries Museum €14.50 • ⓦ princessehof.nl

Just off Oldehoofster Kerkhof, following the line of the track that once connected two of Leeuwarden's original *terpen*, Oldehove and Nijehove, **Het Princessehof** was the birthplace of the graphic artist M.C. Escher. Dating from 1650, the house is now home to Leeuwarden's destination **museum of ceramics**, with an outstanding collection. On the ground floor, you can see the largest collection of tiles in the world, with good examples of all the classic designs – soldiers, flowers, ships and so forth – framed by uncomplicated borders, and a fine array of European ceramics: highlights here include earthenware and majolica from Spain, Delftware naturally, lots of fine porcelain, the creamware of Josiah Wedgwood in Staffordshire, incorporating a nice collection of teapots, and a spectacular collection of Art Nouveau pieces.

On the first floor, the collection of **Chinese**, **Japanese** and **Vietnamese ceramics** is similarly impressive, devoted to the development of **Chinese porcelain** from prehistory to the Ming Dynasty (1368–1644), and from the Ming to the nineteenth century, with powerful, open-mouthed dragons, billowing clouds and sharply drawn plant tendrils. Next door is a room of **Middle Eastern ceramics**, mostly tiles from Iran, Central Asia, Syria and Turkey, beautiful pieces dating from the eleventh to sixteenth centuries.

Boomsma Beerenburg

Bagijnestraat 42a • April–Dec Tues–Sat 10am–5pm; Jan–March Tues–Thurs noon–5pm, Fri & Sat 10am–5pm • Free • ⓦ boomsma.net

Tucked away near Het Princessehof, the delightful small **Boomsma Beerenburg** museum is housed in the old distillery where they used to make the herb-flavoured gin that is a regional speciality. The distillery is still owned by the original family, although the liquor is made in a modern building on the outskirts of town these days. You can taste the gin, which includes a number of other more conventional *jenevers*, in the *proeflokaal* out the back, and if you like it buy a bottle from the museum shop.

The Grote Kerk

Bredeplaats 4 • June Sat 11am–4pm; July to mid-Sept Tues–Thurs & Sat 11am–4pm, Fri 1–4pm • Free

Though restored in recent years, the **Grote** or **Jacobijner Kerk** remains an unremarkable Gothic construction. A victim of subsidence, the whole place tilts slightly towards the newer south aisle, where you can see some fragmentary remnants of sixteenth-century frescoes and a Muller organ dating back to 1727. In front of the church, a modernistic monument remembers Leeuwarden's wartime Jewish community – deliberately placed in front of a building that was until 1943 the Jewish School, it's based on the classroom registers of the previous year.

The Fries Museum

Wilhelminaplein 92 • Tues–Sun 11am–5pm • €10, joint ticket with Het Princessehof €14.50 • ⓦ friesmuseum.nl

As you might expect from the country's proudest and most distinct region, the **Fries Museum** is one of the Netherlands' best regional museums, housed in a spectacular new building on Wilhelminaplein. Founded by a society that was established in the nineteenth century to develop interest in the language and history of Friesland, the museum traces the development of Frisian culture from prehistoric times up until the present day. It also incorporates the Frisian Resistance Museum, with its story of the local resistance to Nazi occupation.

MATA HARI

Leeuwarden's most famous daughter, **Mata Hari** (1876–1917) was born Gertrud Zelle. Hari became a renowned "exotic" dancer after an early but unsuccessful marriage to a Dutch army officer. Although the Netherlands was neutral during World War I, Hari seems to have accepted a German bribe to spy for the kaiser. The French intelligence service soon got wind of the bribe – partly because she was also supposed to be working for them – and she was subsequently arrested, tried and shot. What she actually did remains a matter of some debate, but in retrospect it seems likely that she acted as a double agent, gathering information for the Allies while giving snippets to the Germans. Whatever the truth, there's a small statue commemorating her at her partially clad best on Over de Kelders, erected in 1976 on the hundredth anniversary of her birth.

Among the museum's many highlights is an extensive collection of **silver** – silversmithing was a flourishing Frisian industry throughout the seventeenth and eighteenth centuries, with most of the work being commissioned by the local gentry, who were influenced by the fashions of the Frisian Stadholder and his court. There's also a chronological exhibition tracing the early days of the **Nazi invasion**, through collaboration and resistance and on to the Allied liberation. A range of photographs, Nazi militaria, Allied propaganda and moving personal stories illustrate the text, but the emphasis is very much on the local struggle rather than the general war effort. There are also rooms devoted to the painted **furniture** of Hindeloopen: rich, gaudy and intense, patterned with tendrils and flowers on a red, green or white background.

ARRIVAL AND DEPARTURE
LEEUWARDEN

By train Leeuwarden's train and bus stations virtually adjoin each other, a 5min walk south of the town centre, with regular services to Amsterdam and elsewhere.
Destinations Amsterdam, usually via Zwolle or Lelystad (every 30min; 2hr 30min); Franeker (every 30min; 15min); Groningen (every 20min; 45min); Harlingen (every 30min; 25min); Hindeloopen (hourly; 45min); Sneek (every 30min; 20min); Stavoren, for Enkhuizen ferries (hourly; 55min).

By bus Buses leave from the bus station just outside the train station.
Destinations Dokkum (bus #50, #51, #54 and #60: every 30min; 30–50min); Holwerd (bus #66: hourly; 50min) for boats to Ameland; Lauwersoog (bus #50: 10 daily; 1hr 30min) for boats to Schiermonnikoog.

GETTING AROUND AND INFORMATION

Bike rental You can rent bikes from the Fietspoint next to the train station at Stationsweg 3 (☎058 213 9800, ⓦfietspointleeuwarden.nl) from €8.50/day.
Car rental AutoRent, Celsiusweg 1b (☎085 273 3631, ⓦautorent.nl).
Taxi Taxi Leeuwarden (☎0645 606 616. ⓦtaxi-leeuwarden.nl).
Tourist office The VVV is on the ground floor of the Achmea Tower, a 2min walk from the train station at Sophialaan 4 (Mon noon–5pm, Tues–Fri 9.30am–5pm, Sat 10am–4pm; ☎058 234 7550, ⓦvvvleeuwarden.nl). It publishes a map detailing walking tours of the centre and has a short list of private rooms that covers the whole of Friesland; it also dispenses information on guided boat trips to the Frisian lakes and canal trips through Leeuwarden.

ACCOMMODATION

't Anker Eewal 69–75 ☎058 212 5216, ⓦhotelhetanker.nl. Don't expect any luxury here: the 23 rooms are very basic and simple, as is the breakfast. Its location is good though, and the downstairs bar has atmosphere. It is one of the cheapest options in town, the en-suite rooms being a bit more expensive. **€69.50**
Grand Hotel Post Plaza Tweebaksmarkt 25–27 ☎058 215 9317, ⓦpost-plaza.nl. Shoehorned behind an eighteenth-century facade, this boutique hotel, with spruce rooms finished in a contemporary style, all greys and blacks, is probably Leeuwarden's best place to stay. The rooms are comfortable, and it has a restaurant and a downstairs bar plus a luxurious wellness centre. €98
De Kleine Wielen De Groene Ster 14 ☎0511 431 660, ⓦdekleinewielen.nl; bus #20 or #51 from the train station. About 5km west of Leeuwarden, this is a really nice campsite, beautifully situated by a lake with a shop, bar and snack bar, and with plenty of watersports opportunities nearby. It costs €9.50 for a tent and one person, and €4.75 for each extra adult. For a little more comfort, book a small wooden cabin for €49. April–Sept. **€14.25**

Oranje Leeuwarden Stationsweg 4 ☎058 212 6241, ⓦhampshire-hotels.com. A neat and trim four-star chain hotel right in front of the train station with spacious and comfortable rooms, fairly recently refurbished. It won't win any prizes for originality but the service is great and there's a large bar and restaurant downstairs. Excellent value. **€88**

Stadhouderlijk Hof Hofplein 29 ☎0347 750 424, ⓦhotelstadhouderlijkhof.nl. This place enjoys the best location in town, housed in a former palace with a beautiful inner courtyard. It's incredibly old-fashioned – a bit weary, even – which may not be to your taste, but it retains the grandeur of a palace and some of its rooms have been redone. There are plans to create a terrace at the front as well, though they don't seem to be in a hurry. **€99**

EATING AND DRINKING

RESTAURANTS AND CAFÉS

Eetcafé 't Goede Weerd 13 ☎058 213 6588, ⓦeetcafegoede.nl. Cute little place dishing up mains such as salmon, tenderloin and spare ribs for around €17. Even cheaper is the three-course meal with beer or wine included for €33 or the daily special for as little as €8. Wed–Sun 4.30–10pm.

Eetcafé Spinoza Eewal 50–52 ☎058 212 9393, ⓦeetcafespinoza.nl. One of the most popular places to eat in Leeuwarden, this is a youthful, reasonably priced restaurant with a wide-ranging menu of mainly hearty Dutch food. Main courses run around €15–20 but you can opt for the daily special for €9.95 and there's a good choice of veggie dishes too. The hidden inner courtyard is a well-kept treasure. Daily 10am–10pm.

Eindeloos Korfmakersstraat 17 ☎058 213 0835, ⓦrestauranteindeloos.nl. You get what you're given in this sleek, modern restaurant, with changing set menus featuring the likes of hake ceviche and Friesland lamb. Great food, always seasonal, usually locally sourced, with none of the stress of having to make up your mind – though probably not a place to come if you're in a hurry. Menus start at €37.50 for three courses. Wed–Fri lunch noon–3pm & 6–10pm, Tues–Sat dinner 6–10pm.

De Lachende Koe Grote Hoogstraat 16–20 ☎058 215 8245, ⓦdekoeleeuwarden.nl. A long-time favourite among students, this youthful and unpretentious place has a menu that caters for everyone except die-hard foodies, with all the Dutch staples – satay royal, spare ribs, schnitzels, a decent mixed grill and a couple of veggie and fish dishes, for €15–18. Or you can opt for the three-course dinner with drinks included for €25 – a bargain. Great outside yard in summer. Tues–Sun 5–10pm.

Le Sandre Eewal 54 ☎058 299 84 65, ⓦlesandre.nl. Much lauded and smart fish restaurant with daily fresh catches from the Harlingen harbour. Expect to pay around €22 for excellent cod, sole or oysters or opt for a four-course dinner for €35.50. Tues–Sat 4.30–10pm.

De Vliegende Hollander Berlikumermarkt 15 ☎058 212 1717, ⓦvliegendehollanderlwd.nl. Big place with wooden floorboards and a relaxed eetcafé ambience, a good option for both lunch or dinner, or just a drink, which you can sip on the small terrace that opens onto the secluded alley behind. Decent lunch specials for €8.50, otherwise mains go for €15–20. Mon–Thurs 4–11.30pm, Fri & Sat 11am–11.30pm.

De Walrus Gouverneursplein 37 ☎058 213 7740, ⓦdewalrus.nl. Despite being divided over three storeys, this grand café has retained an intimate feel with oodles of atmosphere plus a huge terrace to catch the late-evening sun. Lunch specials hover around €9, mains such as tournedos, Thai curry or guinea fowl around €17–19. Great for dinner but also just for drinks. Mon & Sun 11am–1am, Tues–Sat 10am–1am; kitchen until 10pm.

BARS

Fire Café Nieuwestad 47–49 ☎058 213 9900, ⓦfire-cafe.nl. Housed in a former police station (the toilets are old cells), this comfortable bar has wooden floors and cosy chairs out in the back room and a front terrace overlooking the canal. Mon–Thurs 9am–1am, Fri & Sat 9am–2am, Sun 9am–midnight.

★**Oranje Bierhuis** Auckamastraatje 2 ☎058 213 0131. Right on the Stadhuis square, this is the old centre's oldest bar, and a thoroughly welcoming place it is too, with a little corner bar and a mixed crowd who have been making themselves at home in this classic brown café for years. Mon 4–8pm, Wed–Sat 4pm–midnight.

Paddy O'Ryan Tweebaksmarkt 49 ☎058 212 2047, ⓦpaddy.nl. OK, it's an Irish bar, but you wouldn't especially know it apart from some of the beers on tap and the fact that it serves Irish stew alongside its other pubby staples. Its grandish main room is very convivial, and it's got a little glassed-in booth for those dying for a cigarette. Its excellent-value mains go for €12–15, mainly consisting of burgers, fish and chips, steaks and the like. Monday is quiz night and there's frequent live music, usually on Wednesdays. Daily noon–1am, Sat & Sun noon–2am.

Sneek

Twenty minutes by train from Leeuwarden, **SNEEK** (pronounced *snake*) was an important shipbuilding centre as early as the fifteenth century, a prosperous maritime town protected by an extensive system of walls and moats. Postwar development has robbed the place of some of its charm but there are still some buildings of interest, notably the grandiose **Waterpoort** at the end of Koemarkt, all that remains of the seventeenth-century town walls. At the beginning of August, crowds flock in for **Sneek Week**, an annual regatta, when the flat green expanses around town are thick with the white of slowly moving sails – and accommodation is almost impossible to find. The town is also known for its regional speciality, Beerenburg, a herb-flavoured gin, that you can buy at the **Weduwe Joustra shop**, at Kleinzand 32, which retains its original nineteenth-century interior, with the old barrels and till.

Martiniplein and around

Sneek's main square is **Martiniplein**, whose ponderous sixteenth-century **Martinikerk** (mid-June to mid-Sept Tues–Sat 2–4.30pm; July also Wed & Thurs 7.30–9pm) is edged by an old wooden belfry, though it's a grand, in-the-round space inside. Around the corner, the **Stadhuis**, Marktstraat 15, is all extravagance, from the Rococo facade to the fanciful outside staircase; inside there's an indifferent display of ancient weapons in the former guardroom.

The Scheepvaart Museum en Oudheidkamer

Kleinzand 16 • Mon–Sat 10am–5pm, Sun noon–5pm • €6 • ☎ 0515 414 057, ⓦ friesscheepvaartmuseum.nl

Expanded over the years to fill several adjoining canal houses, with a modern entrance hall at its centre, this museum has a large and well-displayed collection of maritime miscellanea. A film – in English – gives you a potted history of Sneek and its role in the maritime history of the country, while the same room also displays a model of the town as it would have looked in the seventeenth century. Other rooms exhibit old maps, including a lovely one of Friesland in the eighteenth century, artefacts pertaining to ice-skating and the Elfstedentocht (see p.209), lots of beautiful wooden models of sailing ships, paintings of local scenes and various recreations of domestic settings, including that of a local timber merchant.

ARRIVAL AND INFORMATION SNEEK

By train Sneek's train and bus stations are a 5min walk from the old centre, with regular services to Leeuwarden (every 20min; 20min), and in the other direction to Stavoren (hourly; 30min).

By bus Bus #98 runs hourly between Sneek and Bolsward (20min) then on to Makkum. Bus #99 runs twice per hour between Sneek and Harlingen (30min), also passing Bolsward.

Tourist office The VVV is located inside the Scheepvaart Museum at Kleinzand 16 (Mon–Sat 10am–5pm, Sun noon–5pm; ☎ 0515 750 678, ⓦ vvvsneek.nl). The staff can arrange private rooms for a small fee and give out a free map with an overview of the best ways to explore southwest Friesland, either by foot, in-line skate, horse or canoe – ⓦ routezuidwestfriesland.nl.

ACCOMMODATION

De Domp Domp 4 ☎ 0515 755 640, ⓦ dedomp.nl. Sneek's nearest campsite is 2km northeast of the centre, a right turn off the main road to Leeuwarden; no buses run near, but it's a nice waterside site with decent facilities and its own yacht-filled marina. Tents cost around €15 plus €2.25 per person. April–Oct. **€19.50**

Hostel Sneek Oude Oppenhuizerweg 17 ☎ 0515 412 132, ⓦ stayokay.com. Located on the edge of town, a 5–10min walk from the centre, this is a bright, modern, purpose-built hostel with clean public spaces and a mixture of functional dorms and private rooms. To get there on foot, head east to the end of Kleinzand, turn right down Oppenhuizerweg, and it's the first major road on the left – or take bus # 98 or #99 from the station. Dorms **€18.20**, doubles **€49**

★**Stadsherberg** Lemmerweg 8 ☎ 0515 755 750, ⓦ stadsherbergsneek.nl. This recently opened hotel is probably the best place to stay, located in a monumental building near the Waterpoort. The nine distinctive rooms with high ceilings and many original details have beautiful views over the canal, and the downstairs café serves a decent breakfast or lunch. **€95**

De Wijnberg Marktstraat 23 ☎0515 412 421, ⓦhoteldewijnberg.nl. The twenty-odd rooms are large and decent enough at this lively pub and restaurant, though the ones at the front can be a little noisy. **€88**

EATING AND DRINKING

Kastanje Grote Kerkstraat 12 ☎0515 422 387, ⓦdekastanjesneek.nl. Steaks, brill fillets and venison all feature on the menu here, with starters from €12, mains €20–30. 5–10pm; closed Tues.

Klein Java Wijde Noorderhorne 18 ☎0515 432 498, ⓦkleinjava.nl. Indonesian food served in a pleasant round, light-filled space, with a large terrace outside.

Excellent and authentic food, with *rijsttafels* from €19.75 per person and an eight-course menu from €34.75. Tues–Sun 5–10pm.

Pata Negra Kleinzand 21 ☎0515 439 678, ⓦpatanegrasneek.nl. Lively little place – especially Sunday to Thursday when you can eat as many tapas as your belly can fit in for only €18.50. Daily 5–10pm.

Sloten

With its thicket of boat masts poking out above the rooftops, it's easy to spot **SLOTEN** from afar. It's something of a museum piece, and the village's thousand inhabitants are proud to call Sloten one of Friesland's eleven "cities", and a medieval one at that. Encircled by water, it's a popular spot with Dutch and German tourists alike – the delightful central canal, **Heerenwal**, is flanked by plane trees and pavement cafés. On the bastion at Heerenwal's far end, the **De Kaai** windmill provides a sort of focus, a working mill open on Saturdays for visits (April–Sept Sat 1–5pm; Oct–March Sat 10am–12.30pm). There's also a small **museum**, in the town hall on Heerenwal (April–Oct Tues–Fri 11am–5pm, Sat & Sun 1–5pm; €3; ⓦmuseumsloten.nl), but otherwise it's just a case of wandering the cobbled alleyways and encircling bastions and admiring the gabled facades.

4

ARRIVAL AND INFORMATION
SLOTEN

By bus Reaching Sloten by public transport can be a little awkward; the easiest way is to take bus #42 from Sneek train station to the bus changeover point on the motorway at Spannenburg (takes 35min), where connecting bus #41 continues west to Sloten, while bus #44 runs to Sloten and Bolsward. Alternatively, it's a 19km bike ride from Sneek.

Tourist office The VVV is located with the museum in the town hall at Heerenwal 48 (April–Oct Tues–Fri 11am–5pm, Sat & Sun 1–5pm; July & Aug also Mon 11am–5pm; ☎0514 531 541, ⓦgaasterlandpromotion.nl), and can suggest a few places to stay.

ACCOMMODATION AND EATING

't Bolwerk Voorstreek 116–117 ☎0514 531 405, ⓦrestauranthetbolwerk.nl. Right on the canal in the centre of Sloten, with tables overlooking the water, this is a lovely spot for lunch, with a light menu of sandwiches, salads, *uitsmijters* and pancakes. The short and simple evening dinner menu features dishes like salmon, cod or steak for around €20. April–Oct daily 10am–9pm; Nov–March Wed–Fri 5–9pm, Sat & Sun 11am–9pm.

De Mallemok Baanweg 96 ☎0514 531 300, ⓦmallemok.nl. This old city farm dating back to 1822 has oodles of atmosphere and a romantic garden where you can enjoy dishes such as salmon, duck or rib roast for around €20, all prepared on a charcoal grill. June–Sept daily noon–9pm; Oct–May Thurs & Fri 4–9pm, Sat & Sun noon–9pm.

De Tjasker Iwert 17, Wijkel ☎0514 605 869, ⓦcampingdetjasker.nl. If you have your own transport, it's worth striking out 2km to neighbouring Wijckel and this friendly mini-campsite with its own thatched barn and spotless lawn. Turn left opposite the church, bear right at the first fork, follow the road round, and it's just past the cow postbox. **€12**

Stavoren

Named after the Frisian god Stavo, **STAVOREN** is the oldest town in Friesland and was once a prosperous port; it's now both the end of the train line and the departure point for **ferries** to Enkhuizen (see p.121). Strung out along the coast, Stavoren is an eclectic mix of the old and new: the harbour is flanked by modern housing while the shipyards are linked by cobbled backstreets. Popular with yachtie types, it's a great place to admire the carefully restored seventeenth- to nineteenth-century vessels that once plied the Zuider Zee, now moored up and awaiting rental. On a sunny day, watching the old wooden ships go by and listening to the clink of halyards is as an enjoyable pastime as any. At the southern end of town, massive, squat turbines encased in glass can be seen pumping water out of Friesland and into the IJsselmeer.

ARRIVAL AND INFORMATION   STAVOREN

By train Stavoren's train station is by the harbour and is the terminus of the line that runs to Sneek and Leeuwarden: trains run roughly hourly.

By ferry In season (May–Sept) there are three ferry sailings daily between Stavoren and Enkhuizen at 10.10am, 2.10pm and 6.10pm. Mid-April to late April and Oct ferries run twice daily (10.10am & 5.10pm) but only on weekends and school holidays. The journey takes 1hr 35min. Fares are

€11 one way, day returns €15; €5.30 for bikes. See ⓦ veerboot.info for more information.

Tourist office The Tourist Info Point is on the harbour at Stationsweg 7, a 2min walk from the train station (May–Sept Mon–Sat 9.30am–noon & 1.30–6pm, Sun 9.30am–10.30am, 1.30–2.30pm & 5.30–6pm; ☏ 0514 682 424, ⓦ stavoren.nl); it has details of pensions and private rooms.

ACCOMMODATION AND EATING

Doede's Vishandel Smidstraat 21. A takeaway with a few indoor seats, dishing up tasty fish and chips and lots of other fishy favourites for €5 or less. Mon–Sat 11am–6pm, Sun noon–6pm.

De Vrouwe van Stavoren Havenweg 1 ☏ 0514 681 202, ⓦ hotel-vrouwevanstavoren.nl. Attractively sited

right on the harbour, this is Stavoren's best place to stay, with twenty rooms in a variety of shapes and sizes; if you're not claustrophobic, try sleeping in one of its converted wine-barrels. The restaurant is excellent and well priced, with a dinner menu of good steaks and excellent fish mains at about €20 each. Restaurant daily 10am–10pm. **€70**

Hindeloopen

The exquisitely pretty village of **HINDELOOPEN** juts into the IJsselmeer, and is very much on the tour-bus trail. Outside high summer, however, and in the evening when most visitors have gone home, it's peaceful and very enticing, a tidy jigsaw of old streets, canals and wooden bridges that are almost too twee to be true.

Its attractive **church**, a seventeenth-century structure with a wonky medieval tower, has some graves of British airmen who perished in the Zuider Zee, while the small village museum beside the church, the **Museum Hindeloopen** (April–Oct Mon–Fri

---

THE PAINTED FURNITURE OF HINDELOOPEN

Until the seventeenth century, Hindeloopen prospered as a Zuider Zee **port**, concentrating on trade with the Baltic and Amsterdam. The combination of rural isolation and trade created a specific culture within this tightly knit community, with a distinctive dialect (Hylper–Frisian with Scandinavian influences) and sumptuous local **dress**. Adopting materials imported into Amsterdam by the East India Company, the women of Hindeloopen dressed in a florid combination of colours where dress was a means of personal identification: caps, casques and trinkets indicated marital status and age, and the quality of the print indicated social standing. Other Dutch villages adopted similar practices, but nowhere were the details of social position more precisely drawn. However, the development of dress turned out to be a corollary of prosperity, for the decline of Hindeloopen quite simply finished it off. Similarly, the local **painted furniture** showed an ornate mixture of Scandinavian and Oriental styles superimposed on traditional Dutch carpentry. Each item was covered from top to bottom with painted tendrils and flowers on a red, green or white background, but the town's decline resulted in the collapse of the craft. Tourism has revived local furniture-making, and countless shops now line the main street selling modern versions, though even the smallest items aren't cheap, and the florid style is something of an acquired taste.

11am–5pm, Sat & Sun 1.30–5pm; €5; ⓦmuseumhindeloopen.nl), displays examples of Hindeloopen's unusual furniture (see box opposite).

Schaats Museum

Kleine Weide 1 • Mon–Sat 10am–6pm & Sun 1–5pm • €3 • ⓦ schaatsmuseum.nl

The small **Schaats Museum** is the best kind of local museum, packed full of stuff, lovingly presented, that's utterly unique to its location. It displays skating mementoes relating to the great Frisian ice-skating race "De Friese Elfstedentocht" (see box, p.209), as well as further exhibits on skating in general. Upstairs is plenty of Hindeloopen's unique painted furniture, which is also for sale in the museum shop.

ARRIVAL AND INFORMATION

HINDELOOPEN

By train Hindeloopen is on the Leeuwarden–Stavoren line, with connections roughly hourly: its train station is a 20min walk east of the village centre.

By bus Bus #102 runs to Workum and on to Makkum (Mon–Fri every 2 hr).

By bike From Workum, it's just 6km to Hindeloopen, a pleasant, well-signposted bike ride across fields, past a

windmill and along a dyke. It's a popular route with families as it steers clear of busy roads.

Tourist office Hindeloopen Tourist Info Point is at Nieuwstad 26 (daily 10.30am–3.30pm in summer, irregular hours out of season; ☎0514 851 223, ⓦ touristinfohindeloopen.nl), and can organize the odd private room.

ACCOMMODATION

Camping Hindeloopen Westerdijk 9 ☎0514 521 452, ⓦ campinghindeloopen.nl. Just a kilometre or so south of the village near the coast, this site is set back from the IJsselmeer behind the sea dyke. It's got lots of facilities – shop, restaurant, bike rental, tennis and other sports, and you can go windsurfing on the lake too. April–Oct. €24.50

★**Likhus** Tuinen 5–7 ☎0514 523 208, ⓦhylperhuis.nl. By far the most charming option is this old tiny house that once served as a residence for the wives and children of ships' captains when they were at sea; the entire place is decorated in old Hindeloopen style. It may seem pricey, but the rate

includes champagne, flowers and a DIY breakfast. €250

Pension de Twee Hondjes Paardepad 2 ☎0514 522 873, ⓦdetweehondjes.nl. Right in the heart of the village, this cosy place has five rooms, including two family-sized options, plus free wi-fi and bikes to rent. €80

De Stadsboerderij Nieuwe Weide 7–9 ☎0514 521 278, ⓦwww.destadsboerderij.nl. Part of the *De Brabander* restaurant (see below), this place is right in the centre of Hindeloopen and has simply furnished double rooms at excellent prices. It also runs sailing trips and rents out boats. €78

EATING

De Brabander Nieuwe Weide 7–9 ☎0514 521 278, ⓦwww.hcrdebrabander.nl. Very friendly bar and restaurant that has rooms attached (see above), a garden out the back and serves drinks and a plain but wholesome menu of Dutch dishes for under €20 and *dagschotels* for around €10. Occasional live music, too. April–Sept daily

noon–2pm & 4–9pm; Oct–March Tues–Sat 4–9pm.

Oost Achterom Kalverstraat 13 ☎0514 522 053, ⓦoostachterom.nl. This is a lovely and quite intimate place to enjoy Italian food on the terrace in the evening, just off the harbour. Pizzas €6–14, pasta dishes from €8. Wed–Sun 5–9pm.

Workum

Heavily protected by its sea defences, the town of **WORKUM**, ten minutes southwest of Sneek by train, is a very pleasant place that was until the early eighteenth century a busy seaport. It has a bustling main street and a pretty central square anchored by a seventeenth-century **Waag**, at Merk 4. This is now home to both the tourist office and a small museum exhibiting a standard nautical-historical collection (March Tues–Sat 1.30–5pm; April–Oct Mon, Tues & Sun 1.30–5pm, Wed–Sat 10am–5pm; €3). Immediately behind is Friesland's largest medieval church, the **St Gertrudiskerk** (April–Oct Mon–Sat 11am–5pm), with its enormous stand-alone bell tower and small collection of mostly eighteenth-century odds and ends inside.

Jopie Huisman Museum

Noard 6 • April–Oct Mon–Sat 10am–5pm, Sun 1–5pm; mid-Feb to March & Nov–Dec daily 1–5pm • €7.50 • ⓦ jopiehuismanmuseum.nl

On the opposite side of the square from the church, the likeable **Jopie Huisman Museum** is a sleek modern space devoted to the work of the eponymous local artist who died in 2000. The art on display includes ink drawings, watercolours and paintings – graphic depictions of local people, landscapes and most uniquely the discarded objects of everyday life. Perhaps best is his self-portrait rolling a cigarette.

ARRIVAL AND INFORMATION
WORKUM

By train Workum's station, 2km from the town's main square, is on the main Leeuwarden to Stavoren line, with trains roughly every hour.

By bus Bus #102 runs between Workum, Makkum and Hindeloopen every two hours during the week.

Tourist office The Tourist Info Point is located in the old Waag at Merk 4 (April–Oct Mon & Sun 1.30–5pm, Tues–Sat 10am–5pm; ☏ 0515 541 045, ⓦ vanharteworkum.nl), and has a list of private rooms in the area.

ACCOMMODATION AND EATING

Aan de Wymerts Noard 37 ☏ 0515 540 004, ⓦ hotelaandewymerts.nl. Tucked away off Workum's main street, this is very convenient and very well run, with a cool, contemporary feel and spick-and-span modern rooms. **€109**

Herberg van Oom Lammert & Tante Klaasje Merk 3 ☏ 0515 541 370, ⓦ oomlammertentanteklaasje.nl. It may be a bit cheesy, but sleeping in a *bedstee* (something of an elevated closet, Frisian style) inside a little wooden cabin sure is authentic and relatively cheap. **€65**

It Pottebakkershûs Merk 18 ☏ 0515 541 900, ⓦ itpottebakkershus.nl. One of the most appealing

places to eat in the centre of Workum, right opposite the main square, with short menus of tasty veggie and fish dishes for €19–21, good coffee and high teas. The place doubles as a ceramics factory with a permanent exhibition of antique local pottery. July & Aug daily 10am–9pm; Sept–June Mon & Tues 10am–6pm & Wed–Sun 10am–9pm.

It Soal Suderséleane 29 ☏ 0515 541 443, ⓦ itsoal.nl. This beautifully situated campsite is located right on the IJsselmeer, 3km south of the centre, and has its own beach, marina and lots of opportunities for watersports. April–Oct. **€21**

Bolsward

Some 10km west of Sneek, **BOLSWARD** (pronounced *bozwurt*) was founded in the seventh century and became a bustling and important textile centre in the Middle Ages, though its subsequent decline was prolonged and deep. It's less touristy than the surrounding towns, with a busy and attractive central street, Marktstraat, bisected by a canal, and a couple of especially handsome old buildings.

The Stadhuis

Jongemastraat 2 • April–Oct Tues–Fri 1.30–4.30pm • Free

Your first stop should be the **Stadhuis**, a magnificent red-brick, stone-trimmed Renaissance edifice of 1613. The facade is topped by a lion holding a coat of arms over

---

MUSEUMROUTE ALDFAERSERF

Choosing the scenic route south from Workum to Makkum (see opposite) takes you along the **Museumroute Aldfaerserf**, in which the villages of Allingawier, Exmorra and others serve as open-air museums illustrating Frisian life in the eighteenth and nineteenth centuries. Historic buildings have been restored and refurbished, regaining their historical functions as bakeries, carpenters' shops, farms and smithies, and the 25km route can be done by car or bicycle. Bikes can be rented at the museum route's base at Meerweg 4 in Allingawier (April–Oct Tues–Sun 10am–5pm; €5; ☏ 0515 231 631, ⓦ aldfaerserf.nl).

the head of a terrified Turk, and below a mass of twisting, curling carved stone frames a series of finely cut cameos, all balanced by an extravagant external staircase. Inside there's a small **museum** holding local historical bits and pieces.

The Martinikerk

Groot Kerkhof • May–Sept Mon–Fri 10am–noon & 2–4pm; Oct–April Mon–Fri 2–4pm

Five minutes' walk away from Bolsward's main street, the fifteenth-century **Martinikerk** was originally built on an earthen mound for protection from flooding. Some of the woodcarving inside is quite superb, particularly the choir with its rare misericords from 1470 and the seventeenth-century pulpit, carved from a single oak tree. Its panels depict the four seasons: the Frisian baptism dress above the young eagle symbolizes spring and the carved ice skates, winter. The stone font dates from around 1000 AD, while the stained-glass windows at the back depict the German occupation of World War II and subsequent liberation by the Canadians.

The Friese Bierbrouwerij

Snekerstraat 43 • Thurs & Fri 3–6pm; guided tour at 4pm; Sat 10am–6pm, guided tours hourly • €8.50, drink included • ☏ 0515 577 449, ⓦ bierbrouwerij-usheit.nl

A ten-minute walk from the centre of town, Bolsward is also home to the **Friese Bierbrouwerij**, one of the smallest breweries in the country, producing eight different kinds of "Us Heit" beer and several "Frysk" whiskies. Regular tours of the building take you through a small museum and demonstrate the basics of the production process before you're allowed to sample the product in the clubby *proeflokaal* upstairs.

ARRIVAL AND INFORMATION

BOLSWARD

By bus Buses stop on Bolsward's main street. Services include bus #99 from Sneek train station, which runs on to Harlingen, and bus #98 from Makkum, which runs on to Sneek (both every 30min).

Tourist office Bolsward's Tourist Info Point is located in the small Gysbert Japicxhus museum at Wipstraat 6 (April–Sept Mon 1.30–5pm, Tues–Fri 9am–12.30pm & 1.30–5pm, Sat noon–4pm; hours vary out of season; ☏ 0515 577 701, ⓦ fryslansudwest.nl). It has details of a handful of private rooms.

ACCOMMODATION AND EATING

★**Het Weeshuis** Kerkstraat 53 ☏ 0515 855 666, ⓦ hotelhetweeshuis.nl. Housed in a former orphanage, and with a pleasant garden and courtyard, this is a great-value and very peaceful hotel, a 5min walk from Bolsward's main street, near the church. Rooms are small apartments really, with a sitting room, kitchenette and separate bedrooms. There's free parking and a decent restaurant with a daily-changing menu for €27.50. €80

De Wijnberg Marktplein 5 ☏ 0515 572 220, ⓦ wijnbergbolsward.nl. You can't get more central than this big, busy bar with a terrace right on Marktplein. There are 29 rooms upstairs, all nicely furnished and reasonably up to date decor-wise; and if there's a slightly institutional feel upstairs it's more than offset by the lively bar and restaurant on the ground floor, serving an all-day menu of tapas, croquettes, sandwiches and burgers from around €7.50, plus steaks for €15. €75

Makkum

Just 10km west of Bolsward, **MAKKUM** is a very agreeable place, a collection of immaculate houses, church towers and canals, cobbled streets and wooden boats that's saved from postcard-prettiness by a working harbour. It's long been a centre for the manufacture of traditional, high-end Dutch **ceramics** and is a bit of a magnet for coach parties in summer, as well as a year-round sailing centre, though it never feels overwhelmed.

ARRIVAL AND INFORMATION
MAKKUM

By bus Makkum is served by bus #102 from Workum train station and Hindeloopen beyond (Mon–Fri every 2hr), as well as by the much more frequent bus #98 from Bolsward.
Tourist office Makkum's Tourist Info Point is in the old Waag

at Pruikmakershoek 2 (April, May, Sept & Oct Mon, Tues, Thurs & Fri 10am–noon & 1–3pm; June–Aug Mon–Fri 10am–noon & 1–5pm, Sat 10am–3pm; ☎ 0900 540 0001, ⓦ hetfriesehart.nl.nl), and can arrange private rooms for free.

ACCOMMODATION AND EATING

It Posthus Plein 15 ☎ 0515 231 153, ⓦ itposthus.nl. Housed in an old post office, this is definitely the best place to eat, with mains such as veal, steak and haddock for €19.50 and a decent wine selection. The setting is bright and contemporary, service very friendly and the terrace outside is a lovely place to eat if it's warm enough. Thurs–Sun 4.30–9pm; July & Aug daily 10.30am–9pm.

★**Villa Mar** DL Touwenlaan 5 ☎ 0515 232 469, ⓦ villa-mar.com. There's probably no better place to stay in Makkum than this tastefully renovated old villa

with large, beautifully furnished rooms that have nice bathrooms, a huge kitchen for communal use with a roaring fire that's lit most nights in winter and a lush garden. And the lovely German lady owner rustles up a decent breakfast. €100

De Waag Markt 13 ☎ 0515 231 447, ⓦ hoteldewaagmakkum.nl. Right in the centre of Makkum, this is a welcoming place with fourteen plainish but fairly recently renovated rooms and a nice bar and restaurant downstairs. €70

Harlingen

Thirty kilometres west of Leeuwarden and just north of the Afsluitdijk, **HARLINGEN** is a compelling stop and serves as the ferry terminus for the islands of Terschelling and Vlieland. It's something of a centre for traditional Dutch **sailing barges**, a number of which are usually moored in the harbour. It was a naval base from the seventeenth century onwards, and abuts the Vliestroom channel, once the easiest way for ships to pass from the North Sea through the shallows that surround the Frisian islands and on into the Zuider Zee. Before trade moved west, this was the country's lifeline, where cereals, fish and other foodstuffs were brought in from the Baltic to feed the expanding Dutch cities, and it was also once a centre for the ceramics industry. Its historic importance is reflected in a fine old centre of sixteenth- to eighteenth-century houses, sandwiched between the pretty Noorderhaven and the more functional Zuiderhaven canals. However, Harlingen is too busy to be a twee tourist town: there's a fishing fleet, a small container depot and a shipbuilding yard.

The heart of Harlingen is **Voorstraat**, a long, tree-lined avenue in between Harlingen's two main harbours, Zuiderhaven and Noorderhaven – the latter home to the elegant eighteenth-century **Stadhuis** which faces the water.

Harlinger Aardewerk en Tegelfabriek

Voorstraat 84 • Mon–Fri 8am–6pm, Sat 9am–5pm • ☎ 0517 415 362, ⓦ harlinger.nl

This workshop is worth a peek for its modern-day ceramics, examples of Harlingen's traditional and now resurgent ceramics business, which flourished until tiles were undermined by the rise of wallpaper. The last of the old factories closed in 1933, but the demand for traditional crafts led to something of a recovery, and the opening of new workshops during the 1970s.

The Hannemahuis Museum

Voorstraat 56 • Tues–Fri 11am–5pm, Sat & Sun 1.30–5pm • €5 • ☎ 0517 413 658, ⓦ hannemahuis.nl

Sited in an eighteenth-century merchant's house, the **Hannemahuis** museum concentrates, as you would expect, on Harlingen's long and distinguished, mostly maritime history, and includes some interesting displays on shipping. It also displays seascapes and other paintings by local artists, as well as a lovely array of locally produced tiles.

ARRIVAL AND INFORMATION

By train Trains from Leeuwarden stop on the south side of town at Harlingen's main train station, a 5–10min walk from Voorstraat; there's a second station, Harlingen Haven, right next to the docks.

By ferry Ferries leave for the islands of Vlieland and Terschelling from the dock at the seaward end of Noorderhaven five to six times a day during summer. Cars are not allowed on Vlieland: for more details, check ⓦ rederij-doeksen.nl.

Tourist office Harlingen's VVV is at Grote Bredeplaats 12, a westerly extension of Voorstraat (Mon–Sat 10am–5pm; ☎ 0517 430 207, ⓦ harlingen-friesland.nl): it has a sizeable list of rooms and pensions, many of which are on Noorderhaven.

ACCOMMODATION

Anna Casparii Noorderhaven 67–71 ☎ 0517 412 065, ⓦ annacasparii.nl. Located in three historical buildings, with a cosy lobby, classy restaurant and canalside terrace (see below), this place has one of the best locations in town: the rooms are large and comfortable if blandly furnished, with the best ones boasting views over the Noorderhaven. **€85**

Hotel Almenum Harlingen Kruisstraat 8–14 ☎ 0625 031 173, ⓦ hotelalmenum.nl. Converted from a seventeenth-century warehouse, this has a comfortable and nicely furnished range of budget rooms and apartments, and is a 5min walk from the end of Voorstraat. **€80**

Hotel de Eilanden Noorderhaven 24 ☎ 0517 210 002, ⓦ hoteldeeilanden.nl. Recently opened little boutique hotel with only seven rooms, all very stylishly decorated with lots of wood and beamed ceilings. No reception or breakfast room – for that you need to head towards nearby *Hotel Zeezicht* (see below). **€110**

Hotel Zeezicht Zuiderhaven 1 ☎ 0517 412 536, ⓦ hotelzeezicht.nl. A friendly place, right on the harbour; the best of its 27 rooms are those at the top, which have been refurbished and have nice sea views. **€120**

De Zeehoeve Westerzeedijk 45 ☎ 0517 413 465, ⓦ zeehoeve.nl. Harlingen's nearest campsite is a 20min walk along the sea dyke to the south of town – follow the signs from Voorstraat. April–Sept. **€20**

EATING AND DRINKING

Anna Casparii Noorderhaven 67–71 ☎ 0517 412 065, ⓦ annacasparii.nl. Perhaps the best restaurant in town, with a great range of fish dishes – Dover sole, perch, monkfish – along with steaks, lamb rumps and so on, for €21–25. Daily noon–2pm & 5–9pm.

't Noorderke Noorderhaven 17–19 ☎ 0517 415 043, ⓦ hetnoorderke.nl. At the seaward end of Noorderhaven, this place does good-value daily specials – herring in season, plus baked mussels, sole fillets, steaks, goulash, spare ribs and the like – and a view of the boats passing by

THE ELFSTEDENTOCHT

The **Elfstedentocht** ("Eleven Towns Race") is Friesland's biggest spectacle, a gruelling **ice-skating** marathon around Friesland that dates back to 1890, when one Pim Muller, a local sports journalist, skated his way around the eleven official towns of the province, simply to see whether it was possible. It was, and twenty years later the first official Elfstedentocht was launched, contested by 22 skaters. Weather – and ice – permitting, it has taken place just fifteen times in the last hundred years, most recently in 1997, attracting skaters from all over the world.

The race is organized by the Eleven Towns Association, of which you must be a member to take part; the high level of interest in the race means that membership is very difficult to obtain. The route, which measures about 200km in total, takes in all the main centres of Friesland, starting in Leeuwarden. The first stop is Sneek, after which the race takes in Hindeloopen and the other old Zuider Zee towns, plus Dokkum in the north of the province, before finishing back in Leeuwarden. The event is broadcast live on national TV, the route lined with spectators. Of the 17,000 or so people who take part, usually no more than three hundred are professional skaters. Casualties are inevitably numerous; the worst year was 1963, when 10,000 skaters took part and only seventy finished, the rest beaten by the fierce winds, extreme cold and snowdrifts along the way. Generally, however, something like three-quarters of the competitors make it to the finishing line.

If you're not around for the race itself, the route makes a popular bike ride and is signposted by the ANWB (Royal Dutch Touring Club) as one of its national cycling routes; four or five days will allow enough time to sightsee as well as cycle There's more information on ⓦ nederlandfietsland.nl.

4

from the terrace. Mains go for €18–24. Mon–Thurs 10am–midnight, Fri & Sat 10am–1am, Sun 11am–midnight.

De Tjotter Sint Jacobstraat 1–3 ☎0517 414 691, ⓦdetjotter.nl. Right on one corner of Noorderhaven, this is both a café and a smarter restaurant, with fish snacks and *broodjes* in the café for upwards of €3, as well as fried fish, sole and mussel plates from €9.50. Next door, in the restaurant, the more expensive dinner menu features wonderful oysters, fish soup and cod and monkfish mains for €20–26, with a few meat and veggie options too. Mon & Sun 1–10pm, Tues–Sat noon–10pm.

Franeker

FRANEKER, about 17km west of Leeuwarden, was the cultural hub of the northern Netherlands until Napoleon closed its university in 1810. Today, it's a quiet country town with a spruce old centre, the highlight of which is an intriguing eighteenth-century planetarium.

All Franeker's key sights are beside or near the main street, **Voorstraat**, which runs east–west and ends in the **Sternse Slotland** park – site of a medieval castle. Near the park is the **Waag** of 1657 and, east along Voorstraat, the **Museum Martena** (Tues–Sun 11am–5pm; €5; ⓦmuseummartena.nl) in the old **Martenahuis** of 1498, with bits and pieces relating to the former university and its (obscure) alumni. Past the Martenahuis, on the left, the **Stadhuis** (Wed–Fri 1–5pm; free), with its twin gables and octagonal tower, is a magnificent mixture of Gothic and Renaissance styles built in 1591 and is worth a peek upstairs for the leather-clad walls – all the rage until French notions of wallpaper took hold in the eighteenth century.

The Planetarium

Eise Eisingastraat 3 • Tues–Sat 10am–5pm, Sun 1–5pm; April–Oct also Mon 1–5pm • €4.75 • ☎0517 393 070, ⓦplanetarium-friesland.nl

Most people visit Franeker for its fascinating eighteenth-century **planetarium** opposite the town hall. Now the oldest working planetarium in the world, it was built by a local woolcomber, Eise Eisinga. Born in 1744, Eisinga was something of a prodigy: he taught himself mathematics and astronomy, and published a weighty arithmetic book when aged only 17. In 1774, the unusual conjunction of Mercury, Venus, Mars and Jupiter under the sign of Aries prompted a local paper to predict the end of the world. There was panic in the countryside, and an appalled Eisinga embarked on the construction of his planetarium, completed in 1781, in order to dispel superstition by demystifying the workings of the cosmos.

The planetarium isn't of the familiar domed variety but was built as a false ceiling in the family's living room, a series of rotating dials and clocks indicating the movement of the planets and associated phenomena, from tides to star signs. The whole apparatus is regulated by a clock, driven by a series of weights hung in a tiny alcove beside a half-size cupboard-bed. Above the face of the main dials, the mechanisms – hundreds of handmade nails driven into moving slats – are open for inspection. Beyond, a series of rooms in both the original house and the building next door have displays on Eisinga's work – you can see reproductions of his notebooks as well as the works of other venerable astronomers in the lovely garden room. A detailed guidebook explains every aspect of the place, and there are regular tours and an explanatory film (sometimes in English).

ARRIVAL AND INFORMATION

By train Franeker is on the Harlingen–Leeuwarden line and there are usually two trains an hour in each direction. The train station is a 5min walk southeast of the centre: follow Stationsweg round to the left and over the bridge, first left over the second bridge onto Zuiderkade and second right along Dijkstraat to reach the town.

By bus There are regular buses to Leeuwarden and Harlingen, and they drop off passengers on Kleijenburg, at the northwest corner of the old town centre.

Tourist office Franeker's Tourist Info Point is inside the Museum Martena on Voorstraat (Tues–Sun 11am–5pm; ☎0517 392 192, ⓦbeleeffriesland.nl).

ACCOMMODATION AND EATING

Bloemketerp Burg. J. Dijkstraweg 3 ☎ 0517 395 099, ⓦ bloemketerp.nl. A 10min walk north of the station – head up Stationsweg, Oud Kaatsveld and Leeuwarderweg, then turn left – Franeker's campsite is a nice waterside site with lots of facilities, including a pool, tennis courts and canoes and bikes for rent. **€24.50**

De Doelen Breedeplaats 6 ☎ 0517 383 256, ⓦ dedoelen-franeker.nl. The most central option and although the rooms feel a bit plain and corporate, they're well equipped and have all the mod cons you need. In the sleek downstairs bar and restaurant, you can choose from a wide-ranging menu with main courses such as salmon, veal escalope or cauliflower curry for €15–20. Mon–Thurs & Sun 11am–11pm, Fri & Sat 11am–1am. **€80**

De Grillerije Groenmarkt 14 ☎ 0517 395 7044, ⓦ grillerije.nl. This upmarket, canalside, mainly French restaurant offers main courses such as lamb racks, catch of the day and mixed grill for around €20 in a lovely, eclectically decorated modern interior. Tues–Sun 5–10pm.

Planetarium Café Eise Eisingastraat 2 ☎ 0517 382 106. Beside the planetarium, the building dates back to 1745 and has fine wooden counters, a mosaic floor and original coffee cabinets from 1910, as well as an attractive back garden. And its short menu of soups, salads and sandwiches is always good. Tues–Sat 10am–5pm, Sun 11am–5pm; April–Sept also Mon noon–5pm.

De Stadsherberg Oude Kaatsveld 8 ☎ 0517 392 686, ⓦ stadsherbergfraneker.nl. Situated next to the canal on the continuation of Stationsweg, this is the pick of Franeker's small choice of hotels, a friendly place with ten neat and trim rooms, and a decent restaurant downstairs. **€97.50**

Dokkum

The one significant settlement hereabouts, the town of **DOKKUM**, about 26km northeast of Leeuwarden, made a name for itself when its early pagan inhabitants murdered the English missionary St Boniface and 52 of his companions here in 754. In part still walled and moated, Dokkum has kept its shape as a fortified town, and is best appreciated by the side of the Grootdiep canal, which cuts the town into two distinct sections. This was the commercial centre of the old town and is marked by a series of ancient gables, including that of the **Admiraliteitshuis** which serves as the town's **museum** (Mon–Sat 1–5pm; €4; ⓦ museumdokkum.nl). There's not much else to see beyond a couple of windmills, quiet walks along the old ramparts and all sorts of things named after St Boniface as penance for the locals' early misdeeds. But there are a couple of nice places to stay, and it makes a good base for some *wadlopen* (see p.220), or if you just want to experience small-town Dutch life in one of Friesland's pleasantest provincial centres.

ARRIVAL AND INFORMATION

DOKKUM

By bus Bus #50, #51, #54 and #60 run between Dokkum and Leeuwarden (hours vary but generally every 30min; 30–50min), and there are also buses to Wierum and Moddergat (Mon–Fri 9 daily; Sat & Sun you need to call at least 1hr in advance ☎ 0800 280 2803; 25–35min).

Tourist office The town no longer has an official VVV but the Admiraliteitshuis (see above) doubles as a tourist information point (Mon–Sat 1–5pm; ☎ 0519 293 134) and can help you find accommodation or organize boat trips.

Boat trips Historical tour through the Dokkumer canals; reservations at the tourist information point (April–Oct; Tues, Thurs & Sat 2pm; €5, children free).

ACCOMMODATION

★ De Abdij van Dokkum Markt 30 ☎ 0519 220 422, ⓦ abdij.nl. The top hotel choice in Dokkum, with lovely rooms in the main building – a former abbey – and slightly cheaper ones in the modern annexe next door; many of them are themed according to the eleven Frisian "cities". There's also a great bar and highly recommended downstairs, restaurant serving regional dishes and French classics such as chateaubriand. **€85**

Harddraverspark Harddraversdijk 1a ☎ 0519 294 445, ⓦ campingdokkum.nl. Dokkum's closest campsite is just a 5min walk east of the centre, and is a well-organized site, with good shelter. Not big on facilities though, so just as well it's so near town. **€14**

De Posthoorn Diepswal 21 ☎ 0519 293 500, ⓦ hotel-deposthoorn.nl. This hotel enjoys the town's best position, right on the canal. The rooms are elegantly decorated, good-sized, and pretty good value, either in the main building or in the annexe two doors down. There's also a restaurant with a terrace overlooking the water. **€90**

EATING AND DRINKING

D'Angelo Hoogstraat 27 ☎ 0519 295 097, ⓦ dangelodokkum.nl. Popular pizza joint with kitschy interior and matching frescoes on the walls. The menu boasts eighty different pizzas ranging €8–14, but you can also choose from a decent range of pastas and meat or fish specialities. Nice terrace in summer. Wed–Sun 4–10pm.

De Koffiebranderij Legeweg 5 ☎ 0519 220 045, ⓦ eetcafedekoffiebranderij.nl. Located in a beautifully restored monumental building, this café is known for its great pancakes (around €8) and many coffee varieties. Try the *Dokkumer* coffee with local liquor – a real treat. Next door is a tiny shop selling local products. Mon–Thurs & Sat–Sun 10am–8pm, Fri 10am–9pm.

Stadscafé Artisante Diepswal 1 ☎ 06 5130 8662, ⓦ stadscafe-artisante.nl. Trendy place with lots of wood and industrial artefacts right on the corner of the canal. A three-course menu featuring monkfish, rib-eye or tournedos will set you back €27.50, or there are daily specials for around €20. Kitchen Mon & Sun noon–9pm, Tues–Sat 10am–9pm.

Moddergat and Wierum

Of all the tiny hamlets in north Friesland, two of the most interesting lie on the Waddenzee. **MODDERGAT**, the more easterly of the two, spreads out along the road behind the sea wall 10km northeast of Dokkum, merging with the village of **Paesens**. At its western edge, a memorial commemorates the 1883 tragedy when seventeen ships sank during a storm, with the loss of 83 lives. Opposite, 't Fiskerhuske Museum, Fiskerpad 4–8 (mid-Feb to Oct Mon–Sat 10am–5pm; July & Aug also Sun 1–5pm; €4; ⓦ museummoddergat.nl), comprises three restored fishermen's cottages with displays on the history and culture of the village and details of the disaster: as such small museums go, it's pretty good.

Huddled behind the sea dyke 5km to the west, **WIERUM** has one main claim to fame, its twelfth-century church with a saddle-roof tower and (as in Moddergat) a golden ship on the weather vane. The dyke offers views across to the islands and holds a monument of twisted anchors to the fishermen who died in the 1883 storm and the dozen or so claimed in the century after.

ARRIVAL AND DEPARTURE   MODDERGAT AND WIERUM

By bus Moddergat and Wierum can be reached by bus #52 from Dokkum (Mon–Fri 9 daily; Sat & Sun you need to call at least an hour in advance ☎ 0800 280 2803; 25–35min).

By bike If you've rented a bicycle from Leeuwarden and ridden to Dokkum, follow the signposted cycleway; it's around 12km to Moddergat and a few kilometres more to Wierum.

ACCOMMODATION

Recreatiebedrijf Meinsma Meinsmaweg 5 Moddergat ☎ 0519 589 396, ⓦ recreatiebedrijfmeinsma.nl. This farmhouse pension has six double rooms and a small adjacent campsite with twelve pitches as well as three self-contained four-person bungalows. It's very friendly and in a great location, too. Rooms €59, bungalows €55, tents €15

The Frisian Islands

The four **Frisian islands** preserve an unexpected sense of wilderness in so populated a country: low-lying sandbanks with mile upon mile of hourglass-fine sandy beaches and well-developed networks of cycleways. A tourist magnet in summertime, busy and developed **Terschelling** is large enough to swallow the holiday crowds, while car-free **Vlieland** resembles a grass-covered dunescape and is popular with young families. Both can be reached from Harlingen, while the access point for busy **Ameland** is the port of Holwerd. The smallest of the four islands is **Schiermonnikoog**; this can be reached from Leeuwarden and Dokkum, but the shorter route there is from neighbouring Groningen. One way of reaching the islands is by indulging in **wadlopen**, a hearty walk at low tide across – and often knee-deep in – the mud flats that lie between the islands

and the mainland. See p.220 for ways to do this, but don't attempt it without a qualified guide. The islands have a wide range of **accommodation**, particularly Terschelling and Ameland, but prices rise dramatically in summer, when vacant rooms can be thin on the ground, and you should also always reserve ahead if you're visiting in July or August, or indeed at any time during the summer.

Vlieland

Compared with its closest neighbour, Terschelling, **VLIELAND** is very low-key. All but car-free, it has just one settlement, **Oost-Vlieland**, which has most of the amenities you might need: in fact, it's little more than a tree-lined street with a string of pavement cafés, bike rental agencies and a few hotels and B&Bs. Historically isolated by a complex pattern of sandbanks, the island was of minor importance during the Zuider Zee trade; indeed its only other village was swept away by the sea in the eighteenth century and never rebuilt. These days, there's not much to do but enjoy the country walks and relax along the 12km of sandy beach – a sedate lifestyle that is popular with Dutch families, who load up their bikes with panniers, tents, children and animals, and head for one of the island's campsites. To explore the island's woods and dunes, follow one of the many **bike** routes that run the length of the island, passing close to the wide sandy beach that runs along the north shore. The tourist office can provide you with details in English of two main cycle routes, and there are also plenty of marked **walking** trails.

Centrum "De Noordwester"

Dorpsstraat 150, Oost-Vlieland • July & Aug Mon–Fri 10am–5pm, Sat 2–5pm & Sun 1–4pm; hours vary out of season • €5 • ⓦ denoordwester.nl

Oost-Vlieland is home to a maritime centre mainly geared towards children and displaying an assortment of shells, an explanation of dune formation and a couple of aquariums housing crabs and rays. It also boasts an unexpected elf forest, though information is in Dutch only.

ARRIVAL AND DEPARTURE

VLIELAND

By bus A limited bus service runs along the southern shore from near the ferry terminus.

By ferry Ferries from Harlingen (see p.209) dock at the east end of the island in the village of Oost-Vlieland. There are crossings at least three times a day in summer and twice daily in winter; the journey takes 1hr 45min. A return fare is around €25, plus around €14 for a bike. There's also a fast hydrofoil service from Harlingen (May–Sept 8 weekly, Oct–April 5 weekly), which costs €23 one way but saves you an hour each way in travelling time – perfect for

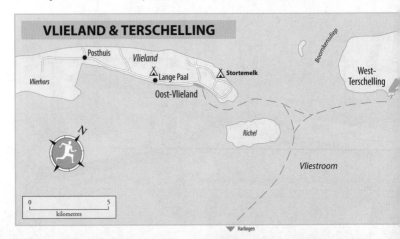

VLIELAND & TERSCHELLING

Posthuis

Vlieland

Vlierhors

Lange Paal

Stortemelk

Oost-Vlieland

West-Terschelling

Boomkensdiep

Richel

Vliestroom

0   5
kilometres

Harlingen

day-trips. In addition, a ferry runs between Terschelling and Vlieland, twice a day in summer, for which tickets cost £8.15 one way (plus roughly the same again for a bike). Check ⓦ rederij-doeksen.nl for the latest schedules and information. You can also travel between Texel and Vlieland twice daily in July and August and three times a week in May, June and September (€18.50 one way, plus €10 for

bikes); see ⓦ waddenveer.nl for more information.

By bike Visitors' cars are not allowed on Vlieland, but in any case the best way to explore is by bike. There are rental companies near the ferry terminal, and you can also rent bikes, tandems and trailers – for kids as well as canines – all over town. Given the sometimes steep, stony hills, it's worth shelling out a bit more for a machine with decent gears.

INFORMATION AND TOURS

Tourist office The VVV, Havenweg 10 (Mon–Fri 9am–12.30pm & 1.30–5pm, also open for brief periods daily to coincide with ferry arrivals; ☏ 0562 451 111, ⓦ vlieland .net), does its best with the island's few private rooms, and will help groups rent apartments and "dune houses"; it also has information on birdwatching expeditions.

Tours Private operators organize day-trips to the northern tip of the neighbouring island of Texel (see p.133 by means of a tractor-like lorry, which crosses the great expanse of sand (the "Vliehors") on Vlieland's western extremity to connect with a boat (May–Sept; €27.50 for a return trip to Texel; ⓦ waddenveer.nl).

ACCOMMODATION AND EATING

Badhotel Bruin Dorpsstraat 88 ☏ 0562 452 828, ⓦ badhotelbruin.nl. This comfortable boutique hotel is a lovely option, with sleek rooms and an excellent restaurant. It's very child-friendly too – unusual for places like this. The restaurant in particular is excellent, perhaps the best place to eat on the island. €99

Duin en Dal Dorpsstraat 163 ☏ 0562 451 684, ⓦ pensionduinendal.vlie.nl. This small pension has just three simply furnished rooms and is right in the middle of town. It's not the most glamorous option, but probably the cheapest. €72

Lange Paal Postweg 1a ☏ 0562 451 639, ⓦ langepaal .com. A really lovely and very peaceful place to camp, set in

the forest clearing of a nature reserve. Facilities are simple but clean and there's a relaxed, friendly atmosphere. Bring some insect repellent though: the mosquitoes here can be ruthless. €21

De Stortemelk Kampweg 1 ☏ 0562 451 225, ⓦ stortemelk.nl. Nicely situated campsite on the dunes behind the beach, about half an hour's walk or a 10min bike ride northeast of the village. April–Sept. €19.60

De Wadden Dorpsstraat 61 ☏ 0562 452 626, ⓦ westcordhotels.nl. There are 22 nicely furnished rooms, some faintly marine in style, in this smartish hotel in Oost-Vlieland. There is a cosy bar and restaurant downstairs, as well as a lovely outdoor terrace. €115

4

Terschelling

Of all the Frisian Islands, **TERSCHELLING** is both the largest – some 30km long and 3.5km wide – and the easiest to reach. Despite its reputation as a summer teenage hangout, it does offer wilderness, peace and tranquillity – you just have to head away from the main

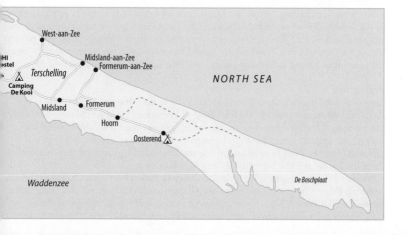

centres to get it. Quite simply, the further east you go the more attractive the island becomes; eighty percent of the island is a nature reserve, dominated by beach, dunes, forest and polder. Although summer temperatures can soar, out of season Terschelling's wild weather seems to mirror its wild landscape, with storms lending it a brooding air.

Most of Terschelling's villages are on the south side of the island, sheltered from winter storms by the sand dunes and occasional patches of forest that lie to the immediate north. Cycle routes are almost always traffic-free hereabouts and you can aim to stay in one of the pensions between the villages of Formerum and Oosterend, far enough east to escape most of the crowds.

West-Terschelling

The ferry docks next to the fishing harbour of **WEST-TERSCHELLING**, a tourist resort in its own right that's packed throughout the summer with visitors sampling the restaurants and bars that line the main streets, Torenstraat in particular. West-Terschelling today is a rather unappealing sprawl of chalets, bungalows and holiday complexes that spreads out from what remains of the old village, belying its past importance as a port and safe anchorage on the edge of the Vliestroom channel, the main shipping lane to and from the Zuider Zee. This strategically positioned town boomed throughout the seventeenth century as a centre for the supply and repair of ships and had its own fishing and whaling fleets; it paid the price for its prominence when the British razed it in 1666. The islanders were renowned sailors, much sought after by ships' captains who also needed them to guide vessels through the treacherous shallows and shifting sandbanks that lay to either side of the Vliestroom. All the same, **shipwrecks** were common all along the island's northern and western shores, the most famous victim being the *Lutine*, which sank while carrying gold and silver to British troops stationed here during the Napoleonic Wars. The wreck still lies at the bottom of the sea, and only the ship's bell was recovered; it's now in Lloyd's of London and is still rung whenever a big ship goes down.

Museum 't Behouden Huys

Commandeurstraat 30–32, near the ferry terminus • April–Oct Tues–Fri 10am–5pm & Sat 1–5pm; Nov–April Wed, Sat & Sun 1–5pm • €4 • ⓦ behouden-huys.nl

The best place to investigate West Terschelling's past is at the excellent **Museum 't Behouden Huys**, near the ferry terminus. Prime exhibits here include maps of the old coastline illustrating Terschelling's crucial position, various items from the whaling fleet, lots of sepia photos of bearded islanders and a shipwreck-diving room.

West-Aan-Zee

From West-Terschelling, plenty of visitors cycle off for the day to the beach 5km away at **WEST-AAN-ZEE**, where there's a beach café, *WestAanZee*, and as much sand as you're prepared to look for. There are two cycle routes to get here, the more northerly passing through a cemetery in a wood, with a small Commonwealth forces graveyard; as ever, the inscriptions make sad reading, with few of the downed airmen aged over 25.

Formerum

Definitely worth a visit should you happen to be in the village of **FORMERUM** is the delightful **Wrakken-museum "De Boerderij"** at Formerum Zuid 13 (March–Nov daily 10am–5pm; €3; ⓦwrakkenmuseum.nl), whose ground floor is an atmospheric bar decked out with all things nautical. Upstairs you can browse a collection of items salvaged from the island's beaches and shipwrecks, including cannons and coins, relics from the *Lutine* and the Netherlands' largest collection of diving helmets.

Another Formerum attraction is the **cranberry factory** at Formerum 51a near the windmill (May–Oct presentation and sampling Mon–Fri at 2pm; €5; shop May–Oct Mon–Sat 10.30am–4.30pm), where you can sample and buy all things cranberry. Cranberries are a major island crop, harvested from September until the first frost.

Hoorn and Oosterend

The island's two final settlements, **HOORN** and **OOSTEREND**, are particularly pleasant and within easy reach of empty tracts of beach and the nature reserve **De Boschplaat**, where thousands of birds, including gulls, oystercatchers, green plovers and spoonbills, congregate in the marshy shallows of the southeastern shore. To help protect the birds, De Boschplaat is closed during the breeding season (mid-March to mid-Aug), although the tourist office runs guided tours for bird enthusiasts.

ARRIVAL AND INFORMATION

TERSCHELLING

By ferry Ferries from Harlingen (see p.209) run to West-Terschelling at least three times a day in summer and twice daily in winter, and the journey takes 1hr 45min. A return fare is €25, plus around €14 for a bike. There's also a fast hydrofoil service from Harlingen (May–Sept 2 daily; Oct–April 1 daily; 45min), which costs €23 one way. In addition, a ferry runs between Vlieland and Terschelling twice a day in summer; tickets cost €8.15 one way, plus €8 for a bike. See ⓦ rederij-doeksen.nl for up-to-date information.

Tourist office The VVV is near the ferry port at Willem Barentszkade 19a (late April to mid-Sept Mon–Fri 9.15am–5.30pm, Sat 10am–3pm; mid-Sept to late April Mon–Fri 9.30am–5pm, Sat 10am–3pm; ☎ 0562 443 000,

ⓦ vvvterschelling.nl). It can provide a full list of pensions and rooms and operates a booking service for the whole island. It also offers a variety of walking tours, sells a good island map that includes towns, beaches and cycleways, and dispenses information on cycling routes and seal-watching excursions.

Environmental information For information about Terschelling's natural environment, visit the Centrum voor Natuur en Landschap, at Burgemeester Reedekerstraat 11 just east of West-Terschelling (April–Oct Mon–Fri 9am–5pm, Sat & Sun 11am–5pm; Nov–March Tues, Sat & Sun 2–5pm; €6; ⓦ natuurmuseumterschelling.nl), which also has a decent aquarium.

ISLAND TRANSPORT AND ACTIVITIES

By bus The island's bus service leaves from right next to the ferry terminus (every 1hr 10min), taking 30min to travel along the south coast to Oosterend.

By bike Haantjes, 50m to the right of the ferry terminal, beyond the VVV (☎ 0562 448 883, ⓦ fietsenopterschelling nl) rents out bikes for €5–7/day, €25–30/week: it also rents tandems and has various drop-off points around the

island, and a handy cycling map. There are more bike rental shops down by the harbour and at the ferry terminal.

Horseriding Rijpaarden Verhuur Lok, 2km west of Formerum in tiny Landerum (☎ 0562 448 188, ⓦ rijpaardenverhuurlok .nl), arranges horseback rides: an hour's ride through the woods for beginners costs €26, but if you're an experienced rider you can set out for the beach (2hr; €37.50).

4

ACCOMMODATION

Camping de Kooi Heester Kooiweg 20, Terschelling-Hee ☎ 0562 442 743, ⓦ campingdekooi.nl. There are a number of shoreside campsites east of town that are popular with the hordes of partying teenagers who descend on the island in summer, and this is one of the best, about 1km inland but near a small lake, with a decent café, bike rental, etc. **€18.10**

Hostel Terschelling 't Land 2, West-Terschelling ☎ 0562 442 338, ⓦ stayokay.com. HI hostel overlooking the harbour with dorm beds and en-suite doubles: it's a 1.5km walk eastwards along the coast from the centre of the village, or you can take any bus to the Dellewal stop.

Dorms **€24.20**, doubles **€59**

Hotel Buren Burgemeester Mentzstraat 20, West-Terschelling ☎ 0562 442 226, ⓦ hotel-buren.nl. Within easy walking distance from the ferry terminus, this small hotel has eleven rooms, all distinctively decorated in different colour schemes and tastefully furnished. **€110**

Pension Altijd Wad Trompstraat 6, West-Terschelling ☎ 0562 442 050, ⓦ altijdwad.nl. Close to the ferry terminal, this is a lovely, bright B&B with five rooms, a cosy studio and small private house to choose from. The furnishings are deliberately marine and minimalist and very nicely done. **€100**

EATING AND DRINKING

De Boschplaat Oosterend 14 ☎ 0562 448 821, ⓦ eetcafedeboschplaat.nl. Hefty Dutch cuisine – lamb shanks, ribs, steaks – at this long-standing Oosterend stalwart. Eat in the cosy interior or on the outside terrace. Daily noon–10pm.

Brasserie de Brandaris Boomstraat 3, West-Terschelling ☎ 0562 442 554, ⓦ brasserie-brandaris.nl. One of

Terschelling's best places to eat, with a suitably nautical atmosphere. It serves *uitsmijters*, sandwiches and pancakes at lunchtime and at dinner main courses such as steak, satay, pork and spare ribs for around €18.50. Daily noon–10pm.

Heartbreak Hotel Strandpaviljoen Oosterender Badweg 71, Oosterend ☎ 0562 448 634, ⓦ heartbreak-hotel.nl. In a superb location overlooking kilometres of

---

THE OEROL FESTIVAL

Every year around the middle of June, Terschelling celebrates the beginning of the warmer season with the **Oerol Festival** (Ⓦ oerol.nl). Oerol – meaning "everywhere" in the Terschelling dialect – is the name of a rural tradition in which the island's cattle were released from their winter stables to frolic and graze in the open fields, an event that marked the changing of the seasons. Today, over 50,000 people head out to the island for the Oerol, transforming Terschelling into a big festival area, with the island serving as both inspiration and stage for theatre producers, musicians and graphic artists. Finding accommodation is almost impossible during the ten-day festival, so book ahead.

---

white sand and sea, this American-style diner is decorated with wall-to-wall 1950s memorabilia. Live music Friday and Saturday. Daily 10am–9pm.

Het Raadhuis Torenstraat 15 West-Terschelling ☎ 0562 850 520, Ⓦ hetraadhuis-terschelling.nl. The former town hall, now a quirky café and restaurant serving mains such as sea bass, cod and rib-eye for around €19.50 as well as a good range of veggie dishes. Daily 10am–10pm.

De Walvis Groene Strand Ⓦ walvis.org. On the western

edge of West-Terschelling, this beach-facing shack is a perfect place to enjoy snacks and drinks while taking in the sea view. Daily 10am–11pm.

't Zwaantje Havenstraat 1, West-Terschelling ☎ 06 1311 5202, Ⓦ cafehetzwaantjeterschelling.nl. Self-proclaimed "brownest" café on the island, with a cosy, dark-brown interior and amenable owner. Seven beers on draught and a good selection of cocktails and whiskies – plus a decent range of bar snacks. Daily 4.30pm–2am.

Ameland

Easy to reach from the tiny port of **HOLWERD**, a few kilometres west of Wierum, the island of **Ameland** is one of the major tourist resorts of the north Dutch coast, with a population that swells from 3000 to a staggering 35,000 during summer weekends. Not that the sun is always shining: at times, clouds jostle for position and the colour of the sky can mirror that of the water. It's during the storms that the island is at its moodiest, the flatness of the land accentuating the action in the sky above.

Ameland is just 2km wide and 25km long, its entire northern shore made up of a fine expanse of **sand** and **dune** laced by foot and cycle paths. The east end of the island is the most deserted, and you can cycle by the side of the marshy shallows that once made up the whole southern shore before the sea dyke was built.

Nes

NES is a tiny place that nestles among the fields behind the dyke. Once a centre of the Dutch whaling industry, it has more than its fair share of cafés, hotels and tourist shops, though quite a bit of the old village has also survived. Mercifully, high-rise development has been forbidden, and there's a focus instead on the seventeenth- and eighteenth-century captains' houses, known as *commandeurshuizen*, which line several of the streets. Perhaps surprisingly, the crowds rarely seem to overwhelm the village, but rather to breathe life into it – which is just as well as there's not a lot to do other than wander the streets and linger in cafés. Even if you do hit peak season, it's fairly easy to

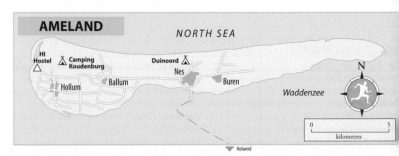

escape the crowds and you can **rent bikes** at a number of shops in the village. If it's raining, you might consider the **Natuurcentrum**, Strandweg 38 (April–Oct Mon–Fri 10am–5pm, Sat & Sun 11am–5pm; Jan–March & Nov–Dec Wed–Sun 1–5pm; €6.25; ⓦamelandermusea.nl), an aquarium and natural history museum – look out for the life-size whale – although there's no information in English.

Hollum

Of the smaller villages that dot the island, the prettiest place to stay is **HOLLUM**, a sedate settlement of old houses and farm buildings west of Nes. There are a couple of small museums here, if you're into all things marine: the **Sorgdragermuseum**, Herenweg 1 (April–Oct Mon–Fri 11am–5pm, Sat & Sun 1.30–5pm; Nov Tues–Sat 10.30am–5pm & Sun noon–5pm; Dec Wed–Sat 1.30–5pm; Jan–March Fri & Sat 1–5pm; €4.25; ⓦamelandermusea.nl), in an old *commandeurshuis*; and the **Vuurtoren**, or lighthouse, dating from 1880, which offers great views over the island (April–Oct Mon 1–5pm, Tues–Sun 10am–5pm; Nov–March Wed, Sat & Sun 1–5pm; €4.50; ⓦamelandermusea.nl).

ARRIVAL AND DEPARTURE   AMELAND

By ferry From Leeuwarden, bus #66 runs to Holwerd (hourly; 30min), from where the connecting ferry departs to Ameland (5–14 ferries daily; 45min); tickets cost €12.45 one way (April–Sept €14.70), plus €7.75–9.30 for a bike: see ⓦwpd.nl for detailed information. Ferries dock near Nes, the main village, and there's a summer bus service from the ferry to the island's other villages.

INFORMATION AND TOURS

Tourist office There are two VVVs: one at Bureweg 2 in Nes (Mon–Fri 9am–5pm, Sat 10am–3.30pm; ☏0519 546 546, ⓦvvvameland.nl); the other in Hollum, at O.P. Lapstraat 6 (Mon–Fri 9am–noon, Sat 10am–noon; ☏0519 546 546, ⓦvvvameland.nl). Both offer the same services and can fix you up with a pension or private room anywhere on the island.
Boat trips A variety of boat trips leave Nes, including excursions to the islands of Terschelling (see p.215) and Schiermonnikoog (see below), and to the sandbanks to watch seals: details from the VVV or tour operators in Nes.

ACCOMMODATION AND EATING

Duinoord Jan van Eijckweg 4 Nes ☏0519 542 070, ⓦcampingduinoord.eu. Ameland's best-appointed campsite is a sprawling affair, 1km north of Nes – head out of town and then follow Strandweg all the way to the sea, bearing left to enter the camping complex. Facilities include a supermarket, restaurant and bike rental. April–Oct. **€14.90**
De Jong Reeweg 29 Nes ☏0519 542 016, ⓦhoteldejong.nl. Central and family-run hotel with comfortable double rooms right in the heart of Nes. There's also a handy café and restaurant on the ground floor, which serves food all day – everything from lunchtime soups and sandwiches to a full dinner menu that includes an inventive array of meat and fish dishes – lamb curry, steak, veal, fish – for €17–22. **€84**
Koudenburg Oosterhiemweg 2, Hollum ☏0519 554 367, ⓦkoudenburg.nl. This well-equipped campsite by the heath to the north of the island is very welcoming and has lots of facilities, including a snack bar, pub and bike rental. Pitches vary in size and cost from €5.15, plus €4.60 per person. **€9.75**
Pension Ambla Westerlaan 33a, Hollum ☏0519 554 537, ⓦambla.nl. Hollum's best-value place to stay is this homely pension, which has a mixture of ordinary rooms and large studios, some with kitchenettes. From **€55**

Schiermonnikoog

At 16km long and 4km wide, **Schiermonnikoog** is the smallest of the Frisian islands, and, once you're clear of the main village, it's a wild, uncultivated place, crisscrossed by cycle paths – a popular spot for day-trippers. Until the Reformation, the island belonged to the monastery of Klaarkamp on the mainland; its name means literally "island of the grey monks". Nothing remains of the monks, however, and these days Schiermonnikoog's only settlement is a prim and busy village, fringed by weekend homes and bordering long stretches of muddy beach and sand dune to the north and farmland and mud flats to the south. At low tide, these motionless pools of water reflect the colours in the sky, particularly atmospheric at dawn and dusk.

4

ARRIVAL AND INFORMATION

SCHIERMONNIKOOG

By ferry Ferries to Schiermonnikoog leave from the port of Lauwersoog, reached by bus #163 from Groningen (4 daily; 1hr), or bus #50 (9 daily) from Dokkum (30min) or Leeuwarden (1hr 30min). Ferries (Mon–Sat; 5 daily, Sun 4 daily; 45min) cost €12.75 one way (April–Sept €15) plus €7.75–9.30 for a bike; see ⓦ wpd.nl for more information. Only residents' cars are allowed on the island. Ferries dock at the island jetty, some 3km from the village; a connecting

bus drops you off outside the VVV in the centre.
On foot It's possible to walk to the island across the mud flats from Kloosterburen, a distance of about 8km, but you must do this accompanied by a guide (see box below).
Tourist office Schiermonnikoog's VVV is at Reeweg 5 (Mon–Sat 9.30am–5pm; ☎0519 531 233, ⓦ vvvschiermonnikoog.nl) and offers the usual services, including booking private rooms around the island.

ACCOMMODATION

Herberg Rijsbergen Knuppeldam 2 ☎0519 531 257, ⓦ rijsbergen.biz. On the east side of the village, a 15min walk from the tourist office, this is an excellent-value and very peaceful hotel, located in a historical building with

lovely gardens and a sun terrace. €105
Hotel Graaf Bernstorff Reeweg 1 ☎0519 820 050. The best pick of the two big hotels in town with seventeen rooms and 27 apartments, all bright and well equipped

---

WADLOPEN

Wadlopen, or mud-flat walking, is a popular and strenuous Dutch pastime, and the stretch of coast on the northern edge of the provinces of Friesland and Groningen is one of the best places to do it: twice daily, the receding tide uncovers vast expanses of mud flat beneath the Waddenzee. It is, however, a sport to be taken seriously, and far too dangerous to do without an experienced guide: the depth of the mud is variable and the tides inconsistent. In any case, channels of deep water are left even when the tide has receded, and the currents can be perilous. The **timing of treks** depends on weather and tidal conditions, but most start between 6am and 10am. It's important to be properly equipped; **recommended gear** includes shorts or a bathing suit, a sweater, wind jacket, knee-high socks, high-top trainers and a complete change of clothes stashed in a watertight pack. In recent years, *wadlopen* has become extremely popular, and as excursions are infrequent, between May and August it's advisable to book a place at least a month in advance. The VVVs in Leeuwarden and Groningen can provide details, or you could contact one of the *wadlopen* organizations direct.

    Prices and trips vary according to location, and how long (and far) you choose to go. You can do a **full trip** crossing to one of the islands – Ameland or Schiemonnikoog – and coming back by ferry, or just do a **circular trip** across the mud flats and back again.

    Another increasingly popular option is to combine a short *wadlopen* trip with a spot of **seal-watching**. The sight of the mud flat covered with hundreds of seals is simply spectacular, especially at sunset, and if you're lucky, you might be able to join the Pieterburen Seal Sanctuary (see p.227) on one of its tours when staff release previously injured seals back into the wild (obviously, tours depend on the health of the seals, so contact ahead).

WADLOPEN GUIDED WALK COMPANIES

Dijkstras Wadlopencentrum Hoofdstraat 118, Pieterburen ☎0595 528 345, ⓦ wadloop-dijkstra .nl. The largest *wadlopen* organization, with tours to Brakzand, Ameland and even Schiermonnikoog for the really fit. A 3hr tour from €12.
Lauwersoog Water Events ☎0519 349133, ⓦ beleefwadenwater.nl. Departing from Lauwersoog harbour, this company offers seal-watching tours by boat, combined, if wanted, with some easy *wadlopen* suitable for families. €14.75.
Stichting Wadloopcentrum Pieterburen Hoofdstraat 105, Pieterburen ☎0595 528 300, ⓦ wadlopen.com. This company has been organizing trips for over fifty years and offers everything from easy

2hr beginners' tours to serious trips for the skilled walker. In season it even organizes night walks, a real experience. From €11.
Tour de Wadden ☎06 2121 7440, ⓦ tourdewadden.nl. An online *wadlopen* travel agency offering day-, weekend- and week-long trips combining *wadlopen* with seal-watching trips. A once-in-a-lifetime experience is releasing a previously injured seal back into the wild. Contact ahead for dates. €39.50.
Wadloopcentrum Fryslân ⓦ www.wadlopen.net. Fourteen tours from 7km to 20km, some easy for the inexperienced, some really strengthening for the diehards. From €11.

nd some with a balcony. The downstairs restaurant has a decent menu with mains such as grilled tuna fish, lamb or ish curry for €19.50. **€140**

Seedune Seeduneweg 1 ☎ 0519 531 398, ⓦ seedune nl. Schiermonnikoog's campsite is in a lovely location, to he north of the main village in the woods just east of Badweg. Many facilities, including bike rental and nidgetgolf. April–Sept. **€17**

De Tjattel Langestreek 94 ☎ 0519 531 133, ⓦ detjattel.nl. Two-star hotel in the heart of the village, with decent but unspectacular rooms. It also has a large

restaurant and bar, which serves meat and fish mains for €18–20 at dinner and a variety of *uitsmijters*, salads, sandwiches, etc, at lunch for €5–10. Restaurant daily noon–3pm & 4.30–9pm. **€125**

Van der Werff Reeweg 2 ☎ 0519 531 203, ⓦ hotelvanderwerff.nl. This long-time favourite, housed in a landmark building, is well overdue a total makeover. The rooms look weary and the downstairs wood-panelled bar is incredibly old-fashioned, as is the adjacent restaurant. Its location is perfect, though, and the atmosphere undeniably nostalgic. **€115**

EATING AND DRINKING

Ambrosijn Langestreek 13 ☎ 0519 720 261, ⓦ ambrosijn.nl. A much-lauded restaurant with super-smart interior and mouthwatering menu. It's not cheap – mains such as lamb, kingfish or cod will set you back €26.50, but there's also a three-course surprise menu for €29.50. There's an adjacent ice cream parlour and three luxurious suites should you be tempted to splash out and stay the night. Daily 6–10pm.

It Aude Beuthus Nieuwestreek 6 ☎ 0519 531 460, ⓦ cafeboothuis.nl. Located in the former rescue

boathouse – the relics reminding of that period – this is now the most atmospheric bar in town with many beers on draught and regular live music. Hours vary but in season generally daily 10.30am–2am, irregular hours out of season.

Tox Bar Reeweg ☎ 0519 7 531 373, ⓦ toxbar.nl. During daytime this is a regular café serving cheap daily specials, but it doubles as the island's only disco on weekends and during summer. Mon–Thurs from 4pm, Fri–Sun from noon, no official closing hours but you can't get in after 2am.

4

Groningen

The most exciting city in the northern Netherlands, **GRONINGEN** comes as something of a surprise in the midst of its namesake province's quiet, rural surroundings. It's a hip, rather cosmopolitan place for the most part, with a thriving student life that imbues the city with vim and gusto. Competitively priced restaurants dish up exotic curries and fresh falafel alongside the standard Dutch staples, and the arts scene is particularly vibrant, especially during the academic year. Virtually destroyed during the Allied liberation in 1945, the city focuses on two enormous squares and is now a jumble of styles, from traditional canalside townhouses to bright Art Deco tilework along the upper facades of the shopping streets – an eclecticism that culminates in the innovative **Groninger Museum** sitting on its own island near the station. Finally, one of the nice things about Groningen is that the centre is almost **car-free**, the result of huge investment in traffic-calming measures and a network of cycle paths and bus lanes. Today two-thirds of residents travel regularly by **bike**, the highest percentage in the country.

Grote Markt

Still encircled by what was once a moat, Groningen's compact city centre is the enjoyable part of town with all the main sights within easy walking distance of each other. The effective centre of town is **Grote Markt**, a wide-open space that was badly damaged by wartime bombing and has been rather unimaginatively reconstructed, though at the time of writing the first bricks were being laid for the **Groninger Forum** (ⓦ groningerforum.nl), a vast cultural centre scheduled to open in 2017, with many postwar buildings being razed for its construction. Costing a staggering 71 million euros, it has been subject of controversy, legal battles and even a referendum. Designed to give the Grote Markt back its intimate prewar feel, it will house a cinema, debate centre, library, museum and a skylounge with restaurant and rooftop terrace.

For now, though, Grote Markt is home to the tourist office at one end and the

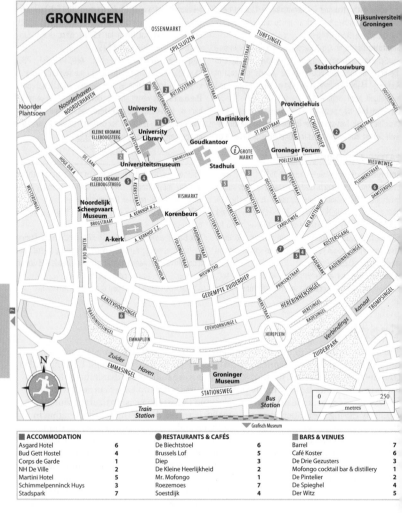

■ ACCOMMODATION		● RESTAURANTS & CAFÉS		■ BARS & VENUES	
Asgard Hotel	6	De Biechtstoel	6	Barrel	7
Bud Gett Hostel	4	Brussels Lof	5	Café Koster	6
Corps de Garde	1	Diep	3	De Drie Gezusters	3
NH De Ville	2	De Kleine Heerlijkheid	2	Mofongo cocktail bar & distillery	1
Martini Hotel	5	Mr. Mofongo	1	De Pintelier	2
Schimmelpenninck Huys	3	Roezemoes	7	De Spieghel	4
Stadspark	7	Soestdijk	4	Der Witz	5

Neoclassical **Stadhuis** at the other, tucked in front of the mid-seventeenth-century **Goudkantoor** (Gold Office); look out for the shell motif above the windows, a characteristic Groningen decoration.

Martinikerk

Martinikerkhof 3 · **Church** Late April to Sept Tues–Sat 11am–5pm; July & Aug Mon–Sat 11am–5pm, Sun 2–5pm · Free · **Tower** April–Oct Mon noon–5pm, Tues–Sat 11am–5pm, Sun noon–4pm; Nov–March Mon–Fri & Sun noon–4pm, Sat 11am–5pm · €3 · ☎ 050 311 1277, 🟦 martinikerk.nl

At the northeast corner of the Grote Markt, the tiered tower of the **Martinikerk** is perhaps Groningen's most significant landmark, and is worth peeking into for its impressive interior. Although the oldest parts of the church were built in around 1180, most of it dates from the mid-fifteenth century, the nave being a Gothicized rebuilding undertaken to match the added choir. Adjoining the church, the essentially eventeenth-century **Martinitoren** can be climbed and offers a view that is breathtaking in both senses of the word. Behind the church is the lawn of the **Kerkhof**, an ancient piece of common land that's partly enclosed by the **Provinciehuis**, a rather grand neo-Renaissance building of 1915, seat of the provincial government.

The Universiteitsmuseum

Oude Kijk in 't Jatstraat 7a • Tues–Sun 1–5pm • Free • ☎ 050 363 5083, ⓦ rug.nl/museum

Northwest of Grote Markt are the main buildings of Groningen's prestigious **university**, one of the oldest and largest in the country, with more than 30,000 students at any one time. Founded in the early seventeenth century, its gabled main building is topped with a bulbous clock tower and normally has a sea of student bikes in front. Around the corner the **Universiteitsmuseum** gives a taste of the university's history, with exhibits ranging from scientific equipment to photos of derby-hatted students clowning around at the turn of twentieth century.

The Vismarkt

Almost as large an open space as the present Grote Markt, the neighbouring Vismarkt is anchored at its far end by the **Korenbeurs** (Corn Exchange) of 1865. The statues on its facade represent, from left to right, Neptune, Mercury (god of commerce) and Ceres (goddess of agriculture), while you can enjoy its wrought-iron-and-glass interior while browsing the aisles of the Albert Heijn supermarket inside. Just behind, the **A-kerk** is a fifteenth-century church with a Baroque steeple, attractively restored in tones of yellow, orange and red. The church's full name is Onze Lieve Vrouwekerk der A ("Our Dear Lady's Church of the A"), the A being a small river which forms the moat encircling the town centre.

Noordelijk Scheepvaart Museum

Brugstraat 24–26 • Tues–Sat 10am–5pm, Sun 1–5pm • €6 • ☎ 050 312 2202, ⓦ noordelijkscheepvaartmuseum.nl

Just west of the A-kerk, the **Noordelijk Scheepvaart Museum** is one of the best-equipped and most comprehensive maritime museums in the country, tracing the history of north Holland's shipping from the sixth to the twentieth centuries. Housed in a warren of steep stairs and timber-beamed rooms, each of the museum's twenty displays deals with a different aspect of shipping, including trade with the Indies, the development of peat canals and a series of reconstructed nautical workshops. The museum's particular appeal is its imaginative combination of models and original artefacts, which are themselves a mixture of the personal (seamen's chests, quadrants) and the public (figureheads, tile designs of ships).

The Groninger Museum

Museumeiland 1 • Tues–Sun 10am–5pm • €13 • ☎ 050 366 6555, ⓦ groningermuseum.nl

The town's main draw is the excellent **Groninger Museum**, set on its own island on the southern edge of the centre, directly across from the train station. Aside from a very cool information lounge with computers and touch screens, the museum is mostly given over to temporary exhibitions and what you see really depends on when you're here. If you're lucky, Rubens' energetic *Adoration of the Magi* will be on display, or Isaac Israëls' inviting *Hoedenwinkel* from a modest sample of Hague School paintings.

Most people, however, visit as much for the building itself as for what's inside: it consists of **six pavilions**, each designed in a highly individual style – think Gaudí on holiday in Miami, and you'll have some idea of the interior decor. Once inside, between the stylish café and museum shop, the striking mosaic stairwell sweeps downwards, depositing you among bulbous lemon-yellow pillars and pink walls, from where moat-level corridors head off to pavilions either side: east to Mendini, Mendini 1 and Coop Himmelb(l)au, west to Starck and De Ploeg.

De Ploeg and the Starck Pavilion
The museum's collection includes a number of works by the Expressionists of the Groningen De Ploeg school, housed in their own pavilion, a trapezium constructed from red bricks. The De Ploeg movement is characterized by intense colour contrasts, exaggerated shapes and depiction of landscapes – often of the countryside north of Groningen. As founding member Jan Altink (1885–1971) put it: "There wasn't much going on in the way of art in Groningen, so I thought of cultivation and thus also of ploughing. Hence the name De Ploeg." As well as Altink, look out for the paintings of Jan Wiegers (1893–1959). Upstairs from De Ploeg, the **Philippe Starck pavilion** is a giant disc clad in aluminium plating and houses the museum's wonderful collection of **Chinese and Japanese porcelain**, beautifully displayed in circular glass cases, softened by gauzy drapes.

The Mendini Pavilions and Coop Himmelb(l)au
On the other side of the mosaic stairway, the **Mendini pavilions** are dedicated to temporary exhibitions, while a large concrete stairway links Mendini 1 to the final, and most controversial, pavilion. Designed by Wolfgang Prix and Helmut Swiczinsky, who together call themselves **Coop Himmelb(l)au**, it's a Deconstructivist experiment: double-plated steel and reinforced glass jut out at awkward angles, and skinny aerial walkways crisscross the exhibition space. It all feels – probably deliberately – half-built. Look out for the glass-walk holes, where the concrete floor stops and suddenly between your feet the canal gapes, two storeys below. This pavilion is also given over to temporary exhibitions.

The train station
Across the water from the Groninger Museum, Groningen's train station was built in 1896 at enormous cost. It was one of the finest stations of its day, decorated with the strong colours and symbolic designs of Art Nouveau tiles from the Rozenburg factory in Den Haag. The grandeur of much of the building has disappeared under a welter of concrete, glass and plastic suspended ceilings, but the old first- and second-class waiting rooms have survived pretty much intact, and have been refurbished as restaurants.

ARRIVAL AND DEPARTURE   GRONINGEN

By train Groningen's grand train station is on the south side of the town centre and is very well connected to the rest of the Netherlands.
Destinations Amsterdam (via Amersfoort or Lelystad; every 30min; 2hr 10min); Assen (every 20min; 20min); Den Haag (hourly; 2hr 40min); Leeuwarden (every 20min; 50min); Rotterdam (hourly; 2hr 40min); Uithuizen (every 30min; 35min); Utrecht (hourly; 1hr 55min); Zwolle (every 20min; 1hr).
By bus The bus station is right next to the train station.
Destinations Emmen (bus #300 and #305: every 20min 1hr 10min); Lauwersoog for boats to Schiermonnikoog (bus #163: 4 daily; 1hr); Zoutkamp (bus #65: Mon–Fri every 30min, Sat hourly; 1hr 15 min).

GETTING AROUND

Bike rental At the train station (€7.50/day; €35/week; ☎ 050 312 4174).
Boat trips Kool, Stationsweg 1012 (☎ 050 312 8379, ⓦ rondvaartbedrijfkool.nl), runs regular trips around the old town moat; tickets cost €12 for an hour-long tour.
Taxis TaxiCentrale ☎ 050 549 7676, ⓦ taxicentrale-groningen.nl.

LIQUOR FIT FOR A KING?
Although Groningen does not have a rich culinary tradition, the **Hooghoudt brewery** (ⓦ hooghoudt.nl) is known throughout the country and dates back to 1888. It's best known for its Graanjenever, but they also produce Beerenburg and other liquors like the Wilhelmus Orange Liquor, which is traditionally served on King's Day.

INFORMATION

Tourist office The VVV is temporarily housed in a hideous building on the main square at Grote Markt 25 until it moves to the new Groninger Forum in 2017 (Mon noon–6pm, Tues–Fri 9.30am–6pm, Sat 10am–5pm; July & Aug also Sun 11am–4pm; ☎ 0900 202 3050, ⓦ tourism.groningen.nl). It offers information on the town and province, online accommodation reservations, tickets for visiting bands, theatre groups and orchestras, and information on exploring Groningen by boat (ⓦ rondvaartbedrijfkool.nl) or canoe. It also sells a brochure of city walks for €1.50, and has a short list of private rooms in both Groningen and the surrounding area, though hardly any are near the centre.

ACCOMMODATION

HOTELS

Asgard Hotel Ganzevoortsingel 2 ☎ 050 368 4810, ⓦ asgardhotel.nl. Very handy for both the train station and the centre of town, this eco-hotel tries very hard, with its untreated Scandinavian wood and bright, simple and contemporary rooms. On the newly added top floor are the more luxurious rooms with balcony, and some with bathtub smack in the middle of the room. An amenable place with friendly service. **€109**

★ **Corps de Garde** Oude Boteringestraat 72–74 ☎ 050 314 5437, ⓦ corpsdegarde.nl. A lovely hotel, probably the city's best choice, with a beautiful, bright breakfast room downstairs and a variety of rooms in a sixteenth-century mansion. No room is the same so prices vary quite a bit. The cheaper beamed rooms are on the top floor, with more contemporary rooms below, with large showers and a modern look and feel that sits well with the ancient building. There's a cosy lounge area in the basement, and the welcome is always warm. **€99**

Martini Hotel Gedempte Zuiderdiep 8 ☎ 050 312 9919, ⓦ martinihotel.nl. A large and central hundred-room hotel in an attractive and quite imposing nineteenth-century building. The rooms vary from standard – dark and rather uninspiring – to the newer "comfort" rooms on the upper floors, which are brighter but still pretty basic. Breakfast costs extra (€12.50) whichever room you choose. There's a large bar and reception downstairs, and a restaurant – *Weeva* – next door. **€74.50**

NH de Ville Oude Boteringestraat 43 ☎ 050 318 1222, ⓦ deville.nl. Although it's now part of a chain, this 65-room hotel has maintained its intimate feel with friendly staff and a fine Baroque interior. The cosy courtyard is also a great location for a romantic dinner, and the downstairs lounge is lovely, very well designed in the context of the old building. **€100**

Schimmelpenninck Huys Oosterstraat 53 ☎ 050 318 9502, ⓦ schimmelpenninckhuys.nl. This place likes to think of itself as the poshest in town, and its faded elegance certainly looks the part, with a lovely downstairs bar and lobby, part of which overlooks a pretty inner courtyard. The rooms vary from grand, antique-filled affairs with large bathrooms in the original old mansion, to simpler, more up-to-date ones in the back annexe. There's a relentlessly old-fashioned restaurant at the front, where a three-course dinner menu costs €27.50. **€100**

HOSTEL

Bud Gett Hostel Rademarkt 3 ☎ 050 588 6558, ⓦ budgethostels.nl. A relatively new hostel decorated in Mondriaan style, smack in the centre of town and offering well-equipped dorm beds as well as simple but functional twin rooms with private facilities. Breakfast is an extra €7.50. Dorms **€25**, twins **€50**

CAMPING

Stadspark Campinglaan 6 ☎ 050 525 1624, ⓦ campingstadspark.nl. Groningen's most obvious option if you're camping, and a pleasant waterside site to boot. It's within a 20min walk of the centre, and located in the city's nicest and largest park. Mid-March to Oct. **€18.50**

EATING

De Biechtstoel Damsterdiep 22–24 ☎ 050 313 8246, ⓦ debiechtstoel.com. Cosy restaurant crammed with holy relics (hence the name "confession chair"). The menu offers everything from spare ribs to Spanish *zarzuela* (richly filled fish soup) for €14–18, and there's always a daily special for €11.50. Also open for lunch. Mon–Sat 11am–10pm, Sun 12.30–10pm.

Brussels Lof A-Kerkstraat 24 ☎ 050 312 7603, ⓦ brusselslof.com. Serves a wide range of vegetarian dishes and good cheese fondues, but also known for its fresh fish; pure, simple and excellent cooking, with veggie mains for €18.50 and fish mains from €19.50. Tues–Sat 5.30–9.30pm.

★ **Diep** Schuitendiep 44 ☎ 050 589 0009, ⓦ dinercafediep.nl. Once a residence for monks, now a stylish restaurant with lime-green hues and a hidden inner courtyard. The friendly staff serve mains such as salmon fillet, duck breast and catfish for around €20, and there's a three-course surprise menu for €32. Daily 5–10pm.

De Kleine Heerlijkheid Schuitendiep 42 ☎ 050 313 1370, ⓦ dekleineheerlijkheid.nl. Located in one of the town's oldest buildings just outside the city walls, the smallest restaurant in Groningen serves mains such as entrecote or lamb shoulder for around €20, in an agreeable atmosphere. Tues–Sat 4–9.30pm.

4

Mr. Mofongo Oude Boteringestraat 26 ☎ 050 314 4266, ⓦ mofongo.nl. The newest hot spot in town with an eclectic kitchen serving exotic dishes such as kangaroo steak and jumbo shrimps prepared on an indoor charcoal grill (around €18). Also fresh pasta and noodles and a daily special for as little as €9.75. Book ahead. Daily 11am–10pm.

Roezemoes Gedempte Zuiderdiep 15 ☎ 050 314 8854, ⓦ eetcafe-roezemoes.nl. If all you want is an original *stamppot* (mashed potatoes with veggies and meat) you're in the right place – they even serve this typical Dutch winter dish in summer, for €12.50 a pop. There are also non-mashed

mains on the menu for around €13–16. Mon & Sun noon–4pm & 5–9.30pm, Tues–Sat 11am–4pm & 5–10pm.

★ **Soestdijk** Grote Kromme Elleboog 6 ☎ 050 314 5050, ⓦ cafesoestdijk.nl. Groningen's closest thing to a gastropub, where you can just as easily sit at the bar and nurse a drink as eat. There are specials on the board from around €15.50 and a decent range of other dishes on the menu – steaks, port satay, a couple of fish options – for €16–21. A really nice feel, and good food too – as at all good gastropubs, simple but well cooked and delicious; they do portions of cheese and various bar snacks, if you don't want a full meal. Kitchen daily 5–10pm, bar till 2–3am.

DRINKING AND NIGHTLIFE

Barrel Haddingestraat 27 ☎ 06 5150 5699, ⓦ barrel-wijn.nl. Atmospheric little wine-bar annexe shop with at least six superb whites and reds by the glass, plus a good selection of full-bodied ports, best enjoyed with an accompanying cheese or meat platter. Thurs–Sat 5pm–midnight, Sun 4–8pm.

Café Koster Hoogstraat 7–9 ☎ 050 314 5217, ⓦ cafekoster.nl. With a dancefloor overlooked by pious figures of Christ, this is central Groningen's old rockers' bar with loud music most nights, and live sounds on Sundays from 4pm. Always fun. Wed 8pm–late, Thurs–Sun 4pm–late.

De Drie Gezusters Grote Markt 39 ☎ 050 312 7041, ⓦ driegezustersgroningen.nl. Perhaps the most historic watering hole in the centre of Groningen, a beautiful *fin-de-siècle* bar and restaurant with a reading bench down the middle and covered booths at the side – quite a Groningen institution, with many of its original fixtures and fittings still in place. Walk through to the rooms at the back, fitted out with old railway seats and luggage racks. Mon & Sun 11am–midnight, Tues–Sat 10am–midnight.

De Pintelier Kleine Kromme Elleboog 9 ☎ 050 318 5100,

ⓦ depintelier.nl. A great long bar with loads of Belgian beers on tap, and a very large selection of whiskies. Popular with students and always crowded. Mon–Wed & Sun 3pm–2am, Thurs–Sat 3pm–3am.

Mofongo Distillery & Cocktailbar Oude Boteringestraat 26 ☎ 050 314 4266, ⓦ mofongo.nl. A must-go, if only to see the automatic robot arm that pours the fifty-plus home-brewed liquors with non-conventional ingredients such as wasabi, truffle and red pepper. Mon–Sat 5pm–late.

De Spieghel Peperstraat 11 ☎ 050 312 6651, ⓦ jazzcafedespieghel.nl. This jazz café has live performances most nights, including some reasonably big names, and a nice terrace in summer. Wed–Sat 8pm–late.

★ **Der Witz** Grote Markt 47 ☎ 050 314 1417, ⓦ derwitz.nl. Cosy, narrow old bar, very comfy and the pick of the many places on the Grote Markt. Even the smokers' booth is better than usual. It serves a good range of Dutch, German and Belgian beers on draught and strong chilled *korns* (the German version of *jenever*). Mon & Sun noon–midnight, Tues–Fri 10am–midnight, Sat 9am–1am.

Around Groningen

Once known as East Frisia, the province of **Groningen** does not have the high tourist profile of many of the country's other regions, but it does boast a large slab of empty coastline where the **Lauwersmeer Nationaal Park** is home to extensive wildlife, the **seal sanctuary** of Pieterburen and the pick of the old manor houses that dot the province, **Menkemaborg** in **Uithuizen**. To the southeast of Groningen, the old frontier village of **Bourtange** has been painstakingly restored, offering an insight into eighteenth-century life in a fortified town, while nearby **Ter Apel** holds a rare survivor from the Reformation in the substantial remains of its monastery.

Menkemaborg

March–June & Sept Tues–Sun 10am–5pm; July & Aug daily 10am–5pm; Oct–Dec Tues–Sun 10am–4pm • €6 • ⓦ menkemaborg.nl

The most agreeable day-trip from Groningen is to the village of **Uithuizen**, 25km northeast, where the moated manor house of **Menkemaborg** is a signed ten-minute walk from the station. Dating from the fifteenth century and surrounded by formal gardens in the English style, the house has a sturdy, compact elegance and is one of

FESTIVALS IN GRONINGEN

Every year in mid-August, Groningen hosts the increasingly popular **Festival Noorderzon** (ⓦ noorderzon.nl), a ten-day blend of theatre, music, film and performance art. About a third of the events are free, many of them staged in the Noorderplantsoen park, a fifteen-minute walk north along Nieuwe Kijk in 't Jatstraat. Come nighttime, food stalls and drinking holes surround the lake in the park, while folk stroll along the lantern-lit paths or chill on the lake's stone steps to the sound of Afrobeat, Latin, funk, rock, jazz or ambient music.

In mid-January, the **Eurosonic Noorderslag festival** (ⓦ eurosonic-noorderslag.nl), a four-day showcase for European pop music, features more than 300 live performances scattered over 36 stages in town and draws at least 35,000 visitors, including many music-industry professionals hoping to discover new talent. You'll need tickets for most of the indoor shows, but you can catch free performances on a huge outdoor stage on the Grote Markt, if you can stand the January chill.

During both festivals, hotels get busy, so if you're planning to visit around these times you'd do well to book in advance.

the very few mansions, or *borgs*, of the old landowning families to have survived. The interior consists of a sequence of period rooms furnished in the style of the seventeenth century, displaying some of the Groninger Museum's applied art and history collection.

The Pieterburen Seal Sanctuary

Hoofdstraat 84a • Daily 10am–5pm • €8 • ☏ 0595 526 526, ⓦ zeehondencreche.nl

Founded almost forty years ago by Lenie 't Hart, a local animal-welfare heroine, the **Pieterburen Seal Sanctuary** rescues abandoned or weak seals with the purpose of releasing them back into the wild. You can view seals – lots of them – in the outside tanks, or on their own in quarantine quarters inside; the best time to see seal pups is during the summer, when many will be nursed and fed until they are strong enough to make it on their own. Look in also on the "kitchen" where they prepare the seals' fish, and take in a permanent exhibition on the work of the centre (info is in Dutch but there is an English booklet), plus naturally there's a shop selling all manner of cuddly seal-related merchandise. Great for kids – and in a very good cause.

The Lauwersmeer Nationaal Park

Lauwersmeer Nationaal Park, some 35km northwest of Groningen, comprises a broken and irregular lake that spreads across the provincial boundary into neighbouring Friesland. Once an arm of the sea, it was turned into a freshwater lake by the construction of the Lauwersoog dam, a controversial 1960s project that was vigorously opposed by local fishermen, who ended up having to move all their tackle to the coast. Spared intensive industrial and agricultural development because of the efforts of conservationists, it's a quiet and peaceful region with a wonderful variety of sea birds,

WALKS AROUND UITHUIZEN

The trip to Uithuizen can be combined with *wadlopen* (see box, p.220) to the uninhabited sand-spit island of **Rottumeroog**, the most easterly of the Dutch Wadden islands; occasional weekend trips are offered in season by local company Stichting Uithuizer Wad (ⓦ wadlopen.nl). Without a guide, it's too dangerous to venture onto the coastal mud flats, but it is easy enough to **walk** along the enclosing dyke that runs behind the shoreline for the whole length of the province. There's precious little to see, but when the weather's clear, the browns, blues and greens of the surrounding land and sea are unusually beautiful. From Uithuizen, it's a good hour's stroll north to the nearest point on the dyke, and you'll need a large-scale map for directions.

THE PIETERPAD

Pieterburen is also the start and end point for the longest unbroken walking route in the Netherlands, the 464km-long **Pieterpad** to Maastricht. More information and a map of the walking route can be obtained at Groningen VVV (see p.225) or at Ⓦpieterpad.nl.

---

and is increasingly popular with anglers, windsurfers, sailors and cyclists. The local villages are uniformly dull. At the mouth of the lake, the desultory port of **LAUWERSOOG** is where **ferries** leave for the fifty-minute trip to the island of Schiermonnikoog (see p.219). The most convenient base for exploring the park is **ZOUTKAMP**, near the southeast corner of the lake on the River Reitdiep.

Bourtange

W Lodewijstraat 33 • April–Oct daily 10am–5pm; Nov–Dec & Feb–March Sat & Sun 11am–4pm • Entry is free but a €7.50 ticket gives admission to specific buildings and exhibitions • ☎ 0599 354 600, Ⓦ bourtange.nl

Some 60km southeast of Groningen, just a kilometre or so from the German frontier, **BOURTANGE** is a superbly restored fortified village. Founded by William of Orange in 1580 to help protect the eastern approaches to Groningen, Bourtange fell into disrepair during the nineteenth century, only to be entirely refurbished as a tourist attraction in 1964. The design of the village is similar to that of Naarden (see p.138) and is best appreciated as you walk around the old bastions of the star-shaped fortress. There are regular events throughout the summer, including mock battles, markets and guided walks, and you can even get married here if you want. Otherwise just turn up: it's tremendously atmospheric, there are usually folk attired in period dress and a cannon is fired at 3pm every Sunday.

Klooster Ter Apel

Boslaan 3–5, Ter Apel • Tues–Sat 10am–5pm, Sun 1–5pm; July & Aug Mon–Sat 10am–6pm, Sun 1–6pm • €7.50 • ☎ 0599 581370, Ⓦ museumklooster-terapel.com

Some 30km to the south of Bourtange, in the small town of **TER APEL**, the **Museum Klooster** is a highlight of this part of the country. This was the monastery of the Order of the Holy Cross – or Croziers – dating back to the Middle Ages and probably unique among rural Dutch monasteries in surviving the ravages of the Reformation. The chapel, superbly restored, preserves a number of unusual features, including the tripartite sedilia, where the priest and his assistants sat during Mass, and a splendid rood screen that divides the chancel from the nave. Elsewhere, the east wing is a curious hybrid of Gothic and Baroque styles, the cloister has a small herb garden, and the other rooms are normally given over to temporary exhibitions of religious art. The monastery is surrounded by extensive beech woods and magnificent old horse chestnut trees; follow one of the marked walks or simply ramble at your leisure.

ARRIVAL AND INFORMATION   AROUND GRONINGEN

By train There are regular trains to Uithuizen from Groningen (every 30min; 35min), and Menkemaborg is a 10min walk from Uithuizen station.

By bus Zoutkamp, for the Lauwersmeer Nationaal Park, is served by bus #65 (Mon–Fri every 30min, Sat hourly; 1hr 15 min) from Groningen. Bus #73 runs from Groningen to Ter Apel hourly: the journey takes a tortuous 1hr 30min. Getting to Bourtange by public transport is even more difficult: take the train from Groningen to Winschoten

(30min), and then bus #14 to Vlagtwedde and change to bus #11 for the short hop to Bourtange (reserve this last leg at least 1hr in advance on ☎ 0900 202 2702). The entire journey will take at least 1hr 30min.

Tourist offices At the time of writing, all official VVV offices in the area had been closed down, so check the website of the Groningen VVV (☎ 0900 202 3050, Ⓦ tourism.groningen.nl) for information on the surrounding area, including *wadlopen* and the Pieterpad.

ACCOMMODATION

PIETERBUREN

De Kromme Raake Molenstraat 5 Eenrum ☎0595 491 600, ⓦhoteldekrommeraake.nl. Just 5km from Pieterburen, the village of Eenrum hosts what is officially (according to the *Guinness Book of Records*) the smallest hotel in the world, an old grocery shop that was transformed into a one-room hotel in 1989 by a former governor of Groningen. The room itself is very nice, if rather eccentrically decorated, but needless to say you have to book a fair way in advance. **€150**

LAUWERSOOG

Camping Lauwersoog Strandweg 5 ☎0519 349 133, ⓦlauwersoog.nl. Located right on the lake, this campsite has all the facilities you can imagine; a restaurant (*Het Booze Wijf* – "The angry woman"), supermarket, boat rental, kiddies' playground and so on. It also organizes seal-watching boat trips, as well as excursions by rescue boat – not for the faint-hearted. **€17.50**

BOURTANGE

Hotel Vesting Bourtange Willem Lodewijkstraat 33 ☎0599 354 600, ⓦhotelvestingbourtange.nl. Right in the middle of the fortified village, this hotel has eight good-sized lodgements with traditional *bedstee* (cupboard bed) and four with a regular bed. Nothing fancy, but being able to walk through the village after the masses have left, makes up for it. **€79**

TER APEL

Hotel Boschhuis Boslaan 6 ☎0599 581 208, ⓦhotelboschhuis.nl. Right opposite the Ter Apel monastery, this is a lovely place to stay if you fancy spending a quiet night in the country. The rooms are comfortable with slightly boutiquey aspirations and there's an excellent restaurant with both atmosphere and good seasonal food. **€87.50**

EATING AND DRINKING

NOORDPOLDERZIJL

't Zielhoes Zijlweg 4 ☎0595 423 058, ⓦzielhoes.nl. This must be the country's remotest café in an amazing spot, where you can climb onto the dyke and look out over the Wadden Sea. It serves a fairly basic but always delicious menu of sandwiches, *uitsmijters*, soup and pancakes at really good prices. April & May Tues–Fri noon–6pm, Sat & Sun 10am–6pm; June–Sept daily 10am–8pm; Oct–March Fri & Sat noon–6pm, Sun 10am–6pm.

PIETERBUREN

Pizzeria Bij de Buren van Pieter Hoofdstraat 82 ☎0595 528 203, ⓦpizzeriabijdeburenvanpieter.nl.

Right in the centre of the village, this cosy joint does all sorts of pizzas from €6.50 – ideal before or after a spot of *wadlopen*. Its speciality is the Waddenpizza, with all sorts of fresh fish and marsh samphire. Daily noon–2am, hours more limited out of season.

BOURTANGE

't Oal Kroegie Marktplein 8 ☎0599 354 580. A little brown café in the centre of the village with oodles of atmosphere and a nice terrace in summer, dishing up simple fare such as pancakes, soups, salads or satay, for reasonable prices. No fixed opening hours but generally 10am–8.30pm.

Drenthe

Until the early nineteenth century, the sparsely populated province of **Drenthe**, by the German border, was little more than a flat expanse of empty peat bog, marsh and moor. In recent decades, it's accumulated a scattering of small towns, but it remains the country's least populated province. Its only conspicuous geographical feature is a ridge of low hills that runs northwest for some 50km from Emmen, its largest town, toward Groningen. This ridge, the **Hondsrug**, was high enough to attract prehistoric settlers whose *hunebeds* (megalithic tombs) have become Drenthe's main tourist attraction. Otherwise, **Assen**, the provincial capital, is a dull place with a good museum, and **Emmen**, its one real rival, can only be recommended as a convenient base for visiting some of the *hunebeds* and three neighbouring open-air folk culture museums.

Assen

About 16km south of Groningen, **ASSEN** is the capital of Drenthe, though you're unlikely to want to stay here long. Its main square, **Brink** is a big, green open space, which was once home to the monastery that gave rise to the town in the Middle Ages, and there are a few scattered remains of this. Off to the left, **Marktstraat** is the town's main shopping street.

Drents Museum

Brink 1 • Tues–Sun 11am–5pm • €12 • ☎ 0592 377 773, ⓦ drentsmuseum.nl

On the southern edge of Brink, spread over a pleasant group of old houses and recently enlarged with an underground exposition hall, the **Drents Museum** is perhaps the only thing that makes a stop in Assen worthwhile. Next to frequently rotating temporary displays, the museum's most important exhibit is its collection of prehistoric skeletons brought here from the neighbouring *hunebeds*. There is also the much-vaunted Pesse Canoe, the oldest water vessel ever found: dating from about 6800 BC, it looks its age.

Herinneringscentrum Kamp Westerbork

Oosthalen 8, Hooghalen • Mon–Fri 10am–5pm, Sat & Sun 1–5pm; April–Sept Sat & Sun 11am–5pm • €8.50 • ☎ 0593 592 600, ⓦ kampwesterbork.nl

Assen's other main sight is a sad one, the **Herinneringscentrum Kamp Westerbork**, a little south of town on the road between the villages of Amen and Hooghalen. It commemorates Holland's largest concentration camp, which was based 3km away and was where the Nazis assembled Dutch Jews before transporting them to the death camps in the east, mainly Auschwitz and Sobibor. The documents and artefacts on display here are deeply affecting, and buses run every twenty minutes to the camp itself. Not much remains of the camp – there is just a watchtower and a stretch of rail line with restored transport wagons, together with a number of monuments, one to the Dutch Resistance in the trees and another a series of coffin-shaped stones remembering those who spent time here before being transported to their deaths.

ARRIVAL AND INFORMATION	ASSEN
By train Assen's train station is on the eastern edge of the city centre, a 5min walk from Brink. There are regular – usually hourly – services to Amersfoort, Hilversum and Amsterdam, and every 30min to Groningen and Zwolle.	**Tourist office** Assen's VVV is at Marktstraat 8–10 (Mon–Thurs 9.30am–6pm, Fri 9.30am–9pm, Sat 9.30am–5.30pm, Sun 1–5pm; ☎ 0592 243 788 ⓦ ditisassen.nl).

ACCOMMODATION AND EATING	
City Hotel de Jonge Brinkstraat 85 ☎ 0592 312 023, ⓦ hoteldejonge.nl. The only hotel in the centre of town divided over two buildings. The budget rooms are right	above the grand café, the more upscale, recently renovated ones are in the annexe and are decent enough if a bit plain. Nice terrace in summer. **€70**

Emmen and around

To all intents and purposes **EMMEN** is a new town, a twentieth-century amalgamation of strip villages that were originally peat colonies. The centre is a modern affair, mixing the remnants of the old with lumpy boulders, trees and shrubs and a job lot of concrete and glass. Emmen is known for two things: its *hunebeds* and its zoo, while the nearby Veenpark is also worth a visit for its giant open-air museum-village.

MOTOR RACING IN ASSEN

Pretty much the only time Assen is the centre of attention is during the **Assen TT** (ⓦ tt-assen .com), the only Grand Prix motorcycle race in the Netherlands, and the British Superbike championships in September. The TT draws in a crowd of around 100,000, making it the largest one-day sports event in the Netherlands. On the three nights leading up to the event, Assen's centre is packed with people enjoying live music and lots of beer. If you are visiting while it's on (the last Saturday in June), make sure you book accommodation well in advance.

The Zoo

Hoofdstraat 18 • Daily: April–June & Sept–Oct 10am–5pm: July & Aug 10am–6pm, Nov–March 10am–4.30pm • €23, children (3–9) €20.50 • ☎ 0591 850 855, ⓦ dierenparkemmen.nl

Emmen's **zoo**, right in the middle of town, is the reason most people visit, and, unusually for a city-centre zoo, boasts an imitation African savanna, where the animals roam relatively freely. It also has a massive sea-lion pool and a giant hippo house, and in the newer part of the park you can find Humboldt penguins. There are plans are to move the zoo to a larger space out of the centre by 2016, where there will be even greater emphasis on recreating the animals' natural habitats.

The Hunebeds

The best of Emmen's *hunebeds* is **Emmerdennen Hunebed**, in the woods 1km or so east of the station along Boslaan. This is a so-called passage-grave, with a relatively sophisticated entrance surrounded by a ring of standing stones. The largest *hunebed* in Drenthe, however, lies 20km northwest of Emmen, in the village of **Borger**, which takes the *hunebed* theme seriously, from street names and pancakes to special menus. On the northeast edge of the village, the **Hunebedcentrum** at Bronnegerstraat 12 (Mon–Fri 10am–5pm, Sat & Sun 11am–5pm; €9.50; ☎0599 236 374, ⓦhunebedcentrum.nl) explains the origins of the massive *hunebed*, which, at 22.5m long, is an extraordinary feat (in prehistoric terms at least).

The Veenpark

Berkenroede 4, Barger-Comapscum • Daily: Easter to Oct 10am–5pm; July & Aug 10am–6pm • €14.50 (under-5s free) • ☎ 0591 324 444, ⓦ veenpark.nl

About 11km east of Emmen, not far from the German border, the **Veenpark** is a massive open-air museum-village that traces the history and development of the peat colonies of the moors of southern Groningen and eastern Drenthe. The colonies were established in the nineteenth century, when labour was imported to cut the thick layers of peat that lay all over the moors. Isolated in small communities, and under the thumb of the traders who sold their products and provided their foodstuffs, the colonists were harshly exploited and lived in abject poverty until well into the 1930s. Built around some old interlocking canals, the museum consists of a series of reconstructed villages that track through the history of the colonies. It's inevitably a bit folksy, but very popular, with its own narrow-gauge railway, a canal barge and working period bakeries, bars and shops. A thorough exploration takes a full day.

ARRIVAL AND INFORMATION   EMMEN AND AROUND

By train and bus Emmen's train and bus stations adjoin each other, a 5min walk north of the town centre: head straight down Stationsstraat into Boslaan and turn left down Zwolle, the main drag. There are trains to Zwolle every 30min, and the journey takes an hour. Buses #300 and #305 run to Borger on their way between Emmen and Groningen and will drop you off at the park &

ride from where it's a 5min walk to the centre. The Veenpark is served by hourly bus #26 from Emmen station (25min).

Tourist information Emmen's VVV is at Hoofdstraat 26 (Mon 1–5pm, Tues–Sat 10am–5pm; ☎0591 649 712, ⓦdrenthe.nl) and can arrange accommodation at pensions, private rooms and hotels.

ACCOMMODATION AND EATING

EMMEN

Stadshotel Boerland Hoofdstraat 57 ☎ 0591 613 746, ⓦstads-hotelboerland.nl. Probably Emmen's nicest place to stay, across the street from the zoo, and with a decent restaurant, serving main courses like schnitzel, steaks and cod fillets for around €18. €87.50

BORGER

Nathalia Hoofdstraat 87 ☎0599 234 791, ⓦhotelpensionnathalia.nl. Pin-neat two-, three- and four-bedded rooms in a delightful shuttered Dutch cottage in the middle of Borger, every one with cable TV and en-suite facilities. There's a lovely welcome, a cosy sitting room, a garden terrace – and parking too. €60

4

The eastern Netherlands

BLOKZIJL HARBOUR

5

The eastern Netherlands

The three provinces that make up the eastern Netherlands – Flevoland, Overijssel and Gelderland – are home to a string of lovely country towns, whose long and often turbulent history is recalled by a slew of handsome old buildings. Among them, Zwolle, Deventer and Zutphen are perhaps the pick, but there are intriguing former Zuider Zee ports as well, most memorably Kampen and Elburg. For British visitors at least, the most famous town hereabouts is Arnhem, site of the "bridge too far" when the Allies tried unsuccessfully to shorten the war with a lightning strike. Art lovers, meanwhile, won't want to miss the outstanding Kröller-Müller Museum set among the sandy heaths and woodland of the Nationaal Park de Hoge Veluwe.

Heading east from Amsterdam, the first province you reach is **Flevoland**, whose three pancake-flat, reclaimed polders – the twin Flevoland polders and the Noordoostpolder – incorporate two former Zuider Zee islands, **Urk** and **Schokland**, both of which are of considerable interest. The boundary separating Flevoland from the province of **Overijssel** runs along the old Zuider Zee shoreline and it's here that the region comes up trumps with a string of one-time seaports, most strikingly the pretty little towns of **Elburg** (in Gelderland), **Kampen** and **Blokzijl**. These three, along with nearby **Zwolle**, the capital of Overijssel, enjoyed a period of immense prosperity from the fourteenth to the sixteenth centuries, but the bubble burst in the seventeenth when the great merchant cities of Zuid- and Noord-Holland simply outplayed and undercut them. Later, these four towns – along with neighbouring **Deventer** and **Zutphen** – were bypassed by the Industrial Revolution, one happy consequence being that each of them boasts a medley of handsome late medieval and early modern houses and churches. Blokzijl also shares its part of the province with the lakes and waterways that pattern the postcard-pretty hamlet of **Giethoorn**.

Further south, **Gelderland** spreads east from Utrecht to the German frontier, taking its name from the German town of Geldern, its capital until the late fourteenth century. As a province it's a bit of a mixture, varying from the uninspiring agricultural land of the **Betuwe** (Good Land), south of Utrecht, to the more distinctive – and appealing – **Veluwe** (Bad Land), an expanse of heath, woodland and dune that sprawls down from the old Zuider Zee coastline towards **Arnhem** and incorporates the **Nationaal Park de Hoge Veluwe**. Anchoring Gelderland is the ancient town of **Nijmegen**, a fashionable university city, with a lively contemporary feel.

Zwolle

Good-looking **ZWOLLE**, the compact capital of **Overijssel** about 85km from Amsterdam, is on the up. Not so long ago, it was a dowdy sort of place, but inward

The onward march of the wind turbine p.244	**Urk irked** p.246
Flevoland rises from the deep p.245	**Cycling the River IJssel** p.252
	Operation Market Garden p.262

GIETHOORN

Highlights

❶ Zwolle Encased within its old fortifications, this engaging town boasts a handsome cityscape not to mention several fine restaurants and bars. **See p.234**

❷ Kampen Lovely little town and former Zuider Zee port hugging the banks of the River IJssel. **See p.241**

❸ Giethoorn Oh-so-pretty hamlet set amid lakes, canals and wetlands; an ideal place for pottering around on the water. **See p.248**

❹ Zutphen Quintessential Dutch country town with a charming, laidback atmosphere and an imposing Gothic church. **See p.253**

❺ Nationaal Park de Hoge Veluwe Spacious area of heath and forest with cycle routes and footpaths galore. **See p.257**

❻ Kröller-Müller Museum Top-notch museum of modern European art, with a large sculpture garden and an impressive collection of works by van Gogh. **See p.257**

❼ Arnhem This industrious riverside city may have had a searing wartime history, but it's a smashing place to hunker down for a few days and it makes a perfect base for exploring the rest of Gelderland. **See p.260**

HIGHLIGHTS ARE MARKED ON THE MAP ON PP.236–237

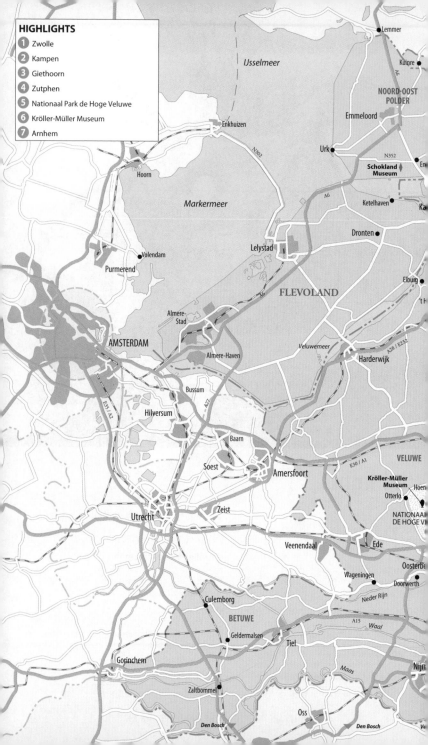

HIGHLIGHTS

1. Zwolle
2. Kampen
3. Giethoorn
4. Zutphen
5. Nationaal Park de Hoge Veluwe
6. Kröller-Müller Museum
7. Arnhem

THE EASTERN NETHERLANDS

5

investment has revived the city and the results are plain to see in a flush of modern buildings – especially on Noordereiland – and the resuscitation of its old harbour, which is now jammed with sailing boats and vintage canal barges.

An ancient town, Zwolle achieved passing international fame when Thomas à Kempis settled here in 1399. Thereafter, it went on to prosper as one of the principal towns of the **Hanseatic League**, its burghers commissioning an extensive programme of public works designed to protect its citizens and impress their rivals. Within the city walls, German textiles were traded for Baltic fish and grain, or more exotic products from Amsterdam like coffee, tea and tobacco. The boom lasted some two hundred years, but by the middle of the seventeenth century the success of Amsterdam and the general movement of trade to the west had undermined its economy – and Zwolle slipped into a sort of reverie from which it is now emerging with much of its old centre intact and well preserved. Unusually, Zwolle's **moat** has survived in fine fettle, encircling the centre and overlooked by nine, seventeenth-century earthen **bastions** that once provided multiple lines of fire for the city's defenders – and little for the enemy's artillery to take aim at. These bastions are seen to fine advantage on the walk in from the train station with fountains playing in the moat and the fortifications clearly visible among the trees.

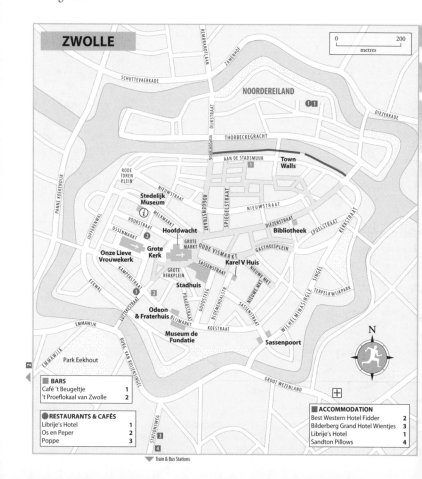

Grote Kerk

Grote Markt • May–Oct Tues–Fri 11am–4.30pm, Sat 1.30–4.30pm • Free • ☎ 038 421 2512, ⓦ grotekerkzwolle.nl

Right in the middle of Zwolle, the **Grote Markt** is a large and somewhat discordant square that surrounds the sandstone mass of the **Grote Kerk,** one of the unluckiest churches in Overijssel: the townsfolk were once inordinately proud of the church's soaring bell tower, but after it had been hit by lightning no fewer than three times (in 1548, 1606 and 1669), they gave up and sold the bells instead. Inside, you'll find the familiar austerity of Dutch Protestantism, with the cavernous nave bare of decoration and the seats arranged on a central pulpit plan. The pulpit itself is an intricate piece of Renaissance carving, but it's the Baroque organ of 1721 that really catches the eye, a real musical whopper with no fewer than four thousand pipes.

Hoofdwacht

Grote Markt 20

Attached to the outside of the Grote Kerk is the **Hoofdwacht**, an ornately gabled building of 1614, which once served as the municipal guardhouse. Public executions took place in front of the Hoofdwacht and the building bears the inscription *Vigilate et Orate* ("Watch and Pray"), a stern warning to the crowds who gathered to witness the assorted mutilations with more or less enthusiasm – the locals once had a reputation for being more preoccupied with money than civic justice. The origins of this reputation lay in a spat with the neighbouring town of Kampen over the sale of some church bells. The bells were faulty, but Zwolle still made Kampen pay, which it did with the lowest denomination of coin possible, obliging the citizens of Zwolle to spend ages counting the pile of copper coins, hence their nickname – **Blauwvingers** (Bluefingers).

The Stedelijk Museum

Melkmarkt 41 • Tues–Sun 11am–5pm • €7.50 • ☎ 038 421 4650, ⓦ stedelijkmuseumzwolle.nl

The **Stedelijk Museum** is divided into two halves – a modern wing, which hosts temporary exhibitions, some of which are very good indeed, and the old wing in the eighteenth-century Drostenhuis. The latter mainly consists of a string of period rooms, enlivened by a modest selection of Golden Age paintings – the highlights being the finely detailed genre scenes of Gerard ter Borch (1619–81) and Hendrick ten Oever (1639–1716).

Onze Lieve Vrouwekerk

Ossenmarkt • April–Oct Mon 1.30–4.30pm & Tues–Sat 11am–4.30pm; Nov–April Mon–Sat 1.30–3.30pm • €2.50, including Peperbus tower • ⓦ basiliekkoorzwolle.nl

The prim-and-proper **Onze Lieve Vrouwekerk**, down an alley off the Grote Markt, has had some hard times: in the sixteenth century, the congregation stuck to their Catholic faith, so the Protestants closed the place down and the last priest had to hotfoot it out of town after he delivered a final sermon in 1580. Thereafter, the church was used for all sorts of purposes – including a cart shed and a musket range – until it was returned to the Catholics in 1809 during the far more tolerant days of the Batavian Republic (see p.327). Today, the interior is firmly neo-Gothic, all ornate paintings and painted walls, but the church does boast an unusual – and especially attractive – tower, called **De Peperbus** (The Pepper Mill) after its distinctive shape.

Museum de Fundatie

Blijmarkt 20 • Tues–Sun 11am–5pm • €9 • ☎ 0572 388 188, ⓦ museumdefundatie.nl

Zwolle's premier art museum, the **Museum de Fundatie**, occupies a grand Neoclassical building from 1841 that began life as the municipal courts. Inside, the ground floor

5

displays a regularly rotated selection from the museum's wide-ranging permanent collection, which includes works by the likes of Turner and Bernini alongside a large collection of modern Dutch art – Mondriaan, Israëls, Toorop and Appel to name but four. Upstairs, the top floor showcases temporary exhibitions.

The old town walls

Like many other towns in the Netherlands, Zwolle was encircled by high **brick walls** until the seventeenth century, when the development of artillery rendered such fortifications obsolete – hence the earthen bastions that replaced them here as elsewhere. Most of Zwolle's medieval wall disappeared centuries ago, but one stretch has survived, complete with defensive parapets and a couple of fortified towers: it stretches out along **Aan de Stadsmuur**, on the south side of the old harbour. The wall is, however, architectural small beer in comparison with the massive **Sassenpoort**, a mighty brick construction whose spiky turrets stand guard over the southern entrance to the old town. Dating from 1409 but extensively restored in the 1890s, this is the town's only surviving medieval gate and Zwolle's main landmark.

ARRIVAL AND INFORMATION   ZWOLLE

By train From Zwolle train station, it's a 10min walk to the Grote Markt: head north along Stationsweg and then proceed east round the old moat.

Destinations Amsterdam CS (1–2 hourly; 1hr 15min); Arnhem (1–2 hourly; 1hr); Den Haag (hourly; 1hr 40min); Deventer (1–2 hourly; 25min); Groningen (3 hourly; 1hr–1hr 10min); Kampen (Mon–Fri every 30min, Sat & Sun hourly; 10min); Leeuwarden (1–2 hourly; 55min–1hr 5min); Nijmegen (1–2 hourly; 1hr 30min); Schiphol airport (1–2 hourly; 1hr 25min); Zutphen (1–2 hourly; 40min).

By bus Located next door to the train station, Zwolle bus station is something of a transport hub for the towns and villages of Overijssel. There is an information kiosk here – or consult ⓦ 9292.nl for route planning.

Destinations Elburg (bus #100; Mon–Sat every 30min, Sun hourly; 40min); Giethoorn (bus #70; Mon–Fri hourly, but no direct service on Sat & Sun; 50min); Vollenhove (bus #71; Mon–Fri every 30min, Sat & Sun hourly; 1hr).

Tourist office There's no VVV in Zwolle as such, but instead there are several Tourist Info Points, including one at the Stedelijk Museum, Melkmarkt 41 (Tues–Sun 11am–5pm; ☏ 038 421 4650, ⓦ zwolletouristinfo.nl).

ACCOMMODATION

Best Western Hotel Fidder Koningin Wilhelminastraat 6 ☏ 038 421 8395, ⓦ hotelfidder.nl. On a suburban sidestreet a 10min walk from the train station, this unusual hotel occupies a big old house dating from the early years of the twentieth century. There are 21 guest rooms here, each decked out with period furniture and assorted knick-knacks. There is also an excellent hotel bar with a good range of bottled beers and an outstanding collection of whiskies. **€90**

Bilderberg Grand Hotel Wientjes Stationsweg 7 ☏ 038 425 4254, ⓦ bilderberg.nl. Housed in a substantial early twentieth-century villa near the train station, this chain hotel offers routine modern bedrooms at competitive prices. It has a pleasant terrace to shoot the breeze on a summer's evening. **€100**

Librije's Hotel Spinhuisplein 1 ☏ 038 853 0000, ⓦ librije.com. One of the region's – if not the country's – most unusual deluxe hotels, Librije's has been shoehorned into Zwolle's old prison, a stern, square stone building dating from the mid-eighteenth century. Many of the prison's original features have been left intact – from the thick wooden doors through to the bars on the windows – and one of the old cells has been left untouched, but nineteen high-spec guest rooms have been added too, each with a large comfy bed, a top-of-the-range bathroom and designer furnishings. Breakfast is taken in the cobbled courtyard, which is covered in the winter, and it's no mean breakfast either – with a series of courses designed to tickle the most jaded of palates. Substantial discounts on the rack rate are often available. **€300**

Sandton Pillows Stationsweg 9 ☏ 038 425 6789, ⓦ sandton.eu. Part of a medium-sized chain, this well-maintained hotel has 43 guest rooms, each of them attractively furnished and brightly carpeted. The hotel is also in a handy location and competitively priced. **€90**

EATING AND DRINKING

RESTAURANTS

Librije's Hotel Spinhuisplein 1 ☏ 038 421 2083, ⓦ librijeshotel.nl. This luxury hotel has two award-winning restaurants – one formal, one more relaxed – but at both the menu is almost self-consciously inventive, featuring such dishes as oxtail with wild mushrooms and piccalilli. Set meals are the order of the day – culminating in an extravagant seven-course dinner costing €160 – and you are expected to linger, dilly and dally. There's also an "atelier" where groups can cook their own meals under a chef's supervision – an extremely popular activity. Reservations are well-nigh essential. Tues–Sun noon–1.30pm & daily 6–8.30pm.

Os en Peper Ossenmarkt 7 ☎038 421 1948, ⓦosenpeper.nl. Attractively chic restaurant in a lovely old building, offering a finely judged menu of both French and Dutch dishes. Both set menus and à la carte – try, for example, the halibut with basil risotto, fried mushrooms, tomato and *beurre blanc* (€25). Tues–Sat 6–10.30pm.

Poppe Luttekestraat 66 ☎038 421 3050, ⓦpoppezwolle.nl. This popular and extremely cosy restaurant, in an old blacksmith's complete with tiled floor and old Dutch photos on the wall, offers a Franco-Dutch menu featuring dishes such as lamb with polenta and aubergine. Mains hover around €25. Reservations recommended – or arrive early. Mon & Sat–Sun 5–10.30pm, Tues–Fri noon–2.30pm & 5–10.30pm.

BARS
Café 't Beugeltje Krabbestraat 63 ☎038 423 6410, ⓦhetbeugeltje.nl. Cleverly shoehorned into a slice of the medieval city wall, this amiable neighbourhood bar looks a bit like a cave – dark, mysterious but still somehow rather cosy. When the sun peeks out, customers migrate to the adjacent terrace, which overlooks the harbour. Daily 5–11.30pm.

't Proeflokaal van Zwolle Blijmarkt 3 ☎038 421 7808, ⓦpfk.nl. Neighbourhood bar, which looks rather like a shop from the outside, but don't let that fool you – the interior is cosy and very brown. Offers five beers on draught plus over thirty *jenevers*, many of which are from the Zwolle region. 4pm–1am; closed Tues.

ENTERTAINMENT

Fraterhuis Blijmarkt 25 ☎038 422 0475, ⓦfilmtheaterfraterhuis.nl. Zwolle's arthouse cinema offers the best in independent films, both Dutch and foreign.
Odeon Blijmarkt 25 ☎0900 1435, ⓦodeondespiegel.nl.

Sharing its premises with the Fraterhuis, Zwolle's main centre for the performing arts offers a lively and varied programme, everything from cabarets and musicals through to contemporary theatre.

Kampen

Pocket-sized **KAMPEN**, just ten minutes by train from Zwolle, strings along the River IJssel, its bold succession of towers and spires recalling headier days when the town was a bustling seaport with its own fleet. The good times came to an abrupt end in the sixteenth century when rival armies ravaged its hinterland and the IJssel silted up – and then Amsterdam mopped up what was left by undercutting its trade prices. Things have never been the same since and, although Kampen did experience a minor boom on the back of its **cigar factories** in the nineteenth century, it remains, in essence, a sleepy provincial town, its medley of handsome old buildings spread over six streets that run parallel to the river – and are themselves bisected by the Burgel canal. It only takes a couple of hours to explore central Kampen and the logical place to start is the **IJssel bridge**, which crosses the river from beside the train station to hit the town centre about halfway along.

Stedelijk Museum
Oudestraat 133 • Tues–Sat 10am–5pm, Sun 1–5pm • €5 • ☎038 331 7361, ⓦstedelijkemuseakampen.nl

From the IJssel bridge, it's a few metres to the **Raadhuis**, which is divided into two: the red-brick Oude Raadhuis, dating from 1543 and topped by a distinctive onion-shaped dome, and the Neoclassical Nieuwe Raadhuis, which was built in the eighteenth century. Together, the two buildings comprise the **Stedelijk Museum**, which is devoted to the history of Kampen with a particular focus on its most prosperous days. The highlight, however, is the **Schepenzaal** (Magistrates' Hall) in the Oude Raadhuis, a claustrophobic medieval affair with dark-stained walls capped by a superbly preserved barrel-vault roof. The hall's magnificent stone **chimneypiece** – a grandiloquent, self-assured work – was carved by Colijn de Nole in tribute to the Habsburg Charles V in 1545, though the chimney's typically Renaissance representations of Justice, Prudence and Strength speak more of municipal pride than imperial glory. To the right,

5

the magistrate's bench is the work of an obscure local carpenter, a Master Frederik, who didn't get on with de Nole at all: angry at not getting the more important job of the chimneypiece, his legacy can be seen on the left-hand pillar, where a minute, malevolent satyr laughs maniacally at the chimney.

The Nieuwe Toren

Oudestraat 146

Just across the street from the Oude Raadhuis is a second tower, the seventeenth-century **Nieuwe Toren**, which becomes Kampen's main attraction for one morning each year, usually in mid-July (check the exact date and time with the VVV), when the "**Kampen cow**" is pulled up to its top. The story goes that when grass began growing at the top of the tower, a local farmer asked if he could graze his cattle up there. To commemorate this daft request, an animal has been hoisted up the tower every year ever since, though thankfully it's now a plastic model rather than a real one.

The Bovenkerk

Koornmarkt • May to mid-Sept daily 10am–4pm; mid–Sept to late Oct daily 1–4pm • Free • ☎ 038 331 3608, ⓦ debovenkerk.nl

Kampen's innocuous main street, pedestrianized **Oudestraat**, runs south from near the IJssel bridge to the **Bovenkerk**, a large and finely proportioned Gothic structure with a mighty spire and an unusual – and architecturally influential – choir with no fewer than thirteen radiating chapels. The choir was the work of Rotger of Cologne, a member of the Parler family of masons who was subsequently to work on Cologne Cathedral. Inside, the nave is light and spacious and although the Protestants jettisoned most of the furnishings and fittings, the fancy sixteenth-century **choir screen** has survived as has the late Gothic limestone **pulpit**. In the south transept, look out also for the urn containing the heart of **Admiral Willem de Winter**, a native of Kampen who loathed the House of Orange. A staunch Republican, he helped the French during the invasion of 1795 and played a leading role in the Batavian Republic thereafter; the rest of him lies in the Pantheon in Paris.

The Old Town Gates

Beside the Bovenkerk is the earliest of Kampen's three surviving **gates**, the fourteenth-century **Koornmarktspoort**, an imposing affair that looks as if it could withstand a fair old battering – not that the townsfolk trusted their defences when a Habsburg army showed up here in 1572: aware of the massacre at Zutpen (see p.253), Kampen's burghers surrendered in double-quick time. The other two gates – the **Cellebroederspoort** and the **Broederpoort** – are of a later, more ornamental design and lie on the west side of town. They are best reached via Vloeddijk, which runs along the west side of the Burgel canal.

ARRIVAL AND INFORMATION

KAMPEN

By train Kampen train station is the terminus of a branch line from Zwolle, with regular services connecting the two towns (Mon–Sat every 30min, Sat & Sun hourly; 10min). From the station, it's a 5min walk over the bridge to the town centre.

By bus Kampen bus station is next to the train station, with a regular service to Urk (Mon–Fri every 30min, Sat hourly; 1hr).

Tourist office There's no VVV in Kampen, but there is a Tourist Info Point. It's on the main street, a 3min walk south of the IJssel bridge inside the Read Shop at Oudestraat 41 (Mon–Sat 9am–5pm; ☎ 038 332 2522, ⓦ ontdekdeijsseldelta.nl).

ACCOMMODATION AND EATING

De Bottermarck Broederstraat 23 ☎ 038 331 9542, ⓦ debottermarck.nl. The best restaurant in Kampen, this is a trim little place with the emphasis on local, seasonal

ingredients, especially seafood – try, for example, the halibut with lobster sauce (€30). Broederstraat begins a few metres from the IJssel bridge, running west from the main street, Oudestraat. Tues–Fri noon–10.30pm, Sat 5–10.30pm.

Hotel van Dijk IJsselkade 30 ☎ 038 331 4925, ⓦ hotelvandijk.nl. Appealing, family-run, three-star hotel in a well-maintained, two-storey modern building just along the riverfront from the IJssel bridge. There are eighteen guest rooms, most of which are quite spacious and the better ones overlook the river. **€90**

Elburg

Once a Zuider Zee port of some renown, tiny **ELBURG**, 17km southwest of Zwolle, abuts the **Veluwemeer**, the narrow waterway separating the mainland from the Oostelijk Flevoland polder. In recent years, the town has become a popular day-trip destination, flush with visitors who come here to wander the pretty little streets, admiring the old brick cottages bleached ruddy-brown by the elements beneath their dinky pantile roofs. Elburg is also awash with cafés and restaurants, some of whom serve the local delicacy, **smoked eel**.

Elburg was a successful port with its own fishing fleet from as early as the thirteenth century, but the boom times really began in the 1390s when the governor, **Arent thoe Boecop**, redesigned the whole place in line with the latest developments in town planning, imposing a **central grid** of streets encircled by a protective wall and moat. Not all of Elburg's citizens were overly impressed – indeed the street by the museum is still called Ledige Stede, literally "Empty Way" – but the basic design, with the notable addition of sixteenth-century ramparts and gun emplacements, survived the decline that set in when the harbour silted up, and can still be observed today. Elburg's two main streets are **Beekstraat**, which forms the northeast–southwest axis, and **Jufferenstraat/Vischpoortstraat**, which runs southeast–northwest; they intersect at right angles to form the main square, the **Vischmarkt**.

Museum Elburg

Jufferenstraat 6–8 • Tues–Sat 11am–5pm • €5, including Kazematten (see p.244) • ☎ 052 5681 341, ⓦ museumelburg.nl

Entering Elburg from the southeast, it's a few metres from the town moat to the **Museum Elburg**, which is housed in a severe-looking former convent and displays a rambling collection focused on the town's history. Of particular interest is the collection of silverware that was once the prized possession of the local sailors' guild, and a small display on the town's maritime hero, **Vice Admiral J.H. van Kinsbergen** (1735–1819). Kinsbergen spent years in the Russian navy before returning to the Netherlands, where he promptly became a hero by defeating an English fleet at the Battle of Dogger Bank in 1781.

St Nicolaaskerk and around

Zuiderkerkstraat • June–Aug Mon–Fri 2–4.30pm, Tues also 10am–noon • Free

From the Museum Elburg, it's a couple of minutes' walk north to **St Nicolaaskerk**, a lumpy fourteenth-century structure that dominates its immediate surroundings even without its spire, which was destroyed by lightning in 1693: the city fathers huffed and puffed about replacing it, but there was never enough money. Close by, just down Van Kinsbergenstraat, is the three-storey, balconied **Stadhuis**, which once served as Arent thoe Boecop's home, and from here it's another short stroll to the town's main square, **Vischmarkt**, a pleasant little piazza overlooked by pavement cafés.

The Vischpoort

Vischpoortstraat leads northwest off Vischmarkt to the best preserved of the medieval town gates, the **Vischpoort**, a much restored brick rampart tower dating from 1594.

5

Behind the Vischpoort, the pattern of the sixteenth-century defensive works is clear to see – from interior town wall to dry ditch, to earthen mound and moat. At the Vischpoort, one of the subterranean artillery casements, the **Kazematten**, is sometimes open to the public in summer: the entrance fee is included in the Museum Elburg ticket (see p.243), but you'll need to check the opening times with the tourist office (see below). It's easy to see why the Dutch called such cramped and poorly ventilated emplacements Moortkuijl, literally "Pits of Murder". From the Kazematten, a lovely, leafy, one-hour stroll takes you right round the old **ramparts**.

ARRIVAL AND INFORMATION

ELBURG

By bus Elburg is not on the train network, but buses drop passengers at the Centrum stop just outside the southern entrance to the old town near the tourist office.
Destinations Nunspeet train station, on the Amersfoort/Zwolle line (bus #100; Mon–Sat every 30min, Sun hourly; 20min); Zwolle (bus #100; Mon–Sat every 30min, Sun

hourly; 40min).
Tourist office Elburg VVV is at Jufferenstraat 8 (Tues–Sat 11am–5pm; ☎0525 681 341, ⍟vvvelburg.nl). It has details of boat trips along the Veluwemeer, as well as information about renting your own sailing boat.

ACCOMMODATION AND EATING

The tourist office has a list of **private rooms and B&Bs** and will phone around to make a booking on your behalf; try to get a room in the old centre and come early in the day in high season, when accommodation can get tight. Expect to pay around €85 for a double, en-suite room. In summer, the town's favourite nibble, **smoked eel in jelly**, is available at any number of pavement stalls and is sold by weight – a *pond* is 500g.

Le Papillon Vischpoortstraat 15 ☎0525 681 190, ⍟restaurantlepapillon.nl. The best of Elburg's many cafés and restaurants, this smart, split-level place offers a satisfying Franco-Dutch menu: try, for example, the tasty coq au vin (€18). Wed–Sun 10.30am–11pm; June–Sept also Tues 10.30am–11pm; kitchen noon–9pm.

Rose Garden Kamperweg 1 ☎0525 685 849, ⍟rose-garden.nl. Of the town's several B&Bs, this one is in a particularly pleasant location just outside (and facing back onto) the old town walls. The rooms are nothing very fancy, but they are well kept and well equipped. **€70**

The Noordoostpolder

Nudging out into the IJsselmeer about 20km northwest of Zwolle, the pancake-flat **Noordoostpolder** was the first large segment of Flevoland to be reclaimed from the ocean (see box opposite). It has the wide skies that characterize the polders (and these can indeed be breathtaking), but – and this is where it really scores – it also incorporates two former Zuider Zee islands. One is home to the engaging fishing village of **Urk** while the other, **Schokland** has been a UNESCO World Heritage Site since 1995 and boasts a particularly fascinating museum.

THE ONWARD MARCH OF THE WIND TURBINE

A small army of **wind turbines** strings out along the shores of the IJsselmeer and the Veluwemeer, but they also pop up on many other rural horizons from Friesland to Zeeland. In the countryside, solitary turbines provide electricity for farmers, while on the coast and out to sea, banks of turbines harness the incoming weather systems, providing electricity for thousands of households. Erected in the 1930s, the first wind turbines provided electricity for remote communities in the US and the Australian outback. However, their full potential wasn't realized until research into cleaner forms of energy, carried out in Denmark and Germany during the 1970s, produced mechanisms that were both more efficient and more powerful. Ideally suited to the flat, windswept polders of the Netherlands, the first Dutch turbines generated 40 kilowatts of electricity; output is now a beefier 600 kilowatts – enough for a single wind farm of fifty turbines to provide power to 6500 households.

FLEVOLAND RISES FROM THE DEEP

Following the damming of the Zuider Zee and the creation of the IJsselmeer (see box, p.112), the coastline east of Amsterdam was transformed by the creation of the Netherlands' twelfth and newest province, **Flevoland**, which was reclaimed from the sea in two major phases. Drained in the early 1930s, the **Noordoostpolder** was the first major chunk of land to be salvaged and during the process two old Zuider Zee islands – Urk and Schokland – were joined to the mainland. The original aims of the Noordoostpolder scheme were predominantly agricultural, with the polder providing 500 square kilometres of new farmland, which the government handed out to prospective smallholders. Yet it soon became apparent that there were design faults: very few trees were planted, so the land was subject to soil erosion, and both the polder and the adjacent mainland dried out and started to sink – problems that persist today.

The Dutch did, however, learn from their mistakes when they came to drain the next large slice of Flevoland in the 1950s and 1960s: they created an encircling waterway, which successfully stopped the land from drying out and sinking, and the government tried hard to make the new polders more attractive to potential settlers, planting mini-forests and setting aside parkland. Together, these two newer polders, the **Zuidelijk Flevoland** and **Oostelijk Flevoland**, now form one large chunk of reclaimed land in front of the old shoreline, effectively a polder-island that comprises the bulk of **Flevoland**. The new polders were also used to house urban overspill with the creation of two new medium-sized towns, **Almere** and **Lelystad**, the latter named after Cornelis Lely (1854–1929), the pioneering engineer who had the original idea for the Zuider Zee scheme.

Urk

Easily the most interesting town on the Noordoostpolder is **URK**, a burgeoning harbour, shipyard and fishing port, where a series of narrow lanes – and tiny terraced houses – indicate the extent of the **old village** before it was topped and tailed by new housing estates. Before it became part of the mainland, centuries of hardship and isolation had bred a tight-knit island community, one that had a distinctive dialect and its own version of the national costume. Most of Urk's individuality may have gone, but its earlier independence does still resonate, rooted in a **fishing industry** that marks it out from the surrounding agricultural communities. One Urk peculiarity that remains today is its addresses: traditionally the village was divided into areas called "Wijks", though nowadays the streets also have names – the tourist office, therefore, is at both Raadhuisstraat 2 and/or Wijk 2-2.

The old village

Wandering the **old village** of Urk, which cuddles up to the north side of the harbour, is a pleasant way to pass an hour or two. Look out for the lakeshore **Vissersmonument** (Fisherman's Monument), where a plaque commemorates local seamen lost at sea and a statue of a woman gazes westward, presumably awaiting the return of her man. There are handsome views out across the IJsselmeer from here, too, with a small sandy **beach** down below. Nearby, the conspicuous **lighthouse** marks the southwesterly tip of the old village – with another, larger sandy beach just along the lakeshore back towards the harbour. From the lighthouse you can see an insignificant-looking rock sticking out of the water about 70m offshore. This is the **Ommelebommelestien**, a rock from where, according to legend, all newly born Urkers spring: all the prospective dad has to do is row out to the rock and pick up a baby – very handy.

Museum Het Oude Raadhuis

Wijk 2-2/Raadhuisstraat 2 • April–Oct Mon–Fri 10am–5pm, Sat 10am–4pm; Nov–March Mon–Sat 10am–4pm • €4.75 • ☎ 0527 683 262, ⓦ museumopurk.nl

In the former town hall, in the centre of the old village, the **Museum Het Oude Raadhuis** is an enjoyably folksy affair with a series of displays devoted to all things Urk-ian. There are examples of the islanders' distinctive traditional costume, down to the fancily painted clogs; a recreated fisherman's home from the 1930s; an old barber's shop, where the men once met to shoot the breeze as confirmed by a set of old photos; fishing tackle; landscape paintings – the best are by Ernst van Leyden (1892–1969); and a small cabinet devoted to Pieter Hoekman, the village policeman who joined the Resistance in World War II, but was betrayed and subsequently shot by the Germans in 1943. There is also a feature on the fishing boats of Urk, unusual in that the inshore boats had small holes drilled into their sides to allow water in, thereby keeping the catch super fresh.

ARRIVAL AND INFORMATION URK

By bus Buses to and from Urk cut a circuitous route through the village's sprawling outskirts, but get off at the Singel roundabout and you'll be just 5min walk from the harbour and the old village. The most useful bus service is the one to Kampen (Mon–Fri every 30min, Sat hourly; 1hr).

By boat In summer, there's a passenger ferry boat service across the IJsselmeer between Urk and Enkhuizen on *De Zuiderzee* (☎ 06 5360 8813, ⊛ de-zuiderzee.nl). Tickets, which can be bought on board, cost €15 one way, €17.50

return). For departure times, consult the company website or visit Urk VVV.

Destinations Enkhuizen (late June to late Aug Mon–Sat 2 daily; 1hr 45min).

Tourist office Urk VVV is in the same building as the Museum Het Oude Raadhuis, in the centre of the old village at Wijk 2-2 (April–Oct Mon–Fri 10am–5pm & Sat 10am–4pm; Nov–March Mon–Sat 10am–4pm; ☎ 0527 684 040, ⊛ touristinfourk.nl).

ACCOMMODATION AND EATING

There are no **hotels** in Urk, but the tourist office does have a list of **B&Bs** with double rooms costing between €65 and €85. As for food, Urk is home to several seafood **restaurants** and these are supplemented by a cluster of seafood kiosks on and around the main street, Raadhuisstraat.

De Boet Restaurant Wijk 1–61/Westhavenkade 61 ☎ 0527 688 736, ⊛ restaurantdeboet.nl. In an old harbourside building, this is the smartest restaurant in Urk, a neat and modern place where they serve the freshest of seafood with main courses averaging around €20. Mon & Sat 5.30–10pm, Tues–Fri noon–2pm & 5.30–10pm.

Pension het Anker Wijk 4–13/Prins Hendrikstraat 13 ☎ 0527 685 307, ⊛ overnachteninurk.nl. Among Urk's handful of B&Bs, this is perhaps the pick, a cosy if

somewhat spartan little place in an old fisherman's cottage a couple of minutes' walk from the tourist office. **€80**

Visrestaurant de Kaap Wijk 1–5/Staverse Kade 5 ☎ 0527 681 509, ⊛ restaurantdekaap.nl. The Urk fishing fleet specializes in sole, plaice and eel, and the best place to sample them is here at this long-established restaurant, near the west end of the harbour on the way to the lighthouse. It's an informal, laidback place with a mini-terrace looking out over the IJsselmeer. Main courses from €15. Daily 10am–10pm, 8pm in winter.

URK IRKED

The damming of the Zuider Zee (see box, p.112) posed special problems for the **deep-sea fishermen of Urk** and it's hardly surprising that they opposed the IJsselmeer scheme from the beginning. Some villagers feared that the disappearance of their island enclave would spell the end of their distinctive way of life (by and large they were right), but it was the **fishermen** who were most annoyed by the loss of direct access to the North Sea. After futile negotiations at national level, the fishermen of Urk decided to take matters into their own hands: the larger ships of the fleet were sent north to fish from ports above the line of the Afsluitdijk and transport was organized to transfer the catch straight back for sale at the Urk fish auctions. In the meantime, other fishermen decided to continue to fish locally and adapt to the freshwater species of the IJsselmeer. These were not comfortable changes for the islanders and the whole situation deteriorated after the Dutch government passed new legislation banning trawling in the IJsselmeer in 1970. When the **inspectors arrived in Urk** to enforce the ban, years of resentment exploded in ugly scenes of dockside violence and the government moved fast to sweeten the pill by offering substantial subsidies to compensate those fishermen affected. This arrangement continues today and the focus of conflict has moved on to **EU quotas** – and attempts to impose them on the deep-sea fleet.

Schokland

The southern reaches of the Noordoostpolder incorporate the former Zuider Zee islet of **Schokland**, a slender sliver of land that was finally abandoned in 1859 by royal decree – the government decided it was just too dangerous for the islanders to soldier on. Given the turbulent waters of the Zuider Zee, it's a wonder that the islanders stayed for as long as they did: approaching from the east or west along the N352, you can only just spot the gentle ridge that once kept the islanders out of the ocean. Neither did their heroic efforts win the respect of their fellow Netherlanders – they were nicknamed *schokker* (literally cow dung) – nor did they breed a sense of community: the north end of the island was Catholic, the south Protestant, and relations were strained, verging on the positively hostile. Schokland's intriguing history is explored at the Museum Schokland (see below) and you can extend your visit by taking the combined **footpath and cycleway** that follows the old Schokland shoreline, a loop trail about 10km long. There's not much to see as such – the islanders didn't leave much behind – but it's a pleasant way to spend a few hours.

Museum Schokland

Middelbuurt 3, 300m south of the N352 • April–June & Sept–Oct Tues–Sun 11am–5pm; July & Aug daily 10am–5pm; Nov–March Fri– Sun 11am–5pm • €6 • ☎ 052 725 1396, ⓦ museumschokland.nl

The main reminder of Schokland's precarious existence is the **Museum Schokland**, a huddle of buildings lying just to the south of the N352 on the site of what was once the island's largest village. The museum kicks off with an excellent film tracking the history of the island and continues with a display of all sorts of bits and pieces found during the draining of the Noordoostpolder – tools, a rusty cannon, pottery and even mammoth bones. Footsteps away from the main museum building, is the old village church, a plain, rather dour building dating from 1834, and a portion of the old stockade that once protected the village from the sea.

ARRIVAL AND DEPARTURE   **SCHOKLAND**

By bus There are no buses to Schokland – the nearest you'll get is Ens, a 50min walk away.

By car Bisected by the N352, the former island of Schokland runs north/south about halfway between the hamlets of Ens and Nagele.

Northwest Overijssel

The closing of the Zuider Zee and the draining of the Noordoostpolder transformed **northwest Overijssel**: not only were the area's seaports cut off from the ocean, but they were placed firmly inland with only a narrow channel, the **Vollenhover Kanaal**, separating them from the new polder. As a result, **Vollenhove** and more especially **Blokzijl**, the two main seaports concerned, reinvented themselves as holiday destinations and today hundreds of Dutch city folk come here to sail and cycle.

Traditionally, both Vollenhove and Blokzijl looked firmly out across the ocean, doing their best to ignore the moor and marshland villages that lay **inland**. They were not alone: for many centuries this was one of the most neglected corners of the country and things only began to pick up in the 1800s, when the "Society of Charity" established a series of agricultural colonies here. The Dutch bourgeoisie were, however, as wary of the paupers as their Victorian counterparts in Britain, and the 1900 *Baedeker*, when surveying the colonies, noted approvingly that "the houses are visited almost daily by the superintending officials and the strictest discipline is everywhere observed." The villagers were reliant on **peat** for fuel and their haphazard diggings, spread over several centuries, created the canals, lakes and ponds that now lattice the area, attracting tourists by the boatload. The big pull is picture-postcard **Giethoorn**, whose mazy canals are flanked by splendid thatched cottages, but try to avoid visiting in the height of the season, when the crowds can get oppressive.

5

Vollenhove

Pocket-sized **VOLLENHOVE** sits on the old Zuider Zee coastline some 30km north of Zwolle, its former role as a busy seaport recalled by the remains of its bastions and ramparts, which now nudge up against the Vollenhover Kanaal - as does its old **harbour**, a cramped, circular affair now encased within steep grassy banks. Overlooking the harbour is **St Nicolaaskerk**, a large, rambling Gothic church that started out as a small chapel in the eleventh century. It backs onto **Kerkplein**, once the heart of Vollenhove and now home to several handsome old buildings, most notably the elegant, arcaded **Raadhuis** and the seventeenth-century **Latin School**, now an antique shop, which boasts charming crow-stepped gables.

ARRIVAL AND DEPARTURE   VOLLENHOVE

By bus Buses to and from Vollenhove stop on Clarenberglaan, a 5min walk from Kerkplein – straight up Doelenstraat and then Kerkstraat.
Destinations Blokzijl (Mon–Sat hourly; 45min, change at Marknesse); Giethoorn (1–2 hourly; 40min, change at Zwartsluis); Zwolle (bus #71; Mon–Fri every 30min, Sat & Sun hourly; 1hr).

EATING

Restaurant Seidel Kerkplein 3 ☎ 0527 241 262, ⓦ seidel.nl. At the very heart of Vollenhove, this is the best restaurant in town, a smart and fairly formal place in the old Raadhuis with charming antique decor. The menu is classic Dutch, featuring such delights as calf liver with bacon and onions. Main courses average €23 at dinner, less at lunch. Tues–Sat noon–2pm & 5–10.30pm, Sun 2–10pm.

Blokzijl

Tiny **BLOKZIJL**, some 5km north of Vollenhove, is the most appealing of the area's former seaports, its cobweb of narrow alleys and slim canals surrounding a trim little harbour, which is now connected to the Vollenhover Kanaal. The town once prospered from the export of peat, an economic boom that accounts for Blokzijl's battery of seventeenth-century buildings, the most conspicuous of which is the **Grote Kerk**, one of the country's first Protestant churches.

ARRIVAL AND DEPARTURE   BLOKZIJL

By bus Buses to and from Blokzijl drop passengers beside the N333 on the western edge of town, a 5min walk from the harbour.
Destinations Giethoorn (Mon–Fri hourly; 1hr, change buses at Steenwijk); Vollenhove (Mon–Sat hourly; 45min; change at Marknesse); Zwolle (Mon–Sat hourly; 1hr; bus to Steenwijk train station and train to Zwolle).

ACCOMMODATION AND EATING

Auberge aan Het Hof Kerkstraat 9 ☎ 0527 291 844, ⓦ aubergeaanhethof.nl. In the centre of Blokzijl, this combined hotel and restaurant offers four bedrooms, each decorated in a spick-and-span modern style. The restaurant serves a well-considered French menu using seasonal ingredients where possible, with mains averaging €24. Mon & Thurs–Sun 6–10pm, daily 6–10pm in high season. **€80**

Giethoorn

GIETHOORN's origins are really rather odd. No one gave much thought to this marshy, infertile chunk of land until the thirteenth century, when the local landowner gifted it to an obscure religious sect. Perhaps to his surprise, the colonists made a go of things, eking out a living from local **peat** deposits and discovering, during their digs, the horns of hundreds of **goats**, which are presumed to have been the victims of the great St Elizabeth's Day flood of 1170; duly impressed, the residents named the place

5

Geytenhoren (goats' horns). Later, the settlers dug canals to transport the peat and the diggings flooded, thus creating the watery network that has become the number one tourist attraction hereabouts – and no wonder: Giethoorn is extraordinarily picturesque, its slender brown-green waterways overseen by lovely thatched cottages, shaded by mature trees and crisscrossed by pretty humpbacked footbridges. The only fly in the idyllic ointment is Giethoorn's popularity: avoid the centre of the village in the summer, when the place heaves with tour groups.

The village's unusual origins account for its **shape**: Giethoorn is about 4km from top to bottom and never more than 900m wide – and it runs parallel to (and just east of) the N334 between Zwartsluis and Steenwijk. Most visitors make a beeline for the centre of Giethoorn, which spreads out along **Ds. Hylkemaweg**, between the N334 and Lake Bovenwijde, but this is in fact the least appealing section. Much more agreeable, with little tourist congestion even in summer, is **northern Giethoorn**, where you'll find pristine thatched cottages, immaculate gardens, the cutest of wooden bridges and the first-rate *Hotel de Harmonie* (see below).

Dwarsgracht

If the watery delights of Giethoorn appeal – and you're after a little more solitude – there's more of the same along **Dwarsgracht**, about 4km to the west of Giethoorn on the other side of the N334. From Dwarsgracht, you can also cycle off into one segment of the **Nationaal Park Weerribben-Wieden** (ⓦnp-weerribbenwieden.nl), which aims to conserve and protect a large area of canal and marshland.

ARRIVAL AND INFORMATION   GIETHOORN

By bus The best bus service to Giethoorn is from Steenwijk train station (bus #70 hourly; 20min). This bus travels the length of Giethoorn, pulling in at several stops, including Ds. Hylkemaweg and the *Hotel de Harmonie* (see below). There are very few direct buses between Zwolle and Giethoorn – you mostly have to change at Zwartsluis – so it's usually quicker to catch the train from Zwolle to Steenwijk (every 15–30min; 25min) and then take the bus. *Destinations* Blokzijl (Mon–Fri hourly; 1hr, change buses at Steenwijk); Steenwijk train station (bus #70 hourly;

20min); Vollenhove (1–2 hourly; 40min, change buses at Zwartsluis).

Tourist office Giethoorn's VVV is at Eendrachtsplein 2 (March Tues–Fri 11am–3pm; April–June & Sept Mon–Sat 10am–5pm; July & Aug Mon–Sat 10am–5pm, Sun 11am–3pm; Oct Tues–Sat 10am–4pm; Nov–Feb Tues 11am–3pm; ☏0521 360 112, ⓦgiethoorn.com), just off the N334 and a few metres from the Ds. Hylkemaweg bus stop. It has all sorts of local information, including several dozen leaflets detailing suggested cycling routes.

GETTING AROUND

The only way to get the real flavour of Giethoorn and its watery surroundings is by **boat or bike** – and fortunately almost every business hereabouts, from petrol stations to hotels, will be able to assist with rentals.

Boat rental Boats in Giethoorn come in a variety of shapes and sizes and although prices vary, reckon on paying around €15/hr for a whisper boat (a quiet, environmentally friendly, electric-powered motorboat) down to €28/day for a kayak.

Water taxis are similarly commonplace and a trip round the village costs about €5/hr.

Bike rental Bicycles start at about €7.50/day. Cycle route leaflets are on sale at the tourist office (see above).

ACCOMMODATION AND EATING

Giethoorn tourist office has a long list of **private rooms** (€50–100), though only a few of them are in the north part of Giethoorn, which is really where you want to stay. Accommodation can get very tight between June and August.

Hotel de Dames van De Jonge Beulakerweg 30 ☏0521 361 360, ⓦdedamesvandejonge.nl. Across the street from the *Hotel de Harmonie* in the northern part of Giethoorn, this appealing canal-side hotel occupies several intelligently converted old buildings and its restaurant has a pleasant terrace. The hotel rooms are modern and smart

(verging on the plush) and there's cycle and boat rental here too. **€90**

★**Hotel de Harmonie** Beulakerweg 55 ☏0521 361 372, ⓦharmonie-giethoorn.nl. Giethoorn's most agreeable hotel is the four-star *De Harmonie*, a warm and friendly modern place at the north end of the village. The hotel consists of two two-storey buildings, one of which is thatched, and although the rooms are not especially stylish, they are attractive, simple and spacious: some have their own canal-side balconies. The hotel also rents out bikes and boats and organizes boat trips from its own jetty. Its attractively decorated restaurant is first-rate too, serving a tasty range of Dutch dishes with main courses costing about €22. This is *the* place to try a local delicacy: perch and pike (*snoekbaarsfilet*) from the IJsselmeer. **€100**

Vakantiepark Giethoorn Binnenpad 49 ☎0521 361 332, ⓦvakantieparkgiethoorn.nl. Short and chubby, Lake Bovenwijde lies immediately to the east of Giethoorn, and its western shore is dotted with campsites and holiday complexes. One of the best equipped is the *Vakantiepark* in a prime spot just north of the village centre, a short stroll from the east end of Ds. Hylkemaweg. The chalets and cottages come in a variety of sizes, but for four people in a two-bedroom chalet (with a minimum stay of two nights) reckon on **€250**

Deventer

Glued to the east bank of the River IJssel, **DEVENTER**, some 35km south of Zwolle, is an intriguing and – in tourist terms – rather neglected town, whose origins can be traced back to the missionary work of the eighth-century Saxon monk, Lebuinus. Subsequently, an influential centre of medieval learning, it was here in the late fourteenth century that Gerrit Groot founded the **Brotherhood of the Common Life**, a semi-monastic collective that espoused tolerance and humanism within a philosophy known as *Moderne Devotie* (Modern Devotion). This progressive creed attracted some of the great minds of the time, and Thomas à Kempis and Erasmus both studied here. Today, Deventer makes for a pleasant stop, with a handful of fine old buildings and a good bar and restaurant scene.

The Brink

Enclosed by the river and the remains of its moat, Deventer's engaging, broadly circular centre has kept its medieval street plan, which zeroes in on the **Brink**, a surprisingly large, cobbled marketplace running roughly north to south. On the west side of the Brink, where it widens out, is the distinctive **Penninckshuis**, whose florid Renaissance frontage is decorated with statuettes of six Virtues. The inscription *Alst*

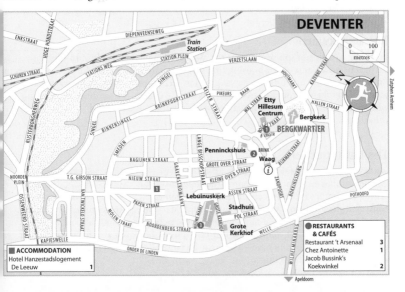

5

CYCLING THE RIVER IJSSEL

Beginning at the **Wilhelminabrug** in Deventer, a signposted **cycleway** follows the banks of the **River IJssel** 20km south to Zutphen. It's a gentle ride through farmland and along quiet, winding lanes, with plenty of places to stop for a picnic and some fine views of the river and the weeping willows that thrive along its banks. Once in Zutphen, the return journey can be made either along the opposite shore, bringing the total distance to around 45km, or direct by train. You can **rent bikes** for the day from both Deventer and Zutphen train stations.

Godt behaget beter benyt als beclaget is smug indeed: "If it pleases God it is better to be envied than to be pitied". Nearby, at the square's southern end is the **Waag**, a late Gothic red-brick structure of 1528, whose good-looking medley of wobbly towers and turrets is fronted by a stone portico that was added a century later. Curiously, the large **pan** nailed to the outside of the Waag's western wall was left there as a warning: when the city council learnt that the mint master was debasing the town's coins, he was put in the pan and boiled alive. The bullet holes weren't an attempt to prolong the agony, however, but the work of idle French soldiers garrisoned here, who were taking, quite literally, "pot shots".

Etty Hillesum Centrum

Roggestraat 3 • June–Aug daily 1–4pm; Sept–May Wed, Sat & Sun 1–4pm; • €3 • ☎ 0570 641 003, ⓦ ettyhillesumcentrum.nl

Just off the Brink, the **Etty Hillesum Centrum** is named after the eponymous Jewish woman (1914–43), who lived in Deventer from 1924 to 1932, before ultimately perishing in Auschwitz. The centre has two permanent displays, one on Etty, the other on Jewish life in Deventer, and also features temporary exhibitions on related topics – racism, religious persecution and the like. A remarkable woman by any standard, **Etty Hillesum** refused to go into hiding during the German occupation and volunteered to work for the Jewish Council instead. Fully aware of the likely consequences, Etty chose to work at the Westerbork transit camp, assisting her fellow Jews as best she could before they were taken to the concentration camps. Etty's wartime diaries and letters have survived – and are still in print (see p.347).

The Bergkwartier

From the east side of the Brink, near the Waag, **Rijkmanstraat** leads in to the **Bergkwartier**, an area of old housing that was tastefully refurbished during the 1960s in one of the region's first urban renewal projects. Centrepiece of the Bergkwartier is the medieval **Bergkerk**. Fronted by two tall towers, the church is a serious-looking affair whose two main stages of construction are clearly indicated by the differences in the colouring of the brickwork.

The Lebuinuskerk

Grote Kerkhof • April–Oct Mon–Sat 11am–5pm; Nov–March Mon–Sat 11am–4pm • Free • ☎ 0570 612 548, ⓦ lebuinuskerk.nl

On the south side of the town centre, the **Lebuinuskerk** is a vast Gothic edifice built during Deventer's fifteenth-century pomp and named after an English **missionary** who converted the locals to Christianity in the middle of the eighth century. Inside, the church's soaring, three-aisled nave, with its high-arched windows and slender pillars, rises to a vaulted ceiling adorned by intricate tracery. Look out also for the medieval murals on the walls of the nave – they may be faded, but enough remains to see the skill of their original execution.

By train Deventer's train station is on the north side of the town centre, a 5–10min walk from the Brink. The bus station is next door.

Destinations Apeldoorn (every 30min; 15min); Arnhem (every 30min; 40min); Nijmegen (every 30min; 1hr);

Zutphen (every 30min; 15min); Zwolle (every 30min; 25min).

Tourist office The VVV is bang in the centre of town, inside the Waag at Brink 56 (Sun & Mon 1–5pm, Tues–Sat 10am–5pm; ☎0570 710 120, ⓦdeventer.info).

ACCOMMODATION AND EATING

't Arsenaal Nieuwe Markt 33 ☎0570 616 495, ⓦrestaurantarsenaal.nl. At the back of the Lebuinuskerk, in what was formerly a church and then the town arsenal, this smart little restaurant offers a short but well-selected, modern menu featuring the likes of prime steak with *pommes fondants* and seasonal vegetables; mains average €25. Mon & Sat 5.30–10pm, Tues–Fri noon–3pm & 5.30–10pm.

Chez Antoinette Roggestraat 10 ☎0570 616 630, ⓦchezantoinette.nl. Appealing Franco-Portuguese restaurant down a side street just east off the Brink. Authentic, tasty dishes – try, for example, the Setubal sardines. After the kitchen closes at 10pm, the places morphs into a bodega – with a first-rate wine cellar. Main courses average €20. Tues–Sun 5pm–1am.

★**Hotel Hanzestadslogement De Leeuw** Nieuwstraat 25 ☎0570 610 290, ⓦhoteldeleeuw.nl. Deventer is short of places to stay, but this lovely

family-run hotel has nine cosy rooms occupying an old terrace house whose stepped gable facade dates back to the 1640s. All the guest rooms are en suite and decorated in an unassuming but pleasant style, and the downstairs breakfast room doubles as a deli-cum-sweet shop (Wed–Sat 11am–5pm) with all manner of regional specialities displayed among the assorted antiques and bygones. €110

Jacob Bussink's Koekwinkel Brink 84 ☎0570 614 246, ⓦdeventerkoekwinkel.nl. Among the platoon of cafés that line up along the Brink, this is perhaps the most distinctive. It's a lovely old-fashioned place – the oldest cake shop in town – where they serve a tasty cup of coffee along with the local speciality, *Deventer koek*, a spiced and very chewy gingerbread biscuit; mind your fillings. Mon 1.30–5.30pm, Tues–Fri 9am–5.30pm & Sat 9am–5pm.

Zutphen

ZUTPHEN, 18km south of Deventer, is everything you might hope for in a Dutch country town: there's no crass development here and the centre musters dozens of old buildings, all set amid a medieval street plan that revolves around three long and very appealing piazzas – **Groenmarkt**, **Houtmarkt** and **Zaadmarkt** – with a seventeenth-century clock tower, the **Wijnhuis**, at the junction of the first two. Much of the centre is pedestrianized and, without a supermarket in sight, the town's old-fashioned shops still flourish, as do its cafés and, in a quiet sort of way, its bars, but not its **pigeons**: Zutphen built itself three pigeon lofts about ten years ago and with the birds happily ensconced, started replacing their eggs with plaster ones – and hey presto, a pigeon is now a municipal rarity.

Zutphen was founded in the eleventh century as a fortified settlement at the confluence of the Berkel and IJssel rivers. It took a hundred years for the town to become an important trading post, but thereafter its very success brought torrid times. **Habsburg armies** sacked Zutphen on several occasions, but the worst came in 1572, when Spanish troops massacred its citizens, an outrage that became part of Protestant folklore, strengthening their resolve against Catholic absolutism right across Europe. It was also here in Zutphen that **Sir Philip Sidney**, the English poet, soldier and courtier, met his end while fighting against the Spanish in 1586. Every inch the Renaissance man, Sidney even managed to die with some measure of style: mortally wounded in the thigh – after having loaned his leg-armour to a friend – he offered his last cup of water to a wounded chum, protesting "thy need is greater than mine."

5

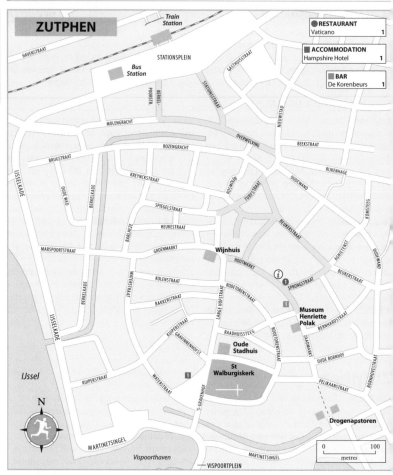

St Walburgiskerk

Kerkhof • Early May to mid–Sept Tues–Sat 10.30–4.30pm, Sun 1–4pm; mid-Sept to early May check diary on the website • €2, €4 with library • ☎ 0575 514 178, ⓦ walburgiskerk.nl

On the south side of the town centre, **St Walburgiskerk** is an immense, Gothic church whose massive, square tower rises high above its surroundings. Inside, the most impressive features are the extravagant brass baptismal font and a remarkable medieval **library**, sited in the sixteenth-century chapterhouse. The library boasts a beautiful low-vaulted ceiling that twists around in a confusion of sharp-edged arches above the original wooden reading desks. It has all the feel of a medieval monastery, but it was in fact one of the first Dutch libraries to be built for the general public, a conscious effort by the Protestant authorities to dispel ignorance and superstition. The library owns over seven hundred items, ranging from early illuminated manuscripts to sixteenth-century books, a selection of which are still chained to the lecterns on which they were once read. Curiously, the tiles on one side of the floor are dotted with **paw marks**, which some contemporaries attributed to the work of the Devil.

Museum Henriette Polak

Zaadmarkt 88 • Tues–Sun 11am–5pm • €3.50 • ☏ 0575 516 878, ⓦ museazutphen.nl

The unassuming **Museum Henriette Polak**, a four-minute walk from St Walburgiskerk, was established in the 1970s largely as a result of the efforts of the eponymous philanthropist and Jewish survivor of the German occupation. The museum is known for its temporary exhibitions of modern and contemporary art, with Dutch artists usually to the fore. The house itself looks nineteenth-century, but is in fact much older, as evidenced by the tiny chapel on the top floor. When the Protestants took control of the Netherlands in the sixteenth century, Catholics were allowed to hold services in any private building provided that the exterior revealed no sign of their activities – hence the development of clandestine churches (*schuilkerken*) all over the country, of which this is one of the few to have survived.

Martinetsingel and the Drogenapstoren

Heading south from St Walburgiskerk, you soon cross the old town moat en route to **Martinetsingel**, which offers delightful views of the town centre as it curves east to the **Drogenapstoren**, one of the old city gates, which takes its unusual name from the time when the town trumpeter, one Thomas Drogenap, lived here. A fine example of a brick rampart tower, it has had some high times, not least during World War II when the Resistance stored ammunition here until an explosion revealed the hideaway to the Germans.

ARRIVAL AND INFORMATION · ZUTPHEN

By train Zutphen's train station is on Stationsplein on the north side of the town centre: from here, it's a couple of minutes' walk south along Stationsstraat to the narrow passageway that leads through the old city wall to the town centre.

Destinations Apeldoorn (every 30min; 20min); Arnhem (every 30min; 25min); Deventer (every 30min; 15min);

Nijmegen (every 30min; 50min); Zwolle (every 30min; 40min).

Tourist office The VVV is in the town centre at Houtmarkt 75 (Mon 11am–4pm, Tues–Sat 9am–5.30pm, plus June–Sept Sun 11am–4pm; ☏ 0575 844 538, ⓦ tipzutphen.nl).

ACCOMMODATION AND EATING

Zutphen is a quiet country town with nowhere particularly inviting to overnight, but it does rustle up a couple of good restaurants.

Hampshire Hotel 's-Gravenhof 6 ☏ 0575 596 868, ⓦ edenhotelzutphen.com. In a fine old, eighteenth-century mansion across from St Walburgiskerk, this hotel should be better than it actually is – most of the rooms are disappointingly routine in terms of both furnishings and fittings – though the location is excellent, and prices are competitive. **€70**

De Korenbeurs Zaadmarkt 84 ☏ 0575 512 423. Endearing, old-fashioned neighbourhood bar, with

well-worn decor, a good range of brews both on tap and in the bottle – and a splendid wooden stairway. Daily from 2pm.

Vaticano Houtmarkt 79 ☏ 0575 542 752, ⓦ vaticano .nl. This large Italian restaurant stands out in quiet Zutphen, not least on account of its decor – the red velvet seats and the open kitchen set the tone. The menu covers all the classics, including pizzas and pastas, with main courses from €16, pizzas €11. Daily 11am–11.30pm.

Apeldoorn

Workaday **APELDOORN**, about 25km west of Zutphen, was no more than a village a century ago, but it's grown rapidly to become an extensive garden city – a rather characterless modern place that spreads languidly into the surrounding countryside. Yet, as the one-time home of the Dutch royal family, Apeldoorn is now a major tourist magnet, particularly popular with Dutch senior citizens, who flock here to

5

visit the town's star turn, the **Paleis Het Loo**, and with families heading for the **Apenheul monkey reserve**.

The Paleis Het Loo

Amersfoortseweg • Tues–Sun 10am–5pm • €14.50 • ☎ 055 577 2400, ⊛ paleishetloo.nl • Bus #102 from Apeldoorn train station (every 30min), or a 15min bike ride

Located on the northern edge of Apeldoorn, and looking something like a glorified military academy, the **Paleis Het Loo** was designed in 1685 by Daniel Marot for William III and his queen, Mary, shortly before they acceded to the thrones of England and Scotland. Later the palace was the favourite residence of Queen Wilhelmina, who lived here until her death in 1962. No longer used by the Dutch royal family – they moved out in 1975 – it was opened as a national museum in the early 1980s to illustrate three hundred years of the history of the **House of Orange-Nassau**. Years of repair work have restored a seemingly endless series of bedrooms, ballrooms, living rooms and reception halls to their former glory. A self-guided tour, with information in English, leads you along a warren of passageways with each room packed with displays of all things royal, from lavish costumes and silk hangings to documents and medals, via roomfuls of sombre dynastic portraits. If you are partial to royalty, it's a fascinating and infinitely detailed snapshot of Orange-Nassau life, and you can view the rooms of William and Mary, including their colourful individual bedchambers, as well as the much later study of Queen Wilhelmina.

Outside, the formal **gardens** (both William and Mary were apparently keen gardeners) are a relaxing place to wander. A maze of miniature hedges and a series of precise and neatly bordered flowerbeds are accessible by long walkways ornamented in the Dutch Baroque style, with tiered fountains, urns, statuettes and portals. The other part of the palace, the **Royal Stables** of 1906, has displays of some of the vintage royal cars and carriages, including a baby carriage that's rigged up against gas attack.

Apenheul monkey reserve

J.C. Wilslaan 21 • April to mid-July & late Aug to Oct daily 10am–5pm; mid-July to late Aug daily 9.30am–6.30pm; €21, children (3–12) €18.50 • ☎ 055 357 5700, ⊛ apenheul.com • Bus #400 from Apeldoorn train station (2 hourly; 10min)

Apeldoorn's second major draw is the **Apenheul monkey reserve** just west of town. The highlight here is the **gorillas** – one of the world's largest captive colonies – living on wooded islands that isolate them from both visitors and the dozen or so species of monkey that roam around the rest of the park. It's best to go early to catch the young gorillas fooling around and antagonizing their elders; as the day warms up they all get a bit more slothful. The park is well designed, with a reasonable amount of freedom for most of the animals (at times it's not obvious who is watching whom), and you'll see other wildlife including otters, deer and capybaras.

ARRIVAL AND INFORMATION   APELDOORN

By train From Apeldoorn train station, it's a 10–15min walk to the town centre straight down Stationsstraat. Destinations Deventer (every 30min; 10min); Zutphen (every 30min; 20min); Zwolle (every 30min; 40min; change at Deventer).

Bike rental Bikes can be rented from the train station.

ACCOMMODATION AND EATING

There's no strong reason to overnight in Apeldoorn, though the town does have a reasonable spread of hotels. The main hive of evening activity is on and around the **Caterplein**, where Hoofdstraat meets Nieuwstraat.

Restaurant Don Quichotte Van Kinsbergenstraat 3 ☎ 055 521 1036 6296, ⊛ restaurant-donquichotte.nl.

Well-established, centrally located restaurant with a French slant to its menu and an ersatz rustic look to it ecor. Mains start at €14, but it's worth paying extra for the ash of the day. 5–11pm; closed Tues.

¹enzez Hotel Canadalaan 26 ☎ 055 522 2433, ⓦ zenzezhotelandlounge.nl. Centrally located hotel with ▮eat and trim modern rooms in a tastefully upgraded Art Nouveau villa of 1904. On a leafy street a 20min walk north of the train station – head up Stationsstraat and its continuation Regentesselaan, and Canadalaan is just after the park. **€100**

The Veluwe

Stretching west of the River IJssel, Gelderland's **Veluwe** (literally "Bad Land") is an expanse of heath, woodland and sandy dune that lies sandwiched between **Apeldoorn** in the east, Amersfoort to the west, **Arnhem** in the south and the Veluwemeer waterway to the north. For centuries these infertile lands lay pretty much deserted, but today they make up the country's busiest **holiday centre**, dotted with a profusion of campsites, bungalow parks and second homes – with the exception of the area's southeast corner, which has been conserved as the **Nationaal Park de Hoge Veluwe**. This slab of protected land lies just to the north of Arnhem and is home – amongst much else – to one of the country's most vaunted art galleries, the **Kröller-Müller Museum.**

Nationaal Park de Hoge Veluwe

The extremely popular **NATIONAAL PARK DE HOGE VELUWE** is an expanse of sandy heath, lake, dune and woodland that is crisscrossed by cycle trails and inhabited by wild game, especially deer, which can be observed from a string of hides. The park was formerly the private estate of Anton and Helene Kröller-Müller. Born near Essen in 1869, **Helene Kröller-Müller** came from a wealthy family who made their money in the manufacture of blast furnaces, while her husband, the ever-so-discreet **Anton**, came from a Rotterdam shipping family. Super-rich, the couple had a passionate desire to leave a grand bequest to the nation, a mixture of nature and culture, which would, Helene felt, "be an important lesson when showing the inherent refinement of a merchant's family living at the beginning of the century". She collected the art, Anton the land and its animals – the *moufflons* (wild sheep) were, for example, imported from Corsica – and in the 1930s ownership of the whole estate was transferred to the nation on the condition that a museum was built inside the park. The resulting **Kröller-Müller Museum** opened in 1938 with Hèléne acting as manager until her death in 1939, and a **Sculpture Garden** was added a few years later.

The Kröller-Müller Museum

Houtkampweg 6 • Tues–Sun 10am–5pm • €8.80, plus €8.80 park admission • ☎ 031 859 1241, ⓦ krollermuller.nl • About 1km from the park visitor centre (see p.260) • Reachable on public transport (see p.260)

At the heart of the Nationaal Park de Hoge Veluwe, the **Kröller-Müller Museum** displays the private art collection of the Kröller-Müllers. It's one of the country's finest art museums, comprising a wide cross-section of modern European art from Impressionism to Cubism and beyond. It's housed in a low-slung building that was built for the collection in the 1930s by the much-lauded Belgian architect Henry van de Velde with a new wing added in the 1970s to create a T-shape: the bulk of the permanent collection is displayed in the original wing, temporary exhibitions are mostly in the other. There's not enough space to exhibit all the museum's paintings at any one time, so what's on show is regularly rotated – though key works by the likes of Mondriaan and van Gogh are pretty much guaranteed to be on display. The works of individual artists are not necessarily exhibited together, which can be frustrating if you are keen to see the work of a particular painter: to help you navigate, the museum supplies a free **plan**.

THE NATIONAAL PARK DE HOGE VELUWE AND AROUND

■ ACCOMMODATION	
Camping Warnsborn	2
Nationaal Park de Hoge Veluwe Campsite	1
Stayokay Arnhem	3

Vincent van Gogh

Helene Kröller-Müller's favourite artist was **Vincent van Gogh**, whom she considered to be one of the "great spirits of modern art", and the collection reflects her enthusiasm: the museum owns 91 of his paintings and 180 drawings, representing the largest collection of his works in the world bar the Van Gogh Museum in Amsterdam (see p.77). Of the earlier canvases, look out for *The Potato Eaters* and *Head of a Peasant with a Pipe*, both rough, unsentimental paintings of labourers from around his parents' home in Brabant. His penetrating *Self-Portrait* from 1887 is a superb example of his work during his years in Paris, the eyes fixed on the observer, the head and background a swirl of grainy colour and streaky brushstrokes. One of his famous sunflower paintings also dates from this period, an extraordinary work of alternately thick and thin paintwork in dazzlingly sharp detail and colour. The joyful *Café Terrace at Night* and *Bridge at Arles*, with its rickety bridge and disturbed circles of water spreading from the washerwomen on the riverbank, are from his months in Arles in 1888, one of the high points of his troubled life (see box, p.78).

The Toorops and Mondriaan

Other highlights of the permanent collection include several revealing self-portraits by **Charley Toorop** (1891–1955), one of the most skilled and sensitive of wentieth-century Dutch artists, as well as a number of key works by her father, **Jan Toorop** (1858–1928), from his early pointillist studies to later, turn-of-the-century works more reminiscent of Aubrey Beardsley and the Art Nouveau movement. **Piet Mondriaan** (1872–1944) is well represented, too: his 1909 *Beach near Domburg* is a good example of his stylized approach to landscape painting, a development from his earlier sombre-coloured scenes in the Dutch tradition. In 1909 Mondriaan moved to Paris, and his contact with Cubism transformed his work, as illustrated by his *Composition* of 1917: simple flat rectangles of colour with the elimination of any identifiable object, the epitome of the De Stijl approach. One surprise is an early Picasso, *Portrait of a Woman*, from 1901, a classic post-Impressionist canvas very dissimilar from his more famous works.

The Sculpture Garden

Houtkampweg 6 • Tues–Sun 10am–4.30pm • Entrance included in Kröller-Müller Museum ticket • ☎ 031 859 1241, ⓦ krollermuller.nl • Free maps of the Sculpture Garden are available at the museum entrance

Outside the Kröller-Müller Museum, the **Sculpture Garden** is one of the largest in Europe. Some frankly bizarre creations are parked within its 25 hectares, as well as more traditional works by, for example, Auguste Rodin, Jacob Epstein and Barbara Hepworth. In contrast to the carefully conserved paintings of the museum, the sculptures are exposed to the weather and you can even clamber all over Jean Dubuffet's *Jardin d'email*, one of his larger and more elaborate jokes.

Museonder

Houtkampweg 9 • Daily: April–Oct 9.30am–6pm; Nov–March 9.30am–5pm • Free with national park ticket • ☎ 0800 835 3628, ⓦ hogeveluwe.nl • Located beneath the Hoge Veluwe Park visitor centre (see p.260) & about 1km walk from the Kröller-Müller Museum • There is no public transport beyond the museum (see p.260)

Beneath the park's visitor centre, the subterranean **Museonder** investigates the distinctive, underground ecosystems that sustain the Veluwe. It's designed for children – hence the interactive displays – but adults will find themselves (morbidly) fascinated too: look out for the giant beetle-mites, a rabbit morgue and a 23m-long beech-tree banister.

The Jachthuis Sint Hubertus

Hertjesweg • Guided tours only (2–8 daily; 45min) • €4 • ☎ 0800 835 3628, ⓦ hogeveluwe.nl • Advance reservations recommended via the website, though you can make a booking on the day at any of the three park entrances (see p.260) • About 3km north of the park visitor centre (see p.260) • No public transport

The **Jachthuis Sint Hubertus**, on the northern edge of the national park, is a hunting lodge and country home built in 1920 for the Kröller-Müllers by the modernist Dutch architect H.P. Berlage. Dedicated to the patron saint of hunters, St Hubert, it's an impressive Art Deco monument, with lots of plays on the hunting theme. The floor plan – in the shape of branching antlers – is representative of the stag bearing a crucifix that allegedly appeared to the saint, and each room of the sumptuous interior symbolizes an episode in his life: all in all, a somewhat unusual commission for a committed socialist who wrote so caustically about the haute bourgeoisie.

Nederlands Tegelmuseum

Eikenzoom 12, Otterlo • Tues–Fri 10am–5pm, Sat & Sun 1–5pm • €5 • ☎ 031 859 1519, ⓦ nederlandstegelmuseum.nl • From Arnhem bus station, take bus #105 (hourly; 30min) to the Onderlangs stop in Otterlo, not far from the park's northwestern entrance

More than a little off the regular tourist trail, the **Nederlands Tegelmuseum** (Dutch Tile Museum) has a first-rate collection of tiles from the sixteenth century onwards. Some of the tiles are from abroad, but the majority are Dutch with the most striking being those from the Golden Age – in particular look out for a set of beautifully executed biblical scenes.

5

ARRIVAL AND INFORMATION

By car/bike The national park has three entrances: one in its northwest corner at the village of Otterlo (on the N310); a second in its northeast corner at Hoenderloo (N804); and a third in the south at Schaarsbergen (N311).

By bus Bus #105 (direction Barneveld via Otterlo) runs from Arnhem train station to the Rotonde bus stop near the park's northwest entrance at Otterlo (Mon–Fri every 30min, Sat & Sun hourly; 30min). Here they connect with bus #106 (direction Hoenderloo) to the Kröller-Müller Museum (Mon–Fri every 30min Sat & Sun hourly; 10min).

Opening times and admission The Nationaal Park de

NATIONAAL PARK DE HOGE VELUW[

Hoge Veluwe (☎ 0800 835 3628, ⓦ hogeveluwe.nl) is ope daily (Jan–March 9am–6pm, April 8am–8pm, May & Au 8am–9pm, June & July 8am–10pm, Sept 9am–8pm, O 9am–7pm). Entry is €8.80 (park only); cars are €6.25; bike are free.

Information The Bezoekerscentrum (Visitor Centre April–Oct daily 9.30am–6pm; Nov–March dail 9.30am–5pm; ☎ 0800 835 3628, ⓦ hogeveluwe.nl) is i the middle of the park, about 1km from the Kröller-Mülle Museum. There are no buses to the visitor centre – th nearest you'll get is the Kröller-Müller Museum.

GETTING AROUND

By bike Visitors can help themselves to free white bicycles at each of the three park entrances and at the visitor centre. Maps of the park are available at all the entrances and at

the visitor centre – and there also are several leaflet suggesting possible cycle routes. Many of the park's road are also open to vehicles.

ACCOMMODATION

Nationaal Park de Hoge Veluwe Campsite Hoenderloo ☎ 0800 835 3628, ⓦ hogeveluwe.nl. The park's only campsite is set amid the woods, close to the Hoenderloo entrance. It comprises a car-free tent site, with

three areas for caravans and campers. There's also children's playground plus power hook-ups. Reservation are not available – you have to turn up on spec. April–Oc A tent pitch for two, including park admission costs **€35**

Arnhem and around

On the south side of the Nationaal Park de Hoge Veluwe, about 30km from Apeldoorn, **ARNHEM** was once a wealthy resort, a watering hole where the merchants of Amsterdam and Rotterdam would flock to idle away their fortunes. All seemed set fair until World War II, when, in what was an unmitigated disaster for the town, hundreds of British and Polish troops died here during the failed Allied airborne operation codenamed **Operation Market Garden** (see box, p.262). Much of Arnhem took a pasting and although some of the key buildings were subsequently rebuilt, today's **city centre** can't but help seem a little patchy and only on its leafy outskirts do you get much of a sense of what Arnhem was like before the war.

Perhaps inevitably, the city is still something of a place of pilgrimage for British visitors, who congregate here every summer to visit the crucial sites of the battle, including Arnhem's **John Frostbrug**, but it's also a lively town with a good selection of restaurants, bars and hotels. What's more, Arnhem makes a first-rate base for visiting a number of neighbouring attractions, most memorably the **Kröller-Müller Museum** in the Nationaal Park de Hoge Veluwe (see p.257) and the Airborne Museum Hartenstein at **Oosterbeek**.

John Frostbrug

Battle of Arnhem Information Centre Rijnkade 155 • April–Oct Mon–Sat 10am–5pm, Sun noon–5pm; Nov–March Mon–Sat 11am–5pm, Sun noon–5pm • Free • ☎ 026 333 7710

Named after the British commander who defended it for four days (see box, p.262), the **John Frostbrug** – the fabled "Bridge Too Far" – is a plain modern bridge, but it remains a symbol of people's remembrance of the battle, Dutch and British alike. Right beneath the north side of the bridge, the **Battle of Arnhem Information Centre** is a modest, one-room affair where the emphasis is on the individuals who participated in the battle – Germans, Allies and Dutch – with a goodly number of potted biographies.

ARNHEM

SHOP
Coming Soon 1

RESTAURANTS & CAFÉS
Eetcafé St Jan 1
Graave 4
La Rusticana 3
Rung Thai 2

ACCOMMODATION
Best Western Hotel Haarhuis ... 6
Camping Warnsborn 2
Hotel Molendal 4
NH Arnhem Rijnhotel 5
Pension Warnsborn 3
Stayokay Arnhem 1

BARS & LIVE-MUSIC VENUES
Café 't Moortgat 3
Le Grand Café 2
Luxor Live 1
Oranje Koffiehuis 4
Roses Lounge 5

5

OPERATION MARKET GARDEN

By September 1944, most of France and much of Belgium had been liberated from **German occupation** and the question for the Allies was how to drive the Germans out of the Netherlands. Fearing that an orthodox campaign would take many months and cost many lives, **Field Marshal Montgomery** decided that a pencil thrust north through the Netherlands and subsequently east into the Ruhr, around the back of the heavily fortified Siegfried Line, offered a good chance of ending the war early. To speed the advance of his land armies, Montgomery needed to cross several major rivers and canals in a corridor of territory stretching from Eindhoven, just north of the front, to Arnhem. The plan, codenamed **Operation Market Garden**, was to parachute three Airborne Divisions behind enemy lines, each responsible for taking and holding particular bridgeheads until the main army could force their way north to join them. On Sunday, September 17, the 1st British Airborne Division parachuted into the fields around Oosterbeek, their principal objective being to seize the bridges over the Rhine at neighbouring Arnhem. Meanwhile, the 101st American Airborne Division was dropped in the area of Veghel to secure the Wilhelmina and Zuid-Willemsvaart canals, while the 82nd Division was dropped around Grave and Nijmegen, for the crossings over the Maas and the Waal.

The Americans were successful, and by the night of September 20, sections of the main British army had reached the American bridgehead across the River Waal at Nijmegen. But the landings around Arnhem ran into serious problems: Allied Command had estimated that opposition was unlikely to exceed three thousand troops, but, as it turned out, the entire 2nd SS Panzer Corps was refitting near Arnhem just when the 1st Division landed. Taking the enemy by surprise, 2nd Parachute Battalion, under **Lieutenant-Colonel John Frost**, did manage to capture the north end of the road bridge across the Rhine, but it proved impossible to capture the southern end. Surrounded, outgunned and outmanned, the 2nd Battalion held their position from September 17th to the morning of the 21st, a feat of extraordinary courage and determination. Meanwhile, other British and Polish battalions had concentrated around the bridgehead at Oosterbeek, which they held at tremendous cost under the command of **General Urquhart**. By the morning of the 25th it was apparent that reinforcements in sufficient numbers would not be able to get through in support, so under cover of darkness, a dramatic and supremely well-executed withdrawal saved 2163 soldiers out of an original force of 10,005. There has been controversy about the plan ever since, with many arguing that it was poorly conceived, while others claim that it might have worked but for a series of military mishaps and miscalculations – the famous 1977 film *A Bridge Too Far* hedged its bets.

Kerkstraat and the Korenmarkt

The north end of the John Frostbrug abuts that part of Arnhem which took the worst punishment in 1944 – and the replacement buildings are singularly unappetizing, mostly clumsy tower blocks that only give way to a more pleasant cityscape as you proceed along **Kerkstraat** with its medley of old shops and stores. From the north end of Kerkstraat, it's a brief stroll to the **Korenmarkt**, a small square that escaped much of the destruction and is now something of a social hub, flanked by several of the city's busiest bars.

Museum Arnhem

Utrechtseweg 87 • Tues–Sun 11am–5pm • €10 • ☎ 026 303 1400, ⓦ museumarnhem.nl • The museum is a 10min walk west of the train station, or take bus #52 (direction Wageningen)

Glued to a bluff above the River Rhine, the **Museum Arnhem** specializes in temporary exhibitions of modern Dutch art, many of which feature prime pieces drawn from the museum's permanent collection, whose forte is the work of the **Magic Realists**. It was the Amsterdam-born artist Carel Willink (1900–83) who popularized the style in the Netherlands in the 1930s, though Pyke Koch (1901–91) was perhaps the most talented practitioner – look out for his *Vrouwen in de Straat* (Women in the Street), a typically disconcerting canvas, where the women's eyes look out from the picture in a medley of contrasting emotions.

Oosterbeek

5

Now a prosperous suburb of Arnhem, leafy **OOSTERBEEK** was a target for Operation Market Garden (see box opposite) on account of its rail bridge over the Lower Rhine. After the failure of the attempt to seize the bridge at Arnhem, it was also where the remains of the Allied forces held out within an ever-shrinking perimeter before their dramatic withdrawal south across the river. The Allied command post at Oosterbeek was in the *Hotel Hartenstein*, which now houses the excellent **Airborne Museum Hartenstein**, whose various displays examine the course of the battle. You might also consider a visit to the **Airborne Cemetery** (open access; free), a neat, symmetrical tribute to nearly two thousand paratroopers, mostly British and Polish, whose bodies were brought here from the surrounding fields. It's a quiet, secluded spot and the personal inscriptions on the gravestones are especially poignant. The cemetery is just a ten-minute walk east of Oosterbeek train station on van Limburg Stirumweg: cross the bridge over the train lines, then turn right.

The Airborne Museum Hartenstein

Utrechtseweg 232, Oosterbeek • April–Oct Mon–Sat 10am–5pm & Sun noon–5pm; Nov–March Mon–Sat 11am–5pm & Sun noon–5pm • €8.50 • ☎ 026 333 7710, ⓦ airbornemuseum.nl • Train from Arnhem to Oosterbeek (every 30min–1hr; 5min) and a 10min walk south along Stationsweg • Bus #52 (direction Wageningen) from Arnhem bus station (every 20–30min; 10min) stops outside

Given the intensity of the battle, it's perhaps surprising that the *Hotel Hartenstein*, the one-time Allied HQ, wasn't razed to the ground, but survive it did and it now makes an appropriate home for the **Airborne Museum**, lying just to the west of the centre of the village. The museum kicks off with a first-rate film of the battle, which makes skilful use of original footage – including the chilling scene where German machine gunners blaze away at paratroopers dropping from the sky. Ensuing rooms hold a series of small exhibitions on some of the individuals who took part, perhaps most memorably Private Albert Willingham who died protecting a Dutch woman from a German grenade. Here too, is a piece of wallpaper, salvaged from the hotel, where British snipers marked up the score of their hits, inscribing it "Fuck the Gerrys". A further display in the basement recreates the scene in the hotel as the Germans closed in – the British were besieged here for a week before finally retreating across the river. The Army Film and Photographic Unit landed with the British forces, and it's their photographs that perhaps stick in the memory most of all: grimly cheerful soldiers hauling in their parachutes; tense, tired faces during the fighting; and shattered Dutch villages.

ARRIVAL AND INFORMATION

ARNHEM

By train Arnhem's large and glitzy new train station is on Nieuwe Stationsstraat at the northern edge of the city centre – around a 10min walk from the river.

Destinations Amsterdam CS (every 30min to 1hr; 1hr 10min); Deventer (every 30min; 40min); Nijmegen (every 30min; 20min); Oosterbeek (every 30min to 1hr; 5min); Zutphen (every 30min; 20min); and Zwolle (every 30min; 1hr).

By bus Arnhem bus station is adjacent to the train station on Stationsplein.

Destinations Kröller-Müller Museum: Bus #105 (direction Barneveld via Otterlo), from Arnhem train station to the Rotonde bus stop at Otterlo (Mon–Fri every half-hour, Sat & Sun hourly; 30min) for connecting Bus #106 (direction Hoenderloo) to the museum (Mon–Fri every half-hour, Sat & Sun hourly; 10min), but not the visitor centre.

Tourist office The VVV is across from the train station at Stationsplein 13 (Mon–Fri 9.30am–5.30pm & Sat 9.30am–5pm; ☎ 0900 112 2344, ⓦ arnhemnijmegenregion.com).

GETTING AROUND

By bus and trolleybus The bus station on Stationsplein is the focus of the city's public transport system, whose buses and trolleybuses are operated by Breng (ⓦ breng.nl). Most services travel from one side of the city to the other, which means there'll often be two buses/trolleybuses at the station with the same number and different destinations, so it's important to get the direction as well as the number right.

5

ACCOMMODATION

Arnhem has a good selection of **places to stay**, but by and large you are better off staying just out of the centre, either down by the Rhine or in one the greener/older districts.

HOTELS

Best Western Hotel Haarhuis Stationsplein 1 ☎026 442 7441, ⓦhotelhaarhuis.nl. Mid-sized hotel in a routine modern low-rise with pleasant public areas and guest rooms that are of a good size and well appointed. The fly in the ointment can be the noise from fellow guests (the hotel is popular with partying weekenders). In a handy location, near the train station. **€90**

★**Hotel Molendal** Cronjéstraat 15 ☎026 442 4858, ⓦhotel-molendal.nl. In a beautifully renovated Art Nouveau villa, this delightful hotel has sixteen guest rooms decorated in soothing tones of white and cream with a selection of antique furniture. Just north of the train station, in a lovely, leafy residential part of Arnhem awash with fine old mansions, the hotel overlooks a slender canal near the assorted greenery of Sonsbeek Park. **€125**

NH Arnhem Rijnhotel Onderlangs 10 ☎026 443 4642, ⓦnh-hotels.com. Medium-sized, four-star chain hotel occupying two adjoining buildings – one an attractive villa with a semicircular wing pushing out above the River Rhine, the other a routine modern block. The well-appointed bedrooms are decorated in pleasant modern style and the best have engaging river views. The hotel restaurant is excellent, offering the likes of steak and chips or sea bass with vegetables: nothing too fancy, just very tasty. Restaurant open daily noon–10pm. Located about 20min walk from the train station. **€100**

★**Pension Warnsborn** Schelmseweg 1 ☎026 442 5994, ⓦpensionwarnsborn.nl. This family-run B&B occupies an attractive old house in a leafy suburb just to the north of the city centre – and within easy reach of the Hoge Veluwe National Park. The guest rooms are homely and distinctly cheerful; most are spacious and some have private balconies. Very competitive prices, too, both en suite (an extra €10 each) and with shared facilities. **€55**

HOSTEL

Stayokay Arnhem Diepenbrocklaan 27 ☎026 442 0114, ⓦstayokay.com; take bus #3, direction Alteveer, to the Ziekenhuis Rijnstate stop, and then follow the signs. In a modern complex on the edge of the Nationaal Park de Hoge Veluwe, some 5km north of central Arnhem, this well-equipped HI hostel has a laundry, a bar, a restaurant, bicycle storage and bicycle rental. Bunk beds, in four- to six-bedded rooms. Dorms from **€20**, doubles **€50**

CAMPING

Camping Warnsborn Bakenbergseweg 257 ☎026 442 3469, ⓦcampingwarnsborn.nl. Large and well-appointed caravan and campsite in a forested setting on the approaches to the Nationaal Park de Hoge Veluwe, 6km northwest of central Arnhem. Electrical hook-up is included in the price. April–Oct. Tent pitch, car and two adults **€22**

EATING AND DRINKING

Arnhem has a particularly good range of reasonably priced café-bars and restaurants plus a platoon of busy bars down on the **Korenmarkt**. There's a further cluster of café-bars and bars beside the river on **Rijnkade**, though things only get going here if the weather is reasonable.

CAFÉS AND RESTAURANTS

Eetcafé St Jan Jansplein 2 ☎026 445 5622, ⓦcafe-sintjan.nl. Beside one of central Arnhem's more pleasant squares, this popular eetcafé, with its Art Nouveau fixtures and fittings, offers tasty Dutch food at economic prices – the mussels with onions, mushrooms and peppers costs just €7.50. Mon–Thurs 11am–11pm, Fri & Sat 11am–2am, Sun 1–10pm.

Graave Kleine Oord 83 ☎026 445 7459, ⓦgraave.com. With its funky modern decor, this pocket-sized café-restaurant has a lively atmosphere and an enterprising menu – try, for example, the chicken satay and scallop risotto. Mains average €13. Wed–Sun noon–midnight.

La Rusticana Bakkersstraat 58 ☎026 351 5607, ⓦrusticana.nl. This well-presented Italian restaurant, in a good-looking older building with wide double windows, offers all the classics, but excels with its inventive pasta and

noodle dishes, the black noodles with shrimp being a prime example. Mains hover around €25. Wed–Sun 5–10pm.

Rung Thai Ruiterstraat 43 ☎026 445 0032, ⓦrestaurantrung.nl. Authentic Thai food in this fashionable, garishly decorated little place with bright pink walls. Does a wicked *Tom Yam Kai* (spicy clear soup). Takeaway also. Main dishes around €16. Mon, Tues & Sun 5.30–9pm, Thurs–Sat 5.30–10pm.

BARS

Café 't Moortgat Ruiterstraat 35 ☎026 445 0393, ⓦmoortgat.nl. This brown-style café, with beer memorabilia on the walls and over a hundred beers to choose from, caters to an older crowd. There's also a billiards table to pass the time on a rainy day. Mon–Fri 3pm–1am, Sat noon–2am, Sun 4pm–1am.

Le Grand Café Korenmarkt 16 ☏ 026 442 6281, ⓦ legrandcafe.nl. Probably the most popular drinking hole on the Korenmarkt, complete with fake palm trees and tacky lampshades – if, that is, you can actually get inside: dense crowds spill out onto the pavement terrace whenever the weather is half decent. Daily noon–1/2am.

Oranje Koffiehuis Arke Noachstraat 7 ☏ 026 351 4081. Tiny café with charming Art Deco interior that – despite its name – also serves stronger drinks. A nice

detail is the miniature glass of liquor served with the coffee. Live music once or twice a week. Tues–Thurs 2pm–1am, Fri & Sat noon–2am & Sun 2pm–midnight.

Roses Rijnkade 49 ☏ 026 351 9491, ⓦ roseslounge .com. Chi-chi lounge bar with kitsch velvet sofas and low lighting plus a riverside terrace that heaves whenever the sun is out. Also restaurant menu and tapas. Mon–Sat 2.30pm–midnight, Sun noon–midnight.

NIGHTLIFE AND ENTERTAINMENT

Focus Filmtheater Korenmarkt 42 ☏ 026 442 4283, ⓦ focusarnhem.nl. Cinema featuring both mainstream and more alternative films, both domestic and international. Themed weeks too.

Luxor Live Willemsplein 10 ☏ 026 351 1660, ⓦ luxorlive

.nl. In a distinctive Art Nouveau building near the train station, Arnhem's live music hot spot has turns from a wide range of bands and solo artists from jazz, soul and funk through to hip-hop and reggae. Times and opening nights vary – see website – but core hours are Thurs–Sat 8pm till late.

SHOPPING

Coming Soon Kerkstraat 23 ☏ 026 370 3044, ⓦ arnhemcomingsoon.nl. In recent years, Arnhem's fashion academy, ArtEZ, has established an excellent reputation, producing a number of young and very

successful designers. Selected work from some of these students is on sale at this city-centre store. Tues–Fri 10.30am–6pm, Sat 10am–5pm.

Nijmegen

Lively and appealing, **NIJMEGEN** sits on the southern bank of the River Waal some 20km from Arnhem, its mostly modern centre a rebuild after the pounding the city took in World War II with many of its key buildings copies of the originals. Nijmegen has a couple of enjoyable sights (principally **Het Valkhof**), a battery of good restaurants and bars and a congenial street life: if the weather is good, be sure to join the locals down by the River Waal, where there is a pleasant **riverside promenade** from which you can observe the barges and boats as they churn along one of the region's busiest waterways.

Brief history

Almost certainly the oldest town in the Netherlands, **Nijmegen** was built on the site of the Roman frontier fortress of Novio Magus, from which it derives its name. The Romans used Nijmegen both as a buffer against the unruly tribes to the east and to awe the locals, though they did come a cropper in 69 AD, when, taking advantage of the confusion in Rome following the death of the Emperor Nero, the "Netherlanders" rose in rebellion under the leadership of **Claudius Civilis**. The story of Civilis's rebellion became a staple of Dutch nationalism, though paintings of it were to cause endless problems for Rembrandt (see p.337).

Long after the Roman Empire had collapsed, **Charlemagne**, Holy Roman Emperor from 800 to 814, made the town one of the principal seats of his administration, erecting the **Valkhof Palace**, an enormous complex of chapels and secular buildings here at the end of the eighth century. Rebuilt in 1155 by another emperor, **Frederick Barbarossa**, the complex dominated Nijmegen right up until 1769, when the palace was demolished and the stonework sold; what was left suffered further deprivations when the French occupied the town in 1796.

In September 1944, the Americans captured the town's bridges during **Operation Market Garden** (see box, p.262), but the failure at Arnhem put Nijmegen on the front line for the rest of the war. The results are clear to see: the old town was largely destroyed, and, give or take the odd survivor, Nijmegen today is almost entirely modern.

5

NIJMEGEN

0   50
metres

Waalhaven

RESTAURANTS & CAFÉS

De Amuse   2
Café de Plak   3
Plaats 1   1
Het Savarijn   4

ACCOMMODATION

Courage   2
De Hemel Hotel Suites 1
Scandic Sanadome   3

BAR

Café in de
Blaauwe Hand   1

Grote Markt

5

At the heart of the town is the **Grote Markt**, a busy open square overlooked by a handsome set of high-gabled buildings that somehow managed to survive World War II. The most conspicuous structure is the red-brick **Waag**, which, with its dormer windows, nifty shutters, decorative gables and double stairway, is a fine example of the Dutch renaissance style dating from 1612. From the Grote Markt, a vaulted passage, the **Kerkboog**, leads through to the precincts of the much-renovated Gothic **Grote Kerk**.

Grote Kerk

St Stevenskerkhof • **Church** March Sat & Sun noon–4pm; April–May & Sept–Oct Mon–Sat 10.30am–4.30pm, Sun noon–4.30pm; June–Aug Mon–Sat 10.30am–5pm; Nov & Dec Mon–Sat 11am–4pm, Sun noon–4pm • Free • **Tower** April–Oct Mon 10.30am–12.30pm, Wed & Sat 2–4pm • €4 • ☎ 024 360 4710, ⓦ stevenskerk.nl

Known as St Stevenskerk until the Reformation, the **Grote Kerk** is of unusual design, without a nave but with a long and lofty, fifteenth-century choir and a chunky transept. Key features of the interior include a massive Baroque organ and a large and ornately carved, semicircular dignitaries bench installed for the Protestant bourgeoisie – just in case anyone thought that there was going to be equality before God after the Catholic priesthood had been ejected. The Protestants also whitewashed the church when they took it over and the conspicuous explanatory plaque inside – and on the left-hand side of – the choir explains their doctrinal reasons at some length. Their efforts were not, however, entirely successful and a few faded medieval **wall paintings** survived and have now been uncovered. The most charming – on the outside, left-hand side of the choir – tells the tale of **St Ontcommer**, a Portuguese princess who refused the marital advances of a pagan king, her resistance helped by divine intervention – she grew a long beard overnight. It didn't do her much good: her father was so angry he had her crucified. In the summer, you can climb the church **tower**, from where there is a commanding view over the surrounding landscape.

The Valkhof

Lindenberg • Open access • Free

In a small park on a hillock overlooking the River Waal lie the scant remains of the **Valkhof Palace** – not Charlemagne's (that disappeared centuries ago), but those of the Holy Roman Emperor Frederick Barbarossa (1122–90), who built a palace here in the 1150s. It's hard to imagine just how imposing the complex once was, but you can view a ruined fragment of the Romanesque choir of the palace chapel, its sturdy design indicative of Barbarossa's monumental efforts. Close by, and in a much better state of repair, is the sixteen-sided **St Nicolaaskapel**, built around 1045 in a similar style to the palatinate church at Charlemagne's capital, Aachen, and originally incorporated within Barbarossa's palace. Perhaps more rewarding, however, are the wide views over the river from the vantage point behind the earlier chapel.

Museum Het Valkhof

Kelfkensbos 59 • Tues–Sun 11am–5pm • €9 • ☎ 024 360 8805, ⓦ museumhetvalkhof.nl

Housed in an attractive modern building a few metres from the Valkhof ruins is Nijmegen's main museum, the **Museum Het Valkhof**. The museum's permanent collection is strong on Roman Nijmegen with a wide range of artefacts from helmets, swords and figurines through to grave monuments, coins and glassware. It also displays lots of paintings of Nijmegen and its environs, most notably Jan van Goyen's wonderful *Valkhof Nijmegen*, which used to hang in the town hall. Painted in 1641, it's a large, sombre-toned picture – pastel variations on green and brown – in which the Valkhof shimmers above the Waal, almost engulfed by sky and river. Supplementing these older

5

paintings are more modern works by the likes of Carel Willink, Pyke Koch and Raoul Hynckes as well as a lively programme of temporary exhibitions of modern art.

Nationaal Fietsmuseum Velorama

Waalkade 107 • Mon–Sat 10am–5pm, Sun 11am–5pm • €5 • ☎ 024 322 5851, ⓦ vvvarnhemnijmegen.nl

Bike enthusiasts shouldn't miss the **Velorama Nationaal Fietsmuseum** (National Bicycle Museum), down by the River Waal. The museum has the largest collection of bicycles and other human-powered vehicles in the Netherlands, over two hundred contraptions dating from the early nineteenth century and displayed over three floors. There are delicately carved wooden bicycles, a bicycle seating five people, penny-farthings, recumbents and quadricycles – anything and everything that has ever helped shape bicycle design. All the exhibits are lovingly restored and beautifully displayed – making this the perfect museum to visit in a country where the bicycle rules.

ARRIVAL AND INFORMATION

By train Nijmegen's train station is on Stationsplein, a 10min walk from the town centre.

Destinations Amsterdam CS (hourly; 1hr 30min); Arnhem (every 30min–1hr; 20min); Deventer (every 30min–1hr; 1hr); Zutphen (every 30min–1hr; 50min); Zwolle (every 30min–1hr; 1hr 30min).

By bus The bus station is on Stationsplein, in front of the train station, with regular local services.

Tourist office The VVV is housed in the Stadsschouwburg at Keizer Karelplein 32, halfway between the train station and the town centre (Tues–Fri 9.30am–5.30pm, Sat 10am–4pm; ☎ 0900 112 2344, ⓦ arnhemnijmegenregion.com).

ACCOMMODATION

★ **Courage** Waalkade 108 ☎ 024 360 4970, ⓦ hotelcourage.nl. In a prime location, beside the River Waal, the *Courage* does itself proud with its distinctively decorated guest rooms, the pick of which have fancy wall paintings. You'll pay a little extra for a river view. **€80**

De Hemel Hotel Suites Franseplaats 1 ☎ 024 365 6394, ⓦ restaurantdehemel.nl/hotel-suites. Near the Grote Markt, one of Nijmegen's oldest and grandest buildings is the Commanderie van St Jan, once a medieval hospital. Today, the building houses several restaurants and bars, as well as the De

Hemel brewery, which operates two guest suites, with a self-service breakfast, in a cosy little annexe. **€95**

Scandic Sanadome Weg door Jonkerbos 90 ☎ 024 359 7280, ⓦ sanadome.nl. Sleek modern hotel with one hundred guest rooms in a glassy, curved building about 4km southwest of the town centre. Apart from its woodland setting, the hotel's main selling point is its thermal waters, which bubble up from deep underground at 23°C, and are then heated up to 34°C. Hotel guests have use of the indoor and outdoor thermal baths at no extra charge. **€120**

EATING AND DRINKING

Nijmegen's **Kelfkensbos** and **Lange Hezelstraat** are good areas for restaurants, while the Waalkade turns into one big riverside terrace on sunny, summer evenings.

De Amuse Lange Hezelstraat 64 ☎ 024 324 5570, ⓦ deamuse.nl. With a menu comprising over fifty small bites (all under €10), this is the ideal finger-food restaurant – and is as trendy as anything you'll find in Amsterdam. Wed–Sun 5pm–midnight; kitchen closes at 10pm.

Café de Plak Bloemerstraat 90 ☎ 024 322 2757, ⓦ cafedeplak.nl. A health-food collective operates this laidback, organic eetcafé, where the menu offers a large selection of vegetarian dishes at very affordable prices. Daily noon–4pm & 5.30–9.30pm.

Café in de Blaauwe Hand Achter de Hoofdwacht 3 ☎ 024 323 2066, ⓦ indeblaauwehand.nl. Footsteps from the Grote Kerk, this is the oldest bar in town, a typical brown café with a lovely wooden facade and offering a wide array of beers and *jenevers*. Has a mini-pavement

terrace, too. Daily 3pm–1am.

★ **Plaats 1** Franseplaats 1 ☎ 024 365 6708, ⓦ plaats1 .com. This is the pick of the several bars and restaurants that inhabit the Commanderie van St Jan: a smart and well-organized restaurant with a delightful tree-shaded courtyard. Creative dishes such as poached wolf fish and a *confit* of duck go for the amazingly low price of €12. Tues–Fri noon–11pm, Sat 10.30am–11pm, Sun noon–11pm.

Het Savarijn Van der Brugghenstraat 14 ☎ 024 323 2615, ⓦ savarijn.nl. Smart but unpretentious restaurant on a side street and with a pleasant pavement terrace. The focus is on French cuisine, with the short but extremely inventive menu featuring dishes such as snails with tapenade, mustard and parsley as a starter. Mains cost €20–25, and reservations are essential. Mon–Fri noon–2pm, Mon–Sat 5–11pm.

The Lux Marienburg 38–39 ☎024 381 6859, ⓦlux-nijmegen.nl. The best mainstream cinema in town, with a good international programme and regular late-night shows.

Villa Lux Oranjesingel 42 ☎024 381 6859, ⓦlux-nijmegen.nl. Sister establishment to *The Lux*, this is Nijmegen's main arthouse cinema, a fashionable and popular spot offering an adventurous programme of independent movies.

Enschede

East of the River IJssel, the flat landscapes of the west give way to the lightly undulating, wooded countryside of **Twente**, an industrial region within the province of Overijssel whose principal towns – **Almelo**, **Hengelo** and Enschede – were once dependent on the textile industry. Hit hard by Asian imports, all three have been forced to diversify their industrial base, with mixed success. The largest of the three is **ENSCHEDE**, some 60km east of Zutphen, whose workaday modern centre is partly redeemed by **St Jacobuskerk**, built in 1933 in neo-Byzantine-meets-Art Deco style with angular copper-green roofs, huge circular windows and a lumpy main tower. The main reason to visit, however, is to see the outstanding collection of fine art gifted to the city by a wealthy mill-owning family, the van Heeks, and now housed in the **Rijksmuseum Twente**.

Rijksmuseum Twente

Lasondersingel 129 • Tues–Sun 11am–5pm • €9 • ☎ 053 435 8675, ⓦ rijksmuseumtwenthe.nl • The museum is a 15min walk north of the train station

Housed in a 1930s Art Deco mansion on the northern edge of town, the **Rijksmuseum Twente** contains two key sections – fifteenth- to nineteenth-century art and modern and contemporary art, primarily Dutch with the emphasis on Expressionism. Among a fine sample of early religious art, two particular highlights are a primitive twelfth-century woodcarving of Christ on Palm Sunday, and a delightful cartoon strip of contemporary life entitled *De Zeven Werken van Barmhartigheid* ("The Seven Acts of Charity").

Of later canvases, the *Portrait of Richard Mabott* by Hans Holbein (1497–1543) is typical of his work, the stark black of the subject's gown offset by the white cross on his chest and the face so finely observed it's possible to make out the line of his stubble. *Winter Landscape* by Pieter Bruegel the Younger (1564–1638) is also fastidiously drawn, down to the last twig, and contrasts with the more loosely contoured figures and threatening clouds of *Landscape* by his brother Jan (1568–1625). Moving on, *The Alchemist* by Jan Steen (1625 –79) is all scurrilous satire, from the skull on the chimneypiece to the lizard suspended from the ceiling and the ogre's whispered advice. Steen also mocks sex, most memorably here in his *Lute Player*, which features a woman with bulging breasts and flushed countenance in the foreground, while on the wall behind is the vague outline of tussling lovers.

High points of the modern and contemporary section include Monet's volatile *Falaises près de Pourville*; a characteristically unsettling canvas by Carel Willink (1900–83), *The Actress Ank van der Moer*; and examples of the work of less well-known Dutch modernists like Theo Kuypers, Jan Roeland and Emo Verkerk.

ARRIVAL AND INFORMATION   ENSCHEDE

By train Enschede train station is on Stationsplein on the northwest edge of the town centre, about 500m from the Markt – just follow the signs.
Destinations Apeldoorn (every 30min; 1hr); Deventer (every 30min; 1hr); Zwolle (every 30min; 1hr 10min).
Tourist office The VVV is at the train station, at Stationsplein 1 (Mon 1–6pm, Tues–Fri 10am–6pm, Sat 10am–5pm; ☎ 053 432 3200, ⓦuitinenschede.nl).

The south and Zeeland

MIDDELBURG STADHUIS

The south and Zeeland

Look at a map and you'll see that the southern part of the Netherlands doesn't make much geographical sense at all: in the west it's all islands and rivers, while in the east a dangling sliver of land hooks deep into Belgium, its shape defined by centuries of dynastic wrangling. The west, which comprises the province of Zeeland, is classically Dutch, the inhabitants of its small towns and villages spending much of their history either at sea or keeping the sea away from hearth and home. Zeeland suffered its last major flood in 1953 and it was this disaster that kick-started the Delta Project, whose complex network of dykes, dams and sea walls, completed in 1986, has prevented any watery repetition. Zeeland has mile upon mile of sandy beach and wide-open landscapes, but many of its old towns and villages have been badly mauled by the developers. Two have, however, survived – Middelburg, with its splendid old centre, and Veere, every inch a nautical, seafaring port.

Inland lies **Noord-Brabant**, whose arc of industrial towns long bore the brunt of the string of invading armies who marched up from the south. Each of these towns has lots of history but not much else, though both **Breda** and **'s-Hertogenbosch** have fine churches. Noord-Brabant's largest town is **Eindhoven**, home to the multinational electrical company Philips, and from here it's just a few kilometres to the region's third province, **Limburg**, which was badly damaged in World War II. Limburg's capital and principal attraction is **Maastricht**, a city of vitality and virtuosity, which comes complete with a lively restaurant and bar scene as well as a set of first-rate medieval buildings.

Maastricht

MAASTRICHT is one of the most vibrant cities in the Netherlands. With its cobbled streets and fashionable boutiques in the old town, contemporary architecture in the Céramique district, a fantastic art fair and excellent cuisine, the city buzzes with excitement and its multilingual, multinational population epitomizes the most positive aspects of the European Union.

Though its claim to be the oldest town in the Netherlands is disputed by Nijmegen, Maastricht was certainly settled by the **Romans**, who took one look at the River Maas and dubbed the town Mosae Trajectum or "Crossing of the Maas". An important stopoff on the trading route between Cologne and the North Sea, the town boasted a Temple of Jupiter, whose remains are now on view in a hotel basement. A millennium later, **Charlemagne** beefed up the city too, though his legacy is ecclesiastical, his two churches representing some of the finest extant Romanesque architecture in the whole of the country.

Preuvenemint p.281
Pinkpop Festival p.282
A scenic cycle ride in South Limburg
  p.284
Middelburg's festivals p.305

Cycling around Middelburg: along the
  Walcheren coast p.308
The Delta Project and the Deltapark
  Neeltje Jans p.314
Cycling around Zierikzee p.315

THE ONZE LIEVE VROUWE BASILIEK, MAASTRICHT

Highlights

❶ Maastricht Alluringly cosmopolitan city in the far south, squeezed between the Belgian and German borders, and known for its mouthwatering regional specialities. **See p.272**

❷ Eindhoven Leading city in modern architecture and design with a vibrant student nightlife and the regenerated Strijp S district. See p.290

❸ 's-Hertogenbosch This bustling market town has a picturesque old quarter of alleys and little bridges. **See p.293**

❹ Breda Pretty town with a stunning Gothic cathedral, lively bar scene and great shopping. See p.300

❺ Carnival at Bergen-op-Zoom If you're around in February, don't miss the country's most exuberant carnival. **See p.303**

❻ Middelburg Attractive maritime town, capital of the watery province of Zeeland and the best place to taste fresh mussels. **p.304**

❼ The Walcheren coast Zeeland's windswept coast has some dramatic footpaths and cycle routes as well as pristine beaches. **See p.308**

❽ Deltapark Neeltje Jans The Delta Project – a monumental engineering project to protect the Netherlands from flooding – is commemorated in this outstanding exhibition. See p.314

HIGHLIGHTS ARE MARKED ON THE MAP ON P.274

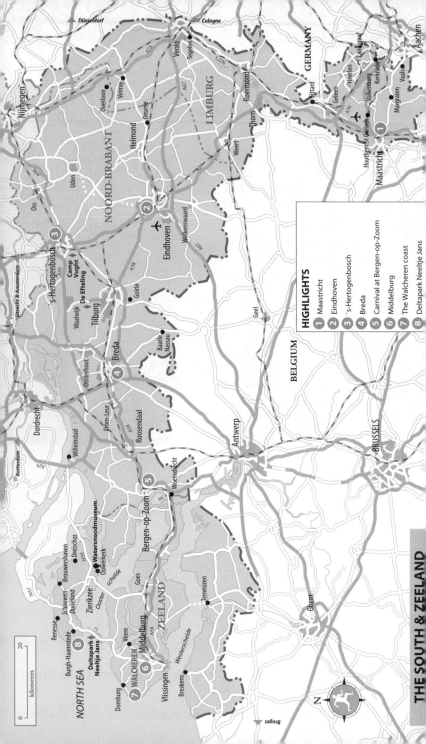

THE SOUTH & ZEELAND

HIGHLIGHTS

1. Maastricht
2. Eindhoven
3. 's-Hertogenbosch
4. Breda
5. Carnival at Bergen-op-Zoom
6. Middelburg
7. The Walcheren coast
8. Deltapark Neeltje Jans

Maastricht has also had its hard times, hitting the economic skids in the 1970s after the last of the region's coal mines closed, but its fortunes have been revived by a massive **regeneration** scheme, which has pulled in foreign investors by the busload. The town is now popular as a day-trip destination with the Dutch, the Germans and the Belgians, and it is also home to students from around the world studying at over forty international institutes, including the European Journalism Centre and the United Nations University. Redevelopment continues apace today around **'t Bassin**, a spruced-up inland harbour north of the Markt, with the conversion of old industrial buildings into cultural attractions. Finally, Maastricht is especially appealing during **Carnival**, with colourful parades and locals and visitors alike dressed up in the most creative outfits, mostly handmade.

Stadhuis

Mon–Fri 9am–12.30pm & 2–5pm • Free

The busiest of Maastricht's squares is the **Markt**, which hosts a general market on Wednesday and Friday mornings. At the centre of the square is the seventeenth-century **Stadhuis**, a square, grey limestone building that is a typical slice of Dutch civic grandeur. Its double staircase was constructed so that the rival rulers of Brabant and nearby Liège didn't have to argue about who should go first on the way in. Inside, the building has an imposing main hall, which leads to an octagonal dome supported by heavy arches.

Vrijthof

Vrijthof, just west of the Markt, is the second of the town's main central squares. It's a large, rather grand open space flanked by a couple of churches on one side and a line of cafés on the other, with tables taking over the wide pavement in summer and a regular venue for the July open-air classical music concerts by local violinist and conductor André Rieu and his Johann Strauss Orchestra. During the Middle Ages, Vrijthof was the scene of the so-called "Fair of the Holy Relics", a seven-yearly showing of the bones of St Servaas, the first bishop of Maastricht, which brought plenty of pilgrims into the town but resulted in such civil disorder that it was eventually banned.

The Basiliek van St Servaas

Keizer Karelplein 6 • Daily 10am–4.30pm • €4 • ⓦ sintservaas.nl

Dominating the west side of Vrijthof is the church that holds the relics of St Servaas today, the **Basiliek van St Servaas**. Dating from 950, it was built on the site of an earlier shrine, which marked the spot where the saint was supposedly buried in c.384. Only the crypt remains of the tenth-century church, containing the tomb of the saint himself, and the rest is mostly of medieval or later construction. You enter on the north side, where a fifteenth-century Gothic cloister leads into the **treasury**, which holds a large collection of reliquaries, goblets and liturgical accessories. Among them a bust reliquary of St Servaas is decorated with reliefs telling the saint's story, which is carried through the town in Easter processions. There's also a coffin-reliquary of the saint, the so-called "Noodkist", dating from 1160 and bristling with saints, stones and ornate copperwork, as well as a jewelled crucifix from 890 and a twelfth-century Crucifixion in ivory. Beyond the treasury is the entrance to the rich and imposing interior, the round-arched nave supporting freshly painted Gothic vaulting. Don't miss the mid-thirteenth-century **Bergportaal** on the south side of the church, the usual entrance during services.

St Janskerk

Vrijthof 24 • April–Oct Mon–Sat 11am–4pm • Free; church tower €1.50

The less prominent religious building on Vrijthof is Maastricht's main Protestant church, the fourteenth-century **St Janskerk**. It was originally built as the baptistery of

6

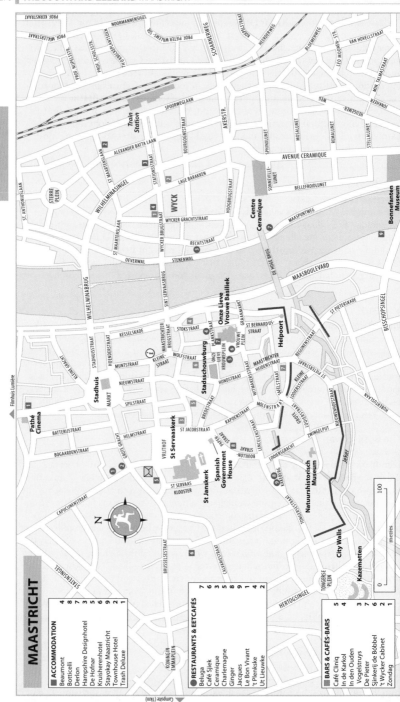

MAASTRICHT

ACCOMMODATION

Beaumont	4
Botticelli	8
Derlon	7
Hampshire Designhotel	3
De Hofnar	5
Kruisherenhotel	6
Stayokay Maastricht	9
Townhouse Hotel	2
Trash Deluxe	1

RESTAURANTS & EETCAFÉS

Beluga	7
Café Sjiek	6
Ceramique	3
Charlemagne	5
Ginger	8
Jacques	9
Le Bon Vivant	1
't Plenkske	4
Ut Lieuwke	2

BARS & CAFÉS-BARS

Café Cliniq	5
In de Karkol	4
In den Ouden Vogelstruys	3
De Pieter	7
Sjinkerij de Bóbbel	6
't Wycker Cabinet	2
Zondag	1

the church of St Servaas when it was a cathedral and now comes complete with its own late-medieval Gothic tower. The church has some medieval murals, but a climb up the tower is its main appeal.

Museum aan het Vrijthof

Vrijthof 18 • Tues–Sun 10am–5.30pm • €8 • Ⓦ museumaanhetvrijthof.nl

On the south side of the Vrijthof square, the sixteenth-century Spanish Government House holds the **Museum aan het Vrijthof**, which has a number of period rooms furnished in Dutch, French and the more local Liège–Maastricht style. Among various exhibits are statues and figurines, porcelain and applied arts and a handful of seventeenth-century paintings.

The Onze Lieve Vrouweplein

The **Onze Lieve Vrouweplein** is a charming, shady square crammed with café tables in summer, and dominated by the large Onze Lieve Vrouwe Basiliek. The portal of the church houses the **Stella Mare** statue, an object of pilgrimage for centuries and one that attracts many devotees. Just north of the square is a small district of narrow streets, the **Stokstraatkwartier**, named after its main gallery- and boutique-lined spine, Stokstraat. This quarter has an intimate feel, with its vermilion townhouses, scattered sculptures and Maasland-Renaissance-style houses in warm Namur stone.

The Onze Lieve Vrouwe Basiliek

Onze Lieve Vrouweplein 7 • **Church** Daily 7.30am–5pm • Free • **Treasury** Easter to mid-Oct Mon–Sat 11am–5pm, Sun 1–5pm • €3

The prominent **Onze Lieve Vrouwe Basiliek** is unusual for its fortified west front, with barely more than one or two slits for windows. First built around the year 1000, it's a solid, dark and deeply devotional place after the relative sterility of St Servaaskerk. The Gothic vaulting of the nave springs from a Romanesque base, while the galleried choir is a masterpiece of proportion, raised under a high half-dome, with a series of capitals exquisitely decorated with Old Testament scenes. Off the north aisle, the **treasury** holds the usual reliquaries and ecclesiastical garments, most notably the dalmatic of St Lambert – the evangelical bishop of Maastricht who was murdered at Liège in 705, allegedly by a local noble whom he had rebuked for adultery.

The city walls and the Natuurhistorisch Museum

On the south side of Onze Lieve Vrouweplein lies another of Maastricht's most appealing quarters, with narrow streets winding out to the remains of the town battlements alongside the River Jeker. The best surviving part of the walls is the **Helpoort** of 1229, close to a stretch overlooking the river at the end of St Bernadusstraat. From here you can walk along the top of the walls almost as far as the **Natuurhistorisch Museum** at De Bosquetplein 6–7 (Natural History Museum; Tues–Fri 11am–5pm, Sat & Sun 1–5pm; €6; Ⓦ nhmmaastricht.nl), where there's a small collection on the geology, flora and fauna of the surrounding area, along with a compact lush garden.

The Kazematten

Tongerseplein 9 • Tours in Dutch; check times with the VVV • €5.50 • Ⓦ maastrichtunderground.nl

A short walk southwest of the Vrijthof square, in the Waldeck Park, the **Kazematten** (Casemates) provide further evidence of Maastricht's once-impressive fortifications. Built between 1575 and 1825, these subterranean galleries are all that remain of a whole network which once protected the garrison from enemy attack and housed a string of complementary gun batteries. The tour takes you through a succcession of damp passages, a mildly interesting way to spend an hour. Trivia buffs might be interested to know that the famous fourth "musketeer", d'Artagnan, was killed here, while engaged in an attack on the town as part of forces allied to Louis XIV in 1673.

Bonnefanten Museum

Avenue Céramique 250 • Tues–Sun 11am–5pm • €10 • ⓦ bonnefanten.nl

Ten minutes' walk south of the St Servaas bridge, the **Bonnefanten Museum** is one of Maastricht's highlights. Named after the Bonnefanten monastery where it used to be housed, the museum now inhabits an impressive modern building on the banks of the Maas. Its space-rocket-style cupola is instantly recognizable, zooming skywards, and is usually devoted to a single piece of art. Inside is a permanent collection of medieval sculptures, Old Masters and contemporary fine art, including works from the Minimal Art and Arte Povera movements. The rest of the museum is given over to various temporary exhibitions, superbly displayed: you could find anything from giant spider installations to Titians.

Centre Céramique

Avenue Céramique 50, at the corner of Plein 1992 • Tues 9am–9pm, Wed–Fri 9am–6pm, Sat & Sun 1–5pm • Free • ⓦ centreceramique.nl

With its low horizons and euro symbols impressed into the paving stones, the **Centre Céramique** is a huge modern building which houses the European Journalism Centre, the city archives and the library. The permanent collection here consists of eighteenth- and nineteenth-century glass and crystal, locally produced ceramics and archeological artefacts, among others. The centre also frequently hosts temporary exhibitions and occasional concerts.

St Pietersberg

North caves Chalet Bergrust, Luikerweg 71 • English tours April–Nov daily 12.30 & 2pm; in combination with Fort St Pieter daily year-round at 12.30pm • €6.20/9.95 • **Zonneberg cave** Buitengoed Slavante • Irregular tours in English • €6.20 • ⓦ maastrichtunderground.nl

There are dank passageways to explore fifteen minutes' walk from the Casemates on the southern outskirts of Maastricht, where the flat-topped hill of **St Pietersberg** rises to a height of about 110m. The galleries here were hollowed out of the soft sandstone, or marl, that makes up the hill – an activity that has been going on here since Roman times. There are more than 20,000 passages, but nowadays only 8000 of them are accessible. The galleries used to claim the lives of people (usually children) who never found their way out, but these days it's almost impossible to enter the caves without guidance. Of the two cave systems, the **Zonneberg** is probably the better, situated on the far side of the St Pietersberg hill at Casino Slavante. These caves were intended to be used as air-raid shelters during World War II and were equipped accordingly, though they were in fact only used during the final days of the German occupation. There is some evidence of wartime usage, plus what everyone claims is Napoleon's signature on a graffiti-ridden wall. Also on the walls are recent charcoal drawings, usually illustrating a local story and acting as visual aids for the guides, not to mention the ten varieties of bat that inhabit the dark (and cold) corridors.

The other, more northerly system of caves, the **Grotten Noord**, is easier to reach (a 15min walk from the centre of town) and also offer regular tours in English. There are panoramic views over the town and surrounding countryside from its entrance on the near side of St Pietersberg. Nearby is **Fort St Pieter**, a low brick pentagonal structure, built in 1702.

ARRIVAL AND DEPARTURE   **MAASTRICHT**

The centre of Maastricht is on the west bank of the River Maas and most of the town spreads out from here towards the Belgian border. You're likely to arrive, however, on the east bank, in the district known as Wyck, that's home to the adjacent train and bus stations and many of the city's hotels. Many local buses run from the station to the Markt, though it's easy enough to walk.

By plane Maastricht airport (🌐 maa.nl) is 12km north of the city at Beek; from here it's a 20min ride on bus #59 to the Markt and the train station; a taxi costs about €25.

By train The train station is about a 5min walk from the St Servaas bridge, which takes you across the river into the centre.

Destinations Amsterdam (every 30min; 2hr 25min); Roermond (every 30min; 40min); Valkenburg (every 30min; 10min).

By bus The bus station is right in front of the train station, on Stationsplein, with services to nearby destinations such as Margraten and Vaals (bus #50; Mon–Sat every 15min, Sun every 30min).

By car Arriving by car, follow the P-Route signs for the most central parking garages; there's no free parking in the town centre, even on Sundays.

6

GETTING AROUND

Bike rental Aon de Stasie, Stationsplein 26 (Mon–Fri 5.15am–1.15am, Sat 6am–1.15am, Sun 7.15am–1.15am; ☎ 043 310 1038, 🌐 aondestasie.nl) rents out bikes from €10/day, plus ID and a €50 deposit.

Car rental Europcar, Sibemaweg 1 ☎ 043 361 2310. The major companies also have desks at the airport.

Taxis Frenske ☎ 043 363 6362.

INFORMATION AND TOURS

Tourist office The VVV (May–Oct Mon–Sat 10am–6pm, Sun 11am–5pm, Nov–April Mon–Fri 10am–6pm, Sat 10am–5pm, Sun 11am–5pm; ☎ 043 325 2121, 🌐 vvvmaastricht.nl) is housed on the west side of the river in the Dinghuis, a tall, late fifteenth-century building at Kleine Straat 1, at one end of the main shopping street. As well as information on the city and on film, theatre and music events around town, it has decent maps and good walking guides. In July and Aug it organizes walking tours in English, which leave from the office daily at 1.30pm (€6.70) and last about an hour and a half; it's best to book online in advance.

City tours From April to Jan, guided tours on the solar-powered Zonnetrein depart from Kesselskade near the St Servaasbrug up to seven times daily (1hr; €6). Slower-paced horse carriage tours are offered by City Tour Maastricht from March to Nov, departing from the Onze Lieve Vrouweplein (Tues–Sun from noon; 45min; €10; 🌐 citytourmaastricht.com).

Cruises Between April and Nov, Rederij Stiphout runs hourly cruises from the bottom of Graanmarkt down the Maas (daily 11am–4pm; check departures out of season; 1hr; €9.25; ☎ 043 351 5300, 🌐 stiphout.nl), as well as trips to the St Pietersberg caves (3hr; €15.45) and to Luik/Liège in Belgium: check which cruises run each day, or ask at the VVV.

ACCOMMODATION

For a small city, Maastricht has a wide range of central hotels, though they do tend to be a tad pricey. Alternatively, the VVV has a list of private rooms, which it can book on your behalf for a small fee. There are also several good pensions and a modern hostel, overlooking the River Maas.

HOTELS

Beaumont Wyckerbrugstraat 2 ☎ 043 325 4433, 🌐 beaumont.nl. This classic example of a contemporary designer hotel combines wooden floors, natural colours and chandeliers with modern elements. It's also home to the excellent *Harry's* restaurant. **€130**

★**Botticelli** Papenstraat 11 ☎ 043 352 6300, 🌐 hotelbotticelli.nl. In a former wine warehouse right in the heart of town, this luxurious hotel, decorated in Italian style, has plenty of atmosphere with an intimate inner courtyard, cosy reception room and wine cellar. **€143**

Derlon Onze Lieve Vrouweplein 6 ☎ 043 321 6770, 🌐 derlon.com. Posh, plush and pricey, with 48 stylish designer rooms and a retro-chic restaurant. It's in a great location on the city's most atmospheric square and there's even a museum of Roman antiquities in its cellar, including the remains of a temple to Jupiter and a well. **€195**

Hampshire Designhotel Stationsstraat 40 ☎ 043 328 2525, 🌐 hampshire-hotels.com. The Netherlands' first design hotel still hasn't lost its spunk. Funky colours and daring art make this one of the trendiest spots in the Wyck area. The adjacent restaurant *Flo* is a great spot for drinks or dinner. **€95**

Kruisherenhotel Kruiserengang 19–23 ☎ 043 329 2020, 🌐 chateauhotels.nl. A fifteenth-century monastery and Gothic church have been transformed into a luxurious design hotel with sixty well-equipped rooms, an inviting wine bar in the former chancel and intimate inner courtyard. Pricey, but worth every penny. **€200**

★**Townhouse Hotel** Sint Maartenslaan 5 ☎ 043 321 1111, 🌐 townhousehotels.nl. This centrally located hotel combines modern design and old-fashioned cosiness with 69 well-equipped rooms in warm beige shades kitted out with flat-screen TVs and comfortable beds. Its sister hotel, *St Martenslane*, across the street has large, stylish rooms. **€102**

B&B, GUESTHOUSE AND HOSTEL

De Hofnar Capucijnenstraat 35 & Keizer Karelplein 13 ☎ 043 351 0396, 🌐 hofnarmaastricht.nl. Cosy B&B divided over two buildings with reasonable rooms, all varying in size and shape. Some rooms have shared facilities and it can be a bit noisy. A very homely atmosphere right in the heart of the city. **€75**

Stayokay Maastricht Maasboulevard 101 ☎043 750 1790, ⓦstayokay.com. Modern hostel sleeping around two hundred, right on the banks of the River Maas and within walking distance of the Onze Lieve Vrouweplein. There's a great terrace overlooking the water in summer. Dorms **€35**.

Trash Deluxe Boschstraat 55 ☎043 852 5500, ⓦtrashdeluxe.nl. The eight en-suite rooms at this quirky boutique hotel, just north of the Markt, are all imaginatively decorated with recycled items – everything from cutlery to industrial conveyor belts. **€90**

6

EATING

Maastricht has some of the best cooking in the Netherlands, so options for good eating abound. Regional delicacies include asparagus, cave mushrooms, *Limburgse vlaai* (fruit tart), *zoervleis* (horse meat stew) and Rommedou cheese. Limburg is also the only wine-producing province in the Netherlands, although not everyone will enjoy its slightly sour taste.

EETCAFÉS

★**Café Sjiek** Sint Pieterstraat 13 ☎043 321 0158, ⓦcafesjiek.nl. Pleasant, welcoming eetcafé serving a wide selection of regional dishes at affordable prices. Its cheese platter is a must for connoisseurs. It's also a great place to try local *zoervleis*. No bookings, just arrive. Mon–Thurs 5pm–2am, Fri–Sun noon–2am.

Ceramique Rechtstraat 78 ☎043 325 2097, ⓦeetcafeceramique.nl. Located in Wyck, the area between the river and the station with many restaurants, this homely eetcafé serves no-nonsense dishes, with main courses such as salmon, steak and scampi for around €20. Daily 5.30–10pm.

Charlemagne Onze Lieve Vrouweplein 24 ☎043 321 9373, ⓦcafecharlemagne.nl. This old favourite has been serving reasonably priced steaks, stews, satay, salads and a wide variety of beers for over a hundred years. Great leaf-covered terrace in summer, and attentive staff. Daily 9am–1am.

RESTAURANTS

Beluga Plein 1992 12 ☎043 321 3364, ⓦrest-beluga .com. A top-notch restaurant, with two Michelin stars, offering exquisite cuisine in a contemporary setting. Lunch is €45 and an eight-course meal will set you back a whopping €155 including wines, but it's worth the splurge. Mon–Sat noon–1.30pm & 6.30–9.30pm.

Ginger Tongersestraat 7 ☎043 326 0022, ⓦrestaurantginger.nl. Contemporary Asian fusion cuisine in a retro-chic setting. Abundant sushi and sashimi as well as main courses such as stir-fried beef or green curry for around €17. Its home-made green tea rice crème brûlée is a must. Mon–Fri noon–11pm, Sat & Sun 5–11pm.

Jacques Tongersestraat 13 ☎06 5423 3085, ⓦrestaurant-jacques.nl. A modest local restaurant serving excellent large portions of Maastricht specialities and French cuisine. Mains start at €18; there's fresh lobster from the tank, home-made foie gras and a set three-course menu for €25 on Wed and Thurs. 6–10pm; closed Tues.

Le Bon Vivant Capucijnenstraat 91 ☎043 321 0816, ⓦlebonvivant.nl. Pure French cuisine such as foie gras, scallops, pigeon and fish soup. A three-course meal in this seventeenth-century vault starts at €35, with main dishes around €24. It also serves an ample selection of regional wines. Tues–Sat 5.30–11pm, Sun 1–9pm.

't Plenkske Plankstraat 6☎043 321 84 56, ⓦhetplenkske.nl. French-inspired cuisine served in a modern restaurant with a young team in the kitchen. There's tenderloin for €30, a half-lobster for €22 and set menus from €28. Tues–Sat noon–2.30pm & 6–11pm.

★**Ut Lieuwke** Grote Gracht 62 ☎043 321 0459, ⓦlieuwke.nl. Great classic Dutch/French cuisine, such as duck breast with mustard sauce or lamb stew, in an informal setting with very amenable owners. Make sure you book as the tiny restaurant fills up fast with regulars. Mon & Thurs–Sun 5.30–10pm.

DRINKING AND NIGHTLIFE

For drinking, head to the bars on the east side of the Vrijthof, particularly in summer when the pavement cafés are jam packed. A more intimate environment can be found around the Onze Lieve Vrouweplein, while heavy night-time entertainment is concentrated around the Platielstraat.

BARS AND CAFÉ-BARS

Café Cliniq Platielstraat 9a ☎043 350 0499, ⓦcafecliniq.nl. This trendy café turns into a vibrant club at night with DJs spinning up-to-the-minute beats and a young and good-looking crowd enjoying a cocktail or two. Tues & Wed 5pm–2am, Thurs 4pm–2am, Fri 4pm–3am, Sat noon–3am.

★**In de Karkol** Stokstraat 5 ☎043 321 7035, ⓦindekarkol.nl. For a truly authentic Maastricht experience, this tiny café has music in dialect by regional artists, which is loudly sung along to by the local crowd. The cosy little inner courtyard makes a pleasant hangout in summer. Mon–Wed noon–midnight, Thurs–Sun noon–2am.

PREUVENEMINT

Maastricht is known as the culinary capital of the Netherlands, and never more so than during **Preuvenemint**, an annual four-day culinary event held on the last full weekend in August (W preuvenemint.nl), when Vrijthof square is filled with more than thirty stands functioning as restaurants. "Preuvenemint" is a contraction of the Maastricht words "*preuve*" (to taste) and "*evenemint*" (event), and it's a great way to explore the richness of Dutch cuisine. The main attraction, though, has to be the crowd the event attracts. Posh Maastricht comes out to show off its latest purchases, but also to contribute to a good cause, since all the proceeds go to charity.

6

In den Ouden Vogelstruys Vrijthof 15 ☎ 043 321 4888, W vogelstruys.nl. One of the nicest bars on the otherwise touristy Vrijthof, just on the corner of Platielstraat, with a dark-brown interior and oodles of atmosphere. Many beers on draught plus regional delicacies to accompany your drink. Try the specialities; nut bread with Rommedou cheese or waffle with cherries. Mon–Fri 9.30am–2am, Sat & Sun 9.30am–3am.

De Pieter Sint Pieterstraat 22 ☎ 043 321 2002, W cafedepieter.nl. Popular with locals, this typical brown café has sand on the floor and a good array of beers. Also serves a simple lunch menu consisting of sandwiches and hefty *uitsmijters* (fried eggs on bread). It hosts regular live jazz, *chanson* and other music, sometimes outside on the nice terrace facing the city walls. Mon 3pm–2am, Tues–Sun noon–2am.

Sjinkerij de Bóbbel Wolfstraat 32 ☎ 043 321 7413, W debobbel.com. This classic bare-boards place is lively in the early evening. Classy Jugendstil interior, waiters in uniform, no music and a favourite with locals. Mon–Wed & Sun 10am–9pm, Thurs–Sat 10am–10pm.

't Wycker Cabinet Wyckerbrugstraat 29b ☎ 043 351 0591, W wyckercabinet.nl. A bustling bistrot-bar on the main street of the Wyck district near the station. There's a selection of beers and wines, light meals, cheese and meats. Daily 10am–2am.

Zondag Wyckerbrugstraat 42 ☎ 043 325 9653, W cafezondag.nl. A trendy little lunchroom-cum-bar, great for a coffee and grandma's apple pie but also suitable for a quick lunch or tapas platter with drinks. Jam-packed at weekends when the DJ takes over. Try its stiff cocktails, if you dare. Daily 10am–2am.

ENTERTAINMENT

Cinema The brand-new Lumière Cinema just north of the centre in the former Timmerfabriek factory at Boschstraat 5–7 (☎ 043 321 4080, W lumiere.nl) has six screens for arthouse movies and a restaurant. Mainstream cinema can be found across the street at the Pathé, Sphinxcour 1 (W pathe.nl).

DIRECTORY

Books Maastricht's largest and best bookstore is Libris, inside the thirteenth-century Dominicanerkerk, at Dominicanerkerkstraat 1, just off Helmstraat: it has a good selection of English-language titles, and you get a great view of the old restored frescoes while you browse.

Exchange office There's a GWK office at the train station (Mon–Fri 9am–6pm, Sat & Sun 10am–5pm).

Markets General market on Markt (Wed & Fri 8am–1pm). Antique and curiosities market on Stationsstraat (Sat 8am–4pm).

Limburg

Pressed between Belgium and Germany, **Limburg**, the Netherlands' southernmost province, is shaped like an hourglass and is only 13km across at its narrowest. By Dutch standards, this is a geographically varied province: the north is a familiarly flat landscape of farmland and woods until the town of **Roermond**, where the River Maas loops and curls its way across the map; in the south, and seemingly out of nowhere, rise rolling hills studded with vineyards and châteaux. The people of Limburg are as distinct from the rest of the Netherlands as their landscape – their dialects incomprehensible to "Hollanders", their outlook more closely forged by Belgium and Germany than the distant Randstad. Nowhere is this international flavour more apparent than in the main city of Maastricht (see p.272), while **South Limburg's** distinctive, and notably un-Dutch, atmosphere makes it popular with tourists from the rest of the Netherlands, who head to its many caves and scenic cycle routes, and visit its resorts such as **Valkenburg**. North and central Limburg are less colourful, but still have some places that are well worth visiting. **Venlo**, with its stunning Stadhuis, is a good starting point for heading on to the **National War and Resistance Museum**, and **Roermond** makes a good base to explore the **Nationaal Park de Meinweg**.

South Limburg

The hilly landscape of **South Limburg** makes a popular holiday destination for Netherlanders who are keen to escape the pancake-flat landscapes of the north. Several long-distance **walking routes** converge on Maastricht, including the popular and scenic Grand Randonné 5 "Traject der Ardennen", the Pieterpad (from St Pietersberg to Groningen's Pieterburen) and the Krijtlandpad, which winds its way to the German border. The countryside is green and rolling, studded with castles (many of which have been converted into hotels), seamed with river valleys and dotted with the crooked timber-framed houses that are unique to this area. **Valkenburg** is the region's main resort, and an easy place to get to as it's on the main train line from Maastricht to Aachen, though it does get packed throughout the summer.

Margraten American War Cemetery

Amerikaanse Begraafplaats 1 • Daily sunrise to sunset • Free • Bus #50 from Maastricht to Aachen stops right outside the cemetery • ⓦ abmc.org

Just outside the town of Margraten, the **American War Cemetery** is a moving memorial to over eight thousand American servicemen who died in the Dutch and Belgian campaigns of late 1944 and 1945. The centrepiece is a stone quadrangle recording the names of the soldiers, together with a small visitors' room and a pictorial representation and narrative describing the ebb and flow of the local campaign; beyond the quadrangle, the white marble crosses that mark the burial places of the soldiers cover a depressingly huge area.

Valkenburg

Set in the gently wooded valley of the River Geul, **VALKENBURG**, ten minutes northeast of Maastricht by train, is southern Limburg's major tourist resort. A medieval castle, its ruins starkly silhouetted on crags above the town, surveys the ersatz castle train station (the oldest in the country) and the garish centre, where busloads of tourists arrive every day throughout the summer. While you probably wouldn't want to stay here, it's certainly a change from the rest of the Netherlands, with a feel more akin to a Swiss or Austrian alpine resort. Valkenburg is famed for its Christmas markets, held in the Fluweelengrot and Gemeentegrot, with all manner of special foodstuffs, decorations and street entertainment. It is also where the **Amstel Gold Race** (ⓦamstelgoldrace.nl), one of the country's leading cycle events, finishes sometime each April.

Theodoor Dorrenplein, five minutes' walk from the train station, is the centre of town, fringed with cafés and home to the tourist office (also the oldest in the country). From here, the main Grotestraat leads up through the pedestrianized old

---

PINKPOP FESTIVAL

What started as a small gathering nearly fifty years ago is now in the *Guinness Book of Records* as the oldest unbroken festival in Europe. Limburg's **Pinkpop** (ⓦpinkpop.nl), a three-day event in June or July, takes place in **Landgraaf**, close to the German border, where it attracts more than 90,000 alternative pop and rock fans every year. It's hosted many big names, from Foo Fighters to Elbow and from Muse to the Rolling Stones, and has always been a trendsetter for other festivals in the region. Tickets are sold out months in advance. Die-hards who don't want to miss anything can stay on the purpose-built campsite on the premises; if that's not your thing, be sure to book accommodation early. During the festival, frequent trains connect Maastricht and Heerlen to Landgraaf station, where there's a shuttle service to the festival site.

6

A SCENIC CYCLE RIDE IN SOUTH LIMBURG

On a leisurely cycle route east from Maastricht to Vaals, right on the German border, scenic villages nestle among vineyards and orchards, linked by quiet lanes dotted with shrines. Cycling is a perfect way to appreciate this rolling landscape and its un-Dutch hills. Pick up a South Limburg map and allow a day for this 70km round trip.

From Maastricht train station, follow the river south to **Gronsveld**, picking up signs to the eleventh-century village of St Geertruid. The road snakes over hills draped with vineyards before swooping into the villages of **Mheer**, **Noorbeek** and **Slenaken** – all very pretty and popular. At Slenaken, the road develops some hairpin tendencies as it climbs the valley side above. Continue through **Eperheide** and **Epen**, with sweeping views across to the rolling valleys of Belgium on the right. Between Epen and **Vaals**, there's a gradual 8km climb on narrow roads, winding between woods of red oaks. From Vaals, you can do an extra 6km round trip to the highest point in the Netherlands (a lofty 321m): follow the signs to the **Drielandenpunt**, where three flags in a graffiti-covered concrete block mark the meeting of the borders of Belgium, Germany and the Netherlands. Otherwise, follow the main road out of Vaals (there's a dedicated cycle lane), turning left to **Vijlen**. Surrounding you is a panoramic view over Belgium, Germany and the Netherlands, beautiful on a clear day. From **Mechelen** and **Gulpen**, you're within striking distance of **Valkenburg** to the north. Climb the steep but brief Cauberg hill to return to Maastricht, enjoying a speedy descent between orchards and farmland with the city locked in your sights. Once on the outskirts, follow the cycle route signs to bring you back to the station.

An alternative (and shorter) return route is to continue from Gulpen to Maastricht on a straight route via **Margraten** and **Cadier-en-Keer**.

centre to the **Grendelpoort** city gate, beyond which is the town's second focal point, **Grendelplein**. Streets lead off from here to Valkenburg's main attractions, many of which are aimed at children, including a bobsleigh run, a fairy-tale wood and a hopeful reconstruction of Rome's catacombs.

Valkenburg castle and caves

Castle Staircase or elevator from Grendelplein 13 • Daily: Feb–June 10am–5pm; July–Aug 10am–6pm; Oct–Dec 10am–5pm • €5 **Caves** Daalhemerweg 27 • Guided tours only: check website for hours • Joint ticket for both caves and castle €9.50 • ⓦ kasteelvalkenburg.nl

Dating from the eleventh century, **Valkenburg castle** was blown up in 1672 on the orders of William III, after he had recaptured it from the French. Repair and restoration began in 1921 and continue still; in the process a series of long-forgotten underground passages has been discovered. These passages form part of the **Fluweelengrot**, a series of caves that were formed – like those of St Pietersberg in Maastricht – by the quarrying of marl, which has long been used for much of the building hereabouts. On the whole they're a damp, cold way to spend an hour, the most interesting features being the signatures and silhouettes of American soldiers who wintered here from 1944 to 1945 and a clandestine chapel that was used during the late eighteenth-century French occupation.

INFORMATION	VALKENBURG

Tourist office The VVV is located on the Theodoor Dorrenplein 5 (Mon–Sat 9am–5pm; July & Aug Mon–Sat 9am–5.30pm, Sun 10am–4pm; ⓣ 0900 555 9798, ⓦ vvvzuidlimburg.nl).

ACCOMMODATION AND EATING

Chateau St Gerlach Joseph Corneli Allée 1 ⓣ 043 608 8888, ⓦ chateauhotels.nl. This beautifully renovated chateau has romantic, spacious rooms and apartments with private terraces, a renowned gourmet restaurant, a spa and pool, lovely estate gardens and the most beautifully frescoed Baroque church in the Netherlands. One stop by train from Valkenburg; alight at Houthem St Gerlach. **€215**

Den Driesch Heunsbergerweg 1 ⓣ 043 601 2025, ⓦ campingdendriesch.nl. The nearest campsite to the centre of town is a short walk up Daalhemerweg from Grendelplein, and attracts a young crowd. Guests have free access to the nearby swimming pool. April–Dec. **€25**

Grand Cafe Tres Luxx Theodoor Dorrenplein 18a ⓣ 043 601 6521, ⓦ tresluxxgrandcafe.nl. Excellent restaurant with a nice location on the main square, right by the River Geul. Set menus start at €30, mains including deer, wild boar, salmon or pasta cost around €20. Tues–Sun 11am–9.30pm.

De Haselderhof Grendelplein 13 ☎043 820 0225, ⓦhaselderhof.nl. The restaurant by the castle ruins is great for a piece of local *vlaai* fruit pie to enjoy along with the views over town. The speciality here is the Wagyu beef

hamburger, and set menus start at €30. Mon–Thurs 10am–6pm, Fri–Sun 10am–9pm.

Hostellerie Valckenborgh Hovetstraat 3 ☎043 601 2484, ⓦvalckenborgh.nl. Family-run hotel where you can choose between classic budget rooms or larger, more modern rooms with rain shower and flat-screen TV. **€83**

Roermond and around

6

ROERMOND, the focal point of central Limburg, is something of an oddity. While not especially exciting, it does have a rich Catholic heritage, as numerous shrines to the Virgin attest – a legacy of several hundred years of Hapsburg hegemony. It was also the home town of that most prolific of architects, Pierre Cuypers, who dotted the whole country with his fancy neo-Gothic structures. Today, the town's greatest asset is its position: Roermond lies on the banks of the **River Maas**, at the point where it meanders around the small, artificial **Maasplassen** lakes. Come summertime, these lakes fill with small boats, windsurfers and waterskiers as holidaymakers take to the water or fish under the town's skyline. The town also has a huge designer outlet centre, attracting busloads of German, Russian and even Chinese tourists shopping for bargains.

Roermond also makes a useful base for visiting **De Meinweg** national park and the nearby village of **Thorn**, as well as being a handy stopover on the way to Maastricht and the south, or Germany.

Munsterkerk

Munsterplein • April–Oct daily 2–5pm; Nov–March Sat only 2–4pm • Free

Built in Romanesque style in the thirteenth century, the **Munsterkerk** was much altered and Gothicized by architect Pierre Cuypers. Inside, the main thing to see is the polychrome thirteenth-century tomb of Gerhard III and his wife Margaret of Brabant.

Around the Markt

The large sloping square of the **Markt** is the town's main plaza. On its eastern side is the early eighteenth-century **Stadhuis**, while the streets leading south from the Markt – Marktstraat, Neerstraat and Minderbroeders Singel – are home to later architecture. Neerstraat 38 and 10 are good examples of Roermond's alluring twentieth-century **facades**, the majority of which are Art Nouveau, often strongly coloured with heavily moulded vegetal patterns and designs, sometimes with stylized animal heads and grotesque characters. Near the river on Brugstraat, there's a fine Gothic house that dates back to the sixteenth century.

The Cuypershuis

Pierre Cuypersstraat 1 • Tues–Sun 11am–4.30pm • €6 • ⓦ cuypershuisroermond.nl

Roermond's principal claim to architectural fame is celebrated at the **Cuypershuis**, the building in which Pierre Cuypers (1827–1921) lived and worked for many years. Cuypers was the Netherlands' foremost ecclesiastical architect in the nineteenth century, his work paralleling that of the British Gothic Revivalist, Augustus Pugin. Almost every large city in the country has a Catholic church by him – those in Eindhoven, Leeuwarden and Hilversum are notable – though his two most famous buildings are secular: the Rijksmuseum and Centraal Station in Amsterdam. Inside the Cuypershuis, you can see exhibits on the architect and examples of his work, as well as a small private chapel, and a large extension in which masses of decorative panels, mouldings and fixtures were produced.

Designer Outlet Roermond

Stadsweide 2 • Mon–Fri 10am–8pm, Sat & Sun 9am–8pm • ⓦ designer-outlet-roermond.nl

Just north of the city centre, Roermond's main tourist attraction is its most

6

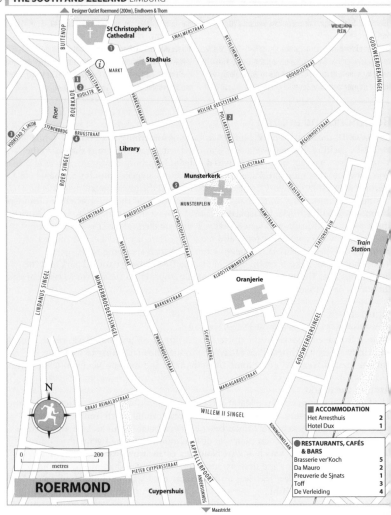

ROERMOND

commercial, an immense designer outlet with over a hundred and fifty stores selling everything from Armani to Burberry and Gucci at sharp prices. The centre is attractively styled like a village and attracts millions of visitors a year. Be prepared for hordes of bargain shoppers and traffic jams at weekends.

ARRIVAL AND INFORMATION

By train The train station is at Stationsplein 8, a straight 5min walk into the centre of town or to the Designer Outlet. Destinations Amsterdam (every 30min; 1hr 55min); Maastricht (every 30min; 30min).
Tourist office The VVV is on Markt 17 (April–Oct Mon noon–5.30pm, Tues–Fri 9.30am–5.30pm, Sat 9.30am–5pm; Nov–March Mon 1–5pm, Tues–Fri

9.30am–5pm, Sat 9.30am–4pm, Sun noon–4pm 0475 335 847, wvvvmiddenlimburg.nl). It ca provide details of fishing and boat trips along the Rive Maas (April–Sept).
Boat rental Watersportschool Frissen, Oolderhuuske (0475 327 873, wwatersportschool.nl), rents out five person boats for €60/day.

ACCOMMODATION

Het Arresthuis Pollartstraat 7 ☎ 0475 870 870, ⓦ hetarresthuis.nl. This former prison has been converted into a stylish and funky hotel. The 105 old prison cells have become 36 luxurious rooms equipped with all mod cons behind the original cell doors. €110

Hotel Dux Roerkade 11 ☎ 0475 300 300, ⓦ hoteldux .nl. An attractive new hotel overlooking the Roer river with a rooftop terrace and 27 spacious rooms with modern bathrooms. There's also a good brasserie restaurant with an inviting terrace. €154

EATING AND DRINKING

Brasserie ver'Koch Munsterplein 22a ☎ 0475 795 861, ⓦ verkoch.nl. Amenable place located in the former residence of local art photographer Victor Mathieu Koch, with kitschy chandeliers and large black and white pictures on the wall. It serves a wide array of coffees, scrumptious club sandwiches and pastas for around €12. Mon–Wed, Fri & Sun 10am–6pm, Thurs 10am–9pm, Sat 9am–6pm.

Da Mauro Roerkade 7 ☎ 0475 317 759, ⓦ damauro.nl. Original Italian specialities such as truffle pasta, *misto di mare* or *scallopine romana* for around €24 per main dish, or large scampi for €6 each. Mon–Thurs 5–10.30pm, Fri–Sun noon–10.30pm.

Preuverie de Sjnats Markt 24 ☎ 0475 331 413, ⓦ desjnats.nl. A locals' hangout with a great terrace right on the bustling Markt square. It serves a good range of beers and simple lunch fare such as hamburgers, toasties and *kroketten* or regional *vlaai* fruit tart. Mon–Fri 10.30am–1am, Sat 10am–2am, Sun noon–8pm.

Toff Voorstad St Jacob 32 ☎ 0475 218 470, ⓦ toffroermond.nl. Overlooking a charming square between the Roer and Maas rivers, *Toff* serves fresh pasta, Thai chicken curry, Indonesian satay and other international dishes for around €19. Three-course set menus are available from €32. Mon, Thurs & Fri 4–11pm, Sat & Sun 3–11pm.

De Verleiding Brugstraat 25 ☎ 0475 332 252, ⓦ deverleidingroermond.nl. A welcoming, homely café filled with historical photos of the city, and a lively terrace overlooking the river. Drinks and snacks only. Mon–Fri & Sun noon–11pm, Sat 11am–1am.

Nationaal Park de Meinweg

Daily dawn to dusk • ⓦ np-demeinweg.nl

Just 10km east of Roermond, the **Nationaal Park de Meinweg** is an excellent region for walking and cycling, with forests and fens that extend to the German border. It comprises sixteen square kilometres of oak, birch and pine trees, dotted with small lakes and heathland, and is home to adders and (shy) wild boar. A network of **cycle paths** crosses the park, all connected and well signposted. For those who feel particularly fit, the 36km **Meinweg** route takes you through the national park and along the Roer valley, crossing the disused "Iron Rhine" railway that was used to transport freight from Antwerp to the German Ruhr from 1877 until 1991. There are also several **walking routes**, ranging between two and seven kilometres.

ARRIVAL AND INFORMATION   NATIONAAL PARK DE MEINWEG

By bus Take the bus from Roermond train station in the direction of Herkenbosch (Mon–Fri bus #78 twice hourly; Sat & Sun bus #178 or the slower #179 hourly). Get off at the Meinweg stop and follow the signs.

By bike Cycling from Roermond is an option; it's a 9km ride

following signs to the village of Herkenbosch, on to Keulsebaan, then turn left down the Meinweg. You can rent a bike from Dirks Rijwielen at Roermond station (€10/day for a three-geared bike).

Thorn

It's easy to see why the village of **THORN** is a favourite on travel agents' posters, and something of a tourist honeypot. Its houses and farms are all painted **white**, a tradition for which no one seems to have a credible explanation, but one which has a striking photogenic effect. The farms intrude right into the village itself, giving Thorn a barnyard friendliness that's enhanced by its cobblestone streets, the closed-shuttered propriety of its houses and, at the centre, the Abdijkerk.

The Abdijkerk

Kerkberg • April–Oct Mon noon–5pm, Tues–Sun 10am–5pm; Nov–March Sat & Sun noon–4pm • €3, joint ticket with the museum €5

The **Abdijkerk** was founded at the end of the tenth century by a powerful count,

6

Ansfried, and his wife Hilsondis, as a sort of religious retirement home after Ansfried had finished his tenure as bishop of Utrecht. Under his control the abbey and the land around it were granted the status of an independent principality under the auspices of the Holy Roman Empire, and it was in the environs of the abbey that the village developed.

The abbey was unusual in having a **double cloister** that housed both men and women (usually from local noble families), a situation that carried on right up until the French invasion of 1797, after which the monks and nuns were dispersed and all the abbey buildings, save the church, destroyed. Most of what can be seen of the church today dates from the fifteenth century, with some later tidying up by Pierre Cuypers. The interior decoration, though, is congenially Baroque, with some good memorials and side chapels and the original fifteenth-century treasury room. If you're into the macabre, head for the Netherlands' only Gothic **crypt**, which has a couple of glass coffins containing conclusively dead members of the abbey from the eighteenth century: this and other highlights are described in the English notes that you can pick up on entry and the audioguide that can be borrowed from the museum.

Museum Land of Thorn

Wijngaard 14 • April–Oct Mon noon–5pm, Tues–Sun 10am–5pm; Nov–March Tues–Sun 11am–4pm • €3, joint ticket with the church €5 • ⓦ museumhetlandvanthorn.nl

Thorn has one small museum, the **Museum Land of Thorn**, in the historic heart of the village. The modern exhibition details the history of Thorn, hosts temporary art exhibitions and houses a three-dimensional model of the village. The permanent collection consists of Gallic coins, Roman ceramics, fossils and objects made of flint, among others.

ARRIVAL AND INFORMATION

By bus Regular buses run from Roermond bus station to Thorn (buses #72 & #73; every 30min; 35min).

By bike The round trip from Roermond train station to Thorn is roughly 30km, along the River Maas, following LF Route 5b (Roermond to Thorn). Take a map (available at the Roermond VVV; see p.286), as the signposting is patchy. To return, follow the 5a signs.

Tourist office The VVV at Wijngaard 8 (April–Oct Mon 1–5pm, Tues–Fri 10am–5pm, Sat & Sun 10am–4pm, Nov–March Tues–Fri 11am–4pm, Sat & Sun 11am–3pm; ⓣ 0475 561 085, ⓦ vvvmiddenlimburg.nl) can help with regional information.

ACCOMMODATION

Bie Os Hoogstraat 42 ⓣ 0475 561 345, ⓦ bedenbotrambieos.nl. A charming family-run B&B with four quirkily themed rooms without TVs but beautifully decorated with local arts and crafts, such as the lace in the white room. Breakfast is served amidst an amazing collection of porcelain, or in the intimate garden. **€84**

Crasborn Hoogstraat 6 ⓣ 0475 561 281, ⓦ hotelcrasborn.nl. Located right in front of the Abdijkerk, with an intimate garden terrace and flat-screen TVs. The restaurant dishes up specialities such as red mullet fillet or traditional meat stew at affordable prices. **€71**

Venlo

Just a few kilometres from the German border, **VENLO** has been repeatedly destroyed and recaptured throughout its history, particularly during World War II, when most of its ancient buildings were knocked down in the Allied invasion of Europe. As a result the town is short of specific sights, but it's pleasant enough to stroll around the cramped streets of Venlo's centre, which wind around the town's architectural highlight, the fancily turreted and onion-domed **Stadhuis**, a much-modified building dating from the sixteenth century.

Limburgs Museum

Keulsepoort 5 • Tues–Sun 11am–5pm • €11 • ⓦ limburgsmuseum.nl

The **Limburgs Museum**, opposite the train station, houses the city's historical artefacts. Its highlight is the largest collection of nineteenth-century kitchenware in western Europe, and it also has an extensive film collection, the oldest of which dates from

1911. The museum is especially suitable for children, with good educational exhibits about life in former eras. Admission includes a drink in the café.

Van Bommel van Dam

Deken van Oppensingel 8 • Tues–Sun 11am–5pm • €8 • ⓦ vanbommelvandam.nl

Limburg's first museum of contemporary art was founded in 1971. Its permanent collection focuses principally on Dutch artists, with work by the CoBrA movement, informal art and the Zero movement. The gallery also hosts regular temporary exhibitions of the contemporary work by mostly local artists. To get here from the train station, take the third right off the roundabout. Admission includes a drink in the café of the Limburgs Museum, next door.

6

ARRIVAL AND INFORMATION VENLO

By train Venlo's train station is south of the centre, a 10min walk from the Markt. Destinations Amsterdam (every 30min; 2hr); Roermond (every 30min; 23min).

Tourist office The VVV is at Klaasstraat 17, 500m north of the train station, towards the Markt (Mon–Wed & Fri 9.30am–6pm, Thurs 9.30am–9pm, Sat 9.30am–5pm, Sun noon–5pm; ☎ 077 354 3800, ⓦ vvvvenlo.nl). It has details of boat trips on the Maas and can help find accommodation.

ACCOMMODATION AND EATING

D'n Dorstigen Haen Markt 26 ☎ 077 354 7397, ⓦ dehaen.nl. Your best bet for a simple meal or drinks in an atmospheric setting, located right in front of the Stadhuis. Its burgers, steaks and schnitzels for around €14 are good value for money – and it also has a huge whisky collection. Mon–Sat 9.30am–10pm, Sun 9.30am–11am.

★ **Puur** Parade 7a ☎ 077 351 5790, ⓦ hotelpuur.nl. The trendiest hotel in town is a hospitable place in the city centre with basic but stylish rooms and a breakfast area with an industrial feel. All the rooms are decorated with a different theme – varying from nautical to cosy – and have colour in abundance. **€71**

Wilhelmina Kaldenkerkerweg 1 ☎ 077 351 6251, ⓦ hotel-wilhelmina.nl. This well-established hotel has been in business for well over a century, with 43 basic but spacious rooms and a decent restaurant serving mainly regional dishes. There's free parking and it's centrally located opposite the train station. **€90**

Noord-Brabant

Noord-Brabant, the Netherlands' largest province, stretches from the North Sea to the German border. Woodland and heath make up most of the scenery, the gently undulating arable land in striking contrast to the watery polders of the west. While it's unlikely to form the focus of an itinerary, the instantly likeable provincial capital of **'s-Hertogenbosch (Den Bosch)** is well worth an overnight visit, as is **Breda**, whose cobbled and car-free centre enjoys a lively market that pulls in the crowds from far and wide. In contrast, **Eindhoven** lacks the historic interest of these towns, as hardly anything here was spared during World War II. It is, however, renowned for its modern architecture and design and has a fairly vibrant nightlife. North of **Tilburg** is the province's other highlight, for kids at least – the **Efteling** theme park, set deep in the woods.

Originally part of the independent Duchy of Brabant, Noord-Brabant was occupied by the Spanish, and eventually split in two when its northern towns joined the revolt against Spain. This northern part was ceded to the United Provinces in 1648; the southern half formed what today are the Belgian provinces of Brabant and Antwerp. The Catholic influence is still strong here: the region takes its religious festivals seriously and if you're here in February and March, the boozy **carnivals** (especially in **Bergen-op-Zoom** and Den Bosch) are must-sees. Towns even change their names for the occasion: Den Bosch becomes Oeteldonk, Tilburg is Kruikenstad and people in Bergen-op-Zoom live in Krabbegat during the festivities. The tradition derives from the Burgundy version of carnival, and the names refer to what the main industry of the cities used to be: Eindhoven, for example, becomes Lampegat, referring to the Philips light bulbs once produced here (see p.290).

Overloon

The affluent little town of **OVERLOON** in Noord-Brabant was rebuilt following its destruction in World War II during a fierce battle in October 1944 in which 2400 men died. The final stages of the battle took place in the woods to the east of the town, where hand-to-hand fighting was needed to secure the area, and it's on this site that a moving museum to commemorate the battle has been built.

Oorlogsmuseum

Museumpark 1 • Mon–Fri 10am–5pm, Sat & Sun 11am–5pm • €15 • ⓦ oorlogsmuseum.nl

Founded with the military hardware that was left behind after the battle, the purpose of the War Museum is openly didactic: "Not merely a monument for remembrance, it is intended as an admonition and warning, a denouncement of war and violence." In showing the machinery of war, including tanks, rocket launchers, armoured cars, a Bailey bridge and a V1 flying bomb, the museum powerfully achieves this, making it a moving experience and a poignant prelude to its excellent collection of documents and posters. Touring the museum takes around a couple of hours.

Eindhoven

EINDHOVEN is not your typical Dutch city and has few historical sights of interest. This is mainly because the town – which was granted city rights in 1232 – only grew to any size in the twentieth century: in 1900 Eindhoven's population was approximately 4700, but a century later it had passed 200,000, making it the country's fifth largest city. What happened in between was **Philips**, the multinational electrical firm: the town is home to Philips' main research centre (the headquarters was lost to Amsterdam years ago), and the name of Eindhoven's benevolent dictator is everywhere – on bus stops, parks, even the stadium of the famous local football team, PSV Eindhoven.

What little there was of old Eindhoven was bombed to smithereens during World War II, but being a very modern city does have its advantages, with a leading modern **design academy** and many high-tech multinationals based here. The annual internationally renowned **Dutch Design Week** attracts almost 80,000 visitors, and all sorts of design projects can be found around town. The technical university draws in many international students, resulting in a vibrant nightlife scene, with plenty of bars and clubs to choose from.

Van Abbe Museum

Bilderdijklaan 10 • Tues–Sun 11am–5pm • €10 • ⓦ vanabbemuseum.nl

Eindhoven's prime attraction is the first-rate **Van Abbe Museum**, founded by a wealthy local cigar producer, with its superb collection of modern paintings that includes works by Picasso, Mondriaan, Klein, Chagall, Kandinsky, Toorop, Appel and Bacon. The museum, built in 1936 by architect Kropholler and expanded with a new wing designed by Cahen (with wonderful singing elevators), is an attraction itself with a very pleasant café overlooking the pretty River Dommel.

DAF Museum

Tongelresetraat 27 • Tues–Sun 10am–5pm • €9 • ⓦ dafmuseum.nl

The least taxing of Eindhoven's museums is the **DAF Museum**, devoted to the history of the Netherlands' only home-grown car and truck manufacturer, and famous for inventing the efficient Variomatic transmission system. There are dozens of cars and trucks on display, as well as some fine examples of unique rally cars, though the museum's pride and joy is its 1968 DAF Siluro: built by Italian car designer Giovanni Michelotti, it is named after and resembles a torpedo.

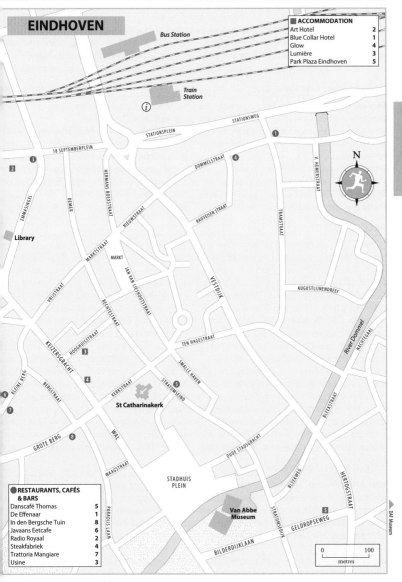

EINDHOVEN

Bus Station

Train Station

■ ACCOMMODATION	
Art Hotel	2
Blue Collar Hotel	1
Glow	4
Lumière	3
Park Plaza Eindhoven	5

6

STATIONSWEG

STATIONSPLEIN

STATIONSPLEIN

18 SEPTEMBERPLEIN

DOMMELSTRAAT

V. HEMERTSTRAAT

N

HERMANS-BOEXSTRAAT

EMMASINGEL

DEMER

NIEUWSTRAAT

RAIFFEISEN STRAAT

TRAMSTRAAT

Library

MARKTSTRAAT

MARKT

JAN VAN LIESHOUTSTRAAT

VESTDIJK

AUGUSTIJNENDREEF

VRIJSTRAAT

RECHTESTRAAT

River Dommel

HOOGHUISSTRAAT

TEN HAGESTRAAT

LACHTEGAAL

KEIZERSGRACHT

SMALLE HAVEN

KLEINE BERG

BERGSTRAAT

KERKSTRAAT

STRATUMSEIND

St Catharinakerk

BLEESTRAAT

GROTE BERG

WAL

OUDE STADSGRACHT

WAAGSTRAAT

BLEEKWEG

HERTOGSTRAAT

STADHUIS PLEIN

PARADIJS LAAN

Van Abbe Museum

STRATUMSEDIJK

GELDROPSEWEG

● RESTAURANTS, CAFÉS & BARS	
Danscafé Thomas	5
De Effenaar	1
In den Bergsche Tuin	8
Javaans Eetcafe	6
Radio Royaal	2
Steakfabriek	4
Trattoria Mangiare	7
Usine	3

BILDERDIJKLAAN

0   100
metres

▶ DAF Museum

Strijp S

Just west of the city centre, the regenerated **Strijp S** district (ⓦstrijp-s.nl) is a former Philips industrial area consisting of dozens of industrial and office buildings dating from the 1920s to the 1970s, such as the NatLab physics laboratory and the landmark Klokgebouw building. Strijp S has recently been opened up and converted into the most creative district of the southern Netherlands, with apartments, galleries, restaurants, design shops, a café hosting live music gigs and even a rock 'n' roll-themed hostel (see p.292). It's well worth a visit during this creative, developmental stage, especially when there are special events on.

6

MU Artspace

Toernallee 40-06, Strijp S • During exhibitions: Mon–Fri 10am–6pm, Sat 11am–5pm, Sun 1–5pm • €3, Wed free • ⊛ mu.nl

Inside the Gerard building in the Strijp S complex, **MU** is devoted solely to contemporary art and design. Its exhibitions frequently rotate, but it usually presents an innovative blend of design, fashion, music, architecture and new media by young and upcoming artists.

ARRIVAL AND INFORMATION   EINDHOVEN

By plane Eindhoven airport (⊛ eindhovenairport.nl), the largest after Amsterdam and a major hub for Transavia and other budget airlines, is 9km northwest of town. Bus #401 runs to the train station via Strijp S and AirExpressBus (⊛ airexpressbus.com) has direct shuttle buses to Amsterdam (11 daily; €22.50 online) via Den Bosch and Utrecht and to Rotterdam via Tilburg and Breda.

By train Eindhoven station is a 5min walk to the Markt and the main shopping precinct and 20min to Strijp S.

Destinations Amsterdam (every 15min; 1hr 20min); Maastricht (every 15min; 1hr).

Tourist office The VVV (Mon 10am–6pm, Tues–Fri 9am–6pm, Sat 10am–5pm; ☎0900 112 2363 ⊛ vvveindhoven.nl), in the kiosk right outside the train station, is a good source of information, maps and walking routes; ask for the city walk booklet (€2.50). It can also book accommodation for a small fee, and has a list of pensions.

ACCOMMODATION

Eindhoven has a wide range of hotels, many of them in the heart of the town. As its hotels mainly cater for a corporate clientele during the week, you can often get a great bargain at the weekends – especially if you don't book breakfast.

Art Hotel Lichttoren 22 ☎040 751 3500, ⊛ arthoteleindhoven.nl. A landmark Philips factory from 1909 is now a funky art hotel with 72 rooms divided over two buildings. Old Philips relics make a nod to its former function, and many industrial elements have been carefully saved. A bargain at weekends and in the summer. **€105**

★ **Blue Collar Hotel** Klokgebouw 10, Strijp S ☎040 780 3334, ⊛ bluecollarhotel.nl. The quirkiest new place to stay is this rock 'n' roll-themed hotel and hostel in the regenerated Strijp S district. The rooms are simple and spacious, but you won't spend much time in them, with an excellent, industrial-looking cocktail bar, a performance space with live music every weekend and an à la carte restaurant all vying for your time. Dorms **€20**, doubles **€55**

Glow Keizersgracht 13 ☎040 782 0078, ⊛ hotelglow .nl. Inspired by the Glow light and colours festival held in Eindhoven every autumn, this city-centre boutique hotel has sleek rooms, accentuated with bright colours, plus all modern comforts. **€99**

Lumière Hooghuisstraat 31a ☎040 239 4950, ⊛ hotellumiere.nl. Right in the heart of town, this boutique hotel with 25 rooms has all the luxury you would expect, with large, comfortable beds and DVD-players in all rooms. Breakfast is served in the next-door bakery. **€99**

Park Plaza Eindhoven Geldropseweg 17 ☎040 214 6500, ⊛ parkplaza.com. This modern hotel offers a high level of comfort, with contemporary rooms, an indoor pool and three Asian fine-dining restaurants. **€80**

EATING AND DRINKING

In central Eindhoven, the Kleine and Grote Berg are the best places for eating: the restaurants here offer a diverse range of international food. Strijp S is an emerging location for new cuisine worth keeping an eye on. The main strip for drinking is Stratumseind, which starts just south of Cuypers' gloomy neo-Gothic St Catherinakerk. This street, with its loud music and cheap beer, has the honour of being the longest bar street in the Netherlands. A little less crowded is the Dommelstraat with a good range of restaurants and trendy bars.

Danscafé Thomas Stratumseind 23, ⊛ cafethomas.nl. A decent student bar and disco on busy Stratumseind, in a monumental building with high ceilings, chandeliers and classy ornaments. Thurs 10pm–2am, Fri & Sat 10pm–4am.

De Effenaar Dommelstraat 2 ☎040 239 3657, ⊛ effenaar.nl. Eindhoven's modern live music venue has regular concerts and parties. The restaurant and café on the ground floor serves tapas and international dishes such as mozzarella quiche for around €17. The set menu is just €20. Mon & Sun 3.30–9pm, Tues–Sat 11.30am–9pm.

In den Bergsche Tuin Grote Berg 17 ☎040 243 7727,

⊛ indenbergschetuin.nl. Cosy eetcafé-cum-restaurant that's very popular with both students and large groups. It specializes in meat dishes (for around €19), or from Tues to Thurs you can eat a three-course meal for a bargain price of €24. Tues–Sun 5–10.30pm.

Javaans Eetcafe Kleine Berg 34 ☎040 245 0097, ⊛ javaanseetcafe.com. Not your typical Indonesian restaurant, as the owner has a passion for Elvis and motorcycles which shows in the interior and choice of music. The menu is authentic though, with a *rijsttafel* of Indonesian delicacies such as *soto ayam*, *babi kecap* and satay from €24. Daily 4.30–10.30pm.

★**Radio Royaal** Ketelhuisplein 10, Strijp S ☎ 040 780 0971, ⓦ radioroyaal.be. Philips' former power plant in the Strijp S district now houses this popular gourmet restaurant, serving three-course menus for €31. Bookings recommended. Daily 4–10pm.

Steakfabriek Dommelstraat 9 ☎ 040 293 9227, ⓦ desteakfabriek.nl. Located in a converted bank, this is one of the trendier spots on the Dommelstraat with a classy black and purple interior, brass chandeliers and decent steaks from €15. Daily 4–9.30pm.

Trattoria Mangiare Kleine Berg 67 ☎ 040 236 7088, ⓦ trattoriamangiare.nl. The best place for authentic Italian specialities, such as truffle spaghetti or ravioli with figs and Parma ham for around €15. The pizza (starting from €11.50) is made in a traditional wood oven. The decor is industrial-style and there's a beautiful inner courtyard for summer. Daily 11.30am–midnight.

Usine Lichttoren 6 ☎ 040 217 1890, ⓦ usine.nl. The city's grandest *grand café* is set in an old Philips factory, directly below the tower where light bulbs were tested. Tasty, fresh food, including good fish options, is served all day, with mains starting at €16. Mon–Fri 9am–1am, Sat & Sun 10am–1am; kitchen closes at 11pm.

's-Hertogenbosch (Den Bosch) and around

Capital of Noord-Brabant, **'s-HERTOGENBOSCH** is a lively town, particularly on Wednesdays and Saturdays, when its Markt fills with traders from all over the province. Better known as **Den Bosch** (pronounced "bos"), it merits a day or two's exploration. The town's full name – "the Count's Woods" – dates from the time when Henry I, Duke of Brabant, established a hunting lodge here in the twelfth century. Beneath the graceful townhouses of the old city flows the Binnendieze, its gloomy depths spanned by small wooden bridges. Staggered crossroads, winding streets and the twelfth-century town walls are vestiges of interminable warfare between the Protestants to the north and the Catholics to the south. The town's history is written into its street and house names – "Corn Bridge", "The Gun Barrel", "Painters' Street" and more. Its most famous son is the fifteenth-century artist **Hieronymus Bosch**; 2016 marks the 500-year anniversary of his death, reason for year-long events and celebrations (see ⓦ jb500.nl).

For the modern side of Den Bosch, cross the brand new Paleisbrug behind the station, a 10m-wide "park bridge" inspired by New York's High Line, to reach a new district with remarkable architecture. Den Bosch also makes a good base from which to visit the chilling **Camp Vught**, nearby.

The Markt

If you were to draw a picture of the archetypal Dutch marketplace, it would almost certainly look like the **Markt** in Den Bosch. It's broad and cobbled, home to the province's largest market (Wed & Sat) and lined with typical seventeenth-century houses. In the middle is a **statue of Hieronymus Bosch**, palette in hand, while the sixteenth-century **Stadhuis** (guided tours Wed 3pm, June–July also Tues & Thurs 2.30pm; €5) has a carillon that's played every Wednesday between 10 and 11am: it also chimes the half-hour to the accompaniment of a group of mechanical horsemen.

Uilenburg

The backstreets of Den Bosch are a mass of intriguing buildings and facades, with the **Uilenburg** quarter being particularly pleasant. Here, pint-sized houses squash up against each other; look out for the restored farmhouse opposite Molenstraat 29, and the picturesque Uilenburgstraatje bridge.

Sint-Janskathedraal

Torenstraat 16 • Daily: April–Oct 11am–5pm; Nov–March 10am–4.30pm; restricted entrance during services • **Western Tower** guided tours April & June–Oct 2.30pm • €5 • ⓦ sint-jan.nl

From just about anywhere in the centre of town it's impossible to miss the **Sint-Janskathedraal**. Generally regarded as the finest Gothic church in the country, it was built between 1380 and 1530. But if Breda's Grote Kerk is Gothic at its most intimate and exhilarating, then St Jan's is Gothic at its most gloomy, with garish stained glass

6

'S-HERTOGENBOSCH

– nineteenth-century or modern. You enter beneath the oldest part of the cathedral, the western **tower**; blunt and brick-clad, it's oddly prominent amid the wild decoration of the rest of the exterior, which includes some nasty-looking creatures scaling the roof – symbols of the forces of evil that attack the church – and modern additions like an angel wearing trousers and holding a mobile phone on the south side.

Inside, there's much of interest. The **Lady Chapel** near the entrance contains a thirteenth-century figure of the Madonna known as *Zoete Lieve Vrouw* ("Sweet Dear Lady"), famed for its miraculous powers in the Middle Ages and still much venerated today. The brass **font** in the southwest corner was the work of Alard Duhamel, who worked on the cathedral in the late fifteenth century. It's thought that the stone pinnacle, a weird, twisted example of Gothicism at the eastern end of the nave, was the sample piece that earned him the title of master mason.

Almost filling the west wall of the cathedral is an extravagant **organ case**, assembled in 1602. It was described by a Victorian visitor as "certainly the finest in Holland and probably the finest in Europe…it would be difficult to conceive a more stately or magnificent design." Equally elaborate, though on a much smaller scale, the south transept holds the **Altar of the Passion**, a retable made in Antwerp in around 1500. In the centre is a carved Crucifixion scene, flanked by Christ bearing the Cross on one side and a Lamentation on the other. Though rather difficult to make out, a series of carved scenes of the life of Christ run across the retable, made all the more charming by their attention to period (medieval) costume detail.

Zwanenbroedershuis
Hinthamerstraat 94 • Tues–Thurs & Sun 1.30–4.30pm • €5 • ⓦ zwanenbroedershuis.nl

Opposite the cathedral, the **Zwanenbroedershuis** has an intriguing collection of artefacts, liturgical songbooks and music scores that belonged to the Brotherhood of which Hieronymus Bosch was a member. Founded in 1318, there's nothing sinister about the Brotherhood: membership is open to all and its aim is to promote and popularize religious art and music.

6

Museum Slager
Choorstraat 16 • Tues–Sun 11am–5pm • €5.50 • ⓦ museum-slager.nl

The **Museum Slager** contains the works of three generations of the Slager family who lived in Den Bosch. The paintings of the family's doyen, P.M. Slager (1841–1912), such as *Veterans of Waterloo*, have the most authority, but some of the other works are competent, encompassing the major trends in European art as they came and went.

Noordbrabants Museum and Stedelijk Museum
Verwersstraat 41 • Tues–Sun 11am–5pm • €12 and €7 each; combined ticket €15 • ⓦ noordbrabantsmuseum.nl or ⓦ sm-s.nl

The **Noordbrabants Museum**, housed in an eighteenth-century building that was once the seat of the provincial commissioner, has recently been enlarged with a superb extension, the **Stedelijk Museum**, which holds temporary exhibitions of modern art; together they cover all aspects of art and culture of the southern Netherlands – from archeology and medieval painting to industrial design. The excellent collection is both good-looking and interesting, with small permanent exhibitions about Vincent van Gogh – with a striking self portrait – and Hieronymus Bosch. There's a good café with a terrace overlooking the quiet sculpture garden too.

Hieronymus Bosch Art Centre
Jeroen Boschplein 2 • April–Oct Tues–Fri 11am–5.30pm, Sat & Sun noon–5.30pm; Nov–March Tues–Fri 11am–5pm, Sat & Sun noon–5pm • €6, includes English audiotour • ⓦ jheronimusbosch-artcenter.nl

The **Hieronymus Bosch Art Centre**, in the striking St Jacobskerk, pays tribute to the life and work of Den Bosch's most prominent native son, the late-Gothic painter **Hieronymus Bosch** (1450–1516), who lived in the town all his life. Bosch's fantastically vivid and tormented religious paintings won him the epithet "The master of the monstrous…the discoverer of the unconscious" from no less than Carl Jung. There are very few original Bosch works in the Netherlands, and the 26 paintings on display in the centre are life-size replicas.

The city fortifications
Bastionder: Zuidwal 58 • Wed & Fri–Sun noon–4pm • ⓦ vestingstad.com

Den Bosch is still surrounded by its impressive seventeenth-century fortifications and some remains of its fourteenth-century city wall, with several restoration projects currently under way. The **Bastion Oranje** once defended the southern section of the city walls and the small underground **Bastionder** exhibition (check the opening hours with the VVV) details its history and displays a rare medieval cannon, **Stuer Ghewalt** ("Great Violence"), cast in 1511 in Cologne and bearing in German the inscription "Brute force I am called, Den Bosch I watch over". The only action it sees now is from the cows, chewing away in the watermeadows of the Bossche Broek nature reserve below.

Camp Vught
Lunettenlaan 600, 9km from Den Bosch • Mon–Fri 10am–5pm, Sat & Sun noon–5pm • €6 • ⓦ nmkampvught.nl • The permanent exhibition is labelled in Dutch, but an English guide is available • Take bus #203 or #213 (2 hourly) from Den Bosch and get off at the Lunettenlaan stop: it's a 20min journey

Opened in January 1943, **Camp Vught** was the only official SS concentration camp in the Netherlands, modelled on camps in Germany. It was divided into two sections, one

6

for political prisoners brought here from Belgium and the Netherlands, the other for Jews, who were, for the most part, subsequently moved to Westerbork (see p.230) before being transported on to the death camps in the east. Predictably, many people died here in the cruellest of circumstances or were executed in the woods nearby. Although it's a reconstruction, and only a fraction of the size it used to be, Camp Vught still makes a vivid impression.

ARRIVAL AND DEPARTURE 'S-HERTOGENBOSCH (DEN BOSCH)

By train Den Bosch's train station is to the east of the centre, about a 10min walk away.
Destinations Amsterdam (every 15min; 1hr); Eindhoven (every 10min; 25min); Tilburg (every 20min; 15min); Utrecht (every 15min; 30min).

INFORMATION AND TOURS

Tourist office The VVV is at Markt 77 (Mon 1–5pm, Tues–Sat 10am–5pm; ☎073 612 7170, ⍟ vvvdenbosch.nl). The office, housed in De Moriaan, the oldest brick building in town, stocks the useful *City walk through 's-Hertogenbosch* (€2.50), which unearths all kinds of historical and architectural nuggets.
Boat trips A good way to see the town is on a boat trip. Open boats do tours of the city-centre Binnendieze canals from Molenstraat 15a, next to *Café van Puffelen* (April–Oct Mon 2–5.20pm, Tues–Sun 10am–5.20pm; every 20min;

€8; reserve online or at ☎073 612 2334, ⍟ kringvriendenvanshertogenbosch.nl). Closed boats tour the lovely surroundings of the city from St Janssingel near the Wilhelmina bridge, taking in the River Aa, Dommel and the Oude Dieze (May & Sept Wed, Sat & Sun noon, 1.30pm & 3pm; June–Aug Tues–Sat also at 4.30pm; Oct Sat & Sun 1.30pm & 3pm; €8). Rederij Wolthuis (☎073 631 2048, ⍟ rederijwolthuis.nl) has information and takes reservations for several other tours too.

ACCOMMODATION

Den Bosch does not have a lot of hotels to choose from in the city centre, so you would be wise to book in advance. If the central hotels are full, there are a couple of large chain hotels just out of the city centre. The VVV has a list of the town's B&Bs.

★**The Duke** Kerkstraat 69b ☎073 369 8332, ⍟ thedukehotel.nl. Seventeen stylish rooms in a brand-new designer hotel on the top floor of the former post office, with plenty of exposed concrete and fabulous views of the cathedral from the corner suite. **€155**
Golden Tulip Central Burgemeester Loeffplein 98 ☎073 692 6926, ⍟ hotel-central.nl. Located smack on the Markt with 125 spacious rooms in warm red and brown shades. Breakfast is served in a

fourteenth-century vault and there's occasional live jazz in one of the bars. **€227**
Stadshotel Jeroen Hinthamerstraat 177 ☎073 610 3556, ⍟ stadshoteljeroen.nl. An appealing option in the old town, located right next to the Hieronymus Bosch Art Centre and with only six rooms kitted out in basic but elegant style. The two suites offer more luxury, with a kitchen and private sauna. Downstairs, the *Brasserie JB* restaurant is a good place to eat. **€146**

EATING AND DRINKING

You can find anything from inexpensive eetcafés to pricey restaurants in Den Bosch. Make sure you try the "Bossche Bol", a local speciality with chocolate and whipped cream – an absolute calorie bomb. Nightlife isn't particularly exciting but it's easy enough to wander up and down Korte Putstraat, Hinthamerstraat or the streets that radiate from the Markt and find somewhere convivial to drink.

BARS AND CAFÉS

't Bonte Palet Hinthamerstaat 97 ☎073 613 2532. A tiny, popular bar with a cornucopia of kitsch hanging from the ceiling, seven beers on draught, an amenable owner and occasional live music. Wed–Sun 3pm–2am.
★**Tapperij het Veulen** Korenbrugstraat 9 ☎073 612 3038, ⍟ hetveulen.nl. Typical brown café with oodles of atmosphere and at least forty beers by the bottle, mainly attracting an older clientele. The peanut shells on the floor add to the atmosphere, and there's an

intimate terrace in summer. Mon–Thurs 3pm–1am, Fri 2pm–1.30am, Sat 11am–1.30am, Sun 1pm–1am.

RESTAURANTS

Brasserie in den Zevenden Hemel Korte Putstraat 13–17 ☎073 690 1451, ⍟ indenzevenhemel.nl. Located in a cosy street, and ideal for a romantic dinner, this restaurant uses seasonal ingredients to produce French dishes with an international twist. Main courses such as cod, black tiger prawns or lamb rack will set you back

ZIERIKZEE (P.313) >

6

around €25 per dish. Daily 5–10pm.

Breton Korte Putstraat 26 ☎073 513 4705, ⓦrestaurantbreton.nl. Soberly decorated restaurant with an intimate terrace. The menu consists of numerous starter-sized dishes inspired by French, Italian and Japanese cuisine, such as fresh tuna salad with wasabi mayonnaise, escargots with garlic and crostini, which cost €4–18. Mon 5–10pm, Tues–Sun noon–10pm.

Da Peppone Kerkstraat 77 ☎073 614 7894, ⓦdappeppone.nl. A little more chic than your standard pizzeria, *Da Peppone* serves tasty pizzas from €10 but also classic dishes such as saltimbocca for around €19. Tues–Sat 5–10pm.

Mariapaviljoen Burg. Loeffplein 70 ☎073 303 1500, ⓦmariapaviljoen.nl. This former city-centre hospital is now a restaurant with an amazing variety of events: films, lectures, exhibitions, theatre shows and barbecue parties. The simple mix-and-match menu allows you to combine three dishes for €16; for example catfish with rice/corn biscuits and bean salad. Wed–Sun 11am–11pm.

★**Noble** Wilhelminaplein 1 ☎073 613 2331, ⓦrestaurantnoble.nl. Star chef Edwin Kats' new "shared dining" restaurant is the most exciting new culinary development in town. Pick a number of small dishes (priced €8–16) with oysters, Peking duck, smoked eel, sea bass, salads or stir-fry and share around. The set five-course menu is €55. Mon–Fri noon–2pm & 6–10pm, Sat & Sun noon–10pm.

Van Puffelen Molenstraat 4 ☎073 689 0414, ⓦlunchdinervanpuffelen.nl. Attractive eetcafé right above the canal, with affordable *dagschotels* and a three-course meal for €24.50. Mains such as cod, mixed grill or Surf & Turf will set you back around €17. Tues–Sun 11am–10pm.

Zoetelief Korte Putstraat 10 ☎073 691 1430, ⓦzoetelief.nu. Large and stylish restaurant with a very decent menu featuring delicacies such as gamba curry and linguine with crab: prices start at €18 for a main dish. Also serves a wide variety of tasty fingerfood and charcuterie, which go down well with a glass of wine. Daily 11am–1am.

Tilburg

Tilburg is a humdrum industrial town, its streets a maze of nineteenth-century houses and anonymous modern shopping precincts. It developed as a textile town, though today most of its mills have closed in the face of cheap competition from India and Southeast Asia. The main reason you might find yourself passing through is on your way to the action-packed **De Efteling** theme park. However, two decent museums within easy walking distance of the train station provide a worthwhile detour. There's no need to explore further – if that's as far as you get, you haven't missed much. That said, thrill-seekers shouldn't miss the largest **funfair** in Benelux (ⓦkermistilburg.nl), a ten-day event held annually at the end of July. Unusually, Monday is the busiest day of the fair as it has long been declared Pink Monday, attracting thousands of gay and lesbian visitors from all over the country.

Textielmuseum

Goirkestraat 96 • Tues–Fri 10am–5pm, Sat & Sun noon–5pm • €10 • ⓦtextielmuseum.nl • From the train station it's a 20min walk; head west along Spoorlaan, turn right along Gasthuisring and continue along Smidestraat; alternatively take bus #5 to Kasteeldreef

The **Textielmuseum** is housed in an old mill with an adjacent modern glass building and displays aspects of the industry relating to design and textile arts. It houses a collection of textile designs by Dutch artists and a range of looms and weaving machines from around the world, and puts on demonstrations of weaving and spinning.

De Pont museum

Wilhelminapark 1 • Tues–Sun 11am–5pm • €10 • ⓦdepont.nl • It's a 15min walk from the station, via Spoorlaan and Gasthuisring

The **De Pont** modern art museum is located in a converted wool-spinning mill north of the station. Its permanent collection features renowned international artists such as James Turrell, Marlene Dumas and Thierry de Cordier, and it also hosts three major temporary exhibitions every year. Its main gallery space is complemented by more intimate side rooms, previously used for wool storage.

Abdij Koningshoeven

Eindhovenseweg 3, Berkel-Enschot • **Tasting room** April–Oct Mon–Sat 11am–7pm, Sun noon–7pm; Nov–March Mon–Sat 11am–6pm, Sun noon–6pm • Free • **Brewery tours** in English Sat 11.30am, booking required; €12, beer included • ⓦlatrappetrappist.com • Bus #141 from Tilburg towards Best, ask to be dropped at the Trappistenklooster

Five kilometres from the centre of Tilburg, **Koningshoeven monastery** is home to the brewery of **La Trappe** Trappist beer. The name does not refer to the type of beer, but to the fact that it has been brewed by a particular order of monks, and Koningshoeven is one of only a handful of Trappist monasteries in the world that brew beer, with nine delicious varieties produced on the premises.

De Efteling

Europalaan 1, Kaatsheuvel • July & Aug Mon & Fri–Sun 10am–8pm, Sat 10am–midnight; Sept–June daily 11am–6pm • €36, reduced online • ⓦ efteling.com • Buses #300, #136 and #800/801 run to De Efteling every half-hour from Tilburg (15min) and from Den Bosch (40min) • The park is well signposted just off the N261 between Tilburg and Waalwijk; parking costs €10

Hidden in the woods fifteen minutes' drive north of Tilburg, the award-winning **De Efteling theme park** is one of the country's principal attractions. It's an excellent day out, and not just for children. The setting is superbly landscaped, especially in spring when the tulips are out. And while it's not Disney, it's certainly vast enough to swallow up the crowds.

Of the rides, Python, Flying Dutchman and Baron 1898 are hair-raising roller-coaster rides, with the Python providing great views of the park before plunging down the track; De Bob, a bobsleigh run, is almost as exhilarating although over far too quickly. Piranha takes you through some gentle whitewater rapids (expect to get wet). Of the quieter rides, Villa Volta is a slightly unsettling room that revolves around you, after a rather lengthy introduction in Dutch. For children, the Fairy-Tale Forest, where the park began – a hop from Gingerbread House to Troll King to Cinderella Castle – is popular. Vogel Rok and Droomvlucht are the best of the rides, and there are afternoon shows in the Efteling Theatre. In addition, there are a number of fairground attractions, canoes and paddleboats, and a great view over the whole shebang and the surrounding woods from the Pagoda. Prepare yourself for long queues on summer weekends; the website indicates which days are relatively quiet.

ARRIVAL AND INFORMATION	**TILBURG**

By train From the train station it's a 10min walk down Stationstraat to the main shopping area.

Destinations Den Haag (every 30min; 1hr 15min); Eindhoven (every 20min; 35min); 's-Hertogenbosch (every 30min; 15min).

Tourist office The VVV is at Spoorlaan 434a (Mon 1–5pm, Tues–Fri 10am–5pm, Sat 11am–5pm; ☎ 013 532 3720, ⓦ vvvtilburg.nl), opposite the train station.

ACCOMMODATION AND EATING	

Het Wapen van Tilburg Spoorlaan 362 ☎ 013 542 2692, ⓦ hetwapenvantilburg.nl. An affordable hotel with five rather bland but perfectly adequate doubles and two family dorms sleeping up to six. There's a lively bar-cum-restaurant downstairs serving dishes such as pasta, schnitzel and steaks for around €18. Dorms €25, doubles €65

Studio Heuvel 9 ☎ 013 543 6016, ⓦ studio-tilburg.nl. Your best bet for some night-time entertainment in a hip and industrial setting with DJs and live jam sessions. Also has a decent restaurant serving main courses for €12.50 and a wicked cocktail list. Mon & Sun 10am–2am, Tues–Sat 10am–4am.

Breda

BREDA, 20km west of Tilburg, is one of the prettier towns of Noord-Brabant, a pleasant, easy-going place to while away a day or two. A magnificent Gothic **cathedral** looms above the three-storey buildings that front its stone-paved main square, which is crammed with stallholders and shoppers on market days. There's a range of well-priced accommodation here too, plus inexpensive restaurants and lively bars, though ultimately it's less appealing than Den Bosch as a base for exploring central Noord-Brabant.

Breda also has an excellent **carnival**, which is celebrated with vim and gusto, and a top-notch, four-day annual **jazz festival** (ⓦ bredajazzfestival.nl), when some twenty stages are scattered around the centre; it usually starts on Ascension Day.

Brief history

While there's little evidence of it today, Breda developed as a strategic fortress town and was badly damaged following its capture by the Spanish in 1581. The local counts were scions of the House of Nassau, which married into the House of Orange in the early sixteenth century. The first prince of the Orange-Nassau line was **William the Silent**, who spent much of his life in the town and would probably have been buried here, had Breda not been in the hands of the Spanish at the time of his assassination in Delft (see p.323). In 1566 William was among the group of Dutch nobles who issued the **Compromise of Breda** – an early declaration against Spanish domination of the Low Countries. The town later fell to the Spanish, was retaken by Maurice, William's son, then captured once more by the Spanish, but finally ceded to the United Provinces in 1648. Curiously, King Charles II of England lived in Breda during part of his long exile and it was here, in 1660, that he issued his **Declaration of Breda**, an offer of amnesty to his former foes that greased the wheels of his return to the English throne.

Around the Grote Markt

The **Grote Markt** is the focus of life, site of a general **market** every Tuesday and Friday morning and a secondhand market every Wednesday morning, when stalls loaded with books, bric-a-brac, clothes and small furniture pieces push up against the **Grote Kerk**. From here, head southbound for Breda's main **shopping street** – the Karrestraat, which turns into the Ginnekenstraat – where you'll primarily find large chain stores and the chic covered mall De Barones. There's more upmarket shopping nearby on Hallstraat, lined with boutique stores.

The Grote Kerk

Kerkplein 2 • Mon–Sat 10am–5pm, Sun 1–5pm • Free • **Tower** Sat 1pm €5 • ⓦ grotekerkbreda.nl

The main attraction on the Grote Markt is the Gothic **Grote Kerk**, whose stunningly beautiful bell tower reaches high into the sky. Inside, the main nave, with its richly carved capitals, leads to a high and mighty central crossing. Like the majority of Dutch churches, the Grote Kerk had its decorations either removed or obscured after the Reformation, but a few murals have been uncovered and they reveal just how colourful the church once was. The Grote Kerk's most remarkable feature is the **Mausoleum of Count Engelbrecht II**, a one-time Stadholder and captain-general of the Netherlands who died in 1504 of tuberculosis – vividly apparent in the drawn features of his intensely realistic face. Four kneeling figures (Caesar, Regulus, Hannibal and Philip of Macedonia) support a canopy that carries his armour, so skilfully sculpted that their shoulders seem to sag slightly under the weight. It's believed that the mausoleum was the work of Tomaso Vincidor of Bologna, but whoever created it imbued the mausoleum with grandeur without resorting to flamboyance; the result is both eerily realistic and oddly moving. During the French occupation the choir was used as a stable, but fortunately the sixteenth-century misericords, showing rustic scenes of everyday life, survived. A couple of the carvings are modern replacements – as you'll see from their subject matter.

The Kasteel

At the top of Kasteelplein sits the **Kasteel** – too formal to be forbidding and considerably rebuilt since the Compromise of Breda was signed here in 1566. Twenty-five years later the Spanish captured Breda, but it was regained in 1590 thanks to a neat trick by Maurice of Nassau's troops using the Trojan Horse strategy. The **Spanjaardsgat**, an early sixteenth-century water gate with twin defensive bastions just west of the Kasteel, is usually (but inaccurately) identified as the spot where this happened. Today the Kasteel is a military academy and there's no admission to its grounds, unless you join one of the VVV tours.

Begijnhof

Catherinastraat 45 • Daily 9am–6pm • Free • ⓦ begijnhofbreda.nl

The **Begijnhof**, built in 1531, was until 1990 the only *hofje* in the Netherlands still occupied by Beguines. Today it has been given over to elderly women, some of whom

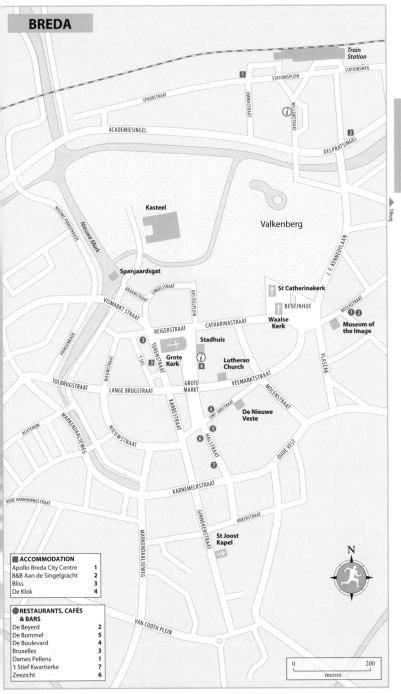

BREDA

6

Train Station

STATIONSPLEIN
STATIONSWEG

SPOORSTRAAT

ACADEMIESINGEL

EMMASTRAAT

WILLEMSTRAAT

DELPRATSINGEL

Tilburg

Kasteel

Valkenberg

NIEUWE PRINSENKADE

Nieuwe Mark

Spanjaardsgat

KRAANSTRAAT
CINGELSTRAAT
KASTEELPLEIN

VISMARKT STRAAT

REIGERSTRAAT
CATHARINASTRAAT

St Catherinakerk

BEGIJNHOF

Waalse Kerk

BOSCHSTRAAT

Museum of the Image

VLASZAK

J. F. KENNEDYLAAN

PRINSENKADE

NIEUWSTRAAT
T SAS
TORENSTRAAT

Grote Kerk

Stadhuis

Lutheran Church

VEEMARKTSTRAAT

MOLENSTRAAT

TOLBRUGSTRAAT
LANGE BRUGSTRAAT

KARRESTRAAT

GROTE MARKT

SINT JANSTRAAT

De Nieuwe Veste

OUDE VEST

ACHTEROM

MARKENDAALSEWEG

NIEUWSTRAAT

HALSTRAAT

KARNEMELKSTRAAT

OUDE VANHOORNESTRAAT

GINNEKENSTRAAT

MARKENDAALSEWEG

AKKERSTRAAT

St Joost Kapel

N

VAN COOTH PLEIN

ACCOMMODATION

Apollo Breda City Centre	1
B&B Aan de Singelgracht	2
Bliss	3
De Klok	4

RESTAURANTS, CAFÉS & BARS

De Beyerd	2
De Bommel	5
De Boulevard	4
Bruxelles	3
Dames Pellens	1
't Stief Kwartierke	7
Zeezicht	6

0 — 200
metres

6

look after the dainty nineteenth-century St Catherinakerk chapel at the rear, and tend the herb garden that was laid out several hundred years ago. To the right of the Begijnhof entrance is the **Waalse Kerk** (Walloon Church), where Peter Stuyvesant (1612–72), governor of New York when it was a Dutch colony, was married.

MOTI (Museum of the Image)

Boschstraat 22 • Tues–Sun 10am–5pm • €7.50 • ⓦ motimuseum.nl

The city's newest museum, **MOTI**, is well worth a visit – and not just for its location in one of Breda's oldest buildings, the Beyerd. Founded as a hospice in 1246 to provide shelter for pilgrims, it later became an old men's home. Inside, the basement of the "Museum of the Image" hosts a permanent exhibition on a hundred years of Dutch graphic design, from magazine covers to old propaganda posters. On the ground floor imaginative temporary exhibitions are held: the displays change regularly, but the theme is always the same – how images affect us and can be interpreted.

ARRIVAL AND INFORMATION   BREDA

By train The train station is at Stationsplein 16: from here, head down Willemstraat and cross the park for the town centre.

Destinations Dordrecht (every 20min; 20min); Maastricht (every 30min; 1hr 50min); Middelburg (every 30min; 1hr 15min); 's-Hertogenbosch (every 30min; 30min).

Tourist office Breda has two VVV offices, one just outside the train station, at Willemstraat 17–19 (Mon 1–5pm, Tues–Fri 10am–5pm, Sat 10am–2.30pm; ☎0900 522 2444, ⓦ vvvbreda.nl), the other at Grote Markt 38 (Wed–Fri 10.30am–5.30pm, Sat 10.30am–5pm; July & Aug also Tues 10.30am–5.30pm).

ACCOMMODATION

Apollo Breda City Centre Stationsplein 14 ☎076 522 0200, ⓦ apollohotelsresorts.com. Conveniently located right next to the train station, this smart hotel has 88 well-equipped rooms in bright colours with funky paintings. It's located in a converted post office, with many relics on the walls reminiscent of its former function. The rooms are well insulated, so you won't hear the freight trains passing at night. Special deals are abundant. **€89**

★ **B&B Aan de Singelgracht** Delpratsingel 14 ☎076 521 6271, ⓦ desingelgracht.nl. Within walking distance of the train station, this small B&B in an old mansion has been elegantly decorated, with an amazing eye for detail. Two of the rooms have original *bedstedes*, beds built in

closets, which was common until well into the nineteenth century. The suite is equipped with a sauna. **€112**

Bliss Torenstraat 9 ☎076 533 5980, ⓦ blisshotel.nl. The place to pick if you want to splash out, with nine luxury themed suites, located in the main shopping street in the centre of town. There's a good restaurant downstairs, and a G&T bar to relax in after a day of shopping. **€180**

De Klok Grote Markt 26 ☎076 521 4082, ⓦ hotel-de-klok.nl. Right in the centre of town, with basic but adequate rooms, some with views over the bustling market square. It's surprisingly inexpensive for the location, but fills up quickly in summer. **€98**

EATING, DRINKING AND NIGHTLIFE

Breda has a decent range of places to eat, many of them located around the Grote Markt and the streets running off it. Kebab joints and Turkish pizzas are plentiful at Havermarkt, a square packed with hole-in-the-wall joints for late-night snacks. This is also the best place for drinking, with plenty of bars that stay open late into the night.

De Beyerd Boschstraat 26 ☎076 521 4265, ⓦ beyerd .nl. The place to be for connoisseurs of Low Countries' beer, with its own on-site brewery. There's also a good restaurant attached, serving main courses such as cod or lamb for €17.50. Mon, Tues, Thurs & Sun 10am–1am, Fri 10am–2am, Sat noon–2am.

De Bommel Halstraat 1 ☎076 521 2429, ⓦ debommel .nl. A large and lively café-bar frequented by a mix of customers – with live music or DJs at weekends. It's extremely popular and often jam-packed. Mon 11am–1am, Tues & Wed 10.30am–1am, Thurs–Sat

10.30–2am, Sun 3pm–2am.

De Boulevard St Janstraat 3 ☎076 514 6399, ⓦ boulevardbreda.nl. Located in an old theatre, this eetcafé mainly attracts families and people on a tight budget with its extremely cheap three-course meals for only €13.50. The café and theatre attract the crowds at weekends with DJs playing everything from disco to drum 'n' bass. Tues–Sun 10am–5pm.

Bruxelles Havermarkt 5 ☎076 521 5211, ⓦ bruxelles .nl. A lively café specializing in Belgian beers which go down well with the cheap daily specials such as spare ribs, steak or satay for around €12–15. They also have an impressive whisky collection, specializing in Scottish malts. Mon–Wed & Sun noon–1am, Thurs noon–2am, Fri & Sat noon–4am.

Dames Pellens Boschstraat 24 ☎076 887 6929, ⓦdamespellens.nl. Modern and classy wine bar, serving French wines and champagne, to accompany the tasty cheese platters or fish pâté. At lunch they also serve salads and sandwiches for around €9. Tues–Sun noon–midnight.

't Stief Kwartierke Halstraat 32 ☎076 522 8493, ⓦstiefkwartierke.nl. Intimate little lunchroom with warm red walls covered with black and white pictures. It mainly serves home-made specialities such as apple pie, chocolate tart, pancakes and salads. Also great for high tea with mouthwatering sweets and a wide variety of teas. Tues, Wed & Fri 9.30am–6pm, Thurs 9.30am–9pm, Sat 9.30am–5.30pm, Sun noon–5.30pm.

Zeezicht Ridderstraat 1 ☎076 514 8248, ⓦcafezeezicht.nl. This upmarket café is good for its large choice of beers, gins and whiskies, its lively terrace and inviting menu consisting of delicacies such as barramundi, lamb stew and stuffed turkey for around €18. Live music on Fridays. Daily 5–10pm.

Bergen-op-Zoom

BERGEN-OP-ZOOM, just 30km north of Antwerp, is an untidy town, a jumble of old and new buildings that are the consequence of being shunted between various European powers from the sixteenth century onwards. In 1576 Bergen-op-Zoom sided with the United Provinces against the Spanish and as a result was under near-continuous siege until 1622. This war-ravaged theme continued thereafter: the French bombarded the city in 1747 and took it again in 1795, though it managed to withstand a British attack in 1814. Bergen-op-Zoom's saving grace is its famous **February carnival** when almost every inhabitant – as well as revellers from all over Europe – joins in the Tuesday procession. It's a great time to be in the town, although you won't find any accommodation – the whole place gets packed out – so just do as the locals do and party all night.

Grote Markt

Walk straight out of the train station and you'll soon find yourself on the **Grote Markt**, most cheerful during summer when it's decked out with open-air cafés and the like. The **Stadhuis** (May–Oct Tues–Sun 1–4.30pm; €1.50) on the north side of the square, is Bergen's most attractive building, spruced up in recent years and comprising three separate houses: to the left of the gateway an alderman's house of 1397, to the right a merchant's house of 1480 and on the far right a building known as "De Olifant", whose facade dates from 1611. All of this is a lot more appealing than the blunt ugliness of the **Grote Kerk**, also on the Grote Markt, an unlucky building that's been destroyed by siege and fire innumerable times over the past four hundred years.

Markiezenhof Museum

Steenbergsestraat 8 • Tues–Sun 11am–5pm • €9 • ⓦmarkiezenhof.nl

Walking northwest of Grote Markt, Fortuinstraat leads to the **Markiezenhof Museum**, a first-rate presentation of a collection that has a little of everything: domestic utensils and samplers from the sixteenth century onwards, sumptuous period rooms and architectural drawings as well as a permanent exhibition on fairground attractions on the top floor. All this is housed in a palace built by Anthonis Keldermans between 1485 and 1522 to a late-Gothic style that gives it the feel of an Oxford college.

Gevangenpoort

Lievevrouwestraat 60 • May–Oct Tues–Sun 1–4.30pm • €1.50

Little was spared of old Bergen-op-Zoom: near the entrance to the Markiezenhof, the **Gevangenpoort** is practically all that remains of the old city defences, a solid-looking fourteenth-century gatehouse that was later converted into a prison which it remained until the 1930s. Today, the gatehouse is used for a small exhibition about archeology for schoolchildren.

ARRIVAL AND INFORMATION

BERGEN-OP-ZOOM

By train The train station is an easy 5min stroll south of the Grote Markt.

Destinations Den Haag (hourly; 1hr 20min); Middelburg (every 30min; 45min); Rotterdam (every 30min; 50min).

Tourist office The VVV, just off the Grote Markt at Kortemeestraat 19 (Mon 1–5pm, Tues–Sat 10am–5pm; May–Oct also Sun noon–4pm; ☎0164 277 482, ⓦ vvvbrabantsewal.nl), has details of private rooms and issues maps of the town centre.

ACCOMMODATION AND EATING

De Bourgondiër Grote Markt 2 ☎0164 254 000, ⓦ grandcafehoteldebourgondier.nl. A centrally located hotel with classy rooms decorated in warm shades. The pleasant café downstairs has a terrace overlooking the market square, and serves great waffles and pancakes as well as a wide variety of beers on draught. **€115**

Hotel Eetcafé van E Beursplein 5 ☎0164 299 500, ⓦ hoteleetcafevanee.nl. Located on the handsome Beursplein near the Markiezenhof museum, this newly renovated hotel offers simple but perfectly adequate rooms. The downstairs restaurant serves snacks, soups, steak, satay and more, with mains around €16. **€112**

Sasa Lounge Steenbergsestraat 1 ☎0164 233 844, ⓦ sasalounge.nl. Stylish Mediterranean tapas and *meze* restaurant with a choice of excellent dishes to share around the table. There's a set menu for €22.50. Tues–Sun 5–11pm.

Stayokay Hostel Boslustweg 1 ☎0164 233 261, ⓦ stayokay.com; take bus #22 from the station and it's a 15min walk from the Ziekenhuis (hospital) stop. Four kilometres out of town, amid the greenery, this hostel is perfectly suited for families with young children with its large forest playground and comfortable facilities. Dorms **€22**

De Teerkamer Grote Markt 13 ☎0164 239 345, ⓦ teerkamer.nl. Smack on the market square this medieval building, with a modern interior combined with plush purple elements, is the place to be for a quick lunch or lingering dinner. The menu features everything from a simple chicken satay to a lip-smacking fish platter. Mon–Sat 9am–10pm, Sun noon–10pm.

Zeeland

Luctor et Emergo, reads **Zeeland**'s slogan: "I struggle and I emerge", a reference to the interminable battle the province has waged with the sea. As its name suggests, the southwestern corner of the Netherlands is bound as much by water as land. Comprising three main peninsulas within the delta of the rivers Rijn (Rhine), Schelde and Maas, this cluster of islands and semi-islands is linked by a complex network of dykes. This concrete web not only gives protection from flooding but also forms the main lines of communication between each sliver of land. The northernmost island, **Goeree-Overflakkee**, a little south of Rotterdam, is connected by two dams to **Schouwen-Duiveland**, while further south are **Noord and Zuid Beveland**, the western tip of which adjoins **Walcheren**. Furthest south of all is **Zeeuws Vlaanderen**, lying across the blustery waters of the Westerschelde attached to Belgium.

Before the Delta Project (see p.314) secured the area, fear of the sea's encroachment had prevented any large towns developing, and consequently Zeeland remains a condensed area of low dunes and nature reserves, popular with holidaymakers escaping the cramped conurbations nearby. The province also has more sun than anywhere else in the Netherlands: the winds blow the clouds away, with spectacular sunsets guaranteed. Getting around is easy, with bus services making up for the lack of north–south train connections, though undoubtedly the best way to see these islands is to **cycle**, using **Middelburg** as a base and venturing out into its environs.

Middelburg

Sitting pretty on Walcheren island, compact **MIDDELBURG**, the largest town in Zeeland, is also its most likeable. The town's streets preserve some snapshots of medieval Holland, its cobbled alleyways echo the sea-trading days of the sixteenth century, and a scattering of museums and churches provide targets for your wanderings. Middelburg's centre holds a large Thursday **market** and if you can only make it for a day, this is the best time to visit. Set against the imposing backdrop of the Stadhuis and packed with local produce, it's an atmospheric event that's guaranteed to draw a crowd – including, quite regularly, elderly couples in traditional costume. With a reasonable range of accommodation, Middelburg also makes an ideal base for exploring the surrounding area, including Veere, Domburg and the Delta Project, with good bus connections and excellent cycling along Walcheren's windswept coast.

Middelburg is an appealing town to explore, small enough to cover on foot and dotted with architectural clues that bear witness to its rich maritime past. The town owes its early growth to its position on a bend in the River Arne, making it easy to defend. The slight elevation on which it was built gave the settlement protection from the sea and its streets slope down to the harbour. Look out for the surviving stone blocks at the end of **Brakstraat**, into which wooden planks were slotted, then bolstered with sandbags, acting as a temporary dyke when floods threatened.

Though its **abbey** was founded in 1120, Middelburg's isolation restricted its development until the late Middle Ages when, being at the western end of the Scheldt estuary, it became rich off the back of the wool and cloth trade with Antwerp, Bruges and Ghent. Thereafter, it became both the market and administrative centre of the region. The town's **street names** – Houtkaai ("Timber Dock"), Korendijk ("Grain Dyke"), Bierkaai ("Beer Dock") – reveal how diverse its trade became, while house names like "London" and "Samarkand" tell of the routes Middelburg's traders plied. Kuiperspoort ("Barrelmaker's Gate") is an alleyway off Dwarskaai along which a string of warehouses have been restored, many of them now occupied by artists and musicians.

The Abdijkerken

Onder Den Toren • April–Oct Mon–Fri 10.30am–5pm; July–Sept also Sat & Sun 1.30–5pm • Free • **Tower** April–June, Sept & Oct Mon 1–4pm, Tues–Sun 11am–5pm; July & Aug daily 11am–5pm • €4

Badly damaged on several occasions, most recently by the Germans in 1940, Middelburg's **Abdijkerken** ("Abbey Churches") complex comprises three churches, parts of which date back to the thirteenth century. Little remains from the abbey's salad days as a centre of Catholic worship, since Middelburg was an early convert to Protestantism following the uprising against the Spanish, and in 1574 William the Silent's troops ejected the monks and converted the abbey to secular use. Thereafter, the complex was used by all and sundry, becoming at one time a gun factory and at another a mint, before the three churches were turned over to the Protestants.

Among the ecclesiastical trio, the **Nieuwe Kerk** has an organ case from 1694; the **Wandel Kerk** holds the triumphalist tomb of admirals Jan and Cornelis Evertsen, brothers killed fighting in a naval battle against the English in 1666; and the **Koor Kerk** retains the oldest decoration, including a fine Nicolai organ of 1479. Best of all, however, is the complex's landmark 91m **tower**, known locally as **Lange Jan** (Long John), whose **carillon** plays every fifteen minutes, with additional concerts year-round. Climb the 207 steps of the **tower** and you'll be treated to some fine views: in clear weather, the view from the top of the tower stretches across Walcheren and as far as the Zeelandbrug and the eastern Scheldt, all of which gives a good idea of how vulnerable the province is to the ebbs and flows of the sea.

MIDDELBURG'S FESTIVALS

One of the town's most colourful **festivals** is **Ringrijderij**, a horseback competition where riders try to pick off rings with lances. It takes place in August at the Koepoort city gate near Molenwater, and in the central Abdijplein on one day in July; check with the tourist office for dates. Another major draw is the annual **Mosselfeesten** (Ⓦmosselfeesten.nl), a weekend in the second half of July devoted to celebrating the arrival of the fresh black mussels, of which Zeeland is particularly proud. The festival takes place around the Vlasmarkt, with live music and restaurants offering their own version of this regional speciality.

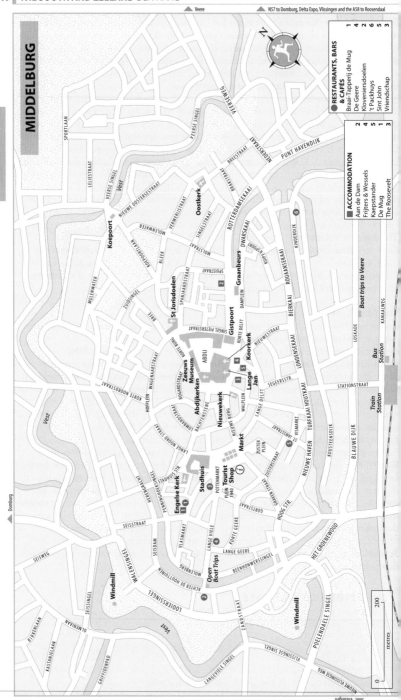

MIDDELBURG

● **RESTAURANTS, BARS & CAFÉS**
Braai-Tapperij de Mug	1
De Geere	4
Kloveniersdoelen	2
't Packhuys	6
Sint John	5
Vriendschap	3

■ **ACCOMMODATION**
Aan de Dam	2
Frijters & Wessels	4
Kaepstander	5
De Mug	1
The Roosevelt	3

0 — 200 metres

The Zeeuws Museum

Abdij • Tues–Sun 11am–5pm • €8.50 • ⓦ zeeuwsmuseum.nl

At the northern tip of the abbey complex, housed in what were once the monks' dormitories, the **Zeeuws Museum** holds a mixed bag of a collection that's regularly changed around for exhibitions. The museum has a small but fine collection of paintings by Adriaan Coorte, Joris Hoefnagel and the twentieth-century Realist painter Charley Toorop. There are also lively tapestries, commissioned by the local authorities between 1591 and 1604 to celebrate the naval battles against the Spanish, and a comprehensive display of local costumes.

Damplein

Exit the abbey complex through the eastern **Gistpoort** gate to reach **Damplein**, which forms a quieter focus for restaurants than the Markt and is the site of the **Graanbeurs**, a grain exchange rebuilt in the nineteenth century. The small alleys east of Damplein are some of Middelburg's quaintest streets, especially Kuiperspoort with its original row of East India Company warehouses dating back to the seventeenth century.

The Stadhuis

Markt 1 • 1hr guided tour of the mayor's office, council chambers, the Vleeshal and various reception rooms; April–Oct daily at 3pm, book in advance for English • €4.25

Middelburg's **Stadhuis** is generally agreed to be Zeeland's finest building, a wonderfully eclectic mix of architectural styles. The towering Gothic facade is especially magnificent, dating from the mid-fifteenth century and built to a design by the Keldermans family from Mechelen in modern-day Belgium. Inside the **Vleeshal**, a former meat hall that now houses temporary exhibitions of contemporary art, which can be visited on the guided tour.

The Stadhuis's impressive pinnacled **tower** was added in 1520, though the current tower, along with the Stadhuis itself and much of the Markt area, is only a reconstruction of the original. On May 17, 1940, this part of the city was all but flattened by German bombing in the same series of raids that destroyed Rotterdam. Restoration of the main monuments was a long and difficult process, with convincing results, but the houses around the Markt were all rebuilt in 1950s style.

Kloveniersdoelen

On the western edge of town, at the end of Langeviele, is the landmark **Kloveniersdoelen** building. Constructed in 1607 in exuberant Flemish Renaissance style, this was the home of the city's civic guard, the arquebusiers, until the end of the eighteenth century, later becoming the local headquarters of the East India Company, and later still a military hospital. It's now an arthouse cinema and restaurant (ⓦ cinemamiddelburg.nl; see p.308). Feel free to climb up the dainty tower for views over the city, and for a peek inside the loft where the local shooting club still regularly practises.

ARRIVAL AND DEPARTURE
MIDDELBURG

By train From the train station it's a short walk to the town centre: cross the bridge on Loskade, head up Segeersstraat and Lange Delft and you find yourself on the Markt.
Destinations Bergen-op-Zoom (every 30min; 40min); Roosendaal (every 30min; 50min).

By bus The bus station is right in front of the train station.
Destinations Burgh-Haamstede and Renesse (hourly; 1hr); Deltapark (Mon–Fri 2 hourly, Sat hourly, Sun every 2hr; 30min); Veere (Mon–Sat hourly; 12min).

INFORMATION AND TOURS

Tourist office Middelburg does not have an official VVV office, but you should be able to find whatever you need at the excellent Tourist Shop inside the Drvkkerij bookshop at Markt 51 (Mon 11am–6pm, Tues, Wed & Fri 9.30am–6pm, Thurs 9.30am–9pm, Sat 9.30am–5.15pm, first Sun of the

month 1–5pm; ☏ 0118 674 300, ⓦ touristshop.nl), which can book all types of tours, has details of events, a list of private rooms and is well stocked with cycling maps for touring Zeeland's coast.
Boat trips Open-top boat trips on the canals depart from

the Langeviele bridge at Achter de Houttuinen 39 (April–Oct daily 11am–5pm; €6.75; ⓦ rondvaartmiddelburg.nl), where you can also rent canoes and pedalos (€15/hr). The return boat trip to Veere (May–Sept daily 10.15am & 2pm; €14.50; ⓦ rederij-dijkhuizen.nl) leaves from opposite the train station.

Tours The Tourist Shop runs a guided walking tour (1 hr 30min; April–Oct daily 11.30am; €5,50, book ahead for English tours), taking in the city's main landmarks. Horse-drawn carriage rides operate from the Markt (May–Sept Wed & Sat 2pm; €8; 1hr).

Taxis Taxicentrale ☎ 0118 612 600.

ACCOMMODATION

Aan de Dam Dam 31 ☎ 0118 643 773, ⓦ hotelaandedam.nl. A well-kept treasure with thirteen suites, all in different styles and varying sizes, but equally elegant and equipped with Auping beds and Bose sound systems. The garden is a real oasis in summer, a great spot to enjoy a high tea after a day of shopping. €110

Frijters & Wessels Reigerstraat 1 ☎ 0118 853 891, ⓦ frijtersenwessels.nl. The perfect combination of a homeware shop and an incredibly stylish B&B. This romantic hideaway with amenable owners has just two rooms and a small studio across the street. Breakfast is served in the shop downstairs. €95

Kaepstander Koorkerkhof 10 ☎ 0118 642 848, ⓦ kaepstander.nl. Small and basic rooms in a seventeenth-century former warehouse, but with great views of the abbey complex and a relaxing café downstairs. Some rooms have shared facilities and the breakfast is very simple. €77

★ **De Mug** Vlasmarkt 54–56 ☎ 0118 614 851, ⓦ demug .nl. By far the most appealing and authentic option in town, these four spacious rooms are located in a renovated building, with a restaurant, popular bar and shop downstairs. €115

The Roosevelt Nieuwe Burg 42 ☎ 0118 436 360, ⓦ hoteltheroosevelt.nl. Opposite the abbey complex, this brand-new boutique hotel has stylish and lofty rooms, many of them split-level, with smart IP-TVs. The presidential suite is twice the price of a regular room, but it's enormous with 8m-high ceilings. €120

EATING AND DRINKING

Most of Middelburg's bars, cafés and restaurants are on or near the Markt. Many are tourist-oriented and pricey for what you get, but there is a sprinkling of top-notch places too. On Thursdays, market stalls supply limitless cheap and tasty snacks, especially fresh fish and seafood. Look out for *bolus*, a circular sweetbread first brought to Middelburg by Portuguese Jews and best served hot with butter and a cup of coffee.

Braai-Tapperij de Mug Vlasmarkt 56 ☎ 0118 614 851, ⓦ demug.nl. Good Dutch-French cooking (mussels in season) at moderate prices, an excellent array of beers including its own "Mug Bitter", and occasional live jazz, all in an old-fashioned setting decorated with aged cognac barrels. Very popular, so book ahead. Tues–Sat 2–10.30pm.

De Geere Lange Viele 51 ☎ 0118 613 083, ⓦ cafedegeere.nl. Daily specials for €8.50 and cheap beer are on offer at this cosy café with red-brick walls and smart chandeliers. Regular main courses, such as rib-eye or a vegetarian dish, are around €16. Visit at the weekend for regular live music or DJ tunes. Tues–Thurs 10am–midnight, Fri & Sat 10am–2am, Sun 3pm–midnight.

Kloveniersdoelen Achter de Houttuinen 30 ☎ 0118 644 969, ⓦ kloveniersdoelen.nl. A large grand café in the historical civic guard building just west of the city centre, which also houses an arthouse cinema and has a lovely and child-friendly garden terrace. There's international cuisine such as lamb burger (€13) and grilled sea bream (€18), and a set menu for €22.50. Mon–Sat 11am-midnight, Sun 2–6pm; kitchen

---

CYCLING AROUND MIDDELBURG: ALONG THE WALCHEREN COAST

The **coast** north and west of Middelburg offers some of the Netherlands' finest beaches and excellent walking and cycling, although on midsummer weekends parts of it are mobbed by crowds of Dutch and German holidaymakers. Countless **cycling options** make the most of Walcheren's handsome coastline, with plenty of refreshments en route. With limited public transport available to carry bikes, most routes are best completed as loops.

Possible **day-trips** include cycling west to Domburg, picking up signs to the Domburg hostel and continuing through the woods to **Breezand**. A cycleway follows the polder to Veere, from where you can ride alongside the Walcheren canal, cutting back to Middelburg. Alternatively, pick up the same canal out of town to Vlissingen, joining the cycleway that runs between dune and woodland to **Zoutelande** and **Westkapelle**: there's a fabulous stretch of dyke to cycle along in the direction of Domburg with spectacular sunsets out to sea and a photogenic lighthouse. A signposted cycle path leads directly back to Middelburg.

open Tues & Wed noon–4pm, Thurs–Sat noon–10pm.

t Packhuys Kinderdijk 84 ☎0118 647 064, ⓦhetpackhuys.nl. Located in an old warehouse with a great waterfront terrace, this maritime-themed restaurant serves fabulous food, such as lobster soup, salads and lambs racks. Main courses are around €19 and a three-course meal costs €32.50. Thurs–Sun 5–10pm.

Sint John Sint Janstraat 40 ☎0118 625 993, ⓦsintjohn.nl. A tasteful mix of a brown café-cum-tearoom, serving artisan beers and a wide variety of

coffee and tea blends. Try the home-made sweets and frozen yoghurt. Regular live jazz, too. Mon–Sat 8.30am–6pm.

Vriendschap Markt 75 ☎0118 612 257, ⓦvriendschapcr.nl. The best of the café-restaurants around the Markt has an extensive terrace and a modern interior. Mains include Camembert cheese fondue and sardines with octopus for around €17. It's also notable as one of the few places that's open and lively on Mondays out of season. Daily 10am–11pm.

Domburg

Sixteen kilometres from Middelburg, **DOMBURG** is the area's principal resort. It's been a favourite haunt for artists since early last century when Jan Toorop gathered together a group of like-minded painters (including, for a while, Piet Mondriaan), who were inspired by the coastal scenery and the fine quality of the light. Aside from a museum that holds a small collection of Toorop's work, the main reason to come to Domburg is to walk over the dunes and through the woods or to cycle the coastal path. It's an easy 7km bike ride southwest of Domburg to the quieter beach resort of **Westkapelle**, with a picturesque lighthouse and a critical spot where the dyke was breached during the 1953 flood (see box, p.314).

Marie Tak van Poortvliet Museum

Ooststraat 10a • April–Oct Tues–Sun 1–5pm • €3.50 • ⓦmarietakvanpoortvlietmuseumdomburg.nl

The **Marie Tak van Poortvliet Museum** is housed inside a pavilion built by artist Jan Toorop (1858–1928) to exhibit his paintings. Today, the museum displays works by members of the Domburg group such as Jacoba van Heemskerck, Ferdinand Hart Nibbrig and Charley Toorop, Jan Toorop's daughter, as well as hosting temporary exhibitions by local, lesser-known artists.

ARRIVAL AND INFORMATION   **DOMBURG**

By bus Bus #53 departs hourly from Middelburg to Domburg, following the longer, more scenic route along the Walcheren coast through Zoutelande and Westkapelle (50min). Bus #52 goes direct from Middelburg to Domburg in approximately 30min.

Tourist office The VVV is at Schuitvlotstraat 32 (April &

May Mon–Sat 9.30am-5.30pm, June & Sept–Oct also Sun 11am–3pm; July & Aug Mon–Sat 9am–6pm, Sun 11am–3pm; Nov–March Mon–Fri 10am–5pm, Sat 10am–2pm; ☎0118 583 484, ⓦvvzeeland.nl). It can help with accommodation and provide a map of the village.

ACCOMMODATION

Duinlust Badhuisweg 28 ☎0118 582 943, ⓦhotelduinlust.nl. Simple but pleasant hotel within easy walking distance of the beach. The rooms are basic but perfectly adequate, most with flat-screens. €85

Slaapzand beach houses Schelpweg 17a, Domburg beach ☎06 5477 7852, ⓦslaapzand.nl. Modern, well-equipped and right on the beach, these unique glass-fronted beach houses have great sea views: they sleep up to five people. €1100 for a week

Stayokay Domburg Duinvlietweg 8, Oostkapelle ☎0118 581 254, ⓦstayokay.com. A particularly scenic

hostel, located in the thirteenth-century Kasteel Westhove which comes complete with a moat and is surrounded by a nature reserve. It's only a short stroll to the beach and less than 2km from Domburg on bus route #53: ask to be dropped off at the castle. Dorms €34

Strandhotel Duinheuvel Badhuisweg 2 ☎0118 581 100, ⓦwilduin.nl. Upmarket establishment – within easy walking distance of the beach – with 35 tastefully decorated rooms in minimalist style, and an art gallery downstairs. Most rooms have balconies, some with a sea view, and all have flat-screens and free wi-fi. €135

EATING AND DRINKING

Badpaviljoen Badhuisweg 21 ☎0118 582 405, ⓦhetbadpaviljoen.nl. Domburg's grandest building, an

1889 hotel perched on a dune top with sweeping views over the beach and the sea, is now a great modern restaurant to

settle down for a drink or a meal. Oysters are €18, venison €16, a four-course dinner €55. July & Aug daily 11am–11pm; Sept–Dec & March–June Thurs–Sun 11am–10pm.
Brasserie Domburg Wijngaardstraat 17 ☎0118 567 989, ⊛brasseriedomburg.nl. A large and lively café and restaurant overlooking a park at the eastern end of Weststraat. Specialities include sandwiches, pasta, six

oysters (€12) or half a lobster (€14). Daily 11am–10pm.
Markt Zes Markt 6 ☎0118 582 373, ⊛marktzes.nl. Right in the centre of town with a pleasant terrace. Wraps, toasties and *uitsmijters* make up the lunch menu, while excellent seafood such as fried sole for €22 is served at dinner. Occasional live music. Daily 10am–midnight.

6

Vlissingen

VLISSINGEN (Flushing), just 5km south of Middelburg, was previously an important ferry terminus, but its role as a transport hub for Belgium has dwindled due to the completion of the tunnel between Ellewoutsdijk and Terneuzen, a little way to the east. There's not a lot to see in the town, although the maritime museum warrants a couple of hours, and the assorted shipping that plies the choppy Westerschelde estuary has an appeal of its own. The Dutch and Belgian pilots who help captains guide their ships to and from Antwerp use the harbour as a base for their speedboats, and have been known to take interested tourists along on trips.

Vlissingen's workaday centre won't detain you long, though you might drop by the improbably named **Cornelia Quackhofje**, an eighteenth-century almshouse for sailors, just north of the Lange Zelke shopping precinct. For more atmosphere, head for the **harbour**, whose bundle of pavement cafés and fresh fish-and-chip stalls is popular with Dutch and German tourists.

MuZEEum

Nieuwendijk 11 • **Museum** Mon–Fri 10am–5pm, Sat & Sun 1–5pm; Oct–March closed Mon • €10, winter €8.50 • **Kazematten** April–Oct only • €4 • ⊛muzeeum.nl

The modern **MuZEEum** maritime museum is partly housed in the grand seventeenth-century mansion of the Lampsins family, who owned the Carribbean island Tobago for eleven years (naming it "Nieuw Walcheren"). Divided into four themes – the sea, trade, glory and adventure – multimedia presentations explain the sea's crucial role in shaping Zeeland's livelihood, while excellent audiovisual displays reconstruct scenes of naval battles to dramatic effect, including those of the brilliant Dutch naval hero Michiel de Ruyter. Exhibits include a rusty wall of shipwrecks, spices shipped along the trading routes of the Dutch East Indies and items brought home by local sailors from as far afield as Easter Island, or salvaged from VOC wrecks. Napoleon's damp Kazematten (casemates) stronghold under the nearby promenade holds an interesting new exhibition about the city's fortifications, along with the original bread-baking ovens.

Het Arsenaal

Arsenaalplein 7 • April–Oct daily 10am–7pm; hours vary outside season but generally Tues–Sun 10am–7pm; last admission 2hr before closing • €15 • ⊛arsenaal.com

Families will enjoy **Het Arsenaal**, a theme park where you can go on a simulated sea voyage, climb an observation tower and walk on a mocked-up sea bed among tanks of sharks. Kids can learn what skills they need to become a real pirate and find out what it was like to live on a pirate's ship. The petting pool where you can touch small sharks and rays is a real attraction.

The Westerschelde

The blustery walk along the Boulevard de Ruyter offers views of the enormous vessels that sail the **WESTERSCHELDE**. Keeping to a narrow, often tortuous route, these container ships must negotiate the shallow waters and shifting sandbanks that sometimes reveal centuries-old wrecks. Further round the harbour, the promenade has a pleasant seaside feel, with a **beach** at the end. Alternatively, you can continue beyond the promenade on the green-signposted cycle path to **Dishoek** and **Zoutelande**; along the way there are plenty of opportunities to hike up and over the dunes, emerging onto a beach that runs for miles – the perfect asset for the Netherlands' sunniest town.

ARRIVAL AND INFORMATION   VLISSINGEN

By train The train station is located in the harbour, next to the ferry terminal to Breskens, a 6min bus ride from the town centre or a 25min walk across the locks and along Piet Heinkade. From Vlissingen regular trains serve Middelburg (every 30min; 7min).

By bus From Middelburg train station, bus #56 runs to the centre of Vlissingen in about 20min.

By ferry The foot passenger and bicycle ferry across the Westerschelde between Vlissingen and Breskens (June–Aug daily 6am–10pm, every 30min–1hr; 25min) departs from next to Vlissingen train station. Tickets are €3, return €5.30 per person, plus €1 for bicycles: check ⓦ westerscheldeferry .nl for up-to-date information. From Breskens bus #42

departs to Bruges in Belgium (hourly; 1hr 30min).

By tunnel The 6.6km-long tunnel beneath the Westerschelde, linking Ellewoutsdijk and Terneuzen, is open 24hr; the toll for cars is €5.

Bike rental You can rent a bike from the train station next to the ferry terminal; the wide selection includes recumbents.

Tourist office The VVV is at Spuistraat 30 (April–Oct Mon 11am–5.30pm, Tues–Thurs 9.30am–5.30pm, Fri 9.30am–9pm, Sat 9.30am–5pm; Nov–March Mon 1–5.30pm, Tues–Thurs 9.30am–5.30pm, Fri 9.30am–9pm, Sat 9.30am–5pm; ☎0118 715 320, ⓦ vvvzeeland.nl). It can provide a list of pensions as well as information on local cycling routes.

ACCOMMODATION

Belgische Loodsensociëteit Blvd de Ruyter 4 ☎0118 413 608, ⓦ bsoos.nl. This newly renovated hotel, originally hosting the Belgian and Dutch pilots who help captains guide their ships to and from Antwerp, offers eleven basic rooms. The seafront ones have fabulous views of the passing ships, easily identified using the interactive radar image on the hotel website. The downstairs

restaurant serves reasonably priced fish dishes. **€105**

City Hostel Vlissingen Kerkstraat 10 ☎0118 415 200, ⓦ cityhostel-vlissingen.nl. Located in two monumental buildings, this backpacker and family hostel has rooms sleeping up to six people. A three-course buffet dinner is served in the cosy downstairs café for only €15. Bicycle rental for €10. Dorms **€23**, doubles **€60**

EATING AND DRINKING

De Beurs Beursplein 11 ☎0118 410 295, ⓦ restaurantdebeurs.nl. In Dutch Renaissance style and dating from 1635, one of Vlissingen's prettiest buildings now houses an agreeable restaurant with a terrace overlooking the harbour. It specializes in seafood and has a good-value three-course meal for €29.50. Mon–Fri 5.30–10.30pm, Sat & Sun 11.30am–10.30pm.

De Gecroonde Liefde Nieuwendijk 13 ☎0118 441 194, ⓦ degecroondeliefde.nl. Attached to the MuZEEum, this is your best bet for lunch or dinner with tasty sandwiches (from €7) and salads followed by home-baked

apple pie, or for afternoon high tea; dinner options incude sea bass for €18. The interior is modern and minimalistic, with a nice terrace in summer. Mon–Thurs 10am–6pm, Fri 10am–9pm, Sat & Sun noon–9pm; July & Aug also open till 9pm on Thurs.

Soif Bellamypark 14 ☎0118 410 516, ⓦ so-if.nl. Located close to the harbour, *Soif* is a cheerful little place with lime-green walls and wooden floors. Like many restaurants in Vlissingen, seafood is its speciality; from fresh oysters and salmon to lobster and shrimps at reasonable prices. Daily noon–midnight, Fri & Sat noon–2am.

Veere

VEERE, some 8km northeast of Middelburg, is an attractive little town by the banks of the Veerse Meer that makes for a pleasant half-day visit. Today, it's a centre for all things maritime, its small harbour jammed with yachts and its cafés packed with weekend admirals, but a handful of buildings and a large church point to a time when Veere was wealthy and quite independent of other, comparable towns in Zeeland.

The town originally made its fortune through a fortuitous Scottish connection: in 1444 a certain Wolfert VI van Borssele, the lord of Veere, married Mary, daughter of James I of Scotland. As part of the dowry, van Borssele was granted a monopoly on trade with Scottish wool merchants and, in return, Scottish merchants living in Veere were granted special privileges. Veere declined economically once the wool trade started to deteriorate. The opening of the Walcheren canal linking the town to Middelburg and Vlissingen, in the nineteenth century gave it a stay of execution, but the construction of the Veersegatdam and Zandkreekdam in the 1950s finally sealed off the port to seagoing vessels, and simultaneously created a freshwater lake ideal for watersports.

The town centre holds many fine old buildings dating from its heyday: their ornate workmanship leaves you in no doubt that the Scottish wool trade earned a bundle for the sixteenth- and seventeenth-century burghers of Veere. Many of the buildings (which are usually step-gabled with distinctive green and white shutters) are embellished with whimsical details that play on the owners' names or their particular line of business.

Museum Veere – Schotse Huizen
Kaai 25–27 • Daily 10am–5pm • €4,50 including Stadhuis, €6 with Grote Kerk • ⓦ museumveere.nl

These two merchants' buildings, **Het Lammeken** (The Lamb) and **In de Struijs** (**At the Ostrich**), dating from the mid-sixteenth century, originally combined offices, homes and warehouses. They now hold a small collection of local costumes, old books and furniture, along with an exhibit on Veere's relationship with Scotland.

Stadhuis
Markt 5 • Daily 10am–5pm • €4,50 including Schotse Huizen, €6 with Grote Kerk • ⓦ museumveere.nl

The town's recently restored **Stadhuis** is a typically opulent building, dating from the 1470s, with an out-of-scale Renaissance tower added a century later. Its facade is decorated with statues of the lords of Veere and their wives (Wolfert VI is third from the left) and inside a modern museum occupies what was formerly the courtroom.

Grote Kerk
Oudestraat 26 • May–Sept Tues–Sun 10am–5pm • €1.50, €6 including Stadhuis and Schotse Huizen

Finished in 1560, Veere's **Grote Kerk** was badly damaged by fire a century later and subsequent restorations removed much of its decoration. In 1808 invading British troops used the church as a hospital and three years later Napoleon's army converted it into barracks and stables, destroying the stained glass, bricking up the windows and inserting five floors in the nave. Despite all this damage, the church's blunt 42m **tower** adds a glowering presence to the landscape, especially when seen from the town's watery surroundings. According to the original design, the tower was to have been three times higher, but even as it stands there's a great view from the top.

ARRIVAL AND INFORMATION   VEERE

By bus Bus #54 runs hourly from Middelburg to Veere.
By bike You can rent a bike from Middelburg train station (€7.50/day) and take either the cycle path to Veere beside the main road or the circuitous but more picturesque route from the north side of town. Local bike rental is available at the Campveerse Toren restaurant (€5–10/day).
By boat The boat from Middelburg to Veere (May–Sept daily 10.15am & 2pm; return €14.50; ⓦ rederij-dijkhuizen.nl)

departs from opposite Middelburg train station, dropping off in Veere beside the *Campveerse Toren* hotel and returning at 11.45am and 3.30pm.
Tourist office Veere VVV is in the Stadhuis at Markt 5 (April to mid-May & Oct Fri–Sun noon–4pm; mid-May to June & Sept Tues–Sun noon–4pm; July & Aug daily 10am–5pm; ☏ 0118 435 858, ⓦ vvvzeeland.nl); it can advise on boat rental and has details of private rooms.

ACCOMMODATION AND EATING

Bed & Brood Kerkstraat 7 ☏ 0118 502 081, ⓦ bed-en-brood.nl. A fourteenth-century house of worship which has been converted into a stylish B&B with very spacious rooms. Classical elements have been given a modern twist and the huge garden is perfect for escaping the tourist crowds. €85
De Campveerse Toren Kaai 2 ☏ 0118 501 291, ⓦ campveersetoren.nl. This 500-year-old inn has rooms in a medieval tower and several adjacent buildings, beautifully located overlooking the water. All the hotel rooms have a

different feel but are equally stylish with an eye for detail. The gourmet restaurant is great for local fresh seafood and ingredients such as samphire, and there's a cheaper café on the top floor too. €120
Suster Anna Markt 8 ☏ 0118 501 557, ⓦ susteranna.nl. A warm and welcoming place dishing up pancakes, sandwiches and cakes in a homely atmosphere. It serves many different blends of tea and has an intimate garden terrace. April–Sept daily 10am–10pm; hours vary out of season.

t Waepen van Veere Markt 23–27 ☎ 0118 501 231, ☺ waepenvanveere.nl. A modern hotel with warm wooden floors, stylish chairs and flat-screen TVs. The classy restaurant serves Zeeland lamb (€25), mussels and regional oysters and has an extensive list of fine wines. **€90**

Schouwen-Duiveland

The storm surge barrier spans the mouth of the Oosterschelde estuary providing easy access over to the island of **Schouwen-Duiveland**. Most of the Dutch and German tourists who come here head directly to the western corner of the island for the acres of beach, pine forest and dune that stretch out between **Burgh-Haamstede** with its quaint town centre and medieval castle, and **Renesse**, two villages situated 6km apart. In the summer, this flank of the island is packed with families and predominantly young holidaymakers, making the most of its waterborne activities. **Zierikzee** further east is a more traditional affair, a miniature Middelburg that makes an appealing base for exploring the area, with some fine trips through the countryside out over one of Europe's longest (and perhaps windiest) bridges nearby.

If you're coming for peace and quiet, you should steer clear of the school holidays. Travel over the season's bookends in June and September and you'll have much of the long, pristine beaches to yourself, though the weather can be unpredictable, facilities dwindle with the approach of autumn, and storms can blot the sky.

Renesse

RENESSE, about 8km north of the Barrier, is a modern sprawl of bungalows just a kilometre from the beach, making an appealing base. Popular with the surfing and windsurfing crowd, its 16km beach is divided in summer into sectors, catering for families, surfers, kite-flyers and naturists. A free, open-top electric **bus** (9am–7pm) plies the length of the beach, linking hotels, campsites and the "Transferium" – the modern bus station on the edge of town that offers changing rooms, showers and bike rental, in an attempt to encourage holidaymakers to abandon their cars at the free car park alongside. Parking at the beach is expensive and time-limited.

INFORMATION

RENESSE

Tourist office The VVV is at Roelandsweg 5a (Mon-Sat 9am-5pm, July & Aug also on Sun; ☎ 0118 630 172, ☺ vvvzeeland.nl), and sells an excellent map of the beach, as well as walking and cycling trails on the island.

ACTIVITIES

Surfing and windsurfing The best spot for windsurfing is at the Brouwersdam, 8km from Renesse, which links Schouwen-Duiveland to Goeree-Overflakkee and offers excellent windsurfing on one side, and one of Europe's cleanest beaches on the other. Windsurfing Renesse, De Room 15 (☎ 0111 462 702, ☺ windsurfingrenesse.nl), has surfboards for around €40/day and offers lessons, as well as renting windsurfing equipment. Halfway along the Brouwersdam, the Zeil- & Surfcentrum, at Ossenhoek 1 (☎ 0111 671 480, ☺ brouwersdam.nl), will rent out a board and wetsuit for €70/day. Tuition, small sailboats, huts (€88 for four) and four-bed dorms (€65) are also available. Take bus #104 from Renesse, and ask the driver for the Port Zélande stop.

ACCOMMODATION

The area is teeming with hotels, campsites and holiday homes and B&Bs. The VVV has a list of available accommodation, or try the English-language website ☺ renesse.com for accommodation and other holiday services. Book accommodation well in advance over the summer.

Hotel de Logerij Laône 15 ☎ 0111 462 570, ☺ delogerij.nl. Within walking distance of both the town and beach, with 22 simple but perfectly adequate and clean rooms. You can rent bicycles at the reception. **€89**

Zierikzee and around

Schouwen-Duiveland's most interesting town, **ZIERIKZEE**, is situated 14km east of the barrier. The town's position at the intersection of shipping routes between England, Flanders and Holland made it an important port in the late Middle Ages and it was

THE DELTA PROJECT

On February 1, 1953, a combination of an exceptionally high spring tide and a powerful northwesterly storm drove the North Sea over the dykes to **flood** much of Zeeland. The results were catastrophic: 1836 people drowned, 47,000 homes and 500km of dykes destroyed and some of the country's most fertile agricultural land ruined by salt water and covered by tonnes of sand. Towns as far inland as Bergen-op-Zoom and Dordrecht were flooded, and Zeeland's road and rail network was wrecked. The government's response was immediate and massive. After patching up the breached dykes, work was begun on the **Delta Project**, one of the largest engineering schemes the world has ever seen and one of phenomenal complexity and expense.

The aim was to ensure the safety of Zeeland by radically shortening and strengthening its coastline. The major estuaries and inlets would be dammed, thus preventing unusually high tides surging inland to breach the thousands of kilometres of small **dykes**. Where it was impractical to build a dam – such as across the Westerschelde or Nieuwe Waterweg, which would have closed the seaports of Antwerp and Rotterdam respectively – secondary dykes were to be reinforced. New roads across the top of the dams would improve communications to Zeeland and Zuid-Holland and the freshwater lakes that formed behind the dams would enable precise control of the water table of the Zeeland islands.

It took thirty years for the Delta Project to be completed. The smaller, secondary dams – the **Veersegat**, **Haringvliet** and **Brouwershaven** – were built first to provide protection from high tides as quickly as possible, a process that also enabled engineers to learn as they went along. In 1968, work began on the largest dam, intended to close the Oosterschelde estuary that forms the outlet of the Maas, Waal and Rijn rivers. It soon ran into intense opposition from **environmental groups**, who pointed out that the mud flats were an important breeding ground for birds, while the estuary itself was a nursery for plaice, sole and other North Sea fish. The inshore fishermen saw their livelihoods in danger too: if the Oosterschelde were closed the oyster, mussel and lobster beds would be destroyed, representing a huge loss to the region's economy.

The environmental and fishing lobbies argued that strengthening the estuary dykes would provide adequate protection; the water board and agricultural groups raised the emotive spectre of the 1953 flood. In the end a compromise was reached, and from 1976 to 1986 the 9km-long Oosterschelde storm surge barrier was built, with a 4km-long series of sluice gates. Constructing the 65 huge, 18000-tonne pillars supporting the 42m-wide sluice doors required new technology and specially designed ships. The gates stay open under normal tidal conditions, allowing water to flow in and out of the estuary, but close ahead of potentially destructive high tides. For more information about the flood and the Delta Project, see ⓦ deltawerken.com.

DELTAPARK NEELTJE JANS

Neeltje Jans, Faelweg 5, Vrouwenpolder • April–Oct daily 10am–5pm; check website for opening hours out of season • €22.50, parking €7, reductions online • ⓦ neeltjejans.nl • Bus #133 (hourly, 1hr 15min) from Middelburg

The pricey but fascinating **Deltapark Neeltje Jans** is located in the middle of the Stormvloedkering dam, on the artificial island of Neeltje Jans. There are seal shows, an aquarium and a waterpark for the children, but it's the exhibition on the Delta Project that is most memorable, with hands-on exhibits and a chance to go inside one of the Stormvloedkering sluice gate pillars, really giving you an idea of the scale of this part of the project. It's best to start with the video presentation before taking in the exhibition, which is divided into three areas: the historical background of the Netherlands' water management problems; the technological developments that enabled the country to protect itself; the environmental consequences of applying the technologies and the solutions that followed. The surge barrier (and the Delta Project as a whole) has been a triumphant success: computer models predict most high tides, but if an unpredicted rise does occur, the sluice gates close automatically in a matter of minutes. A new exhibit lets you feel the full-force scale 12 hurricane winds similar to those that hit this coast in 1953. If you cycle here, you'll run alongside open beaches and dunes, past wind turbines and onto the storm barrier itself, with ample opportunities to peer into the sluice gates: allow for blustery winds on the way back.

amed for its salt and madder – a root which, when dried and ground, produces a brilliant red dye. Today, it's a picturesque town of narrow cobbled streets and traditional gabled facades: encircled by a defensive canal – and best entered by one of two sixteenth-century water gates – Zierikzee's centre is small and easily explored. Although very popular with Dutch, German and Belgian tourists, the town makes a good base for a bike ride in the surrounding area, or a visit to the atmospheric **Watersnoodmuseum**.

Stadhuismuseum

Meelstraat 6 • April–Oct Tues–Sat 11am–5pm, Sun 1–5pm; Nov–March Tues–Sun 1–5pm • €7.50 • ⓦ schouwen-duiveland.nl/museum

Zierikzee's **Stadhuis** is easy enough to find – just head for the tall spire. Inside, the **Stadhuismuseum** has collections of silver, costumes, a regional history exhibition and a collection of maritime memorabilia. Admission to the grand entrance hall, shop and museum café with views of the tower is free.

The Watersnoodmuseum

Weg van de Buitenlandse Pers 5, Ouwerkerk • April–Oct daily 10am–5pm; Nov–March Tues–Sun 10am–5pm • €9 • ⓦ watersnoodmuseum.nl

Six kilometres out of Zierikzee at Ouwerkerk, the impressive **Watersnoodmuseum** (Flood Museum) commemorates the great floods of 1953 (see box opposite), the catalyst for the massive Delta Project. More serious than the Deltapark Neeltje Jans, the museum is atmospherically set in the four huge caissons that were manoeuvred into place to plug the last remaining gap in Zeeland's dykes, nine months after the flood. The first caisson presents the facts about the disaster and the initial rescue missions using photos, documents, objects such as bottles of brandy handed out to traumatized rescue workers), witness interviews and original newsreel footage beamed onto the wall. The second caisson focuses more on the human aspect, with interactive stories and an impressive multimedia memorial to the 1836 victims, with their projected names rippling away on the sandy floor. The third caisson holds draglines, trains and bulldozers used in the 1950s and donations by nations across the world, including complete Scandinavian prefab houses. The fourth caisson has interactive displays giving insight into the future of Zeeland's water management.

ARRIVAL AND INFORMATION ZIERIKZEE

By bus Bus #133 shuttles between Middelburg and Zierikzee every 30min, taking 1hr 10min.

Tourist office The VVV is at Nieuwe Haven 7 (Mon–Sat 9am–5pm; ☎0111 410 940, ⓦvvvzeeland.nl) and can provide you a map of the town as well as details of where to stay.

Bike rental Bike Totaal, Weststraat 5 (☎0111 412 115; ⓦjandejongefietsen.nl) rents out bikes for €7.50/day.

ACCOMMODATION AND EATING

Hotel Van Oppen Verrenieuwstraat 11 ☎0111 412 88, ⓦvanoppenhotel.nl. Simple, comfortable rooms and the big advantage of a large Chinese restaurant downstairs specializing in Cantonese dishes. **€96**

Pension Klaas Vaak Nieuwe Bogerdstraat ☎0111 414 204, ⓦpensionklaasvaak.nl. A sixteenth-century building with seven plain but adequate rooms. The big plus is a huge and lovely garden with a trampoline for kids. **€83**

CYCLING AROUND ZIERIKZEE

There's plenty of scope for exploring the countryside and coastline around Zierikzee by bike. To put colour in your cheeks, you could follow the bike lane over the wind-tunnel-like **Zeelandbrug**, a graceful bridge that spans the Oosterschelde south of Zierikzee, and is one of the longest bridges in Europe, at 5022m. Refreshments are available in Colijnsplaat on the other side: prevailing winds will probably be against you on the way out, so you can expect the journey back to take half the time. Alternatively, **Dreischor**, 8km northeast, makes for a pleasant half-day bike ride from Zierikzee. Here, the fourteenth-century St Adriaanskerk is surrounded by a moat, lush green lawns and a ring of attractive houses. Complete with waddling geese and a restored *travalje* (livery stable), it's an idyllic setting – although busy at weekends.

WILLIAM THE SILENT

Contexts

History

The country now known as the Netherlands didn't reach its present delimitations until 1830. Until then the borders of the entire region, formerly known as the Low Countries and including present-day Belgium and Luxembourg, were continually being redrawn following battles, treaties and alliances. Inevitably, then, what follows is, in its early parts at least, an outline of the history of the whole region, rather than a straightforward history of the Netherlands as such. Please note, incidentally, that the term "Holland" refers to the province – not the country – throughout.

Beginnings

Little is known of the **prehistoric** settlers of the Low Countries, their visible remains largely confined to the far north of the Netherlands, where mounds known as *terpen* were built to keep the sea at bay in Friesland and Groningen. There are also megalithic tombs (*hunebeds*) among the hills near Emmen in the northeast corner of the Netherlands, but quite how these tie in with the Iron Age culture that had established itself across the region by the fifth century BC it is impossible to say.

Clearer details begin to emerge at the time of **Julius Caesar**'s conquest of Gaul (broadly France) in 57 to 50 BC. He found three tribal groupings living in the region: the mainly Celtic **Belgae** (hence the nineteenth-century term "Belgium") settled by the Rhine, Maas and Waal to the south; the Germanic **Frisians** living on the marshy coastal strip north of the Scheldt; and the **Batavi**, another Germanic people, inhabiting the swampy riverbanks of what is now the southern Netherlands. The Belgae were conquered and their lands incorporated into the Roman imperial province of **Gallia Belgica**, but the territory of the Batavi and Frisians was not considered worthy of colonization. These tribes were granted the status of allies and were a source of recruitment for the Roman legions and an object of curiosity for imperial travellers.

Romans and Merovingians

The Roman occupation of Gallia Belgica continued for 500 years until the legions

---

THE DUTCH – ACCORDING TO PLINY

Never overly sympathetic to their unruly "barbarian" neighbours, the Romans were particularly dismissive of the Dutch. As **Pliny** observed of what is now the Netherlands in 50 AD: "Here a wretched race is found, inhabiting either the more elevated spots or artificial mounds… When the waves cover the surrounding area they are like so many mariners on board a ship, and when again the tide recedes their condition is that of so many shipwrecked men."

---

57 BC	406 AD	695
The Romans reach the edge of what is now the Netherlands, but are not impressed by its marshes and bogs.	Barbarians cross the River Rhine in large numbers; the Roman Empire recedes.	Christianity spreads across the Netherlands; St Willibrord becomes the first bishop of Utrecht.

were pulled back to protect the heartlands of the crumbling empire. As the empire collapsed in chaos and confusion, the Germanic **Franks**, who had been settling within Gallia Belgica from the third century, filled the power vacuum, establishing a **Merovingian** kingdom around their capital Tournai (in modern Belgium) with their allies the Belgae. A great swathe of forest extending from the Scheldt to the Ardennes separated this Frankish kingdom from the more confused situation to the north and east, where other tribes of Franks settled along the Scheldt and Leie, Saxons occupied parts of Overijssel and Gelderland, and the Frisians clung to the seashore.

Towards the end of the fifth century, the Merovingian king **Clovis** was converted to **Christianity** and the faith slowly filtered north, spread by energetic missionaries like St Willibrord, first bishop of Utrecht, from about 695, and St Boniface, who was killed by the Frisians in 754 in a final act of pagan resistance before they too were converted. Meanwhile, after the death of the last distinguished Merovingian king, Dagobert, in 638, power passed increasingly to the so-called "mayors of the palace", a hereditary position whose most outstanding occupant was Charles Martel.

Charles Martel

Charles Martel (c.690–741) inherited a large shambolic kingdom, whose military weakness he determined to remedy. Martel replaced the existing body of infantry led by a small group of cavalry with a mounted force of highly trained knights who bore their own military expenses in return for land – the beginnings of the **feudal system**. These reforms came just in time to save Christendom: in 711 the extraordinary **Arab** advance which had begun early in the seventh century in modern-day Saudi Arabia, reached the Pyrenees and a massive Muslim army occupied southern France in preparation for further conquests. In the event, Martel defeated the invaders outside Tours in 732, one of Europe's most crucial engagements and one that saved France from Arab conquest for good.

The Carolingians

Ten years after Martel's death, his son, **Pepin the Short**, formally usurped the Merovingian throne with the blessing of the pope, becoming the first of the **Carolingian** dynasty, whose most celebrated member was **Charlemagne**, king of the west Franks from 768. In a dazzling series of campaigns, Charlemagne extended his empire south into Italy, west to the Pyrenees, north to Denmark and east to the Oder. His secular authority was bolstered by his coronation as the first **Holy Roman Emperor** in 800, a title bestowed on him by the pope in order to legitimize his claim as the successor to the emperors of imperial Rome.

The strength and stability of Charlemagne's court at Aachen spread to the Low Countries, bringing a building boom that created a string of superb Romanesque churches like Maastricht's St Servaas, and a trading bonanza along the region's principal rivers. However, unlike his Roman predecessors, Charlemagne was subject to the divisive inheritance laws of the Salian Franks and after his death in 814, his kingdom was divided between his grandsons into three roughly parallel strips of territory, the precursors of France, the Low Countries and Germany.

814	900s	1083	1432
The Emperor Charlemagne brings law and economic order to the Netherlands; it's short-lived.	Vikings raid the Netherlands by the boatload.	First time "Holland" is used to describe part of the Low Countries.	Philip the Good, the Duke of Burgundy, incorporates the Netherlands within his territories.

The growth of the towns

The tripartite division of Charlemagne's empire placed the **Low Countries** between the emergent French- and German-speaking nations, a dangerous location, which was subsequently to influence much of their history. However, amid the cobweb of local alliances that made up **early feudal western Europe** in the ninth and tenth centuries, this was not apparent. During this period, French kings and German emperors exercised a general authority over the region, but power was effectively in the hands of local lords who, remote from central control, brought a degree of local stability. From the twelfth century, feudalism slipped into a gradual decline, the intricate pattern of localized allegiances undermined by the increasing strength of certain lords, whose power and wealth often exceeded that of their nominal sovereign. Preoccupied by territorial squabbles, this streamlined nobility was usually willing to assist the **growth of towns** by granting charters that permitted a certain amount of **autonomy** in exchange for tax revenues and military and labour services. The first major cities were the cloth towns of Flanders – Bruges, Ieper (Ypres) and Ghent. Meanwhile, their smaller northern neighbours concentrated on trade, exploiting their strategic position at the junction of the region's main waterways – Amsterdam being a case in point.

Burgundian rule

By the late fourteenth century the political situation in the Low Countries was fairly clear: five lords controlled most of the region, paying only nominal homage to their French or German overlords. In 1419 **Philip the Good** of Burgundy succeeded to the countship of Flanders and by a series of adroit political moves gained control over Holland, Zeeland, Brabant and Limburg to the north, and Antwerp, Namur and Luxembourg to the south. He consolidated his power by establishing a strong central administration in Bruges and by restricting the privileges granted in the towns' charters. During his reign Bruges became a showcase for the **Hanseatic League**, a mainly German association of towns that acted as a trading group and protected their interests by an exclusive system of trading tariffs. Philip died in 1467 to be succeeded by his son, **Charles the Bold**, who was killed in battle ten years later, plunging his father's carefully crafted domain into turmoil. The French seized the opportunity to take back Arras and Burgundy and before the people of Flanders would agree to fight the French, they kidnapped Charles's daughter, Mary, and forced her to sign a charter that restored the civic privileges removed by her grandfather Philip.

The Habsburgs

After her release, Mary married the **Habsburg** Maximilian of Austria, who assumed sole authority when Mary was killed in a riding accident in 1482. **Maximilian** continued to implement the centralizing policies of Philip the Good, but in 1494, when he became Holy Roman Emperor, he transferred control of the Low Countries to his son, Philip the Handsome. The latter died in 1506 and his territories were passed on to Maximilian's grandson **Charles V**, who also became King of Spain and Holy Roman Emperor in 1516 and 1519, respectively. Charles was suspicious of the turbulent burghers of Flanders and, following in Maximilian's footsteps, favoured Antwerp at

1482	1517	1555
Mary of Burgundy killed in a riding accident; Netherlands absorbed into the Habsburg empire.	Luther nails up his 95 theses against the sale of indulgences by the Catholic church; Catholics anxious.	The resolutely Catholic Philip II of Spain prepares to weed out his Protestant subjects; Protestants anxious.

their expense; it soon became the greatest port in the empire, part of a general movement of trade and prosperity away from Flanders to the cities to the north.

Through sheer determination and military might, Charles bent the merchant cities of the Low Countries to his will, but regardless of this display of force, a spiritual trend was emerging that would soon question not only the rights of the emperor but also rock the power of the Catholic Church itself.

The Reformation

An alliance of Church and State had dominated the medieval world: pope and bishops, kings and counts were supposedly the representatives of God on earth, and they combined to crush any religious dissent. Much of their authority relied on the ignorance of the population, who were dependent on priests for the interpretation of the scriptures, their view of the world carefully controlled. The **development of typography**, therefore, was a key factor in the **Reformation**, the stirring of religious revolt that stood sixteenth-century Europe on its head. For the first time, printers were able to produce relatively cheap Bibles in quantity, and religious texts were no longer the exclusive property of the Church.

Consequently, as the populace snaffled up the Bibles, so a welter of debate spread across much of western Europe under the auspices of theologians like **Erasmus of Rotterdam** (1465–1536), who wished to cleanse the Catholic Church of its corruptions, superstitions and extravagant ceremony; only later did many of these same thinkers – principally **Martin Luther** (1483–1546) – decide to support a breakaway church. In 1517, Luther produced his 95 theses against indulgences, rejecting – among other things – the Church's monopoly on the interpretation of the Bible and the Catholic view of Christ's presence in the Eucharist. There was no way back, and when Luther's works were disseminated his ideas gained a Europe-wide following among reforming groups that were soon branded **Lutheran** by the Catholic Church. Luther asserted that the Church's political power was subservient to that of the state, whereas the supporters of another great reforming thinker, **John Calvin** (1509–64), emphasized the importance of individual conscience and the need for redemption through the grace of Christ rather than the confessional.

The Revolt of the Netherlands

These seeds of **Protestantism** fell on fertile ground among the Low Countries' merchants, whose wealth and independence could not easily be accommodated within a rigid caste society. Similarly, their employees, the guildsmen and their apprentices, had a long history of opposing arbitrary authority, and were soon convinced of the need to reform an autocratic, venal church. In 1555, **Charles V abdicated**, transferring his German lands to his brother Ferdinand, and his Italian, Spanish and Low Countries territories to his son, the fanatically Catholic **Philip II**. In the short term, the scene was set for a bitter religious confrontation, while the dynastic ramifications of the division of the Habsburg Empire were to complicate European affairs for centuries.

Philip II decided to teach his heretical subjects a lesson they would not forget. He garrisoned the towns of the Low Countries with Spanish mercenaries, imported the

1566	**1578**	**1579**
Rebellious Protestants smash up hundreds of Catholic churches in the Iconoclastic Fury – the *Beeldenstorm* ("statue storm").	Amsterdam finally breaks with the Habsburgs, declaring for the rebels and switching from Catholicism to Calvinism in the *Alteratie* (Alteration).	The seven provinces of the Netherlands break with Habsburg Spain, establishing the United Provinces; Protestants relieved.

nquisition and passed a series of anti-Protestant edicts. However, other pressures on he Habsburg Empire forced him into a tactical withdrawal and he transferred control o his sister, **Margaret of Parma**, in 1559. Based in Brussels, the equally resolute Margaret implemented the policies of her brother with gusto. In 1561 she reorganized he Church and created fourteen new bishoprics, a move that was construed as a wresting of power from civil authority, and an attempt to destroy the local aristocracy's ights of religious patronage. Protestantism (and Protestant sympathies) now spread to he nobility, who formed the "**League of the Nobility**" to counter Habsburg policy. The League petitioned Philip for moderation, but its request was dismissed out of hand by one of Margaret's Walloon advisers, who called them *ces gueux* ("those beggars"), an epithet that was to be enthusiastically adopted by the rebels.

The Iconoclastic Fury

n 1565 a harvest failure caused a winter famine among the workers, and, after years of epression, they struck back. A Protestant sermon in the tiny Flemish textile town of Steenvoorde incited the congregation to purge the local church of its "papist idolatry"; he crowd attacked the church's reliquaries and shrines, smashed the stained-glass windows and terrorized the priests, thereby launching the **Iconoclastic Fury**, which pread like wildfire. Within ten days churches had been ransacked from one end of the Low Countries to the other.

The ferocity of this outbreak shocked the upper classes into renewed support for Spain, and Margaret regained the allegiance of most nobles – with the principal exception of the country's greatest landowner, Prince William of Orange-Nassau, known as **William the Silent** (though William the Taciturn is perhaps a better translation). Of Germanic descent, William was raised a Catholic but the excesses and rigidity of Philip had caused him to side with the Protestant movement. A firm believer n individual freedom and religious tolerance, William became a symbol of liberty, but after the Fury had revitalized the pro-Spanish party, he prudently slipped away to his estates in Germany.

The Duke of Alva dispatched

Philip II was encouraged by the increase in support for Margaret and so, in 1567, he sent the **Duke of Alva**, with an army of 10,000 men, to the Low Countries to suppress his religious opponents conclusively. Margaret was, however, not at all pleased by Philip's decision and, when Alva arrived in Brussels, she resigned in a huff, thereby abandoning the Low Countries to military rule. One of Alva's first acts was to set up the Commission of Civil Unrest, which was soon nicknamed the "**Council of Blood**", after its habit of executing those it examined: no fewer than 12,000 citizens were polished off by the commission, mostly for participating in the Fury. Initially the repression worked, and in 1568, when William attempted an invasion from Germany, the towns offered no support. William withdrew and conceived other means of defeating Alva, sponsoring a band of Protestant privateers, the so-called **Waterguezen** or sea-beggars, who took their name from the dismissive epithet given them by Margaret's adviser. At first, the Waterguezen were obliged to operate from England, but it was soon possible for them to secure bases in the Netherlands, whose citizens had grown to loathe the autocratic Alva and his Spanish army.

1606	1625	1632	1648
Rembrandt born in Leiden, the ninth child of a miller.	Dutch found "New Amsterdam" – the forerunner of New York.	Johannes Vermeer born in Delft.	The Peace of Westphalia heralds Amsterdam's Golden Age.

The revolt spreads

The revolt spread rapidly. By June the rebels controlled most of the province of Holland and William was able to take command of his troops in Delft. Alva and his son Frederick fought back, but William's superior naval power frustrated him and a mightily irritated Philip replaced Alva with **Luis de Resquesens**. Initially, Resquesens had some success in the south (today's Belgium), where the Catholic majority were more willing to compromise with Spanish rule than their northern neighbours, but the tide of war was against him – most pointedly in William's triumphant relief of Leiden in 1574.

The Spanish Fury and its aftermath

When Resquesens died in 1576, the (unpaid) Habsburg garrison in Antwerp mutinied and assaulted the town, slaughtering some eight thousand of its people in what was known as the **Spanish Fury**. The massacre alienated the south and pushed its inhabitants into the arms of William, whose troops now swept into Brussels, the heart of imperial power. Momentarily, it seemed possible for the whole region to unite behind William, and all signed the **Union of Brussels**, which demanded the departure of foreign troops as a condition for accepting a diluted Habsburg sovereignty. This was followed, in 1576, by the **Pacification of Ghent**, a regional agreement that guaranteed freedom of religious belief, a necessary precondition for any union between the largely Protestant north (the Netherlands) and Catholic south (Belgium and Luxembourg).

The end of the Revolt

Philip II was, however, not inclined to compromise, especially when he realized that William's Calvinist sympathies were upsetting his newly found Walloon and Flemish allies. The king bided his time until 1578, when, with his enemies still arguing among themselves, he sent another army from Spain to the Low Countries under the command of Alessandro Farnese, the **Duke of Parma**. Events played into Parma's hands. In 1579, tired of all the wrangling, seven northern provinces (Holland, Zeeland, Utrecht, Groningen, Friesland, Overijssel and Gelderland) broke with their southerly neighbours to sign the **Union of Utrecht**, an alliance against Spain that was to be the first unification of the Netherlands as an identifiable country – the so-called **United Provinces**. The agreement stipulated freedom of belief within the provinces, an important step since the struggle against Spain wasn't simply a religious one: many Catholics disliked the Spanish occupation and William did not wish to alienate this possible source of support. Meanwhile, in the south – and also in 1579 – representatives of the southern provinces signed the **Union of Arras**, a Catholic-led agreement that declared loyalty to Philip II in counterbalance to the Union of Utrecht in the north. Parma used this area as a base to recapture all of Flanders, but he was unable to advance any further north and the Low Countries were, de facto, divided into two – the Spanish Netherlands and the United Provinces – beginning a separation that would lead, after many changes, to the creation of **three modern countries** – Belgium, Luxembourg and the Netherlands.

1652–54	1654	1665–67
First Anglo-Dutch War takes place.	Carel Fabritius, potentially an artist of the first order, is killed in a gunpowder explosion in Delft aged just 32.	Second Anglo-Dutch War: the Dutch fleet sails up the Thames; Charles II humiliated.

The United Provinces takes shape

Throughout the late sixteenth and seventeenth centuries, **Holland** (today's Noord- and Zuid-Holland) dominated the **United Provinces**, both economically and politically: it's true that the individual provinces maintained a degree of decentralized independence, but as far as the country as a whole was concerned, what Holland said pretty much went. The assembly of these United Provinces was known as the **States General** and it met at Den Haag; it had no domestic legislative authority, and could only carry out foreign policy by unanimous decision, a formula designed to make potential waverers feel more secure. The role of **Stadholder** was the most important in each province, roughly equivalent to that of governor, though the same person could occupy this position in any number of provinces – and mostly did, with the Orange-Nassaus characteristically picking up five or six provinces at any one time. The **Council Pensionary** was another major post. The man who held either title in Holland was a centre of political power. Pieter Geyl, in his seminal *Revolt of the Netherlands*, defined the end result as the establishment of a republic which was "oligarchic, erastian [and] decentralized".

Oldenbarneveldt steadies the ship

In 1584, a Catholic fanatic assassinated William the Silent at his residence in Delft (see p.167). It was a grievous blow to the provinces and, as William's son **Maurice** was only 17, power passed to **Johan van Oldenbarneveldt**, the country's leading statesman and Council Pensionary of Rotterdam and ultimately Holland. Things were going badly in the war against the Spanish, but Oldenbarneveldt, somewhat to his own surprise, drove the Spanish back. International events then played into his hands: in 1588, the English defeated the Spanish Armada and the following year the powerful king Henry III of France died. Most important of all, Philip II of Spain, the scourge of the Low Countries, died in 1598, a necessary preamble to the **Twelve Year Truce** (1609–21) signed between the Habsburgs and the United Provinces, which grudgingly accepted the independence of the new republic.

Toil and trouble: the early seventeenth century

In the breathing space created by the Twelve Year Truce, the **rivalry** between Maurice and **Oldenbarneveldt** intensified and an obscure argument within the Calvinist church on predestination proved the catalyst for Oldenbarneveldt's downfall. This quarrel, between two Leiden theologians, began in 1612: one of them, **Armenius**, argued that God gave man the choice of accepting or rejecting faith; **Gomarus**, his opponent, believed that predestination was absolute – to the degree that God chooses who will be saved and who damned, with man powerless in the decision. This row between the two groups (known respectively as **Remonstrants** and **Counter-Remonstrants**) soon became attached to the political divisions within the republic. When a synod was arranged at Dordrecht to resolve the doctrinal matter, the province of Holland, led by Oldenbarneveldt, refused to attend, insisting on Holland's right to decide its own religious orthodoxies. At heart, he and his fellow deputies supported the provincial independence favoured by Remonstrant sympathizers, whereas Maurice sided with the Counter-Remonstrants, who favoured a strong central authority. The Counter-Remonstrants won at Dordrecht, and Maurice,

1672	1688	1700s
End of the Golden Age: the United Provinces is assailed on all sides in the so-called *Rampjaar* (Disaster Year).	William III of Orange successfully invades England – and adds "King of England" to his several titles.	Nautical folklore proclaims the legend of "The Flying Dutchman", who captains a ghost ship that can never make port.

with his troops behind him, quickly overcame his opponents and had Oldenbarneveldt arrested. In May 1619 Oldenbarneveldt **was executed** in Den Haag "for having conspired to dismember the states of the Netherlands and greatly troubled God's church".

The Thirty Years War (1618–48)

With the end of the Twelve Year Truce in 1621, fighting with Spain broke out once again, this time as part of the more general **Thirty Years War** (1618–48), a largely religious-based conflict between Catholic and Protestant countries that involved most of western Europe. In the Low Countries, the Spanish were initially successful, but they were weakened by war with France and by the fresh attacks of Maurice's successor, his brother **Frederick Henry**. From 1625, the Spaniards suffered a series of defeats on land and sea that forced them out of what is today the southern part of the Netherlands, and in 1648 they were compelled to accet the humiliating **Peace of Westphalia**, the general treaty that ended the Thirty Years War. Under its terms, the independence of the United Provinces was formally recognized and the Dutch were even able to insist that the Scheldt estuary be closed to shipping, an action designed to destroy the trade and prosperity of Antwerp, which – along with the rest of modern-day Belgium – remained part of the Habsburg Empire. By this act, the commercial expansion and pre-eminence of Amsterdam was assured, and the Golden Age began.

The Golden Age

The brilliance of **Amsterdam**'s explosion onto the European scene is as difficult to underestimate as it is to detail. The size of the city's merchant fleet carrying Baltic grain into Europe had long been considerable and even during the long war with Spain it had continued to expand. Indeed, not only were the Spanish unable to undermine it, but they were, on occasion, even obliged to use Dutch ships to supply their own troops – part of a burgeoning cargo trade that was another key ingredient of Amsterdam's economic success.

It was, however, the emasculation of Antwerp by the Treaty of Westphalia that launched the so-called **Golden Age**, a period of extraordinarily dynamic growth with Amsterdam becoming the emporium for the products of north and south Europe and the new colonies in the East and West Indies. Dutch banking and investment brought further prosperity, and by the mid-seventeenth century Amsterdam's wealth was truly spectacular.

Civic pride and religious toleration

Taking their new-found riches as a sign of God's pleasure, Amsterdam's Calvinist bourgeoisie indulged in fine canal houses and commissioned images of themselves in group portraits. Civic pride knew no bounds: great monuments to self-aggrandizement, such as Amsterdam's new town hall, were hastily erected, and, if some went hungry, few starved, as the poor were cared for in municipal almshouses. The arts flourished and religious tolerance extended even to the traditional scapegoats, the **Jews**, and in particular the Sephardic Jews, who had been hounded from Spain by the Inquisition, but were guaranteed freedom from religious persecution under the terms

1713	1750	1795
Treaty of Utrecht: Spain finally abandons the Spanish Netherlands (Belgium), which is passed to the Austrians.	Handel visits Amsterdam to gee up its musical scene.	Napoleon's Revolutionary army occupies the United Provinces.

of the Union of Utrecht of 1579. By the end of the eighteenth century, Jews accounted for ten percent of Amsterdam's inhabitants. Guilds and craft associations thrived, and in the first half of the seventeenth century the city's population quadrupled. Furthermore, although Amsterdam was the centre of this boom, economic ripples spread across much of the United Provinces. Dutch farmers were, for instance, able to sell all they could produce to the expanding city and a string of Zuider Zee ports cashed in on the flourishing Baltic trade.

The Dutch East and West India companies

Throughout the Golden Age, the **Dutch East India Company** (Vereenigde Oost-Indische Compagnie; VOC) kept the country's coffers brimming by controlling the immensely profitable trade with the East. Formed in 1602, this Amsterdam-based enterprise sent ships to Asia, Indonesia, and China to bring back spices, woods and other assorted valuables. The States General granted the company a trading monopoly in all lands east of the Cape of Good Hope and, for good measure, threw in unlimited military powers over the lands it controlled. As a consequence, the company became a colonial power in its own right, governing, at one time or another, parts of Malaya, Sri Lanka and parts of modern-day Indonesia. Perhaps inevitably, the success of the VOC led, in 1621, to the creation of the **West India Company** (Geoctroyeerde Westindische Compagnie or GWIC), which was designed to protect Dutch interests in the Americas and Africa. In the event, it proved a failure, expending most of its energies in waging war on Spanish and Portuguese colonies from its base in Suriname, but it did make handsome profits until the 1660s. The company was dismantled in 1674, ten years after its nascent colony of New Amsterdam had been ceded to the British – and renamed **New York**.

Political squabbling

Although the economics of the Golden Age were dazzling, the **politics** were dismal. Interminable wrangling dogged the United Provinces with one faction wanting a central, unified government under the pre-eminent **House of Orange-Nassau**, the other championing provincial autonomy. In 1647, Frederick Henry, the powerful head of the Orange-Nassaus, died, and his successor, William II, lasted just three years before he succumbed to smallpox. A week after William's death, his wife bore the son who would become William III of England, but in the meantime the leaders of the province of Holland seized their opportunity. They forced measures through the States General that abolished the position of Stadholder, thereby reducing the powers of the Orangists and increasing those of the provinces, chiefly Holland itself. Holland's foremost figure in these years was **Johan de Witt**, Council Pensionary to the States General.

THE FLYING DUTCHMAN

The speed of the VOC's vessels amazed the company's competitors, giving rise to the legend of the **Flying Dutchman**. One story has it that the fastest VOC captain of them all, a certain Bernard Fokke, only achieved the sailing times he did with the help of the **devil** – and his reward was and is to sail the seven seas forever; another has the VOC's Captain Hendrik van der Decken sailing round the Cape of Good Hope for eternity after blaspheming against the wind and the waves. Whatever the truth, it was certainly a myth born of commercial envy.

1815	**1830**	**1853**
Belgium and the Netherlands (forcibly) united as the "United Kingdom of the Netherlands".	Belgium revolts – and the Netherlands goes it alone.	Vincent van Gogh born in a village near Breda.

Johan de Witt

In control, **Johan de Witt** guided the country through wars with England and Sweden, concluding a triple alliance between the two countries and the United Provinces in 1668. This was a striking reversal of policy: the economic rivalry between the United Provinces and England had already precipitated two **Anglo-Dutch wars** (in 1652–54 and 1665–67) and there was much bitterness in Anglo-Dutch relations – a popular English pamphlet of the time was titled *A Relation Shewing How They* [the Dutch] *Were First Bred and Descended from a Horse-Turd Which Was Enclosed in a Butter-Box.* England's Charles II, who certainly knew how to bear a grudge, was particularly irritated by an embarrassing defeat in the second Anglo–Dutch war, when **Admiral Michiel de Ruyter** had sailed up the Thames and caught the English fleet napping.

William III of Orange saves the day

Charles II had his revenge in 1672, when, breaking with his new-found allies, he joined a French attack on the United Provinces. The republic was now in deep trouble – previous victories had been at sea, and the army, weak and disorganized, could not withstand the onslaught. In panic, as the so-called **"Year of Disaster"** unfurled, the country turned to **William III of Orange** for leadership and Johan de Witt was brutally murdered by a mob of Orangist sympathizers in Den Haag. By 1678 William had defeated the French and made peace with the English – and was rewarded (along with his wife Mary, the daughter of Charles I of England) with the English crown ten years later.

The eighteenth century: the French covet the Low Countries

Though William III had defeated the French, **Louis XIV** retained designs on the United Provinces and the military pot was kept boiling in a long series of dynastic wars that ranged across northern Europe. In 1700, Charles II of Spain, the last of the Spanish Habsburgs, died childless, bequeathing the Spanish throne and control of the Spanish Netherlands (now Belgium) to Philip of Anjou, Louis' grandson. Louis promptly forced Philip to cede the latter to France, which was, with every justification, construed as a threat to the balance of power by France's neighbours. The **War of the Spanish Succession** ensued, with the United Provinces, England and Austria forming the **Triple Alliance** to thwart the French king. The war itself was a haphazard, long-winded affair that dragged on until the **Treaty of Utrecht** of 1713 in which France finally abandoned its claim to both the United Provinces and the Spanish Netherlands, which reverted to the Austrian Habsburgs (as the Austrian Netherlands).

Dutch stagnation: 1713–95

All this warfare had drained the United Provinces' reserves and a slow **economic decline** began, accelerated by a trend towards conservatism. This in turn reflected the development of an increasingly socially static society, with power and wealth concentrated within a small, self-regarding elite. Furthermore, with the threat of foreign conquest effectively removed, the Dutch ruling class divided into two main camps – the **Orangists** and the pro-French **"Patriots"** – whose endless squabbling soon

1863	**1872**	**1890**
The Dutch finally abolish slavery in their assorted colonies.	Piet Mondriaan born in Amersfoort; his father is a teacher.	Vincent van Gogh shoots himself – and dies 29 hours later.

brought political life to a virtual standstill. The situation deteriorated even further in the latter half of the eighteenth century, and the last few years of the United Provinces present a sorry state of affairs.

French occupation

In 1795 the **French** invaded and swiftly swept their opponents aside. They were welcomed by the Patriots, who helped them dismantle the entrenched privileges of the merchant oligarchy, dissolving the United Provinces and establishing the **Batavian Republic** in its stead – named after the warlike Germanic Batavi who had inhabited the area around Nijmegen in classical times. Now part of the Napoleonic Empire, the Dutch were obliged to wage unenthusiastic war against England, and in 1806 Napoleon appointed his brother **Louis** as their king in an attempt to unite the rival Dutch groups under one (notionally independent) ruler. Louis was installed in Amsterdam's town hall – hence today's Koninklijk Paleis (Royal Palace; see p.53) – but in the event Louis wasn't willing to allow the Netherlands to become a simple satellite of France; he ignored Napoleon's directives and after just four years of rule his brother forced him to abdicate. The country was then formally incorporated into the French Empire, and for three gloomy years suffered occupation and heavy taxation to finance French military adventures.

The United Kingdom of the Netherlands

Following Napoleon's disastrous retreat from Moscow, the **Orangist faction** surfaced to exploit weakening French control. In 1813, Frederick William (1772–1843), son of the exiled William V, returned to the country and eight months later, under the terms of the **Congress of Vienna**, he was crowned **King William I of the United Kingdom of the Netherlands**, incorporating both the old United Provinces and the Austrian Netherlands. A strong-willed man, the new king spent much of his time trying to control his disparate kingdom but failed, primarily because of the Protestant north's attempt – or perceived attempt – to dominate the Catholic south. The southern provinces rose against his rule, and in 1830 the separate **Kingdom of Belgium** was proclaimed.

The Netherlands reconfigures

In 1839, a final fling of the military dice gave William most of Limburg, and all but ended centuries of territorial change within the Low Countries. The Netherlands benefited from this new stability both economically and politically, emerging as a unitary state with a burgeoning industrial and entrepôt economy. The outstanding political figure of the times was **Jan Rudolph Thorbecke**, who formed three ruling cabinets (1849–53, 1862–66 and 1872, in the year of his death) and steered the Netherlands through these changes. The political parties of the late eighteenth century had wished to resurrect the power and prestige of the seventeenth-century Netherlands; Thorbecke and his allies resigned themselves to the country's reduced status and eulogized the advantages of being a small power. For the first time, from about 1850, liberty was seen as a luxury made possible by the country's very lack of power, and the malaise that had long disturbed

1914	1917	1932
The Netherlands stays neutral in World War I.	Dutch Parliament passes the Act of Universal Suffrage.	Afsluitdijk completed, thereby separating the old Zuider Zee (now the IJsselmeer) from the North Sea.

public life gave way to a positive appreciation of the very narrowness of its national existence. One of the results of Thorbecke's liberalism was a gradual extension of the franchise, culminating in the **Act of Universal Suffrage** of 1917.

The war years

The Netherlands remained neutral in **World War I** and although it suffered privations from the Allied blockade of German war materials, this was offset by the profits accrued by continuing to trade with both sides. Similar attempts to remain neutral in **World War II** failed: the Germans invaded on May 10, 1940, destroying Rotterdam four days later, a salutary lesson that made prolonged resistance inconceivable. The Dutch army was quickly overwhelmed, Queen Wilhelmina fled to London to set up a government-in-exile, and members of the **NSB**, the Dutch fascist party, which had welcomed the invaders, were rewarded with positions of authority. Nevertheless, in the early stages of the occupation, life for the average Netherlander went on pretty much as usual, which is just what the Germans wanted – they were determined to transform the country by degrees. Even when the first roundups of the **Jews** began in late 1940, many managed to turn a blind eye, though in Amsterdam the newly outlawed Dutch Communist Party did organize a widely supported strike to protest, a gesture perhaps, but an important one all the same.

The Germans tighten the screws

As the war progressed, so the German grip got tighter and the Dutch **Resistance** stronger, its activities focused on destroying German supplies and munitions as well as the forgery of identity papers, a Dutch speciality. The Resistance also trumpeted its efforts in a battery of underground newspapers, most notably *Het Parool* (The Password), which survives today. Inevitably, the Resistance paid a heavy price with some 23,000 of its fighters and sympathizers losing their lives, but Amsterdam's Jews took the worst punishment: in 1940, Amsterdam's Jewish population, swollen by refugees from Hitler's Germany, was around 140,000, but by the end of the war there were only a few thousand left, rendering the old Jewish quarter – the Jodenhoek – deserted and derelict, a rare crumb of comfort being the survival of the diary of a young Jewish girl – **Anne Frank** (see p.62).

Liberation

Liberation began from the south in the autumn of 1944. To speed the process, the Allies determined on **Operation Market Garden** (see p.262), an ambitious plan to finish the war quickly by creating an Allied corridor stretching from Eindhoven to Arnhem. If it had been successful, the Allies would have secured control of the country's three main rivers and been able to drive on into Germany, thereby isolating the occupying forces in the western Netherlands in double-quick time. On September 17, 1944, the 1st Airborne Division parachuted into the countryside around Oosterbeek, a small village near the most northerly target of the operation, the **bridge at Arnhem**. However, German opposition was much stronger than expected and after heavy fighting the paratroopers could only take the northern end of the bridge. The advancing British army was unable to break through fast enough, and after four days the decimated battalion defending the bridge was forced to withdraw.

1940	1944	1944/5
The Germans occupy the Netherlands in World War II.	Betrayal and capture of Anne Frank in Amsterdam.	Allied forces liberate the Netherlands, but not fast enough – hundreds starve and/or freeze to death in the *Hongerwinter* (Hunger Winter).

With the failure of Operation Market Garden, the Allies were obliged to resort to more orthodox military tactics. In their push towards Germany, they slowly cleared the east and south of the country in the winter and spring of 1944–45, leaving the coastal provinces pretty much untouched, though here lack of food and fuel created the **Hongerwinter** (Hunger Winter) in which hundreds died of hunger and/or hypothermia, their black cardboard coffins being trundled to mass graves. Finally, on **May 5, 1945**, the remains of the German army in the Netherlands surrendered to the Canadians at Wageningen.

Reconstruction

The **postwar years** were spent patching up the damage of occupation and liberation: Rotterdam was rebuilt at speed, the dykes blown during the war were repaired, and the canals and waterways were soon cleared of their accumulated debris. At the same time, the country began a vast construction programme, with modern suburbs mushrooming around every major city, especially Amsterdam, where almost all the land projected for use by the year 2000 was in fact used by 1970. The late 1940s also saw the Dutch launch a disgraceful colonial war, which could not prevent them from losing control of their principal Asian colonies, which were incorporated as **Indonesia**, in 1950.

Floods and sea defences

Tragedy struck the Netherlands on February 1, 1953, when an unusually high tide was pushed over Zeeland's sea defences by a westerly wind, flooding around 150 square kilometres of land and drowning over 1800 people. The response was to secure the area's future with the **Delta Project**, closing off the western part of the Scheldt and Maas estuaries with massive sea dykes. A brilliant and graceful piece of engineering, the main storm surge barrier on the Oosterschelde was finally completed in 1986. Elsewhere, Amsterdam and the old Zuider Zee coast had already been secured by the completion of the **Afsluitdijk** between Noord-Holland and Friesland in 1932. This dyke separated the North Sea from the former Zuider Zee, which now became the freshwater **IJsselmeer**, and in 1976 a second dyke was added, carving the Markermeer from the IJsselmeer.

Counter-culture

The radical and youthful mass movements that swept across the West in the 1960s transformed Amsterdam from a middling, rather conservative city into a turbo-charged hotbed of **hippy action** – and where Amsterdam led, all the big cities of the Randstad followed. Initially, it was the **Provos** (see box, p.330) who led the counter-cultural charge, but in 1967 they dissolved themselves and many of their supporters moved on to the **squatter movement**, which opposed the wholesale destruction of low-cost (often old) urban housing as envisaged by many municipal councils. For many squatters, it seemed as if local councils were neglecting the needs of their poorer citizens in favour of business interests, and in Amsterdam, the epicentre of the movement, there were regular confrontations between the police and protestors at a handful of symbolic squats.

1947	**1953**	**1975**
Johan Cruyff, arguably the greatest European footballer of all time, born in Amsterdam.	Hundreds die when the country's sea defences are breached; the Dutch pause for thought – and plan the Delta Project.	The Netherlands wins the Eurovision contest with the timeless *Ding-a-dong* (or in Dutch *Ding dinge dong*), sung by Teach-In.

Police v squatters

The first major incident came in Amsterdam in March 1980 when several hundred police evicted squatters from premises on **Vondelstraat**. Afterwards there was widespread rioting, but this was small beer in comparison with the protests of April 30, 1980 – the **coronation day of Queen Beatrix** – when a mixed bag of squatters and leftists vigorously protested against both the lavishness of the proceedings and the expense of refurbishing Beatrix's palace in Den Haag. Once again there was widespread rioting and this time it spread to other Dutch cities, though the unrest was short-lived.

At its peak, Amsterdam's squatter movement boasted around ten thousand activists, many of whom were involved in two more major confrontations with the police – the first at the Lucky Luyk squat, on Jan Luykenstraat, the second at the Wyers building in February 1984, when the squatters were forcibly cleared to make way for a hotel. Thereafter, the movement faded away, partly because of its failure to stop the developers, who could now claim, with limited justification, to be sensitive to community needs.

Into the twenty-first century

In the 1990s, the country's street protests and major squats became a distant memory, though some of the old ideas – and ideals – were carried forward by the **Greens**, who

---

THE PROVOS

In 1963, one-time window cleaner and magician extraordinaire **Jasper Grootveld** won celebrity status by painting "K" – for *kanker* ("cancer") – on cigarette billboards throughout Amsterdam. His actions inspired others, most notably **Roel van Duyn**, a philosophy student at Amsterdam University, who set up a left-wing-cum-anarchist movement known as the **Provos** – short for *provocatie* ("provocation") – and organized street "**happenings**" that proved fantastically popular among young Amsterdammers. The number of Provos never exceeded about thirty and the group had no coherent structure, but they did have one clear aim – to bring points of political or social conflict to public attention. More than anything they were masters of publicity, and pursued their "games" with a spirit of fun, promoting policies such as the popular **white bicycle plan**, which proposed that the council ban all cars in the city centre and supply 20,000 white bicycles for public use instead.

A puzzled Amsterdam police force reacted aggressively and there were regular confrontations, but it was the **wedding of Princess Beatrix** to Claus von Amsberg on March 10, 1966, that provoked the most serious unrest. Amsberg had served in the German army during World War II and many Netherlanders were offended by the marriage. Consequently, when hundreds of Provo sympathizers took to the streets to protest, pelting the wedding procession with smoke bombs, a huge swathe of Dutch opinion supported them. Amsberg himself was jeered with the refrain "Give us back the bicycles", a reference to the commandeering of hundreds of bikes by the retreating German army in 1945. The wedding over, the next crisis came in June 1966, when it appeared that students, workers and Provos were about to combine. In panic, the government in Den Haag ordered the dismissal of Amsterdam's police chief, who was deemed to be losing control, but in the event the Provos had peaked and the workers proved far from revolutionary, settling for arbitration on their various complaints instead.

1976	1980	1984
Another decade, another dyke: the Houtribdijk carves the Markermeer from the IJsselmeer.	The coronation of Queen Beatrix is marked by mass protests against the lavishness of the proceedings.	The last mass squat in Amsterdam meets a troublesome end.

attracted – and continue to attract – a small but significant following in every national and municipal election. One of the recurring political problems was the country's finely balanced system of **proportional representation**: time and again major issues became mired in long inter-party wheeling and dealing, and politics often appeared little more than a bland if necessary business conducted between the three main parties, the Protestant-Catholic **CDA** coalition, the **Liberal VVD** and the **Socialist PvdA**.

A jolt came in April 2002, when the country's political class was deeply embarrassed by the publication of a damning report on the failure of the Dutch army to protect the **Bosnian Muslims** ensconced in the UN safe haven of **Srebrenica** in 1995. The report told a tale of woeful incompetence: the UN's Dutch soldiers were inadequately armed but refused American assistance, and watched as Serb troops separated Muslim men and women in preparation for the mass executions, which the Dutch soldiers did nothing to stop (though they were never involved). In a country that prides itself on its internationalism, the report was an especially hard blow and the Socialist PvdA-led government, under **Wim Kok**, promptly resigned.

The rise and fall of Pim Fortuyn

In the **national elections of May 2002**, the three main parties suffered a further shock when a new Rightist grouping – **Lijst Pim Fortuyn (LPF)** – swept to second place, securing seventeen percent of the national vote. The LPF was named after its founder and leader, Rotterdam's **Pim Fortuyn**, who was stylish and witty, openly gay, a pipe smoker and a former Marxist. Fortuyn managed to cover several popular bases at the same time, from the need for law and order through to tighter immigration controls, but most crucially he also attacked the liberal establishment's espousal of **multiculturalism**, claiming that many representatives of minority ethnic groups were deeply reactionary, anti-gay and sexist. Politically, it worked a treat, but in the event Fortuyn's assassination by Volkert van der Graaf, an animal rights activist who claimed to have killed Fortuyn to stop him exploiting Muslims as scapegoats, holed the LPF. Without its leader, the LPF rapidly unravelled, breaking up the governing coalition which had taken office after May 2002 and then losing most of its seats in the general election of January 2003.

The murder of Theo van Gogh

The general election of 2003 saw a **Rightist alliance** led by the VVD and the CDA cobble together an administration under the leadership of **Jan Peter Balkenende**, a plain-speaking Harry Potter lookalike, described by a leading newspaper as "dull but 200 percent reliable". In practice, this coalition proved most unstable, but Balkenende soldiered on (with various partners) until the national election of November 2006. Superficially, therefore, it seemed that normal political service had been resumed, but in truth there was an uneasy undertow, with the success of the LPF pushing certain social issues, particularly **immigration**, to the right. The situation got much worse – and race relations more tense – when, in late 2004, the film-maker **Theo van Gogh** was shot dead on an Amsterdam street by a Moroccan who objected to *Submission*, a film van Gogh had made about Islamic violence against women. Sensing the danger, Amsterdam city council in general – and the mayor, **Job Cohen**, in particular – handled the situation with great aplomb, coining the slogan "keeping things together" (*de boel bij elkaar houden*) and organizing several, candlelit vigils.

1986	1990	2001
The major part of the Delta Project is completed; the Dutch hope their western coast is secure from the perils of the sea.	World Cup: Dutchman Frank Rijkaard hits Germany's Rudi Völler with an amazingly accurate, long-range spit that passes into Dutch folklore.	The Netherlands is the first country in the world to recognize same-sex marriages.

AYAAN HIRSI ALI

Shown on Dutch TV in 2004, Theo van Gogh's film *Submission* was scripted by **Ayaan Hirsi Ali**, a one-time Somali refugee, who had successfully sought asylum in the Netherlands in 1992. Hirsi Ali had progressed through Dutch society, obtaining a degree at Leiden University, working as a translator and becoming an MP for the VVD in 2003. She renounced Islam in 2002 and thereafter received death threats, obliging her to seek police protection and even forcing her into hiding. Hirsi Ali refused to be cowed and her pronouncements on Islam were hard-hitting and headline-grabbing. In an interview with the UK's *Daily Telegraph* in December 2004, she said: "But tell me why any Muslim man would want Islamic women to be educated and emancipated? Would a Roman voluntarily have given up his slaves?" Unfortunately for Hirsi Ali, she was engulfed by controversy of a different kind in 2006, when it turned out that her **application for asylum** had not been entirely truthful. Some supported Hirsi Ali, others argued that she should be stripped of her parliamentary seat, and the furore brought the governing coalition down amid an avalanche of mud-slinging. In the meantime, Hirsi Ali decided to parachute out of the whole mess and now lives in the US. Her autobiography, *Infidel* (see p.346), was published in September 2006.

Balkenende again

After the crisis over Ayaan Hirsi Ali's less than straightforward asylum application had brought the government down (see box above), the **national election of November 2006** saw modest gains for the far right and left, but not enough to unseat Balkenende, who proceeded to weld together yet another coalition. This unwieldy alliance did its best to cope with the banking crisis of 2008, when the government nationalized failing and flailing parts of the banking industry at huge cost to the taxpayer: there is now wide agreement that Dutch banks should be kept under much tighter legislative control with savings ultimately separated from speculation.

To the present day

The Balkenende coalition held together until February 2010, when the PvdA refused to prolong the Dutch army's engagement in Afghanistan. Following the ensuing elections **Mark Rutte**, the leader of the VVD, became the prime minister of a minority right-of-centre administration in coalition with the CDA and with the tacit support of a newly emergent right-wing party the **Partij voor de Vrijheid** (Party For Freedom; PVV). The PVV took fifteen percent of the popular vote under the leadership of **Geert Wilders**, a controversial figure (to put it mildly), who is, amongst much else, an outspoken Eurosceptic and a man whose views on Islam are often regarded as inflammatory. The coalition didn't last long, however: in April 2012, Wilders stormed out of a meeting, refusing to support the government's plan to slice €16bn off the national budget.

In the run-up to the **national election of September 2012**, the established parties were notably apprehensive, but in the event the PVV was unable to hold onto a large slice of its vote and the Wilders threat was contained, maybe for good. By contrast, both the VVD and the PvdA did well and afterwards **Mark Rutte** formed a new governing coalition, which remains in power at time of writing despite moments of acute shakiness, especially over a controversial healthcare bill.

2002	2004	2007
Controversial politician Pim Fortuyn is assassinated in Hilversum; the guilder is replaced by the euro.	Film-maker Theo van Gogh is murdered on an Amsterdam street.	Amsterdam city council moves to restrict and reduce its Red Light District.

Into the future

The PVV may be on the wane, but there is no denying that Wilders – like Fortuyn before him – tapped a populist vein fuelled by a general sense of angst as to how the Dutch conceive of themselves and how things seem to be turning out. The vast majority want their country to be liberal and tolerant, and yet there are undoubtedly racial tensions; nearly everyone wants the Netherlands to be prosperous, and yet they have been stung by the worldwide recession; and while most of the Dutch are still proud of the progressive social policies they introduced in the 1960s and 1970s, these very policies are not wearing too well. The best illustration is in Amsterdam, where the country's liberal attitude to **soft drugs and prostitution** may once have seemed sane and pragmatic, but the result has been to turn the city into a target for thousands of tourists hell-bent on pursuing the city's twin indulgences. To a solid bloc of Amsterdammers, the Red Light District now seems unpleasant, if not downright offensive, and the city council has made repeated efforts to reduce its size and curb its excesses. Neither have the country's **coffeeshops** avoided attention, prompting endless discussions about the need – or not – for IDs and other such legislative tinkering. Indeed, although it's true that in any "happiness poll" the Netherlands is always reckoned to be in the top ten of desirable places to live, many locals are clearly not convinced. Most still hope for better times, but others have simply given up and are voting with their feet: in 2014, 144,000 mostly middle-class Dutch citizens emigrated, one of the largest numbers ever.

2008	**2013**	**2014**
Work is halted on Amsterdam's subterranean Noord-Zuidlijn when buildings start to collapse on the Vijzelgracht; consternation all round.	Queen Beatrix abdicates after 33 years on the throne and is succeeded by her eldest son, Willem-Alexander.	Amsterdammers wonder if the Noord-Zuidlijn will ever be finished: completion date moved back to 2017.

Dutch art

The following is the very briefest of introductions to a subject that has rightly filled volumes. Inevitably, it covers artists that lived and worked in both the Netherlands and Belgium, as these two countries have – along with Luxembourg – been bound together as the "Low Countries" for most of their history. For in-depth and academic studies, see "Books" (p.345).

Beginnings: the Flemish Primitives

Throughout the medieval period, **Flanders**, in modern-day Belgium, was one of the most artistically productive parts of Europe, and it was here that the realist base of later Dutch painting developed. Today, the works of these early Flemish painters, the **Flemish Primitives**, are highly prized, and although examples are fairly sparse in the Netherlands, all the leading museums – especially Den Haag's Mauritshuis and Amsterdam's Rijksmuseum– have a healthy sample.

   Jan van Eyck (1385–1441) is generally regarded as the first of the Flemish Primitives, and has even been credited with the invention of oil painting – though it seems more likely that he simply perfected a new technique by thinning his paint with turpentine (at the time a new discovery), thus making it more flexible. The most famous of his works is the altarpiece in Belgium's Ghent Cathedral, which was revolutionary in its realism, for the first time using elements of native landscape in depicting biblical themes. Van Eyck's style and technique were to influence several generations of the region's artists.

Bouts and Goes

Born in Haarlem but active in (Belgium's) Leuven, **Dieric Bouts** (1415–75) was one of the most talented painters of his generation. Bouts is recognizable by his stiff, rather elongated figures and penchant for horrific subject matter – the tortures of damnation for example – all set against carefully drawn landscapes. **Hugo van der Goes** (d.1482) was the next Ghent master after van Eyck, most famous for the Portinari altarpiece in Florence's Uffizi gallery. Van der Goes died insane, and his later works have strong hint of his impending madness in their subversive use of space and implicit acceptance of the viewer's presence.

Memling, David and Bosch

Active in Bruges throughout his life, **Hans Memling** (1440–94) is best remembered for the pastoral charm of his landscapes and the quality of his portraiture, much of which survives on the rescued side panels of triptychs. **Gerard David** (1460–1523) was a native of Oudewater, near Gouda, but he moved to Bruges in 1484, becoming the last of the great painters to work in that city, producing formal religious works of traditional style. Strikingly different, but broadly contemporaneous, was **Hieronymus Bosch** (1450–1516), who lived for most of his life in the Netherlands, though his style is linked to that of his Flemish contemporaries. His frequently reprinted religious allegories are filled with macabre visions of tortured people and grotesque beasts, and appear faintly unhinged, though it's now thought that these are visual representations of contemporary sayings, idioms and parables. While their interpretation is far from resolved, Bosch's paintings draw strongly on subconscious fears and archetypes, giving them a lasting, haunting fascination.

The sixteenth century

At the end of the fifteenth century, Flanders was in economic and political decline and the leading artists of the day were drawn instead to the booming port of **Antwerp**, also in present-day Belgium. The artists who worked here soon began to integrate the finely observed detail that characterized the Flemish tradition with the style of the Italian painters of the Renaissance. **Quentin Matsys** (1464–1530) introduced florid classical architectural details and intricate landscapes to his works, influenced perhaps by the work of Leonardo da Vinci. As well as religious works, Matsys painted portraits and genre scenes, all of which have recognizably Italian facets – and in the process he paved the way for the Dutch genre painters of later years. **Jan Gossaert** (1478–1532) made the pilgrimage to Italy too, and his dynamic works are packed with detail, especially finely drawn classical architectural backdrops. He was the first Low Countries artist to introduce the subjects of classical mythology into his paintings, part of a steady trend towards secular subject matter.

The Bruegels and Pourbus

The middle of the sixteenth century was dominated by the work of **Pieter Bruegel the Elder** (c.1525–69), whose gruesome allegories and innovative interpretations of religious subjects are firmly placed in Low Countries settings. Pieter also painted exquisitely observed peasant scenes, though he himself was well connected in court circles in Antwerp and, later, Brussels. Bruegel's two sons, **Pieter Bruegel the Younger** (1564–1638) and **Jan Bruegel** (1568–1625), were lesser painters; the former produced fairly insipid copies of his father's work, while Jan developed a style of his own – delicately rendered flower paintings and genre pieces that earned him the nickname "Velvet". Towards the latter half of the sixteenth century highly stylized Italianate portraits became the dominant fashion, with **Frans Pourbus the Younger** (1569–1622) the leading practitioner. Frans hobnobbed across Europe, working for the likes of the Habsburgs and the Medicis.

The Dutch emerge

Meanwhile, there were artistic rumblings in the province of Holland. Leading the painterly charge was **Geertgen tot Sint Jans** (Little Gerard of the Brotherhood of St John; c.1460–90), who worked in Haarlem, initiating – in a strangely naive style – an artistic vision that would come to dominate Dutch painting in the seventeenth century. There was a tender melancholy in his work, which was very different from the stylized paintings produced in Flanders, and, most importantly, a new sensitivity to light. **Jan Mostaert** (1475–1555) took over after Geertgen's death, developing similar themes, but the first painter to effect real changes in northern painting was Leiden's **Lucas van Leyden** (1489–1533). Leyden's bright colours and narrative technique were refreshingly novel, and he introduced a new dynamism into what had become a rigidly formal treatment of devotional subjects. There was rivalry, of course. Eager to publicize Haarlem as the artistic capital of the northern Netherlands, **Karel van Mander** claimed **Jan van Scorel** (1495–1562) as the better painter, complaining, too, of van Leyden's dandyish ways.

Scorel and Heemskerck

Jan van Scorel's influence should not be underestimated. Like many of his contemporaries, van Scorel hotfooted it to Italy to view the works of the Renaissance, but in Rome his career went into overdrive when he found favour with Pope Hadrian VI, one-time bishop of Utrecht, who installed him as court painter in 1520. Van Scorel stayed in Rome for four years and when he returned to Utrecht, armed with all that papal prestige, he combined the ideas he had picked up in Italy with those underpinning Haarlem realism, thereby modifying what had previously been an independent artistic tradition once and for all. Among his several students, probably the most talented was **Maerten van Heemskerck** (1498–1574), who duly went off to Italy himself in 1532, staying there for five years before doubling back to Haarlem.

The Golden Age

The seventeenth century begins with **Karel van Mander** (1548–1606), Haarlem painter, art impresario and one of the few contemporary chroniclers of the art of the Low Countries. His *Schilderboek* of 1604 put Flemish and Dutch traditions into context for the first time, and in addition specified the rules of fine painting. Examples of his own work are rare – though Haarlem's Frans Hals Museum (see p.107) weighs in with a couple – but his followers were many. Among them was **Cornelius Cornelisz van Haarlem** (1562–1638), who produced elegant renditions of biblical and mythical themes; and **Hendrik Goltzius** (1558–1616), who was a skilled engraver and an integral member of van Mander's Haarlem academy. The enthusiasm these painters had for Italian art, combined with the influence of a late revival of Gothicism, resulted in works that combined **Mannerist** and **Classical** elements. An interest in realism was also felt, but, for them, the subject became less important than the way in which it was depicted: biblical stories became merely a vehicle whereby artists could apply their skill in painting the human body, landscapes, or copious displays of food. All of this served to break the religious stranglehold on art, and make legitimate a whole range of everyday subjects for the painter.

North and South diverge

The break with tradition that started in Haarlem and spread across the Netherlands was compounded by the **Reformation** – and this was where the north and the south finally diverged: the austere Calvinism that had replaced the Catholic faith in the United Provinces had no use for images or symbols of devotion in its churches. Instead, painters catered to the burgeoning middle class, and no longer visited (Catholic) Italy to learn their craft. Indeed, the real giants of the seventeenth century – Hals, Rembrandt, Vermeer – stayed in the Netherlands all their lives. Another innovation was that painting split into more distinct categories – genre, portrait, landscape – and artists tended (with notable exceptions) to confine themselves to one field throughout their careers. So began the **Golden Age** of Dutch art.

Historical and religious painting

The artistic influence of Renaissance Italy may have been in decline, but Italian painters still had clout with the Dutch, most notably **Caravaggio** (1571–1610), who was much admired for his new realism. Taking Caravaggio's cue, many artists – Rembrandt for one – continued to portray classical subjects, but in a way that was totally at odds with the Mannerists' stylish flights of imagination. The Utrecht artist **Abraham Bloemaert** (1564–1651), though a solid Mannerist throughout his career, encouraged these new ideas, and his students – **Gerard van Honthorst** (1590–1656), **Hendrik Terbrugghen** (1588–1629) and **Dirck van Baburen** (1590–1624) – formed the nucleus of the influential **Utrecht School**, which followed Caravaggio almost to the point of slavishness. Honthorst was perhaps the leading figure, learning his craft from Bloemaert and travelling to Rome, where he was nicknamed "Gerardo delle Notti" for his ingenious handling of light and shade. In his later paintings, however, this was to become more routine technique than inspired invention, and though a supremely competent artist, Honthorst is somewhat discredited among critics today. Terbrugghen's reputation seems to have aged rather better; he soon developed a more individual style, with his later, lighter work having a great influence on the young Vermeer. After a jaunt to Rome, Baburen shared a studio with Terbrugghen and produced some fairly original work – work which also had some influence on Vermeer – but today he is the least studied member of the group and few of his paintings survive.

Rembrandt as an historical and religious painter

Without doubt, **Rembrandt** (see box below) was the most original historical artist of the seventeenth century, also chipping in with religious paintings throughout his career. In the 1630s, Huygens procured for him his greatest religious commission – a series of five paintings of the Passion, beautifully composed and uncompromisingly realistic. Later, however, Rembrandt drifted away from the mainstream, ignoring the smooth brushwork of his contemporaries and choosing instead a rougher, darker and more disjointed style for his biblical and historical subjects. This may well have contributed to a decline in his artistic fortunes and it is significant that while the more conventional Jordaens, Honthorst and van Everdingen were busy decorating the Huis ten Bosch near Den Haag for the Stadholder Frederick Henry, Rembrandt was having his monumental *Conspiracy of Julius Civilis* – painted for Amsterdam's brand-new Stadhuis – thrown out. The reasons for this rejection have been hotly debated, but it seems likely that Rembrandt's rendition was thought too suggestive of cabalistic conspiracy – the commissioners wanted to see a romantic hero and certainly not a plot in the making: Julius had organized a revolt against the Romans, an important event in early Dutch history, which had obvious resonance in a country just freed from the Habsburgs. Even worse, perhaps, Rembrandt had shown Julius to be blind in one eye, which was historically accurate but not at all what the city's burghers had in mind.

REMBRANDT'S PROGRESS

The gilded reputation of **Rembrandt van Rijn** (1606–69) is still relatively recent, but he is now justly regarded as one of the greatest and most versatile painters of all time. Born in Leiden, the son of a miller, he was a boy apprentice to local artist Jacob van Swanenburgh, before heading to Amsterdam to study under the fashionable **Pieter Lastman**. Soon he was painting commissions for the city elite and became an accepted member of their circle, with the poet and statesman **Constantijn Huygens** acting as his agent. In 1634, Rembrandt married **Saskia van Uylenburgh**, daughter of the burgomaster of Leeuwarden and quite a catch for a relatively humble artist. Five years later, the couple moved into a smart house on Jodenbreestraat, now the Rembrandthuis museum (see p.69), though these years were marred by the death of all but one of his children in infancy, the sole survivor being his much-loved **Titus** (1641–68).

In 1642 Rembrandt produced his most famous painting, **The Night Watch**, on display in the Amsterdam Rijksmuseum (see box, p.75), but thereafter his career went into decline, essentially because he forsook portraiture to focus on increasingly sombre and introspective **religious and historical works** that did not prove especially bankable – though his personal irascibility did not help. Traditionally, Rembrandt's change of direction has been linked to the death of Saskia in 1642, but he was also facing increased competition from a new batch of portrait artists, including Ferdinand Bol and Govert Flinck. Whatever the reason, there were few takers for Rembrandt's later works, and in 1656 he was formally declared insolvent: four years later he was obliged to sell his house and goods, moving to much humbler premises in the Jordaan. By this time, he had a new cohabitee, **Hendrickje Stoffels** (a clause in Saskia's will prevented them from ever marrying), and in the early 1660s, she and Titus took Rembrandt in hand, sorting out his finances and his work schedule. With his money problems solved, a relieved Rembrandt then produced some of his finest paintings, emotionally deep and contemplative works with a rough finish, the paint often daubed with an almost trowel-like heaviness. One of his very last and most exquisite pictures, finished in 1668, is *The Jewish Bride*, now exhibited in Amsterdam's Rijksmuseum. Hendrickje died in 1663 and Titus in 1668, a year before his father.

Genre painting

Often misunderstood, the term **genre painting** initially applied to everything from animal paintings and still lifes through to historical works and landscapes, but later – from around the middle of the seventeenth century – referred only to **scenes of everyday life**. Its target market was the region's burgeoning middle class, who had a penchant for non-idealized portrayals of common scenes, both with and without symbols – or subtly disguised details – making one moral point or another. One of its early practitioners was Antwerp's **Frans Snijders** (1579–1657), who took up still-life painting with vim and gusto, amplifying his subject – food and drink – on large and sumptuous canvases. Snijders also doubled up as a member of the Rubens art factory (see p.341), painting animals and still-life sections for the master's works. In Utrecht, Hendrik Terbrugghen and Gerard van Honthorst adapted the realism and strong chiaroscuro learnt from Caravaggio to a number of tableaux of everyday life, though they were more concerned with religious works (see p.336), while Haarlem's Frans Hals dabbled in genre too, but is better known as a portraitist (see opposite).

Brouwer, Teniers and Ostade

One of Frans Hal's pupils, **Adriaen Brouwer** (1605–38), chose to concentrate on genre painting and his riotous tavern scenes were well received in their day and collected by, among others, Rubens and Rembrandt. Brouwer spent only a couple of years in Haarlem under Hals before returning to his native Flanders, where he influenced the inventive **David Teniers the Younger** (1610–90), who worked in Antwerp and later in Brussels. Teniers' early paintings are Brouwer-like peasant scenes, although his later work is more delicate and diverse, including *kortegaardje* – guardroom scenes that show soldiers carousing. **Adriaen van Ostade** (1610–85), on the other hand, stayed in Haarlem most of his life, skilfully painting groups of peasants and tavern brawls – though his later acceptance by the establishment led him to water down the realism he had learnt from Brouwer.

Jan Steen

The English critic E.V. Lucas dubbed Teniers, Brouwer and Ostade "coarse and boorish" compared with **Jan Steen** (1625–79) who, along with Vermeer, is probably the most admired Dutch genre painter. Steen's paintings offer the same Rabelaisian peasantry in full fling, but they go their debauched ways in broad daylight, and nowhere do you see the filthy rogues in shadowy hovels favoured by Brouwer and Ostade. Steen offers more humour, too, as well as more moralizing, identifying with the hedonistic mob and reproaching them at the same time. Indeed, many of his pictures are illustrations of well-known contemporary proverbs – popular comments on the evils of drink or the transience of human existence that were supposed to teach as well as entertain.

Gerrit Dou, his pupils and Nicholas Maes

Leiden's **Gerrit Dou** (1613–75) was one of Rembrandt's first pupils – and surprisingly enough nineteenth-century connoisseurs actually preferred his work to that of his master. That said, it's difficult to detect any trace of Rembrandt's influence in his paintings as Dou initiated a (genre) style of his own: tiny, minutely realized and beautifully finished views of a kind of ordinary life that was decidedly more genteel than Brouwer's – or even Steen's for that matter. He was admired, above all, for his painstaking attention to detail and he would, it's said, sit in his studio for hours waiting for the dust to settle before starting work. Among Dou's students, **Frans van Mieris** (1635–81) continued the highly finished portrayals of the Dutch bourgeoisie, as did **Gabriel Metsu** (1629–67) – perhaps Dou's most talented pupil – whose pictures often convey an overtly moral message. Another pupil of Rembrandt's, though a much later one, was **Nicholas Maes** (1629–93), whose early works were almost entirely genre paintings, sensitively executed and with an obvious didacticism. His later paintings show the influence of a more refined style of portraiture, which he had picked up in France.

Gerard ter Borch and Pieter de Hooch

As a native of Zwolle, **Gerard ter Borch** (1619–81) remained very much a provincial painter, despite trips to most of Europe's artistic capitals. He depicted the country's merchant class at play and became renowned for his curious doll-like figures and his ability to capture the textures of different cloths. His domestic scenes were not unlike those of **Pieter de Hooch** (1629–84), whose simple depictions of everyday life are deliberately unsentimental and have little or no moral commentary. De Hooch's favourite trick was to paint darkened rooms with an open door leading through to a sunlit courtyard, a practice that, along with his trademark rusty-red colour, makes his work easy to identify and, at its best, exquisite. Nevertheless, his later pictures lose their spartan quality, reflecting the increasing opulence of the Dutch Republic; the rooms are more richly decorated, the arrangements more contrived and the subjects less homely.

Johannes Vermeer

It was **Johannes Vermeer** (1632–75) who brought the most sophisticated methods to painting interiors, depicting the play of natural light on indoor surfaces with superlative skill – as well as creating the tranquil intimacy for which he is now internationally famous. Like de Hooch (see above), Vermeer was an observer of the well-heeled Dutch household without a moral tone and today he is regarded (with Hals and Rembrandt) as one of the big three Dutch painters – though it seems he was a slow worker: only about forty paintings can be attributed to him with any certainty. Living all his life in Delft, Vermeer is perhaps the epitome of the seventeenth-century Dutch painter – rejecting the pomp and ostentation of the High Renaissance to record quietly his contemporaries at home, painting for a public that demanded no more than that: bourgeois art at its most complete.

Portraiture

Predictably enough, the ruling bourgeoisie of the United Provinces was keen to record and celebrate its success, and consequently **portraiture** became a reliable way for a painter to make a living. **Michiel Jansz Miereveld** (1567–1641), court painter to Frederick Henry of Orange-Nassau in Den Haag, was the first real portraitist of the Dutch Republic, but it wasn't long before his stiff and somewhat formal figures were superseded by the more spontaneous renderings of **Frans Hals** (c.1580–1666). Hals is perhaps best known for his "corporation pictures" – **group portraits** of the Dutch Civil Guard regiments that had been formed in most of the larger towns during the war with Spain, but subsequently became social clubs. These large group pieces demanded superlative technique, since the painter had to create a collection of individual portraits while retaining a sense of the group, and accord prominence based on the relative importance of the sitters and the size of the payment each had made. Hals was particularly good at this, using innovative lighting effects, arranging his sitters subtly, and putting all the elements together in a fluid and dynamic composition. Hals also painted many individual portraits, making fleeting and telling expressions his trademark; his pictures of children are particularly sensitive. Later in life, however, his work became darker and more akin to Rembrandt's, spurred – it's conjectured – by his penury.

Verspronck and van der Helst

Johannes Cornelisz Verspronck (c.1600–62) and **Bartholomeus van der Helst** (1613–70) were the other great Haarlem portraitists after Frans Hals – Verspronck recognizable by the smooth, shiny glow he always gave to his sitters' faces, van der Helst by a competent but unadventurous style. Of the two, van der Helst was the more popular, influencing a number of later painters; he left Haarlem as a young man to begin a solidly successful career as portrait painter to Amsterdam's upper crust.

Rembrandt as a portraitist

Rembrandt's early portraits and self-portraits show the confident face of security, when he was on top and sure of his direction – the exquisite detail and half-smile in the *Portrait of Maria Trip* being a case in point. Rembrandt would not always be the darling of the Amsterdam merchants, but his fall from grace was still some way off when he completed his most famous painting, *The Night Watch* (see box, p.75), a group portrait whose fluent arrangement of its subjects was almost entirely original. The painting was once associated with the artist's decline in popularity, but this is incorrect and there's no evidence that the military company who commissioned it was anything but pleased with the result.

Rembrandt's pupils

The early work of **Ferdinand Bol** (1616–80) was heavily influenced by Rembrandt, so much so that for centuries art historians couldn't tell the two apart, though Bol's later paintings are readily distinguishable, blandly elegant portraits which proved very popular with the wealthy. At the age of 53, Bol married a rich widow and promptly hung up his easel – perhaps he knew just how emotionally tacky his work had become. Another pupil was **Govert Flinck** (1615–60), formerly an apprentice silk mercer and perhaps Rembrandt's most faithful follower. In 1659, as a sign of Rembrandt's fading fortunes, Flinck was given the job of decorating Amsterdam's new Stadhuis in preference to his master, but died before he could execute his designs; the commission passed to Rembrandt, whose *Conspiracy of Julius Civilis* was installed in 1662, but discarded a year later. Like Bol, Flinck married into money and his best paintings date from the 1630s. Most of the pitifully scarce extant work of **Carel Fabritius** (1622–54) is portraiture, but he also died young, before he could properly realize his promise as perhaps the most gifted of all Rembrandt's students. Generally regarded as the teacher of Vermeer, he forms a link between the two masters, combining Rembrandt's technique with his own practice of painting figures against a dark background, prefiguring the lighting and colouring of Vermeer.

Landscapes

Aside from Pieter Bruegel the Elder (see p.335), whose depictions of his native surroundings make him the first true Low Countries landscape painter, **Gillis van Coninxloo** (1544–1607) stands out as the earliest Dutch landscapist. He imbued his native scenery with elements of fantasy, painting the richly wooded views he had seen on his travels around Europe as backdrops to biblical scenes. The quaint and unpretentious scenes of **Esaias van der Velde** (1591–1632) show the first real affinity with the Dutch countryside, but while his influence was considerable, his pupil, Jan van Goyen, soon overshadowed him.

Van Goyen and the van Ruysdaels

A remarkable painter, **Jan van Goyen** (1596–1656) belongs to the so-called "**tonal phase**" of Dutch landscape painting. His early pictures were highly coloured and close to those of his teacher, Esaias van der Velde, but it didn't take long for him to develop a marked touch of his own, using tones of green, brown and grey to lend everything a characteristic translucent haze. A long-neglected artist, van Goyen only received recognition with the arrival of the Impressionists, when his fluid and rapid brushwork was at last fully appreciated.

Another "tonal" painter, Haarlem's **Salomon van Ruysdael** (1600–70) was also directly affected by Esaias van der Velde, and his simple and atmospheric, though not terribly adventurous, landscapes were for a long time consistently confused with

THE GOLDEN AGE: THE DUTCH ARTIST AS SPECIALIST

Most of the leading Dutch painters of the seventeenth century could, if push came to shove, try their brush at pretty much anything, but some preferred to specialize. Among them, **Paulus Potter** (1625–54) came up trumps with his animals, producing a string of lovingly executed paintings of cows and horses. **Pieter Saenredam** (1597–1665), on the other hand, zoned in on architecture, becoming famous for his finely realized paintings of Dutch church interiors, as did **Emanuel de Witte** (1616–92), though his churches lack the austere crispness of the former. Architecture was the interest of Haarlem's **Gerrit Berckheyde** (1638–98) too, but he limited his views to the outside of buildings, painting glossy townscapes with a precise eye and cool detachment. Nautical scenes in praise of the Dutch navy were the speciality of **Willem van der Velde II** (1633–1707), whose melodramatic canvases, complete with churning seas and chasing skies, are a delight. Two Haarlem painters dominated the field of still life – **Pieter Claesz** (1598–1660) and **Willem Heda** (1594–1680) – in which objects were gathered together to remind the viewer of the transience of human life and the meaninglessness of worldly pursuits. Thus, a skull would often be shown alongside a book, pipe or goblet, and some half-eaten food.

those of van Goyen. More esteemed is his nephew, **Jacob van Ruysdael** (1628–82), often considered the greatest of all Dutch landscapists, whose fastidiously observed views of quiet flatlands dominated by stormy skies were to influence European landscapists right up to the nineteenth century; John Constable certainly acknowledged a debt to him.

Rubens and his followers

Down in the south, in Antwerp, **Pieter Paul Rubens** (1577–1640) was easily the most important exponent of the Baroque in northern Europe. Born in Siegen, Westphalia, he was raised in Antwerp, where he entered the painters' guild in 1598. Thereafter, he travelled extensively in Italy, absorbing the art of the High Renaissance, and by the time of his return to Antwerp in 1608 he had acquired an enormous artistic vocabulary with the paintings of Caravaggio especially influential. His first major success came shortly after his return and this prompted a string of commissions that enabled him to set up his own studio.

The division of labour in **Rubens' studio** – and the talent of the artists working there (who included Anthony van Dyck and Jacob Jordaens) – ensured an extraordinary output of outstanding work. The degree to which Rubens personally worked on a canvas would vary – and would determine its price. From the early 1620s onwards he turned his hand to a plethora of themes and subjects – religious works, portraits, landscapes, mythological scenes – each exhibiting an acute **sense of light**, in association with colour and form. The drama in his works comes from the vigorous animation of his characters: his large-scale allegorical works, especially, are packed with heaving, writhing figures that appear to tumble out from the canvas.

In the 1630s, **gout** began to hamper Rubens' activities, and his painting became more domestic and meditative. **Hélène Fourment**, his second wife, was the subject of many of these later portraits and she also served as a model for characters in his allegorical paintings, her figure epitomizing the buxom, well-rounded women found throughout his work.

Anthony van Dyck and Jacob Jordaens

Rubens' influence on the artists of the period was enormous. The huge output of his studio meant that his works were universally seen and also widely disseminated by the engravers he employed to copy his work. Chief among his followers was the portraitist **Anthony van Dyck** (1599–1641), who worked in Rubens' studio from

1618, often taking on the depiction of religious figures in his master's works, or at least those that required particular sensitivity and pathos. Eventually, van Dyck developed his own distinct style and technique, establishing himself as court painter to Charles I of England, and creating portraits of a nervous elegance that would influence the genre there for the next 150 years. **Jacob Jordaens** (1593–1678) was also an Antwerp native who studied under Rubens. Although he was commissioned to complete several works left unfinished by Rubens at the time of his death, his robustly naturalistic works have an earthy – and sensuous – realism that is quite different and distinct in style and technique.

The eighteenth century

In the eighteenth century, the Netherlands' economic decline was mirrored by a gradual deterioration in the quality and originality of Dutch painting. The subtle delicacies of the great paintings of the Golden Age were replaced by finicky still lifes and minute studies of flowers, or overly finessed portraiture and religious scenes: the work of **Adriaen van der Werff** (1659–1722) is typical. Of the era's other big names, **Jacob de Wit** (1695–1754) painted burgher ceiling after ceiling in a flashy, romantic style. He also benefited from a relaxation in the laws against Catholics, decorating several of their (newly legal) churches. The eighteenth century's only painter of any real talent was **Cornelis Troost** (1697–1750) who painted competent portraits and some neat, faintly satirical pieces that have since earned him the title of "The Dutch Hogarth".

The nineteenth century

Born in Overijssel, **Johann Barthold Jongkind** (1819–91) was the first important Dutch artist to emerge in the nineteenth century, painting landscapes and seascapes that were to influence Monet and the early Impressionists. He spent most of his life in France and his work was exhibited in Paris with the Barbizon painters, though he owed less to them than to van Goyen and the seventeenth-century "tonal" artists of the United Provinces. Jongkind's work was a logical precursor to the art of the **Hague School**. Based in and around Den Haag between 1870 and 1900, this prolific group of painters tried to re-establish a characteristically Dutch school of painting. They produced atmospheric studies of the dunes and polders around Den Haag, nature pictures that are characterized by grey, rain-filled skies, windswept seas and silvery, flat beaches. **J.H. Weissenbruch** (1824–1903) was a founding member, a specialist in low, flat beach scenes dotted with stranded boats. The banker-turned-artist **H.W. Mesdag** (1831–1915) did the same but with more skill than imagination, while **Jacob Maris** (1837–99), one of three artist brothers, was perhaps the most typical, with his rural and sea scenes heavily covered by grey, chasing skies.

Mauve and Israëls

More talented than many of his contemporaries, **Anton Mauve** (1838–88) was an exponent of soft, pastel landscapes and an early teacher of van Gogh. Profoundly influenced by the French Barbizon painters – Corot, Millet et al. – he went to Hilversum near Amsterdam in 1885 to set up his own group, which became known as the "**Dutch Barbizon**". **Jozef Israëls** (1826–1911) has often been likened to Millet, though it's generally agreed that he had more in common with the Impressionists, and his best pictures are his melancholy portraits and interiors.

Toorop and Breitner

Very different, and slightly later, **Jan Toorop** (1858–1928) went through multiple artistic changes, radically adapting his technique from a fairly conventional pointillism through a tired Expressionism to Symbolism with an Art Nouveau feel. Roughly contemporary, **George Hendrik Breitner** (1857–1923) was a better painter, and one who refined his style rather than changed it. His snapshot-like impressions of his beloved Amsterdam figure among his best work.

Vincent van Gogh

Vincent van Gogh (1853–90) was one of the least "Dutch" of Dutch artists, and he spent most of his relatively short painting career in France. After countless studies of Dutch peasant life – studies which culminated in his sombre *Potato Eaters* – he went to live in Paris with his art-dealer brother Theo. There, under the influence of the Impressionists, he lightened his palette, following the pointillist work of Seurat and "trying to render intense colour and not a grey harmony". Two years later he went south to Arles, the "land of blue tones and gay colours", and, struck by the brilliance of the Mediterranean light, began to develop his characteristic style. A disastrous attempt to live with Gauguin, and the much-publicized episode in which he cut off part of his ear and presented it to a local prostitute, led to his committal in an asylum at St-Rémy. Here he produced some of his most famous, and most Expressionistic, canvases – strongly coloured and with the paint thickly, almost frantically, applied. Van Gogh is now one of the world's most popular – and popularized – painters, and Amsterdam's **Van Gogh Museum** has the world's finest collection of his work (see p.77).

The twentieth century

Each of the major modern art movements has had – or has – its followers in the Netherlands and each has been diluted or altered according to local taste. Of many lesser names, **Jan Sluyters** (1881–1957) stands out as the Dutch pioneer of Cubism, but this is small beer when compared with the one specifically Dutch movement – **De Stijl** (The Style).

De Stijl: Piet Mondriaan

De Stijl's leading proponent was **Piet Mondriaan** (1872–1944), who developed the realism he had learnt from the Hague School painters via Cubism – which he criticized for being too cowardly to depart totally from representation – into a complete abstraction of form which he called **Neo-Plasticism**. Mondriaan was something of a mystic, and this was to some extent responsible for the direction that De Stijl – and his paintings – took: canvases painted with grids of lines and blocks made up of the three primary colours plus white, black and grey. Mondriaan believed this freed his art from the vagaries of personal perception, making it possible to obtain what he called "a true vision of reality". Mondriaan split with De Stijl in 1925, going on to attain new artistic extremes before moving to New York in the 1940s and producing atypically exuberant works such as *Victory Boogie Woogie* – named for the artist's love of jazz.

Van Doesburg and van der Leck

Theo van Doesburg (1883–1931) was a De Stijl co-founder and major theorist. His work is similar to Mondriaan's except for the noticeable absence of thick, black borders and the diagonals that he introduced into his work, calling his paintings "contra-compositions"; he argued these were both more dynamic and more in touch with the twentieth century. Meanwhile, De Stijl's **Bart van der Leck** (1876–1958) was identifiable by white canvases covered by seemingly randomly placed interlocking coloured triangles. De Stijl took other forms too; there was a magazine of the same name, and the movement introduced new concepts into every aspect of design, from painting to interior design and architecture. Yet in all these media, lines were kept simple, colours bold and clear.

The Bergen School, De Ploeg and Magic Realism

During and after De Stijl, a number of other movements flourished in the Netherlands, though their impact was not so great and their influence was essentially local. The Expressionist **Bergen School** was probably the most localized, its best-known exponent, **Charley Toorop** (1891–1955), daughter of Jan, developing a distinctively glaring but strangely sensitive realism. Otherwise, **De Ploeg** (The Plough), centred in Groningen, was headed by **Jan Wiegers** (1893–1959) and influenced by Ernst Ludwig Kirchner and the German Expressionists; the group's artists set out to capture the remote landscapes around their native town, and produced violently coloured canvases that hark back to van Gogh. Another group, known as the **Magic Realists**, surfaced in the 1930s, painting quasi-surrealistic scenes that, according to their leading light, **Carel Willink** (1900–83), revealed "a world stranger and more dreadful in its haughty impenetrability than the most terrifying nightmare".

CoBrA, Karel Appel and Escher

Postwar Dutch art began with **CoBrA** – a loose grouping of like-minded painters from Denmark, Belgium and the Netherlands, whose name derives from the initial letters of their respective capital cities. Their first exhibition at Amsterdam's Stedelijk Museum in 1949 provoked a furore, at the centre of which was **Karel Appel** (1921–2006), whose brutal abstract Expressionist pieces, plastered with paint inches thick, were, he maintained, necessary for the era – indeed, inevitable reflections of it. "I paint like a barbarian in a barbarous age," he claimed. In the graphic arts, the most famous twentieth-century Dutch figure was **Maurits Cornelis Escher** (1898–1972), whose Surrealistic illusions and allusions were underpinned by his fascination with mathematics. Many remain unconvinced by Escher, but the Dutch took a liking to his work and he now has his own museum in Den Haag (see p.155).

Contemporary art

The Netherlands boasts a vibrant art scene with all the major cities possessing at least a couple of art galleries that showcase regular exhibitions of **contemporary art**, but it's Amsterdam that takes the artistic biscuit with its three prestigious museums supplemented by several smaller, avant-garde galleries. Among modern Dutch artists, look out for the abstract work of **Edgar Fernhout** (1912–74) and **Ad Dekkers** (1938–74); the reliefs of **Jan Schoonhoven** (1914–94); the multimedia productions of **Jan Dibbets** (b.1941); the imprecisely coloured geometric designs of **Rob van Koningsbruggen** (b.1948); the smeary Expressionism of **Toon Verhoef** (b.1946); the exuberant figures of **Rene Daniels** (b.1950); the exquisite realism of **Karel Buskes** (b.1962); the unsettling photographic portraits of **Rineke Dijkstra** (b. 1959); the blending of art and engineering in the work of **Theo Jansen** (b.1948); and the witty, hip furniture designs of **Piet Hein Eek** (b.1967) – to name just eleven of the more important figures.

Books

Most of the books listed below are in print and in paperback, and those that are out of print should be easy to track down either in secondhand bookshops or online. While we recommend all the books listed below, we have marked our particular favourites with ★.

AMSTERDAM

Fred Feddes *A Millennium of Amsterdam*. Inventive, well-illustrated book comprising forty studies of the Amsterdam landscape – its reclamation, building and rebuilding. Starts at the Dam and ends at the beach in IJburg.

★**Geert Mak** *Amsterdam: A Brief Life of the City*. First published in 1995, this infinitely readable trawl through the city's past is a simply wonderful book – amusing and perceptive, alternately tart and indulgent. It's more a social history than anything else, so – for example – it's here you'll find out quite why Rembrandt lived in the Jewish quarter and why the city's merchant elite ossified in the eighteenth century. It's light and accessible enough to read from cover to cover, but its index of places makes it easy to dip into as well. If you liked this, try also Mak's *An Island in Time*, an evocative (but never sentimental) native-son return to the small and flailing Frisian village of Jowert.

ART

Svetlana Alpers *Rembrandt's Enterprise*. Intriguing 1988 study of Rembrandt, positing the theory – in line with findings of the Leiden-based Rembrandt Research Project – that many previously accepted Rembrandt paintings are not his at all, but merely the products of his studio. Bad news if you own one.

Anthony Bailey *A View of Delft*. Concise, startlingly well-researched book on Vermeer, with an accurate and well-considered exploration of his milieu.

Walter Bosing *Bosch: The Complete Paintings*. Attractive little book in the Taschen art series that covers its subject in just the right amount of detail (it's 96 pages long). Well conceived and illustrated.

Wayne Franits *Dutch Seventeenth-century Genre Painting: Its Stylistic and Thematic Evolution*. Well-argued, immaculately researched and attractively illustrated book – the best on its subject. Hardly deckchair reading, perhaps, but fascinating all the same. Also *Vermeer*, a thorough examination of the artist's milieu and technique alongside an attempt to unravel the meanings behind the paintings.

★**R.H. Fuchs** *Dutch Painting*. As complete an introduction to the subject – from Flemish origins to the postwar period – as you could wish for, in just a couple of hundred pages. Published in the 1970s and sadly out of print, there's still nothing better.

Melissa McQuillan *Van Gogh*. A small army of books examine van Gogh's paintings, life and hard times, but this superbly researched and illustrated version is hard to beat – and comes in at a very manageable 216 pages. Last published in 1989.

Steven Naifeh & Gregory White Smith *Van Gogh: The Life*. Published in 2011, this serious tome has received mixed reviews, but it is a thunderous volume, whose 992 pages explore the man's life, times and art in exhaustive detail.

Susie Nash *Northern Renaissance Art*. Erudite, 368-page book examining how art was made, valued and viewed in northern Europe from the late fourteenth to the early sixteenth century. All the leading Netherlandish figures are discussed – and Nash argues that it was these painters, rather than the Italians, who set the artistic tone of the Europe of their day.

Simon Schama *Rembrandt's Eyes*. Published in 1999, this detailed work received good reviews, but it's very, very long – and often very long-winded.

★**Gary Schwartz** *Rembrandt's Universe: His Art, His Life, His World*. Beautifully illustrated and well-considered account of the artist's life and work, written by a well-known authority on Dutch art.

★**Mariet Westerman** *The Art of the Dutch Republic 1585–1718*. This excellently written, immaculately illustrated and enthralling book tackles its subject thematically, from the marketing of works of art to an exploration of Dutch ideologies. Highly recommended, but sadly out of print. Also by Westerman is an all-you-could-ever-want-to-know book about *Rembrandt*.

Christopher White *Rembrandt*. Now well into his 80s, Christopher White has long been something of a Rembrandt specialist, responsible for a series of well-regarded books on the man and his times. Most of these books are expensive and aimed at the specialist art market, but this particular title is perfect for the general reader. It's well illustrated with a wonderfully incisive and extremely detailed commentary, though the index is poor. Published in 1984, but still very much on song – though there is tough competition from Gary Schwartz (see p.345).

Frank Wynne *I was Vermeer: The Forger who Swindled the Nazis*. The art forger Han van Meegeren fooled everyone, including Hermann Goering, with his "lost" Vermeers, when in fact he painted them himself. This story of bluff, bluste and fine art is an intriguing tale no doubt, but Wynne' book of 2007, though extremely well informed, is overl written.

BIOGRAPHY

Ayaan Hirsi Ali *Infidel: My Life*. This powerful and moving autobiography, written by one of the Netherlands' most controversial figures, begins with Ali's harsh and sometimes brutal childhood in Somalia and then Saudi Arabia, where – among other tribulations – her grandmother insisted she have her clitoris cut off when she was 5. Later, in 1992, Ali wound up in the Netherlands at least partly to evade an arranged marriage. Thereafter, she made a remarkable transition from factory cleaner to MP, becoming a leading light of the rightist VVD political party and remaining outspoken in her denunciations of militant Islam (see box, p.332), a theme she returned to recently in her *Heretic: Why Islam Needs a Reformation Now*. Ali now lives in the US.

A.C. Grayling *Descartes: The Life and Times of a Genius*. One of the greatest philosophers of all time, René Descartes (1596–1650) was a key figure in the transition from medieval to early modern Europe. He also made key contributions to optics and geometry and, among his miscellaneous travels, spent time living in Amsterdam (see box, p.63). This crisply written biography deals skilfully with the philosophy – Grayling is himself a philosophy professor – and argues that Descartes was almost certainly a Jesuit spy acting on behalf of the Habsburg interest during his time in Amsterdam.

Carol Ann Lee *Roses from the Earth: the Biography of Anne Frank*. Among an army of publications trawling through the life of the young Jewish diarist, this is probably the best, written in a straightforward and insightful manner without sentimentality. Lee's *The Hidden Life of Otto Frank* is equally clear, lucid and interesting. The first was first published in 1999, the second four years later.

HISTORY

Leo Akveld et al. *The Colourful World of the VOC*. Beautifully illustrated, coffee-table sized book on the VOC – the East India Company. The subject is dealt with in a series of intriguing essays on the likes of the uses of Eastern spices, Indonesian fashion and furniture, rituals and beliefs.

★ **Paul Arblaster** *A History of the Low Countries*. Welcome addition to the limited range of English-language books on this wide-ranging subject. Arblaster covers the ground methodically, with impeccable research, and has added lots of fascinating detail – and all in just 322 pages. An excellent survey.

J.C.H. Blom (ed.) *History of the Low Countries*. Books on the totality of Dutch history are thin on the ground, so this heavyweight volume fills a few gaps, though it's hardly sun-lounger reading. A series of historians weigh in with their specialities, from Roman times onwards, and its forte is in picking out those cultural, political and economic themes that give the region its distinctive character. First published in 1999, a partly revised version appeared in 2006. Blom has also edited a second, top-notch volume, *The History of the Jews in the Netherlands*.

Mike Dash *Tulipomania*. Dash examines the introduction of the tulip into the Low Countries at the height of the Golden Age – and the mind-boggling speculative boom that ensued. There's a lot of padding and scene-setting, but it's an engaging read, with nice detail on seventeenth-century Amsterdam, Leiden and Haarlem. Also by Dash is *Batavia's Graveyard*, a tale of mutiny and cannibalism among the shipwrecked crew of the East India Company's *Batavia*.

Pieter Geyl *The Revolt of The Netherlands 1555–1609* and *The Netherlands in the Seventeenth Century 1609–1648*. These detailed accounts of the Netherlands during its formative years chronicle the uprising against the Spanish and the formation of the United Provinces. First published in 1932, they have long been regarded as classic texts on the subject, though they are a hard and somewhat ponderous read.

Lisa Jardine *The Awful End of Prince William the Silent*. Great title for an intriguing book on the premature demise of one of the country's most acclaimed heroes, who was assassinated in Delft in 1584. At just 160 pages, the tale is told succinctly, but – unless you have a particular interest in early firearms – there is a bit too much information on guns and more guns.

John Nichol & Tony Rennell *Arnhem: The Battle for Survival* Operation Market Garden (see box, p.262) has attracted a good deal of attention over the years, both as history and memoir. This addition leaves no parachute unfurled.

Henk van Nierop *Treason in the Northern Quarter* Thoughtful, studious account of the reasons for – and ideologies behind – the Revolt of the Netherlands. The chapter on "Treason" – who to did what to whom and why – is especially illuminating.

★ **Geoffrey Parker** *The Dutch Revolt* and *The Army of Flanders and the Spanish Road 1567–1659* (o/p). The first of these two titles provides a compelling account of the struggle between the Netherlands and Spain and is quite the best thing you can read on the period. The second may sound academic, but it gives a fascinating insight into the Habsburg army that occupied the Low Countries for well over a hundred years – how it functioned, was fed and moved from Spain to the Low Countries along the so-called Spanish Road.

★**Simon Schama** *The Embarrassment of Riches: An Interpretation of Dutch Culture in the Golden Age*. Long before his reinvention on British TV, Schama specialized in Dutch history, and this chunky volume draws on a huge variety of archive sources. Also by Schama, *Patriots and Liberators: Revolution in the Netherlands 1780–1813* focuses on a less familiar period of Dutch history and is particularly good on the Batavian Republic set up in the Netherlands under French auspices. Both are heavyweight tomes, and leftists might well find Schama a tad reactionary. See also Schama's *Rembrandt's Eyes* (p.345).

LITERATURE

A.C. Baantjer *De Kok and the Mask of Death*. An ex-Amsterdam policeman, who racked up nearly forty years' service, Baantjer is one of the most widely read author in the Netherlands. This rattling good yarn, perhaps the best in the Inspector De Kok series, has all the typical ingredients – crisp plotting, some gruesomeness and a batch of nice characterizations on the way. Baantjer died in 2010.

Tracey Chevalier *Girl with a Pearl Earring*. Chevalier's novel is a fanciful piece of fiction, building a story around the subject of one of Vermeer's most enigmatic paintings. It's an absorbing read, if a tad too detailed and slow-moving for some tastes, and it paints a convincing picture of seventeenth-century Delft, exploring its social structures and values.

★**Anne Frank** *The Diary of a Young Girl*. Lucid and moving, the most revealing book you can read on the plight of Amsterdam's Jews during the German occupation. An international bestseller since its original publication in 1947.

★**Willem Frederik Hermans** *The Dark Room of Damocles*. Along with Jan Wolkers, Mulisch (see below) and Gerard Reve, Hermans is considered one of the four major literary figures of the Dutch postwar generation. This title, first published in 1958, is about the German occupation and its concomitants – betrayal, paranoia and treason. Indeed, the reader is rarely certain what is truth and what is false. Hermans died in 1995.

Etty Hillesum *An Interrupted Life: the Diaries and Letters of Etty Hillesum, 1941–43*. The Germans transported Hillesum, a young Jewish woman, from her home in Amsterdam to Auschwitz, where she died. As with Anne Frank's more famous journal, penetratingly written – though on the whole a tad less readable.

★**Arthur Japin** *The Two Hearts of Kwasi Boachi*. Inventive re-creation by Haarlem-born Japin of a true story in which the eponymous Ashanti prince was dispatched to the court of King William of the Netherlands in 1837. Kwasi and his companion Kwame were ostensibly sent to Den Haag to further their education, but there was a strong colonial subtext. Superb descriptions of Ashanti-land in its pre-colonial pomp. Also, Japin's *Lucia's Eyes*, an imaginative extrapolation of a casual anecdote found in Casanova's memoirs and set for the most part in eighteenth-century Amsterdam.

★**Otto de Kat** *Julia*. From one of the country's most praised contemporary novelists, this is perhaps de Kat's best novel so far, an engaging exploration of love and regret in which a suicide leads back to the events of World War II. Also, the comparable *Man on the Move*, set in the Dutch East Indies as the Dutch face the Japanese, and *News from Berlin*, also with a World War II setting and exploring guilt, memory and collaboration. De Kat is the pseudonym of Rotterdam-born Jan Geurt Gaarlandt.

Sylvie Matton *Rembrandt's Whore*. Taking its cue from Chevalier's *Girl with a Pearl Earring* (see opposite), this slim novel tries hard to conjure Rembrandt's life and times, with some success. Matton certainly knows her Rembrandt – she worked for two years on a film of his life. First published in 2001.

Sarah Emily Miano *Van Rijn*. Carefully composed re-creation of Rembrandt's milieu, based on the (documented) visit of Cosimo de Medici to the artist's house. As an attempt to venture into Rembrandt's soul it does well – but not brilliantly.

Deborah Moggach *Tulip Fever*. At first Deborah Moggach's novel seems no more than an attempt to build a story out of her favourite domestic Dutch interiors, genre scenes and still-life paintings. But ultimately the story is a basic one – of lust, greed, mistaken identity and tragedy. The Golden Age Amsterdam backdrop is well realized, but almost incidental.

Marcel Moring *In Babylon*. Popular Dutch author with an intense style spliced with thought-provoking, philosophical content. *In Babylon* has an older Jewish man and his niece trapped in a cabin in the eastern Netherlands and here they ruminate on their family's history. Moring's *Dream Room* is also gracefully nostalgic in its concentration on the family of Boris and his son, David, while the author's *In a Dark Wood*, is set in the town of Assen, again in the east of the country, during the annual Dutch TT motorbike races.

Harry Mulisch *The Assault*. Set part in Haarlem, part in Amsterdam, this novel traces the story of a young boy who loses his family in a reprisal raid by the Nazis. A powerful tale, made into an excellent and effective film. Also, *The Discovery of Heaven*, a gripping yarn of adventure and happenstance; *The Procedure*, featuring a modern-day Dutch scientist investigating strange goings-on in sixteenth-century Prague; and *Siegfried: a Black Idyll*, whose central question is whether a work of imagination can help to understand the nature of evil in general and Hitler in particular. Mulisch died in Amsterdam in 2010 at the age of 83.

Multatuli *Max Havelaar: Or, The Coffee Auctions of the Dutch Trading Company*. Classic nineteenth-century Dutch satire on colonial life in the East Indies. Eloquent and intermittently amusing. If you have Dutch friends, they will be impressed (dumbstruck) if you have actually read it, not least since it's 352 pages long.

Saskia Noort *Back to the Coast*. One of the most popular/populist contemporary novelists in the Netherlands, Noort sets this thriller on the Dutch coast where all sorts of fear and loathing ensue. There are more thrills and spills, murder and adultery in *The Dinner Club*.

Cees Nooteboom *Rituals*. Nooteboom (b.1933) published his first novel in 1955, but only hit the literary headlines with this, his third novel, in 1980. The central theme of all his work is the phenomenon of time; *Rituals* in particular is about the passing of time and the different ways of controlling the process. Inni Wintrop, the main character, is an outsider, a well-heeled, antique-dabbling "dilettante" as he describes himself. The book is almost entirely set in Amsterdam, and although it describes the inner life of Inni himself, it also paints a strong picture of the city.

Donna Tartt *The Goldfinch*. Tartt's Pulitzer Prize-winning, sprawling third novel is partly set in Amsterdam and tells the story of Theo Decker, who, aged 13, loses his mother in a New York art gallery explosion but escapes with one of the world's most famous paintings, the titular 1654 masterpiece by Delft's Carel Fabritius (now safely on display in Den Haag's Mauritshuis; see p.153). The bereaved Theo's possession of – and failure to return – the painting leads to much soul-searching, reckless drug-taking and ultimately into the criminal art underworld.

Jeroen Thijssen *Solitude*. Two brothers living in a squat discover their family's less than wholesome history as plantation owners in the Dutch East Indies (Indonesia). Thijssen interweaves the colonial past and the brothers' impoverished present with considerable skill.

Dutch

It's unlikely that you'll need to speak anything other than English while you are in the Netherlands: the Dutch have a seemingly innate talent for languages, and your attempts at speaking theirs may be met with some bewilderment – though this can have as much to do with your pronunciation (Dutch is very difficult to get right) as their surprise that you're making an effort. That said, the Dutch words and phrases below are useful, especially in the more rural parts of the country, and we have also included a basic food and drink glossary, though menus are nearly always multilingual: where they aren't, ask and one will almost invariably appear. As for phrasebooks, the *Rough Guide to Dutch* is pocket-sized, with a good dictionary section (English–Dutch and Dutch–English) as well as a menu reader; it also provides a useful introduction to grammar and pronunciation.

Pronunciation

Dutch is **pronounced** much the same as English. However, there are a few Dutch sounds that don't exist in English, which can be difficult to get right without practice.

Consonants

Double-consonant combinations generally keep their separate sounds in Dutch: kn, for example, is never like the English "knight". Note also the following consonants and consonant combinations:

j is an English y

ch and **g** indicate a throaty sound, as at the end of the Scottish word loch

ng as in bring

nj as in onion

y is not a consonant, but another way of writing ij

Vowels and diphthongs

A good rule of thumb is that doubling the letter lengthens the vowel sound.

a is like the English apple

aa like cart

e like let

ee like late

o as in pop

oo in pope

u is like the French tu if preceded by a consonant; it's like wood if followed by a consonant

uu is the French tu

au and **ou** like how

ei and **ij** as in fine, though this varies strongly from region to region; sometimes it can sound more like lane

oe as in soon

eu is like the diphthong in the French leur

ui is the hardest Dutch diphthong of all, pronounced like how but much further forward in the mouth, with lips pursed (as if to say "oo").

WORDS AND PHRASES

BASICS

		hello	hallo *or* dag
yes	ja	**good morning**	goedemorgen
no	nee	**good afternoon**	goedemiddag
please	alstublieft	**good evening**	goedenavond
thank you	dank u *or* bedankt	**goodbye**	tot ziens

DOUBLE DUTCH???

Dutch is a Germanic language – the word itself is a corruption of "Deutsche", a label inaccurately given by English sailors in the seventeenth century – and indeed if you know any German you'll spot many similarities. Spoken Dutch, however, is far from consistent, with a hatful of regional dialects: the inhabitants of Amsterdam have a very different accent and slang to someone, say, from Den Haag, while in Limburg the dialect is closer to German and Flemish than to Dutch. The Netherlands has a second official language too, **Fries**, the pride and joy of the people of Friesland – and incomprehensible to everyone else.

see you later	tot straks
Do you speak English?	Spreekt u Engels?
I don't understand	Ik begrijp het niet
women/men	vrouwen/mannen
children	kinderen
men's/women's toilets	heren/dames
I want…	Ik wil…
I don't want to	Ik wil niet…(+verb)
I don't want any…	Ik wil geen… (+noun)
How much is…?	Wat kost…?

TRAVEL, DIRECTIONS AND SHOPPING

How do I get to…?	Hoe kom ik in…?
Where is…?	Waar is…?
How far is it to…?	Hoe ver is het naar…?
When?	Wanneer?
far/near	ver/dichtbij
left/right	links/rechts
straight ahead	rechtdoor
airport	luchthaven
post office	postkantoor
post box	postbus
stamp(s)	postzegel(s)
money exchange	geldwisselkantoor
cash desk	kassa
railway platform	spoor or perron
ticket office	loket
here/there	hier/daar
good/bad	goed/slecht
big/small	groot/klein
open/closed	open/gesloten
push/pull	duwen/trekken

new/old	nieuw/oud
cheap/expensive	goedkoop/duur
hot/cold	heet or warm/koud
with/without	met/zonder
North	noord
South	zuid
East	oost
West	west

USEFUL CYCLING TERMS

brake	rem
broken	kapot
chain	ketting
cycle path	fietspad
handlebars	stuur
pedal	trapper
pump	pomp
puncture	lek
tyre	band
wheel	wiel

MONTHS OF THE YEAR

January	januari
February	februari
March	maart
April	april
May	mei
June	juni
July	juli
August	augustus
September	september
October	oktober

SIGNS AND ABBREVIATIONS

AUB Alstublieft: please (also shown as SVP, from French)
BG Begane grond: ground floor
BTW Belasting Toegevoegde Waarde: VAT
geen toegang no entry
gesloten closed
ingang entrance
K kelder: basement
let op! attention!

heren/dames men's/women's toilets
open open
T/M Tot en met: up to and including
toegang entrance
uitgang exit
VA vanaf: from
VS Verenigde Staten: United States
VVV Tourist office
ZOZ please turn over (page, leaflet, etc)

November	november
December	december

DAYS AND TIMES

Monday	maandag
Tuesday	dinsdag
Wednesday	woensdag
Thursday	donderdag
Friday	vrijdag
Saturday	zaterdag
Sunday	zondag
yesterday	gisteren
today	vandaag
tomorrow	morgen
tomorrow morning	morgenochtend
year	jaar
month	maand
week	week
day	dag
hour	uur
minute	minuut
What time is it?	Hoe laat is het?
It's…	Het is…
3.00	drie uur
3.05	vijf over drie
3.10	tien over drie
3.15	kwart over drie
3.20	tien voor half vier
3.25	vijf voor half vier
3.30	half vier
3.35	vijf over half vier
3.40	tien over half vier
3.45	kwart voor vier
3.50	tien voor vier
3.55	vijf voor vier
8am	acht uur 's ochtends
1pm	een uur 's middags
8pm	acht uur 's avonds
1am	een uur 's nachts

NUMBERS

0	nul
1	een
2	twee
3	drie
4	vier
5	vijf
6	zes
7	zeven
8	acht
9	negen
10	tien
11	elf
12	twaalf
13	dertien
14	veertien
15	vijftien
16	zestien
17	zeventien
18	achttien
19	negentien
20	twintig
21	een en twintig
22	twee en twintig
30	dertig
40	veertig
50	vijftig
60	zestig
70	zeventig
80	tachtig
90	negentig
100	honderd
101	honderd een
200	twee honderd
201	twee honderd een
500	vijf honderd
525	vijf honderd vijf en twintig
1000	duizend

MENU READER

BASIC TERMS

boter	butter
boterham/broodje	sandwich/roll
brood	bread
dranken	drinks
eieren	eggs
groenten	vegetables
honing	honey
hoofdgerechten	main courses
huzarensalade	potato salad with pickles
kaas	cheese
koud	cold
nagerechten	desserts
patat/friet	chips/french fries
peper	pepper
pindakaas	peanut butter
sla/salade	salad
slagroom	whipped cream
soep	soup
stokbrood	french bread
suiker	sugar
uitsmijter	ham or cheese with eggs on bread
vegetarisch	vegetarian
vis	fish
vlees	meat

voorgerechten	starters/hors d'oeuvres
vruchten	fruit
warm	hot
zout	salt

MEAT AND POULTRY

biefstuk (duitse)	hamburger
biefstuk (hollandse)	steak
eend	duck
fricandeau	roast pork
fricandel	frankfurter-like sausage
gehakt	minced meat
kalfsvlees	veal
kalkoen	turkey
karbonade	a chop
kip	chicken
kroket	spiced veal or beef hash, coated in breadcrumbs
lamsvlees	lamb
lever	liver
ossenhaas	tenderloin beef
rookvlees	smoked beef
spek	bacon
worst	sausages

FISH

forel	trout
garnalen	prawns
haring	herring
kabeljauw	cod
makreel	mackerel
mosselen	mussels
oesters	oysters
paling	eel
schelvis	haddock
schol	plaice
tong	sole
zalm	salmon

VEGETABLES

aardappelen	potatoes
bloemkool	cauliflower
bonen	beans
champignons	mushrooms
erwten	peas
hutspot	mashed potatoes and carrots
knoflook	garlic
komkommer	cucumber
prei	leek
rijst	rice
sla	salad, lettuce
stampot andijvie	mashed potato and endive
stampot boerenkool	mashed potato and cabbage

uien	onions
wortelen	carrots
zuurkool	sauerkraut

COOKING TERMS

belegd	filled or topped
doorbakken	well-done
gebakken	fried or baked
gebraden	roast
gegrild	grilled
gekookt	boiled
geraspt	grated
gerookt	smoked
gestoofd	stewed
half doorbakken	medium-done
rood	rare

SWEETS AND DESSERTS

appelgebak	apple tart or cake
drop	Dutch liquorice, available in *zoet* (sweet) or *zout* (salted) varieties
gebak	pastry
ijs	ice cream
koekjes	biscuits
oliebollen	traditional sweet sold at New Year – something like a doughnut
pannenkoeken	pancakes
pepernoten	Dutch ginger nuts
poffertjes	small pancakes, fritters
(slag)room	(whipped) cream
speculaas	spice and cinnamon-flavoured biscuit
stroopwafels	waffles
taai-taai	spicy Dutch cake
vla	custard

FRUITS AND NUTS

aardbei	strawberry
amandel	almond
appel	apple
appelmoes	apple purée
citroen	lemon
druiven	grape
framboos	raspberry
hazelnoot	hazelnut
kers	cherry
kokosnoot	coconut
peer	pear
perzik	peach
pinda	peanut
pruim	plum/prune

DRINKS

anijsmelk	aniseed-flavoured warm milk	melk	milk
appelsap	apple juice	met ijs	with ice
bessenjenever	blackcurrant gin	met slagroom	with whipped cream
chocomel	chocolate milk	pils	Dutch beer
citroenjenever	lemon gin	proost!	cheers!
droog	dry	sinaasappelsap	orange juice
frisdranken	soft drinks	thee	tea
jenever	Dutch gin	tomatensap	tomato juice
karnemelk	buttermilk	vruchtensap	fruit juice
koffie	coffee	wijn	wine
koffie verkeerd	coffee with warm milk	(wit/rood/rosé)	(white/red/rosé)
kopstoot	beer with a jenever chaser	vieux	Dutch brandy
		zoet	sweet

DUTCH GLOSSARY

Abdij Abbey.

Amsterdammertje Phallic-shaped bollard placed in rows alongside many Amsterdam streets to keep drivers off pavements and out of the canals.

Begijnhof Similar to a *hofje* but occupied by Catholic women (*begijns*) who led semi-religious lives without taking full vows.

Belfort Belfry.

Beurs Stock exchange.

Botermarkt Butter market.

Brug Bridge.

Gasthuis Hospice for the sick or infirm.

Gemeente Municipal, as in Gemeentehuis (town hall).

Gerechtshof Law courts.

Gilde Guild.

Gracht Canal.

Groentenmarkt Vegetable market.

Grote Kerk Literally "big church" – the main church of a town or village.

Hal Hall.

Hijsbalk Pulley beam, often decorated, fixed to the top of a gable to lift goods and furniture. Essential in canal houses with steep staircases.

Hofje Almshouse, usually for elderly women who could look after themselves but needed small charities such as food and fuel; usually a number of buildings centred around a small, enclosed courtyard.

Jeugdherberg Youth hostel.

Kasteel Castle.

Kerk Church.

Koning King.

Koningin Queen.

Koninklijk Royal.

Kunst Art.

Lakenhal Cloth hall: the building in medieval weaving towns where cloth would be weighed, graded and sold.

Markt Central town square and the heart of most Dutch communities, normally still the site of weekly markets.

Molen Windmill.

Nederland The Netherlands.

Nederlands Dutch.

Omgang Procession.

Paleis Palace.

Plein A square or open space.

Polder An area of land reclaimed from the sea.

Poort Gate.

Raadhuis Town hall.

Randstad Literally "rim-town", the urban conurbation that makes up much of Noord- and Zuid-Holland.

Rijk State.

Schepezaal Alderman's hall.

Schone Kunsten Fine arts.

Schouwburg Theatre.

Sierkunst Decorative arts.

Spionnetje Small mirror on a canal house enabling the occupant to see who is at the door.

Stadhuis The most common word for a town hall.

Stedelijk Civic, municipal.

Steeg Alley.

Steen Stone.

Stichting Institute or foundation.

Straat Street.

Toren Tower.

Tuin Garden.

Vleeshuis Meat market.

VOC (Vereenigde Oost-Indische Compagnie) The Dutch East India Company, a major force in Dutch colonialism. Also, the much less successful GWIC (Geoctroyeerde Westindische Compagnie or GWIC), the Dutch West India Company.

Volkskunde Folklore.

Waag Old public weigh house, a common feature of most towns.

Weg Way.

Wijk District (of a city).

Small print and index

A ROUGH GUIDE TO ROUGH GUIDES

Published in 1982, the first Rough Guide – to Greece – was a student scheme that became a publishing phenomenon. Mark Ellingham, a recent graduate in English from Bristol University, had been travelling in Greece the previous summer and couldn't find the right guidebook. With a small group of friends he wrote his own guide, combining a highly contemporary, journalistic style with a thoroughly practical approach to travellers' needs.

The immediate success of the book spawned a series that rapidly covered dozens of destinations. And, in addition to impecunious backpackers, Rough Guides soon acquired a much broader readership that relished the guides' wit and inquisitiveness as much as their enthusiastic, critical approach and value-for-money ethos.

These days, Rough Guides include recommendations from budget to luxury and cover more than 120 destinations around the globe, as well as producing an ever-growing range of ebooks.

Visit **roughguides.com** to find all our latest books, read articles, get inspired and share travel tips with the Rough Guides community.

Rough Guide credits

Editor: Ann-Marie Shaw
Layout: Ankur Guha
Cartography: Lokamata Sahu
Picture editor: Aude Vauconsant
Proofreader: Jennifer Speake
Managing editor: Monica Woods
Senior editor: Natasha Foges
Assistant editor: Sharon Sonam

Production: Jimmy Lao
Cover design: Nicole Newman, Ankur Guha
Photographers: Tim Draper, Natascha Sturny, Mark Thomas
Editorial assistant: Freya Godfrey
Senior pre-press designer: Dan May
Programme manager: Gareth Lowe
Publisher: Keith Drew
Publishing director: Georgina Dee

Publishing information

This 7th edition published March 2016 by
Rough Guides Ltd,
80 Strand, London WC2R 0RL
11, Community Centre, Panchsheel Park,
New Delhi 110017, India
Distributed by Penguin Random House
Penguin Books Ltd, 80 Strand, London WC2R 0RL
Penguin Group (USA), 345 Hudson Street, NY 10014, USA
Penguin Group (Australia), 250 Camberwell Road,
Camberwell, Victoria 3124, Australia
Penguin Group (NZ), 67 Apollo Drive, Mairangi Bay,
Auckland 1310, New Zealand
Penguin Group (South Africa), Block D, Rosebank Office
Park, 181 Jan Smuts Avenue, Parktown North, Gauteng,
South Africa 2193
Rough Guides is represented in Canada by DK Canada, 320
Front Street West, Suite 1400,Toronto, Ontario M5V 3B6
Printed in Singapore
© Rough Guides 2016
Maps © Rough Guides

368pp includes index
A catalogue record for this book is available from the
British Library
ISBN: 978-0-24120-447-4
The publishers and authors have done their best to ensure
the accuracy and currency of all the information in
The Rough Guide to The Netherlands, however, they
can accept no responsibility for any loss, injury, or
inconvenience sustained by any traveller as a result of
information or advice contained in the guide.
1 3 5 7 9 8 6 4 2

MIX
Paper from
responsible sources
FSC
www.fsc.org   FSC™ C018179

Help us update

We've gone to a lot of effort to ensure that the seventh
edition of **The Rough Guide to The Netherlands** is
accurate and up-to-date. However, things change – places
get "discovered", opening hours are notoriously fickle,
restaurants and rooms raise prices or lower standards. If
you feel we've got it wrong or left something out, we'd like
to know, and if you can remember the address, the price,
the hours, the phone number, so much the better.

Please send your comments with the subject line
"Rough Guide Netherlands Update" to mail
@uk.roughguides.com. We'll credit all contributions and
send a copy of the next edition (or any other Rough Guide
if you prefer) for the very best emails.

Find more travel information, connect with fellow
travellers and plan your trip on ⊕ roughguides.com.

ABOUT THE AUTHORS

Vicky Hampton, a British-born Amsterdammer, is a writer, cook and avid foodie who has lived and worked the Netherlands since 2006. Her website, ⓦamsterdamfoodie.nl, focuses on reviews and recommendations of Amsterdam restaurants, as well as other culinary travel writing.

Phil Lee, a one-time deckhand in the Danish merchant navy, has been writing for Rough Guides for well over twenty years. His other books in the series include Norway, Amsterdam, Norfolk & Suffolk, Mallorca & Menorca and Belgium & Luxembourg. He lives in Nottingham, where he was born and raised.

Suzanne Morton-Taylor has been working as a travel writer for Rough Guides since 2006 and has contributed to the Amsterdam, Australia, Norway and Belgium & Luxembourg guides, among others.

Emma Thomson is an award-winning freelance travel writer and a member of the British Guild of Travel Writers. She lives in Aalst, Belgium, and visits "rival nation" the Netherlands as frequently as she can after developing a covert love affair with its effortless mix of culture and bohemia.

Jeroen van Marle grew up in England, studied Human Geography in the Netherlands, learnt Romanian and moved to Eastern Europe where he hitchhiked from St Petersburg to Bulgaria and founded a city guide company in Romania. After moving 25 times and living in nine countries, for now he's based in Berlin where he's the Dutch editor for SecretEscapes.com. He has most recently worked on the Rough Guides to Bali & Lombok, South Africa and Germany.

Acknowledgements

Phil Lee would like to thank his editor, Annie Shaw, for her expert editing and cheerful conversation during the preparation of this new edition of the Rough Guide to The Netherlands. Thanks also to my ever-helpful co-authors, Suzanne Morton-Taylor and Jeroen van Marle; Susanne Canisius of Tourism Utrecht; Nel van der Maarel of Delft Marketing; Bert-Jan Zoet of Rotterdam Partners; Petra Hullen of Hanzesteden Marketing; and last but certainly not least, the excellent Dewi van de Wal of Den Haag Marketing.
Suzanne Morton-Taylor would like to thank Wouter Steenhuisen of Marketing Groningen and Rens Kalsbeek

of Tour de Wadden for their hospitality and help with all sorts of queries. Special thanks to Ann-Marie Shaw for an excellent job editing this seventh edition, and of course to my co-authors Phil Lee and Jeroen van Marle.
Emma Thomson Thanks to Machteld Ligtvoet of Amsterdam Marketing.
Jeroen van Marle Many thanks to Phil, Suzanne, Natasha and Annie at Rough Guides. Also thanks to David Koren in Middelburg, Karin, Roland & Sam, Theo Leerintveld of InYourPocket, Jan-Paul Kroese at Chateau St Gerlach. And to Soulafa, who loves sniffing new books – like this one.

Readers' updates

Thanks to all the readers who have taken the time to write in with comments and suggestions (and apologies if we've inadvertently omitted or misspelt anyone's name):

Mette Adegeest; Arda Akin; Kevin Blanking; Maaike Bloem; Brenda Bonte; Tessa Boon; Les Bright; Joyce Brouwer; James Cruickshank; Iacopo Dalu; Stephan Dekker; Floor van Ede; Eep Francken; Kim Gaarthuis; Imogen Gardam; Sean Gostage; Tony Hadland; Brian Hayfield; Dave Himelfield; Marten Hoeksma; Diana Hooper; Helen Jackson; Jamie Jenner; Jo Jones; Martin Jones; Klaas de Jong; Lotte Keess; Dr Mary Ellen Kitler; Marianne de Kuyper; Hans Langenhuijzen; Gordon Leadbetter; Danielle Linscheer; Steve Longo; Gary Low; Mette Luiting; Joe

Luttrell; Colm Magee; Rodney Mantle; Daniel May; Antoon Meert; Roy Messenger; Phil and Diane Moss; Lisa Mottram; Christine van Muiswinkel; Sara Muldoon; Paul Mundy; Brian Musgrave; Janneke van Nunen; Shanice Ofosu; Chantelle Parsons; Arianna Piccione; Maria Pooley; Ellie Ratcliffe; Jan Willem Sanderse; Maarten Schiethart; Richard Shaffer; Duncan M Small; Peter Roald van Stijn; Stoakley; Sabien Stols; Matt Thomson; Laura Tobin; Irene Vriends; David Watkins; Stephen Williams; Dwaze Zaken.

Photo credits

1 Corbis/Jason Langley
2 Alamy Images/Mediacolors
4 Alamy Images/Frans Lemmens
5 4Corners/Sandra Raccanello/SIME
9 Getty Images/Chris Hill (tl); Gallo Images /Neil Overy (tr); SuperStock/Frans Lemmens (b)
11 Corbis/Frank Krahmer (t); Will Pryce (c); Robert Harding Picture Library/Dreamtours (b)
12 Robert Harding Picture Library/Michael Zegers
13 Visit Holland/Den Haag Marketing (t); Dreamstime.com/Kityyaya (c)
14 Corbis/Marianne Hope/RooM the Agency (c); Visit Holland (t & b)
15 Visit Holland/Fotograf Bruno Ehrs (t); Corbis: Keren Su (b)
16 Visit Holland (tr & bl)
17 Alamy Images/David Robertson (t); Corbis/Steppeland – Lutgarde De Brouwer (b)
18 Alamy Images/Frans Lemmens (t); Picture Contact BV (b)
19 Visit Holland (tl)
20 Corbis/Ethel Davies/Robert Harding (c); Visit Holland (l &r)
22 Corbis/David C Phillips
47 Corbis/Sylvain Sonnet
55 Corbis/Jose Nicolas (bl); Robert Harding Picture Library/Hans Zaglitsch (br)

100–101 Corbis/Frank Krahmer
115 Getty Images/Bjorn Svensson (tl); SuperStock/Travel Library Limited (tr); Corbis/Manfred Mehlig (b)
140–141 Corbis/Gary Cook
169 Robert Harding Picture Library/Riccardo Sala (tr); Corbis/Hollandse Hoogte (b)
183 123RF.com/Rostislav Ageev (b)
192–193 SuperStock/Richard Semik
195 Alamy Images/Erik Lam Boats
213 Alamy Images/Lourens Smak (tr); Visit Holland (b)
232–233 SuperStock/Frans Lemmens
235 Dreamstime.com/Antonel
270–271 SuperStock/van der Meer Rene
283 SuperStock/imagebroker.net (t); Malherbe Marcel (b)
297 Alamy Images/Scott Hortop Travel
316 Corbis/Alfredo Dagli Orti

Front cover & spine Bicycle park in Centraal Station, Utrecht © AWL Images/Hemis
Back cover View from canal, Amsterdam © Corbis/Image Source (t); Windmill, Marken © AWL Images/Peter Adams (bl); Tulips at Keukenhof Gardens © AWL Images/Nadia Isakova (br)

Index

Maps are marked in grey

Map symbols

The symbols below are used on maps throughout the book

International boundary	Wall	Point of interest	Campsite
State/Province boundary	Airport	Statue	Hostel
Chapter division boundary	Bus/taxi stop	Museum	Synagogue
Motorway	Parking	Metro station	Church
Pedestrianized road	Post office	Tram stop	Building
Road	Hospital	Bridge	Cemetery
Path	Information office	Gate	Park
Railway	Telephone office	Garden	Beach/dune

Listings key

- Accommodation
- Eating
- Drinking & Nightlife
- Shops

Discover The Netherlands

17th century buildings, picture-postcard canals, fields of tulips and some of the Europe's finest museums can be found in The Netherlands. Discover bustling cities, rolling landscapes, historic sites and beautiful vistas on a tailor made holiday with Railbookers.

Amsterdam City Break

02 nights | from **£269**pp

Bursting with energy and a world-famed artistic scene, Amsterdam boasts several eccentric architectural styles and a wealth of celebrated museums that make the city a must visit on any trip to the continent.

Amsterdam and Utrecht

04 nights | from **£459**pp

Explore the fascinating cities of Amsterdam and Utrecht on a four night holiday by rail. From gondola trips along the historic canals of Utrecht to the exquisite period buildings of Amsterdam, there is plenty to enjoy here!

railbookers

Holidays inspired by you

Let us tailor make your perfect break to The Netherlands, call **020 3780 2272** or visit **www.railbookers.com**

Prices shown are per person, based on two people travelling and sharing a room, subject to availability, correct as of 30/09/2015 and may vary seasonally. Standard terms and conditions apply.